How Philosophy Became Socratic

How Philosophy Became Socratic

A Study of Plato's
Protagoras, Charmides, and *Republic*

LAURENCE LAMPERT

The University of Chicago Press
Chicago & London

Laurence Lampert is professor emeritus of philosophy at Indiana University–Purdue University Indianapolis and the author of *Leo Strauss and Nietzsche*, also published by the University of Chicago Press.

The University of Chicago Press, Chicago 60637
The University of Chicago Press, Ltd., London

Printed in the United States of America

18 17 16 15 14 13 12 11 10 1 2 3 4 5

ISBN-13: 978-0-226-47096-2 (cloth)
ISBN-10: 0-226-47096-2 (cloth)

Library of Congress Cataloging-in-Publication Data

Lampert, Laurence, 1941–
How philosophy became socratic : a study of Plato's Protagoras, Charmides, and Republic / Laurence Lampert.
p. cm.
Includes bibliographical references and index.
ISBN-13: 978-0-226-47096-2 (cloth : alk. paper)
ISBN-10: 0-226-47096-2 (cloth : alk. paper) 1. Socrates. 2. Socrates—Political and social views. 3. Plato. Protagoras. 4. Plato. Republic. 5. Plato. Charmides. 6. Philosophy, Ancient—History. 7. Philosophy, Ancient—Political aspects. 8. Political science—Philosophy. I. Title.
B317.L335 2010
184—dc22

2009052793

♾ The paper used in this publication meets the minimum requirements of the American National Standard for Information Sciences—Permanence of Paper for Printed Library Materials, ANSI Z39.48-1992.

CONTENTS

ACKNOWLEDGMENTS

I am grateful to George Dunn for the help he has given me with this book. His acute insights, exegetically grounded and far reaching, illumined many passages of Plato for me, and he generously permitted me to incorporate them as I saw fit. In addition, the two readers for the Press did me the great service of providing detailed criticisms from deeply informed perspectives; their work greatly improved the finished version of this book.

INTRODUCTION

Plato spread his dialogues across the temporal span of Socrates' life, setting some earlier, some later, inducing their engaged reader to wonder: Does that span map a temporal development in Socrates' thought? Did Plato show Socrates *becoming* Socrates? Yes, this book answers, the dramatic dates Plato gave his dialogues invite his reader to follow a now little-used route into the true mansion of Socrates' thought. Following that route, the reader accompanies Socrates as he breaks with the century-old tradition of philosophy, turns to his own path of investigation, and enters, over time, the deepest understanding of nature, and then, gradually again, learns the proper way to shelter and transmit that understanding in face of the threats to philosophy that Plato made so prominent. The plan of Plato's dialogues shows Socrates becoming *Socrates*, "the one turning point and vortex"[1] of the history of philosophy—and of the history of political philosophy, philosophy's quasi-philosophical means of sheltering and advancing philosophy. Plato's chronological record of Socrates becoming who he was has a significance far transcending philosophy's existence in Socrates' or Plato's time, for it is the enduring record of philosophy becoming Socratic, taking the shape that came to dominate the spiritual life of the West. A study of Plato's dialogues that pays close attention to their chronology and settings sees one of the roots of our civilization being formed, over time, in the mind and actions of a wise man in imperial Athens, a man intending that his wise thoughts and actions colonize the wider world from there.

1. Nietzsche, *Birth of Tragedy*, ¶15.

The question of how Socrates became Socrates arises late in a study of Plato's writings and is meant to arise late: only after Socrates has actually won in Plato's reader a portion of the admiration due him does that question arise. "How did Socrates become himself?" is a question asked by those whom the dialogues have already drawn to that seemingly most public of philosophers. Wanting with some urgency to know just how their own special teacher became himself, such readers will interrogate their primary source on Socrates and only then begin to discover just how Plato wove into his dialogues the answer to a question they were crafted to generate.

Plato's Socrates in Time and Place

Plato assigned most of his dialogues a specific dramatic date, showing Socrates conversing at a particular time and place with a particular person or persons. Platonic scholarship of the last century and a half has paid relatively little attention to these dramatic dates compared with the effort expended on determining composition dates, the time at which Plato might have written them. Scholars assign composition dates on the basis of some theory of *Plato's* development; Plato assigned dramatic dates pointing to stages in *Socrates'* development. By inquiring into the latent significance of the patent dramatic dates, we can reconstruct Plato's account of how Socrates became himself, for Plato did not describe Socrates' development in any straightforward way but instead communicated it indirectly through the dramatic dates. He indicated thereby that Socrates' development did not occur in a vacuum—it was not simply a movement of thought; instead, it was a series of conscious gains by a mind that, in its devotion to thinking, came to recognize the situatedness of thinking in a person in space and time. Plato's dialogues show Socrates to be a most remarkable man in a most remarkable place and time, for Plato set his life history of Socrates against the background of the larger life history of Athens, the city in which Socrates spent his life, whose wars he fought, whose festivals he celebrated, whose young he counseled, whose history and politics he measured, whose laws he obeyed until finally submitting, at age seventy, to its death sentence even though his oldest friend offered him easy escape from prison the day before the sacred ship returned from Delos, releasing his city from sacred restraint and freeing it to kill him.

Plato's dialogues, written in the fifty years after Socrates' death in 399, all reach back to the past. With the possible exception of the *Laws* and *Epinomis* they all look back to the life of Socrates, a life begun in 469 and lived out in a most memorable, spectacular setting: Athens, the dynamic imperial city at the center of Greek civilization, a wealthy democracy led during Socrates' youth and early maturity by its first citizen, Pericles. It was a city made glorious by Pericles' unprecedented public building program of magnificent temples rising atop the acropolis at its center and visible for miles around; a confident, even arrogant city with impregnable defensive walls running five miles down to the sea, where the mightiest fleet in the Mediterranean was housed in luxurious ship sheds; a city still living in conscious exultation of victory over the invincible Persians a decade before Socrates was born; a city of festivals to its gods, including the festivals to Dionysos that produced the unique Attic spectacles of tragedy and comedy witnessed by all male citizens and in at least one of which Socrates was the leading character; a politically experimental city of reasoned public talk, with a one-hundred-year-old tradition of deciding all major matters of policy through public debate and secret vote and of deciding all important judicial cases before huge juries of citizens drawn by lot and voting only after hearing the best case put forward by both sides. Finally, it was a city aware of itself as the center of the Greek enlightenment, which had sprung forth in the eastern and western extremities of greater Greece but now flourished, as nowhere else, in the imperial center, which drew to itself the best minds from all over Greece, with whom Plato showed Socrates in conversation. This was the city aglow with glory and grandeur that suffered, for the last half of Socrates' life, a twenty-seven-year war with Sparta that ended in defeat and civil war. The longer-term consequences of the civil war arguably cost Socrates his life, partly because of suspicions aroused even before the war broke out by his active pursuit of the two talented youths who matured into Athens' two greatest criminals, Alcibiades and Critias.

How could the life of the Athenian philosopher Socrates not be placed against this background? It was the actual background of his life, and by alluding to it Plato gave Socrates' life a setting that had every chance of remaining memorable not only in its marble buildings but in the written record of its tragedies and comedies and in particular in a writing that recorded the history of the war and was written explicitly to be "a possession for all time," Thucydides' history. Against the background of that particular possession for all time, the historical settings for Plato's dialogues win color and focus, for he seems to have had Thucydides in mind when making many spare remarks to locate Socrates' conversations in Athenian history. Another permanent possession of historical writing, Herodotus's history of the war with the Persians—his account in fact of Greekness, of the way of the Greeks—had been published in Athens during the first decade of the war with Sparta and itself presented a lesson in what is timeless in history and what was uniquely Greek, and it too proves illuminating for Plato's historical settings.

When attention is paid to the timely setting of the dialogues via the chronological arrangement Plato gave them, another historic event begins to emerge, an event that would make the time in which they are set all the more memorable because all the more catastrophic. As a time of splendor that passed into a time of decay and loss, the time in which Plato set his dialogues suffered what could be thought the ultimate loss, the unprecedented, once-for-all-time death of the gods of Homer and Hesiod. That dying would be slow—when gods die, men play with their shadows in caves for centuries, said Nietzsche the philosopher of the death of our God[2]—but the essential events in the death of the Homeric gods occurred during Socrates' lifetime. It was not only the war and the plague that cost the young men of Athens their belief in its gods, it was the Greek enlightenment as well, for it actively schooled the best Athenian young in a lightly veiled skepticism about the gods while mocking ancestral or paternal submission to them and counseling its students on just how to make the best use of the piety of others. How does Plato's Socrates stand to Homer and Hesiod, the poets who, Herodotus said, "created for the Greeks their theogeny, gave to the gods the special names for their descent from their ancestors and divided among them their honors, their arts, and their shapes"?[3] A chronological study of the dialogues shows that question rising to singular importance for Socrates in his public presentation of philosophy.

By tying the life of Socrates to the life of Athens, Plato did the opposite of tying the timeless things of philosophy to the merely ephemeral. Instead, he displayed the life of a wise man thinking and acting within a paradigm time of human attainment and human crisis—and responding with paradigm wisdom. Plato set his dialogues in a time and place that would last if human things were to last at all, for he set them at the turning of an age as the Homeric passed to something yet to be named because just being born, just being set afloat on the river of time through the thoughts and deeds of a post-Homeric wise man schooled by Homer. Plato's dialogues were written as a possession for all time *because* they are set within a particular time

2. Nietzsche, *Gay Science*, ¶344.
3. Herodotus 2.53.2.

and present the thoughts and deeds of a particular man as he grew into what seemed the only adequate response to the crisis of his time.

Philosophy in Plato's Chronological Arrangement of the Dialogues

Plato gave his dialogues a structural or taxonomic feature that adds complexity to their settings: he made nine of them *narrations* by a speaker to some audience, while the others are simply *performed* like plays set before the reader with no intervention by a narrator. Each of the performed dialogues occurs at a single point in Socrates' life, and their dates can be determined with more or less exactitude from the historical cues Plato chose to give them: *Euthyphro* occurred on the day of the preliminary hearing on Meletus's charges; the *Hippias* dialogues occurred during the diplomatic congress called by Alcibiades in the summer of 420. The narrated dialogues, however, have two temporal settings, the time of the narration and the time of the conversation narrated. The separation between the two settings can be as brief as that of *Protagoras*, a few minutes or hours, or as long as that of *Parmenides*, six decades.

The nine narrated dialogues are split by a noteworthy feature: Socrates narrates six,[4] while Phaedo narrates *Phaedo*, Cephalus *Parmenides*, and Apollodorus the *Symposium*, all three of these narrators being, in their various ways, devoted followers of Socrates. These three dialogues, exceptional in form as narrations by others, are exceptional too with respect to the question of Socrates becoming Socrates: all three contain retrospective recoveries of a philosophic turning point in the life of a young Socrates, younger than the Socrates of all the other dialogues, which begin with Socrates mounting the stage, so to speak, in *Protagoras* around 433 when he was about thirty-six. It cannot be an accident that Plato made a younger Socrates accessible only in retrospective reports passed on much later by devotees and in all three dialogues narrated by devotees.[5] Readers

4. *Protagoras, Euthydemus, Lovers, Lysis, Charmides, Republic*. Two of these, *Protagoras* and *Euthydemus*, have frames introducing a core discussion; the other four are narrated by Socrates from beginning to end. *Theaetetus* is an interesting variant: it has a frame and a core, but its core discussion is not narrated but *read* as a text that Socrates first narrated to Euclides to write down; its frame discussion between Euclides and Terpsion introduces a reading, long after Socrates' death, of Euclides' writing of Socrates' narration.

5. Plato's *Apology of Socrates* contains an important addition to these three accounts of a younger Socrates; there, in the only speech Socrates ever gave to the collected "men of Athens,"

who notice this feature discover that the three reports fall easily into their proper sequence: the youngest Socrates of all is available through Phaedo's report of Socrates' last day—Plato so arranged things that the oldest possible Socrates, hours before his end and as an introduction to the last argument of his life, tells of his earliest beginnings in philosophy. Chronologically next comes the young Socrates reported by Cephalus, a Socrates avid to challenge old Parmenides and his student Zeno during their visit to Athens in 450 with his own new theory of ideas. That event allows the philosophic biography of the young Socrates to be dated: he was about nineteen in 450, and his new theory must have been devised after the impassioned pursuit of the investigation of nature he reported in *Phaedo*—so the report in *Phaedo* is of a teenager absorbing the whole century of Greek philosophy preceding him and already setting out on what he later called his "second sailing," his turn to the speeches or *logoi*, the turn that led him to the ideas.[6] In the third dialogue narrated by another, Apollodorus's report in the *Symposium*, Socrates relates to a most sophisticated audience an event of learning in which a wise woman named God's-honor, Diotima, led him to the truth about the deepest things, surely the greatest philosophical event of his life, an event that perhaps occurred around 441 when Socrates was about twenty-eight.

The three dialogues narrated by devotees report the essential steps in Socrates' entry into Socratic philosophy—they show Socrates developing his views on the questions of being and knowing fundamental to philosophy itself. Plato gave one of these, Cephalus's report on the conversation of the nineteen-year-old Socrates with Zeno and Parmenides, a most remarkable introduction. It shows that a record of that conversation exists now for one reason alone: certain men of Clazomenae, having heard a rumor of such a conversation, sailed across the Aegean to Athens in order to hunt down the one man alive who might still have memory of it and be able to relate it to them. Plato makes their zeal particularly arresting by contrasting it with the indifference of certain Athenians: it is perhaps ten years after Socrates' death, and when they arrive in the Athenian agora they chance to run into certain former associates of Socrates well known

a Socrates soon to die frees himself to speak mythically and provides the Athenian public with a way for them to think of the most important "turn" in his life (*Apology* 21b). But a turn to the kind of philosophy the public would recognize as his, a turn based on the reason he gives, implies a pre-"Socratic" wisdom: the sole grounds on which the Delphic oracle could acknowledge that no one was wiser than Socrates was a wisdom prior to the turn described in the *Apology*, a wisdom about which Socrates chose to remain silent in his public speech while pointing to it this way.

6. *Phaedo* 99d.

indeed to Plato's readers: Adeimantus and Glaucon. Encountering them simplifies matters for the men of Clazomenae because the man they seek happens to be their half-brother, Antiphon. Adeimantus and Glaucon lead them to their brother's house to see if Antiphon can remember the conversation told to him by an old lover and now some sixty years distant in the past. He can remember despite his loss of interest in anything it contains, but he has to be persuaded because at first he balks, saying it is a lot of work. That travelers from Clazomenae must persuade a reluctant Antiphon to tell the tale he alone remembers is a little revelation: why haven't Adeimantus and Glaucon seen to the preservation of this tale, which they know their brother practiced thoroughly when he was a boy? Saved by the efforts of anonymous men of Clazomenae, Antiphon's memorized tale would have died with him for all Adeimantus and Glaucon cared—they couldn't be bothered to ask their own brother to tell them the story of a life-altering experience of the young Socrates.

An ancient commentator speaks of Plato, "even at the age of eighty, never letting off combing and curling his dialogues, never letting off re-plaiting them,"[7] and the dialogues give every evidence of constant care. The way Plato opened *Parmenides*, stunningly by contrasting the anonymity and zeal of travelers from Clazomenae with the indifference of Adeimantus and Glaucon of all people, cannot be incidental. Instead, his opening seems paradigmatic for the whole question of recovering the young Socrates or learning how Socrates entered Socratic philosophy: his opening suggests that the question of Socrates' entry into philosophy is truly of interest only to anonymous latecomers, travelers from afar bent on recovering what familiars would let fall; they may initially act on mere rumor, and the sequence of transmission may pass through questionable hands, but if they expend the necessary effort they may discover something of the highest interest to *them*. Those willing to let it fall include those privileged to have heard Socrates that night in the Piraeus unfold the *Republic* to them. And rightly so: those charmed as Adeimantus and Glaucon were charmed by the Socrates of the *Republic* quite fittingly feel no need to inquire further. But a tale of his beginnings was saved by anonymous men of Clazomenae. And how did it come down to us? Through a talking head, a *kephalê*, through written spoken words preserved not by Antiphon or Adeimantus or Glaucon but by another brother, a talking head indeed, who cared enough to learn what he could about Socrates young and old and to make his words continue to speak. Plato preserved what he teaches some

7. Dionysius of Halicarnassus, "On Literary Composition," *Critical Essays*, 2:225.

to care about, preserved it in a way that keeps preserving it for nameless future travelers.

And political philosophy? Cicero credited Socrates with being the inventor of that second and indispensable aspect of philosophy, the public shape it would have to take if it was ever to flourish in human culture.[8] Plato showed Socrates entering that too by the chronological arrangement he gave his dialogues, entering it later, of course, than philosophy proper. But the opening of *Parmenides* suggests to me the fitting way to treat Plato's chronology of Socrates' life: consider first the public Socrates and only then trace the way back to a Socrates both younger and more private, the Socrates to whom Plato gave access only through the three dialogues narrated by devotees. Accordingly, I will consider first Socrates' mature attainment of an adequate political philosophy and only then his prior entry into philosophy itself, into that permanent possession and its ongoing investigations around which a politic shelter had to be constructed. The three dialogues I treat in this book, *Protagoras, Charmides*, and the *Republic*, all deal with Socrates' concern for the public appearance of philosophy. They presuppose but do not discuss a nonpublic Socrates whose primary concern is the investigations basic to philosophy, of nature and human nature. To treat the political philosopher before the philosopher seems to me to accord with Plato's chronological arrangement of his dialogues and his assignment of narrators, and to accord as well with what seems to be the principle that structures the chronology and narrations, namely, that politic philosophy be visible and powerful before that other, deeper, perhaps impolitic philosophy is suspected at all—or that the impolitic in philosophy always only be accessible through the politic. *Phaedo, Parmenides*, and the *Symposium*, the dialogues that lead back to a younger Socrates concerned most directly with nature and the possibility of humans coming to know nature, I will treat in a second book, *How Socrates Became Socrates*.

Parmenides himself suggests the two different tasks separated into the two books of my two-part work. Having just destroyed the view that the young Socrates presented so aggressively—that there are "ideas of the beings" and that one must "distinguish each form on its own" (135a)[9]—he describes how the advocate of such a view might react to its refutation: he could "hit a dead end and argue that these things *are* not" or, if they *are*, are necessarily unknown to human nature. But he pictures a different reaction possible for "a naturally gifted man"; he "could learn that there is a cer-

8. Cicero, *Tusculan Disputations* 5.4.10.

9. Translations by Albert Keith Whitaker, *Plato's Parmenides*.

tain kind and beinghood, in itself, for each thing." And above and beyond even such learning, Parmenides points to a still higher attainment: "Only a prodigy more remarkable still will discover all these things and be able to teach someone else to judge them clearly and sufficiently for himself" (135b). At age nineteen, suffering the demolition of his vaunted solution, high-reaching Socrates hears the great Parmenides goad him with the peak of possible attainment for a thinker, the peak of discovery and teaching that Plato will show him actually attaining. This book, *How Philosophy Became Socratic*, aims to show how Plato's chronological arrangement of his dialogues portrays the remarkable prodigy Socrates, having discovered all these things, learning to teach someone else how to judge them clearly for himself. The second book, *How Socrates Became Socrates*, aims to show how Plato's chronological arrangement of his dialogues portrays the naturally gifted Socrates learning that there is a certain kind and beinghood for each thing.

Political Philosophy in Plato's Chronological Arrangement of the Dialogues

I begin this book then with the chronologically first of Plato's dialogues, where *first* refers to the dramatic setting of the dialogue or of the frame that opens it. Viewed this way, *Protagoras* is the chronologically first dialogue, set around 433.[10] A dialogue narrated by Socrates, it displays Socrates setting out to win a certain public name for himself, for he takes the trouble to tell an audience not all that interested in intellectual matters (as will be seen) a conversation among the wise that just took place in private behind closed doors in which he whipped in argument the man his audience thinks is the wisest man in Greece. How fitting that *Protagoras* be chronologically first: it is the dialogue in which Socrates mounts the public stage bent on winning a reputation for himself in Athens as the first man ever to defeat the great Protagoras in argument. Winning a reputation for himself means winning a reputation for what he represents: by going public with his victory over Protagoras, he aims to give philosophy a Socratic public face that will eclipse its Protagorean public face. *Protagoras* leads naturally

10. This date and others asserted in this section are not free of controversy. Warrant for the dramatic dates here simply announced is supplied in two ways. First, within the exegesis of each of the dialogues I emphasize the particular historical cues that Plato offers his readers for determining just when they occurred. Second, I append a "Note" to the end of the discussions of *Protagoras, Charmides*, and the *Republic* dealing in more detail with the dramatic date of each.

(as will be seen) to *Alcibiades I*, a performed dialogue with no introduction but a dialogue closely related to *Protagoras* chronologically and in theme. It shows that Socrates' politics for philosophy around 433 has a related and apparently more overtly political aim: private guidance of the politically most gifted and ambitious young Athenian. Part One of this book, "Philosophy in a Time of Splendor," deals with *Protagoras* and *Alcibiades I* as Socrates' initial way of establishing a responsible public presence for philosophy.

By setting *Protagoras* and *Alcibiades I* around 433, Plato set them shortly before both Socrates and Alcibiades left Athens with the army that eventually besieged Potidaea. This northern city on the isthmus of Pallene in Chalcidice was a tribute-paying member of Athens' empire that had been led to revolt by Corinthians bent on kindling war between Athens and Sparta, the war that broke out in earnest while Socrates was away with the army. He was away for two and a half or three years, returning to Athens only after the Athenian defeat near Potidaea in the spring of 429. When he finally returned, it was to a city enduring its second season of devastating plague and just learning about its defeat at Potidaea after years of siege.

Plato set *Charmides*—a dialogue Socrates narrates to a nameless "friend"—on the day after Socrates' return to Athens from Potidaea: it is late May 429. That date of return announces, by itself, that Socrates returned to a city transformed by war and plague, and he says in *Charmides* that he returns transformed himself, having learned something of high importance while he was away. The transformed Socrates in transformed Athens begins the conversation of *Charmides* by saying he wants to learn something about "things here"—he wants to discover the state of philosophy in Athens and whether any of the young have grown beautiful and wise during his absence. He fully satisfies himself in both respects, and that means, primarily and with respect to the first matter, that Socrates learns what Critias did with his philosophy in his absence—Critias, his prewar associate glimpsed in *Protagoras*; Critias, the man who will become famous as a sophist and, much later, notorious as one of the Thirty Tyrants; Critias, the young man along with Alcibiades for whose corruption Socrates was most blamed right down to his trial and execution. *Charmides*, with fitting restraint, shows Socrates learning that in his absence Critias turned philosophy into an instrument that justified and advanced his own passion to rule. Socrates learns in *Charmides* that the way he transmitted his philosophy to Critias requires of him new modes of transmission entirely.

Plato made the dramatic date of *Charmides* prominent by placing in its first sentence information from which its date can be inferred if other information, offered later, is added. Plato treated the dramatic date of the *Republic* in a similar way: announcing in its first sentence that it occurred on the day Athenians introduced the goddess into Athens, he has Thrasymachus state at the end of his conversation with Socrates that that goddess is Thracian Bendis. The dramatic date of the *Republic*, then, is early June 429. Plato set the *Republic* a few weeks after *Charmides* and indicated the dates of each in the same way, prominently but incompletely in the first sentence of each. Plato seems to want his reader to discover what he refused to say explicitly: *Charmides* and the *Republic* are twinned dialogues with *Charmides* serving as a kind of introduction to the *Republic*. The *Republic* too, then, is a dialogue of the returned Socrates, homecoming after a long absence at war, having learned something significant in his absence, and returning now to a city become different.

The dramatic dates Plato gave his dialogues leads to the conclusion that the origin of Platonic political philosophy is itself a Platonic theme: by placing a gap between *Protagoras* and the *Republic* Plato shows Socrates learning that he will have to undertake a far more radical defense of philosophy than the one he gave in *Protagoras*. The *Republic* will repeat on a grander scale all the themes of *Protagoras,* and a great sophist will be there to take it all in and be reformed by it, young men of political ambition will be there to be transformed by it, and it will all be narrated to an Athenian audience who will be led to think well of philosophy by it. In all essentials, the returned and different Socrates of *Charmides* and the *Republic* is the Socrates who from that point on, publicly at least, remained the same till the end, "always saying the same things about the same things."[11] Part Two of this book, "Philosophy in a Time of Crisis," will deal with *Charmides* and the *Republic*.

Chronology and Exegesis

The chronological arrangement Plato gave his dialogues is prominent in the following chapters partly because it has been neglected but mostly because it serves as one of many tools for a more adequate exegesis of the dialogues, an exegesis that better recovers what Plato placed in them. But if the chronology serves the exegesis, the contrary is also true: the exegesis, in its persuasiveness, its capacity to display Plato's purpose, serves to

11. *Gorgias* 490e.

confirm the importance of the chronology and even the accuracy of particular chronological claims. That the exegesis can support the chronology means more for us than it would for Plato's contemporaries, because chronological cues that sufficed for them are often no longer enough. Plato secured the dramatic date of *Protagoras* for all interested contemporaries by setting it at that moment in Athenian history when three famous sophists were in Athens, a year after a certain comedy by Pherecrates was performed at the Lenaia festival. Exactly when that was may now be impossible to determine—"around 433" may have to suffice for us, whereas Plato's contemporaries could be sure they knew the exact date. But even if the exact date of *Protagoras* is irrecoverable for us, the most important fact about its date is secure: it is set shortly before the war. And exegesis of *Protagoras* can confirm its prewar setting, because exegesis shows a Socrates setting out to instruct Protagoras and lure Alcibiades—and his manner of proceeding in both tasks fits the times, a time of splendor and promise that nevertheless carries with it shadows of what is to come. Exegesis can show that the measures Socrates takes in *Protagoras* for the protection and advancement of philosophy are insufficient for the coming crises, half-measures that will have to be supplanted by more adequate measures that become visible in the first dialogues set in the crisis years.

The chronology of Plato's dialogues serves the exegesis of the dialogues. *Exegesis* is the sustained effort to pursue every detail of the text with a view to a reasoned recovery of everything Plato intended to communicate. Exegesis is what Leo Strauss, its master practitioner and teacher, said it was, "the very long, never easy, but always pleasant work"[12] of studying a great thinker's text in order to advance a reader's conversation with its author, a conversation driven forward by a reader's expectation that the author's generosity has not yet granted everything it wants to grant. By giving his dialogues a chronological order, Plato allows the true magnitude of Socrates' teaching and Socrates' task to rise before his reader's eyes without his having to put it into explicit words; he communicates just who Socrates became by showing him becoming himself. "Become who you are"—Nietzsche used Pindar's words as a sign for his own becoming who he was, a philosopher who gained insight into the fundamental way of all beings and found a mighty task thrust on him.[13] Just so, the chronology Plato gave his dialogues allows him to show Socrates becoming who he was, a philosopher and a political philosopher, a thinker who gained

12. Strauss, *Persecution and the Art of Writing*, 37.

13. Pindar, *Pythian Odes* 2.73; Nietzsche, *Gay Science*, ¶270; *Ecce Homo: How One Becomes What One Is*.

insight into the fundamental way of all beings and subsequently discovered just what fell to him, the task of ensuring that that insight be carried forward on the river of time.

A Nietzschean History of Philosophy

This book too then is an installment in the new history of philosophy made possible by Friedrich Nietzsche.[14] My *Nietzsche and Modern Times* showed how Bacon and Descartes were genuine philosophers in Nietzsche's sense; this book—it might have been called *Nietzsche and Ancient Times*—shows how Plato is a genuine philosopher in Nietzsche's sense. These books take Nietzsche to be the great event in recent philosophy partly because he opened a fruitful and true perspective for our study of the greatest philosophers: they were "commanders and legislators," philosopher rulers who said to their age, "We have to go that way," a different way, an untrod way.[15] Nietzsche shows that philosophic rule is no Platonic dream; it's a Platonic reality made actual again and again by the series of great Platonic political philosophers among whom it is fair to number Nietzsche the latest and Plato the first. Plato came to rule, my book hopes to show, in precisely the way he knew Homer ruled, Homer, "the educator of Greece."[16] The Plato of my book is the Plato Nietzsche recovered, the founding educator of Western civilization, a Platonic civilization whose long, slow rise Nietzsche charted as culminating in those "Platonism[s] for the people" that are Christianity and Christianity's nontheistic extension, modern times, and whose long, slow demise Nietzsche traced in his vivisection of modern nihilism, his "history of the next two centuries,"[17] and whose post-Platonic possible successor Nietzsche had his Zarathustra glimpse from a long way off.

A Nietzschean history of philosophy recovers in Plato what is fundamental to all the greatest philosophers, what ultimately moves or motivates them. Most fundamental are two passions or loves. Philosophy is the passion to understand the whole rationally, the love of wisdom that is, Socrates indicated in the *Symposium*, the highest eros of a whole that can be understood as eros and nothing besides. Political philosophy, the acts of communication and legislation undertaken on behalf of that pri-

14. Lampert, *Nietzsche and Modern Times*, 1–13.
15. Nietzsche, *Beyond Good and Evil*, ¶¶211–12; see Lampert, *Nietzsche's Task*, 196–203.
16. *Republic* 606e.
17. Nietzsche, *Kritische Studienausgabe* 13.11 [411].

mary passion, is driven by love of the human, philanthropy, as Socrates indicated in *Phaedo* where Plato has him pause at the center to state that the greatest evil facing humanity is misology, hatred of logos or reason that entails misanthropy and stems from reason's inability to prove that the world is what the heart most desires it to be. The fundamental connection between these two passions, love of wisdom and love of the human, can be demonstrated exegetically in Plato only through detailed study of the *Symposium* and *Phaedo*, the study to be undertaken in the book to follow this one. The present book concerns Plato's presentation of Socrates' philanthropy. Philanthropy, a now common word, has an uncommon sense in the philosophers, for it denotes action on behalf of the human in its highest reach, its reach for understanding. A Nietzschean history of political philosophy studies the actions undertaken by the greatest thinkers to further the human through the advancement of philosophy. The history of political philosophy, whose opening chapter this book chronicles, is ultimately the history of philosophic philanthropy, philosophic rule on behalf of philosophy.[18]

A Nietzschean history of philosophy explicitly exposes another indispensable element in philosophy: the distinction between exoteric and esoteric known to all philosophers before the modern Enlightenment.[19] When Nietzsche said, "I'm a complete skeptic about Plato" and added, "he's so moralistic,"[20] he offered a key to understanding Plato: Plato's moralism is exoteric, a salutary teaching that must be read skeptically as Plato's instrument to edify or ennoble society and shelter it from philosophy's conclusions, which Plato knew (in Nietzsche's words) were "true but deadly."[21] In all three dialogues discussed in this book the esotericism of the wise emerges as a primary theme. In *Protagoras*, at the opening of his public teaching as Plato presents it, Socrates set out to school Protagoras in a more effective esotericism than the one he was proud of inventing—Protagoras whose very first speeches trumpet his novel solution to the necessity that a wise man speak artfully in order to allay the suspicions he unavoidably triggers. Protagoras and Socrates both know that esotericism—salutary opinions sheltering less than salutary truths—is

18. The theme of philanthropy as the fundamental motive of political philosophy is basic to my previous books. See especially *Nietzsche and Modern Times*, 126–37 (Plato), 137–41 (Bacon), 196, 204–5, 259–71 (Descartes); *Leo Strauss and Nietzsche*, 18, 122–23, 159–61; *Nietzsche's Task*, 71–75, 127–28, 176–79, 301–3.

19. Nietzsche, *Beyond Good and Evil*, ¶30.

20. Nietzsche, *Twilight of the Idols*, "What I Owe to the Ancients," ¶2.

21. Nietzsche, *On the Use and Disadvantage of History*, ¶9.

necessary not only because of persecution: it is dictated above all by "the fundamental requirements of the city," in Leo Strauss's phrase. "Socratic rhetoric is meant to be an indispensable instrument of philosophy. Its purpose is to lead potential philosophers to philosophy both by training them and by liberating them from the charms which obstruct the philosophic effort, as well as to prevent the access to philosophy of those who are not fit for it." This dual function of leading and preventing makes Socratic esotericism "emphatically just. It is animated by the spirit of social responsibility."[22]

For a Nietzschean history of philosophy Leo Strauss is a virtually indispensable resource: he is the first thinker in the long history of esotericism to set out explicitly the reasons why esotericism is inescapable, to list explicitly the many devices of esoteric practice, and to write commentaries on esoteric writings like those of Plato that demonstrate the difference between the exoteric lines and the esoteric sense between them. Strauss's writings—particularly on Plato, Xenophon, and Aristophanes but including his whole body of writings—were indispensable for my book. Also important were the many commentators on Plato who recognize in Strauss a singular teacher; of these by far the richest and most authoritative is Seth

22. Strauss, *On Tyranny*, 6. In *Plato's Philosophers: The Coherence of the Dialogues*, Catherine Zuckert argues that a chronological reading of Plato's dialogues provides new insights into Plato's philosophy; she offers an interpretation of all the dialogues to prove that thesis and show its interpretive worth. I share Zuckert's thesis, but our approaches diverge in important ways. For me, the single most important gain from studying the dialogues chronologically is insight into Socrates becoming Socrates and philosophy becoming Socratic. For Zuckert, the most important gain is indicated by her title, *Plato's Philosophers*: the chronology of the dialogues, she argues, allows Plato to show how Socrates stands to Plato's four other philosophers, the Athenian Stranger of the *Laws*, the Parmenides of *Parmenides*, the Timaeus of *Timaeus-Critias*, and the Eleatic Stranger of the *Sophist* and the *Statesman*. Our books also diverge on the dramatic dates themselves as Zuckert exhibits an unexpected casualness in assigning dramatic dates to some of the dialogues, often accepting consensus views on inadequate grounds; as a result she misdates many dialogues (e.g., *Republic, Timaeus-Critias*, the *Hippias* dialogues) and misses the significance of their chronological settings. But the greatest divergence in our accounts and by far the most important is just who the Socrates is who emerges from a chronological reading of Plato. Hers is a Socrates without irony and therefore without esoteric intent, having no need to shelter a less than salutary true teaching within a salutary exoteric mask. Zuckert reads the words of Plato's Socrates with a relentless literalism that combines close attention to detail with loyalty to first impressions as if they were all that Socrates' exact words imply, as if his words did not also trigger second and third impressions that are co-implied, implied by puzzles or oddities that induce wonder. Because she does not pursue Socrates' esoteric intent into his true radicalism, Zuckert can place Plato's other philosophers on a level with Socrates; she loses Socrates' singularity and fascination by judging him merely a moralist. Still, Zuckert's book (which was published after my book was complete) is an observant, instructive account of the dialogues that offers many new insights from a chronological perspective.

Benardete, who wrote commentaries on Plato but also extended the range of "Platonic" political philosophy back to Homer: his *The Bow and the Lyre: A Platonic Reading of the "Odyssey"* shows Odysseus to be the ancestor of Plato's Socrates in ways that bring to light an unimagined community of kin among the Greek wise made hard to recover by Plato's recognition of his need to break Homer's hold.

Nietzsche is omnipresent in this book if infrequently named on its pages. He properly measured Plato's sway over Western civilization and just what was needed in the cultural catastrophe superficially named "the death of God" but actually the death of Platonism. What was needed was philosophic rule of Platonic dimension and anti-Platonic intent to break Platonism's hold while bringing into the open what Plato believed had to be kept hidden, philosophy's genuine understanding of the way of all beings as eros. A Nietzschean history of philosophy serves the Nietzschean goal for the human future by displaying the kinship of the great Western philosophers, the Platonic-Nietzschean character of their legislative aspiration to rule for the well-being of reason in the world and then, primarily, the Platonic/Nietzschean understanding of what that legislation advanced, insight into the way of all beings as eros or will to power.

PART ONE

Philosophy in a Time of Splendor: Socrates in Periclean Athens before the War, c. 433

CHAPTER 1

Protagoras: Socrates and the Greek Enlightenment

Prologue: Great Protagoras

Historical research plus an act of imagination is now necessary for Plato's *Protagoras* to have its proper shock: Protagoras, widely held by his contemporaries to be the wisest man in Greece, honored and trusted enough to have been invited by Pericles himself to draft the laws of the pan-Hellenic colony of Thurii, old enough now to be father of anyone present at Plato's *Protagoras*, appealing enough to be the main attraction to ambitious young Athenians drawn that day to the house of the richest man in Athens to hear him—that fabled man is defeated in argument by a relatively young Athenian and defeated so soundly that he is reduced at the end to proclaiming his victor his proper successor.

The unrivaled success of Plato's dialogues has transformed Protagoras's word of praise, *sophist*, into a term of abuse and made Socrates philosophy's hero—now everyone expects Protagoras to lose and Socrates to win. And the loss of Protagoras's books, the reduction of his life's work to a few sentences, makes him defenseless before Plato's presentation of Socrates and allows every reader to feel superior to Protagoras in every respect: in moral decency, for Protagoras is now thought morally disreputable even though "virtually everything known of Protagoras suggests that ethically he was a conservative and a traditionalist";[1] in intellectual

1. Schiappa, *Protagoras and Logos*, 107. Among the many accounts of Protagoras, Schiappa's is most effective in showing that Protagoras's high reputation had legitimate grounds; for indica-

acuity, for Protagoras is now imagined to be an intellectual lightweight even though he was the chief founder of the Greek enlightenment, lionized in his own time and long after honored with statues placing him alongside Plato, Heraclitus, and Thales;[2] in the power to attract ambitious young men, even though *Protagoras* itself opens with a young man wanting to use Socrates for nothing more than to introduce him to Protagoras.

Protagoras is the chief founder of the Greek enlightenment, though its roots lie in the investigation of nature that began in Ionian Greece almost a century before Protagoras opened his public career around 460. Although he had precursors, Protagoras was the first to systematically apply the principles of rational or scientific investigation to the natural phenomena of human nature and human culture. He wrote the books that first interpreted humans as that part of nature naturally inclined to develop unnatural or supernatural misunderstandings of nature. Those books spread enlightenment to a wider public beginning to become literate. He was the first to openly call himself a sophist and to travel to the leading cities of greater Greece, setting a pattern for spreading the enlightenment to young men wealthy and ambitious enough to pay for his mentoring. His success generated younger rivals who strove to outdo his books and lectures by producing their own, creating thereby the larger movement of enlightenment out of what started with one man from Abdera.

Plato indicated the singular importance of Protagoras by his chronological ordering of the dialogues. He put Socrates' debate with Protagoras first, at the very opening of his public career, and he put it last as well: *Theaetetus* has a frame set in 369 to introduce the reading of a written dialogue dictated by a Socrates now long dead. Within that dialogue Socrates calls Protagoras back from the dead to defend his views better than his followers can. Socrates debates Protagoras from the beginning of his career to its end; and in written form the debate is perpetual, stretching out into the future as Socratics debate Protagoreans.[3]

---

tions of just how great Protagoras's stature and fame were, see 3–19. With respect to Protagoras's reputation for decency, Walter Burkert, the leading modern authority on Greek religion, comments on his being made the lawgiver of Thurii by Pericles: "Clearly Protagoras' morality was above suspicion" (*Greek Religion*, 312).

2. Schiappa, *Protagoras and Logos*, 15; Schiappa's recovery of Protagoras's reputation includes his reputation as a thinker: his work "was as 'philosophical' (truth-seeking) as it was rhetorical (success-seeking)" (40).

3. Nietzsche enters the debate on the side of Protagoras and states Protagoras's continued importance for the enlightenment: "the Greek culture of the sophists grew out of all the Greek instincts [as that of Plato did not] . . . and it has ultimately shown itself to be right . . . our way of thinking today is to a high degree heraclitean, democritean and protagorean . . . it suffices to say

Only after recovering the greatness of this historic figure in the rational approach to human nature can Plato's *Protagoras* have its proper shock: Socrates is greater still. But in what does Socrates' superior greatness consist? The following account of *Protagoras* pursues that question.

The dramatic date of *Protagoras* places it before the war between Athens and Sparta broke out in 431. For reasons that the details of the dialogue make plausible, that date is uncontroversially set around 433.[4] Thucydides shows that by 433 attentive Athenians could know that war was inevitable, for the Corcyraean ambassadors say so explicitly.[5] Plato set *Protagoras* in prewar Athens with Socrates about thirty-six and Protagoras in his mid-sixties. Hippocrates is about seventeen, as is Callias; Alcibiades is not yet twenty, and Critias somewhat older at twenty-seven; Prodicus and Hippias are both about Socrates' age.

1. First Words

"From where, Socrates, are you appearing?"[6] The Platonic corpus opens with the appropriate question. It is put by a nameless Athenian, a "comrade," like a shipmate or messmate—not *friend*.[7] The nameless questioner leaps to the answer he believes he already knows: "Or isn't it plain that it's from the hunt for the vernal beauty of Alcibiades?" This question and this answer, both made so prominent as the chronologically first question and answer put to Plato's Socrates, appear as the question and answer Athenians in general would naturally have in 433 about their odd countryman and the attentions he so evidently and for such a long time paid to their most spectacular offspring.[8] They are, in a way, also the last question and answer Athenians had about Socrates, the fatal question and answer about Socrates' corruption of Alcibiades and other young Athenians, which they

that it is *protagorean* because Protagoras took both pieces, Heraclitus and Democritus, together into himself." *KSA* 13:14 [116]; *Will to Power* ¶428.

4. See below, "Note on the Dramatic Date of *Protagoras* and *Alcibiades I*."

5. Thucydides 1.31–36; see below, 48–49.

6. I have benefited greatly from a privately printed translation of *Protagoras* by Leon Craig; it is rigorous in being "as literal as possible consistent with grammatical English and intelligibility" (1); it is superior to all the existing English translations I know. I have modified it slightly on occasion.

7. The list of characters calls him *hetairos* (comrade, companion, fellow, mate); Socrates calls him *makarios* (309c), "blessed, happy, fortunate," a member of the upper classes.

8. *Alcibiades I* opens stating that Socrates consistently and openly observed Alcibiades from the time of his earliest youth without actually addressing him until the occasion of that dialogue itself.

acted on by indicting, convicting, and executing him some thirty-four years later.

But the question itself, allowed to stand alone, freed from the rush to the common answer and instead put slowly as a true interrogative asked by those made friends of Socrates by Plato's dialogues—that question is the essential question: from where did Socrates, that singularity in the history of Greek philosophy, appear? Out of what did he arise, or what was the occasion of his arising and growing into himself? The question asks, further, how did Socrates, having become himself, *appear* or let himself be seen? Posed this way, the question that opens *Protagoras* and the whole Platonic corpus does not lead immediately to his hunt for Alcibiades. Its first word—*From where?* (*Pothen*)—leads backward to the Socrates who has already become himself before the Platonic dialogues begin: by posing that question on behalf of their devoted readers, Plato's dialogues open on a question to which the dialogues themselves will offer a different answer from that of his Athenian contemporary, one that readers can recover only retrospectively, by looking backward through the dialogues themselves into what they offer about Socrates' true origins as a philosopher.

As for the second part of the question—from where are you *appearing?*—*Protagoras*, both in its frame and in its core conversation, urges a different answer on the questioner from the one he so automatically supplied. Socrates actively diverts his questioner's attention away from his pursuit of Alcibiades to fix it on a different pursuit, a contest he ignited between himself and Protagoras, who the questioner thinks is the wisest man of their time. Socrates makes that contest originate in his concern about the education of another young Athenian, Hippocrates, whom Socrates introduces uninvited into his narration of the conversation from which he is appearing. He makes it appear that he is appearing from a contest that serves a civic purpose: sheltering young Athenians from the whole set of suspected corrupters, foreign sophists eager to attract Athenian young. When Socrates first appears, *Protagoras* suggests, he looks to his appearance.

Before Socrates says a word, his questioner adds the accusation of his second question; while playful enough and merely a question, it carries an undercurrent of menace as a harbinger of the accusation for which Socrates will be executed: "And he certainly did appear to me still a beautiful man when I saw him the day before yesterday, but a *man* for all that, Socrates, strictly between ourselves, and already sprouting a beard." Having sprouted a beard, Alcibiades is beyond the age during which Athenian custom permitted older males decently to pursue adolescent males: Socrates' pursuit of Alcibiades borders on the criminal or at least the disreputable.

Socrates' very first words are also a question that leads to a further question. "What of that?" he asks first, a response of mild defiance that puts a question to Athenian custom. But if this question too is allowed to stand alone, it too seems definitive, wholly appropriate as Socrates' first words. Here is the interrogating attitude with which Socrates approached everything he encountered; here is the refusal to take as settled even the settled things of customary practice and conviction. His next question implies that he follows a higher authority than Athenian custom: "Are you not then a praiser of Homer who said that youth has the highest grace in him with the first down upon his lip, which Alcibiades has now?" This judgment by Homer appears in each of his poems and each time describes Hermes in disguise coming to the aid of an older man undertaking a harrowing task, Priam in the *Iliad* (24.348) and Odysseus in the *Odyssey* (10.279). It is Hermes in the *Odyssey*, Hermes with Odysseus that adds startling gravity to Socrates' first words.[9] For the event in the *Odyssey* to which Socrates refers in his first speech in the Platonic corpus provides an uncanny portrait of just who Socrates himself is at this point and what his purpose is. Hermes with the first down upon his lip appears to Odysseus just after Odysseus made his decision to come to the aid of his men, a decision that followed the disaster with the Laestrygonians in which he lost eleven of his twelve ships and their crews because of what must be judged his "criminal negligence."[10] Circe's drug has transformed half of Odysseus's remaining men into swine with human minds, and Odysseus is on his way to help them somehow when Hermes appears suddenly and gives him the one gift that will enable him to resist Circe's enchantment. It is perhaps the single most important moment in Odysseus's odyssey to wisdom when, resolved to help his men, he is favored by Hermes who shows him the nature (*physis*, appearing only here in the Homeric corpus) of a plant "black in its root and its flower like milk; the gods call it *moly*, but it is hard for mortal men to dig up, but the gods can do everything."[11] Armed now with what is hard to dig up, a knowledge of nature, immunized, that is, against the enchantment before which his men have no defense, Odysseus succeeds in delivering them from Circe's drug. Who is Socrates at the opening of the

9. Segvic, "Homer in Plato's *Protagoras*," 247–51, also interprets Socrates' words as referring to the events in the *Odyssey* and not to Hermes' appearance in the *Iliad*, though for slightly different reasons.

10. See Benardete, *Bow and the Lyre*, 114; see 84–89 on Hermes' gift to Odysseus. Benardete's guidance to the *Odyssey* is indispensable in bringing to light Homer's oblique and profound teaching.

11. *Odyssey* 10.304–6.

Platonic corpus? He is a praiser of Homer who is like Homer's Odysseus in having been favored with a knowledge of nature. And what is Socrates doing at the opening of the Platonic corpus? He is resolutely turning to an act of rescue that he alone, because of his knowledge of nature, can perform.

Can all that actually be intended by Plato in a citation from Homer? Plato never let off combing and curling his dialogues, paying special attention to their openings, and this is the chronological opening of his whole corpus. When the first words of other dialogues are studied, their art of allusion helps confirm the importance of this allusion—as does Plato's treatment of Homer in the three dialogues studied in this book: Plato comes to light as "a praiser of Homer" like no other. While it need not be fully credited at the beginning, there it stands, glorious, in Socrates' first speech in the Platonic corpus, a claim to the most supreme achievements of knowledge and rescue attained by Homer's Odysseus. A more awesome opening to the Platonic corpus is scarcely imaginable. From where, Socrates, are you appearing? From an understanding of nature on the way to delivering my people from enchantment.

2. The Frame Conversation (309a–310a)

The frame conversation opens *Protagoras* with a brief performed dialogue[12] that sets the conditions under which the long core conversation—a narrated dialogue—is spoken and establishes to whom it is spoken: the nameless questioner and others not identified in any way. After both the questioner and Socrates have made their initial speeches, the questioner responds to Socrates' invocation of Homer's authority by yielding entirely: having just referred to Alcibiades twice as a man (*anêr*), he now calls him a youth (*neanias*, 309b). Still, he speaks like an inquisitor, insistently putting three questions to Socrates: "How are things now? Are you in fact just appearing from him? And how is the youth disposed toward you?" Socrates answers all three questions but puts his answer to the central question last: "Well disposed, it seemed to me, and not least on this very day, for he spoke up a lot as my ally, coming to my aid, and in fact I only just left him" (309b). It is that last fact that Socrates addresses, beginning to cast doubt on his questioner's insinuation that he's coming from a hunt for Al-

12. See *Republic* 392d–394d where Socrates uses the opening of the *Iliad* to explain to Adeimantus the difference between a narrative that is simple and one that is produced by imitation or by both together (392d). On those terms, *Protagoras* is like the *Iliad* in beginning with simple narrative and switching to imitation.

cibiades. He wants to tell him "something rather strange": even though Alcibiades was present, "I not only paid him no attention, several times I quite forgot about him." His questioner can hardly believe it but assumes that if Socrates forgot about beautiful Alcibiades, it could only be because of the presence of someone more beautiful. Through his insistent questions he learns that there is someone, some foreigner from Abdera, more beautiful even than Kleinias's son because "how could the greatest wisdom not appear more beautiful?" (309c). Baffled by Socrates' drawn-out withholding of the name of the competing beauty, the questioner asks: "So it's having just met someone wise that you're present with us then, Socrates?" Socrates employs the superlative, "the wisest of any now living, it may be," but he adds a conditional: "if, that is, it seems to you that the wisest is—Protagoras." Having finally heard the beauty's name, the questioner asks: "What are you saying? Protagoras has come to town?"

The questioner learns only now that Protagoras is in town, Protagoras, the most famous wise man in the Greek world, a former resident of Athens, visiting now after many years' absence and staying at the home of the richest man in town along with other famous, younger wise men. The questioner has betrayed a truth about himself: he cannot belong to the intellectual circles of Athens and so not to Socrates' circle. Not only does Socrates know how long Protagoras has been in Athens, he knows where he's staying, who's with him (314b–c), and that he spends most of his time there (311a).[13] Two salient features of the anonymous audience to whom Socrates narrates the core conversation of *Protagoras* thus come to light: limited interest in intellectual matters coupled with considerable interest in Socrates' love affairs.[14]

Plato's indications about Socrates' audience take on their appropriate weight only as Socrates' narration advances, for both Protagoras and Socrates state that there is a problematic relation between the wise and the public to which the wisest have devoted considerable thought. That relation becomes one of the great themes of the chronologically first dia-

13. When Hippocrates doesn't know that Protagoras is in town Socrates expresses surprise: "You've only just found out?" (310b), and Hippocrates has to explain that he has been away from Athens proper hunting down a runaway slave. Protagoras was likely in Athens last in 443 when, at Pericles' direction, he developed the laws of Thurii, a panhellenic colony in Italy (Diogenes Laertius 9.50; see also Ehrenberg, "Foundation of Thurii"; and Muir, "Protagoras and Education at Thurii."

14. For a chronological study of the dialogues it is important that the interests of the frame audience of *Protagoras* are similar to those of the frame audience supplied twice in the *Symposium*: from the beginning to the end of Socrates' career he faced publics more interested in his love affairs and his practices than in philosophy.

logue, and it focuses on the calculations the wise must make in allowing their wisdom to become public—the *exotericism* of the wise, their studied, cosmetic appearance. But then the whole of Socrates' narration falls under a very precise suspicion: Is Socrates' narration itself an example of how he thinks the wise should make their private words and deeds public? After Socrates' indications about esotericism become visible, the only reasonable answer is Yes. Plato opens his corpus fittingly: a narration presenting itself as an open report to the public on private events that happened behind locked doors has its own ways of locking up its private contents.

But Socrates' questioner was right—he *is* just coming from Alcibiades. The very first words ("From where, Socrates, are you appearing?") dovetail with the very last words of Socrates' narration—"Saying and hearing these things, we departed." Plato makes the whole dialogue seem to cycle back on itself, its opening and closing words making it appear as a closed circle consisting of a private event and its immediate public retelling. Before that retelling Socrates redirects his questioner's attention away from Alcibiades and on to Protagoras, that allegedly wisest man of his time. "And it's from being with *that* one that you now come?" the questioner asks (309d). "Yes indeed, having said and heard much," Socrates answers, using the same verbs he will use to end his narration. Socrates thus creates the impression that yes, he's just come from Protagoras rather than from Alcibiades, and that he has a greater interest in the more beautiful Protagoras than in Alcibiades.

The questioner seems in fact to regard Protagoras as the wisest of any then living, for he is interested enough in what Socrates said and heard with Protagoras to ask him to "narrate to us the being-together—if nothing prevents you" (310a). Nothing prevents him for he does what his questioner told him to do: make the questioner's slave boy give up his sitting place and sit there himself. It is from the seat of the questioner's slave that Socrates narrates the whole conversation: Socrates seems to have been placed under a kind of compulsion to obey what the slave's master asked of him. Is Socrates' narration of what he said and heard compelled or voluntary? It seems he *wanted* to narrate it, given the inducements he offered his questioner about the beauty of the wisest man now living; it seems he wanted to be compelled. His whole narration from the slave's seat will indicate that Socrates narrates under *self*-compulsion, for he brings to light just what it was that forced him, a private man, to go public.

Nothing prevents Socrates from narrating the whole conversation. If his auditors listen at all attentively they will notice that twice in his narration, at its center and at its end, Socrates states that he has business to attend to and must leave the gathering: if they listen attentively they learn that Socrates misled that earlier audience because nothing prevents his relating the whole conversation to them. The frame audience might also notice that Socrates misled his questioner: he tells Hippocrates that he does not think Protagoras is wise, so he can hardly think him more beautiful than Alcibiades—the reason he gave his questioner for forgetting Alcibiades does not hold up. As for Socrates forgetting, he reports the whole conversation, and when once he alleges forgetfulness (334c–d) Alcibiades assures everyone that Socrates has not forgotten (336d).[15] By leading his audience to think he forgot Alcibiades, he leads *them* to forget Alcibiades. He never forgets Alcibiades, and his narration, heard with attention to Alcibiades, proves the questioner right: Socrates *was* returning from a hunt for Alcibiades. It proves too that Alcibiades is a quarry worthy of a hunt, for although he is not yet twenty, he listens better than anyone else and reacts with a confidence that allows him to take charge.

Chronologically Plato's dialogues begin with Socrates mounting the stage to report to a wider Athenian audience events that just transpired in private, events of great public interest showing the next generation of Athenian leadership eagerly seeking out foreign teachers about whom Athenians had naturally grown suspicious. Plato begins with a fitting act for the Athenian philosopher who became famous for being open and public: he narrates for an Athenian public a private conversation displaying the gripping, intensely important relation between foreign sophists and potentially powerful young Athenians. And Socrates? He mounts the Platonic stage to betray that privacy and to show publicly that he faced down the great man of the Greek enlightenment and defeated him in the presence of the best Athenian young. He flaunts his victory to a public that began by expressing suspicions about his pursuit of the most gifted of the Athenian young. In *Protagoras* Socrates mounts the stage to win Athenians over to him; his first public narration in the Platonic dialogues, like his last, is an apology, a public defense of himself and philosophy.

In the final exchange of the frame Socrates says he "will be grateful if you [all] listen"; his gratitude is understandable given the necessity of allaying their suspicion about his pursuit of Alcibiades. His questioner states that

15. Other instances of forgetting occur in the dialogue. Alcibiades accuses all but Socrates of forgetting (336d). Protagoras accuses Simonides of forgetting his point in a poem Socrates defends as consistent (339d). Hippocrates forgot to tell Socrates that he left town in pursuit of his slave Satyrus (310c). The actions of Epimetheus involve forgetting (321b–c, 361c–d), and the actions of Prometheus seem not to.

they will be grateful if he speaks; their gratitude is understandable because their interest in his pursuit of Alcibiades has become an interest in learning how the wisdom of the wisest can be more beautiful than Alcibiades. Each is grateful to the other at the start; each will be satisfied with the other at the end, Socrates satisfied that he allayed their suspicion, his audience satisfied that their original suspicion has been replaced by the salutary opinion that Socrates defends Athenian youths against foreign wise men. Each will be able to be grateful to the other at the end because obedient Socrates in fact takes command from the slave's seat: "But now listen."

3. Socrates with a Young Athenian (310a–314c)

Wholly on his own initiative and before telling the frame audience anything he promised them, Socrates takes them into the privacy of his own bedroom before dawn that morning to tell them how he dealt with an ambitious young Athenian eager to be taught by Protagoras. He thus takes an audience suspicious of his hunt for Alcibiades into what they could think his deepest privacy, in bed in the dark, alone with a young follower feeling around for him.[16] And they hear him speak in an edifying way, warning the young Athenian to be wary of what he may buy from a foreign sophist unknowingly, possibly taking evils into his soul that may harm it. Hippocrates is unknown to the frame audience, for Socrates has to identify him not only by his patronym, as the son of Apollodoros, but also by his brother's name.[17] Unknown Hippocrates comes vividly to life in the events and speeches Socrates narrates about him—making it all the more puzzling that he disappears after Socrates introduces him to Protagoras except for a single early mention (327d).

Hippocrates hammers at Socrates' door before dawn and when he is let in rushes to Socrates' room demanding in a loud voice if he is awake or asleep. Groping in the dark for Socrates' bed, he sits down by his feet to relate his tale. He was away from Athens chasing down his runaway slave, and when he returned and his brother told him Protagoras was in town, he rushed off immediately toward Socrates' house even though he had been getting reading for bed. He wanted Socrates to introduce him to Protagoras—he is no more loath to use Socrates for his ends with Protago-

16. Cf. *Symposium* 219b–d.

17. An Apollodoros narrates the *Symposium* and is present at Socrates' trial (*Apology* 38b) and at the discussion narrated in *Phaedo* (59b, 117d). Debra Nails, *People of Plato*, 169f., presents evidence for Hippocrates' being the nephew of Pericles, but this clashes with his evident obscurity.

ras than he would be to use his friends' money to pay Protagoras (310e). He restrained himself last night because he was tired (310c), not because it was an inappropriate time to visit either Socrates or Protagoras. So he slept briefly before rushing to Socrates before dawn, and dawn comes early on a summer day in Athens. Socrates identifies him as courageous and vehement (310d): his vehemence or excitability seems to be the ground of his courage. Socrates knows Hippocrates well enough to recognize his voice in the dark (310b), and he asks the natural question at being so rudely awakened: is anything wrong? He neither rebukes Hippocrates nor dismisses him when told his reason for being there so early. Instead, he asks what Protagoras's presence in Athens has to do with him: "Has Protagoras done you some injustice?" Hippocrates responds with a laugh and a little joke: "Yes, by the gods, Socrates. Because he alone is wise, but is not making me so." Hippocrates' laugh is the first of three reactions Socrates reports, and the three mark the changes in Hippocrates as Socrates' questioning subtracts his outrageous self-indulgence and fits him to listen to Socrates' instruction.[18]

"Let's go!" Hippocrates says, after informing Socrates of how he intends to use him. Socrates restrains him, for not only does he know that Protagoras is staying at Callias's house, he knows as well that they will likely find Protagoras at home for he usually stays indoors. Instead of leaving in the predawn darkness, Socrates suggests they stroll around in the courtyard until it is light and then go. He informs the frame audience but not Hippocrates of his intention in examining Hippocrates: "to test the strength of Hippocrates' resolve" (311b)—his *resolve* and not his competence, for Socrates seems to know that already. His examination of Hippocrates is chronologically the first Socratic examination in the Platonic corpus; introduced wholly on Socrates' initiative, it is a paradigm examination even if Hippocrates is not a paradigm student.

Socrates presses a twofold question: Hippocrates will pay Protagoras a fee "in his capacity as a *what*?" and "in order to *become what*?" (311b). The

18. These opening events of the first day of Socrates' public life as recorded by Plato resemble events that opened one of the last days Plato records of Socrates' life: when Crito turns up before dawn in Socrates' cell, he too gropes for the end of Socrates' bed. Both dialogues show Socrates in complete privacy speaking to a countryman, one young, one old, and both show Socrates speaking as a loyal citizen, giving lessons of loyalty to one's own. From start to finish of Plato's record of Socrates' public life in Athens, he shows him speaking in private of public loyalty. On similarities between the scene with Hippocrates and the opening of *Crito*, see Strauss, "Plato's *Apology of Socrates* and *Crito*," *Studies in Platonic Political Philosophy*, 54–55; and Landy, "Virtue, Art, and the Good Life in Plato's *Protagoras*," 303–4.

questions seem impossibly hard for Hippocrates who, for all his impetuous action, is slow to answer simple questions. To clarify his twofold question Socrates has to supply three examples, beginning with Hippocrates' renowned namesake from Cos, the founder of Greek scientific medicine. In the course of his questioning, Socrates invents a "someone" to pose the questions, a device that allows him to become Hippocrates' ally, uniting the two of them in face of a common adversary with hard questions, a device Socrates will employ with Protagoras. Socrates pictures them going to Protagoras to pay him—and being willing to spend their friends' money as well—and his "someone" asks them together (311d): "you are intending to spend money on Protagoras in his capacity as a *what*?" Laborious prompting is still necessary before Hippocrates answers: "'Well,' he said, 'a sophist is what they call the man, Socrates.'" Finally. The "someone" can now pose the second part of the question in the singular: "You are going to Protagoras with a view to becoming *what*?" The answer almost dictated by the previous examples is obvious even to Hippocrates, but before Socrates reports his answer he tells the frame audience the second of Hippocrates' three reactions to his questioning: "And he said *blushing*—for enough of the day was dawning that he became fully visible." It is this blush, this sign of Hippocrates' shame, that Socrates emphasizes in his response, though he well knows that Hippocrates has no intention of becoming anything so unmanly as a sophist and is embarrassed even to think of it: "But in the name of the gods!"[19] he says, "wouldn't you be ashamed to present yourself to the Greeks as a sophist?" "Yes, by Zeus, Socrates," Hippocrates says, "if I must say what I think!" And the sophist Protagoras? He is the only other person in *Protagoras* said to be ashamed (348c), but he does not blush—does he say what he thinks? He indicates that he says only what he thinks is *necessary*. Socrates' question was narrow: the shame is "presenting yourself to the Greeks as a sophist." Greeks regard sophistry as shameful and Hippocrates shares that sense, but Protagoras is proud to present himself as the founder of sophism, having given himself that name and applied it to others. Still, he knows what the Greeks think and that he cannot simply say what he thinks.

Socrates gives Hippocrates a way out of the shameful thought, suggesting that Hippocrates is going to Protagoras for the kind of learning he

19. Socrates utters his only two oaths in their exchange in connection with Hippocrates' first two reactions, first, "by Zeus" and here "by the gods." See Coby, *Socrates and the Sophistic Enlightenment*, 28–29. Coby's commentary on *Protagoras* has something useful to say on almost every aspect of the dialogue.

received from his writing teacher or athletic trainer: he did not learn from them how to practice their *technai* but learned the education befitting a layman and a free man (312b). Hippocrates welcomes this escape only to be faced with another question. Socrates describes what Hippocrates is about to do: "place your own soul in the care of a man who is, as you declare, a sophist, yet I'd be filled with wonder if you knew just what a sophist is. And yet, if you don't know that, you don't know whether the business to which you have entrusted your soul is good or bad." Socrates said that he was testing Hippocrates' resolve, and Hippocrates shows he can still be resolute: "I think I do know," he says, unwittingly betraying that worst of all conditions, thinking he knows what he doesn't know.[20] "All right, tell me," Socrates says. Poor Hippocrates. It's inevitable now that his ignorance come into the open. Still, he does his resolute best to defend his claimed knowledge. His first stab merely shuffles the letters of "sophist": "one who's knowledgeable about the *sophôn*"—the wise things. "One could say as much of painters and carpenters," Socrates says, but again he takes Hippocrates' side, calling in that "someone" to question them both about the claim Hippocrates alone made. Socrates even answers his invented questioner, leading Hippocrates to answers he is unable to muster on his own: they should tell their questioner that painters are knowledgeable about "the production of images, and so on with the others." But what a sophist is knowledgeable about Socrates leaves to Hippocrates, while giving him considerable prompting: "But what if someone were to ask, 'As for the sophist, what are his wise things?' What would we answer him? Knowledgeable for making what product?" Hippocrates is tentative and answers questioningly with his last positive contribution: "What should we say, Socrates, except that he knows how to make one clever at speaking?" Here is what he's rushing off to Protagoras to receive, as Socrates knew. His response is gracious: "Likely what we would say is true," but he adds that it is not sufficient for it raises the further question "as to *what* the sophist makes one clever at speaking about" (312d). Socrates' prompting now gives Hippocrates all the words and he can say only "Yes" and "Likely" to the suggestions. Finally Socrates puts the question directly: "But what *is* this about which, being knowledgeable himself, the sophist makes his student knowledgeable as well?" Resolute Hippocrates is finished: "By Zeus, I have nothing left to say to you!" The question should be simple enough for a young man bent on becoming notable in the city (316c); he should be able to examine himself and give a simple answer to what he so passionately

20. *Apology* 21d.

wants from Protagoras. But he is speechless; his resolute insistence that he knew has been exposed as actual ignorance.

With Hippocrates' surrender, Socrates can speak didactically; he is severe in chastising him for risking the care of his soul to "this foreigner who has just arrived" (313a–b). Socrates derides a *foreigner* while elevating the familial and the local: he's not reluctant, for Hippocrates' sake and for the sake of his Athenian auditors, to appeal to the common prejudice in favor of one's own and against the foreign, though he can hardly share that prejudice as the measure of a teacher's worth. Socrates' rebuke becomes a tongue-lashing, relentless in picking up every item of their exchange and throwing it back at Hippocrates in accusation (313b–c). He does so now and not then, back in his room in the dark, for Hippocrates was not ready to attend to it. Can Hippocrates benefit? His response is meek: "So it seems, Socrates, from what you've been saying." Far more telling than his yielding words is Socrates' preface to them, his third and final report on Hippocrates' reactions: "And he, listening, replied." Hippocrates *laughed*. Then he *blushed*. Finally he *listened*.[21] The paradigm sequence of responses sets a pattern, for Socrates will lead Protagoras himself through these stages. Protagoras's resolve will be greater; he will offer incomparably better resistance for he is a man of extreme competence with a reputation to defend—and he is not betrayed by a blush. Still, Socrates moves him too from an initial self-confidence, through shame, to a position of listening achieved only at the very end.

Socrates' instruction now becomes explicit as he asks a Hippocrates who knows he does not know just what a sophist is: "some sort of merchant or dealer in wares by which the soul is nourished?" Hippocrates responds perfectly, with the last words he is to utter in the dialogue, unattributed words that ask of Socrates what can best be asked of him: "But a soul is nourished, Socrates, *by what*?" Hippocrates is not a model learner, being far too slow on the uptake, but here he models the appropriate learning and asks Socrates a Socratic question, a "What is . . . ?" question, the kind of question he has heard Socrates asking from the beginning that morning. In response to a now listening Hippocrates, Socrates becomes the teacher

21. Plato's exact words for these three events indicate that they belong together. Each begins a sentence with *kai* (and), each follows with the demonstrative pronoun *hos* (that one or he), and each adds an aorist participle describing Hippocrates' reaction. The "and" binds the reaction to what preceded; the "he" makes it emphatically Hippocrates' action; the participles state the decisive progress in Socrates' examination.

Hippocrates did not seek out. But instead of saying what nourishes the soul, Socrates says what a sophist is. His lesson is based on a simple but memorable analogy distinguishing those who sell wares that nourish the body and those who sell wares that nourish the soul: like the former, sophists are merchants and hucksters who do not know which of the wares they peddle is useful and which is worthless; they praise everything they sell, and the buyer needs to be guided by someone who does know, some "doctor of the soul," for the sophist's wares are carried away in the very soul of the hearer. He ends his speech uniting with Hippocrates, "let's examine these matters further with our elders," alleging that they are both "still rather young to exercise discretion over such an important matter." "Let's go, just as we started to do." But now that he has shown the danger, why would Socrates expose Hippocrates to it? Because exposing his soul to Protagoras's soul-damaging wares leads to exposing it to a soul doctor who knows what is useful for it: Socrates takes Hippocrates to Protagoras to hear what Socrates has to sell.

The chronologically first Socratic examination in the Platonic corpus is a model of Socratic success. Yet it ends atypically on a didactic speech in which he tells his listener what to learn. Perhaps this feature can be accounted for by another difference, the presence of an *audience* suspicious of Socrates' pursuit of Alcibiades. "Listen," Socrates told them just before giving them privileged access to his privacy, and they hear Socrates warn a young Athenian of the dangers of consulting foreigners rather than family and countrymen. Socrates' gratitude for their listening must stem at least in part from his felt need to alter their view of him.

"Let's go," Socrates says to Hippocrates, and he mentions others who are there: Hippias of Elis, and "Prodicus of Ceos too, I think—and many others, also wise" (314c). Knowing this much about who's there, Socrates certainly knows that other young Athenians will gather at Callias's house, as eager as Hippocrates to learn from the greatest wise men of Greece. He may even know that that young Athenian will be there who complains at the opening of their very first conversation together that Socrates has always taken "such trouble to be present wherever I happen to be,"[22] the young Athenian whom Socrates is suspected of hunting down at the opening of *Protagoras*. "Let's go"—could Socrates' own eagerness to go be partly because he's on a hunt for the vernal beauty of Alcibiades?

22. *Alcibiades I* 104d.

4. Socrates in Hades (314c–316b)

When Socrates and Hippocrates arrive at Callias's house, Socrates reports, they do not enter immediately but stop in the doorway to complete an argument they began on the way. He does not say what the argument was, but he does speculate on its effect: he thinks Callias's doorkeeper must have overheard it and concluded that they were sophists wanting to see Callias. The doorkeeper forcibly slams the door in their faces and locks it against them, only reluctantly granting them admission after being told that they are not sophists and have come to see Protagoras. Socrates seems indistinguishable from a sophist; and the discussions he will report to the frame audience take place behind closed doors. The difficulties they face in entering contribute to what Socrates will suggest is happening: they are entering Hades, whose entryway is guarded by Cerberus.

Entering Callias's house, they pass into what must be a magnificent courtyard befitting the wealthiest family of the richest city in Greece—an interior familiar to Socrates, for he knows that Callias's father used to use as a storeroom the room in which Prodicus reclines (315d). He describes the strikingly different stations and stances of the three sophists: Protagoras strides up and down the portico with three followers on each side and more behind, all streaming in choreographed precision; Hippias is seated in the opposite portico, his followers sitting in front of him asking questions he answers from on high; Prodicus is reclining under blankets in a room off to the side, discussing with followers reclining beside him. Protagoras speaks to worshipful listeners, and Socrates says he is "like Orpheus" in bringing order to those he enchants; Hippias authoritatively answers questions about nature and the things aloft; Prodicus, protected under blankets, is protected as well in what he says, for the deep resonance of his voice echoes in the chamber, making his words indecipherable by one "standing outside" (315e)—a significant detail given what Socrates later says about the need for the wise to shelter their words. Perhaps that is part of the reason Socrates singles Prodicus out: "he seems to me to be a very wise man and divine" (315a).

After describing Protagoras, Socrates names Homer again and quotes phrases that make him Odysseus in Hades. "'After him I beheld,' as Homer says"[23] (315b)—Homer's Odysseus says this when he beholds the last of the twenty-six shades he names in Hades, Heracles, or rather his image,

23. *Odyssey* 11.601.

as Heracles himself is on Olympus. Protagoras would then be the twenty-fifth, Sisyphus, the wise man punished by the gods for scorning them.[24] "Tantylus then I espied"[25] (315c)—Socrates uses Odysseus's words to make Prodicus the twenty-fourth shade seen by Odysseus. He thus links the three sophists with all three Odysseus saw last in Hades. Socrates' first words quoted Homer and suggested that he likened himself to Odysseus; his final naming of Homer will suggest that he assumes the role of Odysseus (348d); and here he likens himself to Odysseus in Hades. In the chronologically first dialogue, as in *Charmides* and the *Republic*, Odysseus is the paradigm figure Plato evokes as a means for measuring Socrates in both his nature and his ambition.[26]

Present with the three sophists in this underworld of instruction is the cream of Athenian aristocratic youth mixed with foreigners who have already been made followers of sophists. The list of young Athenians present will interest the auditors because it names the offspring of some of the oldest and most powerful Athenian families. In the two lines of three marching alongside Protagoras are Callias, their host, his maternal half-brother Paralus, one of the two sons of Pericles,[27] and Charmides, Plato's uncle, a mere boy now but a young man grown beautiful when Socrates returns from Potidaea in *Charmides*. The other line includes Pericles' other son, Xanthippus, and Philippides, scion of a wealthy Athenian family. The Athenians seated in front of Hippias are Eryximachus and Phaedrus, who appear together again in the *Symposium*, and Andron, a future member of the oligarchy of the Four Hundred in 411. Those Socrates names as reclining beside Prodicus are all Athenians: Pausanias and Agathon, who are again paired in the *Symposium*,[28] and "the two Adeimantuses," one of whom, the son of Cepis, is otherwise unknown, whereas the other, the son of Leucolophides, became an Athenian general late in the war.[29]

24. At the end of his final speech in Plato's *Apology*, Socrates names Sisyphus last (after Odysseus) among those he would examine in Hades; examining them, he says, would be "immeasurable happiness" (41c).

25. *Odyssey* 11.582.

26. Planinc, *Plato through Homer*, 13: "The *Odyssey* is not the only source text used in composing [Plato's] dialogues, but it is by far the most important."

27. The younger son of Pericles and Xanthippus, named after Pericles' father. The sons' mother later married Hipponicus and bore him Callias. See Nails, *People of Plato*, 224, "The Stemma of Pericles."

28. None of the Athenians around Protagoras appear in the *Symposium*.

29. It is noteworthy that many of these young Athenians are included in the lists of those suspected of the two great religious crimes of 415, the profaning of the Mysteries and the mutilation of the Herms. See Andocides, "On the Mysteries," 101–40.

But where is Alcibiades? The frame audience expressed great interest in him, and Plato's readers will share that interest. Nothing about him in this dialogue is incidental, including the way he enters. "We"—Socrates and Hippocrates—"had only just come in when behind us came Alcibiades, the beautiful, as you say, and I am persuaded, and Critias son of Callaeschrus" (316a).[30] For the only time in his narration Socrates directly addresses his auditor—"you" in the singular—acknowledging his great interest in Alcibiades. And those already present in Callias's house? From their perspective the entry of these two young men just after Socrates' entry with Hippocrates would look like the arrival of a fourth group of teacher and pupils, a local group, arriving late with Socrates leading three young Athenians, Alcibiades, Critias, and Hippocrates. Socrates' report on the entry of Alcibiades and Critias contains a small ambiguity: he has just used *we* (*hêmeis*) to designate himself and Hippocrates, and he uses *we* again after stating that Alcibiades and Critias had just come in: "We had entered then, and having paused over some small matters and examined them, then went up to Protagoras." Is this *we* still just Socrates and Hippocrates, or does it include the two whose arrival he has just inserted? Socrates quietly resolves what he made ambiguous after the first exchange with Protagoras, for he describes how all three groups came together: the group around Protagoras including himself and Hippocrates decides they will gather the others, and "Callias and Alcibiades came bringing Prodicus" and his group (317e). Callias had been with Protagoras, and it seems that the only reason for mentioning Alcibiades with Callias is to indicate that he had also been with the group around Protagoras. The *we* who paused over "small matters" before going to Protagoras therefore included Alcibiades—he was present at the first, critically important conversation with Protagoras, present when Socrates spoke of matters bound to excite and goad him.

By making it possible to infer the presence of Alcibiades at the first conversation with Protagoras—and by making it necessary to merely infer it—Socrates offers an early sign of a whole array of coming signs: the ser-

30. Plato thus places together at the chronological beginning of his dialogues the two associates of Socrates who later became famous Athenian criminals and did Socrates the greatest damage. In his *Memorabilia* Xenophon also introduces Alcibiades and Critias as a pair, the only two "the accuser" names in the second charge against Socrates, his corruption of the young: "Critias was the most thievish, violent, and murderous of all in the oligarchy, and Alcibiades the most incontinent, insolent, and violent of all in the democracy" (1.2.12). Xenophon prepares his defense by describing them together as "by nature the most honor-loving [or ambitious] of all the Athenians. They wished that all affairs might be conducted through themselves and that they might become the most renowned of all" (1.2.14).

vice Socrates ostensibly performs for foolish young Hippocrates he in fact performs for a young Athenian of far greater promise to whom Protagoras's wares are a far greater threat both to himself and to Athens. Socrates' vagueness about his association with Alcibiades confirms what he suggested by his frame conversation: he is chary about making his interest in Alcibiades evident to an audience unlikely to appreciate its character.

5. Protagoras Introduces Himself (316b–318a)

Because he knows Protagoras from previous meetings, Socrates does not need to introduce himself, just the one he's representing: "Protagoras, this Hippocrates here and I have come to see you" (316b). Protagoras's first words of the dialogue seem out of keeping with the portrait Socrates just painted of an entrancing speaker leading a charmed band of followers: "Which would you prefer, to discuss with me alone or with the others too?" He leaves the decision on privacy to them, but Socrates hands it back—"For us it makes no difference"—and invites him to decide "after you've heard why we've come." Privacy, made so prominent by being their first decision and by being handed back and forth, is a theme of *Protagoras* but, as is fitting, in a way that is secret and retired, out of the main focus of their discussion though haunting it at every point. A second matter is evident in this first little exchange, a tactical maneuvering between Protagoras and Socrates. From the beginning Protagoras is bent on gaining conversational advantage, here ceding to them the choice of how to conduct the conversation, as if it were a matter of indifference to him, as if he can adapt to all circumstances and under the way chosen by others still provide a winning performance. But Socrates will prove the superior tactician.

Socrates states why they've come by describing what Hippocrates *is* (he's an aristocratic youth from a great and prosperous family); how he *seems* (he "seems to be by nature a match for those his age"); how he seems *to Socrates* ("it seems to me he desires to become notable in the city"); and what *Hippocrates thinks* ("he thinks he would most likely become [notable] by consorting with you") (316c). Socrates makes Hippocrates of interest to Protagoras as a paying customer while making himself seem a friendly procurer for Protagoras. Protagoras responds to this gesture with gratitude: "Rightly, Socrates, are you forethoughtful [*promêthêi*] on my behalf"—he compliments Socrates on being "promethean," on thinking ahead, thinking strategically, but his compliment is a little exercise in forethought, for it prepares his report on his own lifelong strategy of exercising forethought, and that in turn prepares what must be his oft-told tale of Forethought himself, Prometheus. Protagoras thus initiates a contest of forethoughtfulness: who will prove the more promethean as a wise bringer of gifts to humans?

In order to ground his preference for a public exchange, Protagoras makes a speech that outlines first the dangerous situation the wise face:

> when a foreign man visits great cities and in those cities persuades the best of their youths to forsake meeting with others, whether family or outsiders, old or young, and to be together with him, through this meeting to become better, the one doing these things must take precautions. For no little envy arises about him and other ill will and even plots. (316c–d)

The wise need to take precautions—what is Protagoras's precaution? He seems to come forth candid, lavishing his candor on a privileged few: here, among ourselves, behind closed doors in Callias's house, I can openly state the difficulty that I and all the wise have faced. He outlines concisely what he himself does in the face of an animosity he fully understands: "I myself however declare the sophistical art to be ancient." His art is not an innovation, he asserts, it belongs to the long and famous tradition of wisdom of which Greeks are so rightfully proud; he is simply the latest figure in that proud tradition. He isolates its shared feature: "those ancient men who pursued [this ancient art], fearful of its offensiveness, fashioned a cloak [an outward ornament] and put a veil over themselves [as women do]"—the ancient wise all practiced timid concealment, hiding themselves out of servile fear; *courage* evidently marks him off from all his predecessors. He lists four types of fearful concealment and names nine concealers, and his list is anything but haphazard for it includes the chief elements of Greek education—poetry, religion, gymnastics, and music—and some of the most honored names. "For some [the veil] was poetry," poetry being the "greatest part of education," he will maintain (338e). His examples are Homer and Hesiod, the highest possible examples, the most honored poet-founders of Greekness, plus Simonides, a poet of more recent times who died around the time Protagoras was beginning his public career—the sophists of the whole poetic tradition are guilty of fearful concealment. "[F]or others in turn [the veil] was mystery rites and prophecies, such as Orpheus and Musaeus and those around them." Sophists were thus responsible for "the most radical transformation of Greek religion,"[31] Or-

31. Burkert, *Greek Religion*, 296.

phism or the mystery cults that had become popular and powerful, like the one at Eleusis that claimed Orpheus as its founder and played a central role in Athenian religious practice. Protagoras then claims that the uniquely Greek practice of gymnastics, naked athletics, was part of the wise tradition of sophists, and he names two, one a contemporary who "is as able a sophist as any." He ends with music and names teachers well known in Athens, "your own Agathocles, who made music his veil" and was the teacher of Damon,[32] and "Pythocleides of Ceos" who, like Damon, was a teacher of Pericles[33]—Protagoras himself being famously a teacher of Pericles. He ends his list saying, "and many others," and summarizing what all these sophists share: "All these as I say fearing the envy made use of these arts as curtains."

Protagoras thus applies the label he gave himself to the whole tradition of Greek wisdom while indicting all its members. He is different: "But I don't concur with any of them in this," for not only were they timid concealers, they failed, "they did not pass undetected by those who have power in the cities, for whose sake they put up these cloaks" (317a). The wise all thought that it was the powerful (or the capable—*dunamenous*)[34] they had to fool, but, Protagoras charges, the wise were not wise enough to do it, not wise enough to overcome the suspicion with which the powerful viewed the wise. He is different, he inaugurated a way for the wise and the powerful to coexist by being useful to one another—and in 433 in Athens it was apparent that wise Protagoras had been useful to powerful Pericles in ways helpful to both.[35]

Protagoras's claim to success in harmonizing the interests of the wise and the powerful depends on understanding an element of the city that he mentions next, the Many. He has understood them: they differ from the powerful because "the Many notice, so to speak, nothing, but merely repeat whatever these leaders proclaim" (317a). His sole remark on the Many is almost parenthetical, a mere aside, it seems, tossed in before he moves to his main lesson about the failure of the wise with the powerful. In fact, however, his little remark indicates that he knows where he is: in

32. *Laches* 180d.

33. *Alcibiades I* 118c.

34. See Morgan, *Myth and Philosophy*, 137 on this ambiguity in *dunamenous* and the care with which Protagoras uses it here and at $319a_1$. He will exploit its ambiguity in his long speech as well.

35. Not only for projects as important as writing the founding laws for a new city but for matters as comprehensive as instructing Pericles on the uses of civil religion, see below, section 7, "Protagoras's Display Speech." On the relationship between Protagoras and Pericles as one of "mutual influence" see Schiappa, *Protagoras and Logos*, 176–89.

democratic Athens, the great city that thinks itself ruled by the Many. In Athens the issue of the power of the Many has to be touched with some delicacy, and Protagoras does it swiftly. The Many notice nothing—their being ruled by the powerful (or capable) exceeds their capacity to notice. The Many simply repeat what the powerful proclaim—their vaunted autonomy or freedom is illusory for they can be made to think and say what they're told. Protagoras knows he's in a democracy, but he knows too that he's behind closed doors with an audience of young Athenians of high ambition aspiring to become powerful: his view of the Many will not shock them because they are all already schooled in the ongoing Athenian debate about oligarchy and democracy that stretched back to the very beginnings of the democracy.[36] Protagoras's little remark is calculated to lure the aspiring powerful to him, for even Hippocrates was able to state that Protagoras knows how to make one clever at speaking. In his double comment on the Many, Protagoras the wise offers the aspiring powerful ways of effectively exploiting the democratic Many who seem to rule in Athens but notice nothing and repeat what they're told by those they come to esteem as they esteem Pericles. Protagoras knows where he is and knows how to speak. Or does he? Socrates is in his audience, and Socrates will attempt to school *him* on wisdom and power, on the wise treatment of the Many and the wise treatment of the powerful—and the wise treatment of the wise.

Protagoras makes his judgment on the failure of the fearful wise emphatic: "For one to steal away and not be able to escape, but to be conspicuous in doing so, shows sheer folly in the attempt, and necessarily makes people even more suspicious since they regard such a one to be, whatever else, a scoundrel" (*panourgon*, "one who will do anything," 317a–b). Forced to conceal themselves, the wise, sophists all, did it foolishly as well as fearfully: they were fools as well as cowards. The first sophist to call himself one calls all the other wise by the same name while claiming to be differ-

36. That debate had been at the heart of Athenian politics since the establishment of the democracy under Cleisthenes in 507 and its extension in the reforms of Ephialtes in 462; Pericles seems to have played a role in the latter and then added further democratic reforms in an Athens that was, Thucydides judged, "nominally a democracy [that] was becoming in his hands government by the first citizen" (2.65.9). On the limits of Athenian democracy, see Rahe, *Republics Ancient and Modern*, vol. 1, chap. 7, "Athens' Illiberal Democracy." Discussion of the role of democracy in all aspects of Athenian life are found in Boegehold and Scafuro, *Athenian Identity and Civic Ideology*, and Boedeker and Raaflaub, *Democracy, Empire, and the Arts in Fifth-Century Athens*. Particularly instructive for the roots of democracy in the agrarian practices of the Greeks is Victor Davis Hanson, *The Other Greeks: The Family Farm and the Agrarian Roots of Western Civilization*. See also the review of Hanson by Paul Rahe in the *American Journal of Philology*.

ent from them, to be, that is, courageous and wise. Protagoras's very name means "the first to speak out," and here he proclaims that he was the first to break with the whole tradition of timid wise whose cloaks failed to deflect suspicion. "I have taken the completely opposite course." He openly admits "to being a sophist and to educate humans, thinking this a better precaution than theirs." Protagoras's open admission makes him look wholly frank, but he shares the common lot of the wise and needs precautions; his frankness is a tactic of caution, the appearance of incaution is caution itself; he cloaks himself in openness. He adds a pleasant little remark that points to one of his main precautions: "And in addition to this, I have taken other [precautions] which, please god, ensure that I suffer nothing terrible from my admission that I am a sophist." *Please god?*—one of his precautions is his mastery at feigning a kind of piety in speech.

In his chronologically first dialogue Plato arranged to have the first exchange between men of the enlightenment, between "wise" men, focus on the common situation of the wise. He has Protagoras give a speech presenting the problem they all faced and his own particular solution to it. The problem is the disproportion between the truths the inquirers uncover and the needs of society—the powerful and the many—the problem that such truths can be "true but deadly." The solution must be a veil of some kind, caution or thrift in communicating such truths. Plato thus made *esotericism* the first topic shared by men of the enlightenment. He allowed Protagoras to state in an appropriately indirect fashion that the whole tradition of Greek wisdom is an esoteric tradition that knew it faced a strategic problem in presenting itself to the public, in securing and transmitting itself. He allowed Protagoras to claim to be superior to all other wise men in the very speech in which he acknowledged that they are all the same in a crucial respect: all must be circumspect, all must veil themselves. Plato allowed Protagoras to come forth veiled in candor, to flaunt his abandonment of masks and have that be his pleasing, winning mask. For Protagoras will make an exhibition speech that shows just how deeply he understood the problem and how comprehensive his solution was. Yet Socrates will condemn his solution, judging it to be dangerous to society and to the wise; the problem intimated in Protagoras's first speech will prove to be the continuous background theme of *Protagoras*: the problem of esotericism is the first and abiding problem of Socrates' confrontation with Protagoras.

Protagoras's proof of the rightness of his own new way is that he has been practicing it for many years and reached an age at which he's old enough to be the father of anyone present (317c); his experience tells him he will "suffer nothing terrible" from his increased frankness.[37] Protagoras ends his speech claiming that the evident success of his new tactic gives him good grounds for preferring to speak with Hippocrates publicly: "much more pleasing for me would be to make my discourse about this in front of the others indoors here." The others here are still a select, semi-private company consisting of ambitious young Athenians and the "wise" competing to become their teachers. But their meeting is now over, and Socrates is reporting it to an outside audience; he helps Protagoras with his candor: he relates Protagoras's indoor speech to an audience he has just made suspicious of foreign hucksters. And what Socrates says next proves he is capable of his own concealment: inside Callias's house he seemed to defer to age and success, but to his audience outside he says what he really thought of Protagoras's preference: Protagoras "wanted to show off to Prodicus and Hippias and preen himself on the fact that the new arrivals were lovers of him." But for both the inside and outside audiences, forethoughtful Socrates may be deflecting attention away from his own interests when he says, "why don't we call over Prodicus and Hippias and those with them, so they can listen to us?" (317d). By the end of *Protagoras* it will be evident that it served a purpose of Socrates' to have both the sophists and all those with them "listen to us."

When all are gathered and seated where Hippias has been holding forth, Protagoras makes a request that confirms Socrates' charge that he wants to preen himself: he asks Socrates to repeat what he said on behalf of Hippocrates (318a). Socrates declines Protagoras's invitation to praise him in front of his rivals; he says that "the beginning for me is exactly the same as before regarding our coming," but then he omits the flattering words he spoke on Hippocrates' behalf, saying only that "it so happens that Hippocrates here desires to meet with you. So he would be pleased to ascertain what, if he does join with you, will result." He ends his stripped-down, flattery-free version emphatically, as if Protagoras were waiting for more: "That's all we have to say." Forced to be content with that introduction, Protagoras does not answer Socrates but turns instead to Hippocrates, addressing him directly and offering a vague promise that he will

37. In *Meno*, set in 402, long after Protagoras's death, a Socrates grown old attests to the success of Protagoras's protective strategy: he informs one of the three men who will be his own accusers that "Protagoras, who corrupted those who associated with him and sent them back in a worse condition than when he received them for more than forty years, escaped the notice of the whole of Greece . . . and in all this time, still to this very day, he hasn't ceased being well thought of" (*Meno* 91e). Just how he *escaped notice* will become evident in his exhibition speech.

get better every day if he consorts with him. Hippocrates has been directly addressed, but he remains mute as Socrates speaks in his stead.

6. Socrates' Challenge and Invitation: Can the Political Art Be Taught? (318a–320c)

Hippocrates was asked but Socrates answers—and the event seems indicative of them both: Hippocrates has nothing to say, while Socrates has an agenda of his own. He asks Protagoras similar things to those he asked Hippocrates—*for* what does one study with him and with a view to *becoming* what (see 311b)? Socrates has shown that he knows the answers, but he evidently wants Protagoras to give his own answers before this company. While the little questions Socrates poses are similar to those he put to Hippocrates and on similar topics, he answers them himself: he does not submit great Protagoras to the indignity of answering questions like a schoolboy, at least not yet.

Protagoras congratulates Socrates on his way of questioning and says he's always gratified to answer those who question nobly[38]—a noteworthy remark for one whose later annoyance with Socrates' way of questioning leads Socrates to threaten to leave. Just as he earlier distinguished himself from the ancient wise, Protagoras distinguishes himself from other sophists—they maltreat the young who have just "escaped from technical subjects" by forcing new technical subjects on them. He would inflict no such hardship on Hippocrates, who would learn from him "only that for which he came"—and Socrates told him in the smaller group that Hippocrates came to learn how to become notable in the city (316c). What Protagoras would teach is *euboulia*, good counsel (318a), applied to two different matters: "his own affairs, how he would best manage his household (*oikeiôn*), and . . . the things of the city, how he would be most powerful regarding the things of the city, both in deed and speech" (319a). Protagoras's words hide a little dissimulation dictated by circumspection: while saying that he teaches how the economic or private things can be *managed*, he drops that strong word for the public things, exercising the rhetorical subtlety of not flaunting the fact that the city can be managed by the clever rhetoric he teaches.[39] Socrates provides the label for what Protagoras promises—"It

38. Diogenes Laertius records that Protagoras was the first to introduce the Socratic form of questioning (9.53).

39. See Morgan, *Myth and Philosophy*, 137.

seems to me that you are speaking of the political art [*technê*]"[40]—and he continues in a way that shows his willingness to be an accessory to Protagoras's circumspection: "and promising to make men *good citizens*," a benevolent interpretation of Protagoras's promise by one who spoke differently in private with Hippocrates.

Socrates then makes the decisive speech. It sets the course for the rest of the dialogue by challenging Protagoras and then inviting him to deliver a long speech to justify himself and his whole purpose as a sophist, for Socrates' speech gives reasons for doubting that Protagoras's art, the political art of making good citizens, can be taught. "It is noble," Socrates begins, reciprocating the apparent praise Protagoras himself just indulged in (318d), "this artwork you have acquired."[41] And what he says next—"For you will get from me nothing less than what I think"—again repeats Protagoras, this time by likewise avowing candor, an almost necessary avowal here in order to excuse himself for the apparent discourtesy of challenging the very possibility of what Protagoras has made his life work. Yet Socrates' avowal of candor is no more believable than Protagoras's. The irony of his very next sentence would be obvious to the frame audience privileged to have heard his earlier exchange: "For I didn't suppose, Protagoras, that this is something which could be taught; but I don't know how I can distrust what you have said" (319a). Really? Moments ago, alone with Hippocrates, he said how much he distrusts what Protagoras says. If the latter part of Socrates' sentence is ironic, what about its first part: does he really think the political art is unteachable? To Hippocrates he spoke as if he thought it was teachable. And the dialogue ends with him arguing that it *can* be taught. But the clearest evidence of irony in Socrates' claim that virtue is unteachable is the very premise of his argument on behalf of that view: "I say, as do all other Greeks, the Athenians are wise" (319b). Could Socrates really believe that Athenians are wise? His argument assumes it and offers two examples of Athenian practice that he has observed, both showing that Athenians don't believe the political art can be taught—and if wise Athenians don't believe it can be taught, how could Athenian Socrates believe it can? His first example concerns what the wise Athenians do collectively in their ruling democratic assembly: when the issue is technical they

40. Protagoras himself earlier spoke of the *sophistical* art (316d).

41. Socrates' apparent flattery may be compromised by his choice of words: at $319a_4$ Socrates spoke of a *politikê technê*, but here he makes the political art a *technêma* ($319a_8$), a word suggesting trickery and artful devices.

pay attention to those who have learned the relevant art,[42] but when the issue is political they attend to everyone equally, thus attesting in practice to their disbelief in the teachability of the political art.[43] For his second example, Socrates turns from the Athenian public to what he has observed of the failure of "our wisest and best citizens . . . to pass on this virtue that they have to others" (319e). He gives two instances, both concerning Pericles' failure to teach his own mastery of the political art, first to "these two young fellows, here," Paralus and Xanthippus, Pericles' two sons, and then to the absent Kleinias, "younger brother of Alcibiades here," Kleinias and Alcibiades being Pericles' two wards.[44] Socrates is specific, pointing to three of the young Athenians present and giving the details of Pericles' failure with Kleinias: "fearing that he be corrupted by Alcibiades, Pericles dragged him away and placed him in Ariphron's household to be educated," but Ariphron sent him back, not knowing what to do with him (320a–b).

Socrates must be aware of the tension between his two points: the very existence of a Pericles in Athens, his success over three decades and his now unrivaled supremacy, indicates that Athenians in the Assembly in fact distinguish among speakers when the issue is political. Moreover, Socrates never claims that Pericles does not believe that his political virtue can be taught—in fact, he shows that Pericles made every effort to teach Kleinias. He claims only that Pericles' failure leads *him* not to believe in the teachability of virtue: "With these things in view, Protagoras, I don't believe that virtue can be taught" (320b). Preparing to end his speech, he repeats the flattery of his opening: "When I hear the things said by you, I am swayed." *Swayed*? The man who privately warned Hippocrates to be on guard against what is said by hucksters who don't know what is useful and what is worthless in what they sell? A Socrates credulous enough to believe that Athenians are wise and gullible enough to let Protagoras's words sway him is an ironic Socrates. The purpose of his irony is only slightly less obvious: a young Athenian philosopher speaks up in Athens on Athenian practice to a famous old foreign wise man who presumes to teach Athenians the political art; he speaks as a loyalist of his own polity, avowing its wisdom while seeming to yield to the old wise man but in fact

42. Socrates' shift from "*we* convene in assembly" to "*they* consider can be learned and taught" (319b) may suggest the limits to his agreement with the Athenian Assembly.

43. Socrates speaks of "managing the city" (319d$_1$), thereby combining what Protagoras kept separate, managing the household and becoming powerful in the city (319a).

44. Kleinias and Alcibiades were the sons of a noted Athenian general, Kleinias, killed in the battle of Coronea in 446. The wife of the elder Kleinias, Dinomache, was a first cousin of Pericles.

issuing him a serious challenge. Protagoras is no fool—the whole purpose of the dialogue presupposes the superiority that his coming performance will make indisputable. He will have recognized Socrates' irony and seen clearly the dilemma that his challenge poses for him: he cannot openly contest Socrates' premise of Athenian wisdom before an Athenian audience to which he wants to ingratiate himself. Nor can he openly challenge the wisdom of the Athenian Assembly or the capacity of Pericles. But if he does not, how can he make a case for *himself* as the indispensable teacher, not of good citizens simply but of effective political tacticians whose art, his art, will enable them to sway the Assembly and win renown for themselves, making them the new Pericles?[45]

It is clear where Protagoras stands on Socrates' premise of Athenian wisdom: speaking with Socrates and Hippocrates, he drew his fundamental distinction between the powerful few who are perceptive and the Many who notice nothing and repeat what they're told (317a). His distinction suggests that in a democracy like Athens, Protagoras, while willing to take money from anyone who can pay, seeks out especially those few young men whose nature enables them to notice what the Many do not, the capable few fit to become powerful. Recognizing the irony in Socrates' embrace of Athenian practice, Protagoras will have recognized that Socrates veiled his own judgment against it. He will have recognized as well that his response here in Athens has to be on Socrates' terms: his proof of the teachability of virtue has to submerge his real judgment against the Athenian Many yet make him seem indispensable to the young Athenians he wants to attract.[46]

Socrates' speech is a challenge, but it ends on an invitation that Protagoras will be eager to accept because it fulfills his purpose in coming to Athens: "If, therefore, you can *exhibit* to us more explicitly that virtue can be taught, please don't begrudge us but give an *exhibition*." Protagoras would begrudge this least of all: give us an *epideixis*, Socrates says, give us the speech you sophists train yourselves to give, the speech employing the

45. Coby calls the dilemma Socrates poses for Protagoras an "entrapment" (*Socrates and the Sophistic Enlightenment*, 51); for a concise statement of the dilemma, see Morgan, *Myth and Philosophy*, 138.

46. It may even be that Protagoras would recognize that Socrates' challenge, with its premise of Athenian wisdom and examples of Athenian practice, is meant as a reminder to him that he is in the most democratic of cities and should speak accordingly—for Socrates will later intimate that he regards Protagoras as kin and that he therefore treats him as a kinsman should. Leo Strauss treats Socrates' challenge as a friendly warning, unpublished transcript of a seminar on Plato's *Protagoras*, 6/13–16. See also Strauss, *Liberalism Ancient and Modern*, 55.

common coin of mythology and history that all sophists give in order to sell themselves to prospective students—give us the *epideixis* that concerns the political art you promise to teach.[47] Protagoras cannot but be grateful for the rare opportunity Socrates' invitation affords him to address the now collected company of all the young Athenians plus his younger rivals and give the speech that most serves his purpose in coming to Athens. Socrates' challenge and invitation sets the whole dialogue in motion, but it is a forethoughtful offer: while offering Protagoras the opportunity to give the speech he most wants to give to the group to which he most wants to give it, it sets up a most rare opportunity for Socrates: to give the *counter*-speech he most wants to give to the group to which he most wants to give it.

Socrates makes his speech on behalf of wordless Hippocrates, but his audience of young Athenians is much broader; the whole band of young Athenians who came to Callias's house to seek out these foreign teachers, for reasons that cannot have been that different from Hippocrates' reasons, listen as Socrates gives his Athens-centered challenge. To hear that speech from their perspective is to hear a loyal elevation of their own things. But one single young Athenian will hear it with special attention, the one most obviously "beautiful and wealthy and well-born,"[48] the one Socrates prominently *excluded* from the list of those Pericles failed to educate while naming him twice and explicitly saying he was the one Pericles feared would corrupt Kleinias: the speech inviting Protagoras to speak seems calculated to arrest Alcibiades. How could he, at his age with his aspirations, *not* be arrested by Socrates' emphasis on the issue that consumes him—the Assembly that rules Athens and who it pays attention to, the Assembly he yearns to address though he is still too young? And how could he not be both stung and goaded by Socrates' intimation of his singular place in Pericles' household, he who already has a reputation for being a corruptor while knowing himself to be the sole fit heir of Pericles' greatness—and his brother to be an idiot and Pericles' sons useless?[49] Socrates seems in fact to be on the hunt for the vernal beauty of Alcibiades while being

47. *Greater Hippias* and *Lesser Hippias* are concerned with the *epideixis* Hippias customarily gave, and *Gorgias* with Gorgias's. Protagoras is allowed to give his speech, whereas Socrates arrives too late for those of Hippias and Gorgias, on purpose. One of many parallels between *Protagoras* and the *Republic* is that the latter begins allowing Thrasymachus to give his *epideixis*. Kathryn Morgan is illuminating on sophistic *epideixeis* and on Protagoras's *epideixis* in particular (*Myth and Philosophy*, 89–131, 132–54).

48. See 319c and *Alcibiades I* 104a–c.

49. *Alcibiades I* 118e.

compelled to deny it to the frame audience. He told that audience that the contest for his attention had been won that day by Protagoras. But his little act of playing down his interest in Alcibiades by playing up his interest in Protagoras seems to be refuted by what begins in this speech, a challenge to Protagoras aimed at arresting Alcibiades. With respect to the frame audience an initial conclusion can be drawn: Socrates goes public in a way that is calculated to serve his public image—he persuades them that he does not improperly pursue the most spectacular young Athenian but defends an Athenian youth like Hippocrates even in private; and even in private he defends the wisdom of Athens and its Assembly and challenges foreign wise men come to prey on Athenian young. Socrates carries out his hunt for Alcibiades before their eyes but beyond their notice.

Socrates' speech has a final audience, Plato's contemporary readers who know that Socrates is speaking in prewar Athens, shortly before the war. For them, Socrates' speech on the purported wisdom of the Athenians—how the Athenian democracy decides political matters and Pericles' failure with his sons and wards—is noteworthy for being a speech on Athenian political decision making set shortly before the outbreak of the war that will bring disaster to Athens, to these young Athenians, and eventually to Socrates himself. For this audience, looking backward through the future of all those present that day, forethoughtful Socrates raises, wholly on his own initiative, the most far-reaching political question facing Athens in 433: what can the future of Athenian democracy be if, facing war with Sparta, its Assembly attends equally to all speakers and Pericles cannot pass on his political virtue to his sons and wards? Pericles' early policy of carrying forward Themistocles' bold plan of naval expansion enabled Athenian democracy to gain its powerful empire; his policy of public funding for great building projects made Athens the architectural jewel of the world—the Parthenon itself is just being completed when Plato presents Socrates first speaking up in Athens—and Pericles' policy of openness to the Greek enlightenment drew the greatest minds of Greece to Athens, justifying Hippias's praise of Athens as "the very hearth of the wisdom of Greece" (337d). What can the future of Athenian democracy be if the greatness, splendor, and enlightenment to which Pericles led it now incite the envy and fear in others that will, as Thucydides argued, force them into war against it?

But could Socrates or anyone else in 433 anticipate that war was coming? Thucydides begins his history by saying that he believed from its beginning that it would be a greater war than any that had preceded it. And he identifies its cause: "The real cause I consider to be the one which was formally most kept out of sight. The growth of the power of Athens, and the alarm which this inspired in Sparta, made war inevitable" (1.23.6). After calling attention to the presence of speeches in his history (1.22.1), he makes the very first speech the Corcyraean address to the Athenian Assembly in the summer of 433. The Corcyraeans speak of war as inevitable: "if any of you [Athenians] imagine that that war is far off, he is grievously mistaken, and is blind to the fact that the Spartans out of fear of you want war" (1.33.3). They go on to say that the summer of 433 is "a time when you are anxiously scanning the horizon that you may be in readiness for the breaking out of the war which is all but upon you."[50] When the Athenians decide to make a defensive alliance with the Corcyraeans, they do so because "it appeared to them that there really would be a war with the Peloponnesians" (1.44.2). *Protagoras*, set in that summer, may be "a sun-lit dialogue,"[51] but it anticipates the coming disaster in Socrates' speech on the "wise" Athenians and their most powerful leader.[52]

Socrates' speech inviting Protagoras to deliver his *epideixis* is heard one way by Protagoras, another by Hippocrates, another by Alcibiades, another still by its frame audience—but those in the best position to attend to its full implications are the audience that can read it as Socrates' public challenge in the first dialogue in Plato's corpus set shortly before the war. A spectacular sight rises before our eyes: Socrates challenges the wisest man of the time on the most important political question of the time in the presence of the most promising political leader of the time on the eve of the war that will change everything. What will the opening dialogue of Plato's corpus show Socrates *doing* about the political future of Athens in its moment of impending crisis? For Socrates challenges Protagoras on what he *does*: to challenge him on the teachability of virtue is to call his whole career as a teacher into question, and to challenge him in relation to Pericles is to call his greatest political success into question. By placing his chronologically first dialogue at the high point of Periclean democracy and by having Socrates challenge Protagoras on the teachability of virtue and in relation to Pericles, Plato forces the question: What will Socrates *do*?

50. The Corcyraeans' argument for the inevitability of war is self-serving because they came to Athens seeking to gain Athenian assistance in their conflict with the Corinthians: if war with Sparta was inevitable, Athenians would be induced to ally with Corcyra because of its powerful navy and its strategic location astride the shipping lanes to Italy and Sicily. Nevertheless, their argument for the inevitability of war would have to be plausible for their general case to carry.

51. Allen, *Ion, Hippias Minor, Laches, Protagoras*, 89.

52. Intimations of war become more overt later in the dialogue when Socrates, again wholly on his own initiative, praises Spartan wisdom and by implication criticizes Athenian wisdom.

7. Protagoras's Display Speech: Why the Political Art Is Teachable (320c–329b)

Before delivering his invited display speech Protagoras employs his tactic of deferral, inviting the others to decide "which of two ways I shall present my epideixis to you" (320c). Because *you* is plural, he must be looking around at his whole audience, giving the choice not to Socrates alone but to the whole group. He doesn't simply state the two choices but manipulates[53] his hearers by reminding them of his authority: should he speak "as an elder to the younger telling a story [*mythos*], or shall I expound an argument [*logos*]?" "Many of the assembled company" respond as they've been told, leaving to their elder the choice of doing what he wishes—and he wishes to speak as an elder to the younger for he chooses to begin with *mythos* and conclude with *logos*. Protagoras would surely have found a way to give his display speech in both methods regardless of what others chose for him; he would have given the mythos and logos he actually gives, for it's not likely that even Protagoras, with all his experience and finesse, long accustomed to speaking in democracies, is inventing on the spot a new myth of origins in defense of democratic belief plus its accompanying arguments. By inviting him to give a display speech, Socrates invites the founder of sophism to give a speech he's trained himself to give and is a master at giving. If it must answer the specific question of the teachability of his own art, it does so within Protagoras's standard advertisement for himself.[54]

Protagoras of Abdera does not confine himself to local affairs as Socrates of Athens did; he speaks as an observer of universal human nature who applies his observations to what you Athenians believe and do. And he speaks as one who proclaimed himself superior to the whole tradition of Greek wisdom from Homer to the present: he must live up to the role he assigned himself as the new educator of Greece. Can he do it? His myth utilizes elements of popularly believed stories of Homer and Hesiod, bending them to his own purpose of providing a divine rationale for democratic theory

53. Morgan, *Myth and Philosophy*, 138.

54. The scholarly consensus that developed on the basis of Werner Jaeger's arguments seems reasonable: the speech Plato gives Protagoras faithfully represents the historical Protagoras's views. See Jaeger, *Theology of the Early Greek Philosophers*, 189–90; Guthrie, *Sophists*, 63–64. Schiappa offers a useful short summary of the reasons in favor of authenticity (*Protagoras and Logos*, 146–48). A chronological reading of the dialogues can offer an additional argument: for Plato to have Socrates mount the stage in Athens in 433 in order to counter the Protagorean enlightenment, and then not to represent Protagoras faithfully would render his whole effort useless.

and practice; his logos summarizes the whole process of education Greeks undergo, indicating with proper caution that Greekness is the result of social conditioning, which, because he understands it, he can shape for the benefit of all: the Many, the would-be powerful, and himself. His combination of myth and logos responds with precision to Socrates' challenge: his myth deals with Socrates' first proof of the unteachability of virtue, the Athenian Assembly's practice of attending to all on political matters; his logos deals with Socrates' second proof, the failure of the most powerful Athenians to teach their offspring. Protagoras splits myth and logos in a way that mirrors the division he drew between the Many and the powerful: his myth edifies the undiscerning Many while instructing those who notice; his argument, while open to the Many, serves especially the very fewest of those who notice. But his split is not clean: he adds two logical considerations to his myth and only then says, "now I shall leave off telling you a myth and give an argument" (324d). Once noticed, Protagoras's compromised split between myth and logos helps show what the new educator means to convey to Socrates about his educational project: Protagoras, proper heir to the whole of Greek wisdom, welcomes those like Socrates to share in what he founded. Yes, he can do it.

Why Do Athenians Believe All Are Fit to Speak on Political Matters?

To defend Athenian democratic belief Protagoras begins at the beginning with a story of human origins. His myth lightly veils a natural history that demarcates the main stages of human development, attributing them mythically to different supernatural powers. First, nameless subterranean gods molded the kinds of mortal species under the earth. Before sending the kinds up into the light, they charged Prometheus and Epimetheus with furnishing and distributing the powers to the kinds. As a further sign of the blindness or lack of thought in a process that takes place in darkness under the earth, Forethought himself, Prometheus, caved in to his brother, Afterthought, Epimetheus, and let him assign the powers to the kinds. Protagoras acknowledges that Epimetheus "was not very wise" (321b) but refrains from acknowledging Prometheus's own lack of forethought. After Afterthought assigned all the powers, he saw that he had left humanity without powers. At this point Prometheus comes and sees that the other animals have been carefully provided for but humanity is "naked, unshod, unbedded, and unarmed" (321c). Prometheus, a pre-Olympian Titan, is "perplexed as to what preservation he should find for humanity," and he turns to the Olympians whose rule succeeded Titan rule and he turns to theft: he "steals from Hephaestus and Athena artful wisdom [*entechnon sophian*] along with fire . . . and gives them to humanity. In this way humanity got the survival wisdom [*ton bion sophian*] but did not get the political, for that was in the keeping of Zeus" (321d). Describing Prometheus's actions, Protagoras switches from the past tense to the present: Prometheus *comes, sees, steals*, and *gives*—the present suggests that the inventive actions necessary for new technical skills are something humans will always have to receive as gifts in fending for themselves against a nature that the myth allows to be seen as niggardly and blind; there is, the present tense suggests, continuous technological progress available to humanity.

Having told the story of Prometheus, Protagoras tells it a second time in order to explain the limits of Titan Prometheus's gifts and the hierarchy among the Olympians. Prometheus had evidently already violated Olympian order, for it is said that "he was no longer permitted to enter the Acropolis which is the dwelling place of Zeus, and in addition the guards of Zeus were terrible." Denied access to the source of political wisdom, Prometheus was able secretly to enter "the building shared by Athena and Hephaestus in which the two liked to practice their arts, and he stole the fiery art of Hephaestus and the other belonging to Athena and gave them to humanity" (321e). Protagoras's twice-told tale of Prometheus's theft and gift makes it clear that humanity owes no gratitude to the Olympians for the technical arts that make survival possible; survival against nature is a pre-Olympian gift of technical skills. Protagoras ends this portion of his myth referring for the only time in his myth to "it is told": "But afterward Prometheus, it is told, thanks to Epimetheus, was put on trial for theft." What was told is in fact different from what Protagoras tells, for what was told did not blame Epimetheus, as Protagoras does, and to say only that Prometheus was put on trial is not enough: Protagoras refrains from passing on what was told about Zeus's convicting Prometheus and punishing him most cruelly for his philanthropy. Protagoras expunges Olympian punishment of Prometheus from his tale even though he will make punishment an important theme in explaining his mythos. Protagoras will make Olympian Zeus, keeper of political wisdom, at least Prometheus's equal in philanthropy.

The stage of human development beyond technical skill requires of Protagoras a more detailed picture of human natural history prior to its attaining the political art. First he summarizes a key result of Prometheus's gifts: "Having acquired a share in the divine portion." Then he describes a further result: humanity, "alone of animals, through kinship with the god, believed in god and endeavored to build altars and images of gods" (322a).

Protagoras's wording allows one to conclude, as Patrick Coby argues, that Protagoras is suggesting that *technê* "is the source of religion . . . it is what links man to *the god*, for it is the cause and origin of his divine portion; and the divine portion, or man's kinship with the god, is the cause of his worshipping *gods*; hence *technê* produces religion."[55] Humanity then quickly "invented by art articulate speech and names, dwellings and clothing and shoes, beddings, and nourishment from the earth." But humans lived scattered, "there were no cities." Prometheus's gifts, adequate for survival, are inadequate for the human war against wild beasts; lacking "the political art of which the skill of war is a part" (322b), they failed in their war against wild animals. Therefore they sought safety by founding cities; but these cities in turn failed because "wherever they gathered together, they were unjust to one another, lacking the political art, so that they once again dispersed and began to be destroyed."

Only at this point of failed cities do the Olympians intervene. Zeus, fearing that "our species might perish utterly, sent Hermes to humans bringing a sense of shame [*aidôs*] and right [*dikê*] so that there might be order in cities and aggregating bonds of friendship" (322c)—right or the just is a moral system of right and wrong, the sense of shame an impetus to do the right and shun the wrong. Protagoras offers no reason for Zeus's action, but coming just after Prometheus's benevolence on behalf of human survival and after the failure of cities, Zeus's act seems to be benevolent action on behalf of human flourishing.[56] Hermes asks Zeus to tell him in what manner Right and Shame are to be distributed, but for Zeus to answer, Hermes must first tell him the manner in which technical skills have been distributed, with single skilled individuals serving many. Are Right and Shame to be distributed this way or among all? Protagoras, that famed public speaker, must be imagined as equal to the fine theatrical moment he has arranged for himself: he must draw himself up in all grandeur to pronounce the ruling of dread Zeus with majesty and force: "Among all," Zeus replies, "and let all have a share. For there could be no cities if but a few shared in them." Zeus's next sentence proves that he knows his distri-

55. Coby, *Socrates and the Sophistic Enlightenment*, 55–56. The same point is made by Ira Mark, quoting Müller ("Protagoras über die Götter," 140): "The relatedness of god and man means no other . . . than that conceptions of the divine are projections and reflections of the mortal." Mark comments: "It is the concept of *homo mensura* applied to theology." "Gods of the East Frieze of the Parthenon," 323 n. 159.

56. In the myth that occupies a corresponding place in the *Symposium*, Aristophanes gives a less philanthropic reason: Zeus saves humanity from perishing in order to keep the supply of sacrifices flowing (*Symposium* 190c).

bution to all is unlikely to succeed, for he orders Hermes to supplement that distribution with a law and a punishment for those who break it: "Yes, and put it as my law that he who is not able to share in Shame and Right is to be killed as a pestilence to a city" (322d). Protagoras knows that a myth of divine grace must be supplemented with a myth of divine anger.

The myth is ended. Hidden within it, if barely hidden, is the actual harshness and penury of human origins as blind forces shaped all species and left ours with no resources but a native ingenuity. Learning by necessity to fend for itself through the inventiveness of a few great individuals, our species created comfort and civility for itself in two great forms of invention. Prior to any Olympian caring, it wrested fire and *technai* from grudging nature by the invention of tools. Stuck nevertheless in rude primitiveness owing to an incapacity to organize into large stable groups, our species was rescued by the invention of moral gods who forged justice and a sense of shame in a naturally unsociable and recalcitrant species through the powerful medium of belief, belief in observant gods as overseers capable of inculcating justice and shame and of punishing injustice and shamelessness. Just where does Protagoras, inventor of the mythos, fit into his natural history of our species? A latecomer, appearing within the civil rule of Zeus, he surpasses "Prometheus," for he succeeded in entering the Acropolis of Zeus, braving his terrible guardians to steal the secret of political wisdom that the ruler of the gods kept to himself. And he surpasses "Zeus" as well for he wrested from the ruler of the gods the ultimate secret that the wisest human rules through rule of the gods. Enlightened Protagoras saw how the gods of Homer and Hesiod could still be useful to rule, his rule, rule though their ruling. Within the naturalistic cosmology being developed by Greek science, wise Protagoras judged that rule by Olympians still belonged to the fundamental requirements of the city. Who is Protagoras in his mythos? He is the founder of the enlightened city, enlightened by a rising science while enlightened as well about the indispensability of Olympian gods. Protagoras teaches the truly capable how to rule both the powerful and the Many: rule through ruling gods. The mythos shows how a Protagoras who flaunts his candor goes further in his precautions than the occasional "please god."

Protagoras has completed his edifying myth gentling a nonedifying natural history, but it is not here that he says he will "leave off telling a myth" and turn to logos—that comes later (324d). First he must supplement his myth with matters based wholly on reasoning, for the myth has not answered the first part of Socrates' challenge—so little is his myth, that staple of his *epideixis*, itself a response to Socrates' challenge. For Socrates claimed that virtue is unteachable, arguing on the grounds that Athenians are wise and that they believe that anyone is fit to give advice on political matters. Protagoras's myth gave divine sanction to such a democratic politics, for Zeus's gift of justice and shame to all justifies seeking the advice of all when the "deliberations involve political virtue, and must be conducted entirely on the basis of justice and moderation . . . because all partake of this virtue" (322e–323a). That political virtue is teachable, however, he has not yet shown. But he did just shift from *dikê* and *aidôs* to *dikaiosunê* and *sôphrosunê*, the first of a number of shifts that transform the language of myth into the language of teachable political virtue. Such shifting language is no flaw: Protagoras knows the need for a certain imprecision in order to convey in a single speech both the edifying and the true. With a view especially to the latter, Protagoras adds a "further proof" to the claim of his myth that "all humans really do believe that justice and the rest of political virtue is something in which every man shares" (323a).

His further proof is that people judge it so necessary that all share in justice that they think it mad to tell the truth about one's injustice, if one is unjust, counseling that one lie to cover up one's injustice (323a–c). Is this "further proof" really just another proof that all share in political virtue? Protagoras ended his myth proper singling out Socrates (322d), and he goes on addressing him in the singular, isolating him as one who, he suggests, could think his myth misleading (323a). What does his further proof prove for someone like Socrates? On closer inspection the further proof can be seen to alter the *issue*, the *judges*, and the *action*. The *issue* is no longer an Athenian practice but what "all humans really do believe [namely] that every man shares in justice and the rest of political virtue"—more exactly, the issue is that "everyone must claim to be just, whether he is or not," that everyone "must put up some show of being just" (323b). And the *judges* are no longer the Athenian Assembly or even "all humans" but a select group, one's kin (*oikeioi*, 323a): if anyone claims to be good at one of "the other virtues," a technical subject like flute playing, when he is not, people treat him with derision and annoyance and his kin "take him aside and warn him that he is mad" (323b). And the *action* is not "managing the city" or practicing an art, but truth telling: "where justice and the rest of political virtue is concerned, even if one is known to be unjust, if one tells many the truth about oneself, then that very truthfulness, which in the [case of flute playing] was regarded as moderation, in this case they treat as madness." Here *they* must still be one's judging kin: while approving truth telling with respect to the technical arts, kin regard truth telling as mad for a kinsman known to be unjust. To such a kinsman, kin "say that everyone must claim to be just, whether he is or not, and that the one who doesn't put up some show of being just is mad, as of necessity no one can fail to partake in justice somehow, or else he will not remain among humans."

Addressed to Socrates in the singular, these alterations make the "further proof" a new point entirely; it is Protagoras's admonition, even his appeal, to his kinsman among the Athenians: we truth seekers must know the place of truth telling in the city: the priority of justice, the necessity that all appear just, dictates a limit on truth telling. The unjust man who must claim justice or be exiled from human company can be none other than Protagoras, and the judging kin who is to allow this claim is Socrates. Protagoras began by noting the danger faced by a foreign sophist while claiming to be the first sophist to tell the truth. And he just told an edifying tale in Athens that supports Athenian democratic practice but invites demythologizing by the truth seeker. His "further proof"—ostensibly of his myth—is in fact further proof of the need for strategic care by the wise, by inquirers made kin by their truth seeking: they must put limits on their truth telling in the face of the vast majority not of their kind, and they must recognize a duty to one another to sustain this masking strategy. Fresh from a beautiful fiction that edifies what is untrue but indispensable in a democracy, Protagoras's "further proof" forestalls objection by making it betrayal. It is the fitting addition to his myth addressed in the singular to his kin by a teller of tales for the Many. Justice is a necessary façade for him, and he can imagine that Socrates will know it, for Socrates is another of those capable inquirers who, having seen through the mythic character of justice and shame, see too the self-interest in maintaining universal respect for them and in protecting their own kind. Protagoras's final sentence of his further proof, in all its ambiguities, confirms his point: "I say these things" (I add this "further proof") "to establish that it is reasonable for them" (*them* now meaning the Athenians) "to accept every man as an advisor [on matters] related to virtue, given their belief that all have a share in it" (323c)—a fine sentence for a man whose art is selling himself as advisor to the actual advisors of the city that imagines it listens equally to every man. Detecting deception in a wise foreigner, the capable[57] few hear a "further proof" that is actually a reminder to them of the necessity

57. Protagoras's word *dunamenous* (317a5) thus proves its useful ambiguity in meaning both powerful and capable: in the past, foreign sophists "did not pass undetected by the *dunamenous* human beings in the city," and neither does this present foreign sophist pass undetected by capable Socrates.

of deception and of protecting the deceiver. As for the Many who notice nothing, they would take the myth to be proof of what they already believe and the "further proof" to be further proof.

For a second time, then, wise Protagoras alludes to the need for circumspection in the wise, the need to know who and where they are and to act on that knowledge. The second time adds to the first: not only do the wise face dangers from the powerful, but the wise, always foreigners, are kin only to one another, related by shared practices and shared interests that forge them into a community in which each looks to the well-being of the other, avoiding above all the betrayal of kin regarding what all must seem to share, justice and the rest of political virtue. Returned to Athens after a long absence and meeting again an Athenian inquirer who impressed him before, Protagoras appeals to him as a kinsman with every right to expect that his appeal will fall on receptive ears. And Socrates? He will, in what lies ahead, prove that he takes the duties of kinship even more seriously than Protagoras does, for kinship will color every aspect of his treatment of Protagoras. One of Socrates' two great aims in the chronologically first dialogue in Plato's corpus is to instruct the sophists, an aim of historic importance, for the sophists are the face of the Greek enlightenment to the Greek public and Socrates will intimate that sophism threatens enlightenment itself. To his kin by custom, the Athenians to whom he narrates the exchange, Socrates masks his kinship by nature with the sophists; to them he speaks of Protagoras as a foreigner (309c). But Protagoras opens the essential element in Socrates' relation to the sophists by intimating how Socrates stands to him: we are kin, and kin do not betray to nonkin the necessary injustice of our kind—that would be madness and you and I are sane.

Now that he has secured his myth for the Many against destruction by his kin, Protagoras can turn at last to Socrates' specific challenge to the teachability of virtue, that is, to Protagoras's life work. Political virtue is Zeus's gift to all; still, people do not consider it to be "by nature" or to "arise spontaneously" but instead believe it to be "a teachable thing" (323c). To prove this Protagoras appeals to the practice of people generally, not simply Athenians. If people think someone's badnesses are by nature or chance, they don't get angry or admonish or teach or punish (323d); but if someone lacks the good things that people think come through care and exercise and teaching and has instead their opposite badnesses, they do get angry and punish and admonish (323e). His examples are injustice, impiety, and all that is opposed to political virtue—here piety enters his account as the third indispensable social virtue.[58] Protagoras can now conclude that "where everyone becomes thoroughly angry and admonishes, they obviously do so as something that can be acquired by care and learning." He isolates one part of this demonstration, punishment, choosing to make punishment especially prominent as the final issue of the mythic part of his speech (324a). He begins by inviting Socrates, "if you will," to consider punishment: the power punishment has over those who commit injustice will itself "teach you" that humans regard virtue as something that can be acquired. The lesson Protagoras offers is noteworthy because it distinguishes between punishment administered by one "who sets out to punish rationally" and irrational punishment, the vengeance of a wild beast. In teaching Socrates this lesson Protagoras acts as if all human beings punish rationally, but he has just emphasized the roots of punishment in anger,[59] and the mythic part of the speech was meant especially for the Many: does Protagoras consider the Many rational? On the contrary, just as his previous rational reflection on his myth singled out his rational kin, so here his suggestion to the rational is that power can be exercised over the irrational, the angry Many, through rational use of punishment. "He who sets out to punish rationally does not inflict vengeance because of the past injustice." The rational punisher punishes for a rational reason: "what has been done cannot be undone," and the rational punisher acts "for the sake of the future: to deter from further injustice either the perpetrator or someone else who sees the punishing" (324b).

The Protagoras capable of inventing edifying myths of the divine origin of political virtue does not leave myth before teaching his rational lesson on punishment. He refrains here from bringing in punitive gods as the ultimate enforcers of punishment for those who act like wild beasts, but he can afford to: he already had Zeus author a law that "he who is not able to share in Shame and Right is to be killed as a pestilence to the city" (322d). The ultimate rational punisher is the wise legislator who calls in Zeus the Punisher. The new educator of Greece legislates rationally, employing irrational powers to punish the irrational. Ending his lesson on the utility of punishment, Protagoras weaves this point into his general argument on the teachability of virtue: virtue can be seared into the irrational by having them observe the penalties of vice. He speaks of all humans when drawing his concluding generalization: that punishment is inflicted for the sake

58. Seth Benardete observes that "*Protagoras* differs from all other Platonic dialogues in consistently adding piety as the fifth virtue to the classical four" (*Socrates and Plato*, 45).

59. Protagoras spoke of anger three times in close succession, $323d_2$, $323e_2$, $324a_2$.

of deterrence "is the opinion of all those who inflict retribution whether in public or in private." If old Protagoras really believes this, he has been a most inattentive observer of public and private life; but he cannot be burdened with that slur, given the precision with which he spoke about anger. Instead, Plato allows him to speak ironically as one who recognizes the indispensability of rational, vengeance-free punishment for ruling the less than rational vengeful Many.

Protagoras brings the mythic part of his speech to a fitting close by moving from all humans to "the Athenians, your fellow citizens," and by calling what he just said about punishment a "logos." Because they too punish those they believe guilty of injustice, "it follows from this logos that the Athenians are also among those who believe that virtue is something that can be acquired and taught" (324c). Protagoras's response to Socrates' challenge on the teachability of virtue thus ends with a master teacher communicating a private point to a capable auditor: you must know, he says in effect, complimenting his select audience, that virtue is teachable through the threat of punishment for the potentially vicious; you must know that our myths of punishing gods teach that way, helping to form populations of law-abiding citizens whose decency is sustained by fear of retribution, divine or otherwise. We both know that logos about mythos. Now let's move on to your second point.

Protagoras's mythos in *Protagoras* stands as a great moment in the history of philosophy, for with that myth Plato allows the greatest of sophists to tell his edifying tale at the chronological beginning of his presentation of Socrates, the teacher who will counter Protagoras so successfully through Plato's writings that he will eclipse Protagoras forever. That eclipse has cost us memory of Protagoras's greatness, and it is useful to linger over his myth with a view to recovering some appreciation of that lost greatness.

Protagoras's myth attributes to gods, Titan Prometheus and Olympian Zeus and Hermes, the two forms of inventiveness responsible for human survival and civility. He cannot have believed in these gods, as the first sentence of his book *On the Gods* attests: "On the gods I am unable to know whether they exist or whether they do not exist or what they are like in form; for there are many hindrances to knowledge, the obscurity of the subject and the brevity of human life."[60] Why did Protagoras the unbeliever spin pleasing tales attributing benevolence to gods he did not know existed? The answer is easily inferred from his myth: he understood the social role of religion and saw how the existing religion, gripping his

60. Translation by Schiappa, *Protagoras and Logos*, 142.

contemporaries as if they knew it were true, could be usefully modified by a speaker as gifted as he was to serve ends wholly his own. Protagoras is not just enlightened about religion and its human sources, he aspires to use religion to advance enlightenment by civilizing and tempering the religion of the vast majority who would not be well served by being enlightened about religion. Civil gods could serve a civil order, promoting justice and moderation among the Many who notice almost nothing but merely repeat whatever their leaders proclaim. Let their leaders proclaim a Protagorean civil religion that underwrites enlightenment.

But wasn't Protagoras famous for being an outspoken atheist? Even in antiquity the first sentence of *On the Gods* was taken as evidence that he was a public atheist,[61] and it was said that the Athenians banished him and burned his books.[62] That view prevailed in modern times until Werner Jaeger argued in the Gifford Lectures of 1936 a more plausible case befitting the thinker whose first speech in Plato's *Protagoras* acknowledges the dangers foreign teachers faced. Jaeger argued that Protagoras was not a public atheist at all.[63] His agnostic sentence at the opening of *On the Gods* created space for the presentation of an anthropocentric, humanistic religion that knows—not the gods but the good things the gods bring. Abstaining from an older debate on the existence or nonexistence of gods, Protagoras treated religion "as an anthropological fact"; he undertook a "phenomenology of religion."[64] Plato's *Protagoras* supports this view: in his exhibition speech, Protagoras indicates the social role of religion, its indispensability and its malleability to thought, and he presses Homer's gods into service for a humanistic perspective. Protagoras's theology, or rather his appreciation of the social utility of religion, allowed him to use Homer's gods to advance his enlightenment project; he knew exactly what he was doing when he used the already existing divine names to honor the founders of human technical ingenuity and social virtue; and he knew exactly what he was doing when he made punishment—that natural upsurge of irrational anger and rage—a function of divine powers who punish only in order to school. Plato's *Theaetetus* further supports the view that Protagoras was not a public atheist. When Socrates brings Protagoras back

61. Sextus Empiricus, *Against the Physicists* 9.50.

62. Cicero, *On the Nature of the Gods* 1.63; Diogenes Laertius 9.51–2.

63. Jaeger, *Theology of the Early Greek Philosophers*, 189–90. Schiappa's discussion of Jaeger's argument (*Protagoras and Logos*, 143–48) accounts for the ancient misunderstanding of Protagoras's atheism (144–45).

64. Jaeger, *Theology of the Early Greek Philosophers*, 176, 189.

from the dead to defend his view, he allows him to object when Socrates introduces the gods as exemplars of "Protagorean measure": "Noble children and elders," Socrates' Protagoras says, "you're sitting down together and making a public speech, and you bring gods into the middle, though I except them from my speaking and writing."[65] Plato's Protagoras can use gods in a mythos, but he refrains from reasoning about them. As to whether the Athenians banished him and burned his books, Plato's *Meno* is against it: Socrates there (91e) reports that Protagoras maintained a good reputation during his whole forty-year career and continued to be thought well of many years after his death—not a likely fate for an outspoken atheist.

Of all the scholarly gains made in the train of Jaeger's recovery of Protagoras, one in particular strikes me as having singular importance for appreciating Protagoras's view of religion and how that view shaped the political aspirations of the thinkers of the Greek enlightenment. Ira S. Mark discovered the now generally accepted view of Protagoras's enlightened understanding of religion in a quite unexpected medium: chiseled and painted marble. He demonstrated that the gods on the east frieze of the Parthenon embody Protagoras's understanding of the indispensability of gods and of the role these imaginary exemplars can play in civilizing humanity and sustaining virtue in a great civil order: "Protagoras' theology determines the selection of the gods [on the east frieze], their iconographies, their seating, and the design of the whole";[66] Protagoras's Parthenon gods are exemplars of "the essential institutions of civilized society"; at the same time, they are depicted as "unresponsive to prayer," "aloof and self-concerned"; they are displaced from the center, with their backs to the human act of religious devotion at the center of the scene; the divine remains "imperceptible to man"; "the gods are apparent rather than true objects of ritual"; "at the center of religion is not the divine *per se* but the human act of piety."[67]

65. *Theaetetus* 162d–e.

66. "Gods of the East Frieze of the Parthenon," 330.

67. Ibid., 312, 335, 336. In a series of brilliant readings Mark shows how the fourteen figures on the frieze are placed in "divine groups that mirror the essential institutions of civilized society" (312): Aphrodite as mother [!] of Eros as child [!],supported by Artemis not as a chaste virgin but with sexual or fertility powers—"the Olympians as protectors of the bearing and raising of children" (302); Hera as bride and Zeus as consort with Nike, victory, "as the victory of marital union . . . the Olympians as the models for and protectors of marriage" (312); Hermes, Dionysos, and Demeter, patrons of the rural technai of animal husbandry, viticulture, and agriculture; Ares linked with Demeter but leaning away as war arises from and defends the appropriation of land;

What Mark recovers is a most remarkable exhibition of the power of Protagoras's thought: the Panathenaia, the Athenian festival depicted on the frieze, "is serving as a vessel, a context through which to render philosophy in visual form."[68] Protagoras's humanistic view of the gods was carved in stone in a prominent place: above the entrance way into the most magnificent—and newly completed—temple to Athenian greatness atop the Acropolis for all the world to gaze at and be amazed. How could that come to pass? Mark shows that Protagoras's teaching must have taken hold in the highest reaches of Athenian decision making. Depending in part on ancient documentary evidence, he makes the plausible case that Protagoras, during his long stay in Pericles' Athens, won over that notoriously enlightened leader, patron of the building program that culminated in the Parthenon. It is entirely reasonable that the Pericles who commissioned Protagoras to write the laws of Thurii in 444 would, in commissioning the great frieze that depicted the Panathenaia with its central event, the annual replacement of Athena's peplos, commission Protagoras to help design the arrangement of the gods that frames that central human act of Athenian pious devotion.[69]

No wonder Protagoras returned to Athens in 433 secure in his superiority: his effective wisdom was carved in stone in the new centerpiece of Athenian religious art high over the entrance way of the most spectacular temple in Greece. No wonder Hippocrates wanted to use Socrates to get to *this* teacher: he was not as foolish as he now looks to a world in which Socrates has so completely won the victory over Protagoras. But Socrates will criticize this great and successful thinker; he will attempt to school him, school the one who so effectively recast Homeric religion for a humanistic imperial empire. What could be wrong with the Protagorean enlightenment that forced an enlightened Socrates to criticize it in the moment of its greatest success?

Athena and Hephaestus, patrons of the urban technai and of metallurgy; Apollo the patron of political technê and Poseidon, Mark argues, as the sole representative of an earlier, more primitive stage of human development, now aged and worn. Only with Poseidon would one like to demur: given the noteworthy absence of Hades, the third of the ruling brothers (and therefore the absence of the whole realm of Hades), and given too the link with Apollo, wouldn't Poseidon—once an avenging punisher full of rage—represent that other aspect of political technê, the justice of rational punishment attested by Protagoras himself in explaining the mythos of *Protagoras*?

68. Ibid., 336.

69. Mark makes his case through the historical evidence for Protagoras's stays in Athens and his relationship with Pericles (336–42). Schiappa discusses Protagoras's relationship with Pericles in detail to determine their "mutual influence" (178ff.). On viewing the Parthenon frieze, see Osborne, "Viewing and Obscuring of the Parthenon Frieze."

Why Is Pericles Unable to Pass on His Virtue?

In turning to the second issue Socrates raised regarding Athenian belief in the teachability of virtue, Protagoras refers twice to the "perplexity" that "perplexes" Socrates ($324d_{3-4}$, $324e_3$), puckishly assigning foresightful Socrates the quality that marked Epimetheus ($321c_3$).[70] He says explicitly that he will "no longer tell you a *mythos*, Socrates, but a *logos*" (324d), even though he has long since left off telling his myth and has addressed Socrates with reasoned comments explaining his own stance toward his myth. The shift to Socrates' second issue allows Protagoras to leave mythmaking for the unnoticing Many entirely behind. Now he develops an argument for the capable few to show that he is not like the wise of the past whose secrecy led the powerful in the city to view them as a threat; he will show the capable few that he has a proper place in the city as the enlightened educator of the powerful.

Protagoras's logos posits one fundamental requirement of the city, "one thing of which all citizens must partake if there is to be a city" (324e); that one thing, political virtue, now has three components, "justice, moderation, and the pious [*to hosion*]." Zeus said the political virtue that "All" were to have consisted of the *dikê* and *aidôs* he gave (322a); when Protagoras applied his myth those two became "justice and moderation" (322e); and when he spoke of the opposites of political virtue he said that "one of those evils is injustice and impiety" (323e). The first sentence of the logos gives his final statement on the content of political virtue; by adding *the pious*, it adds to what Zeus gave the belief that Zeus gave it. Piety ties the actions of justice and moderation to powerful internal hopes and fears attached to invisible but gift-giving and punishing gods.

Protagoras states his claim in a long sentence with many conditionals: if "justice, moderation and the pious" taken together, "what I call manly virtue," is the one thing needed, and if all must share it, and if every man must act in accord with it or be taught and punished until he does or else be expelled or killed, "and if good men teach their sons everything *but* this," then "consider what surprising beings the good must be" (325a–b). Protagoras has already demonstrated that they think it *can* be taught; yet they teach other things the lack of which does not entail death or exile or the confiscation of their property or the total ruin of their households—and they don't teach *that*? "One must think they do, Socrates" (325c). Of course they do, as Socrates acknowledged by describing what Pericles tried to do

70. See Morgan, *Myth and Philosophy*, 153.

with Alcibiades' brother. The failure of the sons must lie in the inability of the good men to teach or in the inability of their sons to learn, not in the unteachability of the virtue the good have themselves learned.

Socrates challenged the teachability of that peculiar, exceptional political virtue that Pericles has and Hippocrates wants. Protagoras is discussing the teachability of the common, universal political virtue that everyone must have for the city to exist, and he continues with that until the end of his argument; only then does he open a small space for himself to imply that he could be the exceptional teacher of the exceptional because he understands the common. To reach that point, he describes what he has observed of the whole process of Greek education—he who said at the start that it is the business of sophists to educate human beings (317b). His observations begin at home in earliest childhood with the family, move through the stages of public schooling that honor the poets, and end with what the city teaches in its laws, which stem from "good lawgivers of ancient times"—reverence for ancient poets and ancient lawgivers is as indispensable to society as reverence for gods.[71] Protagoras observed running through this whole concerted communal effort of education a compulsion and punishment that transformed a natural savage into a civil, tamed beast. He thus allows it to be seen that Zeus's gift of a sense of shame and justice, which he expanded into justice, moderation, and the pious, is the product of social compulsion, long schooling relentlessly compelled and relentlessly enforced with punishment and the threat of punishment.[72] All citizens participate in this compelled education, but the longest exposure to it is the privilege of the especially powerful and "the wealthiest are especially powerful" (326c). In the presence of sons of the wealthiest hoping to continue their education with him, Protagoras now tells Socrates why good fathers fail.

So far, he has shown only that good fathers do in fact attempt to pass on their manly virtue to their sons. His explanation of why they fail calls on what he has observed of all skills and of the capacity of the skillful to pass their skillfulness on to their sons. He explains his key point in a pleasing image: imagine flute playing to be the one fundamental requirement of the city instead of justice, moderation, and the pious; schooling would then compel every youth to become an adequate flute player with punishment

71. See Strauss, *Liberalism Ancient and Modern*, 56.

72. "By repeating six times the word *anankazô* (to force, compel) Protagoras leaves little doubt that compulsion is the salient feature of this kind of education and that moral habituation, therefore, is its principal result" (Coby, *Socrates and the Sophistic Enlightenment*, 64).

for those who don't. Would the really good flute players be able to pass on their special talent to their sons?[73] Not necessarily, for in the flute-playing city competence in flute playing would be distributed naturally across a range from best to acceptable irrespective of what the father was. In the flute-playing city only the "most naturally gifted . . . would become notable" (327b)—*becoming notable* being what Socrates told Protagoras Hippocrates desired in seeking him out (316c). The best flute players would certainly *try* to make their sons the best, but because of the natural distribution of skills, they would frequently fail, and sons of the merely competent could be the most gifted. "Nevertheless," Protagoras says, "all would be *adequate* flute-players compared to laymen who had never learned flute-playing" (327c). "Similarly," he says, applying this basic adequacy to all cities, even "the most unjust human among those brought up amid laws and humans [is] just and even a craftsman of" justice compared with "humans who have neither education nor law courts nor laws, nor any compulsion of any kind to compel them to care for virtue" (327c–d). This is what Protagoras's long account of Greek education aimed to show: in the flute-playing city all are flute players; in the actual city all are just, moderate, and pious; all who have undergone the compulsion and punishment of a city's schooling are adequate in the virtue necessary to the city—it being understood without his having to repeat it that Zeus already legislated that those who simply can't blow a moral note are to be exiled or killed (322d, 325b).

Protagoras, the student of education, reports that the city's system of education straightens the naturally bent and twisted, turning them into something comparable to flute players. Like the edifying myth, the edifying logos employs pleasing images to tell of a transformation of the natural human into the citizen. The logos now suggests what Protagoras really holds about the human animal, because now he speaks of humans as the chorus of a comedy and can dare to speak of natural savages. Turning to comedy, he turns with the same finesse to the local, to what the Athenians gathered around him experienced in the comedy that "the poet Pherecrates presented last year at the Lenaia" (327d). Protagoras cannot have seen that performance: he researches his speeches to have them fit his local audience. You live in a civil order here in Athens, he says in effect, amid humans straightened into decency by education, law courts and laws, and if you had to live among savages like Pherecrates' "chorus of mis-

73. Socrates is narrating Protagoras's long speech and now, near its end, adds for the first time a "he said" (327b) and adds one more just before the end (328b). Is he beginning to break the charm of Protagoras's speech?

anthropes then you'd be delighted to fall in with Eurybatus or Phrynondas"—local bad boys who became the butt of Athenian comedy and whose names world-traveling Protagoras troubled himself to remember.[74] The civility brought about by the justice, moderation, and piety distributed to all straightens the bent and twisted natural savages all would be without them—Protagoras restrains himself from openly telling the truth about the natural history of the human species for that truth is deadly; it must be concealed not simply by edifying myths but concealed in his logos as well. As the logos reaches its deepest level of severity in its judgment on the human animal, it turns to comedy and local miscreants, availing itself of a share in the immunity of the comic poet who by sweetening the truth with laughter can tell the truth as if it were mere comic excess.

Well-briefed on local examples, Protagoras brings the Athenian Socrates onto his comic stage: "You're spoiled, Socrates: given that *all* are teachers of virtue as far as each is able, it appears to you that no one is." He presses his point of universality with another example: "Just as if you were to ask who teaches Greek, no one would appear," for all teach Greek as all teach virtue (328a). After a further example, Protagoras speaks finally of himself: he ends his long account of how the city civilizes through various individuals and institutions—of how all share the teaching role—creating a modest little space for himself: "If anyone among us excels even a little at advancing others toward virtue, be glad." And who, after being treated to a speech like this, would not be glad that Protagoras excels more than a little? Having charmed every ambitious young Athenian present to seek *him* out to become notable in the city, he helpfully adds a little advertisement for himself as someone who is "distinguished among humans at helping some toward becoming noble and good" (328b). He even tells the charmed how to pay him—in this as in everything else, in a studied manner uniquely his own that defers to the decency and gratitude of those he teaches or sends them to the temple.

A little hint hides in this ending of his *epideixis* to suggest just how singular the seemingly modest Protagoras in fact is. By saying that all teach virtue as all teach Greek, he indicates his unique merits as a teacher of virtue,

74. Aristophanes, *Women at the Thesmophoria* 861 (staged in 411); Isocrates 8.57. Pherecrates was an Athenian comic poet who first won the prize for comedy in 438. The comedy Protagoras refers to is now unknown, but by having him say that Pherecrates' comedy was produced last year, Plato again makes exact the dramatic date of *Protagoras* for contemporaries familiar with the history of comedy. Writing around 200 CE, Athenaeus places the performance of this comedy in 421, creating a stumbling block for the modern dating of *Protagoras*; see below, "Note on the Dramatic Date of *Protagoras* and *Alcibiades I*."

for who *are* the teachers of Greek? All, yes, but one man alone pioneered the study of the Greek language and can teach it like no other: Protagoras founded the study of Greek from the tenses of Greek verbs and the gender of Greek nouns,[75] through his famous ability to "make the weaker speech stronger,"[76] and all the way up to the relation of language to reality.[77] He, the founding teacher of the Greek language, thus lays quiet claim to being the founding teacher of the nature and necessity of the social virtues, justice, moderation, and piety. And courage and wisdom? He has not forgotten the other two virtues but allows them to stand apart, unmentioned, genuinely different, the virtues that he, the founding teacher of the nature of virtue, embodies in a unique way: in his first speech, introducing himself as a wise man different from the whole tradition of Greek wisdom (316c–317c), he showed his courage as the founding teacher of the Greek enlightenment, the courage to make wisdom public in a new way. His omission of courage and wisdom from his display speech is a measure of his calculation that keeps unspoken the two virtues exemplified, put into action, in his speech on the indispensability of the social virtues. Protagoras's display speech shows that the courageous founder of the Greek enlightenment is wise enough not to believe in general enlightenment but to be capable of spreading enlightenment in the edifying vehicles of myth and logos that keep the harsh truth from the multitude while making it available to the spiritually courageous. The first man to study and teach the Greek language is the first man to study and teach justice, moderation, and piety in a way that gives access to the true courage of wisdom.

But what about that failure of Pericles that Socrates made his single example of the failure of the Athenian great to teach their virtue to their sons? Finally, having saved this local issue till the end, Protagoras rescues the sons of Pericles from the embarrassment and injured pride Socrates

75. "Protagoras was the first recorded Greek thinker to treat language per se as an object of study." Schiappa, *Protagoras and Logos*, 97. See Diogenes Laertius 9.53–54; Aristotle, *Rhetoric* 1407b.

76. Schiappa shows how this phrase, twisted into accusation by Aristophanes and others, designates in fact the effective power of rational argument; his translation replaces the now customary pejorative translations and "understands 'making the weaker account [*logos*] stronger' as advocating the strengthening of a preferred (but weaker) *logos* to challenge a less preferable (but temporarily dominant) *logos* of the same experience" (*Protagoras and Logos*, 113).

77. "Of everything and anything the measure [truly-is] humanity: of that which is, that it is the case; of that which is not, that it is not the case." In his analysis of Protagoras's famous statement of relativity, Schiappa shows how it and the book for which it was the opening line were a response to Eleatic monism (*Protagoras and Logos*, 121–30) and a logical extension of the teaching of Heraclitus on flux and the unity of opposites, an extension that focused on the relationship between language and reality (90–100).

inflicted on them by holding them up as examples of their father's failure. Protagoras refuses to admit that Pericles failed, Pericles with whom he was famously friendly during his previous long stay in Athens. And he refuses to grant that his sons are failures: "it's not fair to denigrate them just yet; there's still hope for them; they're young" (328c–d). Coming so graciously to the aid of twenty-two-year-old Paralus and twenty-seven-year-old Xanthippus, Protagoras ends on a note calculated to charm all the Athenian young into thinking well of an elderly foreigner who shows how understanding he is of youth and how permissive he is of their ways.

What does Protagoras's great display speech display him to be? Some new Prometheus come to bring humanity the gift of a craft to survive and prosper despite being left by nature in precarious defenselessness? In part, yes, for he teaches a political *technê* that makes him appealing to all the Athenian young from Hippocrates up to Alcibiades. Some new Zeus come to bring humanity a gift of virtue enabling them to live in harmonious communities when once they used to tear one another apart? In part, yes, for he teaches justice, moderation, and piety with what has now been decades of unsurpassed superiority in storytelling and logical argument. But he is more than these imaginary beings. He knows himself to be a latecomer to a human world already made productive and civil by the gifts of Prometheus and Zeus. Indebted to them—to the practitioners of productive trades and a whole society of schoolers and enforcers of civility—Protagoras comes when he could only come, late but with understanding, and bringing the gift of understanding to others who are capable of it. He generously pays his debt to those whose work he needs: he does not betray Prometheus and Zeus but tells edifying tales that allow their civilizing work to continue. But he reaps his own reward: while edifying those who notice nothing and bringing to the sons of the powerful a knowledge of how they are to employ the powers that came to their fathers naturally, he offers to the best of those sons the gift of understanding; he reaps the reward of being the founder of a new tradition of Greek enlightenment. Part Prometheus, a forethinking master craftsman bringing a novel craft of persuasive speaking, part Zeus, a natural ruler bringing civility to those he rules with his teaching on divine exemplars, Protagoras is, he wants it known by the knowers, primarily an innovator, the first man to teach the enlightened way of enlightenment.

Protagoras's myth and logos must be judged a great success. They do not resolve the tension between the two parts of Socrates' challenge, but Socrates knew that there is no resolution: his challenge fused two matters that simply are in tension; the democratic mythology of the Many and the actual rule of the powerful coexist in irresolvable tension in a democratic polity. The incoherences of Protagoras's speech that have drawn scholarly disdain dissolve into the incoherence of the belief he is glad to defend in democratic Athens. The incoherence cannot be abolished, and Protagoras's purposes require that it not be. It needs only to be understood and exploited; his speech shows that he can do not only that but also communicate his understanding to a fit listener while edifying the rest.

Socrates reports to the frame audience that when Protagoras concluded his speech, having "displayed" (*epideixamenos*) so much, he "went on looking at him for a long time, enchanted [*kekêlêmenos*], as though he'd say something more, desiring to hear it" (328d). Socrates enchanted?—he seems rather to be mirroring the enchantment of everyone else, those not immune to the charms of a speaker like Protagoras. For it is impossible to believe that he too is enchanted, he who reported being witness to an earlier enchantment when he entered Callias's house (*kekêlêmenos*, 315b), he who warned Hippocrates to be on guard against Protagoras's power as a salesman (313c–e). Instead, Socrates seems to be doing here what he admits doing later (339d–e), indulging in a little feint to win time to collect himself for a proper response. When he does collect himself he turns to Hippocrates[78] and flatters Protagoras, who must be basking in the success of a great speech. Socrates' flattery puts a new challenge to Protagoras: his speech, he says, was like similar speeches one could perhaps hear from "one of our public speakers [like] Pericles," but the difference with Protagoras is that he's not "like a book" with nothing to answer or ask himself, and he's not "like a gong" that once struck rings on till someone puts his hand on it. Protagoras can also answer a question briefly, Socrates says, setting him up for what Socrates will now require of him; and he can, when he asks a question, wait and receive an answer, setting him up for the long alternative answer Socrates will now provide to his great speech.

Protagoras did magnificently what Socrates challenged and invited him to do: he supported the Athenian democratic prejudice with an edifying myth, and he absolved the Athenian leaders of supposed incompetence or irresponsibility in rearing their young by praising Athenian education and all Athenians as participants in it. And he did as well what Socrates warned Hippocrates he would do: he charmed the Athenian young into a state of involuntary subjection to his mastery, and he did it while offering Socrates and other capable listeners private insight into just how to

78. Socrates calls Hippocrates simply "son of Apollodorus" in this his final reference to Hippocrates (328e), his ostensible reason for being there at all.

do it. By inviting such a speech, by inviting Protagoras to lead with his strength, Socrates risked putting Athenian youth under the charm of Protagoras—but he must have calculated that there was no ultimate risk: in his confidence that he could counter and surpass any speech by Protagoras however great, Socrates arranged that his resultant victory over great Protagoras would put Athenian youth under his own charm. And his charm too, like Protagoras's, will charm the young while conveying its own private lesson to the capable.

8. Socrates' Display Speech, Part I: The Wise Must Teach That Virtue Is Unitary (329b–334a)

Socrates does not take explicit issue with any item in Protagoras's display speech; he delivers instead a competing speech of his own, a speech in his own manner. Addressing Hippocrates, he says that "a certain small obstacle" (328e) stands in the way of his being persuaded by Protagoras that the good become good by human care. Beginning with this obstacle about which Protagoras is supposed to persuade him, Socrates sets out to persuade Protagoras. Who will persuade whom? And of what? Having granted Protagoras the right to speak in his way, Socrates must win for himself the right to speak in his, the way of short answers or dialectic.[79] Therefore, addressing Hippocrates, he flatters Protagoras as the master of both long speeches and short speeches: now Protagoras must defend his reputation as a short answerer by giving short answers.

Socrates turns from Hippocrates to Protagoras and in the only direct reference he ever makes to Protagoras's display speech notes that Protagoras said Zeus sent "justice and shame" to humans and that Protagoras himself spoke of "justice, moderation, and piety" (329c)[80] and spoke of all three as if they were one thing, virtue. What Socrates explicitly wants from him is not anything addressed in his display speech but an explanation for the way in which these virtues are one thing: "is it that justice, moderation, and piety are part of" virtue, or are all three "names for one and the same thing," virtue? "Well, that's easy to answer," Protagoras replies, as if relieved at not being asked something far harder to answer, such as a restatement of Socrates' original challenge, which he knows he has not

79. Giving short answers is called *brachulogia* at 335a–b; Coby calls it the "code word in the *Protagoras* for philosophical dialectics" (*Socrates and the Sophistic Enlightenment*, 72).

80. Protagoras said Zeus gave "shame and the just [*dikê*]" (322c)—Socrates says *dikaiosunê*; Protagoras spoke of "justice, moderation, and the holy [*to hosion*]" (325a)—Socrates says *hosiotês*.

met. His easy answer to the easy question is that they are parts of virtue. Are they parts of virtue as mouth, nose, eyes, and ears are parts of the face, or as parts of a lump of gold are parts?[81] As parts of a face, he says. Socrates then puts the question that moves them to the theme of all their coming arguments, the unity of the virtues: do some people have one part of virtue and others another, or is it necessary that a person who has one has all? Protagoras answers that the virtues are not unitary, but to make his point he introduces the two virtues he omitted from his speech: courage and wisdom.[82] "Many are courageous but unjust, whereas others are just but not wise" (329e). In his speech, he used justice as shorthand for all three socially conditioned virtues (326e, 327c); to add courage and wisdom only now and to separate them from justice implies that for him courage and wisdom not only differ from the socially conditioned virtues but may even require a break with them. Are wisdom and courage then also parts of virtue? Protagoras elevates both above the other three, making wisdom the greatest of all. Socrates then secures Protagoras's assent to the view that each of the five is different from the others with respect to its power (*dunamis*).[83]

Socrates' next step proves to be a revelation of his aim with Protagoras. Employing the little tactic of questioning he used in private with Hippocrates (311b–d), he invents a nameless interrogator to put questions to the two of them, forcing them to unite facing a single inquisitor—whose questions are not easy. Just before introducing their questioner, Socrates uses another little device of dialogue he frequently employs with the questioner's questions: he says what *he* thinks the answer should be and prompts Protagoras's agreement. His question is: "Is justice something, or not at all something?" And he adds: "For it seems so to me. What about you?" (330c). When Protagoras agrees, he introduces their inquisitor to interrogate them on the matter they agreed on: "this something, as you two just named it, justice, is it itself just or unjust?" Socrates says he would reply that it is just and asks, "Which way would you cast your vote, the

81. Coby shows the inadequacies of these analogies (*Socrates and the Sophistic Enlightenment*, 74).

82. Protagoras mentioned cowardly at 326b; before giving his speech he implied his own courage and wisdom by impugning the courage and wisdom of the whole tradition of Greek wise men.

83. For the first time Socrates does not quote Protagoras's response in direct speech, saying only "He agreed it was not" (330b). Perhaps the use of indirect speech here and later in this exchange (330d, 332a, 332b$_{5,7}$, 332c$_{1,3,4,8}$, 332d$_{1,6,8,10}$, 332e, 333b) allows Socrates as narrator to control his presentation of just how Protagoras is reacting to what he is asked. His first announcement of Protagoras's annoyance, for instance, comes as something of a surprise (332a), and it is in a direct speech by Socrates. His report on Protagoras's "great reluctance" to agree (333b) is, on the other hand, narrated to the frame audience.

same as me or otherwise?" Protagoras would say the same as Socrates, and Socrates repeats the little exercise: "Then in answer to the questioner, I would say that justice is of such a sort as to be just. Would you also?" Having set this little pattern, Socrates has their questioner turn to piety to ask if it is a something (330d).

Socrates has engineered a special setting for posing hard questions about justice and piety: somebody else puts the question and the two of them answer together, responding as a little community of answerers giving the same answer to the hard questions. In private, in Callias's house, Socrates has arranged a scene that matches the actual questioning the two of them in fact face outside that privileged privacy: outside they are treated as one, as the wise, the sophists, and they are questioned on the great issues of justice and piety. Where do you, the "wise," stand on justice and piety, on law and the gods, the two things our city is founded on? Faced with such questioners, Socrates and Protagoras share a community of interests, they whose courage led them to investigate justice and piety and whose wisdom led them to conclude that they are socially conditioned virtue, whereas their questioners regard justice and piety as founded by wise ancestors favored by the gods—as Protagoras's speech acknowledged. In the little partnership formed by inventing a questioner, Socrates assigns himself a position of leadership: he may have something to teach Protagoras about answering questions on virtue. How can the wise best answer the questions put by citizens suspicious of the justice and piety of the wise? Having prompted the great speaker Protagoras to give short answers, Socrates now leads him to the answers he himself thinks fitting. Will Protagoras allow himself to be led by Socrates, Protagoras who boasts of having pioneered a new way, decades ago, for the wise to present themselves to the Many and to the powerful?

The Unity of Justice and Piety (330d–332a)

Protagoras agrees with Socrates' prompting on the initial questions about piety: he too would answer by saying that "they speak of a certain piety" (330d) and that piety is a something. But then Socrates has their questioner ask if they say this something piety "is itself by nature an impious kind of thing or a pious kind of thing" (330d). Socrates suggests not only their answer but their attitude in answering: he would be indignant or moved to anger by the question. But is Socrates ever really indignant—and at a question? Feigning anger, we must suppose, Socrates would rebuke their questioner, saying literally, "Speak well, human," or figuratively, "Don't blaspheme." The blasphemy is in the very question for "there could hardly be anything else which is pious if piety itself is not pious." The nature of the pious, the piousness of the pious, seems to be something about which Socrates judges it not pious even to ask—or at least that's how he would answer their interrogator. "What about you, would you not give the same answer?" "Absolutely." But it was Protagoras who, with respect to the most basic issue of piety, gave a famous answer in writing, daring even to make it the first sentence in one of his books: "On the gods I am unable to know whether they exist or whether they do not exist or what they are like in form." He wouldn't answer like that anymore if he answered as Socrates thinks he should answer.

The questioner's questioning takes an odd turn when he poses his next question (330e). Socrates pictures him listening to what he and Protagoras said earlier but listening imperfectly: "it seemed to me you two were saying that the parts of virtue are so related that no one of them can be like another." His observation draws a little instruction from Socrates: "You heard quite correctly, except for your thinking that I also said it; there you misheard. For Protagoras here answered that, I having questioned." Socrates *spoke* those words (330b) but only to spell out the implication of Protagoras's judgment that each of the virtues differs with respect to its powers. And those words were Socrates' last words before he invented the questioner—*that precise issue*, then, the unity of the virtues, is the issue on which Socrates wants their community to be formed; he wants Protagoras to withdraw his judgment about how the parts of virtue are related and, in answering a questioner, say what Socrates would say. Socrates makes the questioner turn to Protagoras: "Is what he says true, Protagoras? Do you in fact say that no part of virtue is like another? Is that in fact your argument?" (331a). Socrates insists that Protagoras answer the insistent questioner: "How would you answer him?" "'It is necessary,' he said, 'to agree.'" It's not necessary to agree. Socrates would not agree. He would answer differently—and his whole exercise on what they should answer about the unity of the virtues aims to persuade Protagoras to answer differently.

Socrates gives their questioner one last question, a knotted, poorly constructed little question that commits the fallacy of concluding that if justice and piety are not alike, they are logical contradictories, each, in not being like the other, being its negation: "So piety is not like a just something, nor justice like a pious one, but such as to be *not* pious; while piety is such as to be *not* just, but therefore unjust, and the other impious?" (331a). The question betrays the questioner: he's not well schooled in logic if he thinks that things that are not alike contradict each other. His mistake in logic seems more serious than his mistake about who said what, yet Socrates does not correct it, does not say that something could well be just without being impious or pious without being unjust. Instead, were he to respond for himself to the logically defective question, he would simply say "both that justice is pious and that piety is just" (331b). But he doesn't want to speak for himself, he wants to speak for Protagoras too: "I would give the same answer on your behalf as well, if you would permit it"—if you let me speak for you, I would reverse the answer you gave a moment ago and say instead "that justice is the same as piety, or as similar as it can be, and above all that justice is like piety and piety like justice." This speech offered on Protagoras's behalf brings Socrates' exercise of creating a questioner as far into the light as he dares: Here's the proper answer to an unschooled questioner, Protagoras, not the one you just gave. If you are questioned on justice and piety by someone like that, you should say they are the same or as near to the same as you can bring yourself to say. As their dialogue proceeds, Socrates proves very inventive in suggesting speeches for Protagoras, suggesting how the great teacher of speaking should *alter* his speech to leave the proper impression with questioners who wonder how he really stands on law and the gods. Here's how I'd answer, and it's how you should answer too: the greatest teacher of speaking in Greece is going to get annoyed at having words put into his mouth by a young upstart.

Protagoras refuses Socrates' suggestion. "It seems to me there's a difference here. But what difference does it make?" (331c). Easygoing Protagoras doesn't think it's all that important that the questioner be answered in either of the opposite ways—"if you wish, we can take it that justice is pious and piety just." Socrates grows stern at such indifference and in his severity makes the questioner disappear: there's no use for him if his partner doesn't take up his suggested answers with some conviction. "I don't want this 'if you wish' or 'if it seems to you' to be examined but me and you. I say 'me and you' because I believe that the argument will best be examined if one removes the 'if.'" The "if" will be removed by Socrates' questioning Protagoras directly; but Protagoras first makes a peevish little speech on difference that deep within it turns on an "if you wish": claiming that there is "a certain similarity between anything and anything else," Protagoras says that "you could, *if you wished*, show that everything is like everything else." But he objects to such obliterating of difference and even invokes justice: "It's not just to call things similar that have merely some similarity, however small the similarity" (331e)—his justice seems to dictate that he give his questioner an honest answer. His wording invites a reply that Socrates could have made the questioner's accusatory reply: "Oh, so according to you the just and the pious have only a small similarity to each other?" Protagoras's response—"Not quite that, but not as you seem to me to suppose, either"—would be hard to interpret if Socrates had not made a comment that leaves no doubt about how Protagoras feels about his interrogation at this point: "you seem to me annoyed with this" (332a). Having annoyed Protagoras and failed to persuade him to answer as he does on the unity of justice and piety, Socrates drops the unity of these virtues, having proven nothing. But he later acts as if he has proven it or nearly proven it (333b, 349d), and he'll act as if he has proven the other unproven unities as well, for from here on the dialogue itself possesses a clear unity: Socrates adheres tenaciously to his purpose of proving the unity of the five virtues, developing four separate arguments that together prove the unity of all the virtues. But the way he proves the first proves something about his proofs: what matters is acting as if the virtues are a proven unity for a questioner interrogating the wise on what the wise hold about what matters most to the questioner.

The Unity of Wisdom and Moderation (332a–333b)

Having shown his purpose in establishing the unity of justice and piety, Socrates turns to a virtue that had no place in Protagoras's display speech but that he identified afterward as the greatest or most important part of virtue, wisdom. To show that wisdom and moderation are identical Socrates develops a simple argument based on opposites. Wisdom, Protagoras agrees, is opposite to foolishness. Socrates then sets out to show that moderation (or sensibleness)[84] is opposite to foolishness. He offers five sets of opposites before asking Protagoras to agree that "for each opposite there is only one opposite and not many" (332c). Maybe Protagoras was deflected by the five examples, but after he agrees, Socrates "adds up our agreements" and easily concludes that they have to give up one of their two theses: "that one thing is the opposite of only one thing, or the claim that wisdom differs from moderation" (333a). Which to give up? Socrates asks twice ($333a_{1,\,6-7}$) without getting an answer from Protagoras. Socrates then restates the problem and asks about the *problem*: "or would you have it otherwise?" (333b). Socrates reports that "He agreed, though with great

84. "Foolishness" is *aphrosunê*: it is obvious in Greek that *sophrosunê* is the opposite of *aphrosunê*. Understanding the argument in English is simplified if *sophrosunê* is here translated *sensibleness*, as is fitting for its Greek meaning.

reluctance." He agreed to the presence of a problem, not to any solution, yet Socrates acts as if his agreement dissolved the problem, indulging in complex sleight of hand. First he asks a question, "Then would moderation and wisdom be one thing?" Then he treats the question as an affirmative answer and adds, "we have already brought to light that justice and piety are nearly the same thing." Two nonproofs become two proofs, and he adds: "Come, Protagoras, let's not falter till we've completed our investigation," moving seamlessly to the third pair whose identity is to be proven, justice and moderation.

Thus it is that Socrates on his own decides for the two of them that wisdom and moderation are identical—on the basis of a more than questionable premise that a thing can have only one opposite, and of a comically incomplete argument. Socrates is still acting under the conditions set down by his invention of a questioner for their first argument, still leading Protagoras to answer as he himself answers. The issue is wisdom and moderation. Protagoras kept wisdom out of his list of socially conditioned virtues, but Socrates makes wisdom the same as moderation. Socrates cannot actually hold that wisdom is the same as moderation, wisdom which depends on a radically immoderate questioning of everything. Still, if a wise man were to be questioned on wisdom and he proved that it was the same as moderation, his questioner would have nothing to fear either in wisdom or in the wise man. Socrates' effort with his second pair serves the same purpose as his effort with the first: this, Protagoras, is how it would be wise to speak in public about wisdom.

Socrates expressed gratitude to Hippocrates for having induced him to come to Protagoras and hear his great speech. But Socrates is showing that he came with his own agenda and came well briefed. He is on a campaign to alter Protagoras's way of speaking, to have him adopt a way of speaking different from the one he has pursued so successfully for so many years. Can Protagoras allow himself to be counseled by his younger interlocutor? The annoyance he already expressed will become more acute with Socrates' next proof.

The Unity of Justice and Moderation (333c–335b)

Socrates' argument on the unity of justice and moderation is preceded by another little debate about how Protagoras should answer. Socrates asks: "Does it seem to you that a human who does injustices is being moderate"—*sensible*—"in committing injustice?" (333c). Protagoras deflects the focus away from himself: "For my part, I would be ashamed to agree to this, but many humans say so." Could his avoidance mask his sharing the shameful view that injustice can be sensible or that there is no unity of justice and moderation? "To which shall I make my argument, to [the many humans] or to you?" "If you wish," Protagoras says (using the concession Socrates requested he avoid [331c]), "address yourself first to the thesis of the Many." Protagoras will answer but on behalf of the others he introduced. But Socrates does not wish Protagoras to disappear behind the Many and requires "that you answer whether it seems so to *you* or not." "It is the thesis itself" that he will be especially testing, he says, while granting that "it's likely that both I who ask and the respondent are also tested"—and his argument will in fact test the respondent. Socrates reports resistance: "At first, Protagoras preened himself, claiming that the argument was too annoying" (333d); he does not say why Protagoras found it annoying, leaving it to be inferred that Protagoras is wary of being questioned on the shameful view of the sensibleness of injustice.

Socrates demands Protagoras's own view: "Do some who commit injustice seem *to you* to be sensible?" "Let it be so," Protagoras says, withholding his view. From here the questioning is swift, and Protagoras must continue to assent: by "sensible" he must mean that those who commit these injustices "think well" (*eu phronein*); and by "think well" he must mean they "deliberate well" (*eu bouleuesthai*) or are well counseled; and if they are well counseled, they "do well"; and if "some things are good," are they those "which are beneficial to humans"? Right here Protagoras must put a stop to the reasoning, for he sees that he, the teacher of good counsel,[85] is in danger of being exposed. He stops Socrates' course of reasoning with some vehemence by swearing his first oath and attempting to deflect the issue of the good away from human benefit: "Yes, by Zeus, and even if they're not beneficial to men, I call them good." Socrates informs his frame audience that Protagoras became "riled up and contentious" and drew "himself up into battle array to refuse to answer" (333e). Faced with a Protagoras he has provoked to anger, Socrates says he continued "with caution and asked gently." His gentle question invites Protagoras to continue the deflection he just initiated—"Do you mean what is not beneficial to any man, or what is not beneficial to anything at all?" Protagoras accepts the invitation, giving a little speech on the relativity of good that would be standard material

85. There is a verbal connection between "well counseled" (*eu bouleuesthai*) and the "good counsel" (*euboulia*) Protagoras claims to teach (318e).

for him, though perhaps his annoyance on this occasion can be felt in his first example of things that are good for some things but worthless for others—"things like shit" (334a).

What would the nongentle question have been, the attacking question averted by a Protagoras drawn up in battle array because of the line of questioning? It would have been the question that closed the trap Socrates set so carefully, the question swift Protagoras sees coming: Injustice, then, Protagoras, when well counseled, is the good thing beneficial to those few your good counsel counsels while not being beneficial to men in general—and it's sensible for those few to act unjustly while concealing it from the just Many?

Socrates' questioning must feel like betrayal to Protagoras, whose "further proof" of his mythos appealed to kinship to compel Socrates, his kin as inquirer, to permit his show of being just to mask his necessary injustice. But it is not betrayal, because Socrates, having all but closed his trap, invites a threatened Protagoras to escape. The subtitle of *Protagoras* is *Sophists: An Arraignment*,[86] and Protagoras is put on trial—but his accuser lets him off just before bringing his indictment into the open, leaving unspoken the charge that the arraigned *must* hide: you are a teacher of the sensibleness of injustice. Everyone recognizes that it is mad to declare oneself unjust (323b), and Protagoras, not mad, reasonably lies about his injustice. He does not follow the policy of immoderation that Thrasymachus will cultivate in his more open declaration to young Athenians that he gives good counsel on the benefits of injustice,[87] but Socrates' argument comes that close to removing Protagoras's cautious cover of pleasing tales like that of Prometheus and Zeus and their divine gifts. Zeus may give all a sense of shame and justice, but Protagoras offers his students the means to exploit those universal gifts. No wonder he draws himself up into battle array. He thinks he might be losing his cover if not his argument, and his cover is more important than his argument.[88]

But Socrates does not violate the community of kin to which Protagoras appealed, the community he himself has aimed to establish in the face

86. It is uncertain if the subtitles stem from Plato, but this one is particularly apt.

87. Thrasymachus, however, openly states his position in a private home after the elder of the house has departed; it is Socrates who betrays Thrasymachus's view to a wider public the next day for reasons that will have to be considered.

88. Socrates' argument would have ended in the disunity of justice and moderation: his argument leads to Protagoras's winning. But by stopping just short of this conclusion, Socrates wins by proving the unity of justice and moderation to Protagoras, that is, proving the desirability of claiming their unity and opposing the shameful opposite view of the Many.

of the hostile questioner he supplies. He *stays* his attack, he allows the injustice of Protagoras to remain hidden from all, perhaps, but himself and Protagoras, swift old Protagoras who has a right to his reputation and who would now know that his adversary has exercised restraint at just that point where he has the least right to expect it: the Athenian philosopher, at home among the best young Athenians, does not press his advantage on the point of greatest vulnerability for a foreign sophist and greatest concern for a citizen. Instead, Socrates tips his hand, as it were, to show Protagoras that he holds the winning cards—and has refrained from playing them. Released just prior to exposure, watching as Socrates goes on to feign a crisis over a secondary matter, Protagoras is granted a privileged perspective on Socrates' methods. He watches Socrates prove his kinship, prove that he is one of those kin Protagoras spoke of who would think it mad for a kinsman not to "claim he is just, whether he is or not" (323b). Can Socrates' now-evident kinship succeed in creating the kind of community with the beneficiary of his restraint that his previous efforts failed to create, a community of like-answerers? For Socrates' concern with Protagoras-as-answerer is not about how he answers *his* questions but about how he answers the questions of a public inquisitor on the virtues. Socrates makes his case to Protagoras for a community of wise answerers to *that* questioner by showing him that he does not press his advantage when he is kin to the answerer.

Socrates pursued his apparently aggressive course of questioning at some cost to himself: when Protagoras finishes his irate little speech on the relativity of the good, the onlookers "shouted in applause as if he had spoken well" (333c). An audience that applauds that speech and not his display speech seems to have been moved to sympathy for him in his annoyance at Socrates' questioning. *They* do not understand Socrates' gracious restraint, his embrace of Protagoras's kind of kinship.

9. Socrates Stages a Crisis (334a–338e)

Socrates' questioning has turned gentle, and Protagoras used the opportunity to make an entertaining speech on the relativity of good, a little gem of a speech he must have made many times before, given its studied examples of how different kinds of things benefit from different materials. His speech works its charm on his applauding audience, but even though it is not particularly long, Socrates makes its *length* the issue: he's a "forgetful sort of person," and if spoken to at length, "I forget what the argument is about," so because of his "poor memory" Protagoras should "cut down your answers to me" (334d). Socrates of the poor memory is now reciting that very speech plus everything else that was said at that meeting. It's not possible that *he* forgot what the argument was about, his own argument that stopped just short of indicting Protagoras, but alleging that he forgets allows him to point to Protagoras's success: he charmed the applauders into forgetting what the argument was about. It was about the sensibleness of injustice and it had Protagoras pinned; but instead of reminding the applauders what the argument was about—instead of doing what he could have done if his aim was to win—Socrates stages a crisis.

For a second time, he invokes Protagoras's reputation: "I've heard" that you can speak either at length or with great brevity and teach others to do so as well (334e). By appealing to Protagoras's reputation for mastery at both kinds of speaking and conceding his superiority on long speeches, Socrates justly claims a right to insist on short speeches. Protagoras's response concedes that their exchange has been a "contest of speaking" and shows that he knows his reputation is in jeopardy: "if I had done such as you bid me, which is to discuss in the way my opponent bids me discuss, I would never have appeared better than anyone else, nor would the name of Protagoras have become known among the Greeks" (335a). The threat is dire and the solution desperate: rather than have them return to what the argument was about, he's willing to lose half his reputation as a speaker; victory in this contest before such a notable crowd of rivals, followers, and prospects is now possible only if he concedes he's losing on Socrates' ground.

Socrates tells his frame audience two conclusions he drew from Protagoras's maneuver. First, "he was not satisfied with his answering thus far"—Socrates knows Protagoras knows his situation. Second, "he would not be willing *voluntarily* to continue the discussion as answerer"—Socrates knows Protagoras is resolute, and if his questioning is to continue, *Protagoras will have to be compelled*. Replying to Protagoras, Socrates again refers to his reputation: "it's said of you, and you yourself say, that you can converse making both long speeches and brief speeches" (335c). And he restates the decisive issue still more clearly: "But it is for you, who are capable of both, to concede to us, and adopt the way suited to both of us, in order that our conversation continue." Then comes the claim that jeopardizes his candor: he says he has other business that makes it impossible for him to stay for long speeches so he must leave, a claim refuted in the act of narrating it to his frame audience whom he assured that "nothing prevented him" from telling the story of where he's coming from (310a). Socrates stands up to leave. Not only is he willing to appear forgetful, he appears willing to abandon the whole argument, to lose the contest he himself arranged with the dangerous huckster he warned Hippocrates about. Why put Hippocrates at risk by letting Protagoras appear to defeat him?

Three young Athenians, none of them Hippocrates, act to keep Socrates there. Callias, the host, seated next to Socrates, grabs him, seizing his arm with his right hand and "this old cloak of mine with his left" (335d); he implores him to stay, saying that "there is nothing I would hear with more pleasure than you and Protagoras discussing." Standing, Socrates addresses their host and likens his situation with Protagoras to what he would face were he to run with a competitive runner, the famous Olympic victor, Crison of Himera:[89] for them to run together Crison would have to slow down and run alongside him. "So if you desire to hear Protagoras and me," Socrates tells their host, "beg him to answer me as before, with brevity, and with respect to what he is presently asked" (336a). Socrates will stay if Protagoras is compelled to answer. But Callias can't see the point and appeals to what seems to him to be just: "But you must see, Socrates, it seems just that Protagoras deserves to discuss in the manner he wishes, and you likewise in the manner you wish" (336b).

Justice is the issue, and the young Athenian who would spend the most on getting an education from sophists[90] judges Socrates unjust in his demand. But the next young Athenian to speak corrects Callias's misjudgment, and in speaking up speaks as Socrates said he would, on his behalf. Alcibiades "broke in" (*hupolabôn*): "Not beautifully [nobly] do you speak, Callias."[91] He gives Callias a lesson in the justice of contests, restating Socrates' position in a way that emphasizes its fairness: Socrates is willing to concede Protagoras's supremacy in long speeches, "so if Protagoras agrees he's inferior to Socrates in short speeches, Socrates is satisfied" (336c). But if Protagoras wants to continue to claim supremacy on short speeches too, "let him discuss by means of question and answer, instead of spinning out long speeches in response to every question." Alcibiades sees that Protagoras's attempt to evade Socrates' argument costs him half his title as world champion of speech, and he won't permit such a dodge. He also saw through the strategy of Protagoras's long speech and dares to accuse great Protagoras of "avoiding the arguments by not being willing to

89. Crison of Himera was the Olympic victor at the Olympics of 448, 444, 440 (Diodorus Siculus 12.5, 23, 29).

90. *Apology* 20a.

91. Alcibiades' first speech is beautiful with its musical *ou kalôs . . . ô Kallia*: not beautifully do you speak, beautiful one.

give an argument, and instead going on until the Many among his hearers *forget* the point of the original question" (336d). Alcibiades knows that the applauded speech merited no applause; the applauders are a mere Many who notice nothing; the applauders forgot what the question was. As for Socrates, Alcibiades knows: "I assure you, he won't forget, despite his little joke about being forgetful." Alcibiades did not forget either; he was not charmed as the applauders were. He ends his intervention on justice: "So it seems to me that what Socrates says is more equitable." Alcibiades is no partisan; he judges by the standard of fairness. He concludes displaying a natural political aptitude: having just told them all what fairness dictates, he says, "now each ought to show what he thinks"—this is a democracy and all are free to show what they think, but if fairness rules all will think as Alcibiades has shown them to think: the young man seems to be fit by nature for democratic rule.

"After Alcibiades, *I think*, Critias spoke"—Socrates makes another little joke about his memory just after Alcibiades assured everyone that Socrates has not forgotten. He knows Critias spoke next—Critias who arrived paired with Alcibiades, Critias who will be paired with Alcibiades for Socrates' whole life as the two young Athenians he corrupted into Athens' two greatest criminals. Here at the center of his chronologically first dialogue, Plato allows Socrates' two most notorious associates to speak up together, each speaking on behalf of Socrates, each speaking characteristically. For if Alcibiades brashly broke in to correct Callias, criticize Protagoras, and invite everyone to follow him, Critias the future sophist and tyrant addresses only the leading men present. "Prodicus and Hippias," he says, "it seems to me that Callias is on the side of Protagoras"—Callias is a mere partisan—"whereas Alcibiades is always a lover of victory in whatever he undertakes" (336e). Alcibiades is a partisan of contest, a lover of victory who knows when victory is merited and when not and who, like Critias himself, can see the fraudulence of Protagoras's appeal to fairness as Callias can not. "But we shouldn't be partisans of either Socrates or Protagoras," says Critias, speaking up not as an open ally of Socrates but in a way that serves Socrates' interests. Critias invites the two sophists to intervene: "but beg them both in common not to break up our meeting in the middle." Critias invites the wise to resolve the situation—Critias who will, as a future sophist, become an advocate of rule by experts and eventually take charge of Athens himself as the ruling expert who imagines he can solve its postwar problems. But here any resolution that resumes the conversation can benefit only Socrates—for although Socrates is standing up to leave, it's Protagoras who wants it over.

Young Athenians speak up at the center of *Protagoras* to resolve the crisis Socrates generated by threatening to leave. Prominent by his absence from these interventions, and from every subsequent event in the dialogue, is Hippocrates. Yet Socrates led his frame audience to believe that it was for Hippocrates' sake that he was there at all. The total disappearance of Hippocrates and the rise of other young Athenians invite an inference about Socrates' real reason for being there: inept young Hippocrates is not the young Athenian who most concerns Socrates; instead, young men of the aptitude and promise of Alcibiades and Critias are his concern, and Alcibiades is the more important of the two, as the opening of *Protagoras* suggested. Socrates was forced to allege to countrymen who gossip about his hunt for Alcibiades that Alcibiades was less attractive to him than wise Protagoras. But at the center of his narration Alcibiades rises to his central role in Socrates' actions in the first of Plato's dialogues. Willing to abandon the whole conversation, Socrates shows himself a worthy hunter of a worthy quarry. He has observed Alcibiades since he was a child and seen his sense of fairness[92] as well as his superior intelligence and brashness. Counting on what he has observed in Alcibiades—the intelligence to secure him against the charm of speeches, the sense of fairness to trigger outrage at an unfair appearance of fairness, the brashness to speak up for what others fail to see—Socrates makes the dramatic gesture of leaving to compel young Alcibiades to speak out on his behalf, compel Alcibiades to compel Protagoras to continue. Alcibiades' two subsequent interventions, both on Socrates' behalf, will confirm the suspicion that Socrates is at Callias's house on the hunt for Alcibiades.

Invited by Critias to solve the crisis of Socrates' threatened departure, Prodicus and Hippias offer characteristic advice. Prodicus makes useful distinctions about how they should all act (the listeners are to listen to both in common but give more weight to the wiser, and the two speakers are to dispute but not wrangle)[93] and about what will result (the speakers will be heard with respect and not merely praised in words, and the listeners will be delighted to learn something that engages the mind and not be merely pleased as at a bodily sensation). "Very many of those present accepted" what Prodicus says, and what follows fills his prescription. Still, his advice contains no compulsion. "Hippias the wise"[94] picks up on

92. *Alcibiades I* 110a–c.

93. Socrates uses dispute (*amphisbêteô*) and wrangle (*eridzô*) as synonyms when describing Simonides' way of addressing Pittacus (343d).

94. The opening words of *Greater Hippias* are: "Hippias, the beautiful and wise."

earlier suggestions of kinship to suggest that among those made kin by nature and not by laws a middle course is possible. But he can say that "all present" are kin by nature and make them all "we who know the nature of things . . . the wisest of the Greeks"—a lax standard of kinship with no test of fitness to belong.[95] He ends by suggesting that Socrates and Protagoras moderate their respective speeches and submit to "an umpire and overseer and president" to watch over the discussion (337c–338a).[96] Who will rule their discussion? On that question Socrates' threat to leave ends.

Socrates responds to Hippias's suggestion by posing the problem of an arbiter: "it would be shameful to choose a judge of the speeches" because all four possible options fail. If the one chosen is inferior, the worse would oversee the better; if he's equal he would be superfluous; if he's better—"but it's impossible for you to choose anyone wiser than Protagoras," and if you choose someone who is no better but you claimed he was, "it's an insult, as though you were choosing an overseer for an inferior" (338c). The only fit arbiter is the wise man, but the "wisest" is party to the dispute. Having described the rule of the wisest as facing an insurmountable impasse, Socrates says what he's willing to do: have Protagoras ask questions first and he'll answer in a way that shows how an answerer should answer—he's willing to instruct Protagoras in one of the ways of speaking of which he is allegedly master. Then, when Protagoras has asked all he wishes to ask, he will answer Socrates. Protagoras will thus be compelled into answering, and Socrates states the consequence: if Protagoras is not eager to answer, "both I and you can beg him, just as you did me, not to ruin our meeting." Socrates rules: he has just compelled them to compel him to continue, and he'll continue under terms that compel them to compel Protagoras to continue. Wanting to continue, Socrates arranges that they continue by having them compel Protagoras who does not want to continue. "And for this there is no need of one single overseer; all will oversee in common" (338d). Everyone agrees, compelling Protagoras to agree, reluctantly, for the time will come for him once again to answer Socrates' questions.

So they proceed with all overseeing in common. And what happens? Socrates shows how to answer by giving a very *long* answer, and when he's done, an overseer appoints himself without claiming to, for the discussion threatens to take a course different from the one agreed upon: Alcibiades intervenes, this time to preside as overseer, speaking up twice on Socrates'

95. See Strauss, *Liberalism Ancient and Modern*, 59.

96. Hippias's use of three words to name a single functionary seems to be a little joke at Prodicus for his distinctions among near synonyms.

behalf to keep the company to the common agreement. "There is no need of one single overseer," Socrates alleged, but this democracy too needs a leader. Young Alcibiades, like Pericles, does not have to be named presider to preside.

10. Socrates' Display Speech, Part II: A Wiser Stance toward the Wise (338e–347a)

Socrates' threat to leave was a complete success: Protagoras, "though very unwilling, was compelled to agree to be questioner . . . and to take his turn at giving only a short speech in answer" (338e). Socrates has maneuvered Protagoras into a crisis where everything is at stake for him,[97] facing as he does eventual questioning by one who has been outsmarting him while refraining from making his victories public. Compelled to question but free to choose his subject matter, Protagoras chooses the topic most advantageous to him: education, the most important part of which, he says, is to be clever in what is said by the poets, "to understand what is correctly composed and what not and to know how to differentiate them, giving a reasoned account [*logon*] when asked" (339a).[98] Here if anywhere he will be able to defeat Socrates and save his reputation. As implied in his very first speech, Protagoras as educator takes on the poets, the educators of Greece. And Socrates indicates that the whole tradition of Greek wisdom is at stake: Is Protagoras's stance toward the ancient wise wise?

Free to choose any text after elevating the study of poetry, Protagoras chooses a passage from Simonides,[99] the poet he named with Homer and Hesiod as sophists who hid their sophism (316d):

> Hard it is on the one hand truly to become a good man
> In hands and feet and mind foursquare well wrought without flaw.

97. Woodbury, "Simonides on *Aretê*," 135.

98. "Plato's account of Protagoras analyzing epic poetry is the earliest recorded instance of textual criticism" (Schiappa, *Protagoras and Logos*, 161). Schiappa argues that "*how* Protagoras taught is at least as important as *what* he taught" (158); he taught by "critically analyzing the epic poets" (161), shifting authority from the mythopoetic to the literate, a revolution connected to the shift from an oral to a literate culture. The importance Protagoras placed on literacy is suggested by his law for Thurii that "the sons of all citizens should be taught to read and write at the public expense" (160). Schiappa argues that Protagoras was the "principal founder" in the formation of a "metalanguage," the language about language that Plato and Aristotle further developed.

99. Simonides of Ceos belonged to an earlier but post-Homeric generation of wise Greeks, c. 556–c. 466; his death occurred a few years after Socrates was born and about when Protagoras began his public career.

After reciting these opening lines he asks Socrates if he knows the poem. It may surprise him to hear that Socrates not only knows it but has studied it carefully. Protagoras's questions elicit exemplary short answers from Socrates, which state his view that the lines are beautifully and correctly composed and would not be so if the poet contradicted himself. Protagoras then quotes lines from later in the poem (339c):

> Nor do I deem harmonious the word of Pittacus[100]
> Albeit spoken by a wise mortal: "Hard," he said, "it is to be goodly."

Socrates sees no contradiction between the two quotations, but Protagoras triumphantly claims that Simonides forgot what he said earlier and criticizes Pittacus for saying what *he* said, contradicting himself. Socrates is a poor student of the most important part of education if he holds a poem that contradicts itself to be beautiful and correct.

Protagoras's speech "met with clamor and praise from many of those listening," testimony to the partisanship the contest has generated and to the effect of Protagoras's seeming discovery of a contradiction in a well-known poem by a revered authority. Socrates reports that "like a man struck by a good boxer, my eyes went dim and I was made dizzy by his words and by the clamor of the others" (339e). But he confesses that he immediately devised a little ruse: "Then—and to be truthful with you, I was trying to gain time to think out what the poet did mean—I turned and called on Prodicus." He is undazed enough to stage a little comedy with Prodicus as ally that exhibits great presence of mind in showing up Protagoras as a student of poetry and preparing his own knockout blow. Socrates says to Prodicus that as a citizen of Ceos,[101] like Simonides, "it is just for you to rescue the man." To form an alliance with Prodicus, Socrates names Homer and appropriates a Homeric alliance: Socrates is like the river Scamander, which called upon the river Simois to withstand Achilles, saying, "Dear brother, let us together check the mighty strength of the man."[102] Scamander's next words, left unquoted, are: "since soon he

100. Pittacus, ruler of Mytilene, was more than a century older than Simonides (650–570). He was said to have resigned his rule upon hearing that Periander of Corinth had turned an office similar to his own into a tyranny: he said upon resigning, "Hard it is to be goodly."

101. Ceos is an island off the southeast coast of Attica. Prodicus was often in Athens on diplomatic missions as well as to earn money teaching (*Greater Hippias* 282c). Socrates calls him his teacher (*Meno* 96c) and consistently speaks well of him (*Phaedrus* 267b–c, *Laches* 197d, *Euthydemus* 277e, *Theaetetus* 151b).

102. *Iliad* 21.308–9. Is Socrates referring to a discussion in one of Protagoras's books? According to a papyrus from the first century CE, "Protagoras says that the purpose of the episode im-

will lay waste the great city of Priam." Socrates' next words are: "So I call upon you lest Protagoras *lay waste*[103] Simonides for us." As Achilles threatened Troy, Protagoras threatens Simonides, and only an alliance can save the threatened. The allied rivers failed because Hera called in Hephaestus to resist the rivers and aid Achilles. Can Socrates allied with Prodicus be more successful against Protagoras? Allegedly dazed, he has, in a contest Protagoras turned into a contest about poetry, struck upon a most apt allusion in Homer to make clear what is at stake in this new battle: Protagoras is like the Achilles described by Scamander: a "wild warrior who now has the upper hand and is eager to act equally to the gods";[104] *this* new wild warrior threatens to lay waste not Simonides alone but the whole sacred tradition of Greek wisdom from Homer onward. Socrates' "restoration of Simonides" (339e) prepares his defense of the whole tradition of Greek wisdom against the wild warrior of the sophistic enlightenment threatening to lay it waste.

To restore Simonides against Protagoras's threat requires the special "musical skill" Prodicus just exhibited, a capacity to distinguish between things as similar as "wishing and desiring." What Protagoras made the same points to a very great difference: "Prodicus, give me your judgment, do these seem to you to be the same, becoming [*genesthai*] and being [*einai*], or different?" (340b). Prodicus proves a fine short answerer: "Different, by Zeus."[105] Simonides gave his own view, then, when he said that *becoming* good is hard and criticized Pittacus for the very different claim that *being* good is hard.[106] Turning to Protagoras, Socrates cites Prodicus as his authority: "But as Prodicus here says, Protagoras, being and becoming aren't the same thing"[107] (340c). It's not only Prodicus that Socrates can call to his aid: "Prodicus and many others besides would say along with

mediately following the fight between the river and mortal men is to divide the battle and make a transition to the theomachy, perhaps also to glorify Achilles." Guthrie, *Sophists*, 269.

103. This Homeric verb, used sixteen times in the *Iliad, ekperthô*, "destroy utterly, sack," occurs only here in Plato.

104. *Iliad* 21.314–15.

105. *Genesthai* often means "to be" in general usage.

106. Simonides' word for good is *agathon*, the standard term, whereas Pittacus's is *esthlon*, but nothing is made of any difference between these words despite Prodicus's propensity to find near synonyms different.

107. *Protagoras* thus merely touches the distinction between becoming and being (in connection with becoming good and being good), whereas *Theaetetus* makes that the very core of Protagoras's view of reality—all is becoming, *Theaetetus* 152c–e, 180d–181b. Socrates' first engagement with Protagoras in the Platonic corpus downplays the ontological element; his last engagement with him—at a very different time and place with a very different audience—plays up that element.

Hesiod that it is hard to become good, 'For before virtue the gods have placed sweat,' but when someone 'Attains its summit, it is henceforth easy to possess, though it was hard before."[108] Bringing in Hesiod completes Socrates' use of all three poets disparaged by Protagoras as lying sophists (316d). He ends with these words of Hesiod, refraining from quoting the famous next lines about the virtue in question, insight: "Best is the man who thinks for himself and sees how things will turn out at the end. Noble too is the man who listens to good advice. But useless is the man who has no brains of his own and, worse yet, pays no heed to the words of others." Nor does Socrates indicate that Hesiod's words were an admonition addressed to a single man, his brother. "When Prodicus heard these things he praised" Socrates—he must remember Hesiod's next words and hear the blow against Protagoras.

Protagoras does not directly answer Socrates' argument about becoming and being; he even abandons Simonides' poem and poetry generally, appealing instead to the opinion of all humans: "Great would be the ignorance of the poet if he says that virtue is so paltry a thing as to be easy to possess, when it is the hardest of all, as it seems to all humans." Are "all humans" right in judging virtue hardest of all? Socrates' argument against this claim takes a wholly new tack while still making use of Prodicus, this time as a teacher from whom Protagoras himself ought to learn as Socrates learned. For Prodicus, Socrates says, belongs to the ancient line: his "divine wisdom" is "ancient, originating in the time of Simonides, or perhaps in an even more ancient time" (341a)—perhaps back through Pittacus to Hesiod and Homer, then. Protagoras, on the other hand, is "inexperienced" in this, whereas Socrates experienced it as a student of Prodicus and so himself stands in the ancient line.

Socrates' next argument belongs in comedy as he enlists Prodicus as an ally to interpret a word from Simonides' first line (hard, *chalepos*) that Protagoras repeated (hardest, 340e). "Maybe Simonides didn't conceive 'the *hard*' the way you conceive it"—maybe he used the word in a local, Cean sense. Maybe he used the word *hard* as Socrates used the word *terrible* (*deinos*): "Prodicus admonishes me each time I use the word to praise someone like yourself and say that 'Protagoras is a *terribly* wise man.' . . . For 'terrible,' he says, is bad." Socrates gets to call Protagoras a *bad* wise man to his face and in this company, and does so with the immunity of a comedy writer. If Prodicus the Cean claims that "terrible" is bad, maybe Simonides the Cean used "hard" to mean bad (341b). "Let's ask Prodicus,

108. Hesiod, *Works and Days*, 289–94.

for it's just to ask him about Simonides' dialect. What did Simonides mean by 'hard,' Prodicus? 'Bad.'" No wonder Socrates studied with Prodicus, a sophist with a sense of humor willing to play the stooge while watching to see just where Socrates' wicked response to Protagoras leads. So Simonides "criticized Pittacus, for saying 'It's hard to be good,' as though he heard him say that it's bad to be good"—as though Simonides heard Pittacus say what Socrates hears Protagoras daring to say to young men in Athens: it's bad to be good—and good to be bad, to break courageously and wisely with the justice, moderation, and piety you've been taught. Prodicus is a fine comedy partner: "But what do you think Simonides means, Socrates, other than this? Wasn't he reproaching Pittacus for not knowing how to differentiate words correctly, being from Lesbos and educated in a barbarous dialect?" (341c). Being from Abdera, how can Protagoras answer *that*? He answers soberly if correctly with mere assertion again based on what is generally thought: "That's way off, Prodicus. I well know that Simonides also meant by 'hard' just what we others mean: not 'bad' but that which is not easy and is accomplished only with much trouble" (341d).

Of course he meant that, Socrates admits, and Prodicus knows it because Prodicus was *joking*—and Socrates acts as if Prodicus was joking in order "to *test* whether you can rescue your own argument." *Socrates* is the jokester and *Socrates* the tester, and he announces to all that Protagoras flunked: "the great proof" that Simonides did not mean 'bad' by 'hard' is the very next line of his poem: "god alone would have this prize" (341e)—he can't mean the good is bad if god has this prize. This is *crushing* victory: what kind of student of poetry is Protagoras if he can't even refute an outrageously incorrect interpretation of a line of a poem *he* introduced by citing its next line? And Socrates? He performed a masterful little trick of exegetical acuity against the sophist who claimed that being clever in poetry is the most important part of education. Socrates the jokester can make jokes sting.[109]

Socrates' alliance with Prodicus continues for one last blow, as he assigns Prodicus the words to be used of Simonides if in fact he meant that it's bad to be good and then said that the good belongs to god alone: Prodicus would say Simonides is "some sort of profligate[110] and in no way a

109. Meanwhile a problem has arisen, an apparent conflict between wise Hesiod and wise Simonides: If god alone can have the prize of virtue, how can it be said to be easy to possess after attaining it? Perhaps the conflict could be settled by asking what a god is.

110. *Akolaston*, lit. "unrestrained," undisciplined, debauched, and in some uses, uneducated.

Cean." By denying Simonides citizenship in his own city, would Prodicus be denying Simonides citizenship in that city to which Prodicus most belongs, the "city" in which Hippias said the wise share citizenship (337c)? And Protagoras, then, who seems to suggest that it's bad to be good? Is he in no way a "Cean"?

Socrates now seems to have gained enough time "to think out what the poet did mean" (339e), for he ends his use of Prodicus and submits to Protagoras's testing. "But what it seems to me Simonides intends in this ode I'm willing to tell you, if you wish to test what experience I have concerning verses, as you said." Socrates keeps to the agreement he engineered by inviting Protagoras to continue questioning him "if you wish" (342a). All Protagoras can say in response is "If you wish, Socrates," repeating the phrase Socrates just used twice despite his earlier prohibition on Protagoras's use of that phrase (331c). Matters are not left simply with their wishes, for "Prodicus and Hippias strongly bid me to go ahead"—they smell blood in the water, the blood of their founding rival.

Having won the right to continue questioning Protagoras by staging a crisis over Protagoras's long answer, having then fashioned the resolution that required him to give the model short answers, and having brought in Prodicus as a short-answerer, Socrates delivers a very long answer. It is an interpretation of the poem Protagoras introduced to defeat him, an interpretation intricate in detail, comprehensive in scope, and totally twisted to the service of his own ends, for Simonides cannot possibly have meant what Socrates will say he meant. Still, his interpretation is an unassailable argument against Protagoras, for it outdoes Protagoras in what Protagoras does best: interpret the poets to his own advantage. No wonder Protagoras will again have to be compelled to speak after this display speech by Socrates: he knows how to measure mastery in his field.

Socrates delays his exposition of the poem in order to set out a comic prologue that highlights a single feature of the tradition of Greek wisdom, its esotericism. He dramatizes his point in a memorable, hilarious claim: "Philosophy is most ancient and abundant among the Greeks in Crete and Sparta" (342b). Sparta! Athens' rival since the Persian wars, the city famous for dour militarism, self-serving piety, and lack of modern education, the Greek city *least* open to philosophy.[111] In an Athens famous for the *parrhêsia* or free-speaking that allowed foreign sophists to speak their radical thoughts with the least amount of veiling, and in a house full of

111. For what a sophist had to surrender to speak in Sparta, see the measures Hippias was forced to take and willing to take, *Greater Hippias* 283b–286a.

foreign sophists speaking freely to young Athenians, Socrates' claim about Sparta could not fail to bring major amusement.[112] His story explicitly recalls Protagoras's earlier story of Greek wisdom (342b, see 316c–e): each tells a tale of the tradition of Greek esotericism, with Socrates' praise of it aiming to supplant Protagoras's scorn.[113] The Spartans deny that they are philosophers, Socrates says, "and pretend that they're ignorant"; they do so to hide the genuine superiority that is due to their wisdom and to make their superiority seem due to "their fighting ability and courage."[114] When the Spartans wish to consult their wise, having grown weary of meeting them in secret, they expel all Sparta-lovers and strangers and meet their wise unbeknownst to any foreigners (342c). Socrates suggests a test for his claim that the Spartans are the best educated in philosophy and argument: they will know what he says is true when they meet with even the most inferior Spartan and discover that at some chance point he "will throw out a worthy saying, brief and pithy, like a clever [*deinos*][115] shot," making his interlocutor seem no better than a child (342e). Brevity, not long speeches, is the sign of wisdom, and "there are those, both now and in the past," who know "that the uttering of such sayings bespeaks a perfectly educated man." He gives a list of seven Greek wise men with no overlap with the nine Protagoras cited in his list (316d–e). Socrates' list of those who practiced Cretan and Spartan wisdom has noteworthy features: it contains no Cretan, centers on "our own Solon," and ends with the seventh only "*said to be* the Spartan, Chilon."

As his final and most telling point about the Spartan wise, Socrates says "they went together in common to Delphi and dedicated to Apollo the first fruits of their wisdom, putting up on the temple there what is now on every man's lips, 'Know thyself' and 'Nothing too much.'" The ancient wise were united and acted in common to shelter their shared wisdom by mak-

112. See *Republic* 557b on the *parrhêsia* that characterizes the democratic city; *parrhêsia* is "claimed by Athenians as their privilege" (Euripides, *Hippolytus* 422). See also *Gorgias* 487d. Monoson (*Plato's Democratic Entanglements*) argues for translating *parrhêsia* as "frank speech" rather than "free speech," and her chapters on the topic emphasize truth telling and risk taking as constantly reinforced by Athenian experience in the Assembly and in the theater ("Citizen as *Parrhêsiastês*," 51–63, and "Philosopher as *Parrhêsiastês*," 154–80).

113. Most of Socrates' audience will not have heard Protagoras's story, told before the three groups united.

114. The two special virtues of wisdom and courage, introduced late by Protagoras and soon to be examined by Socrates as the final part of his examination of Protagoras, are thus coordinated in Socrates' story, courage being the open virtue that serves to conceal wisdom.

115. Socrates' own throwing out of *deinos* after just making a joke with its ambiguity (341a–b) may be an indication that Spartan education in philosophy and argument is really *terrible*.

ing it public in a laconic, Delphic form that became sacred and authoritative for everyone; they became powerful by making it seem that Apollo himself spoke their wise words. Protagoras's condemnation was therefore both right and wrong: it's true that the wise "did not pass undetected by those who have power [*dunamenous*] in the city" (317a), but those *having power* in the deepest sense were the wise who put up words that bore the god's authority; it's true that "the Many perceive, so to speak, nothing, but merely repeat whatever these leaders proclaim," but real leaders *proclaim* through the voice of the god what the Many *repeat* in obedience to sacred commands.[116] The ancient wise were wise and effectual in the way they sheltered their wisdom and in the way they proclaimed it: Protagoras is more than wrong about them, he's foolish and ineffective to proclaim himself wise and to prove it by claiming that the reputed wise were foolish. Let the ancient wise be seen as Spartanizers, laconic and powerful in speech, and models for the present.[117]

"Why do I say these things?" Socrates asks (343b). He says them as the indispensable prologue to his interpretation of Simonides' poem, for Pittacus's words, "It is hard to be good," took their place, Socrates claims, among the terse sayings of the ancient wise. Simonides, being "a lover of honor as regards wisdom, realized that if he overthrew this saying, just as if it were a famous athlete, and prevailed over it, then he would become famous among the people of his own time" (343c). Socrates' thus claims a singular place in Simonides' corpus for this poem: it opened his campaign to be counted among the wise; with this poem Simonides mounted the stage. Socrates is emphatic: "It was against this saying, and for the sake of this, that he composed the entire poem, as a plot to discredit it."

Socrates begins his exegesis doing violence to the first line of the poem, violence that allows him to argue—quite fictitiously—that the whole poem is a contest Simonides picked with Pittacus. It also allows him to cast much of Simonides' indictment in first-person direct speech: "I" accuse "you."

116. Critias is in the audience for this claim about what wise humans "put up" at Delphi. *Charmides* will show how memorable Socrates' words were for him, for he recites them back to him, using the same verb Socrates used, *anatithêmi*, and to telling effect (*Charmides* 164d–165a).

117. Plato's two *Hippias* dialogues, set in Athens in 420 during the great diplomatic congress arranged by Alcibiades, also have as a major theme the wise stance toward the ancient wise, *Greater Hippias* opening on Hippias's belief in the progress in wisdom (281a–283b). In these dialogues too the attitude toward the ancients hinges on esotericism: *Lesser Hippias* is an effort to prove that polytropic Odysseus is wiser than truth-telling Achilles and that the author of both is wisest. Socrates' artful exegesis of Homer in *Lesser Hippias* proves that it's possible to recover what the ancient wise meant in their poems, despite their esotericism and despite Socrates' statement to the contrary (*Lesser Hippias* 365d).

He begins by construing two words in the first line, the particle *men* and the adverb *alêthôs* (truly), in unnatural ways.[118] This frees him to "imagine" (343e) that Pittacus's words opened the poem and that Simonides replied with an accusation. The imagined poem begins with Pittacus saying: "O humans, it is hard to be good" and Simonides saying, "O Pittacus, what you say is not true" (344a). Pittacus addressed all humans, Simonides addresses Pittacus alone on what he said to all. Only then did Simonides speak his first line, which Socrates fits into the opening stanza:

> Whereas not to be,
> But to become a good man, in hands and feet and mind foursquare
> Well wrought without flaw, that is the hard thing truly.

Having altered the first stanza to show a rising wise man address an older one on the truly hard thing, Socrates makes a claim about the "general character and intention" of the rest of the poem: "in its entirety, [it is] above all a refutation of Pittacus' saying" (344b, 343c). Simonides speaks in his poem "as if he were speaking an argument [*legei logos*]," (344b) which Socrates reconstructs: whereas *becoming* a good man is truly hard but possible for a time, to remain or *be* so, "as you say, Pittacus," is impossible and not human, for god alone can have this privilege (344c):

> But a man cannot be not bad
> Whom unmanageable [*amêchanos*] catastrophe has brought down.

Just who can be brought down by unmanageable catastrophe? Socrates makes Simonides' words apply first to one who rules, the pilot ruling a ship, then to the resourceful (*eumêchanos*) in contrast to the resourceless (*amêchanos*). Giving as examples of the resourceful the pilot, the doctor, and the farmer, Socrates summarizes the traits of the one who cannot be not bad when unmanageable catastrophe brings him down: "resourceful,

118. The conjunctive particle *men* typically anticipates a *de* as "on the one hand" anticipates "on the other hand." Socrates' imaginative exegesis treats *men* as itself an "on the other hand" introducing Simonides' response to Pittacus's saying. He makes *alêthôs* (truly) modify *hard* instead of *good* in order to prepare his main point; that *alêthôs* actually modifies *good* and not *hard* is clear from the lines that follow immediately for they describe what *truly good* really means. For more detailed explanations of Socrates' exegetical sleight of hand, see Taylor, *Protagoras*, 144–45, and Coby, *Socrates and the Sophistic Enlightenment*, 114–15. Adam Beresford ("Nobody's Perfect") argues for a reordering of the lines of Simonides' poem that makes Socrates' twisted use of it more fully intelligible.

wise, and good" (344e). "But you say, Pittacus," that it is merely hard to be good, not *impossible* as is actually the case:

> For whereas when doing well every man is good
> If doing bad he's bad.

Socrates asks what doing well "at letters" or at doctoring or carpentering means: it means *learning*; those alone can become bad who have, through learning, become good. Socrates gives possible causes of becoming bad: time or toil or illness or some other calamity, all such causes sharing one general feature: "doing bad is this alone: to be lacking in knowledge" (345b). "All these things were said against Pittacus," he claims, the ostensible reason being Simonides' desire to be counted among the wise by defeating one of them. But isn't the genuine reason for Socrates' violence to the poem slowly dawning? All the points of his argument share a common feature: all are arguments that he, a rising wise man, wants to address to Protagoras, an older one. They concern the rule of the wise who put up brief statements addressing all humans but who, being themselves human, cannot be simply wise, simply good. Protagoras demands the impossible of them, that they *be* good or beyond the reach of his self-advancing criticisms. "All these things were said against Pittacus," Socrates says, " and the following passages in the ode . . . make the point even more plainly" (345c). In fact they confirm the suspicion that Protagoras is Socrates' object, that his Simonides stands to his Pittacus as he stands to Protagoras.

Claiming that "throughout the poem" Simonides "advances against the saying of Pittacus" (345d), Socrates does his final violence to the poem, arguing again that a word with a clear referent refers in fact to something else. Simonides said he praises and loves whoever *willingly does nothing shameful*, and Socrates transfers *willingly*: Simonides *willingly praises and loves* whoever does nothing shameful. Socrates can then say that Simonides, like all the wise, knows that "all who do shameful and bad things do so unwillingly" (345e)—all are teachable if their shameful actions are made clear to them. Transferring agency and making the bad unwillingly bad leads Socrates to a new claim about Simonides: he "believed that a noble and good man often *compels himself* to become the friend and praiser of someone, as often occurs to a man estranged from mother or father or fatherland or other such thing" (345e–346a)—estranged from kin and country. When the bad suffer such estrangement, "it's as if they observed with glee the worthlessness of their parents or fatherland, and *make a display* [*epideiknunai*] of blaming and reproaching, in order to avoid criticism from humans for neglecting them; they even increase their blame and *willingly* add enmities to those that arise of necessity." Here Socrates' violence to Simonides' poem almost states its purpose: Protagoras acts like a bad estranged man, estranging himself from the "parents and fatherland" that generated him as a wise man, the tradition of wisdom that schooled him but to which he now paints himself wholly superior, delighting in display speeches that blame and reproach what are like parents and fatherland to him; he willingly adds enmities to those that arise out of necessity among the wise—and because none can simply *be* wise, disputes always arise.

What do the good do in unavoidable estrangement? They "compel themselves to conceal and praise"—the opposite of what "Pittacus"/Protagoras does. Socrates emphasizes the need for self-compulsion: "should the good become irritated at some *injustice* inflicted by their parents or their fatherland, they appease themselves and are reconciled, compelling themselves to love and praise *their own*" (346b). In his myth Protagoras made the injustice of kin the occasion for appealing to his wise kin for restraint in handling his own unavoidable injustice: everyone agrees that it is mad to tell the truth about one's injustice. Socrates here responds: kinship among the wise entails a self-restraint that you, Protagoras, violate by elevating yourself through unrestrained blame of the kin who generated you. Socrates' criticism of Protagoras, restrained by concealment in the exegesis of a predecessor's poem, is a model of a family member's self-appeasement and reconciliation.

But if restraint is needed, why did Simonides blame and accuse Pittacus throughout his poem rather than exercise the self-compulsion of the wise to praise and love their own? Socrates ends by saying why. Reverting to direct speech,[119] Socrates has the young wise man address the older: "'Pittacus, I'm not blaming you because I'm a lover of blaming [*philopsogos*]'" (346c). Socrates cites three lines about what suffices Simonides in a man and leads him not to censure. Socrates then almost repeats himself—"'I'm no lover of censure [*philomômos*].'" Simonides is not looking for perfection, Socrates says, but "accepts without blame the middling things" (346d), and he recites again the lines he recited earlier that a "wholly blameless human" is not to be found (346d, 345d). Repeating too the decisive verse in which he changed the referent of *willingly* (346e)—"I praise and love all willingly . . . who work nothing shameful"—Socrates repeats his essential addition: "there are those I praise unwillingly." Within

119. He last used direct speech at 344e.

his reestablished context of praise and love—unwilling praise and love—Socrates makes a place for blame with words wholly his own: "As for you, Pittacus, if what you said had been even middlingly equitable and true, I would never have blamed you." With his final naming of Pittacus (346e) Socrates frees himself to use nothing but pronouns to the end. His blame is severe: "But as it is, you lie, vehemently in fact, and about the greatest things, seeming to speak the truth—because of this, you I blame" (347a). Such blame blames a blaming that blames its own kin; such blame blames a liar who, seeming to speak the truth, speaks a lie about the greatest things, which can only be the things of wisdom. In these bare pronouns *I*, Socrates, blame *you*, Protagoras, as Socrates closes his case. The last three words he speaks as "Simonides" are an emphatic "*you I blame*,"[120] you, Protagoras, I, Socrates, blame. The blow is stunning. Young Socrates dares to blame the old founder of sophism for words like those Protagoras spoke first in the dialogue, characteristic words that threaten to lay waste the whole tradition of Greek wisdom in the service of elevating himself. Socrates blames Protagoras for violating the natural kinship of the wise, recklessly making all the previous wise seem fools and cowards to a public only too willing to believe it. Socrates' blame, for all its power, is veiled; he keeps it in the family. Such loyalty to kin invites Protagoras to reciprocate in kind—to prove teachable in his treatment of the wise.

Socrates' "analysis" of Simonides' poem makes Simonides address Pittacus with the critique Socrates wants to address to Protagoras—*does* address to Protagoras, wisely or in the Spartan manner, having, in the subtlety of his words, expelled the foreigners. Like his earlier blame of Protagoras for giving good counsel for injustice, Socrates' blame for threatening to lay waste the whole tradition of Greek wisdom avoids what it blames Protagoras for, criticism of the wise within hearing of the public. Defeating Protagoras in this manner, and in the very skill he judged "the most important part of education" (338e), and in a *long* speech, Socrates has good reason to think he could be successful.

Adopting Simonides' role, Socrates does what he says Simonides did: take a calculated step to enter the company of the wise by defeating a famous wise man (343c). While this can hardly describe Simonides' situation,[121] it describes Socrates' exactly. But if the situation fits, can the mo-

120. *Se egô psegô*. Adding the first-person-singular pronoun to a first-person-singular verb that can stand alone is a standard way of giving emphasis to the pronoun.

121. Little is known about the occasions for Simonides' surviving poems, but Protagoras reported that Simonides addressed this poem to Scopas, the son of Creon of Thessaly (339a), where

tive? Socrates said Simonides was a lover of honor. But he qualified that claim, making Simonides a lover of honor *as regards wisdom*. And that describes Socrates' action in *Protagoras* exactly, as he makes clear at the very end. Having insisted on making his victory so painfully obvious that Protagoras called him a lover of victory (360e), Socrates narrates that Protagoras himself, in his last words, acknowledged what such a victory could mean for Socrates: "it would not surprise me if you became famous among men for wisdom" (361e). And Socrates *narrates* those private words, makes them public to a mildly interested audience: he *wants* to become famous for wisdom. Socrates is a lover of honor *as regards wisdom*, judging it better that the public view the wise as Socratic rather than Protagorean—better for wisdom. Socrates is willing to take on the burden of fame in order to give wisdom a defensible public face.

But if Socrates uses his victory to win a reputation for wisdom with the Athenian public, what about his reputation with the Athenian young who came to Callias's house seeking a wise teacher? Hippocrates wanted to use Socrates merely as a means of access to Protagoras. Will what is happening before his eyes lead him to reconsider and recognize that the teacher he needs is Socrates? The question cannot be answered for Hippocrates, who has dropped out of the dialogue, replaced by young Athenians of greater promise. It may not escape *their* notice that the teacher they seek is not one of these great sophists who came to town seeking them but their own fellow citizen. Among these young men one stands out, as was clear from the very opening. In fact hunting the vernal beauty of Alcibiades, Socrates hunts with wisdom's weapons to win honor as regards wisdom with Alcibiades. Hunting Alcibiades, he camouflages his hunt from those who first accused him of that by reporting on his defeat of the wisest man of their time; he persuades those auditors that he is not a hunter of Alcibiades with the very words that may make his hunt successful. He hunts hiding that he's a hunter.

In the chronologically first of his dialogues, Plato shows Socrates mounting the stage as a politic philosopher who knows he must act to preserve Greek wisdom from the Greek enlightenment, act to restrain a flawed esotericism. Protagoras, "wisest of our generation," is a genuine intellectual prodigy who endangers Greek wisdom by a reckless and self-serving assault on the wise that ridicules their esotericism as fearful and

---

Simonides is known to have spent some years. Because his statement serves no particular purpose of Protagoras's, it is a much more likely occasion than the one to which Socrates twists the poem: that it was an address to wise Pittacus.

ineffective and as hiding nothing more than sophism. Socrates praises esotericism in the only way true to it, esoterically, inventing salutary tales about the famous wise while recommending laconic brevity. But what does *he* hide? A Socrates who praises ancient esotericism invites a close examination of all his speeches. They're speeches that by their very nature expel foreigners and communicate a private wisdom to those avid to speak with him in private about it. The wise way to speak of the wise includes a wise invitation to wisdom.

11. Alcibiades Presides (347a–348c)

Socrates ends his long speech by addressing Prodicus and Protagoras. But a long time passes before Protagoras speaks up again, and even then he speaks reluctantly and under the duress of being shamed into speech by Alcibiades (348c). Protagoras seems to have suffered in fact what Socrates feigned suffering; he's like a man struck by a good boxer, his eyes growing dim, made dizzy by Socrates' words (339e). Beyond having been delivered a possible knockout blow in that half of his acclaimed mastery still remaining to him, long speeches interpreting poetry, Protagoras will know that he has been addressed in the Spartan manner, one wise man to another; he will know that Socrates intimated far more than he stated openly, and even quick Protagoras needs time to sort out the implications of Socrates' gracious way of smashing him. Socrates gives him time, for he makes a speech about speeches and reports that he said even more than he reports (348b).

With Protagoras silent, Hippias leaps in, praising what Socrates said and offering a display speech he was evidently accustomed to giving on that very poem (347a). He is eager to enter the competition to stake out his own claim now that Socrates has shaken the authority of old Protagoras.[122] But he's not permitted to begin: "Some other time, Hippias," Alcibiades says. Who appointed this youngster overseer? He's not the host; he's not a peer of the famous sophists gathered here to contest for superiority; no vote was taken. Alcibiades simply orders Hippias not to make a speech. He does not speak as a partisan; he enforces what Socrates established

122. Competitive Hippias later adopted the practice of going to the Olympics to make display speeches that would prove he was the wisest man in Greece (*Lesser Hippias* 363d–364a; set in 420 shortly before the Olympics that year). Did Hippias understand what Socrates so subtly implied to Protagoras? *Lesser Hippias* shows he is not given to subtlety or indirect speech, for he judges Achilles a better man than Odysseus because Achilles says what is on his mind and does not indulge in the evasive speaking that made Odysseus repellant to him.

and all agreed to (338e), restating that agreement and invoking the justice of holding to what has been established. For the second time, then, Alcibiades speaks up as the spokesman of justice: "But right now, the just thing, according to Protagoras' and Socrates' agreement with each other, is for Protagoras, if he wishes, to question, Socrates answering, or if he wishes to answer Socrates, for the other to do the questioning" (347b). Socrates stated the reasons why they could not appoint any single overseer, suggesting instead that they all oversee together (338e). Alcibiades, invoking the prior agreement, simply rules Hippias out of order. He takes command as the presiding judge Socrates said it would be impossible to find.

With Alcibiades having again come to his aid, Socrates assumes that the order Alcibiades restored will be followed and leaves it to Protagoras to choose whether he will question or answer. But he wants to "give up odes and epics" and return to "the things I first asked you about, Protagoras, for I would be pleased to bring their examination with you to a completion" (347b). The things he first asked about, the unity of the virtues, remain Socrates' theme to the end, though incompleteness in treating it would have resulted from his earlier threat to leave: he knew he would be stopped. Abandoning display speeches on poetry has advantages, for such discussions of poetry are like the drinking parties or symposiums of the uneducated, who "are not able to be together just by themselves, through their own voices and speeches of their own" (347c); instead, they "hire the extraneous voice of the flutes and carry on their intercourse through these other voices" (347d). Those who "have been educated" speak in their own voices; "there is no need for an extraneous voice or for poets who cannot be asked to explain what they say" (347e)—but before he returns to the things he first asked about, he too employs the allegedly extraneous voice of the flute, bringing in Homer to represent or misrepresent what he wants to do with Protagoras (348c). When the Many introduce poets into their speeches, they put forward different interpretations that they are not able to test—he does not say that the interpretations are beyond testing or that what the poet meant is beyond recovery.[123] But "you and I" should set aside the poets and "make speeches of our own to ourselves, putting ourselves to the test of truth" (348a). Socrates repeats Alcibiades' repetition of their previous agreement, inviting him to continue question-

123. At a similar turning point in *Lesser Hippias* (365d) Socrates says, "Let us leave Homer aside, since it is impossible to ask him what he was thinking when he composed these verses." Socrates' subsequent argument depends on his having understood perfectly what Homer had in mind when he composed these verses.

ing if he wishes, or begin answering him if he wishes. He reports that he said more such things with the same aim but Protagoras stayed silent.

The silence of Protagoras provokes Alcibiades to a third intervention. As in his first, he addresses Callias: "Callias, does it seem to you that Protagoras is acting nobly, not being willing to make it clear whether he will give an argument or not?" Callias is a partisan of Protagoras (336b), but he can offer no defense of his master now. Alcibiades renders judgment against Protagoras: "It doesn't seem [noble] to me." And he says what Protagoras must do: "Let him either take up the discussion or say he's not willing to discuss, so we can collectively understand his position"—sixty-five-year-old Protagoras, greatest of sophists, sits in silence as an Athenian too young to address the Assembly pronounces on how he should speak. If Protagoras remains unwilling to keep to the rules, Alcibiades says, "Socrates can then discuss with someone else, or another with someone else who wishes to" (348b). We don't need Protagoras, Alcibiades says in effect, making it clear that *he* has no need of him, I'm ready to preside over new alignments within the rules we agreed on. All this is addressed to Callias, but its true audience is Protagoras and all the others listening in—young Alcibiades knows how to play to the crowd to give his speech maximum effect.

And Socrates reports that Alcibiades' speech had its intended effect: "Protagoras was shamed, or so it seemed to me, by the things Alcibiades had said." Alcibiades already knows the uses of shame, a gift of Zeus to all, according to Protagoras, who implied that the wise and courageous could learn from *him* how to manipulate it (322c–d). Alcibiades already employs it effectively, for his theatrical little aside is a complete success: "Callias and nearly all of the others present" add their pleas to have Protagoras continue under the rules (348c).[124] "Reluctantly," but given no choice except a still more shameful surrender, Protagoras "brought himself to take up the discussion," and Socrates reports that he chose to finally face up to Socrates' questioning: "he bade me ask him questions which he would answer" (348c). As befits an assembly that Socrates made democratic, Alcibiades' forceful clarification of the situation for all as overseers, plus his reasonable setting forth of new, if less attractive, options, leads to popular persuasion—all within the rules set down by Socrates and now with their agreement enforced by an unelected but natural leader, some Pericles rising in the midst of their little democracy, untaught by his guardian.

124. A disappointed Hippias perhaps being the exception?

Alcibiades never has to intervene again, but the strength of his presiding continues to exercise its force: knowing that a watchful and severe judge presides over their exchange, Protagoras keeps to the argument all the way to its bitter conclusion. But if Alcibiades presides, what brought him to preside? Socrates. Having provoked reaction by threatening to leave, Socrates set the rules of questioning and answering under which Protagoras would have to proceed. He then arranged that all would preside in common, knowing full well that such an arrangement would result in a few presiding, knowing full well that Alcibiades above all was fit to act—*compelled* to act, compelled by his nature, a nature well known to Socrates who has observed him since he was boy.[125] To preside, one would have to be capable of recognizing what was happening, committed to fairness, and bold enough to intervene. Socrates' long, close observation of Alcibiades taught him that he is a most intelligent observer fiercely committed to fairness and lacking least in boldness—Socrates would know that Alcibiades would preside even though he is not yet twenty.[126] By setting the rules under which the conversation would proceed, Socrates rules by ruling Alcibiades.

Socrates led the frame audience to believe that he forgot about Alcibiades in the presence of Protagoras, "more beautiful" because more wise—but introducing Hippocrates enabled him to show that he did not hold Protagoras to be wise. It also enabled him to lead his frame audience to conclude that he conducted his whole conversation with Protagoras for the sake of a young Athenian, hoping to cure him of his desire to learn from Protagoras. But Hippocrates has disappeared, replaced by the young Athenian Socrates wanted his suspicious auditors to believe he had forgotten. He hadn't forgotten. Instead, he seems to have conducted his conversation with Protagoras in part for the sake of Alcibiades, the young Athenian who matters most, the one whose corruption by Protagoras would most damage Athens, the young Athenian Socrates had long hunted but whom he has learned he must hunt while seeming not to. Allied now with a forceful leader manipulated into his camp, Socrates can proceed with his examination of a Protagoras shamed into responding. No wonder Xenophon said, when speaking of Critias and Alcibiades, that they knew that Socrates could do what he wanted with any interlocutor.[127]

125. *Alcibiades I* 103a–b, 106e, 109d, 110b.
126. See especially the incident with a playmate that Socrates describes at *Alcibiades I* 110b.
127. *Memorabilia* 1.2.14.

12. Socrates' Display Speech, Part III: A Wiser Stance toward the Many (348c–359a)

Having regained at last the right to continue the argument he interrupted with his threat to leave, fully in command having shown Protagoras that he can defeat him in short speeches and long and that he practices restraint by not exposing his injustice and by speaking as a Spartan—now, after all this maneuvering, Socrates can give his reason for wanting to speak with Protagoras. He alleges that it is "to investigate things which constantly perplex me" (348c), but he brings in the allegedly extraneous voice of a poet (347e) to point to the real reason: to instruct Protagoras on a matter he has investigated himself.

A Homeric Alliance

Socrates calls in Homer for the final time in order to intimate in the appropriate laconic manner who he is and what he's doing, adjusting Homer's words just enough to make his point (348c–349a). He speaks of what "Homer said," but it's what Diomedes said when he chose Odysseus as his companion for his dangerous spy mission into the enemy camp of the Trojans. The leading Achaians were present, gathered by Agamemnon, Menelaus, and Nestor to plan what to do on that desperate night after the Trojans had driven them back to their ships, there to await the onslaught expected on the following day, when, they feared, the Trojans would burn their ships and massacre them wholesale. Socrates quotes the words Diomedes spoke before choosing a companion to accompany him on the mission he volunteered for, an alliance of two that just might be able to learn what the enemy planned for the next day: "when two go together, one observes before the other."[128] But Socrates omits Diomedes' next words, "how profit may be had," and substitutes his own: "for thus somehow all we humans are more resourceful [*euporôteroi*] in every deed and speech and thought" (348d). Socrates replaces Diomedes' words with words that ring of Odysseus the resourceful. Returning to Diomedes' words, he quotes his opening phrase of why he needs a companion—"If one observes by himself"—but not his next words: "yet is his discernment the shorter, and but slender his device." No such disparagement of the solitary observer passes Socrates' lips; instead, when one observes by himself, he says, "he immediately goes around searching for someone to whom he can show his

128. *Iliad* 10.224.

discovery and thereby confirm it" (348d). Diomedes mistrusted his capacity to observe and chose Odysseus to aid him in discernment; Socrates fully trusts his capacity to observe and chooses Protagoras to aid *Protagoras'* discernment, to show *him* what Socrates observed on his own. Yet how fitting Homer's scene is: the two of them must become allies, for the wise have no choice but to enter the camp of a dangerous enemy that could destroy them tomorrow. This was the first thing Protagoras said to Socrates: when the wise enter a city, the powerful always regard them as a threat, and they must take precautions. Homer's scene gives Plato a graphic image for Socrates' basic reason for wanting to speak with Protagoras: the future of the Achaian cause, the future of Greek enlightenment, hangs in the balance.[129]

Why does Socrates choose Protagoras? "Who else but you?" he asks, as Diomedes asked why he chose Odysseus.[130] He gives two reasons: First, Protagoras considers himself noble and good (*kalos k'agathos*), but unlike others who are good but unable to make others good, "you are yourself good and are able to make others good in the same way" (348e). This flattery must be measured against Socrates' private judgment to Hippocrates: the great risk is that Protagoras will make others worse, particularly the impressionable young. His second reason is that "you have such faith in yourself that, while others conceal this art, you have openly proclaimed yourself to all Greeks by the name of *sophist*, declaring yourself a teacher of education and virtue" (349a): taking Protagoras back to his first speech, this reason points to Protagoras putting his *kin* at risk in face of the enemy camp. "How could I not then invite you to investigate these matters, and ask questions and consult with you? There's no way I could not" (349a). Deep within *Protagoras* Socrates intimates to Protagoras that he is under a strong compulsion to speak with him, a self-compulsion generated by the harm Protagoras could inflict on the young and on the tradition of Greek wisdom. Compelled to intervene, Socrates speaks as resourceful Odysseus to needy Diomedes; he acts to forge an alliance between kindred Achaian heroes that will alter the reckless way the wild warrior enters what both know is an enemy camp.[131]

129. Socrates names and quotes Homer three times to suggest an alliance: with Alcibiades (309a–b; *Odyssey* 10.279), with Prodicus (340a; *Iliad* 21.308–9), and here with Protagoras. He also names and quotes Homer to suggest that he, like Odysseus, has descended to Hades (315b; *Odyssey* 11.601). Socrates names Homer one other time (311e), and Protagoras names him once (316d).

130. *Iliad* 10.242–47.

131. Many are eager to be chosen by Diomedes but Agamemnon urges him to choose the best man; Diomedes gives his reason for choosing Odysseus: "wise above all is he in discernment"

Why would Protagoras listen? He's seen Socrates point to his injustice yet refrain from exposing it. He's seen Socrates' view of the kinship of the wise mask his criticism of him in Simonides' criticism of Pittacus. He's seen Socrates surpass him in what he himself called the most important part of education and then set such a use of poetry aside. And now he hears a Homeric invitation to learn what Socrates observed about the wise way to enter the enemy camp, a wise way to do what Protagoras thought he was already doing wisely. How could he not listen?

Going Back to the First

Socrates wants to get back to "those things I first asked about" (349b, see 347c), "back to the beginning." He holds out hope that Protagoras will now, finally, relent on the unity of the virtues already discussed and unite courage and wisdom to them. He lists the five virtues, again putting courage at the center (349b; see 330b), courage being what Protagoras said his predecessors particularly lacked (316d). Protagoras maintained that the five had no underlying essence or being (*ousia*, 349b$_6$), each name denoting a unique something with all being parts of virtue like parts of a face, not like parts of gold (349c). Having reviewed their argument under the new conditions set by his sequence of self-disclosures to Protagoras, Socrates invites him to abandon his former position: if things "still seem to you as before, say so; but if somehow otherwise, explain it precisely." He fashions his invitation to help his potential ally know exactly what to do: "I'm not holding you to any view, if you now say something else; for I wouldn't wonder if when you said those things you were testing me." Here's how to abandon what you said earlier and become an ally in saying that the virtues are one: say you were just testing me, do as I did when I led Prodicus in a test of you: say you were joking (341d). If he says he was just testing Socrates, Socrates passed, and he can say that he was the first to hold what Socrates says he holds: all the virtues are the same, all golden. A graceful invitation.

Protagoras refuses. Unwilling to play Diomedes to Socrates' Odysseus, he grants only that "four are fairly close to each other," the four previously discussed. Wisdom, moderation, justice, and piety may be as close as Socrates' arguments made them seem, but the one not yet discussed, courage, "is very much different from all of them" (349d). Obstinate Pro-

(10.247). Odysseus in fact saw everything first; he set their strategy (e.g., in capturing Dolon); he conducted the inquiry of Dolon that gained them knowledge of the enemy camp and the enemy's intentions. Diomedes performs the physical deeds.

tagoras offers a proof: "You will find among humans many who are very unjust, very impious, very unrestrained, and very ignorant, but who are distinguished by being very courageous." He seems to be launching into a long speech, for Socrates has to say "Stop!" before saying, "what you say deserves thorough investigation" (349e).

Socrates' investigation of the singular character of courage consists of a brief argument to show that courage is the same as wisdom, and therefore the same as the other virtues. His argument is his fourth and final attempt to persuade Protagoras to present the virtues as a unity. Can it persuade him? Socrates gains the following agreements:

- the courageous are bold, even impetuous or rash, Protagoras adds;
- courage is most noble, purely noble, noble to the highest degree;
- some bold men act knowledgeably; Protagoras generalizes, saying that in all cases the knowledgeable are bolder than the nonknowledgeable, and themselves bolder after having learned than before;
- some of the nonknowledgeable are also bold, even overbold, Protagoras adds.

Given these agreements Socrates can ask if these overbold, nonknowledgeable ones are also courageous, and Protagoras must answer that courage would then be a base thing, for the overbold are mad—not courageous. Socrates has him: if the courageous are bold and the overbold mad, knowledge alone separates them; therefore, the wisest are also the boldest. "According to this argument, wisdom would be courage." This leap to the *identity* of wisdom and courage fits the pattern of Socrates' three earlier arguments, for the identity of courage and wisdom hardly follows from his argument, however much it establishes a certain overlap of knowledge and courage. As with the other three arguments, the desirability of identifying these two virtues derives from the setting imagined at the very beginning, where Socrates pictured the two of them being questioned on what they, as wise, held with respect to justice and piety, a setting reinforced and made more ominous by their Homeric alliance.

Socrates' argument is more than a logical exercise: it is an uncanny mirror of his judgment against Protagoras's practice. The contrast Socrates elicits at the end forces Protagoras to utter the judgment against himself: his boast of a novel boldness in telling the truth about his wisdom is in fact the rash act of one who lacks knowledge—it's even mad. If kin say to their own that it's mad to tell the truth about one's injustice, as Protagoras urged in his own defense (323b), so too, Socrates urges in his veiled attack, is it mad and base and neither courageous nor wise to tell the truth about one's wisdom. Bold Diomedes-Protagoras is not courageous, he's only overbold, says Odysseus-Socrates, who combines courage with observant wisdom.

Protagoras does not yield. Instead, arguing with genuine acuteness, he shows that Socrates' argument could equally well, by a substitution of terms (strength for courage and power for boldness), demonstrate that *strength* is wisdom. All that is required is the fallacious assumption of the coextension of strength and power, as Socrates fallaciously assumed the coextension of courage and boldness. Socrates tacitly acknowledges the correctness of Protagoras's rebuttal: he moves to what looks like a different argument entirely. But it was never the *logic* of his arguments that Socrates meant to be decisive, it was their *utility* in the face of a hostile questioner—and Protagoras has again refused to form a united front for safety despite the added gravity of the Homeric setting. Socrates wants to give him a lesson in salutary arguments, but Protagoras insists on giving him a lesson in logic, as if Socrates were unaware of the fallacy in his argument. Still, Protagoras has shown his mastery of short argument by showing how Socrates manipulated his correct answers into a conclusion that seems persuasive while being invalid. By showing up Socrates as arguing manipulatively and invalidly, Protagoras seems still to be aiming to *win* where Socrates is aiming at agreement in the face of a common enemy.[132]

Protagoras's rebuttal does not lead Socrates to threaten to leave, even though it is longer than the speech that did. Instead, Socrates opens a new line of questioning (351b), preparing his argument for hedonism. Once he completes that argument he returns to the very point here suspended (359a), the identity of courage and wisdom, and develops an argument that mercilessly crushes Protagoras, leading him to put a stop to their discussion. They've arrived at a turning point, small in appearance but major in impact, a new tactic by which Socrates may succeed where he has failed till now: persuading Protagoras to teach the unity of the virtues. The whole sweep of the dialogue comes into clearer focus. For what just happened? Protagoras just made clear that he has no intention of doing what he was invited to do, change his position on the unity of the virtues, treating his

132. Protagoras rebutted Socrates' argument at the cost of contradicting his premise that courage was different from all the other virtues (349d). His rebuttal concluded that courage must be distinguished from mere boldness and that while boldness can come from art (*technê*), it "can also come from anger [*thumos*] and from madness;" courage on the other hand "comes from nature and the well-nurturing of souls" (351b). Courage demands the wisdom that comes from well nurturing.

earlier position as a joke to test Socrates. Instead, he insists that the virtues are different, refusing to embrace what Socrates has unremittingly offered as the salutary view. He has just made his final refusal to act as if the virtues are unitary, and Socrates initiates a novel way of schooling the founding sophist in a less dangerous and more successful way to make a trade of enlightenment. His new tactic rises as what Odysseus observed and can pass on to Diomedes; courage unites with wisdom to produce a new strategy for enlightenment in the face of an enemy Many.

Hedonism

Socrates opens his new line of questioning by gaining Protagoras's agreement that some humans live well but others badly (351b), that a human would not be living well if in pain and misery, that living life to the end pleasantly is to have lived well. Finally, he asks if living pleasantly is good and unpleasantly bad. Protagoras can agree to this claim only with a proviso: a life of pleasure would be good "if he lived taking pleasure in noble things" (351c). Having introduced *pleasure* and *good*, Socrates introduces the other element essential to his new argument, the *Many*, for he refuses Protagoras's qualification on pleasure: "Surely you don't, as the Many do, call some pleasant things bad and some painful things good? I mean, insofar as they are pleasant are they not good, if nothing else arises from them?" Socrates is forcing them onto treacherous ground; to claim that pleasure is simply good is to approach the disreputable doctrine of hedonism that sophists were accused of teaching. Protagoras answers with appropriate wariness, "I don't know whether I ought to answer so absolutely as your question invites me to." He looks to his safety, as he always must, saying that "with respect to the present"—our little gathering here—"but also with respect to all the rest of my life, it would be *safer* to answer" in a way that is consistent with what Socrates said the Many hold: "that some of the things that are pleasant are not good, that again some of the painful things are not bad and others are, and that there is a third kind which is neither, neither good nor bad" (351d).

Socrates insists: "Are things not good insofar as they are pleasant—that is, I'm asking about pleasure itself—is it not good?" Protagoras stalls but in a manner that yields to Socrates: "Just as you always say, Socrates, let us investigate this." And he defines what they are to investigate: "whether pleasure and the good appear to be the same" (351e). A master of short argument has seen where Socrates is moving, and he communicates his insight masterfully. Using the same language he just used to rebut Socrates' argument—"power and strength are not the same" (351a$_1$), "boldness and courage are not the same" (351a$_4$)—Protagoras completes what Socrates has been suggesting about pleasure and good: let us investigate "whether pleasure and the good appear to be the same" (351e). Protagoras takes them definitively into an investigation of hedonism, knowing full well that he is doing with pleasure and good what he was unwilling to allow with courage and boldness because it involved the fallacy of identifying a predicate with the subject of which it is predicated. He commits neither himself nor Socrates to the doctrine of hedonism, only to its investigation. Socrates responds, "Do you wish to lead the investigation, or am I to take the lead?" Will Protagoras raise the objection with respect to pleasure and good that he just raised with courage and boldness? He will not: "It is *just* for you to take the lead, after all, you began the argument." Unyielding Protagoras yields. Why? His novel yielding suggests that his interest has been piqued: what might Socrates say on the identity of pleasure and good, on the dangerous topic of hedonism? He will have recognized that an argument that begins with similarity in form promises similarity in intention: its aim is not logical validity but safety in the face of a common enemy—and because Socrates has trod so often on dangerous ground without betraying Protagoras or himself, Protagoras can trust him on this one. Socrates is willing to lead in a new argument about pleasure and good, and Protagoras is willing to listen because of what he just expressed: safety, and for them both. Let's investigate it and you lead: Protagoras invites Socrates to dive into the dangerous waters of hedonism on the basis of a possible fallacy of the kind he just pointed out. Maybe on this topic Socrates' overriding interest in an alliance will be shared by Protagoras.

To yield leadership to Socrates requires yielding more: Socrates investigates not just hedonism but also Protagoras. Casting himself as a doctor who has observed face and hands, he says, "Come, uncover and display [*epideixon*] to me your chest and back as well so that I may examine you more thoroughly" (352a). The doctor is observant. "Having observed your relation to the good and the pleasant to be just as you say"—having observed your shift from pleasure is good to the good is pleasure, having observed your move to hedonism[133]—he demands more: "come now,

133. Socrates does not have to be so indirect about Protagoras's true position on hedonism in the *Theaetetus*: Protagoras is dead and no longer put at risk by his defense of hedonism. Leo Strauss indicates how hedonism can be a respectable philosophical position even for Socrates in the chapter of *On Tyranny* entitled "Pleasure and Virtue" (92–102).

Protagoras, uncover your thought for me on this: how do you stand on *knowledge*?" Knowledge and pleasure is the decisive issue in the inquiry Socrates now opens on hedonism. Before forcing Protagoras to uncover his stance on knowledge, Socrates assumes his role in the proposed Homeric alliance—Odysseus reports to Diomedes what he observed by himself in the enemy camp: how the Many stand on knowledge. They do not hold knowledge to be "a strong, or a guiding, or a ruling thing" (352b); they hold that even for one who has knowledge, it's not knowledge that rules but "sometimes anger, sometimes pleasure, sometimes pain, other times eros, and often fear." The Many think knowledge is a slave to the passions, the five primary passions Socrates named. The doctor wants to uncover Protagoras's view of *the power of knowledge to rule*. Does he side with the Many on the rule of the passions over knowledge? The doctor poses his well-prepared question to his patient: "Do you think knowledge is noble and able to rule a human being so that if someone knows the good things and the bad things he will not be overpowered by anything, so as to do anything other than what knowledge commands, wisdom [*phronesis*] being sufficient aid to the human?" (352c).

This decisive question draws a two-part answer from Protagoras: first he says, "It seems to me as you say," and then he adds, "it would be *shameful* if I, of all people, were to say that wisdom and knowledge were not the mightiest of all human things" (352d). Once before the patient invoked shame in his response (333c): he cited many humans as holding a shameful view from which he wanted to keep his distance, the view that injustice can make sense, a view that Socrates' questioning showed he actually held. Does shame hide his sharing what the Many hold on the power of the passions to rule knowledge? The answer seems to be no, for his doctor responds to both parts of his patient's declaration, first to its second part: "*Nobly*"—not shamefully—"do you speak," then to its first: "and also *truly*." To speak both nobly and truly uncovers Protagoras's chest and back on the power of knowledge: Protagoras shares Socrates' view that knowledge can rule the passions—after all, the great exhibition speech by the founding investigator of the Greek enlightenment showed that he, a knower of the truth about religion, knew too how to rule through religion. From this point on Socrates speaks as one of an allied pair over against the Many: "You know that the many humans are not persuaded by *you and me*, but say that many who know what the best things are are not willing to do them, though it is possible for them, but do other things."

You and Me and Hedonism

Socrates-Odysseus and Protagoras-Diomedes can speak as one, as "you and me," in the enemy camp, arguing that knowledge *can* rule the passions. They can, Socrates promises, come to rule the enemy camp, rule as welcomed educators of the ruled.

Acting as if he and Protagoras are already one in persuading the Many, Socrates shows that they differ in their interest in the Many: *he* has actively investigated their opinions. "*Whenever I ask them* what on earth the cause of this is [that passions rule knowledge], *they say* that those who act this way do so because they are overcome by pleasure or pain or one of those things I just mentioned." Protagoras, who believes that they "merely repeat what [their] leaders proclaim" (317a), answers: "They say many other things too that are not correct" (352e)—why even bother asking what they hold on this one? To a Protagoras displaying his lack of interest in the Many, Socrates, their investigator, makes his invitation: "*Join me* in the attempt to persuade the humans[134] and to teach what this experience of theirs is" (352e). Here, so beautifully prepared by the Homeric alliance, is the breathtaking core of Socrates' mission for philosophy: he, a young philosopher, invites the famous founder of the Greek enlightenment to become his ally in a mission to persuade and teach all humans a new interpretation of their basic moral experience. Socrates steps forward in *Protagoras* to form an alliance that will give the enlightenment a new public face, one geared to reverse the public suspicion of the wise by making them useful to the public.

A new ally must first be taught, and Socrates turns to that. Humans tell him that their experience of knowing the good and not doing it is "being overcome by pleasure." Socrates and Protagoras will contest their interpretation: "What you say is not correct, you humans, but false." This claim will provoke humans to question them, Socrates says: "probably they would ask us, 'But Socrates and Protagoras, if this experience is not that of being overcome by pleasure, then what on earth is it? What do you say it is? You two tell us" (353a). Those two, Socrates and Protagoras, kindle a dialogue with humans in which humans urgently desire their answer. Why would they care? Because those who claim to be wise promised them a new interpretation of their characteristic moral anxiety, their felt vulnerability to anger, pleasure, pain, eros, and fear, powerful forces that overpower

134. *Tous anthropous*, humans generally, "the world," says Lamb in the Loeb translation, indicating the range of what Socrates is inviting Protagoras to do.

their desire to do the good they know to be good—for they know what gods and forefathers gave them of justice, moderation, and piety. "You two tell us" what our experience really is so we can remedy it and do the good. Socrates offers Protagoras an alliance that promises that the whole world will seek him out if they believe that they can learn from him how the good they know to be good can rule their passions.

Protagoras sees no reason to engage the Many: "But Socrates, why do we have to investigate the opinion of the many humans who say just whatever happens to occur to them?" (353a). Not having bothered to study the Many, Protagoras is wrong about them; Socrates, having observed and questioned them, learned that they have in fact very settled opinions that he can report. For Protagoras to become Socrates' ally in teaching humans the power of knowledge, he must not only be taught what to say, he must also be taught why he should be concerned about the views of the Many. What Socrates says is brief but telling: "it is relevant to our inquiry about courage, regarding how it relates to the other parts of virtue." The unity of the virtues has been Socrates' concern from the beginning, and he just interrupted their argument on the unity of courage and wisdom to school Protagoras in teaching the Many the power of knowledge to rule the passions—but Protagoras sees no point in consulting the Many. Socrates insists on his continuing leadership: "If it seems best to you to abide by our previous opinion that I should lead however I myself think will in the most noble way make the matter become clear, then you follow." He adds a threat: "But if you don't wish to, then, as you like, I'll bid farewell" (353b). So indispensable is Socrates' argument with the Many on the power of knowledge that without it he'll leave. He earlier threatened to leave, and Protagoras would have welcomed it. That crisis was resolved but without eliminating the threat of shameful defeat for Protagoras when his opponent would again question him. That questioning has begun, but Socrates makes it an occasion to form an alliance. There's no need for Socrates to leave—Protagoras *wants* to hear him out: "Finish as you began." And Socrates literally finishes as he began, again supplying an interrogator to question the two of them and again recommending that they answer in one voice. The unity of Socrates' whole pursuit of unity on the unity of the virtues is apparent as he repeats his tactic from the very start of his dialogue with Protagoras. Protagoras resisted a unity of voices at every step, but in the coming dialogue with the Many he will only agree. The one who now interrogates the wise speaks for the whole human race outside the few wise; those ruled by the passions ask the few ruled by knowledge, and their questions are no long hostile, for the answers they eagerly seek could perhaps cure the deep moral malaise that makes them slaves to passions that keep them from doing what they know to be good.

Free to pursue what he started, Socrates once again has the many humans "ask us" their heartfelt question about the meaning of their experience of being overcome by pleasure. Socrates answers that "Protagoras and I will try to explain it to you" (353c). The method they use is no sophistic display speech but a questioning and answering in which the two of them question the Many, drawing out from them the proper interpretation of their experience. Showing Protagoras how to proceed in a Socratic manner, Socrates conjures an elaborate theater-piece. A teachable Many learn from themselves, as it were, via questions put by Protagoras and Socrates. They learn that they are hidden hedonists. What they really believe is that "good and bad" are terms that can be replaced by "pleasure and pain"; the replacement would become obvious to them if they simply considered the long-term effects of what they call good and bad: by *good* they really mean productive of long-term pleasure and by *bad* productive of long-term pain. Twice Socrates invites the many humans to give some other explanation of good and bad, and twice he answers for them, "But you can't" (354d, e). "What you're saying is true," Protagoras grants (354e).

Having taken Protagoras with him this far, Socrates suddenly changes the scene: no longer do the humans "ask *us*," nor do the replies come from Protagoras and Socrates; now they "ask *me*" and Socrates alone replies. And he no longer asks Protagoras to agree on what they would reply, he simple says what they would reply, leaving Protagoras to observe. The scene change begins with a rebuke: "you humans" criticize "me" for being so tediously long-winded in explanation. But he can't help it: "it isn't easy to demonstrate what you mean by being overcome by pleasure," and everything depends on that. He even challenges the many humans to take back their agreement that good and bad really mean pleasure and pain and give some other explanation; if they can't, if in fact it "satisfies you to live out your life pleasantly and free from pains," and if "you have nothing else to say good and bad is," then "listen to what follows. For I say to you all . . ." *This* is what Socrates knows about his audience; *this* is why humans will pay close attention: the vast majority are hidden hedonists who would like nothing more than to live out their lives pleasantly and free from pains. Because pleasure means *that* to *them*, they're ready to submit to what he now says to them—more tedious long-windedness. He will demonstrate to them how their hedonism, hitherto suppressed because they judged it immoral, can lead them to live pleasantly, free from pain and doing the good they know to be good. To achieve that goal they have to be taught to believe in the power of knowledge to rule their passions: only then can knowledge become what Socrates says it can be, the very "salvation of our lives" (356d). For salvation by knowledge to be secure, knowledge must seem trustworthy, seem to be an "art of skilled-measuring" with the power to overcome the deceptive "power of appearance." Pleasures and pains are powerful when close at hand; that power confuses us and leads us to change our minds and to perform actions and make choices we regret. Saving knowledge has to be skilled-measuring that can battle the power of immediate pleasures and render them powerless.

In this long-winded little play—this setting out of the doctrine of hedonism which so many readers of *Protagoras* suppose Socrates or Plato simply *holds* at this point—Socrates leads the many humans to a belief in salvation by knowledge. The play is theater for an audience of one, Protagoras; it puts on stage those slower at learning than he is in order to school him, a quick-witted sophist who paid little attention to the Many. After Socrates completes his play, after he persuades the many humans of the saving knowledge of skilled *measuring*, he can invite Protagoras back on stage, for who is he? He's the famous author of the famous saying on *measure*: "Of everything and anything the measure truly is humanity: of that which is, that it is the case; of that which is not, that it is not the case."[135] New content can now be poured into his famous words, and to that end Socrates invites the teacher of measure to rejoin him in speaking with the many humans. Their joint speech is as didactic as Socrates' solitary one and demonstrates that "salvation in life" (357a) depends on skilled measuring of pleasure and pain, skilled measuring being an art (*technê*) and a knowledge (or science, *epistêmê*, 357b). The many humans to whom they speak seem poor at remembering, for Socrates has to remind them that his whole demonstration arose because of what "you asked Protagoras and me to demonstrate" (357c): "We two were agreeing with each other that nothing is mightier than knowledge and that wherever it is present it rules pleasure and all the other things. But you said that pleasure often rules even the knowing human. And when we did not agree with you, you next asked us . . ." Socrates indulges in a word-for-word repetition of the initial speech of the many humans (353a), and now it can be heard for what it was, a *plea* to be shown how the wise might save them from the passions that

135. Schiappa translation, *Protagoras and Logos*, 121; Schiappa offers persuasive arguments for translating Protagoras's famous words just this way. They are thought to be the opening sentence of Protagoras's book, *Truth*.

thwart their desire to do the good. Now Socrates can offer the welcome word that they are ruled by passions because of ignorance, a deficiency they can remedy if they attend to "Protagoras here" (357e).

Socrates played the doctor, but now he puts his patient forward as a doctor. Seek out Protagoras, he recommends, he knows the cure for the ignorance that overcomes you and keeps you from doing the good you want to do. There are more doctors, Prodicus and Hippias here are doctors (357e). Socrates could not be more helpful: you many humans ignorant of the fact that you're overcome by ignorance in doing the bad, "you neither go yourselves nor send your sons to these teachers of these things, sophists, as if it were not teachable; and because you prefer to hoard your money rather than give it to them, you do badly both in private and in public life." The blame is all yours; you're as miserly as you are ignorant in not seeing that all your problems would be solved if only you paid these foreign doctors. Socrates draws Hippias and Prodicus on stage to answer with Protagoras: "Have I spoken truly or have I lied?" He reports that "it seemed to all that the things said were surpassingly[136] true." He leads the three sophists to reverse Protagoras's initial qualification on the goodness of pleasure: instead of the *noble* making pleasure good, pleasure as the good determines the noble (358b).[137] Socrates concludes with revelatory wording: "If the pleasant is good, no one who either knows or *believes* that other things are better than those he is doing, and are within his power, will ever do what he is doing, the better being open to him" (358c)—the distinction between knowledge and belief is irrelevant. Belief is sufficient for right action, for it is not "in human nature . . . to go willingly toward what one believes are bad things in preference to good things" (358c). To end his discussion with all three, Socrates turns to *wrong* action and emphasizes the dreaded:[138] "What human being would be willing to go toward that which he dreads, when it is open to him not to?" (358e). Again, it is not necessary to *know* the dreadful: "what is dreaded are *thought to be* bad things; but of things *thought to be* bad, no one willingly either goes toward or takes them." As teachers

136. *Huperphuôs*: super-naturally true, true beyond nature, impossibly true.

137. Unlike every other response of the three sophists, this one is not said to include *all*. Does the more conventional Protagoras withhold assent to this correction of his initial statement? Socrates asks Prodicus to waive his distinctions regarding the pleasant (358a), for Prodicus distinguished the *delights* of knowledge from the *pleasures* of eating (337c), a genuine distinction but irrelevant for their present purposes with the Many.

138. Socrates notes a distinction between fear and dread that Prodicus rightly insists on (Coby, *Socrates and the Sophistic Enlightenment*, 166), but he treats it as irrelevant: avoidance of the feared or dreaded is what counts.

of right action, sophists are teachers of right belief; they instill socially beneficial beliefs in the dreadful, beliefs in Zeus and his power of punishment, beliefs in the laws and customs and their power to punish. Fear of punishment returns as a tool to move hedonists.

"These are our answers to the Many" (358a). What Socrates has said in this part of his display dialogue—dialectic with the Many—completes what he fought all day to win the right to say. This is the last new point in the agenda that began when he invited Protagoras to share his answers to a hostile interrogator. That lone questioner has expanded into the Many whom Socrates investigated by studying their speeches, their logoi. Behind the tedium of Socrates' laborious demonstrations for the Many lie implications easily inferred by a Protagoras, or by a Prodicus or Hippias, kin to whom he communicates by indication. Here is what Socrates-Odysseus observed on his own and can show Protagoras-Diomedes; here is what will enable them all to enter the enemy camp and, in time, subdue and conquer it, making a place for enlightenment by having it serve the unenlightenable as well.

Questioning the many humans and attending to their answers schooled Socrates in their profound need for a means to exercise control over their passions. Protagoras is aware of that need: his myth and logos showed that justice, moderation, and piety are trained into human populations to make them civil and that punishment is the indispensable enforcer of the power of custom. Socrates goes well beyond Protagoras, offering the sophists collected in Athens a public teaching that is an improved version of what Protagoras offered in his myth and logos. The great advance of Socrates' public teaching is that it reinforces the civic virtues bred into the moral not solely with a threat of punishment but with a belief in the power of knowledge. It recognizes that the Many are hidden hedonists while recognizing that they desire to be moral, to have the good rule their passions. Their moral experience is the experience of the human *sickness*, of being a slave to inner powers greater than one can resist, of knowing the good but not being able to do the good. Socrates' new medicine is founded on knowledge of that experience, but his medicine cannot be knowledge simply—knowledge is hard to attain, requiring the intelligence of a Protagoras. The medicine is *belief* in knowledge, belief in the *power* of knowledge, a belief that can extract the sting of scandal from hedonism, transforming it into something other than indulgence in gluttony or sex. If the *good* of pleasure is attainable only through knowledge, the new hedonism taught by reformed sophists can subject the power of pleasure to a greater power: enlightened pleasure, belief in a long-term life of ease and freedom from pain. The power of knowledge can be effective even when it's only "knowledge," as Protagoras knew when he made Prometheus and Zeus divine dispensers of *technê* and civic morality. Still, Socrates shows Protagoras a nontraditional supplement to belief in the power of "knowledge."

By making knowable virtue the means to the knowable good of pleasure, Socrates makes virtue teachable; he shows how to do what he earlier said he doubted could be done. Teachable virtue can reform Athenian practice, which acts as if virtue were unteachable. Now there are experts in virtue to whom Athenians can turn both in the Assembly and in private. An Assembly once willing to listen to every carpenter, smith, cobbler, merchant, or sea captain can now restrict advice on matters of politics and virtue to experts as it already restricts advice on building and ship construction. Pericles and other leaders can now entrust their sons and wards to experts who know how to pass on their expertise. "Wise" Athens has not been at all wise; reform by one of its sons makes it wise.

Socrates' teaching for the public on their experience of being overcome by pleasure is a teaching offered to Protagoras—and to Prodicus and Hippias, to the sophistic enlightenment as a whole. It gives enlightenment the best possible public defense: knowledge saves. By peddling a certain kind of gnosticism, Socrates redirects the Protagorean enlightenment. He, a private investigator, sells the salesmen of knowledge a better way to sell themselves, better by knowing its buyers. Socrates' offer of hedonism takes its place in the suite of recommendations he attempts to sell to Protagoras. Hedonism with its attendant doctrine of an art of measure or the indispensability of sophists is the selling point that may lead sophists to adopt Socrates' teaching on the unity of the virtues and the unity of the wise on that unity. One step remains to make the package complete, the unity of courage and wisdom.

Socrates Rules

Socrates' purpose in seeking out Protagoras can now be inferred, even if Socrates can never pronounce it: his purpose is rule. Were Protagoras to become his ally in teaching humans the power of knowledge to rule, Socrates would rule in the way wise Greeks have ruled since Homer. The one in whom knowledge rules would rule the whole sophistic movement that learned its self-interest from him. It in turn would rule those humans in whom passion rules knowledge. The rule of knowledge as belief in knowledge is rule by an actual knower over the most-acknowledged knowers, who make it effective among the nonknowers. Wise Socrates remains the Spartan solitary who knows the uses of the public esteem of wisdom. If Hippocrates sought out *this* Protagoras, he would not have to know on his own whether what he carried home in his soul helps or harms.

Socrates' advocacy of hedonism interrupted his effort to prove the unity of courage and wisdom to Protagoras; it is itself courage and wisdom united in action. Socrates' display speech at Callias's house shows a wise man courageously intervening in order to establish, *re*establish, wise practice. What Socrates advocates would result in a society stratified as a hierarchy of teachers and taught, all ruled by knowledge, now known to be the ruling power. The city would be a unitary population consisting of a knower, the famous knowers, and the many "knowers," a republic of knowers. Courage and wisdom unite to establish an idealized or imaginary republic. *Protagoras* shows Socrates imagining something like the modern Enlightenment, a society of pleasure seekers enlightened by those who know the true pleasures and teach the means to attain a version of those pleasures. Socrates does more than imagine an "enlightened" society—he acts to establish it in the only way it can be established, through the acknowledged wise who already gain a hearing just by coming to town and attracting the most ambitious of the rising young.

13. The Final Tribunal: Courage and Wisdom (359a–360e)

Socrates proved his goodwill by refraining from revealing Protagoras's injustice and proved his kinship and capacity to lead by offering a favorable alliance; but now the good-willed kinsman-leader seems willing to crush Protagoras in a final, devastating argument. Is he just a lover of victory after all?

Socrates can properly conduct his crushing argument with Protagoras only after he has, as it were, dismissed the Many and renewed the debate among the wise in their absence. In that restored semiprivacy, Socrates separates the three sophists whom he drew together for the "common argument" (358a) that concluded his offer of the hedonism teaching (358a–359a): he and Prodicus and Hippias are to form a tribunal before which Protagoras is called to defend himself against a charge (359a) regarding "the first things he answered." Prodicus and Hippias are never mentioned again as Socrates alone prosecutes Protagoras for those "first things." But *first* is a little verbal mistake that the prosecutor throws in to give himself a chance to review his whole case against the defendant on the overarching issue: the wise presentation of the unity of virtue. He doesn't mean "the *very* first things" Protagoras said because he came around on those:

he first said that the five parts of virtue are all different but later granted that "four of them were fairly close to each other" (359a). Socrates thus calls attention to Protagoras's surrender on his first three arguments, though they were hardly demonstrations and the surrender was grudging and less than total. Still, Protagoras will be tried not on the *first* things but on "the things he said afterward," for if Socrates can act as if Protagoras willingly came around on those first arguments, Protagoras insisted that courage was different from the other virtues.[139]

Socrates is meticulous and exacting, proceeding in the lawyerly way a prosecutor must. He repeats what Protagoras said to prove that courage "very much differed from the others" (359b)[140] and emphasizes that he "was quite surprised at his reply, all the more so after having gone through these things with you." Of course he found it surprising after twisting Simonides' poem so arrestingly into wise blame of Protagoras's rashness; he had a right to expect Protagoras to accept his offer to treat his earlier, unwise position as a mere test of Socrates. But no, he insisted on the difference of courage.[141] Socrates restates exactly how he began his argument for the unity of courage and wisdom with the premise that courageous men are bold; he even quotes Protagoras's response, "and he said, 'and even impetuous'" (cf. 349e). Socrates thus continues the argument from the same premise, but he can proceed differently because of the agreements won by his argument for hedonism. Protagoras's enthusiastic endorsement of every step of that argument allows Socrates to continue his previous argument successfully.

Having repeated the opening premise, Socrates has Protagoras agree that the courageous do not go toward the same things as the cowardly (359c). Do the cowardly, then, go toward the emboldening things and the courageous toward the terrible things? Protagoras, that inveterate shelter

139. Socrates' inaccurate reference to "the first things he answered" is a reminder of his earlier reference to the "things I first asked about" (347c, 349a); it was there that Protagoras insisted that courage is different. At the end of the argument he again refers to what he said about the difference of courage as "the first" (360e).

140. His repetition is exact except that he reverses the order of unjust and impious (see 349d).

141. The two turning points in the dialogue linked by the "surprise" Socrates expresses reward close attention for they point to the structural unity of *Protagoras* as Socrates' campaign to persuade Protagoras: Protagoras's surprising speech on the singularity of courage occurred after Socrates' long exposition of Simonides' poem; having finished that exposition, Socrates told Protagoras his reasons for seeking him out (348d–e) and asked him to "go back to the beginning" (349a) and review his resistance to the unity of the virtues; he then offered Protagoras the opportunity to treat his earlier resistance as a test for Socrates. How surprising, after all this schooling on Socrates' part, that Protagoras still insists on the difference of courage.

seeker, tries his old dodge of hiding behind what people say (359c), but Socrates won't permit it; he demands that he speak for himself and alters his question in a way that brings in their agreements on hedonism: do the courageous go toward the terrible things *believing* them to be terrible? Protagoras answers as he must: "But this was just now demonstrated to be impossible by the arguments you spoke" (359d). Does the hedonist view that "no one goes toward what he believes to be terrible" mean that the courageous and the cowardly go toward the same things? They go toward completely opposite things, Protagoras answers, offering the obvious example that the courageous go willingly to war whereas the cowardly are not willing to go. From here, the prosecutor's task is easy, and Socrates performs it with excruciating exactitude. Is it noble or shameful to go to war, he asks, bringing in the standards of nobility and shame that Protagoras made so prominent throughout their discussion by claiming the noble and avoiding the shameful.[142] It's noble, Protagoras answers, and therefore it's good, Socrates adds in accord with their previous agreement (cf. 358b). And if noble and good, it is also pleasant (360a). What about the cowardly, then, are they "knowingly not willing to go toward what is more noble and better and more pleasant?" To say that would violate their previous agreements, Protagoras says. And the courageous? They go toward what is more noble and better and more pleasant. They do not fear shameful fears, nor are they emboldened by shameful emboldenings.

Is it yet dawning on Protagoras that here, again, Socrates is doing what he has consistently done in such uncanny fashion in all his arguments until now, referring obliquely to Protagoras himself, here to his very first speech where he indicted all the earlier wise? Maybe not, for his agreements seem wholehearted enough. The courageous, then, when they feel fear, fear noble fears and are emboldened by noble emboldenings, and if noble, then good (360b). When Socrates turns back to the cowardly to contrast their shameful fears and emboldenings, he makes them more than simply cowards; now they are rash and mad, reminders of the rash and the mad earlier referred to to distinguish them from the wise.[143] These rash, mad cowards are emboldened by the shameful and bad only through "not knowing [*agnoian*] and ignorance [*amathian*]"; they are "cowardly through their ignorance of what the terrible things are" (360c).

Now is it dawning on Protagoras that Socrates means *him*?—means

142. See 333c, 348c, 349e, 350b, 352c as the occasions on which shame dictates Protagoras's response.

143. The merely bold or rash, 350b; the mad, 323b, 349e, 350b.

that *he* is the rash mad ignorant coward who thinks he is avoiding war by following a course different from all previous wise men? As Socrates draws out the details of the coward acting out of ignorance and cowardice, Protagoras's replies grow less assured; for the first time, he merely nods his agreement (360c$_8$). Courage is the opposite of cowardice—Protagoras can say this is so (360d$_1$). Then is *wisdom*—wisdom here introduced in place of knowledge, wisdom being the virtue whose unity with courage the argument means to prove—"is wisdom of the things that are terrible and not terrible the opposite of ignorance of these things?" Protagoras again merely nods assent. "But ignorance of these things is cowardice?" Protagoras's nodded assent comes this time with "much reluctance" as he must be recognizing that *he* is being convicted of ignorant cowardice, and not for some minor slip but for his whole life's practice as the first sophist to declare himself courageous and wise and all his forebears cowards and fools.

Socrates is not shy about legalistically drawing out the obvious conclusion: "Therefore wisdom of the things that are terrible and are not terrible is courage, whose opposite is ignorance of these things?" But he does shy away from stating the nonobvious implication that the one he is questioning is guilty of that ignorance—it thus begins to become visible that even a conviction can be gracious toward kin. Protagoras's response bespeaks his recognition of the unspoken charge against him: "he was no longer willing even to nod but was silent." When the prosecutor asks Protagoras why he neither affirms nor denies what he was asked, Protagoras says: "Finish it yourself." Socrates does not finish it; he lets the question stand unanswered even though its answer is the essential conclusion that wisdom and courage are inseparably linked and that the five virtues therefore share a unity. Instead of drawing the dialogue-long argument to the explicit conclusion at which it has arrived, Socrates puts a different question. Before posing it, however, he says explicitly that it is the last question he will put: "I have only one question still to ask you: whether you are still of the same opinion as you were at the first, that there are some humans who are very ignorant yet very courageous?" (360e). Protagoras does respond to this question, for Socrates made a response easier by informing him that there will be no more questions—there will be no question about what has dawned on Protagoras as Socrates' unspoken indictment of him. Socrates proves again that he is kin by doing what he said kin do: he compelled himself to conceal and not make a display of blaming and reproaching (346a–b).

Before actually giving his answer to what he knows is the final question, Protagoras characterizes his questioner: for Socrates to demand that he answer this question makes him seem to Protagoras *philonikein*, one who loves being victorious. Conceding victory he can say: "I shall gratify you and say that from what has been agreed, this seems to me impossible." He concedes, at least overtly, that with respect to what Socrates asked in his *final* question, he is not "still of the same opinion as [he was] at the *first*" (360e). First and last unite to confirm that Protagoras's surrender is complete: not only are four of the virtues "fairly close to each other" (359a), all five are, and what he said at the *very* first about his superior courage and wisdom can no longer stand.

The tribunal has completed its work and forced Protagoras to pronounce himself guilty of being wrong from the first. Losing an argument is an unprecedented experience for him, and to lose before this assembly must seem especially shameful. But he was forced into the bitter admission that he was wrong because the indictment Socrates left unspoken is far worse: it condemned his whole proud career as a sophist as criminally mistaken. How much better to concede defeat on a particular thesis about virtue than risk opening up Socrates' unspoken question whether now, after these arguments, he judges himself guilty in his whole career of being a rash mad ignorant coward, guilty from the *very first* in his choice of a novel strategy of enlightenment, guilty of entering the enemy camp in a way that could doom the whole Achaian enterprise.

14. Socrates the Victor (360e–362a)

Three speeches and a final narrative sentence bring *Protagoras* to a close. Socrates makes a long speech that begins by denying that he questioned out of a love of victory, claiming instead that he desires "to investigate the things pertaining to virtue and what virtue itself is." He claims knowledge: "I know" that once it has become apparent what virtue is, it will be plain whether it is teachable or not. And he treats their lengthy arguments as if he had been saying throughout that virtue was not teachable while Protagoras had been saying it was. Socrates then introduces a judge who accuses and laughs at them both. He thus graciously submerges the tribunal's judgment against Protagoras by inventing a judge who convicts him too. Who is this judge? Not the argument itself, as is often said, but the *exodos* of the arguments, their exiting as at the end of a tragedy or here at the end of a comedy. Socrates gives a human voice to the recessional music of this comedy, the voice, it seems, that Socrates so often introduced as the questioner of the two of them, the public voice, the voice of the Many now heard at the end in judgment, accusing and laughing at them, beginning with a summary judgment: "How strange [*atopoi*, out of place] you are, Socrates and Protagoras" (361a). "You," Socrates, who said virtue is not teachable, now you are "attempting to demonstrate that all things are knowledge"—the voice lists only "justice, moderation, and courage"—"which would make it appear that virtue especially must be teachable." So Socrates is confused. As for Protagoras, he first established that virtue was teachable and now he's going to the opposite extreme, making it appear to be something other than knowledge and thus the thing least teachable. So Protagoras is confused. Socrates was right: disagreements among the strange wise before an audience of the nonwise leads to their condemnation; the wise are condemned if they do not speak in a unitary way.

Socrates responds to the condemning voice with the courage of one who knows he's going to war: "seeing these things confused so *terribly* [*deinos*]," he goes toward them with eagerness (361c). He sets out in an ordered sequence of inquiries just what he goes toward: first, he will go through these things again to gain clarity, then go through what virtue is, and then go back to consider whether it is teachable or not. Going through "these things again" means going through what Socrates laid out in his consistent argument with Protagoras that showed what they should say together to a questioning public. Those who judge the wise strange and confused on the basis of "these things" will not be inclined to go back through them, but those who seek understanding and have the courage to go toward the terribly confused may be eager to do just that. In these things they will discover what virtue is and the desirability of teaching teachable virtue in the way Socrates, never confused, suggested throughout, as a unity on which the wise are united.

If Socrates' order is not followed, "that Epimetheus of yours" who you say neglected us in his distribution may baffle us with deceptions in these investigations too: your way of treating virtue, Protagoras, is Epimethean, it lacks foresight in kindling conflict in public among the wise. Socrates dares to claim to be Promethean: "for I, making use of him and taking forethought for my entire life, am myself occupied with all these things" (361d). Socrates claims at the end what became evident underway: he came well briefed, having worked out in forethought just what he was compelled to say to the founder of sophism at a meeting with young Athenians. He could direct the conversation as he did, he could rule it, because through forethought he knew what he would have to convey. A more than strategic claim is also implied in Socrates' assertion that he is Promethean: *he* is the teacher of virtue who had the forethought to think through the whole nature of virtue and the manner in which to teach it. The last words of his speech extend an offer to Protagoras: "I would be pleased to investigate these questions together with you." Socrates has already put his last question to Protagoras and knows this conversation is over. Still, it is of great importance that Protagoras accept Socrates' offer to meet "whenever you wish."

Protagoras's final speech is a portrait in urbanity. The world-famous wise man who has just suffered the first defeat of his long life praises Socrates for the "eagerness" he just claimed and for his "way out [*diexodos*] of the arguments." As for himself, he is "the least envious of humans," a claim one could doubt were envy not so absent from his final speech and praise of his victor not so free—his next sentence virtually anoints Socrates his worthy successor: "And I have said of you to many, that of all those I have happened to meet, particularly of your own age, you are by far the one I most admire" (361e).[144] And the most famous of Greek wise men then adds, "And let me say that I would not be amazed if you became famous among men for wisdom." These are more than generous words: they acknowledge at the end that Protagoras knew from the start that when Socrates appeared in Callias's house, everything changed; he knew he would be dealing with a rival of the highest competence. His forethought told him that arranging for all the sophists and their followers to meet as one (317c) was arranging a showdown with his true rival before an audience of special judges. As a final note of admiration at Socrates' victory, Protagoras says, "And at some other time, whenever you wish, let us indeed examine these things." *Protagoras* ends with Protagoras expressing his willingness to listen and perhaps learn more from a kinsman who displayed such mastery and such restraint. His response bespeaks more than lack of envy and recognition that Socrates acted as kin should act: it permits the inference that Protagoras would perhaps be pleased to examine with Socrates in private and not in front of the others indoors here (317c) his view that the wise must unite in teaching the unity of virtue.

"But now it is time to turn to something else," Protagoras says in his last words, bringing their present conversation to an end. Socrates yields: "That must indeed be done, if it seems so to you." But he adds two remarks: "it's long since been time for me to be where I said." That alleged appointment, first claimed when he stood up to leave in the middle (335c), stands refuted by the fact that he is narrating their hours-long conversation to those he happened to meet afterward. "I stayed behind to gratify Callias the Beau-

144. It is therefore clear that Socrates and Protagoras met on Protagoras's earlier visit or visits to Athens and that Socrates deeply impressed him.

tiful." No he didn't. When Callias spoke up to keep Socrates from leaving, his misunderstanding of what happened was not what persuaded him to stay. Socrates' last reported words to those gathered at Callias's house are a parting civility to their host. Socrates' last speech thus contains two polite little lies whose falsity is visible; they seal the dialogue with Socrates' manner of speaking throughout: there is deception here, deception that is more than merely polite, deception of a very high order, Spartan deception required of a wise man who knows where he is and knows how to speak.

15. Last Words

Is there deception in Socrates' parting too, then, as his two parting politenesses may suggest, deception driven by necessity as he retells the day's conversation for the sake of his frame audience? His last words address that audience and lead Plato's reader back to the first words: "Having said and heard these things, we departed"—"From where, Socrates, are you appearing?" The frame audience has listened silently as Socrates narrated his long answer to their question, a fully satisfying answer that refutes their suspicion that he is appearing from a hunt for Alcibiades. But could deceptive Socrates be deceiving them about his parting to deceive them about his appearing? *We departed*. Who departed? The frame audience could naturally suppose after hearing the narration that Socrates departed with Hippocrates. But: "Having *said* and heard these things"—Hippocrates said nothing at all, so Socrates' exact words exclude him. Nor is Hippocrates with Socrates when he meets the questioner at the beginning, a questioner who imagines he's coming from Alcibiades.

Could Socrates have left Callias's house with Alcibiades?[145] If he does, *Protagoras* ends as its opening suggests it should, the hunter Socrates having successfully hunted down the vernal beauty of Alcibiades. An odd little shift in Socrates' wording during the opening conversation suggests that he acts to cover up the fact that he just came from Alcibiades. When he first tells his questioner, "[I]n fact, I only just now left that one [*ekeinou*]," *that one* is Alcibiades (309b$_7$). After he alleges that he forgot Alcibiades in the presence of the more beautiful Protagoras, his questioner almost repeats Socrates' statement, "So it's from being with that one [*ekeinôi*] that you now come?" (310d$_6$). *That one* is now Protagoras, and Socrates lets that impression stand: Socrates led his questioner to forget Alcibiades while

145. The possibility is recognized by Coby, who sketches some of its implications (*Socrates and the Sophistic Enlightenment*, 202–3 n. 83).

alleging that *he* forgot him—an unlikely forgetting by a Socrates who remembers everything and who indulges in the little deception of alleging Protagoras's greater beauty as wise even though he does not believe Protagoras to be wise. An odd nuance in Socrates' last words at Callias's house reinforces the suggestion that he left with Alcibiades: "I stayed to oblige Callias the Beautiful." That polite lie recalls words Socrates used in his only direct address to his original questioner in his whole narration: describing Alcibiades' arrival he said, "Alcibiades the Beautiful, as you said and I don't disagree" (316a). Socrates stayed to gratify—*charizomai*, show favor to—Alcibiades the Beautiful. Having succeeded in that, he left with him.

But if Socrates left Callias's house with Alcibiades, the questioner is dead right: Socrates is coming directly from a successful hunt of the vernal beauty of Alcibiades. Taking this as a fact fully explains all the nuances of the opening conversation. Having just left Alcibiades, Socrates is confronted by a reminder that his hunt for Alcibiades has become a subject of public gossip. The goals of his private hunt would be compromised by such gossip, and now, if it has in fact been successful, it is imperative that its success be hidden from a leering and potentially censorious public. Socrates must manage his public image wisely, like the admirable Spartan wise he invented; he must hide his effective wisdom, expelling foreigners from the private consultations between the wise and the powerful, keeping them as secret as possible. So he leaves the impression that he left the gathering in the company of Hippocrates. Socrates arrived with Hippocrates, but Alcibiades eclipsed him completely and showed himself to be the young Athenian of outstanding merit. He understood the fairness issue engineered by Socrates in his staged departure. He provided the supervision that kept the conversation to its agreed-upon course. He shamed Protagoras into continuing by his contrived little aside to Callias. It is Alcibiades and no one else whose insight and leadership abilities were drawn out by Socrates in the conversation he reports. "We departed." "In fact, I only just now left that one." If these two statements from the end and beginning of *Protagoras* are meant to suggest that Socrates left with Alcibiades, they demonstrate *Plato's* Spartan wisdom, his sheltering of Socrates' wise enterprise with the powerful. For then some time would have elapsed between the end of *Protagoras* and its beginning, time enough for Socrates to have his first private conversation ever with Alcibiades, a conversation made compelling for Alcibiades by his own interventions on Socrates' behalf at the great meeting of sophists. Perhaps, in the semiprivate setting of *Protagoras*, we've just witnessed the events that set up the completely private exchange of *Alcibiades I*, a dialogue that begins abruptly with no introduction.

Did Plato, an author rumored to have written tragedies before meeting Socrates, indulge in a little piece of dramatic poetry to begin and end his comedy *Protagoras*? Did he quietly suggest that the study of his chronologically first dialogue be followed immediately by the study of another dialogue? If so, *Protagoras* most pleasingly nests within itself the other dialogue argued to be chronologically first, *Alcibiades I*, and Socrates' rumored hunt for Alcibiades is covered over by a deception in order to hide its complete success. If so, Socrates' first private conversation with that most exceptional young Athenian occurred moments after his successful hunt in *Protagoras* and moments before he is asked about his relations with Alcibiades by an overcurious questioner. If *Alcibiades I* is in fact nested within *Protagoras*, then Plato opened the chronological order of his dialogues in a sporting mood, almost jesting, certainly teasing, with a possibility rich in implication.[146] That possibility cannot be proven in the lawyerly manner Plato shows his Socrates practicing in the final tribunal of *Protagoras*. Let it be entertained as a dramatic poet's playfulness, his unprovable sport on that deadliest of themes for Socrates' biography, his relationship with the spectacular Alcibiades, sport that will always fall short of what a prosecutor needs to prove guilt. Imagining that Socrates is guilty of hunting down his beautiful quarry, we see that he has reason to repeat at the end what he said in the middle—that he has other business to attend to (335c): now he really *does* have other business to attend to, business arranged by the hunt the dialogue portrays, business completed by the time he claims that he has leisure to narrate the events of the day, business with Alcibiades.[147]

If Socrates goes to Callias's house to continue his hunt for Alcibiades, if the core conversation of *Protagoras* is in part for him, then what better way for the Athenian philosopher to win the attention of this singular young Athenian preparing to mount the public stage than to do what he actually

146. In any case *Alcibiades I* must be later than *Protagoras* because at its end Alcibiades announces that "we will probably be changing roles, Socrates, I taking yours and you mine, for from this day nothing can keep me from attending on [*paidagôgêsô*] you, and you from being attended upon [*paidagôgêsêi*] by me" (135d): the hunter of *Protagoras* becomes the hunted because of the private conversation of *Alcibiades I*. *Alcibiades I* emphasizes at its opening that this is the first private conversation between the two. The familiarity Alcibiades exhibits with Socrates' ways in *Protagoras* in no way contradicts this: Socrates has been hanging around him for years, making a nuisance of himself but never having a private conversation with him (*Alcibiades I* 104d). Catherine Zuckert (*Plato's Philosophers*, 217–18 n. 4) also argues that *Alcibiades I* must occur after *Protagoras*.

147. If *Alcibiades I* and *Protagoras* are connected this way, both dialogues can be dated in 433 with some probability. See below, "Note on the Dramatic Date of *Protagoras* and *Alcibiades I*."

did? For he began by asking what Hippocrates could expect to gain from Protagoras in becoming "most powerful in the affairs of the city both in action and speech" (318e)—and Plato pointed only slyly to Alcibiades' presence when that question was asked. Socrates then described the Athenian Assembly that Alcibiades was longing to address: it accepts the opinion of the expert on technical matters, he said, and ignores that of the nonexpert even if he's "quite handsome and rich and well-born" (319b–d). And what better way to intensify the youth's arrested attention than to speak in his presence of his guardian, Pericles, as unable to teach the political art of which Pericles is the master, the art of directing the Athenian Assembly (319d–320b), and then to speak of the education of Pericles' two sons, Paralus and Xanthippus, and one of his two wards, Kleinias, Alcibiades' brother, and to mention that Pericles sent him to be educated by his own brother, Ariphron, fearing that he would be corrupted by Alcibiades—and *not* to speak of Alcibiades' education? And what better way to tap what he knows is Alcibiades' passion for fairness than to make himself seem the victim of unfairness in his contest with Protagoras? And what better way to make this natural young leader actually lead than to set the conditions for continuing the discussion and then practically compel Protagoras not to continue? And what better way to cement Alcibiades' attention than to show himself a student of the Many who has learned what rules them and therefore what it would take to rule them in the Assembly? Rule of the Many would be made easier if those who aspired to rule them knew that the Many are ruled by pleasure while thinking themselves virtuous; rule over them would require rule over oneself, not allowing oneself to be "overcome by pleasures," as was so often alleged of Alcibiades, even by himself. If being overcome by pleasure is in fact being overcome by ignorance, then it is important to know just what that experience is or to have wise counsel on the art of measure that would make it possible for knowledge to rule the passions. The long-winded explanations for the Many would not have been long-winded at all for one who yearned to address the Many in the Assembly. And if Socrates closes his account of the Many by recommending the sophists to them as their doctors, anyone who is paying attention and is willing to spend his money on sophists would be learning that he should spend it not on these doctors but on *their* doctor. And what better way for Socrates to end his hunt for Alcibiades than by suggesting that he who began by saying that virtue is unteachable ends by attempting to demonstrate that virtue is teachable? The one to whom Socrates could teach it could then teach the Athenian Assembly, Pericles-like, to respect his expert opinion in matters of policy, reaching even the *demos* with the powers of persuasion Alcibiades just displayed by taking control over the assembly at Callias's house.

The debate Socrates directed with Protagoras aimed to educate the sophists and establish an alliance with them. But when heard from Alcibiades' standpoint, Socrates' efforts seem to have been directed at him. Socrates' agenda for the day seems to have had a second aim, hunting down young Alcibiades in order to teach him. But is Alcibiades in all his brashness at all teachable? If *Protagoras* shows Socrates successfully pursuing Alcibiades and turning him into an ally who presides over the conversation, what would he do with him if he were given the choice he gave Protagoras, speaking alone rather than in the company of others (316b)? Being a follower of the Spartan wise, Socrates would not choose as Protagoras chose but would speak with Alcibiades in private as he did in *Alcibiades I*.

Alcibiades I opens suddenly, with no apparent introduction.[148] To start their wholly private conversation (118b), Socrates penetrates to the most private matter, Alcibiades' secret ambition to rule, which he has told no one. Having discerned those ambitions, Socrates neither tempers them nor chastises Alcibiades for entertaining them but encourages and expands them while claiming that he alone and "no guardian or relative or anyone else" has the power to help him realize them (105e). He must still break down Alcibiades' arrogant bearing that held all other suitors or teachers at bay, and he does so by spending the whole first half of their discussion on the very issues he raised in *Protagoras*, now, however, approaching them from the opposite direction: Alcibiades is unfit to give counsel to the Athenian Assembly before he is educated (106c–118c), and it is unlikely that Pericles could educate him, given his failure with his own sons and with Kleinias (118c–119c). In *Protagoras*, with a large company of the best teachers and best students present, Socrates questions whether the political virtue is teachable; in *Alcibiades I*, where the best of teachers is alone with Athens' most promising political leader, he simply sets out to teach Alcibiades political virtue. Because Alcibiades is too brash to suppose he needs counsel—in that way sharing Athenian belief in the unteachability of political virtue—Socrates shames him into admitting that he never had a teacher and never learned it on his own. Alcibiades is reduced to begging Socrates for counsel after Socrates charms him with a display of his

148. *Alcibiades II*, another private conversation between Socrates and Alcibiades, must occur later than *Alcibiades I* because Socrates has already won Alcibiades' confidence. Accordingly, *Alcibiades II* is given an introduction: Socrates encounters Alcibiades who is on his way to make a sacrifice and attempts to teach him what to wish or what to pray the gods will give him.

capacity to provide it and shames him with awareness of his ignorance: as happened with Hippocrates and with Protagoras himself, Socrates breaks an initial confidence, induces shame, and wins a willingness to listen. *Protagoras* provides a context for interpreting *Alcibiades I*—a dialogue without a setting seems in fact to enjoy a very elaborate setting.[149]

If *Protagoras* and *Alcibiades I* are connected this way, *Protagoras* opens just after Socrates has succeeded in private with Alcibiades. Having just left him, he encounters a questioner who leers at Socrates' inappropriate interest in their most promising young countryman. Such questioners have no need to know what passed between the two of them or that there even was a private meeting between them: Spartan practice dictates that the wise meet with the powerful in a way that leaves "foreigners" unaware that such meetings occurred. It's enough that they be entertained by what he's willing to do for Hippocrates in showing him the dangers of foreign sophists, and by what he flaunts of himself as the Athenian superior to the sophists who can whip even the best of them. He's really good, this Socrates of ours, coming to the aid of young Hippocrates and putting those foreign "wise men" in their place. Socrates' love of honor with respect to wisdom works its magic—he will be honored where at first he was thought suspicious.

But would Plato really choose to open something so momentous as the whole public career of Socrates with a little sleight of hand, inserting *Alcibiades I* within *Protagoras*? What does he gain by such a maneuver? The

149. *Protagoras* and *Alcibiades I* are linked by many major themes: Each opens on the question of the appropriateness of Socrates' pursuit of Alcibiades after he has passed the age when custom permits it. *Alcibiades I* shows that Alcibiades has already learned from the sophists that it is better to lie about injustice (109c; cf. *Protagoras* 323b) and that there are advantages in the practice of injustice (113d; cf. *Protagoras* 333b–e). *Protagoras* suggests that the good counsel Protagoras offers is injustice (318e–333e), whereas Socrates' good counsel concerns justice (*Alcibiades I* 125e–127d). The abruptness of the opening of *Alcibiades I* is nicely remedied if it is read as following immediately the "we departed" of *Protagoras*; and its opening exchange about Socrates' annoying silent attentions is given a plausible setting if the whole of *Protagoras* in fact preceded it. The two dialogues are linked by many smaller items: Pericles' education of his sons and of Kleinias (115d–e); long speeches versus short (106b); advising the Athenian Assembly (113b, see 106c); Alcibiades' speaking of learning Greek from the Many, a point Protagoras explicitly made (110e–111a; *Protagoras* 327e–328a). Socrates begins *Protagoras* doubting that virtue can be taught but ends affirming it, and in *Alcibiades I* he sets out to teach virtue to Alcibiades, with justice as its chief component and "Know thyself" as its motto (124b; *Protagoras* 343b). Socrates offers Alcibiades what Protagoras promised, good judgment in his own affairs and the affairs of the city (318e).

Landy raises the issue of the relationship of *Protagoras* to *Alcibiades I*; he places *Alcibiades I* some days earlier than *Protagoras*, supposing, unnecessarily in my view, that Socrates' speaking for the "first time" to Alcibiades requires it ("Virtue, Art, and the Good Life in Plato's *Protagoras*," 302–6). In *Protagoras* Socrates does not speak *to* Alcibiades, however much he speaks for his sake.

gains are offers to his reader, small-scale gains like understanding Socrates' deflection of interest away from Alcibiades at the opening of *Protagoras* and recovering the truth that Socrates *is* hunting Alcibiades, large-scale gains like understanding *Alcibiades I* as a fragment of a larger political project whereby Socrates shelters and advances philosophy by surrounding it with a politic defense. Apart from such particulars, Plato's sleight of hand offers his reader an introduction to the author: he's present in his absence partly as trickster, burying pleasant discoveries about himself and his ways in cleverly marked shallow graves. Homer's Odysseus is the model for Plato's Socrates, but the characters model their authors as well; Plato's tale to Alcinous promises to be as polytropic as Homer's for he knew what Nietzsche knew: "the great sweep of life has always shown itself to be on the side of the most unscrupulous polytropoi."[150]

Still, whether one takes *Alcibiades I* to be dramatically nested within *Protagoras* or insists on the greater sobriety of placing it some time shortly thereafter, Socrates' words and actions in *Protagoras* and *Alcibiades I* remain the same: with these two sequential dialogues to open his corpus, Plato shows Socrates acting on behalf of philosophy to redirect the Greek enlightenment and redirect the ambitions of an Athenian political genius.[151]

16. Socrates' Politics for Philosophy in 433

With the chronologically first of his dialogues Plato shows Socrates mounting the stage—and taking center stage and meaning to dominate it. Concerned that Athenians thought they knew where he came from and

150. Nietzsche, *Gay Science*, ¶344.

151. Catherine Zuckert argues (*Plato's Philosophers*, 53–58) that Plato's *Laws* is the chronologically first dialogue, set after the Persian wars but prior to about 450 when its historical references run out, as do its references to past philosophy. The *Laws* are then pre-Socratic: the Athenian Stranger faces the problems that philosophy raises for a civic order lacking the perspective gained later by Socrates. A comment by Seth Benardete made some years before Zuckert's book adds a supplementary element: "The *Laws* ends up with the recommendation of a nocturnal council, which is to discuss the unity of virtue. If the *Laws* ends with a proposal to introduce philosophy into the city of laws, it is on the way to philosophy. 'On the way to philosophy' is a formula that holds for every Platonic dialogue: no dialogue answers the question 'What is philosophy?' in a completely adequate manner. The *Laws* would be peculiar in starting further back than any other dialogue if it only comes to this question, common to all of the dialogues, at the very end" (Benardete, *Plato's Laws*, 3). If Zuckert's proposal turns out to be correct, then *Protagoras* is the chronologically first dialogue in this sense: after the only dialogues in which Socrates is absent (the *Laws* and the *Epinomis*) have described the civic world faced by the philosopher prior to Socrates, Plato moves to Socrates as the indispensable innovator, beginning with *Protagoras* where Socrates first mounts the public stage with his new politics for philosophy.

what his loves were, Socrates takes steps to create a new public image for himself and thereby for philosophy as he has come to understand it. He speaks in public like a new kind of Spartan wise man, taking on the burden of fame in order to show his Athenian countrymen that philosophy is salutary and public-spirited—for he reports to them how, in private, he defeated the most famous foreign sophist, leading him and the young Athenians present to honor all five virtues. A Spartan wise man, however, speaks laconically in public words sheltering lessons for kin: Socrates' public words contain a private offer to the founder and leaders of the sophistic enlightenment to reform their public teaching. And his public words lure future leaders away from foreign teachers who promised to make them masters of the political art and toward a more salutary teaching. And, most subterraneanly, his public words post signs for the most private of ways, the way up and out to the most private possession, philosophy itself.

Embodying a new public image of philosophy that flaunts its civic responsibility with respect to enlightenment and the young, Socrates comes forth publicly in order to hide—for his political aims with the public, the sophists, and the rising young are ultimately in the service of philosophy itself which can only be solitary and private. While making his privacy seem entirely public, Socrates makes himself compellingly attractive to those with a genuine interest in his true privacy, what he thinks, the wisdom he has gained. Plato has Socrates come forth as a thinker who knows himself to be heir to the long history of Greek wisdom, esoteric wisdom with an edifying face. Counseling the famous wise to honor that esoteric tradition, he speaks esoterically himself, asking to be questioned on what his exoteric appearance shelters. Socrates' ultimate political aim is to transmit the tradition of inquiry and his own advances in wisdom to those whose fitness for it can be proven only by their capacity to use his public words as signposts on the way into it. Plato's Socrates, thought interesting because of an illicit eros, comes forth to make himself boring or moral to the many, the famous wise, and the powerful few, and to make himself erotically alluring to the very fewest.

"Listen," Socrates commands just before beginning his uninterrupted narration, and Plato's artful construction of *Protagoras* allows his reader to listen in as three kinds of supplied auditors hear Socrates from their different perspectives. The frame audience hears a fellow Athenian being anointed successor by the one they think the wisest of their time. Sophists present in Athens to win students for themselves hear a teaching that would make them his students. Young Athenians present to buy the teachings of foreign sophists learn who they should really want as their teacher.

All three kinds of public audience appear repeatedly in chronologically later dialogues as the Socrates here introduced sustains his public defense of philosophy to the end—with the fourth potential audience, the rarest and most private, always also possibly listening in.

Socrates and the Sophistic Enlightenment

The public, like Callias's doorkeeper, did not distinguish between philosophy and sophistry; therefore, to make the city safe for philosophy, Socrates must make sophistry safe for the city. Protagoras, the founder of sophism, dominates that Socratic project, as Plato suggested by the chronology of his dialogues: they begin with a contest between Socrates and Protagoras, and they end by continuing that contest as one that will never end. *Theaetetus* is chronologically the last of Plato's dialogues, its frame set in 369. A Protagoras long dead there returns from the underworld, popping his head out of the ground to help his disciples counter Socrates, an older disciple made by Protagoras when he was still alive and a youthful disciple made Protagorean by the writings in which he lives on. The frame of *Theaetetus* prepares its core as the reading of a writing that is the nearest thing to an authentic writing by Socrates in the Platonic corpus, a dialogue that Socrates, in prison before being executed, took pains to narrate to Euclides and have him write down, even making editorial corrections to get it right during Euclides' visits to his cell. *Theaetetus* thus contains a written text in which Socrates lives on posthumously, contesting with a Protagoras living on in his written texts. *Protagoras* exhibits Socrates' concern for the public reputation of philosophy at the opening of his public career: let it be Socratic, transmitted by his own public narration of his private acts. *Theaetetus* exhibits Socrates' concern for the public reputation of philosophy at the close of his career: let it be Socratic, transmitted by writings taken down by devotees. How fitting that the Protagoras of *Theaetetus* be the posthumous Protagoras living on in his writings, and living well to judge by the fervent loyalty with which disciples young and old defend his teachings. From first to last in Plato's dialogues, living or dead, speaking or present in his books, Protagoras is the Orpheus to young Athenians, the famous wise man, the public intellectual, who will always accompany enlightenment and with whom philosophy will always have to contend. In Plato, a Socrates concerned with the public reputation of philosophy lives on posthumously as truth's champion against his kin, a Protagoras who lives forever.

When the first and last dialogues are read together, parallels surface, one of which may be noted here, basic but not flaunted, as befits its character: both dialogues are deeply concerned with the esotericism of the wise. In *Protagoras*, at the outset of his public work, Socrates recommends an esotericism more ancient and more wise than the novel esotericism of Protagoras, which scorns the past wise, aiming to surpass them by diminishing them. In *Theaetetus*, with the end of his public work in sight, Socrates has Euclides put into writing, if enigmatical, folded writing, just what the secret teaching of the wise from Homer to Protagoras was, a teaching they chose to make "an enigma for us, the vast refuse-heap," while telling "the truth as if it were a forbidden secret" to their pupils (152c). Homer, head of an army of wise enlisting all but Parmenides, put the forbidden secret in images: "Ocean and mother Tethys, the becoming of gods" (152e, cf. 180d)—motion, generating everything, generates what looks permanent and is venerated as permanent. Opening and closing on a contest between Socrates and Protagoras, a partially public contest between philosophy and sophism for talented young Athenians, Plato points to philosophy's essential esotericism as something that enlightenment generally must, in its own way, share.

Socrates' attempt to reform the sophistic enlightenment did not confine itself to its founder and first representatives. He encounters a younger, more radical representative of the enlightenment in the *Republic*; Thrasymachus of Chalcedon is present with the Athenian young whom Socrates finds in Cephalus's house in the Piraeus. What he does with this more outspoken representative of the sophistic enlightenment carries forward what he did with Protagoras: to him too he offers an alliance calculated to win him over. Even Euthydemus and Dionysodorus, those sophistic clowns from Chios, have to be treated with care though it offends his friend Crito: they too give the whole enterprise of enlightenment a bad name, and, *Euthydemus* shows, an attempt must be made to curb them even if it is unlikely to succeed. The great teacher of rhetoric, Gorgias of Leontini, must be engaged when he comes to town in order to make clear to him just what his gift of rhetoric can effect in young Athenians like Polus and Callicles; Socrates invites Gorgias to view their extremism, counting on his self-interest to curb his manner of teaching. When Hippias of Elis comes back to town on a diplomatic mission, he tries to sell himself with a display speech parading himself as the new Nestor; Socrates, schooling the famous diplomat in diplomacy, invites him to see that he needs a more Odyssean diplomacy if he is to avoid falling victim to actors more polytropic than he is: Plato set his two *Hippias* dialogues in the summer of 420 during the momentous diplomatic congress called by polytropic Alcibiades at which he successfully altered Pericles' strategy in the war through alliances with the leading Peloponnesian cities, including Hippias's Elis, aiming for a definitive hoplite battle between Sparta and the new Athenian alliance.

The sophistic enlightenment, a novelty in the public presentation of wisdom, is itself an offspring of the true novelty, the Greek investigation of nature that had begun and made inexorable intellectual advances before Protagoras initiated his novel frankness. Socrates himself began as a passionate student of the investigation of nature and made his own discoveries and advances long before mounting the stage in *Protagoras*. As is so beautifully fitting, Plato made *that* Socrates, the Socrates who matters most, available only through the public Socrates. He traced the coming to be of that Socrates in the three retrospective views of a young Socrates in *Phaedo*, *Parmenides*, and the *Symposium*. *That* Socrates needs the public shelter of a redirected Protagorean enlightenment and of young political men charmed into Socrates' service by a teaching that appeals to them.

Socrates and Alcibiades

Xenophon's defense of Socrates, his *Memorabilia*, put first a defense against the charge that damaged him most: that he corrupted Alcibiades and Critias, "who harmed the city most."[152] Plato put Alcibiades and Critias together in his chronologically first dialogue and wrote dialogues dealing with each, a whole series of dialogues for Socrates' failure with Alcibiades, a single dialogue for his failure with Critias.

In two dialogues named *Alcibiades* Plato gave his readers the opportunity to study Socrates' pursuit of Alcibiades. The dialogues themselves indicate that they closely follow on Socrates' successful hunt for Alcibiades in *Protagoras*, and Alcibiades' speech in the *Symposium* proves it. For Plato's *Symposium* is, among many other things, an elaborate closure of the theme on which his *Protagoras* opened, Socrates' hunt for Alcibiades. It dictates that the two dialogues be studied together: all speakers in the *Symposium* except Aristophanes are present in *Protagoras*. Both dialogues have frames that question Socrates' relation with Alcibiades; both core discussions occur in private Athenian homes and are reported to a wider public; Socrates'

152. These words of Socrates' accuser in the *Memorabilia* are followed immediately by Xenophon's extended defense (1.2.13–47), which ends: "As soon as [Alcibiades and Critias] supposed themselves to be superior to the other citizens, they no longer came to Socrates. For he did not please them anyway; and if they did come to him they were annoyed by being refuted regarding their errors. Rather, they became engaged in the city's affairs, which was why they had in fact come to Socrates."

arrival at the private home, accompanied by a young companion, is delayed in both by an unreported argument that has to be brought to completion before he enters; in both, Socrates stages a protest to win the right to continue in his preferred fashion; in *Protagoras*, Socrates describes how a symposium for gentlemen who are properly educated should be conducted (347b–e), advising among other things that flute girls should be dismissed;[153] the war is an unmentioned but ominous presence in both, *Protagoras* occurring just before the war, the core discussion of the *Symposium* in 416, at a crucial turning point in Athenian war policy as it considered Alcibiades' audacious plan to open a front in Sicily; and, because of the frames, Alcibiades is a constant presence in both, a haunting presence for most of the *Symposium* because he is announced early and arrives late.[154]

The *Symposium* opens with a frame audience expressing interest in Socrates' relation with Alcibiades, and what *Protagoras* intimates, the *Symposium* flaunts: the frame audiences care more about Socrates' pursuit of Alcibiades than about his thought. Plato's presentation of this matter of acute public concern begins and ends in front of publics privileged to hear reports of private events after the limited nature of their interest in Socrates is shown. What these publics are told distances Socrates from Alcibiades, defending him against the charge that damaged him most, while sheltering his most private aims for Alcibiades. There is good reason to hold that the frame of the *Symposium* occurs in 399 when suspicion of Socrates' corruption of Alcibiades and other young Athenians reached its fatal pitch. Just before the trial, perhaps, at which Athenians would be called upon to judge Socrates' alleged corruption, Plato supplies *two* frame audiences, both demanding to hear the tale of Socrates' privacy, both uninterested in philosophy. Plato's final treatment of the explosive theme of Socrates' relation to Alcibiades is thus set at the decisive moment of

153. *Symposium* 176e.

154. Plato goes out of his way to make Alcibiades "present" in dialogues where he is not named. In "Who's Who in Plato's *Timaeus-Critias* and Why," Planeaux and I argue that Alcibiades is the absent fourth in *Timaeus-Critias*, the pair of dialogues set in 421 that open: "One, two, three—but where's the fourth" from yesterday's discussion? Alcibiades' absence from speeches on the cosmology that underlies the city's order and on Athens' historic greatness leads, we argue, to catastrophe for the Athenian adventure in Sicily that Alcibiades set in motion—a catastrophe caused in no small measure by the *absence* of Alcibiades and the *presence* of Hermocrates of Syracuse, who brilliantly led the Syracusan defense and whom Plato placed in Athens eight years earlier, present at the discussions in *Timaeus-Critias* for which Alcibiades was absent. In "Socrates' Defense of Polytropic Odysseus," I argue that Alcibiades is the massive background presence for the two *Hippias* dialogues as the mastermind and master actor of the diplomatic congress that called Hippias to Athens—the spectacular achievement by Alcibiades that Thucydides chose as the moment to introduce Alcibiades into his narrative.

the public judgment on Socrates, and its importunate audiences are taken back to a decisive moment in Athenian history, 416 when Alcibiades was firing Athens with an eros for subduing Sicily. Those audiences hear testimony from the most unimpeachable witness, an Alcibiades speaking from the dead to vouch for Socrates' virtue. Alcibiades leads the company assembled at Agathon's house in 416—plus the publics Plato supplied for Apollodorus's narrations seventeen years later—farther back in time and into the most private possible setting: Socrates and Alcibiades under a blanket together through the night, with an unattended young Alcibiades eager to yield. And Socrates did nothing. Alcibiades kept this *shaming* of his beauty secret for years, but on this night of speeches celebrating eros, drunk, among friends, competing with Socrates for the victorious young beauty Agathon, he tells the shameful truth. Alcibiades intends his revelation, his profaning of Socrates' mysteries, to prove Socrates' guilt, but for the frame audiences it proves his innocence. Without being able to know it in advance, their eagerness to "question [Apollodorus] closely about Agathon's party—the one at which Socrates, Alcibiades and others were then present at dinner together—to question [him] about the erotic speeches,"[155] led to an inquisitor's bonanza: Alcibiades himself, revealing the most shameful secrets of Socrates' pursuit of him, *exonerates* Socrates.

After revealing the horrible truth, Alcibiades says it all happened *before* "the expedition to Potidaea." With this quiet reference, Plato states that what began so successfully in *Protagoras* and *Alcibiades I* and *II* came to an early failure before they left Athens in 432: Alcibiades' whole public career, from Potidaea through the planned expedition to Sicily and after, was conducted without the wise counsel Socrates showed he could give. Plato's *Protagoras* opens with Socrates pursuing Alcibiades, his *Symposium* ends with Alcibiades himself telling why Socrates failed. Socrates stated another reason for his failure before the two of them left for Potidaea. *Alcibiades I* ends with Socrates saying, "I am filled with dread not because I do not have trust in your nature, but rather because, seeing the strength of the city, I fear that it will overcome both you and me." Alcibiades repeats that reason in 416: "whenever I go away [from him], I know within myself that I am doing so because I have succumbed to the honor I get from the Many."[156] The *Symposium* shows why Alcibiades was bound to misunderstand Socrates: absent for Socrates' speech on eros in which he indicated

155. *Symposium* 172a–b.
156. *Symposium* 216b.

his most fundamental learning, Alcibiades reveals in his drunken, truthful speech how he misinterpreted Socrates' eros while admiring his powers of self-control. Socrates did all he could with Alcibiades, but not even his labors based on knowledge of Alcibiades' nature could overcome the greatest sophist.[157]

"What should we do with Alcibiades?"—in Aristophanes' *Frogs*, performed in 405 as Athens debated yet another return of Alcibiades to deliver it in the still-continuing war, Dionysos asked this question to test Aeschylus and Euripides. Aeschylus replied: "It is best not to raise a lion in the city, but if you do, it is best to accede to his ways" (1422–32). Athens raised the lion in its midst inattentively, neither training him nor giving him his due. Plato shows Socrates, like some combination of Zeus and Hermes, making every effort to equip this remarkable growth of political genius with the justice, moderation, and piety that could perhaps turn it civil after it had been corrupted by sophists and the greatest sophist. What should have been done with Alcibiades Socrates tried to do in *Alcibiades I* and *II* after successfully hunting him down in *Protagoras*.

To what end would Socrates pursue his nascent private alliance with Alcibiades? *Alcibiades I* and *II* answer: he would not dream of trying to transform a young political genius into a philosopher, of remaking his nature. Instead, Socrates' pursuit of an inescapably public man aims to make him a public man capable of ruling himself and only then ruling others. Such rule would be just rule, ceding to the god the ultimate outcome while gaining from the god the right to aspire to rule all of Greece and all of Asia, to rule the world. Alcibiades' role in *Protagoras* seems an image in miniature of what Socrates aimed to make of the political genius of Alcibiades: were an Alcibiades to take Socrates' side in the larger setting of the city as he did in Callias's house, he would preside on behalf of philosophy as Socrates practiced it, coming to its aid by leading a whole community to make a place for Socrates' way of speaking while Socrates himself stayed Spartan, concealing his wisdom by denying it and acting as if he were ignorant. Though not made a philosopher by Socrates' successful hunt, Alcibiades would pride himself on his philosophical bent while thinking himself engaged in more important tasks, as Anaxagoras's Pericles did, as Aristotle's Alexander would. *Alcibiades I* shows what could be gained from an

157. *Republic* 492a–e. See Benardete, "On Plato's *Symposium*," *The Argument of the Action*, 183–85 for a persuasive argument that by encouraging Alcibiades to misinterpret him as merely moral and thereby implanting an imitative moderation in him, "Socrates came *that* close to saving Athens."

alliance of Alcibiades and Socrates: Alcibiades' passion to rule, cultivated by Socrates, would make the parts of the world subdued by Alcibiades as friendly to philosophy as Alexander's world came to be.

In the chronologically first of Plato's dialogues Socrates mounts the stage in Athens, the imperial city ruling an empire and made glorious by monuments of art and intellect that carry forward the Homeric. In a city that takes itself to be enlightened and to welcome those who spread enlightenment, Socrates acts to restrain and redirect the founder of sophism—and his famous followers—and to take in hand the education of the young Athenian who matters most to Athens' imperial future, a man less modest than Pericles, less content to merely preserve the already established imperium, a man in whom Socrates himself encourages grander ambition.[158] To mount the stage this way is to mount the stage to rule. Imperial Athens would then itself be ruled by imperial philosophy. Socrates' form of enlightenment would spread out from Athens as other forms of power spread out from an imperial center to the hinterland it rules. By redirecting the best minds drawn inexorably to the imperial center, Socrates sees to the export of his wisdom, to the rule of philosophy wherever Athens rules. At the same time, he sees to the expansion of Athenian rule by planting in the mind of the most ambitious and politically gifted young Athenian the passion to rule Asia. Mounting the stage, Socrates thinks even more imperially than Themistocles did; he thinks on the scale of Homer schooled by what Homer wrought, and Homer wrought Greekness itself, which spread wherever Greeks spread.

Socrates and Critias

Plato's defense of Socrates against the charge that he corrupted Critias, like his defense of Socrates regarding Alcibiades, leads from *Protagoras* to chronologically later dialogues, in Critias's case, to *Charmides*.[159] In *Protagoras*, when Critias first enters Callias's house with Alcibiades, he could be

158. On Alcibiades' imperial ambitions, see his speech to the Spartans, Thucydides 6.90.

159. It is imperative for understanding Socrates' relationship with Critias, son of Callaeschrus, that he be separated from his grandfather, the Critias of *Timeaus-Critias*. One of the small devices Plato used to separate the two was consistently calling the younger "Critias son of Callaeschrus," while calling the aged and honored older man simply "Critias"—everyone knows who that great man was. *That* Critias is already extremely old in 421 when *Timaeus-Critias* occurs, and he is the fit Athenian host during the Peace of Nicias for estimable guests from enemy cities, such as Timaeus of Locri and Hermocrates of Syracuse. On the arguments for separating the two Critiases, a separation familiar to the ancients, see Lampert and Planeaux, "Who's Who in Plato's *Timaeus-Critias* and Why," 95–100.

thought to be a follower of Socrates, for he enters just after Socrates and Hippocrates (316a). He speaks only once but speaks in character, for he addresses Prodicus and Hippias only and calls upon them to solve the problem posed by Socrates' threat to leave (336e): Critias advocated the rule of the capable few. The glimpse in *Protagoras* of this other great Athenian criminal with whom Socrates would be linked in Athenian memory points to a prewar association with Socrates that is greatly elaborated in *Charmides*, where he is Socrates' most important interlocutor. The overt topic of their conversation is *sophrosunê*, moderation or sound-mindedness, but Socrates' covert topic is implied by an intention he states at the opening: returning to Athens after a long absence, he intends to discover how things now stand with philosophy. He satisfies that intention in one way only: by speaking with Critias. Socrates' questioning confirms that Critias paid him very close attention during their prewar association, but it reveals to Socrates that things stand badly indeed with philosophy, with *his* philosophy, if Critias is exemplary of how those who heard him before Potidaea received it.

By spreading Socrates' relation with Critias across the temporal gap separating *Protagoras* from *Charmides*, Plato allows his reader to see Socrates learning from his failure with Critias, a different kind of failure from his failure with Alcibiades: his failure with Critias concerns his effort to transmit his philosophy to a potential philosopher, not his effort to direct a political man in the service of philosophy. A full appreciation of what Socrates learned from Critias requires a detailed study of *Charmides*, but one key feature can be noted beforehand in a striking difference between the Socrates of the prewar *Protagoras* and the Socrates who returns to an Athens devastated by war and the plague in *Charmides* some four years later. In *Protagoras*, Socrates did not, as Protagoras did, speak in the manner of Homer, speak mythically of gods. Protagoras celebrated the philanthropy of Prometheus and of Zeus and Hermes, and his salutary use of Homer and Hesiod's gods led to his humanized, civil version of those gods being chiseled in stone as exemplars of civil human life. In *Protagoras* Socrates made no comment whatever on this prominent aspect of Protagoras's display speech, nor did he speak as a theologian himself. The Socrates who returned in *Charmides* after his years away returned different, he says, having learned a new teaching about the soul from a doctor of the god Zalmoxis. *Charmides* intimates that the pre-Potidaean Socrates taught Critias a skeptical view of the gods and an enticingly positive view of the power of the wise who spoke for them—a liberating and provocative teaching that kindled in Critias the vaunting thoughts and deeds that would characterize his mature acts as a sophist and, finally, as a political leader. The Socrates who says he returned different in *Charmides*, bringing a new teaching on the soul and, by implication, on the gods, does not elaborate that teaching in *Charmides*. A few weeks later, however, in the chronologically next dialogue, the *Republic*, he does set out a new teaching on the soul and he does speak as a theologian, telling his young Athenian audience, while Thrasymachus listens, how they are to think about the gods and how reason can control their spirited natures; and he ends his instruction by making the soul immortal, closely observed by moral gods who reward and punish it. In the gap between his pre-Potidaean and post-Potidaean teachings, Socrates learned the need to speak as a theologian who knows the nature of the soul.

Socrates' Politics for Philosophy in 433 and a Nietzschean History of Philosophy

The politics for philosophy set out in *Protagoras* and *Alcibiades I* and *II* is the strategy of the thirty-six-year-old Socrates in 433, the strategy of an enlightened man in revolt against the sophistic enlightenment because it endangered enlightenment, the strategy of a thinker who took on the responsibility of teaching both sophists and the best young Athenians a better way to advance enlightenment. The temporal gap that Plato built in between the dialogues of 433 and the dialogues of Socrates' return in 429 allows him to demonstrate wordlessly the great strategic advancements Socrates himself learned for his prototype defense of philosophy. That prototype is not finished in 433, but its essential features are set: Socrates must mount the public stage in order to redirect the Greek enlightenment, to charm ambitious Greek young, and to report his doings to the Athenian public. What compels him to such actions? A Nietzschean history of philosophy, schooled to a degree by all the great philosophers and especially by Nietzsche himself, has learned that the fundamental motive for such actions is philanthropy in the special sense of loving the human and desiring its advancement in what most makes the human human, its capacity to understand the world and to inhabit the world as understood. In *Protagoras* Plato allows Protagoras himself to embody such philanthropic effort: Protagoras attributes to Prometheus and to Zeus and Hermes gifts to humanity that he knows can come only from humans, gifts he himself is capable of giving, the technical gift of the art of speech and the civilizing gift of gods who divinize civil human order by exemplifying it themselves. It is Socrates in *Protagoras* who shows that this philanthropy of the wise is particularly focused on the well-being of wisdom and its transmission to potential kin: he can criticize Protagoras for betraying kin to nonkin. Still, the full range of Socratic philanthropy has not been attained by 433 and will be attained only in the dialogues of Socrates' return, *Charmides* and the *Republic*. Nor are the grounds of Socratic philanthropy made visible in the dialogues of 433; only the dialogues that most enter Socrates' privacy, dialogues that show how he came to be himself, *Phaedo* and the *Symposium*, will intimate the full grounds of Socratic philanthropy.

Note on the Dramatic Date of *Protagoras* and *Alcibiades I*

Plato made it easy for contemporaries to figure out exactly when *Protagoras* occurred while choosing not to simply state the date:[160] it was when Alcibiades' growth of beard made him too old for Socrates' pursuit, when Protagoras was old enough to be the father of anyone present, when Protagoras, Prodicus, and Hippias were all in Athens together, when Pericles and his two sons were still alive, when Agathon was just a boy, the year after a certain comedy by Pherecrates was performed at the Lenaia.[161] Plato also made it easy for contemporaries to infer just when *Alcibiades I* occurred: twice Socrates calls attention to the fact that Alcibiades is eager to address the Athenian Assembly for the first time;[162] he is therefore not yet "twenty,"[163] and it was easy to learn when that was. For us, however,

160. Debra Nails made an effort to determine the dramatic dates of all the dialogues that are datable, Appendix I, *People of Plato*, 307–30. As good and as exacting as the rest of her book is, there are difficulties with this appendix and with many of the dates assigned. For a brief assessment of this part of her book, see the review by Planeaux. See also Zuckert's list of the dramatic dates she assigns the dialogues (*Plato's Philosophers*, 8–9).

161. Plato typically uses indirect means of indicating dramatic dates (such as the items here cited), although more direct methods of dating were available to him as they were to Thucydides, who secured the dates of events by Athenian archonships, for instance. The method of securing dates by Olympiads was apparently introduced only after Hippias compiled a list of Olympiads. For general discussions of ancient dating, see Strassler, "Calendars and Dating Systems in Thucydides," 623–25, and Nails, *People of Plato*, xli–xlii. As for the dramatic dates within the calendar years, Plato frequently referred to festivals in the annual calendar of Athenian religious events to secure those more exact dates.

162. *Alcibiades I* 105a–b, 113b.

163. *Alcibiades I* 123d. Becoming "twenty" was a collective experience for young Athenians: it was when the whole cohort of second-year ephebes together celebrated the festival, probably in August–September, that inducted them into adulthood as *neoi* (young men). See Garland, *Greek Way of Life*, 180, 201. It was an important experience because becoming twenty meant being able to serve in the military and attend the Assembly. Because the ages of young men were absorbed into annual cohorts, no exact dating is possible for becoming eighteen or nineteen (the two years spent as an ephebe) or twenty.

separated in time from these details and the exactitude they offer, it is possible to say with certainty only that Plato set *Protagoras* and *Alcibiades I* in prewar Athens, Periclean Athens in the golden age of its attainments, around 433.[164]

A strong reason internal to the dialogues rules out 432. In his speech in the *Symposium* set in February 416, Alcibiades accuses Socrates of having shamefully dishonored him many years ago by refusing his advances, including his final, most provocative effort when he maneuvered Socrates into spending all night alone with him under a blanket—and Socrates did nothing a father or brother would not do (219a–e). While describing that event Alcibiades remarks that "it was winter" (219b), and when he finishes he adds that they went together on the expedition to Potidaea "after this" (219e). To put a winter at the end of his pursuit of Socrates is to make 432 impossible as a date for *Protagoras* and *Alcibiades I*: these summer dialogues necessarily preceded Alcibiades' attempted seduction of Socrates, and, as I will argue, the two of them left together for Potidaea in the summer or fall of 432.[165] Therefore, the winter of Alcibiades' failure to seduce Socrates sets *Protagoras* and *Alcibiades I* in 433 or earlier.

Was it 433 then? Alcibiades' little remarks—it was winter; we went to Potidaea after this—make 433 very likely because they help create a plausible compact chronology for Socrates' effort to win Alcibiades: preceded by long observation of the child and boy, it was initiated with strategic mas-

164. The historical cues for dating *Protagoras* are discussed by Morrison, "Place of Protagoras in Athenian Public Life," 2–3. Morrison concludes that *Protagoras* has "a dramatic date of about 433." That is the consensus view shared by A. E. Taylor, *Plato*, 236 ("cannot be put later than 433"); Guthrie, *History of Greek Philosophy*, 4:214; C. C. W. Taylor, *Protagoras*, 64; Nussbaum, *Fragility of Goodness*, 91; Coby, *Socrates and the Sophistic Enlightenment*, 23–24 ("approximately 432"); and Nails, *People of Plato*, 310. Two weak objections were raised in antiquity to a dramatic date of *Protagoras* before the war broke out—by Athenaeus, writing around 200 CE, in *Deipnosophistai* (The Learned Banquet) 5.218b. One concerned what was interpreted as a reference to the death date of Hipponicus, the father of Critias, namely, "a certain storeroom which Hipponicus had previously used as a treasury" (315d). This need not imply that Hipponicus (who died in 422/421) is now dead and Callias master of the house, only that for the purposes of this great gathering the room has been put to a new use for his son. Furthermore, the doorman who refuses Socrates and Hippocrates entry says, "Yuk! Sophists" and turns them away. It seems unlikely that he could do so for that reason if Callias were his master but quite likely if it were Hipponicus. Second, the date of the performance of the play by Pherecrates referred to by Protagoras as "performed last year at the Lenaia" (327d): Athenaeus's character says that the play was *The Savages* and that it was performed in 421/420. But, as Reginald Allen argues, Pherecrates first won the dramatic competition in 438, and he "may well have returned to such an obvious theme several times. Besides, the title of the play here mentioned seems to have been *The Misanthropes*" (*Ion, Hippias Minor, Laches, Protagoras*, 187 n. 11).

165. See below, "Note on the Dramatic Date of *Charmides*."

tery in the summer of *Protagoras*, advanced in the provocations of *Alcibiades I* shortly thereafter, and foundered the following winter after a whole autumn of mutual striving between the two of them, a striving that can be studied in its essential aspect from Socrates' side in *Alcibiades II*, his effort to teach Alcibiades the Spartan prayer with all that it implies about personal ambition, and from Alcibiades' side in the many stages of his effort to win Socrates erotically that he reports in the *Symposium*. *Alcibiades I*, linked closely in time with *Protagoras* by their similarity of themes large and small, occurs just before Alcibiades first addressed the Athenian Assembly,[166] something he had to be twenty to be allowed to do. Because 432 is ruled out as a date for *Alcibiades I*, and because that dialogue is temporally linked with *Protagoras*, both most likely occur in 433, just before Alcibiades became old enough to address the Athenian Assembly for the first time. Thucydides supplies a reason for not setting them earlier than that: when he first introduces Alcibiades to his narrative in 420, he says he is "a man still young in years for any other Hellenic city"[167]—young to be a commander, that is, and in Athens thirty was the minimum age to be elected one of the generals. Alcibiades' relative youth in 420 argues in favor of placing *Protagoras* and *Alcibiades I* in 433.[168]

Thucydides offers another consideration in favor of setting *Protagoras* in 433: he gives great prominence to the Corcyraean exhortation to the Athenian Assembly in 433 that war with the Spartans is coming. That the Athenian Assembly debated anticipations of war in the summer of 433 makes that a most fitting time for Socrates' contrast in *Protagoras* between the wise policy of the "Spartans," who listen to their wise, and the foolish policy of the Athenian Assembly in listening to anyone equally on matters of peace and war.

It has often been argued that *Alcibiades I* must have occurred before *Protagoras* because *Alcibiades I* opens with Socrates saying that I "have not so much as spoken to you during the many years the others came clamoring to converse with you" (103a).[169] But Socrates does not speak to Alcibiades in *Protagoras*, he merely speaks in his presence. That *Protagoras* precedes *Alcibiades I* is indicated by the end of *Alcibiades I*, when Alcibiades says, "we will probably be changing roles, Socrates, I taking yours and you mine,

166. *Alcibiades I* 105b.

167. Thucydides 5.43.2.

168. The standard date assigned for Alcibiades' birth, based on Plato and Thucydides, is 451. See Nails, *People of Plato*, 13.

169. E.g., Coby, *Socrates and the Sophistic Enlightenment*, 189 n. 18, and Landy, "Virtue, Art, and the Good Life in Plato's *Protagoras*," 302–6.

for from this day nothing can keep me from attending on you and you from being attended on by me" (135d). That reversal of roles seems not to have occurred before *Protagoras*, a dialogue that shows Socrates attempting to win Alcibiades rather than already having won him.[170] Alcibiades speaks up in *Protagoras* on Socrates' behalf but first because fairness dictates it and later because the rules do. Another important indication that *Alcibiades I* follows *Protagoras* is the fact that many points large and small in *Alcibiades I* repeat and enlarge what Alcibiades heard in the conversation between Socrates and Protagoras.[171] Given the repetition of these numerous items, it is most reasonable to conclude that the first private conversation between the two occurred shortly after the conversation Alcibiades was privileged to hear between Socrates and Protagoras.

Even if absolute certainty is not attainable for 433 as the dramatic date of *Protagoras* and *Alcibiades I* and *II*, this much is certain: they are prewar dialogues set before Socrates and Alcibiades depart for Potidaea on what will turn out to be a two-and-a-half- to three-year expedition.[172] By setting *Protagoras* and *Alcibiades I* and *II* in prewar Athens at the height of its Periclean greatness, Plato allowed a gap to open between them and the dialogues of Socrates' return; he exploited that gap by having Socrates return in late spring 429 in *Charmides* and the *Republic*, dialogues in which a different Socrates returns to an Athens made different by war and plague.

170. See also Zuckert, *Plato's Philosophers*, 217–18n4.
171. See above, 126–29.
172. See "Note on the Dramatic Date of *Charmides*."

PART TWO

Philosophy in a Time of Crisis: Socrates' Return to War-Ravaged, Plague-Ravaged Athens, Late Spring 429

CHAPTER 2

Charmides: Socrates' Philosophy and Its Transmission

Prologue: The Return of Socrates

Charmides is the dialogue of Socrates' return. He has been away from Athens for two and a half or three years with the Athenian army besieging rebel Potidaea, and the Athens to which he returns in late May 429 is different from the Athens in which Plato set the prewar *Protagoras*.[1] While it has by no means wholly lost its triumphal self-assurance, Athens has suffered far greater losses than Pericles ever led it to suspect it would. In the first two summers of the war, the Spartan army and its allies invaded Attica, forcing the rural population to take refuge inside the city walls, leaving their homes, crops, olive trees, and fruit trees to be burned or ruined by the invading forces. And in late spring 429, for the second year, a mysterious plague has returned, threatening to destroy the unity of the city and break its will in the face of horrifying suffering and wholesale death. At Potidaea Athens has just suffered its first major defeat of the war, losing not only four hundred and thirty hoplites and all three generals but the immense investment of treasure that the long siege had cost it. The Athens to which Socrates returns is a newly needy Athens faced with the existential crises of the invading Spartans and the plague, but faced as well with a deep spiritual crisis generated by the visible crises and recognizable in these earliest stages only by a person with the widest perspective and deepest insight. As *Protagoras* and *Alcibiades I* showed, Socrates is such a person, and his

1. For the details of the dramatic date see below, "Note on the Dramatic Date of *Charmides*."

attentions have been turned to public concerns with a view to defending the private, investigative concerns of philosophy.

Athens in late May 429 is different. So too is Socrates: he announces in *Charmides* that he returned having learned in his absence a new teaching about the soul, a new medicine that Charmides so desires by the end of the conversation that he is willing to threaten Socrates with violence in order to receive it. Yet the incantations of which that medicine consists are not chanted in *Charmides*.

Charmides almost opens with Socrates stating his intentions after his long absence: he wants to discover the state of philosophy in Athens and whether any young men have become beautiful or wise in his absence. He satisfies his second aim by questioning young Charmides, who is about seventeen at the time; he satisfies the first by interrogating Critias, his prewar associate who is now about thirty. Critias was fated to become almost as notorious as Alcibiades and to do Socrates, his ostensible corrupter, permanent damage. Proper appreciation of *Charmides* depends in part on recognizing who Critias is: perhaps the cleverest of Socrates' prewar associates, he would become a famous Athenian poet and sophist, more radical or outspoken than Protagoras, as was typical of the second generation of sophists. Late in his life, twenty-five years after *Charmides*, he would be one of the Athenian leaders assigned by the victorious Spartans to replace Athens' century-old democracy with an oligarchy more akin to the Spartan polity. Critias became a leader of that group, known to history by the title affixed to it by the Athenian democracy that overthrew it, the "Thirty Tyrants." Xenophon wrote that Critias was the most thievish, violent, and murderous of all in that regime. The man whom Socrates questions about moderation is an extremely capable intellectual, influenced when young by Socrates, now about thirty years old, who will, when called upon to engage in politics, prove appallingly immoderate.

1. First Words (153a–d)

"We came on the day before in the evening, out of Potidaea, from the army camp . . ."[2] These first words of Plato's *Charmides* give great prominence to something Socrates evidently wants his auditor to know first: exactly when the conversation occurred. But saying that it was the day after he returned from Potidaea is not enough to secure the date for his auditor,

2. I use the translation of *Charmides* by Thomas G. West and Grace Starry West because of its accuracy but modified it occasionally.

for a few moments after reporting his own first words, Socrates reports the first words spoken to him on the day after his return, fervent words of his longtime friend Chaerephon, and he finds it necessary to explain Chaerephon's surprise and joy at his return: "A little while before we left, a battle had occurred at Potidaea, which those here had just been learning about" (153b). The auditor can now conclude that Socrates had just returned from the Athenian defeat at Spartolus, the first major defeat in the war that ultimately destroyed the Athenian empire.[3] The auditor can conclude what Plato evidently wanted his reader to be able to conclude: *Charmides* is set in what we call late May 429. When Socrates adds in his very first sentence, "I had been away for some time," Plato's first readers would know that Socrates is returning to Athens after an absence of at least two and a half years and probably three, for Athenians aware of the great events of the history of their city would know that three contingents of hoplite soldiers had been sent to Potidaea in 432 and 431, where they then remained to besiege the city.[4] The dramatic date of *Charmides* assigns it a special place in the chronological arrangement Plato gave his dialogues: *Charmides* is the dialogue of Socrates' return home after a long absence. Separated in time from the prewar dialogues, it calls attention to that separation in its first words.

Charmides is special in other ways: one of six dialogues narrated by Socrates, it differs from the other five in not being narrated on the same day or the next day but at some later time.[5] For Socrates' need to explain that *those here* were just learning of a terrible battle in which friends and family could have fallen removes his auditor from that time and sets the narration at a later time. *Charmides* has two settings, one for the conversation it reports and the later one for its narration. *Charmides* is singular in another, perhaps related way. One of four dialogues that Socrates narrates from beginning to end,[6] *Charmides* differs from the other three, *Lysis*, the

3. The battle of Spartalos was the first battle of the war to inflict major casualties on Athens; Thucydides states that 430 Athenian hoplites and all their generals were killed there (2.79.7). In addition, it was "the most expensive siege in classical Greek history" and "cost Athens 40% of its prewar capital reserves" (Hanson, *War Like No Other* 179, 97).

4. The three Athenian contingents besieging Potidaea went out in the spring of 432, the fall of 432, and the spring of 431; Socrates and Alcibiades likely left with the first contingent under Archestratus. See below, 238–39.

5. Of the other five dialogues Socrates narrates, *Protagoras* is narrated the very day it occurred, *Euthydemus* and the *Republic* the day after each occurred, the *Lovers* and *Lysis* at apparently indeterminate times

6. The other two he narrates, *Protagoras* and *Euthydemus*, have frame conversations that introduce them.

Lovers, and the *Republic*, in that Socrates addresses his auditor or auditors in this one only, calling him "comrade" (154a), "friend" (155c), and "noble one" (155d). The significance of these two special features is recoverable from *Charmides* itself.

As part of his long first sentence, Socrates reports that his extended absence made him glad to go around to the places where he usually spent his time, and the first place he went was "the palaistra of Taureas,[7] the one right across from the shrine of the Queen." When he entered he found some who were unknown to him, though most were known.[8] Entering unexpectedly, he was greeted by acquaintances from all over the palaistra, but one, "Chaerephon that madman," exhibiting his characteristic vehemence and his deep relief at seeing his friend, jumped up, rushed over to him, and seized his hand.[9] After describing Chaerephon's actions, Socrates reports the conversation between the two of them, a private conversation between himself and his longtime associate to which no one in the palaistra was privy but which Socrates wants his auditor to hear. This first reported conversation on Socrates' return is laconic in the extreme as Chaerephon's questions and Socrates' answers move toward maximum brevity, with Socrates' final answer repeating a single word from Chaerephon's question. Why does Socrates think it necessary to relate this odd private exchange to the auditor as prelude to a conversation with another of his associates from before Potidaea?

Chaerephon's first words, "Socrates, how were you saved from the battle?" draw Socrates' first reported words on his return: "Just so, as you see." His words seem wrong, curt, and ungenerous as his first words to his "comrade from youth,"[10] who has just expressed such relief at his return alive from the battle.[11] But perhaps the words would not seem wrong to a

7. Taureas may have been the man slapped by Alcibiades in a public incident recalled in Andocides' speech "Against Alcibiades" (Gagarin and MacDowell, *Antiphon and Andocides*, 165–66).

8. Socrates distinguishes between unknown (*agnôtas*) and known (*gnôrimos*) using forms of *gignôskô*. He will introduce other words for knowing at crucial points in the dialogue as he develops its theme of knowledge.

9. In Plato's *Gorgias* Socrates and Chaerephon are paired at the beginning; Chaerephon shows that he knows how to begin a Socratic investigation, first of Gorgias and then, almost immediately, of Polus, his follower, but Socrates takes over very quickly (*Gorgias* 447a–448d). According to Socrates in the *Apology* Chaerephon was responsible for the reflections that led Socrates to "turn" to the investigations of political men, poets, and manual artisans that confirmed for him that the oracle was right to declare that no man was wiser than Socrates.

10. *Apology* 20e.

11. Lawrence Levine calls Socrates' words "curiously abrupt and inscrutable" ("Commentary on Plato's *Charmides*," 18). Levine's 1975 Pennsylvania State University dissertation on *Charmides* is well worth studying.

Greek reader well schooled in Homer; perhaps they would recall a similar statement made on another occasion of return: "Here am I, such as you see," were the words spoken by Odysseus in response to the first recognition by an Ithacan that he, long-awaited Odysseus, had returned alive.[12] Odysseus addressed those words to Telemachus alone, his son. Could Plato mean to suggest by these first reported words of Socrates upon his return—private words to a close follower—that Socrates' return in 429 is to be thought against the background of that greatest of all returns?

Chaerephon seems unwilling to believe that Socrates was in fact saved from the battle: "And yet it has been reported here that the battle was quite fierce and that many of the known died in it." The word Chaerephon employs for "the known," *tôn gnôrimôn*,[13] is a word used only once in Homer, shortly before Odysseus's recognition scene with Telemachus. Telemachus himself has just returned to Ithaca, and he approaches the house of Eumaeus, the loyal swineherd, where Odysseus is present but unrecognizable as a beggar. Odysseus hears his footsteps and, noticing that the dogs who attacked him on his approach are not barking but fawning, says to Eumaeus: "someone is on his way here who is truly one of yours, or else *known*" (16.8–9). Could Chaerephon be acknowledging that he recognizes Socrates' first words as in fact a reminder of Odysseus's return—he playing Telemachus to Socrates' Odysseus, a spiritual son acknowledging the return of his spiritual father?

"And it is fitting"—with these words Socrates begins his brief response to Chaerephon, and he continues: "what *has been reported* is true." "Reported" is *apaggellô*, to bring tidings, a word used in the *Odyssey* shortly after Odysseus reveals himself to Telemachus: Athena made Odysseus radiant for his disclosure of himself to his son, but she transforms him back to a beggar when Eumaeus returns, "for fear that the swineherd might look upon him and know him and might go *to report* to circumspect Penelope and not hold the secret fast in his heart" (16.454–59). If Chaerephon recognizes the word as a citation from the *Odyssey*, he hears Socrates—in this central speech of their seven-speech private exchange—set him under an imperative: he must hold the secret fast in his heart.

Chaerephon responds with his third speech, which again, by itself, sounds odd: "Were you present at the battle?" The verb he uses for "present" is *paragignomai*, and Socrates' response, his final response, is a single word: *Paregenomen*, "I was present." The extreme economy of these two

12. *Odyssey* 16.205.

13. The word Socrates used when saying that many in the palaistra were *known* to him (153a).

speeches completes their exchange on another remarkable note. For the word Chaerephon chose to pose his final question is again a word used only once in Homer, and again a word associated with Odysseus' return. The suitors who have been engaged in sporting events in front of Odysseus' palace enter the palace for dinner, and "Medon, who of the heralds was most to their liking and was always *present* [*paregigneto*] at their feasts" (17.173), addresses them. Medon is the special herald in the *Odyssey*, "a man of thoughtful mind"[14] who remained loyal to Penelope and Telemachus during Odysseus' long absence, reporting the suitors' plot against Telemachus to Penelope;[15] he is one of the two for whom Telemachus speaks up in order to have his father spare them in the slaughter of the suitors, the one on whom Odysseus smiles and the one to whom he speaks.[16] Loyal Chaerephon announces his continued careful presence at home as a man of thoughtful mind in asking about Socrates' presence at the battle—not "mad" then as he may seem and as Socrates said. Socrates' single-word answer makes their presence to one another fully present.

Chaerephon makes the final speech: "Come here then, sit down, and go through it for us, for in fact we haven't yet *learned about* it all." The last word of their exchange is a verb that Socrates, in his report to the auditor, inserted into the beginning of their exchange in order to explain that the battle was something those here were just learning about. The word thus used twice is a word that appears with great frequency in the *Odyssey: punthanomai*, to learn by inquiry or hearsay, to inquire about, to hear tidings of—a word most often associated with learning about absent Odysseus's possible return. At the opening of *Charmides*, in its rare words and common words, we seem to breathe the atmosphere of Odysseus's return.

Is this all coincidence, an accidental gathering of words important in Odysseus's return? If it is, it is not the end of such coincidences: the sole explicit mention of Homer in *Charmides* accompanied by its sole explicit quotation from the *Odyssey* concerns how Odysseus must act on his return in order not to be recognized by the suitors;[17] the final direct allusion to Homer will be Penelope's distinction between true and false dreams that she tells Odysseus in the encounter that must be her recognition of her long-awaited husband;[18] and the last words of *Charmides* will include

14. *Odyssey* 4.696.
15. *Odyssey* 4.675–714.
16. *Odyssey* 22.354–80.
17. See below on 161a.
18. See below on 173a.

another rare word in Homer used only at the final recognition scene of the *Odyssey*.[19] The opening exchange between Socrates and Chaerephon, that enigmatic, private little exchange between the returned Socrates and his welcoming follower, yields its enigmas when brought into contact with Homer, for it initiates a series of references in *Charmides* to the recognition scenes in the *Odyssey*. And *Charmides* puts them in the right order from the very first to the very last.

The privacy of the opening exchange, and the Homeric event to which it privately alludes, suggest that the public conversation to come will have a private dimension, one to which Chaerephon, schooled in Socrates' pre-Potidaean ways, will be alert and one to which the auditor and the reader must work to become alert if we are to share in Socrates and Chaerephon's private understanding of Socrates' homecoming. Schooled into attention to the private by this private opening, the auditor and reader are given the gift of insight into *Charmides* as a public conversation containing secret and explosive private matters of intimate concern to Socrates and of immense public consequence. The Homeric opening of *Charmides* opens a way into the recognition of just who Socrates is on his return and just what his plans are.

2. Socrates' Intentions (153c–d)

While he and Socrates are conducting their private conversation, Chaerephon takes charge of Socrates and leads him to where he is to sit. He places him next to Critias, son of Callaeschrus,[20] as if that were the place Chaerephon thinks it's necessary for him to be. *Charmides* thus brings together in 429, as associates of Socrates, the democrat Chaerephon, then, like Socrates, about forty, and the aristocrat Critias, then about thirty. Twenty-five years later these two men would find themselves on opposing sides in the events that would make Critias forever notorious as the most forceful and cruel member of the Thirty Tyrants. Critias drove the democrats, Chaerephon among them, into exile;[21] they in turn organized an army that eventually overthrew the Thirty. Chaerephon ensures that Socrates on his return speaks first in public with the future sophist and tyrant and not

19. See below on 176d.

20. The addition, "son of Callaeschrus" does not imply that the auditor is unfamiliar with Critias: other notable Critiases in Athens made it necessary to state which one this was even to an Athenian auditor, as happened in *Protagoras* (316a).

21. See *Apology* 21a.

with faithful Chaerephon himself, the only one in the dialogue to whom Socrates speaks in private.

Charmides also places together in 429 Critias and Charmides, with Socrates himself noting that Critias is guardian to his seventeen-year-old cousin (155a).[22] These two would likewise be linked in the events of 404–403, when the relationship exhibited here, Critias the leader, Charmides the follower, would be repeated as the Thirty Tyrants led by Critias appointed Charmides one of the Ten of Piraeus. The cousins would die together in 403 at the battle of Munychia Hill in the Piraeus, killed by the victorious democratic army that won the city back from the tyranny.[23] The appearance of the cousins Critias and Charmides in Plato's *Charmides* is noteworthy for another reason: this is Plato's family.[24] In the Seventh Letter Plato refers explicitly to the events of 404–403 and the deeds of his family members, particularly their treatment of Socrates, as the cause of his turn away from a political life (324b–326b).[25] In his *Charmides* Plato writes Socrates' conversation with his uncle and his uncle's cousin and alludes to their disastrous turn to the political, an inevitable reminder of their younger relative's turn away from political life toward Socrates and philosophy.

After Socrates has taken his place next to Critias, he relates news of the army camp (153c). He responds to everything anyone asks but reports none of it to the auditor—the concerns of men learning whether their loved ones are alive or dead cannot be the concerns of a later auditor or reader. "When we had our fill of such things," Socrates says, "I in turn asked them about the things here" (153d), but he does not ask them about the corresponding event in Athens, the plague.[26] What he does ask them about is of singular importance for the rest of the dialogue because it defines what he intends

22. Critias's father, Callaeschrus, was an older brother of Charmides' father, Glaucon. If Critias is Charmides' guardian, his father-replacement, Glaucon must have died relatively early, perhaps killed by the war or the plague.

23. Xenophon, *Hellenica* 2.4.11–19.

24. Charmides was Plato's uncle, his mother, Perictione, being Charmides' sister; she was thus also Critias's cousin. See the stemma of Plato's family in Nails, *People of Plato*, 244.

25. On the authenticity of the Seventh Letter and its reference to the events of 404–403, see Rhodes, "Mystic Philosophy in Plato's Seventh Letter," esp. 201–7

26. In May 429, the plague was in its second devastating year as Athenians who lived in rural Attica all crowded inside the walls of Athens under extremely unsanitary conditions, expecting the third consecutive invasion of Attica by the Spartans, which in fact never came: hearing of the plague in Athens, the Spartans ravaged Plataea instead. Pericles himself died of the plague a few months later in the fall of 429, having already witnessed, earlier in 429, the death of his two sons who had appeared in *Protagoras* (Plutarch, *Pericles* 34–36, 38). The Potidaean siege army (and Socrates along with it) had itself experienced the plague when army reinforcements carried

to learn on his return, intentions befitting the Athenian philosopher who, as the prewar dialogues testify, was especially attentive to Athenian youth and to the threat to philosophy represented by rash teachers of enlightenment. Speaking to his auditor and not reporting the words he actually used in the palaistra, Socrates says, "I asked them about the things here: about philosophy, how things stood with it now, and about the young, whether any among them had become distinguished for wisdom or beauty or both" (153d). These two intentions are never referred to again, but they persist as the silent accompaniment of every move Socrates makes in the dialogue, grounding his moves as reasonable steps in fulfilling his once-mentioned aims. Socrates does his auditor a very great favor: he simply tells him why he did everything he did in the dialogue. He did it in order to learn: *Charmides* is the dialogue in which the returned Socrates aims to learn, not to teach—and this is true even though Socrates makes it possible, toward the end, for Critias himself to learn.[27]

Socrates' second intention is addressed first, for Charmides arrives and is said to be the youth who has become most distinguished for both wisdom and beauty during Socrates' absence. An aspect of his beauty will be attested by Socrates himself, but his examination of Charmides allows him to learn that wisdom was attributed to him falsely. He thus satisfies himself with respect to his second intention, at least as far as the youth grown most beautiful is concerned. What about his first intention? The word *philosophy* is spoken only one more time in *Charmides*, by Critias judging Charmides philosophic (155a), but it must be assumed that Socrates has not forgotten the first thing he said he wanted to learn on his return: Socrates' discovery of the state of philosophy in Athens constitutes in fact the main dramatic action of the dialogue, though it is kept offstage. Socrates will prove to be the sole director of the course of the conversation. As he acts to draw out from Critias, his former associate, the words that define *sôphrosunê* for him, it becomes evident that they are Socrates' own words, words he had implanted in Critias before he left and that he now prompts Critias to voice.[28] When Socrates completes his examina-

---

it to their camp in 430; it killed 1,050 hoplites there, fully one quarter of the besieging hoplites (Thucydides 2.58).

27. Levine notes that Socrates later says that his exchange with Critias was primarily "for his own sake" (166d) ("Commentary on Plato's *Charmides*," 8).

28. For the exegesis of *Charmides* I will simply transliterate *sôphrosunê* rather than use any of the English words that translate some aspect of it: sensibleness, moderation, self-control, discretion, sound-mindedness. Only the last of these carries into English the notion of mind or thought present in one of the roots of sôphrosunê (*phron*) and crucial to *Charmides*' investigation

tion of Critias on sôphrosunê he quite forcefully brings their conversation to a close. Socrates satisfied his intention to learn the state of philosophy in Athens in one way only, by discovering the state of his own philosophy in Critias. Critias is as singular in representing Socrates' philosophy as Charmides is in representing beauty, but Critias will come to stand as representative of something more general: Socrates' effort to communicate his philosophy.

By stating his two intentions at the beginning of *Charmides* and never mentioning them again, Socrates leaves to informed inference the underlying theme of *Charmides: Charmides* is about the returned Socrates' discovery of the fate of his philosophy in his absence; *Charmides* is about Socrates' philosophy and its transmission to young associates.[29] Did the philosophy Socrates shared with others before leaving for Potidaea survive his absence? As *Charmides* unfolds, that question gains precision: did Critias, that gifted and ambitious prewar associate, faithfully understand and carry forward what Socrates transmitted to him? And what did Critias transmit of Socrates' philosophy to his beautiful young ward Charmides? By announcing his intention at the beginning and never mentioning it again, Socrates puts in play the underlying character of *Charmides*: it is a dialogue in which he leaves the essential matters to the inferences of his auditor.

In the prewar *Protagoras* Critias and Alcibiades entered Callias's house together just after Socrates, appearing thereby to belong to Socrates' party (316a). These two young men, more than any others, became notorious for causing the debacles and disasters of Athens' ultimate defeat and civil war, and they were the two whom Athenians had most in mind when they put Socrates on trial for corrupting the young.[30] Did Socrates corrupt Alcibiades and Critias? Plato's chronological arrangement of his dialogues makes it possible to pursue a complete answer to that question. *Charmides*, set in 429, takes its reader back before Potidaea to Socrates' prewar teaching as it was taken over by Critias. Returned after his long absence and inquiring about the state of philosophy, Socrates learns how the second-most prom-

of sôphrosunê; but *sound-mindedness* does not directly suggest the moral aspects first heard in the word, thus losing an indispensable first impression of *sôphrosunê*. I will use *sôphrôn* for the state of having sôphrosunê.

29. As Seth Benardete says, "The question of sôphrosunê is a question about the transmissibility of philosophy as self-knowledge" ("Interpreting Plato's *Charmides*," *Argument of the Action*, 233).

30. Xenophon, *Memorabilia* 1.2.12–16; Aeschines says explicitly that the Athenians "put to death Socrates the sophist because he was shown to have educated Critias, one of the Thirty who put down the democracy" (1.173).

ising Athenian of his generation interpreted his prewar teaching. Like the *Alcibiades* dialogues, *Charmides* on its face encourages a forceful denial of the charge that Socrates corrupted the best Athenian young. Yet in allowing its reader to listen in as Socrates hears Critias's interpretation of his own words, *Charmides* allows its reader to learn what Socrates is learning, the liberating and formative role his own teaching played in creating the future sophist and future tyrant.

Because he intends to learn the state of his philosophy in Athens on his return and because he conducts his main discussion with one of his most talented associates, Socrates is free in *Charmides* to speak with a rapidity and brevity that will leave behind all but the most informed and assiduous. Mere phrases serve as stand-ins for extended arguments; what seem like leaps or shifts cover long and logical developments of the reasoning that neither participant needs to explain to the other—and that neither spells out for those who surround them in the palaistra. In its rapidity and compactness *Charmides* is a difficult dialogue. But Socrates narrates it for a sole auditor—if he is the *comrade, friend, noble one* that Socrates calls him, he will want to decipher what Socrates' shorthand covers; he will engage in the long, never easy, but always pleasant work necessary to reconstruct from spare phrases just what Socrates conveyed to his talented pupil a few years ago and what he now learns that pupil has done with it in the meantime. That Socrates narrates it at all carries an implication: he must suspect that his auditor is fit for the work. To him alone Socrates conveys what he aimed to learn from Critias and Charmides about the state of philosophy and the young in Athens on his return from Potidaea. But that means that the very narration of *Charmides* serves its unstated theme: Socrates attempts to transmit his philosophy successfully by narrating his failure to transmit it to Critias. Socrates honors his auditor by presuming that he may be equal to the challenge of piecing together his philosophy from phrases he once transmitted to Critias but that Critias misinterpreted. The reader of Plato's *Charmides* joins a succession of the privileged, listening in as Socrates renews his attempt to transmit his philosophy to a comrade, friend, and noble one.

3. The Spectacle of Charmides' Entrance (154a–155a)

Critias responds to what Socrates asked about, informing him that he will know very soon about "the beautiful ones"—and the uproar at Charmides' arrival submerges Socrates' quiet statement of his intention regarding philosophy. Critias noticed a tumult around the door and knew that it heralded the arrival of "the one who is reputed to be most beautiful, right now at least" (154a). "Who and whose is he?" Socrates asks. "You know," Critias replies, noting that "he wasn't yet mature when you went away" and identifying him as "Charmides, the son of our uncle Glaucon, and my cousin."[31] While claiming the most beautiful as his close relative, Critias does not mention that he is Charmides' guardian; Socrates himself will state this crucial relationship between the two (155a). "Know him I certainly do, by Zeus," says Socrates, adding that Charmides was in no way ordinary as a boy and must now be quite a lad. "Straightaway you will know how mature and what sort he has become," says Critias, sure of his grounds for holding Charmides in high regard. And into this state of expectancy the young beauty enters.

Other youths enter just before Charmides, "taunting one another" as a crowd follows behind (154a). It is a scene highly charged with eros—as is fitting for a dialogue that Socrates will cause to focus on sôphrosunê. The scene is also redolent of a kind of battle as Critias identifies the band of youths entering with Charmides as "heralds and lovers"; their taunting one another bespeaks an epidemic of rivalry, a war of each against all for the affections of Charmides. While presenting Socrates returned from battle to dally once again in the precincts of eros, *Charmides* intimates that he is returning from one war to another, the latter fueled by rivalrous lovers, of which he himself is a special sort, seeking the beautiful and wise.

Before describing Charmides Socrates describes himself, addressing his auditor directly: "Nothing is to be measured by me, comrade [*hetaire*], for I am simply a white line when it comes to those who are beautiful, because almost all who have just reached maturity appear beautiful to me." Socrates' standard of beauty is allegedly less demanding than others', a line as faint as a white chalk line on white marble. But he does say *almost* and he does say *appear*: Socrates' almost invisible standard of beauty may well be far more exacting than that of others, for his standard may hardly appear at all to others and yet be as straight as a chalk line. And he does after all judge Charmides: "he appeared wondrous to me in both stature and beauty." Socrates reports not only his own judgment but that of "all the others": in his opinion, "all the others were in love [*eros*] with him, so excited and confused had they become as he came in." Unconfused Socrates

31. Socrates observed Charmides in *Protagoras* (315a) in one of the lines streaming after Protagoras; his presence in those lines with Callias and the two sons of Pericles attests to his belonging at the forefront of the most aristocratic sons of Athens.

describes the scene for the auditor, as "many other lovers" besides all those already in the palaistra followed in behind Charmides.

Socrates proves his singularity by being the only one able to take his eyes off Charmides to observe the fixation of the others. There was nothing "wondrous" in the fact that "we men" were in love with Charmides, Socrates reports, but he says that when he turned his attention to the boys, he "noticed that none of them, not even the littlest, looked anywhere else." The only one to look anywhere else observes "that all were contemplating [Charmides] as if he were a statue." Through Socrates we observe what we would likely not have seen ourselves, and we see that the desire inspired by Charmides has a mimetic character: the desire of each for Charmides is confirmed and watered by the desire of all the others. The desire for Charmides is universal, but while the men must want to possess him, the boys must want to be him or wholly like him.

And Charmides himself, the title character of the dialogue? In contrast to the excitement and confusion swirling about him, this object of universal desire projects the poised impassibility of a statue. Is he immune to eros? It seems rather that behind his apparent impassibility he is every inch the coquette: his game is to appear desirable without ever once compromising his desirability by betraying desire of his own—"Discovering that his love is returned should really disillusion a lover about his beloved," Nietzsche said.[32] The appearance Charmides gives of self-sufficiency or of being the source of his own satisfaction inflames the desires of others; their desires take their cue from what is apparently his own narcissistic desire for himself. But Charmides is completely dependent on the desires of others, for when Socrates arranges to examine him on sôphrosunê, after Critias has assured him that Charmides "is reputed to be distinguished from those his age [by his sôphrosunê]" (157d), Charmides' self-control will stand revealed as the product of his dependence and his appearance of self-sufficient impassibility as a fraud of dependence. That dependence has political overtones, for Charmides will turn out to be Critias's creature, now and in the events that will define them historically twenty-five years later.

Critias is witness as his glorious protégé makes his appearance. He watches as outside of Charmides' hearing Chaerephon breaks in on Socrates' observation of the others to call out: "How does the youth appear to you, Socrates? Is he not fair of face?" (154d). Socrates replies with a single word, "Supernaturally"—*huperphuôs*. Chaerephon heightens what

32. *Beyond Good and Evil*, 102.

appears to be mere ribald incitement: "But if he should be willing to strip"—and stripping is what is expected in a palaistra—"he will seem to you to be faceless, so all-beautiful is he in his form [*eidos*]." Socrates' friend thus ends his contribution to *Charmides* by goading Socrates to examine Charmides' eidos, employing the word that has had a special meaning for Socrates since he was nineteen, the word made prominent in *Phaedo* and *Parmenides* as what he first pursued after making the turn in philosophy that was wholly his own. Socrates picks up on Chaerephon's use of his special word, employing it for the only other time in the dialogue a moment later in a way that exploits its ambiguity: "Why don't we strip [his soul] and contemplate it before contemplating his form?" (154e). To strip Charmides' soul *is* to contemplate his eidos in Socrates' sense of that word. When Socrates' friend uses their special word to suggest that Charmides' eidos is all-beautiful, he seems to suggest that if Socrates examines him he will learn otherwise. Chaerephon is not incidental to the *Charmides*: after welcoming Socrates in a private exchange of greetings, he sits him next to Critias and invites him to examine Charmides; he has observed what happened to Socrates' philosophy in his absence.

When "the others said the same as Chaerephon," they couldn't have meant the same as Chaerephon, but Socrates exclaims at their collective judgment of Charmides' stripped beauty: "Heracles! The man [*ton andra*] you speak of is not to be withstood, if only he happens to have one little thing besides."[33] Socrates thus introduces the notion on which the dialogue will end, withstanding Charmides (176d)—and the Charmides to be withstood Socrates here calls a *real man* even though he is too young to merit this designation. But Socrates' implication that all-admired Charmides could possibly lack something seems calculated to compel Critias to intervene—and he in fact breaks in. "What?" he asks—what little thing could he yet need? Socrates begins as might be expected, by introducing the notion of the soul—"If in respect of his soul he happens to be of a good nature"—but he adds something that flatters Critias: "Surely it is fitting, Critias, for him to [have a soul of good nature], since he is of your family." By this measure, everything revealed about the soul of Charmides has implications for the soul of Critias: do they share a family resemblance in the nature of their souls? The relation between the two is strengthened and given an additional component when Socrates notes that Critias is

33. Levine notes that Heracles is "one of the tutelary gods of the palestra and wrestling" ("Commentary on Plato's *Charmides*," 26).

Charmides' *guardian*—he is his surrogate legal father and thereby the one responsible for his education (155a).

Critias judges that with respect to his soul Charmides is "altogether beautiful and good," or altogether noble and good, *kalos* and *agathos*,[34] the two words that in a common contraction, *kalokagathos*, form the standard designation for a perfect gentleman (154e). But Critias's unrestrained praise of his relative and ward praises himself, hardly the sign of a good nature. Socrates then sets in motion the rest of the dialogue as an exercise in stripping aimed at learning what he said he intended to learn on his return: "Why don't we strip this part of him and contemplate it" (154e),[35] thus preparing the stripping not only of Charmides' soul but of Critias's, for he, to some degree at least, fathered and formed it.

Stripping Charmides' soul requires a willingness on his part to converse (*dialegesthai*), and Socrates states his confidence that at his age Charmides is willing. "Absolutely," Critias replies, offering a twofold reason: "since he is both philosophic and, in the opinion of others as well as his own, quite poetic" (155a). Critias, a student of Socrates and a future famous poet, assumes his capacity to judge both qualities. By withholding endorsement of others' praise of Charmides' poetic capacity, he not only indicates his reservation but suggests a certain vanity on his cousin's part. Critias's praise of Charmides' philosophic capacity, however, carries no reservation. But is he a capable judge? This second and last mention of *philosophy* in the dialogue (cf. 153d) indicates that Socrates' intention of inquiring about the state of philosophy in Athens will be fulfilled in one way only, through stripping Charmides' soul and then stripping Critias's soul, the natural next step, for Critias is the cousin and guardian responsible for the sole venture into philosophy that Charmides hazards.

Socrates responds with seeming flattery that is as precise in its limitations as was Critias's praise: "This beautiful quality [*poetic* capacity, not philosophic], my dear Critias, is yours [your *family's*] from far back, from your kinship with Solon." Socrates then takes the initiative in suggesting the step that will make the dialogue possible: "Why don't you call the youth over here and show [*epedeixas*] him to me?" *Show* him to me: the coming conversation is a form of *epideixis* in which Critias will display his protégé to Socrates in the expectation that Socrates will judge the soul of

34. This is the first use of *agathos* in the dialogue, a word that will become crucial to their inquiry at its end.

35. On stripping the soul, see *Alcibiades I* 132a.

his ward to be of a beautiful and good nature, particularly with respect to philosophy, and the soul of his guardian like in kind.

With all the erotic excess throbbing in the palaistra Socrates shows himself attentive to the niceties of customary restraint: "For even if he happened to be still younger, surely it would not be shameful for him to converse with us in front of you who are at once his guardian and his cousin." And with that Critias does as Socrates directed him and invites Charmides over. But in doing so he indulges in a little trick of his own invention.

4. Critias Scripts a Play but Socrates Takes It Over (155a–157d)

Socrates initiated the invitation to call Charmides over, but Critias dictates the terms of his coming: as inventive as a future playwright, as peremptory as a future tyrant, he issues orders that play a trick on his teacher and betray his pupil. Within the hearing of the others he tells his slave to call Charmides over with the promise of introducing him to a doctor who may be able to help with the disorder of the head he recently told Critias about (155b). Only after he has publicly issued this order and sent off his slave does Critias turn to Socrates to ask him if anything prevents him from acting the doctor and "pretending to him that you have knowledge of some drug [*pharmakon*] for the head." Critias thus authors a little play to be acted out before him: his adulated protégé appears as defective and needing a cure while his honored teacher is forced to fake being a doctor with knowledge of a drug. All three will know it's a pretense, for none will have forgotten that they were all together at Callias's house for the memorable meeting of sophists before Socrates left for Potidaea.

Critias's little play is powerfully topical: Thucydides' report on the plague states that the symptoms start in the head.[36] Charmides has every right to worry about the heaviness in his head and to welcome attention by a doctor who promises a cure. As for Socrates, forced into a pretense of knowledge of medicine, he makes good use of the opportunity: Socrates the actor will make doctoring his chief example of a knower in his examination of both Charmides and Critias, and he, a fake doctor, will claim that while he was away he learned a whole new medicine to cure the head and not only the head.[37] Assigned to say only that he has a *drug* for the head, he

36. Thucydides 2.49.

37. Critias uses the word *doctor* only once to arrange the roles; Socrates uses it some seventeen times.

will adjust his role to suit his intention by adding an "incantation," curing *words* that by the play's end have wholly replaced the promised drug and leave Charmides begging to be taught the incantation.

There is a second arresting feature in the pretense Critias forces on Socrates: "having knowledge" (*epistasthai*, 155b_6) first appears in the dialogue as Critias's demand that Socrates *pretend* to have knowledge. Once introduced, the word is repeated immediately in a brief sequence of uses: Socrates reports that Critias tells Charmides "that *I* was the one who *had knowledge* of the drug" (155c_8); Charmides asks Socrates "if I *had knowledge* of the drug" (155e_2); and Socrates answers by saying, "*I had knowledge*" (155e_3). What began as Critias's demand that Socrates fake knowledge ends with his unconditional claim to knowledge. Socrates will elaborate that claim in a fabulous tale of what he learned while away. Is his new knowledge fake or genuine? Much later (164c), he will introduce the noun form of the verb for knowledge that Critias here introduces, and the investigation of knowledge as *epistêmê* will, under Socrates' direction, form the very core of the dialogue: Is knowledge that is not pretense at all possible? Does Socrates the fake doctor have it? Does Critias, that presumptuous know-it-all, have it?

When Charmides came over he caused a comic scene as everyone shoved his neighbor hoping to open a space for Charmides to sit next to him, but Charmides chose to sit between Socrates and Critias. Because someone at each end of the bench was pushed off, Socrates and Critias must each have pushed hard to create the space between them where Charmides in fact sits. Given this seating arrangement, when Socrates and Charmides converse, they are face to face, and when Socrates and Critias converse, Charmides is between them as they talk across him and to some degree about him.

In the little scene of seeming self-disclosure that Socrates then reports on himself, he twice addresses his auditor, as "friend" and as "noble one," to claim that he fell into perplexity (*aporia*) and had all his former boldness knocked out of him. When Critias told Charmides that Socrates was the one with knowledge of a drug to cure his head (155c), three things happened: Charmides looked at Socrates in an irresistible way; everyone in the palaistra flowed around them in a complete circle; and "then indeed, O noble one, I saw inside his cloak" (155d). In the presence of beauty involuntarily stripped, surrounded by a large company, erotic Socrates "burned with passion"—had an erection.[38] Socrates tells his auditor that at this mo-

38. For another reference to Socrates' erotic arousal, see *Lovers* 133a.

ment he was no longer in control of himself—literally, "I was no longer in my own." He exaggerates, for he immediately exercised self-control: his thought was not just of Charmides and himself but of the spectacle of Charmides and himself and how a poet pictured such a spectacle. He thought of Cydias[39] and judged him "wisest in erotic matters" because when speaking of a beautiful boy he warned a lover that "a fawn coming opposite a lion should beware lest he be taken as a piece of meat." Kept from becoming a piece of meat by recalling a poet's image, Socrates collected himself, and when the lion asked "if I had knowledge of the drug for the head," Socrates, no fawn, "somehow answered that I had knowledge" (155e).

"What is it then?" Though he says his boldness has been knocked out of him, leaving him in a state of aporia, Socrates plays his assigned role: he invents a little fiction that he will expand and sustain to the end as his means of taking control of Charmides. Of what does the doctor have knowledge? The moment is important: called upon to feign having knowledge, the returned Socrates expands his initial claim to knowledge into a report of something he learned while he was away, a doctor's knowledge of a cure that he is bringing back to Athens. In his first description of it, recovering from a surge of eros, Socrates claims knowledge of a drug that is a certain leaf, but he adds that the drug is not enough: "there was a certain incantation [*epôidê*] in addition to the drug, and if one chanted it at the same time as he used it, the drug would make him altogether healthy, but without the incantation there would be no benefit from the leaf" (155e). Socrates will have to modify what he first manages to blurt out about the leaf and the incantation, but he will do so only after a comic little episode that restores his boldness.

Charmides is eager: "Then I'll write down the incantation from you." Plato's uncle will write down the doctor's cure, write down what Socrates never wrote down? Socrates demurs with a telling reservation: "If you persuade me, or even if you don't?" Would you put my still-secret cure into writing without first persuading me that you're worthy of receiving it?[40] Charmides is forced to laugh at the accusation that he would steal a secret teaching, but he plays along: "If I persuade you, Socrates." *Socrates*? Charmides violates Critias's little play as he draws Socrates out of his role, but Socrates resists: "And do you have my name precisely?" You may know my

39. Presumably a poet but unknown.

40. On Charmides writing it down, see Szlezak, "Die Handlung der Dialoge *Charmides* und *Euthydemos*," esp. 342–46.

name from before Potidaea, but do you really know who I am now, the doctor bringing back the cure you need? "If I am not doing an injustice," Charmides replies, offering evidence for how he knows who Socrates really is, "there's no little talk about you among those of our age." Long-absent Socrates is a topic of gossip among the youth of Athens—his intention of inquiring about them is to some degree matched by their curiosity about him. But do their rumors do him justice? Charmides' talk about Socrates has an identifiable source: "even as a boy I remember your associating with Critias here." As a remembered associate of Socrates, Critias would be an authoritative source in the considerable talk about Socrates spread around by Athenian boys. The little play Critias arranged turns back on its author: does *Critias* have the doctor's name precisely? Does what *he* passed on about Socrates in Socrates' absence do him an injustice?

After this little exchange Socrates says he will "speak more frankly to you about the incantation"—the drug Critias ordered him to speak about is left behind as Socrates explains "what sort [the incantation] happens to be." His alleged greater frankness is an actual alteration of his initial claim that the incantation had to be used at the same time as the drug.[41] He excuses himself for what he first said by confessing to Charmides part of what he confessed to the auditor: "just now I was perplexed [*êporoun*] about how I might show you its power" (156b, cf. 155c). The incantation needs further explanation, he now says, for "it does not have the power to make the head alone healthy." To treat the head requires treating the whole of which it is a part, the body, as "good doctors" generally recognize. Explicitly asked by Socrates if he agrees with this, Charmides enthusiastically approves. And this praise by Charmides "again emboldened" him, Socrates says, and "little by little my boldness rose back and I was rekindled to life" (156d). It is in this state that he expands his story of the incantation: it is the bold tale told by one reborn. The fabulous tale that Socrates introduces with this claim about himself is a report of what he learned while he was away, a report on a Socrates that can be no part of what Athenian boys rumor about him from stories told by prewar associates like Critias. It is a report to which a chronological account of Socrates must pay the closest attention, for it contains the first indication that Socrates returned from Potidaea different.

Bold, revivified Socrates, playing a doctor, tells Charmides "how it is with this incantation" (156d). "I learned it there in the army, from one of

41. On the varying permutations of the combination of drug and incantation, see Coolidge, "Relation of Philosophy to *Sôphrosunê*."

the Thracian doctors of Zalmoxis." Charmides' doctor learned his new medicine from a doctor of a teacher-god whom one could learn more about from Herodotus.[42] Reading Herodotus is practically commanded when Socrates refers a second time to the incantations of Zalmoxis, for he mentions there another tale told by Herodotus, the tale of Abaris the Hyperborean, and alleges that he too taught curative incantations (158b).[43] Socrates follows Herodotus in mentioning first that feature of Thracian medicine that is also its most extreme: the doctors of Zalmoxis, "it is said, even *immortalize* people" (156d).[44] Reading Herodotus, one learns that Zalmoxis was the god of the Getae, "who believe they are immortal" (4.93). They also believe that their god is the only god. Among the Getae customs Herodotus reports is that they "shoot arrows into the sky when thunder and lightning occur, and hurl threats at the god, because they recognize no god other than their own"—their monotheism permits them to ridicule the false gods of others, even the god of thunder and lightning, Zeus himself. Herodotus's report suggests that the beliefs of the Getae are the foundation of virtuous actions: they were the only Thracians who resisted Darius on his way to fight the Scythians, and Herodotus calls them the most courageous and most just of the Thracians. Of particular interest is Herodotus's report that the neighboring Greeks on the Hellespont and the Pontus were skeptical about Zalmoxis, holding that he was a former slave of Pythagoras who deceived the Getae into believing in his immortality by an elaborate trick. The Greeks thus believed that the Thracian teacher of immortality was himself taught by a Greek, perhaps the first philosopher to have claimed a belief in immortality. Herodotus thus implies that the Thracian teacher learned from Pythagoras how to feign immortality and create a whole people whose belief in immortality and a single god made

42. Herodotus 4.93–96. Mark Munn describes Herodotus of Halicarnassus as an important figure in Athens during these years; Munn argues that Herodotus wrote his *Histories* with the conscious intent of providing instruction for an imperial people risking reversals in war, and that the intellectuals paid close attention to his work (*School of History* 2, 41, 43–44, 95, 115–17, 315, 363 n. 78).

43. Herodotus 4.36. Herodotus says nothing about Abaris teaching incantations. In fact, after telling a long tale of the journeys of Hyperborean sacred objects that took them to Delos, birthplace of Apollo, Herodotus explicitly refuses to tell the tale of Abaris, saying only that he carried an arrow all the way around the world without eating anything. Like Zalmoxis, Abaris was connected with the Pythagorean tradition. On Abaris, see Burkert, *Lore and Science in Ancient Pythagoreanism*, 143, 150, 162.

44. On *apathanatizein* (used only here in Plato), see David J. Murphy who argues that it is to be understood as "render immortal from a state of mortality" ("Doctors of Zalmoxis and Immortality in the *Charmides*," 290–91). On Zalmoxis, see Burkert, *Lore and Science in Ancient Pythagoreanism*, 156–59.

them uniquely courageous and law-abiding. Herodotus speaks for himself when he says that he thinks Zalmoxis lived many years before Pythagoras, and when he finally raises the question of whether Zalmoxis was a god or a man—"well, let that be enough about him," he says, ending the whole episode (4.96). This then is the shadowy figure, made vivid and questionable by Herodotus, whom Socrates credits with being the ultimate source of what he learned while he was away, a figure believed by his followers to be the only god, by the Greeks to be a deceiver who learned deception from a Greek wise man, by Herodotus to be—well, let it be enough about him that he taught his followers the monotheism and belief in immortality that made them courageous and law-abiding.[45]

While putting the teaching on immortality first, Socrates chooses to elaborate a second feature of Thracian medicine, also a teaching on the soul and also extreme. Its source is what the Thracian doctor said was said by "Zalmoxis, our king, who is a god." Zalmoxis explicitly corrected Greek medicine, which, with the Hippocratic school, was just beginning to treat disorders of the body properly as disorders of parts of the whole which is the body. Zalmoxis said that Greek doctors are "ignorant of the whole to which care must be given"—the soul, that greater whole of which the body itself is a part. Zalmoxis taught that "everything starts from the soul, both good and evil things for the body and for the entire human being" (156e), and that the soul must therefore be treated for every bodily disorder.[46] The soul, however, can be treated in one way only: with "certain incantations and these incantations are beautiful speeches" (157a). Socrates implies that he no longer shares Greek medicine's ignorance of the soul and that he has learned the incantations that treat it: the pretense Critias forced on him—knowledge of a drug for the head—he has transformed into a claim to knowledge of incantations for the soul. One more modifying step is needed before the role he was assigned can take the shape that enables him to fulfill his intentions.

The incantations, which are beautiful speeches, have a direct product in the soul: "from such speeches *sôphrosunê* comes to be in souls and once it has come to be and is present, then it is easy to provide health both for the head and for the rest of the body." Thus does Socrates introduce

45. On Herodotus's tale, see Benardete, *Herodotean Inquiries*, 109–10.

46. Christopher Bruell characterizes Thracian medicine in a way that isolates its two extreme features: "'Thracian' medicine then is distinguished from Greek by its attempt to immortalize and by its assertion of the power of the soul over the body. . . . If we were not held back by our ignorance as to what moderation is, we would be tempted to say that Socrates' Thracian teacher was not conspicuous for possessing it" ("Socratic Politics and Self-Knowledge," 141–203, 148).

sôphrosunê into their conversation: it is the ultimate product of what he learned while he was away. Having made that final step in his description of what he learned, emboldened Socrates must now correct what he first said to Charmides about the drug and the incantation while still under the influence of his arousal. He quotes his Thracian teacher as saying, "Let no one persuade you to treat his head with this drug unless he *first* submits his soul to be treated by you with the incantation." No longer are drug and incantation to be taken "at the same time" (155e); instead, before the drug is applied (the drug he does not possess, that certain leaf), the soul must be submitted to the teacher and the healing incantations chanted. It is "the error common among human beings," Socrates' teacher said, "that some attempt to be doctors of these things separately, sôphrosunê and health" (157b)—for a second time, Socrates says sôphrosunê is the key to health. Socrates' teacher was strict: "he commanded me quite vigorously to allow no one, however rich, noble, or beautiful, to persuade me to do otherwise"—rich, noble, beautiful Charmides seems to have had a medicine concocted just for him by a doctor who learned the chants of a god. Bold Socrates now risks everything: he says he swore an oath to his Thracian teacher that he will obey, and if Charmides wants the healing drug he must first submit his soul to chant the incantations of the Thracian, "but if not, we would have nothing that we could do for you, my dear Charmides" (157c). The promised drug becomes a mere accessory of the chants that induce sôphrosunê, as Socrates declares himself ready to reject beautiful Charmides if he is unwilling to submit his soul to him: Charmides is becoming *his* piece of meat.

Socrates addressed "my dear Charmides" (157c), but Critias, "hearing me say this," speaks up. Critias is the author both of the roles now being played out and of rumors passed around among the young about Socrates—but Critias has been induced by Socrates to speak up on behalf of his ward about "this very thing for which you say you have the incantation. You say it is for sôphrosunê, don't you?" (157d). Critias can hardly believe his ears: a teaching on sôphrosunê, as will be seen, lay at the heart of Socrates' prewar investigations to which Critias was privy and was part of the rumors Critias passed on about him. But *incantations* for sôphrosunê? *Those* Critias never heard, and he needs confirmation that this is what Socrates actually said. Socrates is proving a most creative actor, using his assigned role to introduce one of his own key words, *sôphrosunê*, and force the play's author to respond. When Critias breaks in (and he must be seen as breaking in from behind Charmides as Charmides and Socrates speak face to face), he says: "A godsend, Socrates, would this illness of the head be for the youth if he will be compelled because of his head to become better also in his thought"—Critias seems dubious about his ward's willingness or ability to think. But he means his intervention to praise Charmides: he "is reputed to be distinguished from those of his age not only in his looks but also in this very thing for which you say you have the incantation" (157d). After confirming that this very thing is sôphrosunê, Critias repeats himself: "he is reputed to be quite the most sôphrôn by far of his contemporaries; and in all other respects, to the extent he has reached maturity, he is second to none."

It cannot be reasonably imagined that Socrates subjected his mind to a foreign teacher whose authority is the word of god; but it can well be imagined that his creative transformation of the role Critias assigned him is more than a playful device to induce Charmides to submit to examination—to submit to satisfying one of Socrates' aims on his return. After the little stumble with the leaf, Socrates has turned his assigned role to his advantage by claiming that he came back different from what any rumor by a prewar associate could have reported about him. The incantations of his new medicine, the "beautiful speeches" that induce sôphrosunê, concern two things only: immortality and the soul as the cause of everything healthy or sick in the body. Nothing in the prewar dialogues hinted at such medicine; on the contrary, in *Protagoras* Socrates used Hippocrates of Cos as an example of a teacher one would go to in order to learn medicine.[47] And nothing in *Charmides* will explain these two teachings further. But the chronological arrangement Plato gave his dialogues suggests that they can be found where he put them, in the dialogue he set a few weeks after *Charmides*, the *Republic*, that other dialogue of Socrates' return.

5. Stripping Charmides' Soul (157d–162b)

Socrates flatters Charmides by praising his lineage, which it is unlikely "anyone here" could rival[48] (157d–158b), and then sets the terms for his ex-

47. Protagoras 311b.

48. In private Socrates did not praise Alcibiades for a lineage far surpassing Charmides' (*Alcibiades 1* 103a, 104a–b, 121a–124b). When Socrates describes the praiseworthy on Charmides' father's side, he implicitly includes Critias, who shared the same grandfather on his father's side, also named Critias. He mentions the praise accorded Charmides' father's family by Anacreon and Solon, naming "beauty and virtue and the rest of what is called happiness" (157e; see also *Timaeus* 20e). On his mother's side he singles out praise accorded Pyrilampes, Charmides' uncle (and second husband of Perictione, Plato's mother), when he was sent on diplomatic missions to the

amination: if Charmides in fact has the sôphrosunê Critias says he is reputed to have, Socrates can skip the incantation and simply administer the drug; if not, Socrates will have to teach him the incantation that will establish sôphrosunê. Socrates has again corrected the formula he blurted out in his eros-induced perplexity: instead of being administered "at the same time" as the drug, the incantation is wholly superfluous if sôphrosunê is already present—the strategy he has now struck upon to use sôphrosunê to discover the state of philosophy in Athens requires this correction. "So tell me yourself whether you agree with [Critias] and say that you already have a sufficient share of sôphrosunê or that your are in need" (158c). Charmides responds to his doctor's request voluntarily and involuntarily; first he blushes, then he speaks. His speech declines an answer, but his blush, that involuntary irruption of self-consciousness and shame, answers for him: he thinks he has it but knows it would be unbecoming, unsôphrôn, to say so.[49] Socrates approves his blush: it makes him "appear even more beautiful, for a sense of shame [*aischuntêlon*] suited his age"—his blush shows he possesses the sôphrosunê of one of the definitions he will offer. Socrates also approves the "not ignoble" words with which Charmides declines to answer, words asserting the unreasonableness of claiming either to have sôphrosunê or to lack it. To say he lacks it would be strange for he would be speaking against himself, and besides, it would give the lie to his guardian and the others who say he has it. And if he says he has it, "perhaps it will appear annoying"—appear like self-promotion in one whom everyone else is willing to promote. Socrates is gracious and does not compel him "to say what you don't wish to" (158e), recognizing his wish as a powerful desire not to say what his blush shows he thinks. Socrates suggests that instead they investigate together whether he has acquired it by inquiring into what he thinks it is.

Charmides' First Definition: Sôphrosunê Is Decorum

Socrates says that if sôphrosunê is present in Charmides, he will be able to offer some opinion about it, because its presence will furnish some

---

Great King—praise not for his diplomacy but for his beauty and stature, the qualities Socrates has already noted in Charmides.

49. Benardete notes that in all six dialogues narrated by Socrates, and only in those dialogues, someone blushes (*Argument of the Action*, 205): Hippocrates in *Protagoras* (312a); Thrasymachus in the *Republic* (350d); one of the boys in the *Lovers* (134b); Kleinias and Dionysodorus in *Euthydemus* (275d, 297a); Hippothales blushes furiously in *Lysis* (204b–d) and Lysis simply blushes (213d).

perception on the basis of which an opinion can be formed and then spoken (159a): from the beginning he treats sôphrosunê as a kind of self-knowledge. Being able to speak Greek, Charmides will be able to say, by examining himself, what his opinion of sôphrosunê is. But Charmides' first answer, *hêsuchia*, a certain quietness or decorum[50] (159b), while it may initially evidence self-examination, comes ultimately from what Charmides learned while learning to speak Greek: Socrates immediately identifies it as what "they say." Charmides' first answer stands as an initial indication that he simply incorporates what they say and that his outward decorum, his walking quietly in the streets while causing a general indecorum, is simply deference to public perception. Charmides' self, along with his sôphrosunê, seems to be a product of his public; his "self"-knowledge can thus take the form only of a report on what "they say." The heat of his blush is what Charmides seems to perceive as the presence of sôphrosunê within him: looking within, he finds his blush confirming what "they say." Socrates acts as if he believes that one first perceives, then opines, and finally says. But that sequence is reversed in Charmides: first comes what they say, which he then internalizes as his own opinion whose presence he then feels in the heat of his blush.

Is sôphrosunê decorum? It is to be counted among the *beautiful* things, Socrates says, but with many examples—very slowly—he persuades Charmides that the things of both body and soul seem more beautiful when done swiftly and keenly, and therefore that sôphrosunê cannot be the unbeautiful quietness and slowness associated with decorum (160b). For if sôphrosunê is always beautiful, and decorum is not always beautiful, sôphrosunê is not decorum. Socrates' conclusion (160c–d), however, acknowledges that some beautiful things are quiet and slow, thus leaving open the possibility that sôphrosunê as what "they say" falls among those beautiful things that are quiet and slow. More importantly, his conclusion points to a sôphrosunê that is swift and keen. What would a swift and fierce, an indecorous sôphrosunê be? Socrates' examples focus on learning, on *swiftness* in learning, recollecting, comprehending, taking counsel, making discoveries. His examples show that he is fulfilling one of his intentions: does the one grown beautiful in his absence possess the qualities of mind necessary for pursuing philosophy, can he become "wise"?

50. *Hêsuchia* (stillness, quiet, peace) is the quality of one whose unhurried manner reflects his relative self-sufficiency and lack of need; "decorum" seems to come closer to its meaning here than the customary "quietness."

Charmides' Second Definition: Sôphrosunê Is a Sense of Shame

"Back again," Socrates says for the first of three times (160d; see 163d, 167a), back to what you were first told to do: look within to find the answer, for if it is present within you it can be perceived and stated. Socrates reports to his auditor that Charmides did look within and did state courageously what he found there: he found sôphrosunê as *aidôs*, a sense of shame or modesty, a sense that there are things that would make one blush if others saw that one had them or did them. Socrates refutes Charmides' second answer swiftly after securing his agreement that sôphrosunê is *good* as well as beautiful. He refutes it by a single citation from authority: "Don't you believe that Homer speaks beautifully when he says, '*Aidôs* is not good for a needy man?'"[51] Agreeing that aidôs, being both good and not-good depending on one's character and circumstances, cannot define sôphrosunê which is simply good, Charmides abandons his second definition. But he abandons it out of the very sense of shame his definition posits, for it would be shameful to contradict Homer who they say is wise. Charmides exemplifies his second definition even as he repudiates it, indicating again the extent to which his actual sôphrosunê is the colonization of his innermost being by the speeches of others.

Charmides' first two answers have a deep fitness about them for they connect the outer and inner qualities basic to the conventional sôphrosunê Charmides seems in fact to have. Whether he recognizes it or not, his own outward decorum is the product of his inward sense of shame, and while his honest introspection detects that inner sense of shame, it probably does not disclose to him that it was planted in him in just the way he learned Greek, planted involuntarily through learning the customs of his people. Charmides' fitting answers strip him, revealing that he has not escaped the conventional and in all likelihood never will. With his surrender of aidôs he simply yields to the authority of Homer or rather to the authority of Homer as Socrates presents it: he lacks the swiftness to object that Homer did not say those words, Telemachus did, and that Telemachus said them as advice for a beggar, and that in not being good for a beggar, aidôs may yet be good for himself and everyone like him. Instead of thinking of a way to object to Socrates' simpleminded refutation through a proof text, Charmides tries to get out of the argument entirely, spontaneously putting forward a third definition, hoping to shift Socrates' discomfiting examination away from himself to his source for that definition, his guardian Critias.

51. *Odyssey* 17.347.

There is more to Socrates' use of Homer than a quick refutation of Charmides' second definition. Only here is Homer named in *Charmides* and expressly quoted, and what Socrates quotes reinforces the impression left by Socrates' first words in *Charmides* that his return to Athens is to be likened to Odysseus's return to Ithaca. For the quoted words are spoken by Telemachus the day after Odysseus revealed himself to him and while he is still the only one to know. Odysseus is unrecognizable, a beggar seated alone just inside the threshold of his palace. Telemachus calls Eumaeus over to give him food to take to the beggar and to tell him that he is to instruct the beggar to beg for more among the suitors, for "*aidôs* is not good for a needy man."[52] This advice for a returned Odysseus, offered by the only one who has so far been allowed to recognize him, tells Odysseus what he already well knows, that he dare not risk recognition by any others: the rightful king must keep begging, for he is still a needy man with a mighty project to complete, and *aidôs* is not good for a needy man. These words of counsel are spoken in *Charmides* by Socrates; "Homer's" words can be heard as Socrates' counsel to himself, for he too has just returned after a long absence and is in his own way a needy man: like Odysseus he has in his absence learned something of the highest importance, like Odysseus he is now attempting to learn the conditions at home on his return, and like Odysseus he will have to act on what he learned both abroad and at home in order to establish something new among those to whom he has returned. *Aidôs* or customary sôphrosunê is not good for a needy man like Socrates; like Odysseus he must be shameless, he must be stealthy, he must appear to be far less than he is, because fulfillment of his purpose on return demands that he not be recognized as who he is. Socrates' project on return, no less than Odysseus's, demands all the polytropic skill at his command, not excluding skill in citing Homer to indicate his own mission.

Charmides' Third Definition: Sôphrosunê Is Doing One's Own Things

Charmides' third definition, unlike his first two, is offered spontaneously. What he wants investigated, however, is not the definition but "whether in your opinion *he who says this* speaks correctly" (162b). Charmides has

52. Eumaeus repeats the words Telemachus told him to say almost exactly (352); Penelope later uses similar words to the beggar (578). Within the *Odyssey* itself Telemachus's advice comes with a certain irony: a few weeks earlier, tongue-tied young Telemachus feared speaking to Nestor, telling Mentor-Athena that "a youth feels *aidôs* when addressing one who is his elder" (*Odyssey* 3.23–24); matured now after visits with Nestor and Menelaus and Helen, he finds himself able to address this advice to his own great father.

had enough self-examination and wants attention directed away from himself to the one who said this. Moreover, he tells Socrates to "investigate *this* statement about sôphrosunê, what it is in your opinion." Charmides does not want his own opinion to be examined: let Socrates give his opinion about someone else's opinion. Charmides says he has "just recollected what I once heard someone say, that doing one's own things would be sôphrosunê." That "someone" is sitting right beside him as Socrates well knows: "You've heard it from Critias here or from another one of the wise." Critias immediately denies being the source: "Likely from another, certainly not from me." Certainly from him as the sequel shows: Socrates learns that Critias in fact transmitted to his beautiful ward wise words that he himself left behind before departing for Potidaea. Having dealt with Charmides' conventional definitions, Socrates can now begin to discover the state of philosophy, his philosophy, in Athens. What he will discover confirms his first word in response to hearing Charmides repeat his own words to him as Charmides' final offer of a definition: "Wretch!" "Wretch!" he will say again when he hears his own words repeated back to him for the last time when he is examining Critias's final offer of a definition (174b)—neither Charmides nor Critias proves to be a fit transmitter of Socrates' words on sôphrosunê.

Charmides' effort to deflect attention away from himself led Socrates to say that Charmides heard the words from Critias or another of the wise. "What difference does it make from whom I heard it?" asks Charmides, who believes every word he hears from Homer even if it's spoken by Telemachus. "None," Socrates answers, "for it must not at all be investigated who said it"—says the one who said it—"but whether or not what is said is true." The one who said it then says that it "looks like a kind of *riddle*" (161c). That itself seems riddling to Charmides, for he asks, What makes it look like a riddle? And the riddler answers: "because surely his words didn't express what he had in mind when he said that doing one's own things is sôphrosunê" (161d). Socrates expressly says that a riddler like himself purposely avoids putting what he has in mind in the words of his riddle—but that too is a riddle, for if a riddler's words are *wise* they must somehow indicate what he has in mind and guide one who hears them to discover what he has in mind. Socrates has just identified the class to which his own pre-Potidaean words belong. At the very beginning of a serial restatement of such words by Critias, Socrates says they are intentional riddles that demand of anyone who wants to understand them concerted effort to discern what a wise man had in mind when he put what he had in mind into riddling words.[53] Contrary to Charmides' statement but consistent with his practice, it matters after all who the words come from; if they come from a wise man it will be worthwhile to work at unriddling them to discover what their riddler had in mind.[54]

Socrates gives an immediate if almost unbelievable intimation of what he had in mind in the whole sequence of riddling words about to be quoted in *Charmides*. He leads Charmides through some examples of an extremely literalist interpretation of "doing one's own things," moving from a writing teacher writing and reading only his own name, through the arts of doctoring and house building and weaving, concluding with the question of whether a city would be well-governed if it made a law that each of its citizens must produce and do all his own things, such as weave and wash his own cloak or cobble his own shoes (161d–e). The opposite to doing your own things is "meddling," writing the name of another or, in the city example, touching the things of others. Charmides agrees that sôphrosunê cannot mean "doing one's own things" in this strict sense because, while the well-governed city must be governed by sôphrosunê, it could not practice "doing one's own things" in this literalist way. What did Socrates have in mind then with his riddling words that sôphrosunê is doing one's own things? His examples suggest that both the wise teacher and wise laws meddle—that the wise man does *his* own things by intervening in the things of others, being meddlesome or touching the things of others in a way that could seem most immoderate or un-sôphrosunê but that is nevertheless true sôphrosunê. Socrates does not simply leave it at the possibility that *this* is what the riddler had in mind: he will end his argument with Critias on the issue of the well-governed city (171e) and suggest a parallel inference about what he had in mind.

Socrates asks Charmides again about the one who said to him that sôphrosunê was doing one's own things: "Or did you hear someone foolish say this, Charmides?" (162b). "Least of all," Charmides replies, "as he was

53. Unriddling riddles again becomes explicit at the end of this argument (162b–c), and once more when Critias claims to have unriddled the riddling words put up at Delphi (164e).

54. On the use of riddles by the Greek wise, see Kingsley, *Ancient Philosophy, Mystery, and Magic*, chap. 4, "The Riddle." Kingsley shows that the extensive use of riddle by Empedocles includes his employment of single, characteristic words from Homer to suggest radical conclusions; regarding the gods, for instance, Empedocles' use of "bright" and "life-giving" (Diels fragment 6) allows the inference that "Zeus" simply *is* air or "Hera" earth (Kingsley, 42–45). Kingsley describes the use of riddle as the "art of allusion . . . an art of speaking indirectly: the art of hinting, of really saying more than one is apparently saying" (43, see 52). Kingsley also refers to "Plato's . . . deliberate art of casual allusion" (129).

reputed to be *quite* wise." Its original author then makes a claim: "in my opinion, he put it forward as a riddle, being aware that it is hard to know [*gnônai*] what doing one's own things is" (162b). "Perhaps," says Charmides, not all that sure that the one *he* supposes is its author put it forward as a riddle. But that Charmides at least has no idea what it means, Socrates now makes clear: "So what would doing one's own things be? Can you say?" "I don't know, by Zeus,"[55] Charmides replies, and he has no inclination whatever to work at it, for he adds a humorous and clever little remark aimed at ending his examination by transferring it to the one he thinks authored the saying: "But perhaps nothing prevents even the one who said it from not knowing what he had in mind." In this fine suggestion that his own ignorance may be shared by the one who told it to him, Charmides shows both presence of mind and insight: he knows his well-reputed guardian well enough to expect that attributing ignorance to him will incite him to defend his words. "And while he was saying this, he laughed slightly and looked at Critias"—Charmides turns his beautiful gaze away from Socrates and toward Critias sitting on the opposite side of him. Looking at him he looks *to* him—the ward has goaded his guardian into bailing him out.

Charmides has been stripped: he has sôphrosunê in the common sense—he's decorous and possessed of a sense of shame. And he lacks any inclination to examine a definition of sôphrosunê whose wise if riddling words came to him through Critias from Socrates. It's a complete riddle to him, even though, in being decorous and having a sense of shame, he *does* his own things, the things befitting a boy of his age and station. In a deeper sense, however, Charmides does not do *his own* things: by introducing the definition *doing one's own things* in order to turn the examination away from himself, he shows that in his decorum and sense of shame he does his own things not *on his own* but only by incorporating the things of others. Stamped by his schooling in conventional sôphrosunê, he refuses the riddling definition that promises to elucidate that stamping; he involuntarily intimates that he will always do the things of others whether they be the conventional things or the things of one who takes authority over him. The first to speak Socrates' words *doing one's own things* shows they are a thing foreign to him, mere words he got from Critias that he neither understood nor felt any need to understand. The end of Socrates' examination of Charmides answers for him the question he posed at its beginning:

55. *Know* here is *oida*, the word used earlier with respect to Socrates' knowing Charmides (154a–b). Its root is *eidenai*, to see, and hence "what one has seen one knows" (Liddell, Scott, and Jones, *Greek-English Lexicon* [LSJ]).

Charmides thinks he has a sufficient share of sôphrosunê and he *has*—it's necessary to be sôphrôn but not necessary to be wisely sôphrôn (158c). Beautiful Charmides will always do the things of others, particularly of his present and future guardian; Charmides stripped is a young man fated to remain a ward of his cousin till they die together in 403.

Just before Charmides gives up and transfers Socrates' inquiry to Critias, Socrates offers him the necessary prompting for pursuing what the original riddler had in mind with sôphrosunê as *doing one's own things*. The author of that view tells him that he is certain of the author's reason for putting it forward as a riddle: he was aware "that it is hard to know [*gnônai*] what doing one's own things is" (162b). The indispensable word for carrying the inquiry forward is contained in that statement: to truly *do* one's own things one must *know* one's own things, know oneself and the things appropriate to such a self; one must have self-knowledge—and that is hard.[56] Socrates prompts Charmides to the hard task of knowing, but that requires a willing respondent and Charmides is unwilling. As befits a young man, Charmides lives an unexamined understanding of his own place; to move from the conventional to the unconventional or Socratic requires a passion to know just what is implied in the conventional, and *that* Charmides shows he lacks.

"Doing one's own things" will appear as less riddlesome a definition of sôphrosunê than first said, for it is the appropriate first step in inquiring into natural sôphrosunê of the sort Charmides embodies. Charmides' three definitions are a natural progression from unexamined convention as prescriptive or moral behavior to inquiry's first generalized conclusion about that behavior. But Charmides is not willing to inquire into "doing one's own things." That is not his own thing; he will have nothing to do with philosophy. Therefore, Socrates will have nothing to do with him. But it is not only Charmides' disinclination to pursue inquiry that leads Socrates to say he would much rather discuss with Critias (162e): if he is to learn the state of philosophy in Athens he must turn from the young man who has become most beautiful in his absence and interrogate the man who passed on his riddling phrases in his absence. It is wise to leave in the form of a riddle what the wise man himself has worked to come to know and knows. Leaving it as a riddle induces would-be unriddlers to attempt

56. *Gignôskein*, the word employed here by Socrates, means *know* in the sense of recognize or "gain knowledge of" (LSJ). Forms of the word have been present from the beginning where Socrates said of those in the palaistra that some "were unknown [*agnôtes*] to me but most of them were known [*gnôrimous*]" (153a).

to know what is hard to know and to prove their capacity or incapacity in the attempt. Charmides is not willing even to start.

What about Critias? Socrates' examination of Charmides ends on the problem of authorship and ownership. Who is the author of the view that sôphrosunê is "doing one's own things," and will he own it? When Charmides supposed that its author was the one who said it to him, he innocently betrayed Critias as falsely claiming that the definition *doing one's own things* was his own. No wonder Critias got angry: his ward exposed him to the real author of the view as falsely claiming as his own what was that author's own. Who did Charmides get it from? Not me, Critias said (161b–c). He was lying, but he was given little choice. This hard beginning for proud Critias—confident originator of the whole play—makes it unlikely that he unriddled "doing one's own things" as its original riddler meant it—the riddler who even now does not own it as his own.

6. What Critias Took from Socrates and What That Riddler Had in Mind (162c–166c)

Socrates' two audiences, those present in the palaistra and the auditor of his narration, now hear a sequence of definitions of sôphrosunê from Critias. None is his own, for each he took over from Socrates before he left for Potidaea. Each appears now because Socrates controls the conversation and prompts Critias to explain the definition Charmides introduced—sôphrosunê is doing one's own things—by using other phrases Critias took over from him. The definitions that Critias voices at Socrates' prompting appear with great rapidity and no explanation: they are completely familiar to Socrates and Critias, who make no effort whatever to clarify them for the others present. As far as their exchange is concerned, those others are present only in the restraint their presence imposes on them both, aware as each is of the necessity for riddling words. From this point on, the dialogue is strenuous and dense, conducted in a shorthand familiar only to those who spent time with Socrates before he left. Is the auditor also familiar with Socrates' views? If not, he, like any reader of Plato's *Charmides*, will have to take care with Socrates' words to make the intricacies of his examination of Critias intelligible.

When Socrates narrates the transition from Charmides to Critias, he favors his auditor with an interpretation of what happened and a sketch of Critias's character (162c–d). He had evidently been observing Critias the whole time—as he could easily do just by looking past Charmides—and it had long been clear to him that Critias was eager to enter the contest, being agonistic and desiring to win honor. Interpreting the play unfolding in front of him as he directs it, Socrates states what is easily inferred: Charmides got his answer that sôphrosunê is doing one's own things from Critias. He also states explicitly that Charmides did not wish to give an account of the view but wanted Critias to do it and "kept prodding him and pointing out that he had been caught out." It is pointless for Critias to deny any longer that Charmides' definition came from him; he must now enter his own play as defender of the definition he passed on to Charmides to Charmides' baffled indifference.

Socrates' characterization of Critias measures his sôphrosunê: Critias has held himself back with difficulty and is unable to do so any longer. The cause of his losing control is Charmides saying he has been "caught out."[57] Critias "did not endure this," Socrates says, and says why not: "it was my opinion that Critias was *angry* with [Charmides], just as a poet is with an actor who recites his poems badly" (162d). Critias *is* a poet, due to become a famous one who will write dramatic poems to be played out by actors;[58] here he has just set a little play in motion and one of his actors is reciting his words badly—and showing him up as a questionable guardian. Critias's anger is the third revelatory irruption of passion that displays the presence of the involuntary and the manner in which each handles it. Socrates is inflamed by eros but controls it, displaying it only to his auditor. Charmides blushes with shame, displaying what he wanted to hide. Critias is taken over by anger and attacks his ward for failing to recite his poem well.[59] But his "poem," like the other phrases to come, is recited by Critias but authored by Socrates: how does *Socrates* respond to an actor's bad recital of his words? Charmides' recital moves Critias to uncontrollable anger, but Critias's recital—his supposing wrongly that he is repeating what the original author had in mind—evokes no anger in Socrates. Instead, it provides Socrates with an event of learning that will move him to prepare more effectual words.

57. Tarrant ("Naming Socratic Interrogation in the *Charmides*," 255) argues that *exelêlegmenos* (used here for the only time in *Charmides*) cannot mean *refuted* but must mean *caught out*. For Critias it's a matter less of logic than of pride: he is "caught out," mirrored in Charmides' ignorance.

58. On Critias's fame, see Sprague, *Older Sophists*, 241–49; Dillon and Gergel, *Greek Sophists*, 217–33.

59. Levine describes the grounds of Critias's anger: he had vouched for Charmides' philosophical ability and he has just been shown up as a bad judge; he doesn't know his own ward; how well has he "done his own things," the things of his guardianship? "Commentary on Plato's *Charmides*," 150–54.

Critias yields involuntarily to anger, but what he says to rebuke Charmides is restrained by his "love of honor" (162c_2), his desire to win honor before Charmides and the others. Still, his rebuke allows Socrates to speak up in defense of young Charmides and become his advocate before his guardian: "it's no wonder that he at his age does not know. But you, no doubt, are likely to know because of your age and the care you have taken" (162d–e). Socrates easily recognizes that seventeen-year-old Charmides has taken no care with his guardian's words, and his praise of thirty-year-old Critias for taking care can only confirm Critias's conviction that he knows what Socrates had in mind when he said those words. Socrates thus prepares his invitation to Critias to "take over the argument" as the one who taught Charmides that sôphrosunê is doing one's own things and who thinks he knows what that means. "I would be much more pleased to investigate with you whether or not what was said was true" (162e). By arranging to investigate the ambitious and intellectual adult who has taken care for Socrates' view, Socrates investigates the state of his own philosophy in Athens on his return.

Critias's First Definition: Sôphrosunê Is Doing One's Own Things[60]

Socrates begins by restating what defeated Charmides: "doing one's own things" forbids *any* doing of the things of others (161d–e). His subtle questioning prompts a distinction that Critias will seem to introduce—for Socrates introduces and repeats three times the word *poiein*, "making" (162e–163a) and moves immediately to the word *prattein*, "*doing* one's own things" and "*do* the things of others" (163a). Critias's defense of the definition distinguishes the two words Socrates just used interchangeably. But first he introduces *working* as synonymous with *doing*, for he needs a famous phrase of Hesiod's for his defense: "Work is no disgrace."[61] Speaking as an expositor of Hesiod who knows what wise Hesiod held, he disagrees with something Socrates just said. He claims that Hesiod would hold, as

60. Socrates' pre-Potidaean private instruction for Alcibiades also included "doing one's own things." Socrates there connected it with justice and made it one of the occasions on which he reduced Alcibiades to saying he did not know what he meant (*Alcibiades I* 127a–d, cf. 116e). Comparing *Alcibiades I* and *II* with *Charmides* provides important access to Socrates' way of teaching the best young Athenians before Potidaea. The two *Alcibiades* dialogues intimate that the differences between the political man Alcibiades and the intellectual Critias dictated the different ways in which Socrates attempted to teach them. The Platonic writings never show Socrates speaking in private to Critias.

61. Hesiod, *Works and Days* 311.

aristocratic Critias does, that it is a "disgrace for someone to be a shoemaker or salt-fish salesman or prostitute"—Socrates used shoemaking as an example of what everyone would do in the city in which everyone does one's own things (161e). Then Critias claims that Hesiod distinguished "making" (*poiein*) from "doing" (*prattein*) or "working" (*ergazesthai*): doing or working is that part of making that produces things in accord with the *kalon* ($163c_2$), whereas making can include the disgraceful.[62] The initial criterion for doing one's own things that Critias draws from Hesiod is the kalon, but he adds a second criterion in Hesiod's name, the "beneficial" (*ôphelimôs*, $163c_3$). Critias's prominent distinction between making and doing somewhat masks his more important claim regarding criteria: one ought to say of Hesiod, he says, that he believed that only the kalon and beneficial are "kindred to oneself" or one's own, "while everything *harmful* is alien" (163c). The harmful, then, is someone else's *kalon and benefit*, someone else's interest. Not only Hesiod teaches this: Hesiod and "anyone else who is sensible [*phronimos*] call that one sôphrôn who does his own things"—who does the kalon and beneficial things while not harming himself by doing things in someone else's interest. Critias invokes the traditional authority of Hesiod and all the wise to interpret traditional virtue, sôphrosunê, as the unwise service of the interests of others, and wise practice as an informed, wised-up pursuit of one's own benefit.[63] Insight into universal egoism liberates Critias into a private, calculating egoism.

It is worth lingering over Critias's first substantial speech. It implies but does not state a comprehensive teaching on human behavior: humans act out of their supposed self-interest; insight into that fact, wisdom about human behavior, frees one to consciously pursue one's self-interest. If such insight and action are implied in Critias's speech, then the speech itself attests to his rhetorical prowess: he is aware of the need for riddling speech that does not fully express what he has in mind, and he is capable of practicing it. He can communicate what he means to Socrates without stating the offensive truth openly in a palaistra full of impassioned lovers of Charmides—*that* would not be in his interest. If Critias speaks that way, what can be expected of Socrates? The auditor and reader are alerted by this speech to a feature of the whole coming exchange: it is riddling short-

62. Critias's argument unavoidably loses focus in English because English cannot reproduce in a single word the multivalence of *kalos*: beautiful, noble, right, good—a rich mix of aesthetic, teleological, and moral judgments. Because any one of the English words buries the other senses, I will simply transliterate *kalon* while discussing this argument.

63. See Levine, "Commentary on Plato's *Charmides*" 160.

hand conducted by speakers who know they are playing with fire. This is no surprise for those who study Socrates chronologically: he mounted the stage in *Protagoras* to reform Protagoras's inadequate esoteric cautions and to help Protagoras learn from the wise the esoteric economy of the whole Greek tradition of wisdom.

Did Critias get his Hesiod interpretation from Socrates? That the famous words of Hesiod came to him through Socrates receives external support from Xenophon, who reports that Socrates' accuser used this very phrase against him to show how he taught tyranny to his pupils: "The accuser said that [Socrates] also would pick out the most wicked passages from the poets held in the highest opinion and, using them as witnesses, teach his companions to be doers of evil and skilled at tyranny—such as the verse from Hesiod: 'No work is disgraceful, but idleness is disgraceful.'"[64] What Critias says he "learned from Hesiod" seems to have begun with what he thought Socrates taught him to learn from Hesiod; he seems to think that Socrates himself implied that sensible human behavior consciously aims at self-benefit because all human behavior implicitly aims at self-benefit. In offering his Hesiod-interpretation, Critias may even believe that Socrates will be pleased to hear how well his former associate understood him.

Socrates' first words in response suggest that he is the source at least of the Hesiod quotation: "Critias, right away, even as you were beginning, I almost understood your argument." But differences are present. The aristocratic sneer that marks Critias's examples of the disgraceful and his explicit disagreement with Socrates over shoemaking indicate that his examples at least did not come from Socrates. What about the core of his argument, his criteria of kalon and benefit? Socrates immediately introduces a new word: after noting that he almost understood from the beginning, he says, "you call things *good* that are kindred to oneself and one's own and you call the making of good things doings" (163d). No, Critias *called* such things kalon and useful. Socrates' substitution of *good* for *kalon and useful* anticipates just where the fundamental difference between them will be found: in their respective notions of the good. But that will come to light only serially.

Putting all the emphasis on Critias's distinction between making and doing, Socrates refers to his experience with Prodicus: he too has heard Prodicus and his "ten thousand distinctions among names" (163d). He evidently learned from this experience, for he gives Critias "leave to set down

64. *Memorabilia* 1.2.56–57.

each of the names however you wish" while making one demand: "only make clear to what you are referring whatever name you say." But he does not stop at this demand; he goes on to show exactly what he means by dictating the next definition. "So now, back again, define it more plainly from the beginning." This is the second or central *back again* in the dialogue, and Socrates does not leave this one to his interlocutor but instead gives as the new definition what he just introduced in substitution for Critias's criteria of kalon and utility—such going *back* must go back to what he said before Potidaea. "The doing of *good things* or making, or however you wish to name it, is this what you say sôphrosunê is?"[65]

"I do," is Critias's one-word response to this statement of the significant change in the definition—whatever verb he might choose, the change is that sôphrosunê as one's own is now defined by the *good* things and not the *kalon and useful*. Socrates states: "Then he who does evil things is not sôphrôn, but he who does good things is." If Socrates has just stated on his own what Critias has long since heard him say, then Critias's response is completely natural: "In your opinion, best of men, isn't it so?" (163e)—you who've just given your own opinion about sôphrosunê and the good, you who've just taken over the argument, why not just say this is your view? "Let that go," Socrates says. "For let's not yet investigate what my opinion is, but what you are saying now." No, you who repeat my words in my absence, you are being investigated here; what's your understanding of this statement of mine about sôphrosunê?

By moving so directly to a new definition, Socrates leaves wholly unexamined the issue he raised with respect to Critias's first definition: What is the *range* of one's own things that being sôphrôn requires of one? What counts as *meddling* in doing the things of others? More specifically, given Socrates' final example with Charmides, who would be a meddler if he touched the things of others and who would be sôphrôn in touching them? Socrates will return to this issue at the end of his discussion with Critias.

Critias's Second Definition: Sôphrosunê Is Doing the Good Things

Critias restates the definition Socrates dictated, and Socrates acknowledges that Critias's statement is true. But he makes no attempt to examine Critias on its content; only much later, when good and evil reappear in Critias's final quotation of words he learned from Socrates (174b), does

65. The criteria governing the first two arguments with Charmides also began with *kalos* and shifted to the good.

Socrates investigate it. For now, his examination indicates only what is implicit in Critias's understanding of *good things*, while at the same time prompting a third definition. But the unexamined definition represents an essential step in the inquiry into sôphrosunê that Critias heard from Socrates, for, like "doing one's own things," it makes explicit an implication of conventional sôphrosunê: decorum and a sense of shame imply not only an implicit knowledge of one's own, one's place, but also an implicit knowledge of moral imperative transcending one's place: whatever one's place, sôphrosunê dictates doing the good appropriate to it. Implicit in conventional sôphrosunê is a supposed knowledge of the good. Socrates' pre-Potidaean inquiry into the grounds of conventional sôphrosunê is a genealogy of morality.

Socrates begins by wondering "if you believe that those who are sôphrôn are ignorant of being sôphrôn" (164a). "Ignorant" is *a-gnoein*, not-knowing: Socrates again turns to *knowing* and again uses both the negative and the positive forms of the word as he did at the very beginning (153a), but now his questioning uses not-knowing and knowing to draw out Critias's understanding of *doing the good things*. Taking advantage of Critias's agreement that sôphrosunê can include craftsmen making the things of others, he asks if "in your opinion a certain doctor who makes someone healthy makes beneficial things both for himself and for him whom he doctors" (164b).[66] Critias agrees that he who does this "does what is needed (or proper)" and in so doing is sôphrôn. "So is it necessary for the doctor also to know [*gignôskein*] when he is doctoring beneficially and when not?" Before allowing Critias to answer his question—which leaves unspecified whether the benefit is to the patient or to the doctor or to both—Socrates asks a question that is both more general and more focused: is it necessary "for each of the craftsmen to know when he is going to profit [*ônesesthai*] from the work he is doing or not?" Critias answers reasonably—"Perhaps not": how could it be expected that every craftsman know not only his craft but just how and when it would bring him gain? But Socrates' sudden shift to *profit* has made gain for the practitioner or agent the sole factor; when he reverts immediately to *benefit* and leads Critias to deny vehemently that the agent is ignorant of benefit, the residual effect of the restriction on

66. Socrates' constant repetition of *doctor* reminds them all of their setting in plague-ridden Athens and keeps constantly before them his claim to have returned with a new medicine. Socrates speaks first of his own doctoring for Charmides ($156b_5$) through a medicine he learned from the doctor of Zalmoxis ($156d_{5,7}$, $156e_4$, $157b_6$); with Critias he uses the doctor as his most frequent example of a knower with beneficial knowledge ($164a_9$, $164b_7$, $164c_1$, $170e_{1,4}$, $170e_7$, $171a_4$, b_5, c_5, $171c_{1,2}$, $173b_2$).

profit seems revelatory: Critias means the gain of *doing the good things* to be restricted to the agent's gain.[67]

But Socrates' Prodicus-like precision with words does more than imply that Critias interpreted *doing the good things* as self-centered gain. Taking advantage of the little opening he made with respect to a possible ignorance of the agent's *profit*, Socrates speaks with an exactitude that practically forces Critias to say what he wants him to say next: "Sometimes then, the doctor though he acted beneficially or harmfully does not *know himself* [*gignôskei heauton*] how he acted/fared."[68] His next speech modifies the crucial word: "sometimes then he who does something beneficially does it in a sôphrôn manner and is sôphrôn, but *is ignorant himself* [*agnoei d'heauton*] that he is sôphrôn?" (164c). Such wording contradicts a definition of sôphrosunê he well knows he left with Critias—how can Critias not say next that sôphrosunê is *knowing oneself*?

Critias's Third Definition: Sôphrosunê Is Knowing Oneself

Before actually repeating the words Socrates prompts, Critias emphatically states the priority of this definition for him: "That would never happen," he declares of the possibility of someone's being ignorant of being sôphrôn, and if anything he has said so far would lead necessarily to that conclusion, "I would rather put one of those things aside, and I wouldn't be ashamed to say that I have not spoken correctly rather than ever to concede that a person who himself is ignorant of himself is sôphrôn" (164c–d). As honor loving as Critias is and as powerfully susceptible to shame,[69] he would unashamedly admit error and abandon the two definitions he has already endorsed rather than concede that one who is ignorant of his own sôphrosunê is sôphrôn. Critias has just differentiated himself from Socrates. Socrates began examining him on sôphrosunê as "doing one's own things" and led him through "doing the good things" to "knowing oneself." The definitions are linked: to truly understand what one's own is, one must know the good things for oneself, and to know that, one must know oneself. In feeding his actor his lines, Socrates supplied the words but not

67. Like Levine, whose persuasive analysis I here follow, Tuozzo emphasizes that Socrates brings to light Critias's view as seeking benefit for the *agent* alone ("Greetings from Apollo," 298–300).

68. 164c$_1$ Benardete translation, "Interpreting Plato's *Charmides*," *Argument of the Action*, 246.

69. Socrates described Critias as "honor loving" at 162c$_2$. At 169c he explicitly calls his auditor's attention to this feature; it is also exhibited in Critias's way of intervening at 161c, 162c, and in his suspicions about Socrates' motives at 166c.

the connecting logic, and his actor betrays his ignorance of that logic: he thinks he can abandon the first two steps and still retain the third.

It is becoming evident that the definitions Socrates prompts from Critias represent not only the path Socrates followed in his pre-Potidaean inquiry into conventional sôphrosunê but the path a philosophical investigator naturally follows in such inquiry. He first discovers that the fundamental features of conventional morality are two kinds of *action*: doing what is appropriate to one's place or station and doing the good things appropriate to that place. Those two kinds of action presuppose two kinds of supposed *knowledge*: of the good and of oneself. If Critias is ignorant of the internal logic of the inquiry as it moves from action to the knowledge presupposed in that action, how likely is it that he has properly understood what the inquiry yields? The speech he now gives states the singularly important thing he learned from Socrates without having learned how and why Socrates arrived at it.

Critias's vehement speech explaining and defending the third definition of sôphrosunê—his longest speech—occurs at the center of the dialogue and appears to be conceptually central as well, both in defining Critias's view and in marking it off from Socrates'.[70] Socrates has prompted Critias to say that self-knowledge defines sôphrosunê. To support the definition, Critias invokes the most authoritative of all statements about self-knowledge, beyond Homer and Hesiod, the Delphic inscription ascribed to the god himself: "For I assert that this is almost what sôphrosunê is: knowing oneself; and I go along with the one who put up such an inscription at Delphi" (164d).[71] Critias speaks very precisely; he never mentions Apollo,

70. Tuozzo argues for the centrality of this central speech on the grounds of its being consistent with what precedes it and follows it; that is, the speech is not what it is customarily accused of being, an unanticipated detour into "epistemology" that breaks with the preceding "moral inquiry" ("Greetings from Apollo," 296–305), a misunderstanding that repeats Critias's.

71. Critias repeats Socrates' words (*gignôskei heauton* 164c$_1$, *gignôskein heauton* 164d$_4$) both here and again as the final words of his speech (165b$_4$). The words of the inscription were *gnôthi sauton* (165a). Socrates' pre-Potidaean private teaching to Alcibiades gave the words put up at Delphi a prominent place—both Critias and Alcibiades were led by the pre-Potidaean Socrates to think about the Delphic inscription. With Alcibiades, Socrates' explanation of "know thyself" shows what Socrates thought it was necessary for Alcibiades to learn: "know thyself" means know who your actual rivals are, those you will have to surpass, in Alcibiades' case, the Lacedaimonian kings and the Great King of Persia (*Alcibiades I* 124b). Socrates went on to show Alcibiades the difficulty of knowing oneself, of knowing one's own things (129a), and that knowing oneself is knowing one's soul (130e). Knowing oneself is explicitly said to be *sôphrosunê* at 131b and 133c. Socrates' final explanation of the words used the image of an eye looking into another eye; for Alcibiades "know thyself" becomes the intimate but shared experience of looking into the eye of the other, of Socrates, that other who just demonstrated his indispensability to Alcibiades (132d–133b). "Know

and he cites the inscription as something he agrees with, not something he obeys. His agreement is with "the one who put up" the inscription, its human author, for he thinks he knows what that wise man was thinking when he put it up. Being wise, the one who put it up said it "in a rather riddlesome way, like a diviner" (164e)—Critias follows Socrates in understanding the wise as riddlers whose sayings must be interpreted (162a–b). The wise riddle "Know thyself" has a rank in wisdom far outstripping what was put up later at Delphi, "Nothing too much" and "Guarantee, and you guarantee disaster," for each of those sayings is mere counsel, whereas "Know thyself" "was put up as if it were a greeting of the god to those entering."[72] The two later sayings are what is commonly taken as sôphrosunê, cautionary counsel warning humans about the propensities of their own kind. By outstripping those later counsels, "Know thyself" outstrips common wisdom with riddling wisdom that may befit a god. What is a god?

Critias states that the god used "Know thyself" as a greeting "instead of '*Xaire*,'" the usual Greek greeting between human beings, meaning "Rejoice." "This greeting, 'Rejoice,' is not correct, and . . . they should not exhort each other to this but to be sôphrôn," to know yourself. "Thus the god addresses those entering the temple somewhat differently than do human beings," says Critias. The god greets, he does not counsel; the god acknowledges likeness, he does not stand superior counseling moderation. "Know thyself" was commonly interpreted to mean "know you are not a god, know your place as a mortal." So understood, "Know thyself" *is* counsel and means the same as "Nothing too much"—it is as far as possible from a greeting between equals, for it is the god's counsel to "Know that you are not my equal." By making "Know thyself" a *greeting* of the god, Critias accepts the greeting from the one who put it up and greets him in return, acknowledging that he knows that the one who put it up acted like a god in giving words to the wordless gods; Critias knows *him* as one who knew himself and knew what gods are. By putting up the riddling words as a greeting of the god to those entering the temple, he put up words inviting their reader to know what he knows, and Critias returns his greeting: he greets the godlike godlike.

---

thyself" appears in the following places in Plato's dialogues: *Alcibiades I* 124a, 129a, 130e, 132c–d; *Hipparchus* 228e; *Laws* 923a; *Phaedrus* 230a; *Philebus* 48c; *Protagoras* 343b; *Lovers* 138a.

72. In *Protagoras* with Critias present Socrates referred to both "Know thyself" and "Nothing too much" as laconic sayings "put up" by wise men at Delphi (343b). Herodotus holds a similar view of Hesiod and Homer as the poets who put up what the gods say for the Greeks: "they were the ones who created the gods' genealogies for the Greeks, gave them their names, assigned them their honors and areas of expertise, and told us what they looked like" (2.53).

What is a god? Critias intimates that he knows that a god is a powerful being come to word in speeches assigned to it by authoritative humans, none more wise than the one who said the god said "Know thyself." Critias returns the greeting: he knows what the one who put up the words knew, and in knowing that knows himself: he knows he is free of the counsel of the gods that comes to others as commands, he knows he is free, if he is able, to put up his own words. Not only does Critias embrace the atheistic teaching, he accepts it as a spur to aspire himself to the only kind of godhood there is.

Critias at thirty displays to an observing Socrates the grounds of his future career as a famous writer, the most important sophist raised in Athens, and at the end of his career as a famous tyrant after a life that was not politically prominent.[73] His months as a tyrant eclipsed his years as a writer to the extreme detriment of his writings: very little survives of the writings of the greatest Athenian sophist. The longest surviving fragment, however, a forty-line speech by the hero Sisyphus, reads like a commentary on Critias's speech in *Charmides* on the Delphic inscription.[74] The atheistic teaching is appropriately put into the mouth of a hero punished by the gods for opposing them—it would not do to put that teaching in the author's own name; let a hero punished by the gods state the true teaching. Critias's Sisyphus argues that the history of the human species has three stages. The bestial, anarchic first stage came to an end when humans established laws for punishment; that reign of justice was precarious, however, because crimes could be committed in the dark and go unpunished. The third and final stage was ushered in by some "clever fellow wise in counsels" who introduced a God who lived forever and could see in the dark, see even into the secrets of human hearts. That wise inven-

73. It is often supposed that Critias played a part in the oligarchic revolution of 411, but his name is not mentioned in the extant records; in his "Ode to Alcibiades" he credits himself with moving the recommendation that Alcibiades be recalled from exile in 407; at some point he was exiled by the democracy, and Xenophon uses this as a partial explanation of his readiness to kill his democratic opponents in 404 (*Hellenica* 2.3.15).

74. The speech was preserved by Sextus Empiricus, who quoted it in a list honoring early Greek atheists (*Against the Physicists* 1.48–54). See Dillon and Gergel, *Greek Sophists*, "Critias of Athens," 250–53. Some assign the fragment to Euripides, but Sextus Empiricus and the historic consensus following him read it as Critias's, and contemporary opinion seems to favor the traditional view. See Burkert, *Greek Religion* (314–15), who reads Critias's statement in *Sisyphus* as a culmination of the atheist teaching developed by Protagoras and Democritus. On the greater radicality of the younger sophists or the products of the sophists in Athens with special reference to Critias, see Forrest, "Athenian Generation Gap"; see also Wallace, "Sophists in Athens."

tor assigned the gods a place in the heavens, the source of both bounty and terror; he thus "extinguished lawlessness by laws."

When Socrates narrates *Charmides* to an unidentified auditor, he puts at its center Critias's exegesis of the Delphic inscription, the guarded but triumphant statement of the atheistic teaching by a young man who would become a well-known intellectual famed for being schooled by Socrates himself. His speech is subtle; he does not say, "Zeus does not even exist," for he knows the usefulness of Zeus. Honor-loving Critias must offer his subtle exegesis to his teacher in pride at his accomplishment, displaying to its ultimate author just how well he learned what Socrates taught him before leaving for Potidaea. But for Socrates, Critias's triumphal reading of "Know thyself" must be a central event in the sobering discovery of the fate of his philosophy in his absence. For he is learning that his pre-Potidaean teaching on sôphrosunê came, for Critias, to focus on his liberation from the gods and on his embrace of a kind of godhood for himself, the only godhood left.

Socrates raises not a word of protest against Critias's reading of the sacred inscription. Instead, directing Critias to the next definition, he will lead him to reveal that a knower who knows himself as he does feels himself freed, in the absence of gods, to act like a god, to rule and rule knowingly through a knowledge of knowledges, or a science of sciences. Released from customary moderation into immoderation, Critias at thirty has already been freed for what his mature career as sophist and political actor displays in full. When Critias the sophist actually attained political power, he outlawed sophistry: "Critias . . . when as a member of the Thirty he became legislator along with Charicles . . . wrote into the laws that one is not to teach an art of speeches."[75] There is no irony in this. Critias simply acts as he knows the powerful must act to protect their interests against sophists like himself who teach a veiled atheism and a consequent freedom to act without restraint.[76]

Critias ends his unriddling of the Delphic inscription by stating explicitly "why I'm saying all this" (165a): it's because he's willing to "take back" everything he said before about sôphrosunê for the sake of clearly defining

75. Xenophon, *Memorabilia* 1.2.31.

76. Had Critias's writings survived, it seems certain that Plato's *Charmides* would be even richer for us than it now is—it must have done with Critias's writings what it did with Herodotus's: allude to them in a way that would allow his core views to come to light. *Charmides* would, on this supposition, provide particular guidance to Critias's aspiration to rule in the way those who put up what the god said at Delphi ruled, spiritual rule that preceded his actual tyranny.

it as "oneself knowing oneself" (165b). "For perhaps in some way you were speaking more correctly about them, perhaps I was, but nothing of what we were saying was quite plain"—for the sake of the speech he just made, Critias is willing to throw away everything said till then. "Know thyself," as Critias understands it, together with its corollary that follows next as the fourth definition, is the core of what he learned from Socrates, and he thinks it stands independent of the path of reasoning that led Socrates himself to it. By stating again his indifference to any connection between the previous definitions and "Know thyself," Critias displays a cardinal feature about himself: he is interested not in the inquiry as such but in what he takes to be an isolated truth of singular importance; his aim is not to know but to use what he thinks he knows to further some project of his own. He is not a philosopher, but what the philosopher concluded and allowed him to see can be of great use to him.

Taking his stand with this definition, Critias challenges Socrates, initiating a moment of drama as the two wrestle for control of what will be said next. Critias offers Socrates a choice: either agree with the definition or he will "give an argument for this." Socrates wants neither to agree with Critias nor to give him the opportunity to make a display speech on knowing oneself that employs the skeptical reading of the Delphic oracle. Socrates wins back control of the argument by postponing any statement of agreement with Critias, a postponement that proves perpetual. "You're coming at me,"[77] he says, "as though I claim to know what I'm asking about. . . . But that's not how it is, for I'm inquiring along with you into what is put forward because I myself don't know" (165b–c). Socrates is not lying; what he does not know—and knows he does not know—will be the chief distinction marking him off from Critias the knower. But Socrates surely knows everything Critias knows, in particular what Critias is putting forward now, for he is its ultimate source, as Critias impatiently acknowledges when he states his next definition (166c). What Socrates does not know right now and must continue investigating to find out is what else Critias has done with his philosophy. Critias, proud of what he has done and wanting to be honored for it, willingly submits to be investigated further. Socrates thus ensures that Critias not give his promised "argument for this," the atheistic teaching, an offer that must have come to Socrates with foreboding, surrounded as they are in the palaistra by known and not-known.

As the radical views of Socrates' former associate collect around phrases prompted by Socrates himself—and as Socrates deflects attention away

77. The verb *prospherô* includes the sense of rushing against or attacking.

from his own views—what is being suggested about Socrates' own view? Nothing is said directly, but in each case so far—human behavior as a universal egoism, the good as one's own benefit, the gods' authority as human based—the views seem in fact to be what a sufficiently radical inquirer into the nature of the human would conclude. It makes all the difference, however, whether these views are held by Socrates, a lover of wisdom schooled in the necessity of distinguishing the exoteric and the esoteric, or by Critias, a lover of honor with both talent and aspirations as a writer and a political actor. The Socrates returned to Athens intent on learning the state of philosophy there is discovering that he was insufficiently esoteric, he who counseled Protagoras to a more careful esotericism.

Socrates renews his investigation of Critias by introducing a final indispensable word in the philosopher's inquiry into sôphrosunê. Till now, the knowledge needed to understand conventional sôphrosunê has been the knowledge denoted by *gignôskein*, knowing as recognizing. On the path Socrates followed, the drive to understand the presuppositions of conventional sôphrosunê submits to an imperative: know yourself. The self-knowledge thus gained drives the inquirer to a further question: is that knowledge *knowledge*? Can the human kind, the knowing kind, truly know what it thinks it knows? Is the knowledge presupposed as the secure ground of customary sôphrosunê in fact available? That is, are the grounds of moral behavior—supposed knowledge of oneself and supposed knowledge of the good—genuine knowledge? Such questions never reach the surface in *Charmides*, but the trajectory of its argument shows them to be the questions Socrates pursued in the inquiry he communicated, riddlingly, to Critias. Commanded now by Critias to investigate after deflecting agreement that sôphrosunê is "oneself knowing oneself," Socrates says that "if sôphrosunê is knowing [*gignôskein*] something, it is clear that it would be a kind of knowledge [*epistêmê*, 165c5] and of something, wouldn't it?" This move to *epistêmê*, knowledge as understanding or scientific knowledge,[78] is the necessary move on the path Socrates followed. For self-knowledge to count as *knowledge* one must know what kind of knowledge it is and how and whether it is at all possible: the philosopher's investigation of sôphrosunê and its presuppositions dictates a turn to "epistemology," study of the nature and limits of human knowing.

To investigate Critias's understanding of sôphrosunê as a kind of knowl-

78. English translations of *Charmides* frequently translate *epistêmê* as *science* (e.g., Jowett, Sprague) to distinguish it consistently from *gignôskein*. Critias introduced the verb form, *epistasthai*, when he asked Socrates to pretend *to have knowledge* of a drug for the head (155b6).

edge, Socrates gains his agreement that doctoring is a kind of knowledge, knowledge of the healthful. He then adopts a little tactic to enable him to direct the discussion to what he wants to consider: he acts as if Critias were investigating him, a device that allows him both to ask the questions and to answer them. Were Critias to ask him in what respect doctoring is *useful* and what it produces, Socrates would say it produces as its *benefit* a *noble* work, health. (The criteria Critias introduced in his Hesiod interpretation persist as part of how Socrates would answer Critias now.) Were Critias to ask him, Socrates would then say that other arts are similar in being of something and producing useful works. Having set matters up, Socrates can ask Critias, "If sôphrosunê is a knowledge of oneself, what beautiful work does it produce for us worthy of its name?" (165d–e)—how is this knowledge like the other knowledges? "But Socrates," Critias replies, "you're not inquiring correctly." The incorrectness of Socrates' inquiry is his acting as if knowledge of oneself is similar in kind to a knowledge like doctoring. No, Critias says, knowledge of oneself is a knowledge like calculation and geometry, which do not generate products like health, and with that he challenges Socrates: show me the product of such knowledges. "But you can't," he adds, confident that what he's saying, Socrates knows. "What you say is true," Socrates grants (166a), but those knowledges are still *of* something that is different from the knowledge itself. Socrates can then pose the question he so carefully arranged: "What then is sôphrosunê knowledge *of* which is different from sôphrosunê itself?" "*This is it, Socrates*," Critias cries triumphantly, "you've come in your search to the very thing by which sôphrosunê differs from all the knowledges" (166b).

Critias's Fourth Definition: Sôphrosunê Is Knowledge Both of Other Knowledges and Itself of Itself

"This is it." The search seems to be over for Critias when Socrates' questioning brings him to the point where he can state that the knowledge in knowing oneself differs from all other knowledges: *they* are all knowledges of something else and not of themselves, whereas sôphrosunê "alone is a knowledge both of the other knowledges and itself of itself" (166c). In Critias's view, Socratic inquiry turns to "oneself" as knower and achieves a kind of ultimate knowledge that differs from all other knowledges in two ways: it is of itself whereas all other knowledges are other-regarding or self-forgetful, and it lacks the specificity of a single domain, for it is the knowledge that ranges over all other knowledges.

But the way Critias states sôphrosunê's uniqueness reverses the proper order of inquiry and states first what seems to be of first importance to him, knowledge of other knowledges. The proper order will be restored a moment later when Socrates requests a restatement of Critias's view (166e). But for Critias, sôphrosunê as the Delphic greeting, "Know thyself," leads directly to what he states first and holds first, that special knowledge that is a knowledge of knowledges, or a "*science of sciences*."[79] Possessing such knowledge would confer on its possessor the right to direct those sciences. Such knowledge would be *ruling* knowledge supposedly transparent to itself and superior to the whole array of other knowledges or expertises whose purposes or ends it could govern. Here is a sôphrosunê fit for an ambitious young sophist eager to rule through his writings or for a future tyrant whose rule would enact his perfect or totalizing knowledge.

But having announced his conclusion, Critias abruptly introduces a different issue entirely because he cannot control his fear that Socrates is manipulating him to do him harm. Having just given a bare statement of his ultimate definition of sôphrosunê, he says, "You are far from being unaware of this" (166c). Sôphrosunê as the special knowledge that leads to the knowledge of knowledges is the core of your teaching on sôphrosunê, Critias says in effect, I know it, I've preserved it, I'm handing it back to you—but why are you questioning me this way? Critias, being Critias, cannot help believing that Socrates is serving some selfish purpose of his own when he forces Critias to voice what Socrates already knows. Suspicion compels him to an attack on Socrates that parallels his earlier anger with Charmides. "You're doing what you just denied you were doing. You're trying to refute me and letting go of what the argument is about." Taking the high ground of concern only for the argument, honor-loving Critias accuses Socrates of trying to make him look bad when he most wants to look good, here in the presence of his beautiful ward to whom he has tried to transmit what his teacher taught, here at the center of a whole circle of onlookers. Why else would Socrates play dumb about what he himself taught Critias except to make Critias look bad and himself look good? Critias knows no reason beyond honor to explain Socrates' actions.

79. This translation conveys more directly an essential component of Critias's understanding of what he gained from Socrates. Socrates introduced the plural *knowledges* at 166a_4, and Critias, taking the prompt, repeated it at 166b_8, 166c_2, and in his definition at 166$e_{5,6}$. After that the plural is used only by Socrates as he examines Critias's claim to a knowledge of knowledges at 167c_1, 168a_8, 170c_6, 171a_8, 174a_{10}, 174$c_{2,4}$, 174$d_{4,9}$, 175b_8.

7. Should Each of the Beings Become Clearly Apparent Just As It Is? (166c–e)

Socrates responds to Critias's accusation with a speech containing the most remarkable sentence in the whole of *Charmides*. He responds to the accusation alone, not to the new definition Critias announced, but it becomes obvious that he responds as he does because of that definition, for his response prepares a definition of his own that marks the decisive turning point in his examination of Critias. As for Critias's accusation, Socrates uses it as an opportunity to explain with all the openness permitted him just why he is proceeding as he is. *Openness* itself has to be one of the themes of his explanation because the openness permitted them is restricted in a public gathering where knowns and unknowns young and old are circled around them. When Socrates told his auditor at the beginning what his intentions were on his return, he indicated in advance that he examines Critias in order to discover the state of his philosophy in Athens; when Socrates tells Critias why he is examining him as he does, he indicates just what his whole enterprise for philosophy is and why it dictates caution.

The first sentence of Socrates' response tacitly and for the first time refuses a definition by Critias while denying that he's investigating simply to refute him: "What a thing you're doing, by believing, even if I do refute you, that I am refuting for the sake of anything other than that for the sake of which I would search through myself as to what I say, fearing that unawares I might ever suppose that I know something when I don't know" (166c–d). Socrates will refute Critias on this definition, but for the same reason that he attempts to know himself: out of *fear* that he might suppose he knows what he doesn't know. His examination of Critias aims to show Critias and himself that they should fear that Critias, with his ultimate definition of sôphrosunê, supposes he knows what he doesn't know.

Socrates begins the chief sentence of his response with an adamant claim—"So I do assert that this is what I am also doing now"—and then he asserts that he's doing exactly what Critias accused him of not doing: he *is* "investigating the argument" and does it for the sake of two different interested parties. First, "most of all for the sake of myself"—Socrates unequivocally has a powerful self-interest in the argument, a self-interest only secondarily concerned with Critias. Socrates the philosopher attained something of the highest value and has a profound interest in transmitting what he attained. His argument investigating Critias serves his self-interest as an interest in the future of his philosophy; he is investigating

Critias as he would himself because by investigating Critias he investigates that part of himself that Critias has taken over—or failed to take over. Second, Socrates is investigating the argument "perhaps also for the sake of others who are fit [*epitêdeiôn*]." *Perhaps also*: Socrates is unavoidably less sure of the benefits actually accruing to others through his investigation. Who are those others? The word he employs, *epitêdeios*, is usefully ambiguous. It means, in the first instance, "fit or adapted for a special purpose," but it can also be applied to "an intimate friend." A combination of both senses seems most apt here: Socrates is conducting his investigation of Critias perhaps also for the sake of those fit to be his intimate friends by virtue of being fit for the special purpose that is philosophy. These words addressed to Critias signal that he is being measured for fitness: Socrates' examination will either prove him fit or refute him, proving him unfit. For it is 429 and Socrates and Critias are not enemies in 429; instead, Socrates the returned teacher exercises a legitimate claim on his former associate, a right to measure him. Whether Critias can pass that test depends wholly on him: is he *epitêdeios*? Socrates' response to Critias's accusation is a teacher's challenge to a former pupil: Show yourself fit if you are fit. *That's* the reason I'm conducting this investigation with you, *perhaps also that*.

Socrates' remarkable sentence is not yet complete. What he adds contrasts sharply with the implication of "the *fit*" that he has just uttered: "or don't you think that it is a *common good for almost all human beings*. . . ." Socrates conducts his investigation for the good of himself and perhaps also for the other fit—and the common good of almost all human beings? How would *that* be served by what Socrates does for the sake of so exclusive a group as himself and the fit? He casts his point as a question that implies the affirmative answer Critias will actually give it. The question that ends his sentence is this: "or don't you think that it is a common good for almost all human beings that each of the beings [*tôn ontôn*] should become clearly apparent just as it is?"

Their theme has been *knowledge*—self-knowledge (*gignôskein*) and then the kind of knowledge (*epistêmê*) self-knowledge would lead to—which Critias claims is a comprehensive knowledge of the knowledges. This is the context in which Socrates mentions—seemingly incidentally—the most comprehensive possible knowledge, the clearly becoming apparent of each of the beings just as it is, the completely successful ontology that would fulfill the ultimate pursuit of philosophy.[80] *This* is what Socrates and

80. Socrates speaks of "the beings" (*tôn ontôn*) three times later (169a$_1$, 174b$_1$, 175b$_3$), each time suggesting the aspiration to an ontology, a comprehensive account of the beings.

his fit friends are ultimately concerned about. But Socrates asks a *question* about such knowledge, and not a question about its possibility but about its possible benefit as the common good for almost all human beings. Here, where Critias has just claimed a comprehensive kind of knowledge, Socrates forces a glimpse of the most comprehensive knowledge that he and his friends seek—clear knowledge of each of the beings just as it is, knowledge of the *kinds* of beings that there are, knowledge of their nature, knowledge of the *ideas* in Socrates' peculiar usage. Socrates forces this glimpse of what he and his friends seek in order to ask one thing only about it: would clarity about what they aim to achieve serve the common good? Socrates himself pursues his questioning for himself and his intimates, knowing—and the prewar *Protagoras* made it clear how Socrates can claim to *know* this—that such knowledge is not a common good for almost all human beings. Why then does he put the question in a form that demands an affirmative answer, making him appear to hold that such knowledge would be a common good for almost all? It must be because he also knows that such appearing is the only way that philosophy can publicly defend itself—it must act as if the knowledge it passionately seeks to acquire is in fact something that would benefit all, all in the palaistra for instance, Charmides for instance.

Socrates' response to Critias's accusation is a defense speech that does three things: limit the number for whom he conducts his inquiry to a few; acknowledge that what he inquires into is unlimited in extent; indicate the necessity that it claim universal benefit. Socrates' inquiry is therefore imperatively esoteric, the nature of his inquiry entailing the exoteric claim that its effort to make each of the beings clearly apparent just as it is is a common good for almost all human beings. Where do *you* stand on such esotericism? That is Socrates' question to his accuser.

Critias answers that "I do very much" think it a common good—and he surely means his affirmative answer to Socrates' affirmative-demanding question to suggest to Socrates its exact opposite. Agreement is Critias's only way to show Socrates that he shares with him a recognition of the necessity of esotericism—therefore he repeats the exoteric claim that a clear knowledge of everything is a common good for everyone. How could Critias mean anything else? He's the one who just indicated the kind of being a god has—it's the kind that exists through words put up for it by human authors. How could Critias think that it is a common good for almost all human beings to make *that* kind of being clearly apparent just as it is? He himself spoke with due circumspection about the gods' words—he who had earlier been exposed to circumspect speech about the gods when he witnessed Socrates investigating Protagoras, for even Protagoras spoke mythically, alleging that Zeus and Hermes were responsible for the justice and sense of shame in human beings indispensable for civil order. Critias knows the uses of gods; therefore he knows the uses of circumspect speech. His affirmative response to Socrates' question communicates his own recognition that it is not a common good for almost all human beings that each of the beings become clearly apparent just as it is—and that in the presence of a public like that in the palaistra, it is a common good to say that it is.

The ontological project alluded to by Socrates, the becoming apparent of each of the beings just as it is, is not a claim to possess a comprehensive ontology. But, coming as it does in the context of the investigation of knowledge as self-knowledge, and coming as a response to what Critias just asserted, and coming in an appeal to caution, it does seem to claim knowledge about a certain kind of being, the highest beings: we can know that the being of the gods arises from reports of authoritative human beings, and we can know that because we know human being. Philosophy's fundamental issues of being and knowing, ontology and epistemology, thus appear momentarily together in *Charmides*, but ontology receives no extended treatment beyond this reminder to Critias of the necessity of caution about what can be known about the highest beings. Having secured Critias's agreement on the necessity of restraint, Socrates can invite him, ironically enough, to "be bold, blessed one, and answer however what is asked appears to you, letting go of whether Critias or Socrates is the one being refuted." "Critias or Socrates"—by naming himself in this either/or pairing, Socrates prepares what comes next: he will contrast Critias's view with his own, and *that* either/or will carry its disjunction through the rest of their exchange. But for now Socrates can give his accuser an instruction that shows that *he* was guilty of what he accused Socrates of, not following the argument: "But apply your mind to the argument and investigate in what way it will turn out under refutation" (166e). Critias responds chastened: "In my opinion you speak with due measure"—a fitting synonym of sôphrosunê and a fitting way for Critias to assure his teacher that he will be mindful of restraint. Having gained this assurance, Socrates can invite Critias to repeat what he said about sôphrosunê.

Why did Socrates issue his words of restraint right here? The answer must be that the high point of dangerous unrestraint had been reached, the point at which a warning was most needed. That means that Socrates must have heard in Critias's bare statement of sôphrosunê as the knowledge of knowledges the full threat of the conclusion he drew from "Know thyself": to understand the words put up at Delphi is to glimpse the ultimate principle of rule over human beings. In Critias's supposed "knowledge of knowledges" lay Critias's own nascent claim to a right to rule: as the knower of knowledges he can order the knowledges rightly, he can rule them in a way that will bring the most benefit to all human beings, himself included. But such a conclusion about rule cannot have been Critias's own invention: the highest point of danger cannot endanger Critias alone. This must have been a step in the reasoning he took over from Socrates: the danger is to Socrates or to philosophy itself in this public forum. Philosophy as Socrates pursued it, inquiry into the kind of being that the human is among the kinds of beings that there are, issued in insight into the kind of being a god is, the kind of being the ultimate rulers are—and therefore into the principle of rule. It thereby opened a possible aspiration to rule. Just here, Socrates' pre-Potidaean inquiry into the very principle of human restraint—sôphrosunê—reached its peak in potential unrestraint. And just here, Socrates must restrain his former associate, and does. There is, then, severity in Socrates' words; Socrates meets Critias's accusation with a rebuke that can still have some purchase on Critias.

But is it just false that it is a common good for almost all human beings that each of the beings become clearly apparent just as it is? Is the claim to common good just an exoteric cover to shelter the truth, which is otherwise? Neither Critias nor Socrates can think so. Each must think that it is a common good for almost all human beings that each of the beings become clear just as it is—clear to *them* and the very few knowers like them. Critias believes (as will become evident) that a knower like himself will rule to the benefit of the ruled as well as the ruler. What Socrates knows is very different from what Critias thinks he knows, as his continued investigation of Critias aims to demonstrate, but he too must think that it is a common good that each of the beings become as clear as possible to *him*. He is a student of the rule of the wise, as *Protagoras* showed, and his changing view of the actions that may be required of him is indicated by the continuous underlying current of *Charmides*: Socrates' return is like Odysseus's return. Benefit is the final issue on which Socrates will examine his student, just how the common good is served by the conception of sôphrosunê ultimately held by Socrates.

Do the fundamental philosophical enterprises of ontology and epistemology serve the common good? Or is enlightenment a private pleasure and a public curse? *Charmides* allows that question to be glimpsed in Socrates' investigation of the possible public curse of Critias's supposed enlightenment.

8. The Final Definition of Sôphrosunê, Socrates' Definition (166e–167a)

Having cautioned Critias by turning Critias's accusation of him into an accusation of Critias for dangerous rashness, Socrates invites him to say again what he was saying about sôphrosunê. Critias's restatement of his final definition alters his wording slightly and puts its two elements in their proper order, highlighting its dual character: sôphrosunê, "alone of the knowledges, is a knowledge both itself of itself and of the other knowledges" (166e, cf. 166c). Socrates fixes on one part only: "wouldn't [sôphrosunê] then be a knowledge also of non-knowledge if it is also of knowledge?" Critias agrees, but the sequel shows that he has given this implication of the knowledge of knowledge little thought. For Socrates now offers a definition of sôphrosunê on his own, the second time he has done so in *Charmides*. On the first occasion, he defined sôphrosunê as doing the good things (163d); on this occasion he emphasizes knowing what one knows and does not know (167a). After stating his definition, Socrates asks what he asked on the first occasion: "Is this what you are saying?" And Critias answers as he did the first time: "I am." These two definitions, then, seem to be singled out as the parts of Socrates' pre-Potidaean inquiry into sôphrosunê that Critias attended to least, for he showed himself ready to abandon the definition that sôphrosunê is doing the good things, and as for his saying that sôphrosunê is knowing what one does not know, Critias did not say it, nor will he ever say it on his own. Socrates will show that this definition, offered on his own, is an essential part of his philosophy that Critias never took seriously enough. The final definition, volunteered by Socrates, will be his means for measuring Critias's final definition and for showing that Critias's supposed knowledge of knowledges is a nonknowledge.

Charmides isolates Critias's third and fourth definitions by little cues of narrative that show them to be the ones most significant to him and to be connected by a logic powerfully attractive to him. They are the two that deal with god and man, with divine authority and the consequences for man of discovering its source in human words alone: "Know thyself" yields the truth about divine authority and leads Critias to envision a knowledge of knowledges, an unrestrained ruling art that he, freed of sacred restraint, would wield like a god. Discovering this in Critias, Socrates begins to introduce restraint, beginning with the great restraint of exoteric caution and leading now to the insurmountable restraint built into the heart of Socrates' own unrestraint in following the command "Know thyself." The conclusion Socrates drew from "Know thyself," *his* ultimate definition of sôphrosunê, sounds like a close cousin of Critias's conclusion, but Socrates will show it to be essentially different in both restraint and unrestraint.

The Final Definition, Socrates' definition: Sôphrosunê Is Knowing Both What One Knows and What One Does Not Know

Socrates alone states the final definition. He elaborates it just after Critias agrees that sôphrosunê is a knowledge of knowledge and *nonknowledge*, even though Critias has never spoken of nonknowledge and never will speak of it (166e). What Socrates does next is significant: he goes back to retrieve the Delphic definition and does so in order to expand it with what he has just introduced, the knowledge of nonknowledge: "Then only the sôphrôn one will himself both know himself and be able to examine both what he happens to know and what he does not" (167a). Like Critias's knowledge of knowledges, Socrates' definition comes directly out of the Delphic definition, but Socrates' definition differs from Critias's in knowing nonknowledge and in a second way that Socrates here adds. Not only is the sôphrôn one able to examine himself and his knowledge, but that very self-examination enables him "in the same way . . . to investigate others in regard to what someone knows and supposes, if he does know, and what he supposes he knows but does not know. No one else will be able to."[81] The other-directed aspect of Socrates' definition differs from the other-directed aspect of Critias's definition: Critias claims a knowledge of other knowledges, Socrates claims a capacity to examine the knowledge claims of others. Critias supposes his knowledge of other knowledges grants him a right to rule other knowers; Socrates demonstrates his capacity to examine Critias's supposed knowledge by laying it bare as nonknowledge. Critias took a right to rule from Socrates' teaching on sôphrosunê, and Socrates' final definition of sôphrosunê will show that he has no right to that right.

Socrates gives no reason why one who knows himself would also be able to examine others, but the reason must be implicit in knowing oneself in Socrates' sense: knowing what one knows and does not know must mean that one has come to know *knowing*. Socrates' sôphrosunê as self-

81. The translation follows the emendation of Bekker (*Charmides, Alcibiades I and II, Hipparchus, The Lovers, Theages, Minos, Epinomis*, trans. Lamb), making the one examined the "someone" just introduced.

examination leads one, leads Socrates, to know himself in a very precise sense: his self-knowledge is human knowledge's knowledge of itself. As knowledge knowing knowledge, it also knows nonknowledge. What it knows therefore are the nature and limits of human knowing. Only one who knows that would be able to examine others to determine if their knowledge claims exceed the limits of possible knowledge. "Knowledge of knowledge" makes possible an appropriate kind of "knowledge of knowledges": it would know the kinds of knowledges that could count as possible knowledge. Socrates' definition therefore retains both prongs of Critias's final definition but puts the first thing first—knowledge itself of itself—and makes *it* the proper tool for testing any claim to a knowledge of knowledges. Socrates' knowledge of knowledges is based on a knowledge of knowledge. It can therefore examine Critias's claim to a knowledge of knowledges: is his kind of knowledge of knowledges at all possible?

Having prepared it this way, Socrates states his own definition of sôphrosunê: "And this is what being sôphrôn, and sôphrosunê, and oneself knowing oneself are: knowing what one knows and what one does not know" (167a). The finality of the final definition is shown by the fact that after receiving Critias's confirmation that this is what he means, Socrates investigates it no further but instead turns immediately to its possibility and benefit. The definition is final, but its initial statement turns out to be partial, for Socrates supplies three later repetitions that complete it in the appropriate ways: first, he adds to what one does not know "*that one does not know it*"; this more complete formulation of the final definition he places at the beginning of his investigation of the possibility of that definition (167b). Then he adds to what one knows "*that one knows it*," placing this complete and final formulation both at the beginning of his investigation of its benefit (171d) and then again at its end, in his final summarizing speech (175c)—knowing that, Socrates is able to examine Critias and discover that what he supposes he knows he does not know. In its pursuit of the definition of sôphrosunê, *Charmides* thus has Socrates himself author the final definition and use it to measure Critias's final definition.[82]

In 429 Socrates returns to Athens and learns that Critias is well on the way to what will become his actual career as a sophist and as a tyrant. As

82. If the six items Alfarabi lists as treated in *Charmides* represent the serial unfolding of the dialogue, then his account accords well with the one given here (Alfarabi, *Philosophy of Plato and Aristotle*, 2:23).

a sophist, he already possesses what is basic to his tyranny: knowing the nature of authority in words put up by human beings and aspiring to authority himself, he can envision a perfection that his knowledge gives him the right to script or found. Such a glorious attainment for one who truly had a knowledge of knowledges would be limited only by his capacity to persuade others to submit to what he knows. If there is a science that rules the other sciences as those sciences rule their subject matters, its perfect practitioner can reap the honor of establishing perfect order. As Socrates causes Critias's dream to come to light under the direction of his inquiry, he learns just how the riddling words of his philosophy corrupted Critias into dreaming. He learns with respect to the state of philosophy in Athens that in the mind of Critias philosophy has attained its end or completion; Critias supposes that in him philosophy has passed into a state of wisdom.[83] Learning that, Socrates is surely learning as well that something must be done about how he communicates his philosophy.

What Socrates is shown learning about Critias in *Charmides* marks an epoch in his life, compelling him to reflect on the consequences of communicating his philosophy to spirited young men with a passion to rule. Once that problem becomes apparent in *Charmides*, the dialogue can be interrogated on a related aspect of that issue: how does Socrates himself stand to the issue of rule? *Charmides* can then be seen almost to begin with Socrates displaying his knowledge of what ultimately rules humans. He had recovered his boldness, he tells his auditor (156d), just before a bold act: he alleged to the company in the palaistra that while he was away he had subjected himself to knowledge claims based on the words of the god Zalmoxis. At its center *Charmides* demythologizes the words of gods, putting that enlightenment in Critias's mouth but intimating that he learned from his teacher Socrates that gods' words are the more or less wise words put up by human authors. Critias recognized that unriddling gods' words need not render them powerless but could hand their unriddler one of the secrets of power: power wielded by gods is power wielded by the one who puts up their words. Critias is eager to exercise such power. And his teacher? Could he aspire—be compelled to aspire—to rule human beings through salutary beliefs?

The philosopher Socrates cannot have submitted his mind to the authority of a god, a god Herodotus showed to be such an effective fraud. That god, the only god, teaches his followers to scorn other gods and to regard themselves as immortal; believing themselves immortal followers of

83. Levine, "Commentary on Plato's *Charmides*," 190.

the one true god, they grow courageous and just—these words put up for the god seem to be wise words in their moral effect. And they ring of the words Socrates himself will soon put up about the gods when he becomes a theologian in the *Republic*, poetizing a theology in the service of justice. The question of Socrates and wise rule through authoritative words put up for the gods will have to be considered further in the *Republic* after *Charmides* raised it as the central issue in what Critias took over from Socrates.

9. The Possibility of Socrates' Sôphrosunê (167a–171c)

For a third and final time Socrates says, "back again," and this time is special for he adds, "'the third one for the Savior'" (167a): like the third and final libation at a banquet offered to Zeus the Savior, it is the lucky time successfully accomplishing something.[84] What allows this to be the final time is the definition they arrived at: they no longer have to go back to recover a new definition as they did the first two times (160d, 163d). Instead, "as if from the beginning let us investigate first whether it is possible for this to be or not—to know what one knows and what one does not know that one does not know [it]" (167a–b). Investigating the possibility of such knowledge opens a further task: "what benefit there would be for us in knowing it." Investigating the possibility and benefit of sôphrosunê as they just defined it carries them to the end of their exchange, to a successful fulfillment of Socrates' intentions; after that there remains only a summary speech by Socrates (175a–176a) and a brief exchange with Charmides (176a–d).

For this third "back again," Socrates goes back[85] and, as if from the beginning, investigates the possibility and benefit—of *what* definition? The extreme complexity of their discussion follows from the complexity of Socrates' aim in going back: he demonstrates the impossibility and harm of Critias's final definition of sôphrosunê by employing his own final definition, proving it both possible and beneficial.

Socrates' argument is an exercise not simply in logic but in learning as well, and to that end he indulges in a little stratagem calculated to force Critias to put his nature on display. He begins by claiming to be perplexed (*aporeô*) about the strange or atypical (*atopon*) character of knowledge as

84. See also *Republic* 583b, *Philebus* 66d, *Laws* 3.692a, and *Letters* 7.334d, 340a.

85. On the first occasion, Charmides went back and stated that sôphrosunê is a sense of shame (160d–e); on the second occasion, Socrates did and stated the definition that sôphrosunê is doing the good things (163d).

they have defined it (167b). Then, having set out his alleged perplexity, he challenges Critias to show the way out (169b), but his own perplexity (he tells his auditor) has made Critias perplexed. There's a difference: Critias refuses to admit perplexity. The sheer mastery of Socrates' questioning proves that he's not perplexed, and he leaves no doubt that Critias is by both reporting it and showing it. In the following argument, then, broken into two parts by Socrates' narrated comment on Critias's perplexity, unperplexed Socrates maneuvers Critias into a revelatory perplexity: he supposes he knows what he does not know, and Socrates comes to know it.

The first part of Socrates' argument (167c–168a) concerns the atypical character of the knowledge of knowledge—it can be knowledge both of itself and of other things like itself (knowledges) but not of what those others are of. Socrates highlights the strangeness of such knowledge by comparing it with other human faculties or powers for which this strange feature is impossible. His list of other powers is a mix of eight items that begins with two faculties of perception (*seeing* and *hearing*), generalizes to *all perceptions*, moves to *desire* and *wishing*, adds two particular passions (*eros* and *fear*), and ends with a cognitive faculty, *opinion*. Immediately after mentioning opinion, Socrates speaks again of knowledge. Seth Benardete claims that the list misplaces opinion, putting it last when it should follow perception.[86] But opinion seems in fact to be in just the right place, last, where it can be paired with knowledge, last, after a whole list of powers similar to the first item on the list, seeing, in the relevant respect: seeing can *not* be of itself and of other seeings and not of what those other seeings see. A list of seven such powers—they can be called "nonreflexive" for convenience—predisposes Critias to suppose that the next item, opinion, like them, is nonreflexive. For Benardete is surely right on his main point: opinion is the special case on the list; there *is* opinion that is of itself and of other opinions and not of what the others opine. Critias's answer implies as much, for when he answers, "In no way," he gives an opinion that proves its contrary: that very opinion is an opinion that is of itself and of other opinions and not of what those opinions opine. Socrates set Critias up; he led him through powers lacking a reflexive quality and then framed his question about opinion as if it were just another one of those.

Socrates' ostensible perplexity and actual clear-headedness lead Critias into the mistake of failing to distinguish cognitive powers from non-

86. Benardete, "Interpreting Plato's *Charmides*," *Argument of the Action*, 250–51.

cognitive powers.[87] Had Critias recognized the reflexivity of opinion, he would be in a position to raise the relevant question about knowledge: if both knowledge and opinion can be of themselves and of other things like themselves but not of what those other things are of, how do knowledge and opinion differ? Could knowledge have a way of knowing what it knows and does not know that opinion lacks, keeping opinion always only opinion? A knowledge of knowledge of Socrates' sort seems to lead him to the knowledge that most "knowledge" is only knowledge so-called, opinion clothed as knowledge, nonknowledge that thinks itself knowledge and serves as a basis for action. Critias's perplexity begins right here, before Socrates calls attention to it; it begins in his false opinion about opinion, his failure to see the kinship of knowledge and opinion in the strange difference they share and the difference between them.

Socrates supplements his argument on the strangeness of knowledge by introducing relations of "multitudes and magnitudes"[88] (greater, double, heavier, older) and showing that it is impossible for such a relation to be of itself and of relations of its kind and not of what those relations are of (168a–d). If knowledge were like these relations, knowledge of knowledge would be impossible. Socrates ends (168d–e) by returning to the perceptual faculties on his previous list. Hearing will be of sound, seeing of color, but hearing would itself have to be a sound for there to be hearing of hearing; seeing would itself have to be a color for there to be seeing of seeing. Yet the verb Socrates uses for noticing the fact that "seeing would never see anything colorless" is *see*: "So you see, Critias . . ." (168e).[89] *This* seeing is of the colorless, *this* seeing is reflexive, but this seeing is an exercise of mind, not of the eye; to speak of *seeing* this way metaphorically transforms a faculty of perception into a cognitive faculty. There is a "seeing" that is of itself and of other seeings and not of what those other seeings are seeings of—as Critias *sees*. But he doesn't see himself seeing it, he doesn't *see* that cognition shares its strangeness with this sort of seeing.

The conclusion Socrates draws classifies "the things we have gone

87. As Benardete puts it, Socrates asks Critias in various ways, "'Have you noticed . . .' This faculty of noticing is not on Socrates' list, for it notices not only all other faculties as well as itself, but it also does not have any range to which it is restricted; we can call it the surveying or enumerating faculty" (ibid., 250).

88. Klein, *Commentary on Plato's "Meno,"* 24.

89. The verb Socrates uses here, *horaô*, is different from the word translated as *seeing* as the first item on Socrates' list of eight, *opsis*, the power of sight (167c). The whole discussion of possibility began with Socrates commanding Critias to "*See* what a strange thing . . ." (167c).

through": some appear impossible (e.g., those concerning multitude and magnitude), while "we vigorously distrust that the others would ever have their own power with regard to themselves" (168e). Had Critias in fact "seen" Socrates' argument, he would be in a position to distrust that vigorous distrust in the appropriate cases, for he would "see" that seeing is reflexive, that he himself offered an opinion about opinions, and that there could, perhaps, be a knowledge of knowledge that would include knowledge of opinions as nonknowledge and of seeings as questionable if unexamined. Because Socrates reports that Critias was in perplexity, it is unlikely that Critias saw that. The intricate argument devised by a Socrates feigning perplexity confirms that Socrates himself sees that there could be knowledge of knowledge, just as there is opinion of opinion and seeing of seeings.

Maybe there are "certain others," Socrates says next, who would not "vigorously distrust" the strange reflexivity of knowledge (169a). Who? "Some great man is needed, my friend," Socrates tells Critias, "who will draw this distinction capably in everything." What distinctions would the great man draw? He would determine "whether none of the beings [*tôn ontôn*] has itself by nature its own power with regard to itself[90] but has it with regard to something else." The great man would engage in ontological inquiry with respect to the nature of beings and their power to do the things they have been discussing, whether it is altogether impossible for there to be this strange thing they have defined knowledge to be, "or whether some have it and others don't"—whether knowing and opining and seeing have it as they seem to—"and again, if there are some things that themselves have it with regard to themselves, whether among them is a knowledge that we assert is sôphrosunê." The great man would do what Socrates began showing he could do in the implied distinctions in the list of examples he gave. But Socrates says that "I don't trust myself to be capable of drawing these distinctions," and that he therefore leaves open the possibility of a knowledge of knowledge, even though his argument with its examples of opining and seeing suggests that he himself possesses a kind of knowledge of knowledge. Why raise "vigorous distrust" in such knowledge? He has just heard an ambitious follower claim for himself a certain kind of knowledge of knowledges; distrust in the knowledge of knowledge would be salutary for a capable lover of honor freed of sacred restraint and believing himself to possess the knowledge of knowledges

90. The logic of the passage argues in favor of Schleiermacher's deletion of the next two words in the manuscripts, *plên epistêmês*, "except knowledge."

that equips him to be like a god in putting up words others are to obey. In a dialogue in which Socrates aims primarily to learn something himself, he here also aims to have Critias learn something, his actual perplexity.

But even if it were *possible*, Socrates says, he would still not accept that knowledge of knowledge defines sôphrosunê until he had investigated whether such knowledge were *beneficial*. Only if it were beneficial could he call it sôphrosunê because "I do divine that sôphrosunê is something beneficial and good" (169b). Socrates' divination appears at the point where he has just suggested how knowledge of knowledge is possible for him while aiming to make it seem impossible to Critias—it appears at the point where he begins to show the benefit of his knowledge of knowledge.

Having said what some great man needs to do and denied he can do it, Socrates challenges "the son of Callaeschrus" to show first that a knowledge of knowledge is possible and then that it is also beneficial. But in challenging Critias Socrates makes an obvious blunder, for he says, "*you* set it down that sôphrosunê is a knowledge of knowledge and *particularly* of non-knowledge." No, Critias spoke only of a knowledge of itself and of other knowledges and did not even mention nonknowledge (166e). Socrates had to add nonknowledge on his own. Critias will not mention nonknowledge even when he restates the definition (169d–e); and he will say again that he regards a knowledge of knowledge as the *same* as knowing what one knows and does not know (170a), thereby canceling again what Socrates here says he, Critias, introduced. By falsely alleging that Critias said what he alone said, Socrates indicates the difference between them that he will soon demonstrate.

At this point, for the only time in his long conversation with Critias, Socrates interrupts his narrative to speak directly to his auditor (169c–d; cf. 162c–d). He uses an image to picture the transmission of his perplexity to Critias: it passed to Critias like a yawn inducing another to yawn. But yawns can be voluntarily induced and voluntarily suppressed: Socrates voluntarily induced his "perplexity," and Critias voluntarily suppresses the perplexity Socrates' "perplexity" induced in him (169c). Critias can control his "yawns," he can render his perplexity invisible. But not to Socrates who reports to his auditor exactly why Critias masked his perplexity: "he is well-reputed on every occasion." Critias at thirty has already gained a striking reputation. Wanting to maintain it, "he was ashamed before those present" at his perplexity, "and he was neither willing to concede to me that he was unable to draw the distinctions I called upon him to make, nor did he say anything plain, concealing his perplexity." Socrates allows his auditor to see Socrates claim perplexity but know more than he says and his perplexed follower claim knowledge but say more than he knows.

Socrates not only breaks into his exchange with Critias to address his auditor, but for the only time in this exchange, he refrains from telling his auditor Critias's own words: Critias's words masking his perplexity are not worth reporting. But by reporting that Critias refused to concede his inability to draw the required distinctions, Socrates invites an inference about the unreported words. To the company collected in the palaistra who hold him in high repute on every occasion, Critias either said or implied: I can make the distinctions that need to be made; I am the great man needed. Socrates did not introduce the "great man" in order to suggest an immodest implication about himself; he introduced him in order to induce Critias to display his view of himself—and the view he needs others to have of him. Critias did what he was scripted to do. He did it naturally, teaching his teacher his nature.

Does Critias know himself well enough to know he does not know? Or is he fooling himself when he fails to fool Socrates? He will soon show that he has in fact persuaded himself at thirty that he possesses the supposed knowledge he acted on both as a famous public intellectual and later when he was given the opportunity to become the great man of Athens, the man needed to solve the political problems of postwar Athens, the man Critias imagined he was because he imagined he possessed the ruling knowledge that knows itself and other knowledges. Socrates does not report to the little crowd in the palaistra that he knows Critias is perplexed. Would they have seen as clearly as he did that Critias's words were unclear? Instead of charging him with perplexity in front of those whose high repute he needs, Socrates makes every effort to induce knowledge of the perplexity in him that would alone enable him to moderate himself in his immoderate claim to an impossible knowledge.

Socrates has refuted Critias, as Critias feared (166c), and done so by keeping to the argument, not, as Critias charged, by abandoning it. He now reports how he recovered the conversation from whatever words Critias used to hide his perplexity (169d). This second phase of his argument shows that Critias's perplexity did not end with the unreported speech hiding it. For Socrates now takes advantage of Critias's not knowing how the power of knowledge is distinguished from the other powers: he shows that Critias does not know how a knowledge of knowledge might extend to a knowledge of knowledges, but not to the technocratic knowledge of knowledges Critias presumes to possess.

Socrates' new beginning (169d) concedes what he in any case knows, that a knowledge of knowledge *could* come to be, and he raises a different question: even if one had a knowledge of knowledge, how would that contribute to knowing what one knows and what one does not know? And he reminds Critias that this is what "we were saying know thyself and being sôphrôn" means. In fact, this is what *Socrates* said it meant, but his inclusive *we* sets up the second part of his argument,[91] because it brings into play both definitions of sôphrosunê stemming from the Delphic "Know thyself": Critias's knowledge of itself and of other knowledges; and Socrates' knowing what one knows and does not know. Critias doesn't think there's a problem here, and his statement shows how he interpreted Socrates' definition: "if someone has a knowledge that itself knows itself, he himself would be of the same sort as what he has" (169e)—I myself know myself because I have the knowledge that knows itself. I don't dispute that, Socrates says, it's something different that I wonder about. That something different concerns the definition of sôphrosunê he introduced and just what it added to what Critias had said: "what necessity is there for him who has this [knowledge of knowledge] to know both what he knows and what he does not know?" Socrates thus asks Critias how he understands the relation between his own supposed "knowledge of knowledge" and Socrates' "knowledge of what one knows and does not know." Critias's response shows that he has thought little about the definition Socrates had to introduce on his own: "this is the same as that" (170a). Critias regards what Socrates added to his own definition as insignificant.

"I'm still the way I always was," Socrates reminds his associate who has not seen him for three years, "for I still don't understand how knowing what one knows and knowing what one does not know are the same." Socrates is still the way he always was, still asking tricky questions as he does here in the most complicated part of their exchange. "What are you saying?" Critias asks—a completely reasonable question, for Socrates has just used the word Critias used, *same* (*autos*), but used it ambiguously: are you saying that you don't understand how the two things you just named are the same as each other or how those two together are the same as a knowledge of knowledge? Socrates meant the latter: if there is a knowledge of knowledge, will it know "anything more than this: that this one of these is a knowledge and that one is not a knowledge?" This is what Socrates is saying and has always been saying: to have a knowledge of knowledge in his sense is to possess the necessary criteria for distinguishing between

91. It suggests too that Critias's unreported words were an unclear effort to show that knowledge of knowledge is possible.

knowledge and nonknowledge, enabling one to say about some knowledge claims, this is knowledge, and about others, this cannot possibly count as knowledge, it's opinion that can't be substantiated. When Critias answers that a knowledge of knowledge will be able to do precisely that (answers in effect that they are the same), Socrates again uses *same* ambiguously: "So are knowledge and non-knowledge of the healthful, and knowledge and non-knowledge of the just the same?" Critias correctly infers that Socrates again means the same as knowledge of knowledge, for his "In no way" leads Socrates to explain what he meant: "One, I suppose, is doctoring, one is politics, and one is nothing other than knowledge" (170b).

Here Socrates' complex, knotted little argument does more than perplex Critias, here it begins to demonstrate that Critias not only lacks a knowledge of knowledge in Socrates' sense but lacks as well the knowledge of knowledges with which his own definitions culminated and, most tellingly, lacks a knowledge of precisely that knowledge which he most decidedly supposes he knows. For Socrates just referred to three subject matters (the healthful, the just, and knowledge) and distinguished those three from the three knowledges that govern them (doctoring, politics, and knowledge, 170b). Socrates' questioning (170b–c) assumes that each of the knowledges is confined exclusively to one subject matter knowable by its knowledge alone: the healthful by the knowledge that is doctoring, the just by the knowledge that is politics, and knowledges by the knowledge that is of knowledge. If that's the case, then sôphrosunê as the knowledge of knowledge cannot know what doctoring or politics knows—their subject matters can be known exclusively by their appropriate knowledges, while a knowledge of knowledge knows exclusively knowledges. Socrates' skillful questioning allows the example of *politics* as a knowledge and the *just* as its subject matter to flash up only once and to disappear again behind two other knowledges and their subject matters, music which knows harmonics, house building which knows house building. In the brief moment when the examples center on politics as the knowledge of the just, Socrates poses no question that would allow Critias to respond regarding his supposed knowledge of the knowledge politics and its subject matter the just, the relevant knowledge of knowledges that Critias must inescapably claim, both as a sophist during his long famous career and as a tyrant in the final disastrous display of his supposed knowledge of politics and the just. Instead, Socrates' questions (170b) are about the knowledge of knowledge. When he finally does pose a question about the possibility that the knower of knowledge knows other knowledges (170c), politics has been supplanted by music and house building, and the question he asks is, if sôphrosunê is a knowledge only of knowledges, how will a person know by sôphrosunê that he knows the healthful or house building? "He will in no way," Critias says (170c), an answer he would have found it more difficult to give had Socrates' question been about the just. Our brilliant questioner is not perplexed.

Socrates' questions in conclusion (170d) draw only conditional answers from a Critias who must be realizing that he has surrendered any meaningful content to "knowledge of knowledges" but is ashamed to show either that he erred or that he is confused. "Then he who is ignorant of this [the healthful and house building] will not know *what* he knows [the healthful and house building] but only *that* he knows [doctoring and the house building art]." "It is likely," Critias grants, as he must. The knower of knowledges seems to know that there are such knowledges but not what they know, to know that there are arts of doctoring and house building without knowing their subjects, the healthful and house building. "Probably," Critias replies, leading Socrates to an additional point (170d): such a knower of knowledges will not "be able to examine whether another claiming to have knowledge of something does have knowledge or doesn't have knowledge of what he says he has knowledge of." "It appears not," says Critias, who claimed to possess the sôphrosunê that is knowledge of knowledges—*he* would not be able to examine any claimant to knowledge to ascertain whether he knows or does not know. Socrates, however, claiming only to be perplexed, is examining a claimant to the knowledge of knowledges and showing that he does not have that knowledge—he is doing with Critias precisely what the argument claims one with a knowledge of knowledge could not do. The action of the argument shows that Socrates in fact possesses the knowledge whose possibility was left an open question (169d).

After drawing his conclusions about the ostensible impotence of a knowledge of knowledge, Socrates drops all the other examples he introduced and concentrates exclusively on the example with special bite because Critias forced him to play it: the doctor (170e–171d). One who lacks knowledge of knowledge "won't be able to judge between one who pretends to be a doctor but is not and one who truly is" (170e). The one pretending to be a doctor addresses this claim to the one who forced him to pretend. Is this pretender a true doctor? *Critias* won't be able to judge. As for Socrates, he now shows how a knower of knowledge would investigate a doctor. He wouldn't converse with him about doctoring—a knowledge—because a doctor doesn't know his knowledge, he knows only the subject matter of his knowledge, the healthful. Just so, the sôphrôn one, knowing only knowledge, will know that the doctor has a kind of knowledge, but how will he investigate what that knowledge is of (171a)? By investigating "what is spoken and done . . . whether what is spoken is truly spoken and what is done is correctly done" (171c). But given what they've assumed about the exclusivity of knowledges, "would someone without doctoring be able to follow either of these?" Perplexed Critias is led to conclude that a knower, knowing only knowledges, cannot know what another knower knows and therefore cannot distinguish a true knower from a fake (171a–c). Critias claims to be a knower of knowledges and Socrates has just shown him to be a fake—and he did it with an argument "proving" that he cannot do what he's doing.

Critias is left in perplexity and makes no speech to hide it. Critias cannot draw the necessary distinctions. In the first part of the argument, he could not give an account of the strange power of knowledge to know itself and other knowings but not what those other knowings know. Lacking that, he could not, in this second part of the argument, show how the knowledge of knowledge is the same as knowing what one knows and does not know—he *said* they were the same, but Socrates showed he did not know how they were the same. Socrates, however, by successfully examining his "patient" not as a doctor with respect to health but as a knower with respect to knowledge, shows how they are the same in his sense and that he himself is a knower—he has the knowledge of knowledge, which knows that this is knowledge and that is not, the knowledge without which it would not be possible to examine others on knowledge as he just examined Critias. The knowledge of knowledge and knowing what one knows and does not know are the same. A knowledge of knowledge, then, is a knowledge of the character of knowledge, of its nature and limits; knowing that, one can examine others and say with respect to their knowledge claims: this is possible knowledge, that is not. Knowing the strange power of knowledge to know itself and other knowings and not what those other knowings are of, Socrates can do what he did with Critias.

But could he, being a knower and not a doctor, do the same with a doctor? He said how it would be done: by examining what the doctor said and did. Without doctoring he could not examine what the doctoring of the other doctored, but as a knower he could examine what that doctor claimed to know in his saying and doing. Having just done what he did with Critias, whose knowing has to do with politics and the just, wouldn't he have done a similar thing with the doctor he introduced earlier, that Thracian doctor who the play-doctor Socrates alleged taught him a new medicine? Socrates' success with Critias invites one to suppose he succeeded too in judging whether the doctor of the god Zalmoxis knew what he was saying and doing as a doctor. Examining him as a knower, the knower Socrates would have concluded about the doctor of Zalmoxis what the source of his tale, Herodotus, says the Greeks concluded about Zalmoxis: he's a fake.

Socrates is the great man needed. He knows what he knows and what he does not know, that he does not know it. He possesses a knowledge of knowledge, the knowledge that knows itself and other knowledges though not what those other knowledges know. Being such a knower, he can examine Critias to discover how his philosophy has fared in his absence. Learning this, he can do what *Charmides* shows him beginning to do: attempt to moderate Critias's misplaced self-assurance as a knower. Beyond that—far beyond—he can do what the *Republic* will show him doing: change the way he presents his philosophy to ambitious young Athenians, wrapping his knowledge in fake knowledge, chanting a new medicine for the soul that he supposedly learned from a Thracian doctor.

Socrates' examination of Critias on the knowledge of knowledge solves the perplexity Socrates alleged and Critias displayed. It shows that a knowledge of *knowledges* is possible in one way only: a knowledge of knowledge knows whether knowledges' claims to knowledge are possible or not. Critias's knowledge of knowledges claimed to know what knowledges are knowledge *of*, but he can know neither the healthful nor the just nor house building. Critias's knowledge of knowledges is impossible. Socrates' knowledge of knowledges is possible and actual, as he shows by demonstrating that Critias's knowledge of knowledges is not knowledge.

"It would be grandly beneficial," Socrates says when this argument is over, if the one with sôphrosunê "knows both what he knows and what he doesn't know—that he knows the one and that he doesn't know the other—and if he were able to investigate someone else in this same state" (171d). Just what would the grand benefits be of the knowledge Socrates just demonstrated he has and Critias lacks?

10. The Benefit of Socrates' Sôphrosunê (171d–175a)

What kind of good is sôphrosunê? As Socrates turns last to the benefit of sôphrosunê, he sets out two different ways of construing its good; one is Critias's, the other his own. The consideration of the *benefit* of sôphrosunê thus repeats the complex operation employed for its *possibility*: Socrates' final definition measures and refutes Critias's final definition. But on the issue of benefit, Socrates' discussion is even more truncated and dense, for it treats a theme they have not even discussed: wise rule.[92] Such rapidity and lack of explanation befit *Charmides* as a master draws out from his pupil what he has made of his teaching. As for the auditor and reader, we are left to infer just how the pupil misunderstood his master's pre-Potidaean teaching on sôphrosunê as the benefit of wise rule.

Socrates takes full charge, making long speeches broken only by responses from Critias that are virtually dictated by Socrates' questions.[93] Socrates now assumes as *possible* what his argument about possibility questioned: the sôphrôn one knows what he knows and what he does not know and can examine others for what they know and do not know (171d). It is this definition, the one Socrates added last, whose benefit they examine—four times he says that this is the definition in question.[94] With the first and last of these repetitions he says that it is this definition that they were setting down "from the beginning"—but Socrates introduced that *last*. This oddity plus repeated vague temporal references to a *then* and a *now* suggests that Socrates is referring back to what Critias heard *from the beginning* of his contact with Socrates, prior to Socrates' departure for Potidaea. The temporal gap is between *that* then and *this* now—what Critias *then* took from Socrates' philosophy forces Socrates *now* to reduce him to perplexity.

With breathtaking suddenness Socrates announces just how "grandly beneficial to us" we assert sôphrosunê to be: "we would live through life without error, we ourselves . . . and all others who were ruled by us" (171d). Perfect knowledge achieves perfect rule as "we ourselves would not attempt to do what we didn't have knowledge of, but we would find those who had knowledge and hand it over to them" (171e), a deferring that requires knowledge of what one does not know. Knowing what we don't know, we yield to superior knowers, but "to others whom we ruled, we would not turn over anything to be done except what they would do correctly when they did it, and this would be what they had knowledge of," a ruling that

92. At the end of his examination of Charmides, Socrates touched the issue of managing the city (161e–162a). *Rule* (*archein*) is used first by Socrates at 171d8.

93. It is characteristic of this long exchange on the good of sôphrosunê that without exception each speech is accompanied by a narrative phrase such as "I said" or "he said" ($171a_9$–$173e_1$). Conversely, the long argument on the possibility of an effective knowledge of knowledge that immediately precedes it began with "'What are you saying,' *he said*" (170a6), ended much later with "'It appears so,' *he said*" (171c9), and contained between these speeches not even one such narrative phrase.

94. 171d, 172a, b, c. After these four, at $173a_{10}$ Socrates refers to sôphrosunê "being such as we now define it," leaving undefined what he has just repeatedly defined.

presumes knowledge of what those others know and do not know. Perfect rule by perfect knowledge is pictured on the modest scale of managing a household and the grand scale of governing a city and "everything else that sôphrosunê could rule." Socrates presents this apex as implied in his own definition of sôphrosunê, which he set out in complete form as the premise to his claims (171d). But it must represent as well what Critias imagined as the benefit of his own supposed knowledge of knowledges.

Socrates completes his sudden portrait of perfect rule by perfect knowledge: "with error taken away and correctness leading, it is necessary for those so situated to do nobly and well in every doing, and for those who do well to be happy" (172a–b)—doing well and being happy is the standard Socrates will repeatedly invoke to measure the benefit of sôphrosunê. The question Socrates finally asks is direct but includes a vague time reference: "Isn't this, Critias, what we were saying when we said how much of a good it would be to know both what one knows and what one does not know?" In fact today they said nothing at all about rule. But Critias betrays by the vehemence of his assent that this "certainly is" what he understood sôphrosunê to imply. Fully familiar with what Socrates has not even mentioned today, Critias confirms that this is the interpretation he placed on Socrates' pre-Potidaean words: supposing that he knows himself and possesses the knowledge of knowledges, Critias imagined himself the perfect ruler of the perfect city. Socrates jerks them from that indefinite past to their immediate present: "*Now*, though, you see that no such knowledge has appeared anywhere." Critias has no alternative but to assent.

Socrates' next speech sharpens his distinction between then and now. He refers to what "we are *now* discovering sôphrosunê to be" and the "good" that it would have ($172b_1$), a different good from the good of perfect rule that followed from "what we *were* saying." The sôphrôn one "will learn more easily whatever else he learns and everything else he learns will appear more distinct to him, since in addition to each thing he learns, he will also discern the knowledge." This good still includes a kind of knowledge of knowledges, but instead of leading to rule it would allow one to "examine others more fittingly [*kallion*] about what he himself has learned"—examine Critias, say, on his supposed knowledge of knowledges. This good is decidedly more modest than what Socrates just caused them to imagine: were they then "looking at something greater and requiring [sôphrosunê] to be something greater than it is" (172c)? "Maybe that's so" is all Critias can manage in response to this reduced benefit of sôphrosunê with its implication that he imagined it to be something greater than it is.

"Certain strange things about sôphrosunê," Socrates now claims, "are becoming clearly apparent to me." Before stating those strange things, he restates what they have been conceding: that knowledge of knowledge is possible and that sôphrosunê is knowing both what one knows and what one does not know (172c–d). This is not strange, though they still need to ask just what its profit for them is. It is the something greater and *its* supposed good that cause strange things to appear: "as to what we were saying just now, how great a good sôphrosunê would be if it is such as this, leading to the management of household and city, in my opinion, Critias, we have not agreed fittingly [*kalôs*]"—*fitting* will ring through the following little exchange as a sign of Critias's incredulity at the strange things he's hearing. How was it not fitting? he asks. They should not have agreed, Socrates replies, that "it is some great good for human beings if each of us does what he knows and hands over what he does not have knowledge of to others who have knowledge" (172d). "And our agreement was *not* fitting?" Critias asks in disbelief. "What you're saying is truly strange, Socrates" (172e). Strange things arise, Socrates says, because of differences between the way he "looked at it then and just now";[95] as a result, "I feared we were not investigating correctly." The strange thing is this precise fear about their investigation: "For truly, even if sôphrosunê is such a thing [as perfect rule], it's not clear in my opinion that it produces a good for us" (173a). The student can't believe his teacher: how could a sôphrosunê that leads to perfect rule not produce a great good for us? "I suppose I'm babbling," Socrates says, while affirming that "it's necessary to investigate just what appears and not to pass by indifferently if one is concerned for oneself even a little." "Now *that's* spoken fittingly," Critias says, though it remains truly strange that Socrates judges their earlier agreement unfitting.

"Hear my dream," Socrates commands, "whether it came through horns or through ivory." "Hear my dream and interpret it," Penelope commanded[96] before relating her dream and her horns-and-ivory distinction between dreams. Socrates chooses to make his whole argument about the benefit of sôphrosunê ride on a dream and on Penelope's principle of interpreting dreams. "Those dreams that come through the gate of sawn ivory deceive bringing words which are unfulfilled; but those that come through the gate of polished horn fulfill true things, when any mortal sees."[97] Penelope tells her dream of the eagle killing her twenty geese in her first conversation with returned Odysseus, still disguised as a beggar. She alleges

95. Following the reading of MS B: *houtôs ei entautha*.
96. *Odyssey* 19.535.
97. *Odyssey* 19.564–67.

to the "stranger" that her dream came through the gate of sawn ivory, but she knows it to be a true dream that came through the gate of polished horn, for it conveys perfectly to the beggar that she has recognized him as her long-awaited husband who will see and fulfill her dream.[98] Resourceful Penelope has just told him of her capacity for guile, her tricking the suitors through weaving and unweaving Laertes' shroud; she is like her husband, who "tells lies like the truth."[99] Telling a fake dream to a fake beggar, she tells her wily husband: I know who you are, I know what you must do, and you can trust that I know that what I know must not be told. Recognizing him and communicating her recognition to him, she then informs him that she will arrange on the next day the contest of the bow that initiates what he must do. Socrates' babbling, his invitation to judge whether "my dream" came through horns or through ivory, invokes the most marvelous recognition scene in all of the *Odyssey*, the most intimate, the most guileful, the heaviest in portent. Penelope's dream is no dream, it is her knowledge parading as a dream, giving itself to be taken as a dream by all but one who will see it and fulfill it—that dream spreads its penetrating light over Socrates' dream.

After his invitation to measure his dream by this Homeric precedent, Socrates states it: sôphrosunê "would rule us totally," sôphrosunê "being such as we now define it" (173a), a vague formulation permitting the dream to represent Critias's claim to a knowledge of knowledges. Rulers ruled by sôphrosunê would know how to detect fakes: anyone claiming to be a pilot while not being one would be unable to deceive them, nor would they be unaware of a doctor or a general or anyone else pretending to know something he didn't know. With knowledge ruling the knowledges, bodies would be healthier, travels and wars safer, all products including "all footwear" technologically more advanced. To cap his dream of perfect rule Socrates adds one more knowledge: "let us concede that divination too is a knowledge of what is to be." Presiding (173d_1) even over that presider, sôphrosunê "would turn away the boasters and establish true diviners for us, prophets of what is to be." Socrates' addition of divination as a knowledge recalls the single previous reference to a diviner: Critias said that the wise man who put up the words "Know thyself" spoke "like a diviner" (164e). Socrates' dream adds the true diviner, the wise man speaking

98. Brann, *Homeric Moments*: "When does Penelope recognize Odysseus? At first sight, of course" (274). Brann goes on to prove most beautifully from Penelope's words that she recognized her husband from the start.

99. *Odyssey* 19.203; Penelope related her guileful weaving and unweaving at 19.137–63.

like a diviner, putting up new words of the gods; the dreamer of perfect rule knows he must rule even the gods. "That humankind so equipped, would act and live on the basis of knowledge [*epistêmonôs*],[100] I can follow," Socrates says, but he ends his dream on a reservation bound to startle Critias: "but that in acting on the basis of knowledge we would do well and be happy—this we are not yet able to learn, my dear Critias" (173d).

Acting and living on the basis of knowledge, acting and living within a hierarchy of presidings in which knowledge always rules—knowledge-governed rule over knowledge-directed *technai—this* dream Socrates suggests may come through sawn ivory. Critias must protest; this is the dream he dreams, believing it to come through polished horn: "But you will certainly not easily find some other delimitation of doing well if you dishonor *by knowledge* [*epistêmonôs*]" (173d). Socrates in no way dishonors *by knowledge*; instead, his caution points to one more knowledge, a knowledge whose presence or absence makes his dream benefit or bane, for his masterful, knowing questioning prompts a final phrase from Critias that names that last knowledge. "Teach me yet a little thing in addition," he says, approaching the biggest thing. "Of what are you saying '*by knowledge*'?" But he gives Critias no chance to answer the general question, for he asks immediately, "Of shoemaking?"—a mischievous first candidate, shoemaking having been Critias's first example of disgraceful knowledge (163b).[101] Critias's emphatic denials that he means knowledges like shoemaking or working in bronze or wool or wood permit Socrates to say that it's not living *by knowledge* in some general sense that makes one happy, but instead "the happy man is defined well as *one* of those who live *by knowledge*." Which one? Could Critias mean the one Socrates just reintroduced, the one "who knows everything that is going to be, the diviner? Are you saying it is he or someone else?" (174a). "Both he and another," Critias replies. "Who?" Socrates asks, but immediately adds, "the one who in addition to knowing everything that is going to be, knows everything that was and everything that now is [*ta onta*] and is ignorant of nothing? Let us set down that someone of this sort exists." We are still in the world of the dream, where such a one can be thought to exist, for Critias thinks it's him. But Socrates asks no question about that postulated perfect knower. Instead, he asks

100. To act and live *epistêmonôs* is the core of Socrates' dream—*epistêmonôs* is the adverbial form of *epistêmê* (knowledge, skill, scientific knowledge) and means knowledgeably, by knowledge, on the basis of knowledge, or in accordance with knowledge. I have unavoidably had to vary the words used to translate *epistêmonôs*.

101. Socrates slyly included "all footwear" in his dream as one of the things that knowledge-based rule would improve (173c).

only if there's anyone more knowledgeable than the perfect knower. "Of course not" is all Critias can say. Again Socrates replaces his general question ("Which of the knowledges makes him happy?") with a particular one ("All of them alike?"), knowing that Critias is bound to answer no. "But which one in particular?" Socrates asks and repeats immediately his list of knowledges of the possible beings: "The knowledge by which he knows *what* among what is (*tôn ontôn*) and what was and is to be?" Critias does not get to answer this question either, for Socrates continues to toy with him: "The one by which he knows draught playing?" Not by that one, of course, and not by calculation. Not even by the *healthful*, though "*More*" that. "Then *most* what that I speak of?" Socrates says. "That by which he knows what?" At last the telling question is allowed to stand: knowledge of *what* makes doing well and being happy possible? And not just for one individual but for what the dream depicts, the knowledge which is the "little thing in addition" that would ensure that all in the dreamed-of order live well and are happy. At last Critias is allowed to answer: "That by which [he knows] the good and the evil.'"[102]

"Wretch!" Socrates says for a second time, chiding Critias for this final quotation from his philosophy as he chided Charmides for the first (161b): Charmides and Critias show what wretches have done to Socrates' philosophy in his absence. Charmides has reputedly become distinguished for both wisdom and beauty but he lacks both the desire and the competence to make Socrates' philosophy his own. Critias had absorbed its phrases before Socrates left, but he distorted Socrates' riddling words for sôphrosunê into an immoderate dream of perfect rule, elevating himself to perfect ruler with a knowledge of knowledges including the knowledge of good and evil.

Now Socrates knows that Critias was set to dreaming by his own words. His teaching on the words put up at Delphi released Critias into the freedom to do his own things as the good things; and his elevation of a ruling knowledge of knowledge led him to dream that a knower of knowledges could effect perfect rule. For Socrates to divine *Critias's* dream is to learn that he himself helped author it, for a dream like Critias's arises naturally when a man of Critias's nature, "anxious to contend and win honor" (162c),

102. With respect to good and evil, Socrates earlier reported that Thracian medicine held that the evil things and the good things all started from the soul (156e). Good and evil also appeared with the second definition Socrates elicited from Critias, the doing of good things; at that point Socrates' second or central "back again" asked for a plainer definition of good and evil things (163d–e).

is led to think of sôphrosunê as Socrates defined it; he is moved to act on what he supposes is knowledge. But a man of Critias's nature, needing to be well reputed on every occasion (169c), resists by nature knowing what he does not know; he is unable to know his own not-knowing. Returning to Athens after a long absence Socrates learns that his own teaching led Critias to dream himself the ideal ruler of a city based on the ideal of knowledge. Examining Critias, the true diviner sees the future tyrant. He does not divine that the soul of Critias is bent on evil; he divines that it is subject to a dream. Critias is not the victim of an evil nature, nor did Socrates corrupt him by an evil doctrine. Instead, Socrates corrupted Critias by opening a path to the natural human dream of an enlightened human community founded and administered by enlightened knowers. Many Athenians will shed their blood because of Critias, and Athenian history will brand him evil. But Critias is not thirsty for Athenian blood, he's thirsty for Athenian perfection under his knowing rule and prepared to sacrifice Athenians who impede his ideal. Returning from Potidaea to inquire about the state of philosophy, Socrates learns that his own philosophy helped corrupt a talented and honor-loving young Athenian by leading him to dream.[103]

By showing Socrates measuring Critias's dream of perfect rule, *Charmides* implies that Socrates measured as well that other dream of perfect rule introduced in the dialogue, one that stands silent in the background until Socrates makes it foreground again at the end: the dream of the doctor of Zalmoxis. His medicine, like Critias's rule, springs from a dream of perfection based on a claim to perfect knowledge by the perfect knower, the god who knows everything and reveals the important knowledges to his followers. When Socrates added divination to the knowledges presided over by the knower of knowledges, he suggested that false divining is boasting. The doctor of Zalmoxis boasts that the only god revealed the truth to him and taught him the incantations that properly treat the immortal soul; one who knows what he knows and does not know can examine that knower's knowledge or nonknowledge. Socrates' dream measures the deceiving dreams of enlightenment generated naturally both by reason and by revelation.

103. On the common judgment against Critias as "evil" see the counterarguments in Notomi, "Critias and the Origin of Plato's Political Philosophy." In his Seventh Letter, Plato refers to the "evil deeds" of the Thirty who included "some of my relatives" (324b–325a). Xenophon makes Critias's vengeance and greed graphic in his history, *Hellenica* II, 3.15–16, 21–22, 43. 4.1, 21, 40; and in his *Memorabilia* calls Critias "the most thievish, violent, and murderous of all in the oligarchy" (1.2.12).

Knowledge of good and evil is the last of six phrases Socrates prompts Critias to speak, the others all being definitions of sôphrosunê. Judging by the sequence of phrases—whose order Socrates alone directs—Socrates' pre-Potidaean investigation of sôphrosunê culminated in the problem of knowledge of good and evil for the wise rule of human beings. Socrates' last argument in *Charmides* shows how a knowledge of good and evil stands to "my dream" of perfect rule through a knowledge of knowledge.

Socrates accuses Critias of dragging him around in a circle (174b), but in fact he drags Critias and not in a circle but in an ever-deepening penetration into what he made of Socrates' philosophy in Socrates' absence. He accuses Critias of concealing from him that it was not living knowledgeably that made one "do well and be happy" but one knowledge alone, knowledge of good and evil. Using three examples just given in his dream (doctor, pilot, and general) but dropping diviner, Socrates argues that they do not need knowledge of good and evil to perform their *technai* expertly but that "we will be deprived of having each of these done well and beneficially if this knowledge is absent" (174d): the ends that the knowledges of doctor, pilot, and general serve, the good and evil they serve, require supervision by the knowledge of good and evil. Socrates' argument retains the hierarchy of knowledges pictured in the dream; the knowledge of good and evil governs the governing arts of medicine, piloting, and generalship, directing them to the good or evil it alone knows. The art of benefit, then, is not "the knowledge of knowledges and non-knowledges but of good and evil." Socrates' argument retains the exclusivity of knowledges and their products—one knowledge, one product: "So if [knowledge of good and evil] is beneficial, sôphrosunê would be something other than beneficial to us" (174d).

Critias is unwilling to surrender the beneficiality of sôphrosunê as he understands it, as the knowledge of knowledges, and for the last time resists what Socrates says. He states his resistance by taking up the verb of governance Socrates introduced in the dream: as knowledge of knowledges, sôphrosunê "*presides over*" (*epistatei*, 174d$_9$; see 173c$_5$) the other knowledges (*epistêmais*). He claims that "since it would *rule* [*archousa*, 174e$_1$; see 171d$_8$, e$_3$] the knowledge of the good, it would benefit us." Critias's objection sounds reasonable and confirms his own aspiration as made evident in *Charmides*: this knower of knowledges believes he can rule knowledge of good and evil by putting up words to define it for all and to "benefit *us*." Given the self-centered way in which Critias already interpreted "one's own" and "the good things," *us* is restricted: his rule serves primarily the advantage of the ruler. Not only does Critias think he is the great man needed to draw the distinctions that in fact perplex him, he thinks the dream Socrates called "my dream" is his. Socrates must now perplex him about his dream.

The terse little argument Socrates now makes (174e–175a) aims to put Critias in as much perplexity about the benefit of sôphrosunê as his previous argument did about its possibility. Socrates speaks of three knowledges only, sôphrosunê, knowledge of good and evil, and doctoring. Each of the three could claim to be the knowledge of benefits: doctoring, the knowledge of health; sôphrosunê, which Socrates identifies as "a knowledge only of knowledge and of non-knowledge but of nothing else," and knowledge of good and evil, which Socrates now argues must alone be the art of benefits. Would sôphrosunê "also make someone healthy rather than doctoring," he asks, "and would it make the other products of the arts too?" (174e). To say so would violate their premise of one knowledge, one product, and they were "long bearing witness that [sôphrosunê] is a knowledge only of knowledge and of non-knowledge": it cannot be "a craftsman of health." Then it cannot be "a craftsman of benefit" either. "How then will sôphrosunê be beneficial if it is a craftsman of no benefit?" "*In no way*, Socrates; *at least as is likely*." Critias's last words in Socrates' examination of him consist of a statement of certainty qualified immediately by a confession of uncertainty: Critias ends in perplexity. And Socrates leaves him in perplexity, permitting him no further speech after his baffled words, for Socrates now closes down his investigation with a long valedictory speech that he ends by turning to Charmides and putting his final questions to him. Socrates ends, no longer allowing Critias to hide his perplexity in unreported speeches but stopping him in his very exhibition of it.

In his brief resistance to Socrates' argument, Critias maintained that the knowledge of knowledges rules the knowledge of good and evil (174d–e). This must be Socrates' view of the hierarchy of knowledges as well. But good and evil is the most powerful thing on earth, ruling the thousand peoples through their thousand tablets of the good, ruling as our belief in what is good for us and evil for us.[104] Knowledge of good and evil rules human beings as the ultimate practical or moral knowledge, but it is not simply ultimate either as knowledge or as rule. As a "knowledge"—a claimed knowledge—knowledge of good and evil is presided over by the unique knowledge, sôphrosunê in Socrates' sense, knowledge of knowledge. Knowledge of knowledge presides over all knowledges by ruling in or ruling out what can count as knowledge (170a); it rules absolutely,

104. Nietzsche, *Thus Spoke Zarathustra*, First Part, "On the Thousand Goals and One."

accepting no supervision from beyond itself.[105] Sôphrosunê in this sense stands to knowledge of good and evil as theoretical knowledge to practical knowledge. As theoretical knowledge, fruit of the passionate pursuit of the knowledge of the beings and of knowledge itself, it is ruled by nothing other than itself, not even by benefit, not even by good and evil; driven solely by the passion to know which directed it to know knowing, it stands beyond good and evil, knowing good and evil and its power to rule. What perplexes Critias in Socrates' argument on benefit is that Socrates' sôphrosunê is *beyond* benefit, whereas his own understanding is enclosed within benefit, within his inescapable subjection to the good of reputation and the evil of shame. Critias's perplexity reflects his failure to penetrate Socratic sôphrosunê in its true radicality, its autonomy beyond good and evil. Socrates is free in a way that Critias can never be.

When Socrates demonstrated the *impossibility* of Critias's understanding of sôphrosunê, he demonstrated the actuality of his own. Does his argument questioning the *benefit* of Critias's understanding of sôphrosunê demonstrate the benefit of his own—despite its being beyond benefit in its ground or reason?[106] The answer hinges on "*my* dream"—is it really *Socrates*' dream? This is the strangest of the "strange things" that Socrates says overtake him when he considers the benefit of sôphrosunê. For what he caused to happen after he described "my dream" of perfect rule showed that the benefit or bane of his dream hangs on one thing only, possessing or lacking knowledge of good and evil. The knowledges considered in his argument arrange themselves hierarchically. Sôphrosunê as the knowledge of knowledge presides over all knowledges; knowledge of good and evil as the knowledge of benefits presides over the benefits any knowledge can bring, whether doctoring, piloting, generalship, or shoemaking. *Charmides* suggests that Socrates has knowledge of knowledge; when he forces the knowledge of good and evil into the discussion, he suggests that as a knower of knowing he knows the knowledge of good and evil. The absence of *one* knowledge prevented Socrates from saying that "we would do well and be happy" in the perfectly ruled city (173d); possession of that knowledge qualifies its possessor to rule for the well-being and happiness of all. Socrates' love of wisdom carried him beyond good and evil to a knowledge

105. "The science of science cannot be subordinate to any science." Benardete, "Plato's *Charmides*," *Argument of the Action*, 256.

106. That its benefit lies in the first instance in its own satisfaction is implied by its being a passion. What is at issue here is its being a benefit for others.

of knowledge and to a true dream of its benefit. The greatest strangeness of "my dream" is this: perfect rule is rule by the philosopher.

The full meaning of Socrates' invitation to measure his dream by Penelope's standard only now comes to light. Her dream of eagle and geese dreams of the restoration of rightful rule through the destruction of pretenders, aspirants to illegitimate rule. The promised benefit of Socratic sôphrosunê is nothing less than the restoration of rightful rule, rule by the wise. Rule by Homer was rightful rule by a wise man, but the demise of Homeric rule has brought a host of pretenders among whom Critias must be numbered. When Socrates presents as a dream his return to Athens to restore the rightful rule of the wise, he does what Penelope did: she acted as if her dream were a deceptive dream whose words would never be fulfilled, but she knew that her dream fulfills the truth for any mortal that sees—and Odysseus saw and fulfilled its truth. As is fitting, almost all will think that Socrates' dream came through the gate of sawn ivory, for after all, didn't Socrates refute it? But a few will see that it came through the gate of polished horn and that Socrates acts to fulfill it.

By showing what Socrates' sôphrosunê is, *Charmides* shows that when Socrates acts he does his own things, the good things, knowing himself, knowing knowledge, and knowing how to examine others to see if what they take to be knowledge is knowledge or nonknowledge. Knowing that most humans act as Critias acts, on the basis of nonknowledge they suppose to be knowledge, Socrates will act to align action-inspiring nonknowledge with what he knows to be good, act to put up the most authoritative words as a new medicine for the soul. And this is sôphrosunê? To think through the fundamental word for human restraint as Socrates does is to be driven by the unrestrained passion to know. At its most extreme that knowing is led to the most extreme acting, action aimed at rule by putting up authoritative words of the gods. Socrates is restrained in his unrestraint: he keeps to the ancient words. It is wholly appropriate that he set the word *sôphrosunê* over his extreme knowing and acting, for while that word hides his unrestraint, it names his true restraint: his knowing and acting are beyond good and evil yet oriented to the good.

Driven to know knowing irrespective of benefit, Socrates learns he is not spared acting with a view to benefit. Returning to Athens after a long absence and learning what was made of his philosophy by the talented Critias, he learns that he must act on behalf of what his inquiry has shown him to be necessary for the good of Critias, Athens, and himself—ultimately for himself and perhaps also for his fit intimates, for philosophy. By ending on a hierarchy of the knowledges, *Charmides* shows that when

Socrates acts he acts with a knowledge of knowledge that presides over all other knowledges, in particular the knowledge of good and evil, benefit-bringing knowledge. When the knower of knowledge acts beneficially in the most comprehensive way, he acts as a legislator who knows how to put the names *good* and *evil* on the appropriate deeds and things (175b). *Charmides* suggests that such actions peak in putting up words in the sacred places where they are taken as counsel from the gods. *Charmides* also suggests that the knower of knowledge, acting in that legislative manner, acts also as a doctor who knows the way to health of the soul and has knowledge of its proper medicine, incantations that induce sôphrosunê.

By intimating these acts of philosophical philanthropy, *Charmides* takes its important place in a Nietzschean history of philosophy: the Platonic precedent for Nietzsche's understanding of the genuine philosopher as commander and legislator, and as physician of culture, reveals itself clearly in the actions of the returning Socrates. And the chronology Plato gave his dialogues becomes particularly instructive here. The *Republic*, which Plato set a few weeks later, makes literally central the dream of *Charmides*, the rule of the philosopher. Because it sets that dream at the center of a huge canvas, it can paint the dream impossible and undesirable in the very act of showing its possibility and desirability. While displaying the philosopher's nature and grounding his right to rule in his nature, the *Republic* shows what compels such a nature to descend to rule at just this point in Athenian and Greek history: Homeric rule is breaking down, the Homeric gods are losing their hold on the young. In that crisis the wise man finds himself compelled to ensure that the Critiases not rule, that the many lovers of honor freed into unrestraint by the Greek enlightenment not rule, because they lack the knowledge possession of which alone can make rule a benefit. The *Republic* will show that "my dream" is Socrates' dream, a knowledge-based, reality-based dream that he can make seem merely imaginary while showing it to be necessary. Nietzsche could speak openly about the rule of the philosopher as legislator and physician and aim to embody it himself; Plato could speak about that only covertly while showing Socrates in action as its embodiment. Nietzsche could state that Socrates was "the one turning point and vortex of so-called world history";[107] Plato could only intimate that Socrates aimed at that as a philosopher who descended to rule, but by writing it he could make that aim his own.

107. Nietzsche, *Birth of Tragedy*, ¶15.

11. Socrates Judges the Inquiry (175a–176d)

Socrates now makes the longest speech of the dialogue, directly asserting the authority he has tacitly exercised ever since Critias assigned him the role of doctor. Now that he has succeeded in discovering the state of philosophy in Athens and done what he could to help Critias know his perplexity, he hides his success in an appearance of failure and blames himself. Again using "see" in a cognitive sense, he asks if Critias *sees* that "my fear was all along a reasonable one and that I was justly accusing myself of investigating nothing useful about sôphrosunê" (175a). There is more to see here than first appears, for Socrates again takes full advantage of the temporal ambiguity he has been exploiting in his references to the past:[108] while referring explicitly to the past of this conversation (172e), he reaches back to that deeper past he shares with Critias, the time before Potidaea when Critias absorbed all these words and phrases. Socrates' final judgment on their conversation, his declaration of failure and acceptance of blame, seem inappropriately harsh, mere irony, given the gains he has made in understanding Critias and conveying to the auditor his own understanding of sôphrosunê. But when these judgments are seen to reach back to that more distant past, failure and blame are altogether fitting; he is right to fear that he did nothing useful in presenting sôphrosunê as he did. Socrates justly accuses himself long before anyone else accuses him.

Socrates focuses his blame: "For surely what is agreed to be most beautiful of all would not have appeared unbeneficial to us if I had been of any benefit with regard to inquiring beautifully." He generalizes his failure: "For as it is now, we are everywhere worsted" (175b). But he also introduces, here at the end, a word for his failure that he never used in their conversation that day: "we are unable to discover upon which of the beings the *lawgiver* set[109] this name, sôphrosunê" (175b). This too must have been part of the pre-Potidaean teaching Socrates shared with Critias. The lawgiver puts up the words that determine what things are sôphrôn; he exercises the ultimate form of rule. *Sôphrosunê*—like the other words for virtue—is a name put up by the most powerful human maker, the legislator who legislates good and evil through names applied to things. More powerful even than the gods whose words are put up at oracles are the good and evil legislated

108. See 171d ("from the beginning"), 172a ("what we were [then] saying"), 172c ("we inquired into nothing useful"), 172c ("from the beginning"), 172e ("when I looked at it then"), 174e ("long bearing witness").

109. Literally, the law*setter* set . . . (*nomothetês . . . etheto*).

by the ultimate legislators—the gods are instruments to police their good and evil. And by referring to the beings (*tôn ontôn*, 175b) for the final time in connection with the ruling words of the lawgiver, Socrates again intimates that his inquiry into sôphrosunê had an ontological as well as an epistemological basis. Among the totality of beings, the law-setting being who comes to a knowledge of knowledge knows himself commissioned to set the name sôphrosunê on these or those beings and to put that up in the sacred places.

We were worsted, Socrates continues to allege, even though "we conceded" a lot that the argument did not demonstrate (175b). He names two concessions and both concern his own final definition. They conceded that sôphrosunê is "a knowledge of knowledge"—but Socrates' action in investigating the possibility of sôphrosunê so defined demonstrated its possibility. And they conceded that this knowledge "knows the works [*erga*] of other knowledges"—a way of phrasing what a knowledge of knowledge knows that they did not use before and that encompasses both Critias's dream of an impossible knowledge of knowledges and Socrates' understanding of a possible one. They conceded all this, Socrates asserts, in order to be able to claim that "the sôphrôn one might become knowledgeable of both what he knows, that he knows it, and of what he does not know, that he does not know it" (175c)—again Socrates gives the definition he added on his own (167a) its complete form (171d; cf. 167b).[110] This final definition did

110. Despite Socrates' explicit statement that sôphrosunê is knowing what one knows that one knows it and knowing what one does not know that one does not know it, Catherine Zuckert repeats in her commentary on *Charmides* her often expressed view that "Self-knowledge as Socrates understands it consists in knowledge of one's ignorance rather than as Critias claims, knowledge of knowledge" (*Plato's Philosophers*, 244), and that "In the *Charmides* Socrates admits that he knows only that he does not know, and he doubts that anyone can know that he knows" (247 n. 60). Misunderstanding Socrates on self-knowledge is by far the most important misunderstanding in Zuckert's interpretation of *Charmides*, but her failure to exploit the chronology of this dialogue of Socrates' return, despite her chronological reading of the dialogues, is also of some importance. Also, referring to one of the arguments on the possibility of sôphrosunê as knowing what one knows, Zuckert says, "no sense or mental operation refers solely to itself" (244), whereas that argument shows in fact the strangeness of knowledge (and opinion and "seeing") in referring to itself. On a smaller scale, a series of little errors shake one's confidence in her reading of *Charmides*. She speaks of "auditor(s)" (237, 245) and Socrates' "anonymous auditors" (246), but Socrates addresses his auditor three times always in the singular. She speaks of Socrates "rushing to the school upon returning to Athens" (238), but he went to the palaistra only on the day after he returned. She says, "as Charmides entered with a group of admirers, [Socrates] looked inside the youth's cloak" (239), but Socrates saw inside Charmides' cloak only after he was called over to sit next to him. She speaks of Charmides' "future tyranny" (240), but he was never himself tyrant, just one of the ten at Piraeus appointed by the Thirty. She speaks of "The Thracian physicians who taught Socrates" (240), but Socrates speaks of only one doctor of Zalmoxis. She says that "Homer's hero, disguised as a beggar, observes that 'shame is not good for a needy man'" (240), but Odysseus did not say this, Telemachus has Eumaeus say it to his father.

not replace the previous four Socratic definitions but augmented and limited them in ways that Critias had not understood, for Socrates' examination showed that Critias thinks that the first two are expendable (164c–d, 165b) and that the one Socrates added last is the same as his own final definition (170a). Critias took from Socrates only the truth about the gods and the seemingly unlimited right to rule that a knowledge of knowledges grants its knower—he took only what allowed him to dream the immoderate dream that he was fit to be the ultimate lawgiver. What "his own" is, what the good things are, a knowledge of what he knows, that he knows it, and of what he does not know, that he does not know it—*that* Critias was unable to take over from Socrates. And as a consequence he understood both "Know thyself" and the knowledge of knowledges in a nonsôphrôn way. Not only did Socrates fail to teach Critias sôphrosunê, he successfully taught him its opposite, a twisted version of the immoderate core of the true understanding of the moderate. No wonder Socrates ends by emphasizing his failure: if Critias in his perplexity can be led to think that he learned something impossible and undesirable from Socrates, Socrates will have remedied his failure.

Socrates lingers over what was conceded in his final complete definition, pointing to what should be investigated in order to test what they conceded: the "impossibility of someone somehow or other knowing what he does not know at all." Is such knowledge impossible? Socrates forces that question by repeating himself: "our agreement asserts that [the sôphrôn one] knows that he does not know this. And yet, as I suppose, nothing would appear more irrational [*alogôteron*] than this" (175c). Is this as irrational as Socrates makes it appear? They have not investigated the issue, he says, but the investigation that he did conduct implies that one who inquired into what he knew and did not know could ultimately arrive at an understanding of the character of human knowledge such that he could know that he cannot know what lies beyond the limits of possible knowledge—and could therefore succeed in examining Critias to show that what he claimed to know in fact cannot be known.

Socrates ends his whole inquiry with Critias by bringing the inquiry (*zêtêsis*) itself on stage to judge and be judged. In a single complex sentence judging the truth they've arrived at, Socrates seems to state his dissatisfaction with what they've achieved. In fact, however, his sentence states the contrary; he can terminate their exchange now because their inquiry has shown him the hard truth about the very thing he set out to learn on his return: what Critias could show him about the state of philosophy in Athens. In the first half of his sentence the inquiry judges them and he judges it; in the second half the inquiry laughs at the truth it has made apparent to them. In that laugh and in that truth lies Socrates' affirmative if rueful judgment on what he has attained (175c–d).

The inquiry judges the two of them "simple, and not hard."[111] Is this true? Socrates judges the inquiry "no more able to discover the truth." Is this true? The falsity of both judgments becomes evident through the inquiry's laughing judgment: "it laughed scornfully at this [truth] that it quite hubristically made apparent to us, [namely] that what we, then agreeing to and fabricating together, were setting down to be sôphrosunê, is unbeneficial" (175d). The inquiry laughs neither at them nor at itself but at the very truth it made apparent to them: that sôphrosunê is unbeneficial when understood as what they agreed to and fabricated together "*then*." That word (*palai*, 175d$_3$) carries into the final judgment the temporal ambiguity Socrates has been exploiting; it could mean what is just past, the beginning of their conversation, but it could also mean what it usually means, *long ago, of old*. And when one considers that Socrates' stated purpose was to discover the state of philosophy on his return, and that he fulfilled his purpose by prompting Critias to say what he made of key phrases he had taken over from Socrates before he left for Potidaea, then the sense of *palai* that must predominate for Socrates if not for Critias is *back then, before Potidaea*. Socrates' final judgment therefore reports the truth the inquiry has made apparent to him: it was unbeneficial, laughably unbeneficial, to attempt to transmit the true understanding of sôphrosunê to Critias in the way he did. The inquiry's final judgment reports Socrates' judgment on his own pre-Potidaean practice. But by pointing to what the inquiry succeeded in showing him, Socrates indicates that the judgment he just made on the inquiry was wrong: it did discover the truth. That in turn means that the judgment the inquiry made on him was wrong: so far from being simple and not hard, subtle and hard Socrates forced himself to view the unbeneficial character of his pre-Potidaean teaching. Learning from his inquiry that his attempt to transmit his philosophy to Critias in fact helped corrupt him, hard and resourceful Socrates learns that he must

111. "Hard" (*sklêrôn*) is the first characteristic of Eros that Diotima lists after describing his birth and before describing him as a philosopher (*Symposium* 203d). Hard, strong, and resourceful, Eros—Socrates—shares all the traits of his mother, Penia, and none of the traits of his drunken, languorous, divine father, Poros, not even his name, for Eros is known by his thousand-fold poverty.

learn to transmit his philosophy in a new way that will not corrupt and will benefit. For now, though, hard and subtle Socrates continues to seem simple and not hard, acting the failure who produced and directed a failed inquiry.

12. Last Words (175d–176d)

Having ended his inquiry with a veiled approbation of it, Socrates turns away from Critias to address Charmides, who has been sitting silently between the two of them for their whole exchange. He fakes annoyance at his inquiry as if it showed sôphrosunê to be unbeneficial. He's less annoyed for himself, he says, than for him, Charmides, if he will not profit from the sôphrosunê reputedly in his soul. But Socrates expresses annoyance for himself after all by invoking the beginning of their conversation: he'll be most annoyed "over the incantation I learned from the Thracian if, when it was for a matter of no worth, I was learning it with such earnestness" (175e). Did Socrates learn the Thracian incantations for nothing? That would be the peak of annoyance. But there's no reason to believe that Socrates is at all annoyed, for his inquiry fulfilled his intentions completely. He has learned that the young man who has become most distinguished for beauty has not and will not become distinguished for wisdom; he has learned that the state of his philosophy in Athens is dire if he leaves it as he left it with Critias; he therefore knows that he did not learn the incantations in vain, and he will see to it that the last words of his narration compel him to teach them.

Sôphrosunê cannot be unbeneficial, Socrates asserts, so an inquiry that ends with that conclusion must show he's a bad inquirer. Because sôphrosunê is a great good, Charmides is blessed if he has it. Does he have it? Or does he need the incantations that impart it? Socrates thus returns to the initial question of the dialogue as if his inquiry with Charmides did not completely settle it. But Charmides is now free to say that he doesn't know whether he has it or not—"how would I know what not even you two are able to discover?" But he doesn't quite believe Socrates when he claims not to know, and that allows him to say unequivocally that he thinks he needs the incantation. The Charmides eager to free himself of Socrates' dialectic is eager to be taught Socrates' chants.

Charmides' guardian breaks in to respond to the plea Charmides addressed to Socrates—and to reassert his authority over his ward. His interruption initiates the last exchanges between him and Charmides and between Charmides and Socrates, exchanges that seem to have been composed by some diviner with a knowledge of what is to be. When Critias breaks in, Charmides must turn his head away from Socrates to face Critias seated on his other side, and Socrates acts as if he was unable to hear what Critias and Charmides were "plotting" together (176c). But he's narrating what he alleged he didn't hear: he has no objection to his auditor's recognizing that he was a trickster to the end. The quasi-private exchange between guardian and ward opens with Critias granting Charmides permission to submit to Socrates' chants, but he's still confused: he thinks that Charmides can show he has sôphrosunê if he submits to the exercise by which alone he is supposed to acquire it. Critias's wish that Charmides submit to Socrates' chant and "not abandon him either much or little" comes to Charmides as a command: "You can count on me to follow and not abandon for I would be doing something terrible if I wouldn't obey you, my guardian, and do what you command." Charmides is sôphrôn in his way: he does his own things as a ward who will always be a ward. Critias responds emphatically with his last words of the dialogue, a commander's words: "But indeed, I do command, I myself." Critias remains Charmides' commander, his director assigning him his roles; he will still be commanding him twenty-five years later when they are killed together on Munychia Hill.[112]

Socrates breaks in on this conspiracy: "Hey, what are you two plotting to do?" But it's too late, Charmides replies, "Our plotting is done." This exchange opens Socrates' control over the last words of the dialogue. He introduces the words they exchange: "plotting," "do violence" (*biazô*), "put one's hand to" (*epicheireô*), and "oppose" (*enantioô*). Charmides and Critias plotted together, but Socrates asks Charmides in the singular, "Will *you* [Charmides] use violence, and not even grant me a preliminary hearing?" "You can count on me to use violence," young Charmides says jokingly to a hoplite just returned from violence, and his reason is telling: "because *he* orders me to." Blame Critias for the violence, says Charmides, and Critias is in fact to blame, though ultimately it was Socrates himself who helped free Critias of restraint in commanding. Charmides is bold in challenging Socrates: "It's up to you to plot as to what you will do in view of this."

112. Alcibiades names Charmides in the *Symposium* as one of the young men betrayed by Socrates. Socrates tells a story about Charmides in the *Theages*, set in 409, twenty years later. Ostensibly to dissuade Theages from associating with him as his student, Socrates tells Theages and his father that he knows nothing except "the erotic matters" in which he is more skilled than any person past or present (128b). He gives examples in which bad things happened to those who disobeyed what his daimonion counseled and Charmides is his first example. The daimonion opposed Charmides' training for the Nemean games and Socrates told Charmides, "just don't train." Charmides rationalized this opposition and trained anyway (129a).

What can Socrates plot in the face of violence plotted against him by Critias and his allies, a commander who will turn on his teacher and liberator with many an obedient tool like Charmides at his command? "No plotting is left," Socrates alleges, speaking still in the singular, "for if you put your hand to [*epicheirounti*] anything at all, especially by violence, no human will be able to oppose you." Charmides' response picks up on *oppose* and not *put your hand to*. But the word not picked up rings with meaning here at the end for the auditor and reader cued by the serial references to the recognition scenes of the *Odyssey*. For them, one word would be enough, and *epicheireô* is that word: it is used only twice in Homer, both times in the last of the recognition scenes at the very end of the *Odyssey*. As Odysseus and his father, Laertes, were "putting their hands" to dinner,[113] old Dolios, a servant especially loyal to Penelope, arrived with his six sons. When they "saw Odysseus and recognized him in their minds, they stood still in the hall in wonder."[114] Odysseus at his most gracious said, "Sit to dinner with us, old man, and let be your wonder; for a long time we have been eager to put our hands to food, but we waited for you in the halls, ever expecting you."[115] Ever so artfully, employing a few words rare in Homer at the beginning and end of *Charmides*, Plato invokes the first and the last recognition scenes of returning Odysseus; and between that beginning and end he invokes two famous statements that cast light on the limits and character of the recognition of returning Odysseus: auditor and reader are to recognize that Socrates' return to Athens must be both recognized and not recognized by those to whom he returns. Returning to those who are both known and unknown to him, he must remain both known and unknown to them. At the end, Plato steps forth as graciously as Odysseus did. Those who see in Plato's word *epicheireô* a returning Socrates as a returning Odysseus will, like Dolios and his sons, stand still in wonder yet feel themselves waited for and welcomed to the feast. And, to go one step further, they will feel themselves invited, as were Dolios and his sons, into willing service for the last battle of the *Odyssey*, after which Zeus called an end to conflict though not an end to Odysseus's mission.

Those who find themselves invited to the feast by the end of *Charmides* can look differently on Socrates' last words. He has just told Charmides that "no human will be able to oppose you." Before meeting the beautiful Charmides that day he said no one would be able to withstand him if

113. *Odyssey*, 24.386.
114. *Odyssey*, 24.391–92.
115. *Odyssey*, 24.394–96.

he had a soul with a good nature (154d). He has learned that Charmides does not have a soul of the very best nature, and he is able to withstand him. But Charmides has now asserted that violence is his means, and he tells Socrates, "Don't you oppose either." "No, then," Socrates says as the last words of the dialogue, "I won't oppose." He *will* oppose and with all the cunning resourcefulness available to him, as the end of *Charmides* just proved. For how did *Charmides* end? With Socrates submitting to a playful threat of violence if he does not teach the Thracian incantation: Socrates has compelled Charmides to compel him to teach the incantation. "I won't oppose." He won't oppose teaching the incantation because teaching the incantation *is* his opposition.

Teaching the incantation is Socrates' plotted opposition to what he sees he set loose in Critias. For what does it mean that *Charmides* ends by promising incantations introduced at its beginning, returned to at its end, no syllable of which it supplies? *Charmides* shows Socrates succeeding in discovering the state of his philosophy in Athens: discovering his failure to transmit his philosophy to Critias, he discovers that the philosophy that led him long ago to the truth about human beings and the highest beings and the truth about human knowledge, when transmitted to Critias, corrupted him into tyrannical ambition. The truth that liberated Socrates was deadly for Critias. For Socrates to learn that the truth of sôphrosunê is deadly for the Critiases is to learn that that truth must be sheltered and that its transmission requires that it be sheltered within a covering that will make it accessible only to those for whom it can be liberating. *Charmides* displays Socrates discovering a necessity: the esotericism required by deadly truth will have to be far more elaborate than what he recommended in *Protagoras*. In the last words of *Charmides* Charmides compels Socrates to teach him the incantations that impart sôphrosunê to the soul, and Socrates does not oppose him. That promise of *Charmides* will be fulfilled: hard and resourceful post-Potidaean Socrates becomes, under compulsion, a teacher of soul-healing chants. *Charmides* says the chants are a medicine for a soul which is immortal and the cause of everything in the human. To hear the incantations in the form in which Socrates actually chants them, one must study the dialogue Plato placed just after *Charmides*, the *Republic*. *Charmides* is an introduction to the *Republic* that gives aid by pointing to its narrator as a returned Odysseus and to its core teachings as the incantations of a reluctant but compelled innovator. It is not for nothing that the *Republic* ends by explicitly pointing to a reformed Odysseus who can only be Socrates.

Charmides displays an indispensable step in Socrates' serial discoveries that philosophy as such always faces an issue that is philosophy only derivatively, the theological-political problem of philosophy or the unlikelihood that philosophy as the passionate pursuit of wisdom could pursue its ownmost problem in peace. *Charmides* shows that the demythologizing Socrates known to Critias has learned that he will have to *remythologize* with a view to establishing philosophy effectively. The Thracian incantations, those mysterious chants that are such an arresting part of *Charmides* while never being voiced there, signal Socrates' mature esotericism. Thracian incantations are the vehicle through which Socrates will transmit the truth; they will secure the state of philosophy in Athens and make it possible that the young who become beautiful, and almost all the young become beautiful for white-line Socrates, may perhaps also become wise, which almost none ever will.

Plato used the recognition scenes of the *Odyssey* to intimate just who stole into Athens when the survivors of the battle of Spartolus made their way back home. Socrates' return is like Odysseus's return, recognized serially by Telemachus, Penelope, and Dolios, and it includes Telemachus's warning (as if Odysseus needed it) to swallow his shame lest he be recognized by the suitors. But do any of those who recognize returned Odysseus *really* recognize who he is? Does even Penelope, as resourceful as she is and as favored as she is with Odysseus's retelling of his odyssey, recognize who her returned husband really is? Homer's *Odyssey* suggests that it would take Odysseus's like to recognize the one who has returned as one who has grown wise in the wisdom of nature and human nature and is now bent on a political project that will establish wisdom in the world in the only way possible, by refounding the Ithacan order already well founded but now threatened and destined to be led by a man who is only good, Telemachus who will never be what his father became. By suggesting that the Socrates who returned to Athens in 429 is to be likened to returned Odysseus, Plato, schooled by Homer, suggests that Socrates is like the Odysseus none would recognize. He comes bringing a new order to be established in the imperial city, an order that sees to its successful succession by transmitting its core only to its like. The new politics for philosophy will be as comprehensive and as poetic as Homer's, for the incantations of Homer, educator of Greece, must now be replaced by the incantations of Socrates.[116]

116. The full extent of wise Odysseus's political project can be read in Seth Benardete's *The Bow and the Lyre*. He shows how Odysseus's odyssey is his entry into philosophy and then, as a

13. Who Might the Auditor of Plato's *Charmides* Be?

Plato had Socrates narrate *Charmides* to a single unnamed auditor addressed as comrade, friend, and member of a noble family (154b, 155c, d). He assigned a clear date, late spring 429, to what Socrates narrated while indicating that the narration occurred at some later, indeterminate date, long enough after 429 to require that Socrates give his auditor some assistance with the details of his return to Athens. The date of narration is uncertain, but does anything in *Charmides* suggest who its auditor might be?

What Socrates narrates in *Charmides* is his discovery that he failed to transmit his philosophy to Critias and that his very attempt corrupted Critias, opening the way for him to become a sophist and tyrant. That Socrates now narrates this event of learning in a private conversation to a single individual suggests that the narration is itself an effort to transmit his philosophy. That Socrates allows his auditor to be party to his discovery that he helped corrupt Critias suggests that he judges his auditor a fit audience for that incriminating fact. And that he narrates their exchange in all its density and complexity suggests that he judges his auditor capable of hearing bare phrases and compact arguments and learning from them what Socrates learned without needing to have everything spelled out. Socrates' narration thus suggests that he narrated *Charmides* to an auditor he judged fit to transmit his philosophy in the oblique way in which he narrated it; he assigns his auditor the responsibility of transmitting his philosophy in a way that will keep it out of the hands of a Critias while holding it open for those who resemble himself.

Who could the auditor be then but Plato? Socrates' narration of his failure to transmit his philosophy to Critias, who failed to transmit it to Charmides, would have as its auditor that member of this very family who transmitted it successfully, who dedicated his life and genius to the successful transmission of Socrates' philosophy. If *Charmides* suggests that Socrates narrates it to Charmides' nephew, then *he* did what he wrote that his uncle was prepared to do, write down the incantations, but he wrote down the arguments as well in all their subtlety, for he understood the arguments as his uncle could not, and he wrote with Socrates' permission for he had Socrates' name precisely and would not do him an injustice (156a).

---

consequence, into political philosophy whose nature he indicates in his final sentence: Odysseus "should now know that his destiny is to establish belief and not knowledge."

And Plato would handle the matter with taste, not mentioning it but leaving it to always tentative, merely pleasant inference.

Plato's report of Socrates' narration would thus allude to what surely happened in any case as Socrates, pursuer of Athenian youth, questioning Charmides' nephew as he had questioned Charmides, found, to his amazement, that he was talking to a *Plato*—the almost disabling surge of eros that Socrates reports on seeing inside Charmides' cloak would actually apply to his almost losing control of himself on seeing within his interlocutor the beauty of a *Plato*. And Plato, for his part, would display even more fire and drive than the men of Clazomenae who sailed across the Aegean on the rumor that they might be able to hear a remembered conversation of the young Socrates. Plato would be *avid* to hear all he could of Socrates' past, and when that past concerned his notorious uncle and his uncle's appalling cousin, well, *this* auditor of the dialogue on sôphrosunê would be rapt indeed.[117]

Let the auditor of *Charmides* be the author of *Charmides*. Let an author who never speaks in his writings show himself listening. The problem of transmitting Socrates' philosophy would thus be transmitted to the one who transmitted it successfully. He solves the problem of transmitting it by transmitting it as a problem that will continue to draw to a Socrates now permanently absent the young distinguished by the beauty of a passion for wisdom. As auditor of Socrates' narration of *Charmides*, Plato would show himself commissioned to transmit the teaching that sôphrosunê is self-knowledge that leads to knowledge of knowledge and of the power of knowledge or "knowledge" to rule. Transmitting Socrates' philosophy, Plato would safely transmit Socrates' discovery of its earlier vulnerability to Critias's criminal version, a great event in the history of Socrates becoming Socrates.

The question of the transmitters of Socrates' philosophy arises in other dialogues. What kind of a transmitter is Phaedo, the young man flattered and stroked at the center of the report he memorized and loves to repeat of Socrates' last day? Or Apollodoros, who is made to seem ridiculous for despising those to whom he narrates the tale of Socrates' secret night when he spoke of Eros with Agathon and Alcibiades? Or Aristode-

117. The date of the narration would then be long after 429, perhaps in the time during or just after the rise to power of Critias and Charmides, when Plato himself was in his mid-twenties, a time which Plato's Seventh Letter records as his time of disillusionment with politics and his relatives' participation in it because of their treatment of Socrates (324b–325c).

mus, from whom Apollodoros got his story and who goes uninvited and barefoot to a party for which invited Socrates put on his fancy shoes? Or Cephalus of Clazomenae, who made the long journey to Athens to hear and memorize a report of an early conversation between Socrates and Zeno and Parmenides that is about to be lost forever through the neglect of Athenians—including Glaucon and Adeimantus, who never bothered to ask their half-brother about the conversation he alone had memorized? Or Euclides, whose role as transmitter of a report that Socrates dictated to him includes a decision on his own part to transform a narrated dialogue into a performed one? Or, to apply the question to an auditor of one of Socrates' narrations, what kind of a transmitter of the Socratic teaching is Crito, father of Critobulus, likely to be as the only one to hear Socrates' report of his reasons for taking seriously the ridiculous sophist brothers Euthydemus and Dionysodorus? Such questions of transmission can arise only in narrated dialogues, though transmission can be an explicit theme in performed dialogues, as it is in *Phaedrus* where it is part of the problem of writing.

Note on the Dramatic Date of *Charmides*

The case for late May 429 as the dramatic date of *Charmides* carries a high degree of probability.[118] I will present that case briefly and then consider how the exegesis of the dialogue supports that date. Again, as with *Protagoras*, it is important to recognize that Plato's contemporaries would have had little difficulty in concluding quickly just when the dialogue occurred. Plato states in his first sentence that the events Socrates' auditor is about to hear occurred on the day after Socrates returned to Athens from the Athenian army camp in Potidaea. Moments later Socrates reports that a severe battle occurred just before his return and that "those here" were hearing some of its details first from him. Plato's contemporaries could easily infer that Socrates was returning from the battle of Spartolus in late May 429, a severe defeat that killed all the generals and left the army disbanded, a memorable event in Athenian history as the first major defeat in the war that was to be disastrous to Athenian greatness.

As Christopher Planeaux demonstrated, all the historical information

118. See Christopher Planeaux, "Socrates, Alcibiades, and Plato's *ta poteideatika*." Planeaux's article argued against the then-prevailing scholarly consensus that placed Socrates' return for *Charmides* in 432 after "the battle of Potidaea" and that assumed that Plato was careless with historical references. See also Nails, *People of Plato*, 311–12, who accepts the arguments of Planeaux's article.

now required to determine the exact dramatic date of *Charmides* can be secured if *Charmides*, along with Alcibiades' speech in the *Symposium*, is read against the background of Thucydides. The following historical events described by Thucydides are relevant for *Charmides*:

Spring 432: Because Potidaea, a member of the Athenian league, had been led by the Corinthians to revolt, the Athenians prepared a force of thirty ships and a thousand hoplites under Archestratus to take hostages from the Potidaeans and raze the city wall (Thucydides 1.57).

Summer 432: Archestratus arrived in Thrace, ignored Potidaea, which was already in revolt, and turned toward Macedon (1.59, 61); the Athenians prepared a second force of forty ships and two thousand hoplites to move north under Callias (1.61).

Fall 432: Callias arrived in Macedon and with the Athenians already there proceeded to Potidaea (1.61); the "battle of Potidaea" took place, and the Athenians succeeded in driving the Potidaeans and their Peloponnesian allies into the city; they raised works against the city wall on the side facing the sea in order to blockade the city (1.62–64). The siege began at this point and continued uninterrupted until the spring of 429.

Spring 431: Phormio arrived in Thrace with an additional sixteen hundred Athenian hoplites and completed the blockade of Potidaea by raising works against the city walls facing the land (1.64).

Summer 430: Hagnon son of Nicias arrived in Potidaea with additional troops but failed in an attempt to take the city; the plague arrived with them and ravaged the besieging army (2.58).

Winter 429: Exhausted by the siege and reduced to cannibalism, Potidaea negotiated a capitulation; the Athenians evacuated the Potidaeans from the city and flattened the city and its walls (2.70).

May 429: Marching out of Potidaea, the Athenians were defeated near Spartolus by Chalcidian hoplites and cavalry and retreated back to Potidaea; all Athenian survivors returned to Athens (2.79).

Thucydides' account implies that the Athenian siege army at Potidaea, like that at Syracuse later in the war, was not relieved by any rotation of forces but remained in place for the whole siege, three years for Archestratus's men, two and a half for Callias's, and two for Phormio's. (The Athenian army invading Sicily remained there for two and a half years before it was wiped out.)

It is most likely that Socrates left Athens with the original contingent under Archestratus in the spring of 432 or the reinforcements under Callias in the fall of 432 because of the report on Socrates that Alcibiades gives in the *Symposium*. He describes how Socrates' pursuit of him became his pursuit of Socrates, a long pursuit that he describes at length and that ended in shaming failure.[119] It ended almost certainly in the winter of 433–432 because Alcibiades then reports that "after this we went together on the expedition to Potidaea."[120] He goes on to tell the story of how Socrates saved him in the battle at which the generals gave him, Alcibiades, the prize for excellence (220d–e). That battle was likely "the battle of Potidaea" in the fall of 432, a battle in which only the forces of Archestratus and Callias took part. Alcibiades also reports on Socrates' feats of endurance at Potidaea, how he was able to go without food on expeditions when they were cut off from others; how he could enjoy festivals without getting drunk; how he withstood winter there "and winters there are terrible"; and also what he did in summer—an account that makes it clear that they were there for a long time.

Considerations internal to *Charmides* confirm a dramatic date of 429. Socrates' stated intentions on his return make it evident that he has been away for some years, for he wants to learn on his return just how things have changed in his absence with respect to the young men and with respect to the state of philosophy. As regards the young men, Charmides "was not yet mature[121] when [Socrates] went away" (154a), but he has become a beautiful young man (*neos*) by the time Socrates returns; for Charmides to have changed from a boy to a young man would have required a passage of some years. As regards the state of philosophy, the main inquiry of *Charmides*, Socrates' examination of Critias, can plausibly be his means of learning the state of philosophy in Athens only if he has been away long enough to allow Critias to develop an interpretation of Socrates' philosophy that Socrates would now want to test. Moreover, Socrates has been away long enough to allow him to reasonably represent himself as having learned a new, Thracian medicine in his absence. And finally, the somewhat subterranean theme of the returned Socrates as a returned Odysseus also suggests a long absence on Socrates' part: only a voyager who has been away on a long odyssey could plausibly merit being compared with Odysseus on his return.

Charmides is made almost overwhelmingly intricate by its chronologi-

119. *Symposium* 216c–219e.
120. *Symposium* 219e.
121. Literally, not yet of an age fit for military service; an age reached by Athenian boys at twenty.

cal tension: it stands as a fixed whole endlessly, fluidly traversing the gap between then and now, pre- and post-Potidaea. From this side of the gap, post-Potidaean Socrates announces being schooled during the gap into a new teaching on the health of the soul; on that side of the gap, pre-Potidaean Socrates comes to light through the responses of a follower reporting what he heard back then. Also on that side of the gap a younger Critias comes to light as an eager recipient of what he heard then, while on this side a more mature Critias appears as transformed during the gap by reflection on what he heard back then, transformed into what he now aspires to become and will become. We watch Socrates drawing out that transformation in his follower, but the transformation he announced in himself remains invisible, awaiting display a few weeks later in the *Republic*. There the transformed Socrates appears as a teacher whose words for the ambitious young will not make of them what his pre-Potidaean words made of Critias.[122]

122. If *Charmides* and the *Republic*, two dialogues that Socrates narrates from beginning to end, are dialogues of Socrates' return, what about the dramatic dates of *Lysis* and the *Lovers*, the only other dialogues Socrates narrates from beginning to end? Are they also dialogues of Socrates' return as that formal feature might suggest? In each of them Socrates does what he said in *Charmides* he was eager to do on his return, go to his usual haunts, a palaistra, seemingly to discover what happened to the young and philosophy in his absence. The cues of dating they contain make it difficult now to determine if they fall before or after Potidaea.

CHAPTER 3

The *Republic*: The Birth of Platonism

Prologue: Socrates' Great Politics

Plato's *Charmides* is the unexpected introduction to the *Republic*, which Plato set a week or two later.[1] *Charmides* shows who the Socrates is who just starts talking in the *Republic* with no apparent introduction: he is the Athenian philosopher returned after a long absence, returning different, having learned during his absence a new teaching on the health of the soul. And he returns as Odysseus returned: the *Republic* is the great deed befitting a returned Odysseus, a deed aimed at establishing a new order in Athens and not only in Athens.

But if *Charmides* introduces the *Republic*, so too do the prewar *Protagoras* and *Alcibiades I*. In these dialogues Socrates set out the political project for philosophy that now, in the *Republic*, he will equip with far more radical means. For the *Republic* shows Socrates transforming the two primary political projects he undertook for philosophy in *Protagoras* and *Alcibiades I*, redirection of the Greek enlightenment and reeducation of Greek youth. What may have sufficed for a time of splendor proves deficient for the extremity that has befallen Athens in late spring 429. Nothing shows that extremity better than Athenian willingness to introduce, for the first time at least since the Persian wars, a foreign god. And on the very night and in the very place that Athenians assemble to introduce Thracian Bendis in hopes of delivery from the curse of plague and war, Socrates introduces his

1. For the details of the dramatic date see below, "Note on the Dramatic Date of the *Republic*."

new teaching in hopes of delivery from the deeper crises made visible by the various beginnings of the *Republic*. And on the next day in Athens, as his countrymen stream back to the high city with their reports of the entry of foreign divinity, Socrates reports his own novel introductions. Plato gave his *Republic* the most auspicious of occasions.

If the extremity of the times calls for extreme measures, the deadliness of truth, known to Socrates from the esoteric tradition of Greek wisdom and indicated in the fitting way in *Protagoras* and *Charmides*, dictates that the new measures be something other than insistence on truth. The new measures must serve the city while serving philosophy, and to do that they must shelter the city from philosophy while sheltering philosophy from the city. What is called for is a new poetry to replace the now-ruined poetry of Homer. In the *Republic* Socrates dares to play the most dangerous of all games: he introduces a new, post-Homeric teaching on god and the soul for the sake of the city and the sake of philosophy. In Athens in late spring 429, in Plato's *Republic*, the soul of Odysseus, made immortal in the only way possible, chooses its new life.

The *Republic*, so complex, so pivotal, so immense, cannot be treated whole as I was able to treat *Protagoras* and *Charmides*. Because the dense web of detail is always what conveys the most significant points, I have chosen to deal in detail with selected passages, those that seem to benefit most from a chronological approach, from the introduction provided by *Protagoras* and *Charmides*. Such selectivity will cost not only some sections of the *Republic*—most notably book 8's analysis of regimes and book 9's contrast of philosophic and tyrannic souls—but also some important themes not integral to the new politics for philosophy. What follows is an event-centered interpretation of the *Republic* where the events are easy-to-ignore little occurrences like Socrates naming Odysseus or noting Thrasymachus's blush or prostrating himself before Adrasteia. Collected together, these events unite into the great event: in the *Republic* the returned Socrates carries into fortified Athens the foreign teachings that came to dominate and in some measure produce Western civilization.

ONE: THE WORLD TO WHICH SOCRATES GOES DOWN

The *Republic* takes a long time to begin. It must first display the world to which Socrates descends by introducing all facets of the crisis to which he responds. Cephalus, Polemarchus, Thrasymachus, and Glaucon and Adeimantus all play their roles in making that world vivid, each showing in his unique way what compels Socrates to act.

1. First Words

"Down I went yesterday to Piraeus with Glaucon, son of Ariston, to offer prayers to the goddess; and, at the same time, I wanted to observe how they would put on the festival since they were now holding it for the first time."[2] These first words of the *Republic* do what the first words of *Charmides* do: give prominence to the day on which the dialogue occurred. And like the first words of *Charmides*, the first words of the *Republic* need additional information to fix the exact day, information that each goes on to supply. For "the goddess" in Athens is *the* Athenian goddess, Athena, while "the goddess" generally is Persephone, goddess of the underworld—and a festival held for either "for the first time" would be an oddity in Socrates' lifetime. "Which goddess?" is a question naturally spurred by the first sentence of the *Republic*. The answer is not given until Thrasymachus, as if by the way, refers to "the Bendideia" at the end of his exchange with Socrates (354a).

Bendis is a Thracian god whose entry marked a revolution in Athenian religion: for the first time in living memory Athenians allowed a foreign

2. Bloom, *Republic of Plato*. I use Bloom's translation with frequent modifications.

god into their civic religion.[3] Plato set the *Republic* on a day of innovation in the religious history of Athens, a day every Athenian could easily identify: early June 429. It was the second summer of the plague and a low point in the war for Athens, and no day more perfect could be imagined for the *Republic*: while Athenians, in a public festival in the Piraeus, introduce a new god to deliver them from the devastation of war and plague, the Athenian philosopher, in the private house of a rich foreigner in the Piraeus, introduces his own new teaching to effect a different kind of deliverance from a greater devastation he is the first to see.[4] And for Plato to set his *Republic* on that historic day is to set it a week or two after his *Charmides*: he gives his interested readers the gift of studying the *Republic* deeply informed about just who Socrates is at that moment: he is the returned Socrates of *Charmides*, returned as some new Odysseus to deliver his Ithaca.[5]

"*Down I went*"—*katebên*. The first word of the *Republic* announces a descent.[6] "*Katebên*," the first-person-singular aorist of *katabainô*, is used once by Homer: Odysseus has just killed the suitors and he speaks with Penelope: their trials are not yet over, he announces; "still hereafter there is to be measureless toil, long and hard, which I must fulfill to the end; for so did the spirit of Teiresias foretell to me on the day when *I went down* into the house of Hades to inquire concerning the return of my comrades and myself."[7] When he adds immediately, "But come, let us go to bed," he must know that Penelope will compel him to tell her first just what their new trial is—it is Odysseus's journey to introduce the religion of angry Poseidon, the punishing god, to a people who do not yet know him. "Down I went," says Homer-quoting Socrates as the first word of the *Republic*: he is like Odysseus in descending to Hades, and he will be like the Odysseus of that final task as well. Socrates' final task that night will relate a tale of Hades that introduces punishing gods to people who did not know them.

Socrates' first word in the *Republic* anticipates a command he will issue after he relates the most famous image in the *Republic*, the image of the cave (520c): "You must go down," he says to those educated by the city he

3. Garland, *Introducing New Gods*, 99, 111–14.

4. The introduction of Bendis was memorable for a second reason: it marked a revolution in the *political* history of Athens by tacitly changing the preconditions of Athenian citizenship, opening a new way for foreigners to become citizens (Planeaux, "Date of Bendis' Entry into Attica").

5. "A week or two" after *Charmides* is as much precision as now seems possible, but Plato's contemporaries could easily have determined the exact number of days between Socrates' return from Potidaea and the introduction of Bendis.

6. The verb *katabainô* is used eight more times in the *Republic*: 328c, 359d, 511b, 516e, 519d, 520c, 539e, 614d.

7. *Odyssey* 23.252.

builds in speech. Socrates' descent is a prelude to future descents that his own descent allows him to command. Socrates' first word sets a pattern—or repeats Odysseus's pattern—for those few who are like him: his descent is the model descent for all political philosophy subsequent to him.

"*Yesterday*." Socrates narrates the *Republic* the day after the conversation occurred. He has returned to Athens from the Piraeus, one of many Athenians to return that day reporting the novelties of the all-night spectacle. Socrates reports not the public innovations but those he himself introduced in private. His auditor(s) are never identified in any way, an indeterminacy that seems the very point: Socrates narrates the *Republic* to any and all or to all and none; it is a public report of a private event whose publicizing may well ensure keeping the private private. As he did in *Protagoras*, Socrates in the *Republic* reports to a wider Athenian audience a private conversation in a rich man's house where he confronted a famous foreign wise man in the presence of Athenian young. His report allows his audience to judge him: the audience of the *Republic* like that of *Protagoras* is given every reason to acclaim Socrates a defender of the moral decency of Athenian youth against corruption by foreign sophists. And yet in being for all, his report is also for none, for that smallest minority who could become like Socrates himself by thinking through what he narrates for all.

"*To Piraeus*." Socrates goes down from the high city of Athens to its port five miles away. The port of the imperial city with its maritime empire is rife with foreign influences like those of Thrace, far to the northeast, which carried on an important trade with Athens in timber and grain, or those of Sicily, far to the west, the home of Cephalus and his family of shield makers who were invited to Athens by Pericles himself. On this night the Athenians introduce a Thracian god—and Socrates said it was from the doctor of a Thracian god that he learned his healing incantations. The very wording, "to Piraeus," with its absence of the customary direct article, suggests, Eva Brann argues, a descent to Hades, for *Piraeus* means "the land beyond."[8] When he ends by introducing a new version of Hades, the returning Socrates brings up into Athens a view of the underworld whose post-Homeric sources within the Greek sphere lay in Thrace and Sicily.[9]

8. Brann suggests that the opening words imply, "I descended yesterday to the land beyond the river." (*Music of the "Republic,"* 117–18).

9. For a report on the splendor of the Piraeus, a most modern city with its grid design laid out less than twenty years earlier by Hippodamus of Milesia, "the world's first professional urban planner," see Hale, *Lords of the Sea*, 112–21. With its three circular, protected harbors and magnifi-

"*With Glaucon, son of Ariston.*" Socrates goes down with Plato's brother, one of the interlocutors with whom he will spend the night conversing, the one directly responsible for there being a conversation at all. Glaucon decides they must stay in the Piraeus; he demands that the conversation continue after Socrates finishes with Thrasymachus; he is Socrates' interlocutor for the issues that touch on philosophy itself; he is singled out by name as the recipient of the lesson at the very end (618b, 621c). Because Socrates fits his words to his interlocutor, Glaucon's identity as revealed by his words and deeds helps interpret Socrates' words. Socrates' failures with Alcibiades and Critias dictate a new approach to politically ambitious young Athenians like Glaucon.

"*To offer prayers to the goddess, and, at the same time, I wanted to observe how they put on the festival.*" Socrates states two purposes in going down to Piraeus, to offer prayers and to observe, and he states them twice ($327b_1$). Does he stay in the Piraeus and say everything he says that night for the same two reasons of piety and observation? He surely observes that the gathering at Cephalus's house affords him a special opportunity, and he explicitly says that he responds to Glaucon and Adeimantus out of piety (368b), repeatedly saying later that he hopes his argument will be more than a prayer (450d; see 456b, 499c, 540d).

"*Since they were now holding it for the first time.*" The opening of the *Republic* shows the Athenians innovating in religion; thirty years later the Athenians will execute Socrates partly on the charge of introducing new gods.[10] The Athenian innovation on the first night of the Bendideia heralds the chief feature of the *Republic*: on the night Athenians innovate, Socrates introduces new teachings on god and the soul, post-Homeric teachings that mark the end of Greek or Homeric religion. The leading contemporary authority on Greek religion, Walter Burkert, states at the end of his book *Greek Religion* just what ended Greek or Homeric religion: "Since Plato and through him, religion has been essentially different from what it had been before."[11]

---

cent ship sheds for triremes, Piraeus was the seat of the Athenian navy, the basis, as Hale shows, of both its empire and its democracy.

10. *Euthyphro* 3b; *Apology* 26c.

11. Burkert, *Greek Religion*, 322. Burkert describes the features of Plato's revolutionary role in religion: "It is Plato who brings about a revolution in religious language and in piety at one and the same time. Thereafter we find faith supported by philosophy, love transcending the world, and hope for an afterlife; there is humility, service of the gods, and at the same time the goal of assimilation to god" (275; see also 199).

2. The Compelled and the Voluntary

In his second sentence Socrates judges the Athenian procession "beautiful," "yet, the one the Thracians sent appeared no less befitting." Socrates' first judgment in the *Republic*, his sole judgment on what he went to observe, makes the Thracian celebration the equal of the Athenian. This judgment on the grave theme of Athenian innovation in religion set at the very opening of this dialogue of innovation seems like a promise for what is to come: observing and judging without the bias of a partisan of his own things, Socrates the innovator can find the foreign as fitting as the Athenian.

"After we had offered prayers and looked on,"[12] Socrates says, "we went off toward town." Socrates' descent was to be followed immediately by an ascent, a return to Athens long before the festival introducing Bendis was over. But their ascent is thwarted "as we were hurrying homewards." Polemarchus's slave boy ran after them and "took hold of my cloak from behind." The first words Socrates reports being spoken are a slave boy's words relating Polemarchus's command: "He orders you, Polemarchus [does], to wait." "Of course we'll wait," Glaucon says, yielding to the command with the first of the decisions he makes for the two of them.

Polemarchus arrives, "apparently from the procession" that Socrates and Glaucon had been observing, and he arrives with Adeimantus and Niceratus, whose father, Nicias, will become a famous general, and some others. Polemarchus takes the lead: "Socrates, I guess you two are hurrying to get away to town." His correct guess implies what the repetition of *hurrying* also suggests: Socrates has a reason to return to Athens. Polemarchus—the name means *Warlord*—makes a playful threat, "Do you see how many we are?" "Well then, either prove stronger than these or stay here." Thrasymachus will define justice as the advantage of the stronger, and the use of the word here as a threat induces Socrates to say, "Isn't there still one other possibility . . . our persuading you that you really must let us go?" Force or persuasion is the first issue of debate that Socrates reports in the *Republic*. From his position of superior force Polemarchus states

12. Socrates' second verb for his intention to observe, *theôreô*, "to look at, especially to be a spectator at the public games and festivals" (LSJ), has a secondary sense meaning "to be sent to consult an oracle" (LSJ; see Plato, Fifteenth Letter, 315b), and is the root of "theory"; it differs slightly from the first, *theaomai*, "to gaze at, behold with a sense of wonder" (LSJ). His second verb for pray repeats the first, *proseuchomai*.

the problem Socrates faces: "Could you really persuade if we don't listen?" Glaucon decides a second time: "No way." Polemarchus and Glaucon see no way, but Socrates? The prominence of this issue at the very opening, plus the fact that Glaucon answers while Socrates stays silent, suggests what the dialogue will show: Socrates has a way to "get around the obstacle of the will that refuses for no reason to listen to reason."[13]

Adeimantus breaks in, employing persuasion on behalf of the stronger: is it possible that Socrates and Glaucon don't know about the spectacle that awaits them if they stay, a torch race on horseback for the goddess? "That is novel," says Socrates, revealing that his knowledge of Bendis is limited. Polemarchus takes up the way of persuasion, saying that there will be an all-night festival and dinner and many young men to converse with. For the third time Glaucon decides and Socrates submits to his decision, using the word to affirm the passing of a law by the Athenian Assembly—"if it is so resolved." At the opening of the *Republic* Socrates yields to Glaucon, who yields to superior force and to the force of persuasion. But it is shortly after Socrates' return in *Charmides*, and the intentions he stated there regarding both philosophy and the young in Athens still obtain: Socrates may have persuaded himself to stay in the Piraeus because it promised fulfillment of his intentions on his return.

When Socrates narrates the opening of the *Republic*, he presents himself submitting to compulsion. Is the *Republic* a dialogue Socrates was compelled to give? He narrates the whole of it the next day, an initial proof of its voluntary character. Moreover, Socrates' actions in *Protagoras* and *Charmides* showed that efforts to compel him are unlikely to succeed because he has the power to adapt circumstances to his own ends. And *Protagoras* and *Charmides* showed as well that what Socrates freely chose is identical with what he compelled himself to do for the sake of philosophy. Socrates' compulsion in the *Republic*, initially wholly external as both raw force and persuasion, becomes internal: the returned Socrates of the *Republic*, led back to Polemarchus's house, finds himself in a setting that could not be more advantageous; in that setting he compels himself to act, to speak the teaching he returned to give.

3. Learning from Cephalus

When the small party from the procession arrives at Polemarchus's house, they find six others already there: Polemarchus's two brothers, Lysias and

13. Benardete, *Socrates' Second Sailing*, 10.

Euthydemus; Thrasymachus of Chalcedon; Charmantides the Paean; Cleitophon, son of Aristonymus; and Cephalus, the wealthy father of the three brothers and host to the whole gathering.[14] Plato set the *Republic* in the comfortable home of a rich Athenian metic from Sicily with a foreign sophist present with Athenian young; he set the prewar *Protagoras* in the comfortable home of the richest man in Athens with foreign sophists present with Athenian young. In these two dialogues with similar settings Socrates pursues the same project: the advancement of philosophy with both sophists and the young. The greater radicality and foreignness of Socrates' measures in the *Republic* seem signaled in the one main difference in the setting: the host and his family are foreign.

In *Charmides* the returned Socrates had spoken with two young men destined to become leaders in a movement that "attempted a political restoration, putting down the democracy and restoring an aristocratic regime dedicated to virtue and justice."[15] Now, shortly after, Plato shows Socrates speaking in the presence of at least three young men who would become victims of that attempt to restore Athenian virtue;[16] their conversation took place in a house that couldn't have been far from Munychia Hill on which the decisive battle was fought that killed Critias and Charmides. Plato's indirect reference to the failed restoration of Critias, a restoration unworthy of success, suggests that the *Republic* is Socrates' worthy restoration of Athenian virtue, impelled in part by his recognition in *Charmides* of what he had made of Critias.

The newcomers at Cephalus's house take seats on stools in a circle around Cephalus, who is seated at the center crowned with a wreath, having just come in from a sacrifice he is conducting in the courtyard. The patriarchal host singles out among his new guests the well-known Athenian wise man and speaks welcoming words, the first words in the place where

14. If the "some others" who originally appeared with Polemarchus (327c) also went to his house, the group was larger than the eleven named, Socrates and the ten in the Piraeus. There has been dispute about Charmantides: is he the treasurer of Athens in 427/426 and about the same age as Cephalus, or is he that man's grandson who may have been the student Isocrates mentions (*Antidosis* 93–94)? If the *Republic* occurs in 429 he must be the older man; Socrates' audience after Cephalus leaves does not consist then simply of young men and the rivals Socrates and Thrasymachus. The *Republic* is the only dialogue to name silent auditors.

15. Strauss, *City and Man*, 63.

16. According to Xenophon, Polemarchus was killed, beheaded, for his money in accord with a policy toward metics advocated by Critias. Niceratus was also killed, and Lysias barely escaped (Lysias, *Against Eratosthenes* 4–23; Xenophon, *Hellenica* 2.3.39, 2.4.19, 38). Perhaps the fate of Niceratus and Lysias at the hands of Critias helps explain their named presence; if so, the presence of the other silent auditors may also have fitting explanations that may be lost for us.

the whole dialogue will occur: "Socrates, you don't come often to us, coming down [*katabainôn*] to the Piraeus, yet it is proper to" (328c). Including a near repetition of the first words of Socrates' narration, Cephalus's words suggest the necessity of Socrates' descent: "If I still had the power to carry myself to town easily, there would be no need for you to come here, but we would come to you." Who can come to whom? Socrates must descend because ascent to him is beyond their power. The last words of Cephalus's speech complete the point. An old man used to authority, Cephalus gives himself the right to order Socrates: "Now do not do otherwise, but be with these youths and come here regularly to us as to friends and your very own kin" (328d). Unable to ascend, the old metic hands over his sons and their friends to Socrates' care, inviting him to be not just their friend but their very kin: the *Republic* opens with an authoritative invitation for Socrates to descend and do what he fully intended to do.

Socrates' first speech is wholly about speaking with Cephalus, not with his sons, and focuses on what he can learn from Cephalus, one thing only: "what sort of road [old age] is, whether rough and hard or easy and smooth" (328e). Cephalus defers to authority for every point he makes, but it is Socrates who first speaks of "the poets," invoking what they call the "threshold of old age," Homer's phrase for the time shortly before death.[17] Cephalus does what he was asked with some enthusiasm, reporting "by Zeus" on his regular meetings with men his own age. He differs from most of them who lament the loss of youthful pleasures, and from others who lament the abuse of relatives. Apparently honored in his old age by relatives, Cephalus finds himself to be like Sophocles, one of the few who are glad to be free of a "frenzied and savage master" like sex, and of the other "very many mad masters" to which he seems to have once been subject (329c). In his first report on the sort of road old age is, he says it brings "great peace and freedom," a state he attributes to "character." For those who are "orderly and content with themselves even old age is only moderately troublesome" (329d).

Socrates narrates that he was full of wonder at this answer and sought to "stir him up," speaking for the Many who would believe that Cephalus's money, his substance (*ousia*), and not his character allows him to bear old age well. Having likened himself to the great Athenian Sophocles, Cephalus likens himself to the great Athenian Themistocles, who claimed a right

17. *Iliad* 22.60 and 24.487 in reference to Priam; *Odyssey* 15.246 refers to Amphiaraos, son of Oikles, ancestor of Theoclymenos, who "never came to the threshold of old age" but was killed in his prime. Cephalus's death is usually placed in 429–428.

to base his fame on himself and not merely on his city: Cephalus bases his serenity on his character. But if his substance is not the foundation of his serenity, Socrates asks him what "is the greatest good that you have enjoyed from possessing great substance?" (330d). Led this way, Cephalus makes his most important speech, giving it two introductions. First: "What I say wouldn't persuade many perhaps"—has he had the experience of being ignored on what he thinks is the greatest good? Second: "Know well, Socrates"—*this* is what a man on the threshold of death thinks he can teach the wise man to whom he hands over his sons: "when someone comes near to the realization that he is coming to the end, fear and care enter him for things to which he gave no thought before" (330e). Cephalus just praised his peace and freedom from the many mad masters of appetite; now he reports agitation and bondage evoked by "tales told about what is in Hades" to which he never gave thought before.

Here is how *justice* explicitly enters the *Republic*: in Cephalus's fourfold repetition of fear of having been "unjust" and "paying the penalty there." "He laughed up to then" at these tales of punishment in Hades, but now they make "his soul twist and turn because he fears they might be true" (330e).

Here is how the *soul* explicitly enters the *Republic*: twisting and turning in Cephalus's fear that his soul might be punished for injustices he might have committed while he was young enough to laugh at tales of Hades.

Cephalus gives two conflicting reasons why fear might arise now: debility of old age, or greater discernment of "the things in that place because he is nearer to them" (330d). Whether he's losing capacity or gaining new capacity, he is now "full of suspicion and terror." Having reported that being "orderly and content with oneself" makes even old age only moderately troublesome, Cephalus reveals that suspicion and terror make one "reckon up his accounts" to discover if he has done anything unjust to anyone. And "he who finds many unjust deeds in his life often even wakes from his sleep in a fright as children do, and lives in anticipation of evil" (330e). This is Cephalus's final report to Socrates about the road that he first made seem easy and smooth: it is rough and hard for it is full of suspicions and terrors over which he has no control and which trouble his waking and sleeping. There is a nurse to these sufferings brought on by old age—money, Cephalus tells Socrates, who has no money. The ability to pay off what one may owe to men and gods allows "sweet and good hope" to replace suspicion and terror. In his speech on Hades Cephalus cites a poet by name only when he turns from fear to hope and recites Pindar's words about hope, which "most of all pilots / The ever-turning opinion of mortals" (331a). Piloted most of all by fear, Cephalus cites lines that feed his money-based hope. The greatest good of money is that it contributes to "not departing for that other place afraid because one owes some sacrifice to a god or money to a human being"—says the man on the threshold of old age during a pause in the sacrifice he must be conducting to pave his way to Hades.

Cephalus's speech on Hades is no incidental matter spoken by an incidental character soon to disappear: not long after he leaves, Adeimantus says out loud in Cephalus's house but out of Cephalus's hearing that he finds ridiculous those whose last resort in persuading the young to be just is to threaten them with Hades (366a). But Socrates will make Hades believable again by reforming the stories children are told about it; and so great will his authority become that he will be able to end his speaking that night relating a tale of Hades identical in its essentials to what Cephalus fears and hopes and be believed as Cephalus complained he never was. "What you say is very fine indeed," Socrates says of Cephalus's speech on Hades. What Cephalus introduces runs far deeper than poets' tales of Hades, for his fears and hopes about Hades imply a moral view of reality, belief in an ultimate payback for human action. For Cephalus's fear and hope to be justified, humans must inhabit an order in which evil is punished and good rewarded, an order in which just gods must watch over immortal souls. Implicit within the first view of things expressed in the *Republic* is the belief that Socrates will persuade the young men to hold, that justice as a retributive order of punishment and reward is built into the nature of things.

Socrates begins to take control of the conversation by abstracting a definition of justice from Cephalus's speech and challenging it: is justice really speaking the truth and giving back what one takes (331b, d)?[18] Socrates makes justice their theme, and because of the example he will give, their discussion of justice begins as a challenge to ancestral and poetic authority that Cephalus cites. His example will echo through the whole *Republic*. It appeals to "what everyone would surely say," namely, that if one takes weapons from a friend who is sane, it cannot be just to give the weapons back when he is mad, nor should one "be willing to tell [the mad] the whole truth" (331c). Socrates' first statement about *justice* avows the justice of withholding weapons owned by the mad; his first statement about *truth* avows the rightness of withholding truth from the mad who have weapons.

18. Socrates' restatement omits a chief element of Cephalus's statement: winning the favor of the gods.

When Socrates says his example proves that the definition of justice cannot be what Cephalus implied it was—"speaking the truth and giving back what one takes"—Polemarchus speaks up on behalf of his father. Cephalus gladly passes on the argument to his firstborn son, "the heir of what belongs to you," as Polemarchus says. And Cephalus departs laughing at his son's remark, laughing as he returns to the sacrifice he hopes will avert the fear and torment that attend his old age.

Crowned with a wreath from a sacrifice to which he returns, old Cephalus stands at the beginning of the *Republic* for ancestral authority but ancestral authority altered. He is not Athenian and his words appeal not to ancestral Athenian religion but to non-Homeric, non-Hesiodic foreign teachings that enter Athens through the Piraeus from their places of origin in Sicily and in Thrace, from which even now a new god is being introduced outside. The tales of Hades that cause Cephalus fear and hope are not Homer's tales, for all share a similar fate in Homer's Hades, where hope is offered to none. Adeimantus will speak of Musaeus and Orpheus, singers of the underworld from Thrace. But the tales of Hades that Cephalus brings to Athens would not be Thracian but Sicilian, for Sicily with its active volcanoes and bubbling hot springs was a source of tales of an active underworld that spread throughout greater Greece.[19] Still, whether Thracian or Sicilian, foreign tales of Hades can gain authority with Athenian young touched by the sophistic enlightenment only when they pass through a teacher they respect. Cephalus is right to return to his sacrifice laughing and to leave Socrates unattended with his heirs, for Socrates will teach them to believe what they ridicule when they hear it from him.

4. Polemarchus and Socratic Justice

Polemarchus invoked the authority of Simonides to defend his father's view of justice, and when Socrates asks him to state Simonides' view he says: "it is just to give to each what is owed." Restating that view, Socrates makes "what is owed" giving "to each what is fitting" (332c). Such justice would require knowledge of what befits each, knowledge of the highest order that only the wisest could possess. The laconic sayings of the wise must be interpreted, Socrates argued in *Protagoras*, and *Protagoras* sug-

19. On Sicily and new teachings on Hades see Kingsley, *Ancient Philosophy, Mystery, and Magic*, 71–78; Kingsley also demonstrates the Sicilian character of the "geography" of Socrates' *Phaedo* myth, 79–111.

gests that Socrates does not disbelieve "wise and divine" Simonides (331e), who speaks in "a riddle, after the fashion of poets" (332b).[20] Socrates' argument with Polemarchus over Simonides' words yields in fact a wise interpretation of them that Socrates leaves in a riddling form by leaving it unspoken.

Polemarchus interprets Simonides' view of justice to mean doing good to friends and harm to enemies. Socrates leads Polemarchus to the conclusion that justice seems useless: its one use is guarding things in their uselessness while the other arts provide everything useful. Socrates concludes: "Then justice, my friend,[21] wouldn't be anything very serious, if it is useful for useless things" (332e). This first conclusion to an argument in the *Republic* seems to be a reductio ad absurdum refutation of Polemarchus, but in fact the apparently absurd conclusion states an exact if riddling truth. For is every good useful? Is *philosophy* useful? Socrates' philosophizing—as distinct from his political philosophy—is pursued not for any use but solely out of a passion to understand, a passion sated simply by understanding. Socrates' first conclusion in his first argument accurately states the solution to philosophy's predicament: useless philosophy needs a defense before the city, which measures the value of everything by its use; philosophy really is nothing very serious where the serious is the useful. It is useful to useless philosophy to appear to have a use. The conclusion of Socrates' first argument about justice signals his primary purpose in the *Republic*: he will do justice to philosophy in its uselessness through a useful political philosophy. His first conclusion signals that he continues to speak as the wise have always spoken, hiding the wise view in plain sight.

The first argument of the *Republic* goes on: "consider it this way," Socrates instructs, explaining that the capacity to do good with an art entails a capacity for its opposite. His examples end on the "good guardian of an army [being] the very same one who can steal the enemy's plans, or defeat their undertakings by stealth" (334a). He generalizes, "Of whatever anyone is a clever guardian, he is also a clever thief," and he names Homer for the first time: "The just person, it seems, has come to light as a kind of thief, and I'm afraid you learned this from Homer," from "the grandfather of Odysseus on his mother's side," Autolycus, Wolf Himself. For Homer admired Autolycus, Socrates claims, and "said he surpassed all men 'in

20. Later in the *Republic*, when Socrates criticizes a statement customarily assigned to Simonides, he does not mention Simonides' name (489b).

21. *Friend* is a significant form of address where the issue is doing good to friends with justice.

stealing and in swearing oaths.'"[22] Thus quoting Homer, Socrates draws his second conclusion: "Justice, then, seems, according to you and Homer and Simonides, to be a certain art of stealing, for the benefit of friends." "No, by Zeus," Polemarchus did not mean that. But Socrates did: according to Socrates and Homer and Simonides, the justice of the wise is the art of the one who gave Odysseus his name, a certain art of stealing for the benefit of friends. Socrates introduces his spiritual forebears while in the act of taking over the heirs of Cephalus, stealing what is not his own and seeing to their benefit. Socrates' second conclusion, like his first, is a literal truth whose apparent absurdity allows it to be stated openly. Socrates is a man of many guiles who, like Homer, admires the grandfather of Odysseus on his mother's side.

Socrates' first reference to Homer resembles his last reference to Homer: they are the only two occasions in the *Republic* on which he names Odysseus. The last falls at the very end, as the final event in Socrates' recasting of Homer's Hades to resemble Cephalus's: the soul of Odysseus, recovered from the love of honor through memory of its former labors, chooses its next life, "the life of a private man who minds his own business" (620c). Naming Odysseus only at its beginning and end, and only in reference to a forebear and a descendant, the *Republic* points to the Socrates promised in *Charmides*, a Socrates who lays claim to being the latest in the long line of Greek wise that Homer alleged stretched back before himself to Odysseus's grandfather. Socrates is the post-Homeric offspring of Autolycus who arises in a crisis time for the sons of Athens raised on Homer. The first two conclusions of the *Republic* confirm what *Protagoras* and *Charmides* showed: Socrates knows how to employ his kin in a way that adds him to their number. But because he does what they did, he has to distance himself from his kin; he even has to blame them, blame even Homer, though he is not a lover of blame.

Socrates' argument left Polemarchus confused, no longer knowing what he meant but loyally standing by justice as helping friends and harming enemies. Socrates' next argument asks who the friends are: those who seem

22. *Odyssey* 19.395–96. Socrates does not add as Homer did that these are the gifts of a god, Hermes. Homer's words are taken from the long pause he forced into the recognition scene of Penelope and her husband: old Eurycleia, Odysseus's childhood nurse, recognizes his scar, and Homer takes his auditor back not only to the event that caused the scar but to Odysseus's naming. He reveals that Odysseus is the only one who did not receive his name from his parents (8.550–55), for Eurycleia set the unnamed child on Autolycus's knees, inviting him to name the child he had prayed much to have (19.404).

to be good or those who are good? Because humans make mistakes and are likely to mistake their friends as good, Socrates induces Polemarchus to change his definition: the friend to whom good is to be done not only seems to be but is good (335e). Socrates then moves to harming enemies. Using examples of domestic animals, he argues that when they are harmed they become worse with respect to the virtue appropriate to them. So too with humans: harming them makes them worse with respect to human virtue; but human virtue is justice; therefore a justice that harms would make others unjust by justice. The second half of Polemarchus's definition must be altered more radically than the first: "it is never just to harm anyone" (335e).

Socrates sums up this argument by returning to Simonides: "if someone asserts that it's just to give what is owed to each [as Simonides did] and he understands by this that the just man owes harm to enemies and help to friends [as Polemarchus did], the man who said that was not wise"—Polemarchus's unwise interpretation does not make Simonides unwise. Gaining Polemarchus's agreement, Socrates conscripts him for an enterprise that befits "Warlord": "We shall do battle then as partners, you and I," and Warlord salutes: "I'm ready to be your partner in the battle." Socrates has stolen the "heir to what belongs to" Cephalus for his side in a battle against the very thing Polemarchus said he inherited from his father, his view of justice. He will fight for Socrates against anyone who says the view he inherited is the view of "Simonides, or Bias, or Pittacus, or any other wise and blessed man." In the first skirmish of the *Republic* Socrates wins a partner for a battle on behalf of the wise as he interprets them.[23] But if the view Polemarchus defended as inherited from his rich father did not come from the wise, who did it come from? Socrates instructs his new partner to think of it as coming from Periander, or Perdiccas, or Xerxes, or Ismenias the Theban, "or some other rich man who has a high opinion of what he can do" (336a).[24]

Having relieved the wise of responsibility for Polemarchus's interpretation of Simonides' statement about justice and assigned its origin to political leaders, Socrates asks, "what else would one say it is?" His invitation hangs unanswered because an event of seeming violence breaks over them,

23. In *Phaedrus* Socrates says Polemarchus turned to philosophy (257b).

24. The four share a quality besides riches and ambition: each was a political leader of Athenian enemies: Periander of enemy Corinth was the wise Corinthian on most lists of the Seven Wise Men of Greece (though not on Socrates', *Protagoras* 343a), Xerxes was the chief enemy from the Persian wars, Perdiccas was the Macedonian king who interfered in the Athenian siege of Potidaea, and Ismenias was from enemy Thebes.

destroying the tranquility in which they discussed friends and enemies. Thrasymachus, "hunched up like a wild beast" but restrained till then, "hurled himself at us as if to tear us to pieces" (336b), an enemy of Socrates, Socrates as narrator leads his auditor(s) to think, bent on harming him. The force of that event redirects the conversation, obscuring the less dramatic but more important event that just occurred. Socrates asked "what else" one would say justice is, an invitation one could take up despite Thrasymachus's intervention, for Socrates prepared a most explicit response to his invitation: what else would one say justice is but what survived his critique of Polemarchus's political interpretation of wise Simonides' saying? Justice as Socrates defined it, giving to each what is fitting, can be said to be: doing good to friends who are good and not harming anyone. The interrupted end of Socrates' argument with Polemarchus does what each previous stage did: silently point to Socrates' view, the view he suggests is simply the view of the wise.

No event in the *Republic* is more important than this one that leaves offstage, leaves to inference, Socrates' view of justice. For Polemarchus's refuted view returns with a vengeance: the city Socrates builds in speech is the one best able and most willing to do good to friends and harm to enemies, and when Socrates caps his instruction that night with a myth of the afterlife, he makes Polemarchus's view cosmic with a myth that portions out good to the just and harm to the unjust. Yet the triumph of Polemarchus's view of justice in the *Republic* does not contradict Socrates' justice: Socrates does good to friends who are good and does not harm anyone; he gives to each what is fitting by openly advocating what he judges to be politically necessary, a moral or punitive city and cosmos, and by covertly indicating the true.

5. Gentling Thrasymachus

Thrasymachus of Chalcedon is not a singularity; he's a representative of the sophistic enlightenment founded by Protagoras, a radical, outspoken representative who says out loud, if in private, what Protagoras put obliquely even in private. Socrates' treatment of Thrasymachus resembles his earlier treatment of Protagoras in the crucial respect: with Thrasymachus too he attempts to redirect the Greek enlightenment. But with Thrasymachus Socrates succeeds in a way he apparently failed with Protagoras, for his most illuminating words about Thrasymachus are uttered late when he tells Adeimantus that he and Thrasymachus have "just become friends though we weren't enemies even before" (498c). Socrates certainly made him seem like an enemy, introducing him as a wild beast who flung himself at them as if to tear them to pieces. But the "wild beast" acts under rational control; he's a calculating actor, and because he is, Socrates can get the better of him.

Thrasymachus's Entry

Thrasymachus enters after Cephalus removed himself and Socrates robbed Polemarchus of his inheritance: Plato's dramatic artistry makes Thrasymachus enter the void created by the departure of traditional authority and the loss of traditional convictions. What justice might be has become an open question, and Thrasymachus enters trumpeting a powerfully attractive but subversive alternative and enters as Socrates' rival just after Socrates cleared the way for asserting his own authority with ancestral authority gone.[25]

In Cephalus's house, Thrasymachus's violent irruption forces Socrates to act in order to win back control of the conversation; but in Athens the next day he has complete control over what he narrates. Free to characterize Thrasymachus's entry for his own purposes, he says that "hunched up like a wild beast, he hurled himself at us as if to tear us to pieces," and he says he was "all in a flutter from fright" (336b). But he later speaks of Thrasymachus's "pretense," and while this refers to Thrasymachus's wanting Socrates to give an answer to what justice is, it applies as well to Thrasymachus's anger: it's fake anger, playacted to evoke anger at Socrates in the others present, for as Socrates says in *Phaedrus*, "the mighty man of Chalcedon" is the master of the art of arousing and assuaging anger.[26] But if Thrasymachus can playact anger, Socrates can act as if that anger were genuine, as if it frightened him—he can act to evoke anger in his audience at Thrasymachus. Leo Strauss warns the reader not to fall prey to Socrates' rhetoric as narrator here: "It is most important for the understanding of the *Republic* and generally that we should not behave toward Thrasymachus as Thrasymachus behaves, *i.e.* angrily, fanatically, or savagely [but

25. Thrasymachus was a well-known figure in Athens at least by early 427, less than two years after the *Republic*, for Aristophanes mentioned him by name on the comic stage as the possible inventor of an unusual word of legal reasoning (in the lost *Symposiasts*; see Dillon and Gergel, *Greek Sophists*, 205). Thrasymachus is assigned an important place in the history of rhetoric by Aristotle (*Sophistical Refutations* 183b28–34; *Rhetoric* 3.8, 3.11) and by Cicero (*Orator* 38–39, 174–76) and other ancient writers on rhetoric with access to Thrasymachus's writings. For collected references see *The Greek Sophists*.

26. *Phaedrus* 267c–d.

instead] look without indignation at Thrasymachus' indignation."[27] The rhetorical power of Socrates' image of the wild beast hides the quieter reality: he and Thrasymachus are men of the enlightenment, rivals for the ears of the young men but kin with shared interests. A chronological reading of the *Republic* makes the kinship of Socrates and Thrasymachus easier to see, for in the prewar *Protagoras* Socrates, with the caution due the subject, claimed kinship with the sophistic movement in his image of family and counseled the fitting way to deal with family members.[28] Socrates and Thrasymachus, mature men schooled in the rhetorical arts, vie with one another in the house of newly pious Cephalus for the young doubtful both of piety and of justice. Socrates claims that because he saw Thrasymachus before Thrasymachus pounced he was able to prepare himself for the attack. His arguments establishing mastery over Thrasymachus prove that he prepared himself very well indeed.

Thrasymachus's first speech is an indictment of Socrates. It attacks his method of questioning, challenges his refusal to give his own answer, and prohibits five possible answers that make justice choiceworthy—five answers that Socrates in fact gives in the long argument that night showing justice to be the needful, helpful, profitable, gainful, and advantageous. In his first speech to Thrasymachus, Socrates affirms his seriousness in searching for justice by using an image: it is more serious that a search for gold. In his last speech in the dialogue Thrasymachus will repeat this image of searching for gold (450b) as he joins the community of those voting to compel Socrates to speak on a topic he left unexplained: Thrasymachus too is serious and lets Socrates know in a fitting way. Socrates' speech contains a still more important word that comes up later that night, for in response to Thrasymachus's accusation of unseriousness, Socrates says, "Don't suppose that, my friend" (336e). *Friend* may sound ironic just after Socrates described Thrasymachus as a wild beast and just before Thrasymachus speaks of Socrates' "habitual irony." But when Socrates later says that they've just become friends, he makes their friendship a result of what he had just then argued: Socrates viewed Thrasymachus as friend from the start, but he had to work to make Thrasymachus see him, a rival, as in fact a friend.

Thrasymachus says he "predicted that you would be ironic," and Socrates says, "That's because you're wise" (337a). And Thrasymachus pre-

27. Strauss, *City and Man*, 74–75; Strauss's "most important" and "and generally" are particularly noteworthy.

28. *Protagoras* 346a–b.

dicted that "you . . . would do anything rather than answer," and Socrates maneuvers Thrasymachus into answering. As Socrates' questions advance, Thrasymachus reveals the "pretense" in his attack on Socrates for not giving an answer: "What if I could show you another answer about justice" different from the five he forbade? Thrasymachus has no interest in hearing Socrates' answer and a powerful interest in giving his own. Of course he asks for money; he's a professional teacher who traveled from Chalcedon at least partly to gain students. Glaucon shows that he has already formed a low opinion of Thrasymachus by breaking in to offer to pay for Socrates: "Now, for money's sake, speak." And Socrates continues to speak ironically: "Don't begrudge your teaching to Glaucon here and the others."

Thrasymachus's Exhibition Speech

Socrates narrates what he has already made evident: "Thrasymachus clearly desired to speak so that he could win a good reputation, since he believed he had a very fine answer" (338a). His very fine answer is that "The just is nothing other than the advantage of the stronger (superior)." Having announced it he asks for the only payment Socrates said he could offer, praise. Instead, alleging he doesn't yet understand, Socrates indulges in a deflating little joke that compels Thrasymachus to make a short speech explaining what he announced. His speech proves to be the first of three that set out his view systematically: taken together his three speeches are a well-constructed exhibition speech of a master sophist. Having stated his thesis, Thrasymachus first shows its political character: whether ruled by tyranny, democracy, or aristocracy, a city's laws serve the interests of its ruler; justice for the ruled is simply obeying the law, serving the interests of the ruler. The duality of justice evident in this statement gives Socrates the opening for his argument: if the ruler makes a mistake, the mistaken law is both just and unjust, just as the law, unjust as contrary to the ruler's advantage.

Thrasymachus seems a trifle slow to grasp the point as Socrates develops his argument, and after Socrates spells it out his partner in battle, Polemarchus, pipes up in triumph to announce that Socrates has got him. Cleitophon speaks up as Thrasymachus's partner, offering a way out; Thrasymachus refuses the offer, for his advantage lies elsewhere: a *ruler*, in the precise sense of the practitioner of the craft of rule, makes no mistakes. This is not an empirical claim about rulers but Thrasymachus's promise to the young men present who aspire to rule: I teach the perfect practice of the craft of rule through perfect knowledge of rule. Thrasymachus's three speeches expounding his definition progressively set forth his sales pitch to the young men, beginning with his promise to teach the means to become that stronger, superior one who serves his own advantage by wised-up, mistake-free rule.

There is again a certain slowness in Thrasymachus's catching on to Socrates' argument against his claim about the benefits of the art of rule: he could have glimpsed its conclusion at its start when Socrates claimed that the art of the doctor cares for the sick and the art of the pilot rules the sailors (341c). When he does begin to resist the drift of Socrates' argument ($342c_7$), Socrates as narrator obscures the exact nature of his resistance by putting each of Thrasymachus's responses in indirect speech right up to his outburst after the argument is lost (343a); he reports "a great deal of resistance" ($342c_7$) and trying "to put up a fight" ($342d_3$), but not his actual words, the only exception being a response to a question that calls for assent only to something agreed on earlier ($342e_1$). Thrasymachus as arguer remains obscured by Socrates' choice not to give the exact form his resistance took: did he express it in words, in gestures, in hesitations?

Socrates' argument leads inexorably to the unstated conclusion that the ruler who practices the art of rule rules for the sake of the ruled (342e). With that conclusion looming, Thrasymachus insults Socrates for the childish innocence of such a view. No innocent, Thrasymachus proceeds to the most important part of his speech, setting out his key selling point by identifying himself and flattering his prospective clients. Assuming Thrasymachus's competence—and we must for both historic and dramatic reasons—he means exactly what he says: he and his art serve "[his] master's good and [his] own" (343b). He is neither the master nor the mastered but stands to master and mastered as a shepherd stands to an owner and his sheep: he possesses the art with which his master, the ruler, can fatten and fleece the ruled. Thrasymachus has made his own role clear: his art is ministerial, it serves his own advantage by serving the city however it is ruled. The reason for his feigned anger at Socrates is clear: he mimics the city's real anger, for the city is justifiably angry at a teacher who criticizes its justice (doing good to friends and harm to enemies) while holding the impractical view that justice does not harm. Thrasymachus knows himself to be a shepherd serving the only master he can imagine; Socrates' aim with him will come to light as an offer to serve a different master.

If justice really is someone else's good, then the ultimate implication is clear: one's own good is served by injustice and best served by complete injustice: not merely contracts, or taxes, or even a ruling office of some kind, the three partial injustices Thrasymachus lists. No, he is speaking of one "who has the ability to get more[29] in a big way" (344a). "Consider him," Thrasymachus says, moving explicitly to "the most perfect injustice, which brings the one who does injustice the greatest happiness . . . and that is tyranny." What follows is Thrasymachus's explicit advocacy of the life of the tyrant as bringing the greatest happiness through "injustice entire." The tyrant takes for himself everything that belongs to others, everything sacred and profane, private and public, and does so "all at once." When the tyrant not only takes the money of the citizens but kidnaps and enslaves them, "he gets called happy and blessed, not only by the citizens but also by whoever else hears that he has done injustice entire." Thrasymachus brings his speech to an end in the rhetorically proper manner, summarizing his key point—"Injustice, when it comes into being on a sufficient scale, is mightier, freer, and more masterful than justice"—and his last words return to his opening words and repeat the memorable phrase that was one half of his teaching on tyranny, but now he adds the other half: "the just is the advantage of the stronger (superior), and the unjust is what is profitable and advantageous for oneself." He ends his speech in the polished way that Socrates refers to in *Phaedrus* just after naming Thrasymachus: "some call it *recapitulation* and others some other name."[30]

"He had it in mind to go away" after his speech, Socrates reports. He would depart not in petulance but with calculation, depart not to disappear but to be sought out for that private tutoring which alone can convey the art of the tyrant—and to avoid having to debate with Socrates about such private matters even before a public as small as that at Polemarchus's house. For no sophist from Chalcedon could ever become tyrant of Athens; he serves his advantage by being exactly what he says he is: first minister to an aspiring tyrant. Are there any takers at Polemarchus's house? He had it in mind to go away because he had given his professional pitch for his ministerial art and made himself as enticing as he could, promising perfect rule by perfect injustice over a willing populace of docile just. He's a shepherd, he's for hire, and anyone interested will know how to reach him. Why does he stay? For the same reason Socrates stays: "those present didn't let him and forced him to stay put." Compelled, Thrasymachus too hears persuasion: Socrates "begged him." Socrates' begging is a speech characterizing what Thrasymachus has just done: he set out "an entire way

29. *Pleonektein* is the crucial word for "the ambition to outdo, to get the better of," the kind of ambition present in the highest degree in an Achilles or in admirers of Achilles like Alcibiades.

30. *Phaedrus* 267d.

of life—how each of us can live his life in the most profitable way." To leave now would show that "you have no care for us." Besides, "it wouldn't be a bad investment for you to do a good deed for so many as we are." Socrates emphasizes that he himself is not persuaded that "injustice is more profitable than justice," and "perhaps someone else among us shares this sentiment." He ends with a challenge: "So persuade us adequately . . . that we are not advised correctly in having a higher regard for justice than injustice." Thrasymachus stays because he must; to leave in the face of general force and Socrates' persuasion would ruin any prospect his powerful speech might have created for him. He must do what he didn't intend to do and face Socrates knowing Socrates' reputation for proving himself the stronger or superior by destroying the views offered by others.

What now transpires is the pivotal matter in their exchange as Socrates and Thrasymachus argue the best way of life for the young men present. Socrates' refutation takes advantage of the "precise sense" of an art in order to introduce an arresting notion about the art of rule: no one rules willingly. Rule, like all other arts, serves the benefit of what it has been set over. There must, then, be an accompanying art that serves the practitioner's benefit, a "wage-earner's art" that pays for the art that benefits those on whom it is practiced. What about rule? Socrates repeats his earlier bare claim: "no one willingly chooses to rule and get mixed up in straightening out other people's troubles." What are the wages of rule? Socrates mentions three: money, honor, or a penalty for not ruling.

Glaucon Interrupts

No wonder Glaucon intervenes: he's a young man with a powerful passion to rule, and his attention has been arrested by Socrates' provocation that no one willingly chooses to rule. He says he understands money and honor as motives to rule, but what could a penalty for not ruling be and how would a penalty be a kind of wage? Socrates is direct, even insulting: "You don't understand the wages of the best on account of which the most fit rule when they are willing to rule" (347b). "Or don't you know," he adds, "that love of honor and love of money are said to be, and are, reproaches?" "I do indeed," says Glaucon, who will show himself to be driven by a certain kind of love of honor for which he must have suffered reproach.[31] The most fit do not rule out of *love of honor* (*philotimos*). Socrates uses this im-

31. Xenophon reports that Glaucon had a desire to preside over the city and that Socrates stopped him all by himself (*Memorabilia* 3.6.1).

portant word here for the first time in the *Republic*[32]—and uses it for the last time at the very end to describe the soul of Odysseus in its choice of a life: from memory of its former labors and recovered from the love of honor (620d), it chose a private life. Why do the most fit choose to rule when they do choose to rule? There is no more important topic in this dialogue on the *politeia*, which reaches its center on the rule of the philosopher.

Here, speaking of the rule of the best and contrasting the best with lovers of honor and lovers of money, Socrates speaks not of the *love* that moves the best but of two movers, "necessity and a penalty." Three times he says *necessity*, but instead of elaborating, here, all that is involved in that necessity—instead of elaborating their motive as a love—he emphasizes the penalty: he cannot yet say that the best are the wise or that love of wisdom grounds the necessity that the wise rule. What is the penalty the best suffer if they do not rule? "The greatest of penalties is being ruled by a worse, if one is not willing oneself to rule." Rule or be ruled. That is the option facing the wise, the fundamental alternative compelling them to rule. Moved by love of wisdom alone, the best are penalized if they do not act to assume rule, penalized by being ruled by the worse, by unwisdom: here at last is Socrates' genuine compulsion in the *Republic*. The principle of Socratic political philosophy, its reason for being, partially surfaces here as Socrates speaks of the rule of the best. Philosophy can exist only if it is free, and it can be free only if it rules. What moved Socrates to aspire to rule in *Protagoras* moves him now to a far more ambitious project of rule in order to succeed where he earlier failed. He announces a principle that precedes philosophy's project of rule: "Every person of understanding would choose to be benefited by another rather than take the trouble of benefiting another"—every person of understanding seeks his own advantage. The best would avoid rule or the advantage of the ruled if that were advantageous. The best rule to the advantage of the ruled in order not to be disadvantaged in what matters most; the best rule for the advantage of themselves and their like. Thrasymachus is not wrong.

Though occasioned by Glaucon's unavoidable ignorance, this speech is part of Socrates' encounter with Thrasymachus: he is its primary audience. Hear this, Socrates says in effect, and know why it is necessary for me to confront you. I, a seeming innocent who seems to you to make way

32. Socrates will contrast love of honor with love of victory as one of the important forms of spiritedness. See Craig, *War Lover* (esp. 24, 75–80), for the differences between the two, particularly as they apply to the difference between Glaucon and Adeimantus.

for the other, confront you and your ministerial art that needs a master to serve: I am that master. The rest of the *Republic*, with all its unexpected and indispensable additions, sets out the means whereby the best assumes rule, having recognized that he must rule or be ruled by a worse. And for Socrates to assume rule, Thrasymachus is as important as Glaucon.

Socrates ends his interlude with Glaucon on a small manipulation that also has Thrasymachus as its audience. About to turn back to Thrasymachus, he calls attention to what he earlier noted (344e): Thrasymachus shifted the argument. He began with a definition of justice but shifted to a "far bigger thing," the way of life implied by his definition: the life of the perfectly unjust man is stronger or better. "Which do you choose, Glaucon?" Socrates asks, forcing into the open the existential choice facing all the young who listen to Thrasymachus or other such teachers of the sophistic enlightenment. Of course Glaucon says, "I choose the life of the just man as more profitable." But has he heard the many good things Thrasymachus listed as belonging to the life of the unjust man? "I heard but I'm not persuaded," Glaucon insists. What Socrates says next makes use of Glaucon to set up the rest of his conversation with Thrasymachus and the rest of the *Republic*: "Do you want us to persuade him, if we're able to find a way, that what he says isn't true?" "How could I not want it?" Glaucon says, tempted as he is by Thrasymachus but still deeply held by justice. Will Socrates be able to find a way to persuade Thrasymachus and thereby persuade Glaucon? His arguments with Thrasymachus completely disappoint Glaucon, leading him to dare to rebuke Socrates for only seeming "to have persuaded us" instead of "really persuading us" (357a)—and then to reveal in his own long speech just how much the tyrant's way of life tempts him and just why he is committed to justice. Socrates heightened Glaucon's expectations for his coming arguments in order to fail to meet them: he must draw out of Glaucon how strongly he is tempted and why he resists, and what he draws out of Glaucon is an indispensable part of his education of Thrasymachus.[33]

Socrates has one other little use to make of Glaucon at this point: *how* shall he attempt to persuade Thrasymachus, by long speeches from each that require adjudication or by continuing his method of questioning to arrive at agreement? Through Glaucon's preference for the latter Socrates places another compulsion on Thrasymachus: he cannot profitably insist on his own method if his prospective clients desire another.

33. See Strauss, *City and Man*, 85: "What Socrates does in the Thrasymachus section would be inexcusable if he had not done it in order to provoke the passionate reaction of Glaucon."

Socrates Examines Thrasymachus on the Best Way of Life

Before embarking on his three arguments to persuade Thrasymachus, Socrates calls attention to just how radical Thrasymachus is. Socrates knows full well "what you want to say" (348e): the tyrannical teaching is no novelty to him; but while others who speak of injustice as profitable agree that it is "vicious or shameful" (others like Protagoras), Thrasymachus is willing to say that justice is vice and injustice virtue, though he also uses euphemisms like "high-minded innocence" for justice and "good counsel" for injustice. Thrasymachus dares to speak more openly in Polemarchus's house than Protagoras did in Callias's house and to speak a more radical view.

Socrates' three arguments repeat the subtlety of his arguments with Polemarchus: each has an implied content open to inference from its obvious content. But the inferable content in these arguments is addressed to Thrasymachus; they are therefore like his earlier arguments with Protagoras: addressed to one with whom Socrates shares an enterprise, they proffer an invitation to perform that enterprise differently in order to avert a shared danger and serve a shared end.

Socrates' first argument is on justice as virtue and wisdom (349b–350d). It focuses on *pleonexia*, the passion to get more, to get the better of, a healthy passion in a culture of admirers of Peleus's advice to his son Achilles to "always be first and excel all others."[34] But *pleonexia* derives from the word for *too much* and denotes a disposition to take more than one's allotted share, to gain inappropriate advantage over another. Socrates' argument treats the *technai* as kinds of knowledge; beginning with the musical art and the medical art, it moves to "every kind of knowledge and lack of knowledge" and shows that the wise and good possessor of knowledge does not aim to get the better of another knower in his field—only the ignorant and bad do that. Socrates wins: "the just [person] has revealed himself to us as good and wise" (350c).

Socrates narrates all his questions and all Thrasymachus's answers in direct speech, with no narrative comment beyond the necessary *I said* and *he said*. Thrasymachus answers every question, and his answers end with the just man being good and wise and the unjust ignorant and bad. But after completing the argument Socrates states that his narration of steady question and answer failed to show what was actually happening: "Thrasy-

34. *Iliad* 11.784, 6.208.

machus did not agree to all of this so easily as I tell it now" (350c). Instead, "he dragged his feet and resisted." Where is there any room for such resistance in the speeches as Socrates narrated them? If he narrated them as they were spoken, Thrasymachus's resistance must have been nonverbal, like the reaction Socrates reports afterward: Thrasymachus "produced a wonderful quantity of sweat, for it was summer. And then I saw what I had never seen before, Thrasymachus blushing." This is Socrates' sole narrative comment in all three arguments, and it calls attention to a resistance invisible in the words. Socrates makes Thrasymachus's resistance visible to an unpresent audience by reporting his involuntary reaction. Why is it important to make that reaction visible?

Socrates had never before seen Thrasymachus blush. Why blush now? It can't be because he lost an argument—he lost every argument till now and never blushed. There must be more to the *pleonexia* argument than first appeared. The argument concerned the ignorance and badness of trying to get the better of someone with whom one shares an art. But the two of them share an art, each in his own way practicing the art of speech. Trying to get the better of Socrates in speech before this audience of young men, Thrasymachus failed at every step: Socrates showed himself Thrasymachus's overwhelming superior in his own art, seeing through him in an instant, establishing his argumentative authority with a brilliance Thrasymachus could not but admire. And hearing the *pleonexia* argument, Thrasymachus blushes: his blush is not mere shame but shame acknowledging the inappropriateness of his *pleonexia* against a superior of his own kind so sovereign in his superiority that he gets the better of him with an argument that rebukes him for even trying to get the better of him. And Socrates got the better of him not out of *pleonexia*, inappropriate striving, but by actually having the mastery Thrasymachus claims but lacks.

Thrasymachus must hear Socrates' *pleonexia* argument personally: by attacking me and trying to get the better of a superior of your own kind, you acted ignorantly and badly, inviting your defeat and ignominy. Socrates communicates his superiority to Thrasymachus as he did to Protagoras, and his one narrative comment during their whole argument about the best life points to the success of his communication. Thrasymachus can be shamed; he is no more a wild beast—no more evil—than Critias, but he has embraced an evil doctrine for his own advantage. If he can be shown that his advantage lies elsewhere, perhaps he can be led to speak otherwise—for the rebuke that brings the blush is the merest beginning of the long process of Socrates' attempt to educate Thrasymachus on justice.

But it's a promising beginning because Thrasymachus's capacity for shame opens the possibility that he could place his always only ministerial art in the service of masterful Socrates.

Socrates closes his narrative comment on what transpired in the moment of the blush by saying, "we had come to complete agreement about justice being virtue and wisdom, and injustice both vice and ignorance" (350d). Is blushing Thrasymachus in complete agreement? "What you're saying now," he says, "doesn't satisfy me and I have something to say about it." He doesn't say it but says instead that the rules Socrates set down with Glaucon forestall his saying it, "for you would say that I'm making a public harangue." After the argument that made him blush, he says, "either let me say as much as I want, or, if you keep on questioning . . . just as with old wives who tell tales, I shall say to you, 'All right,' and nod and shake my head" (350e). His "complete agreement" amounts to this: I heard what you said and will not try to outdo you but will keep to what you set down and keep agreeing—a begrudging enough agreement, but Socrates' next argument will carry his private case forward with a powerful reason to agree completely.

Socrates' second argument, that justice is mightier (351a–352d), would be easy, he says, if he based it on the conclusion of the first argument that justice is virtue and wisdom. But he chooses a harder way, shifting the argument to the city. He knows that Thrasymachus would praise the city that enslaves other cities unjustly, but what he wants to ask about is that city's *internal* justice: "do you believe that either a city, or an army, or pirates, or thieves, or any other group that has some common unjust enterprise would be able to accomplish anything if its members acted unjustly to one another?" (351c). Socrates is precise: if they didn't act unjustly, "wouldn't they be more able to accomplish something?" For injustice "produces factions, hatreds and quarrels among themselves, and justice produces unanimity and friendship." Socrates is insistent: when injustice comes into being "both among free and slaves, will it not also cause them to hate one another and to form factions, and to be unable to accomplish anything in common with one another?" The same thing would happen "between two" and even "within one." Injustice "possesses a power such that, wherever it comes into being, be it in a city, or a family [*genos*],[35] or an army, or whatever else, it first makes it unable to accomplish anything . . . and then makes it

35. *Genos* (race, clan, kind) is made particularly prominent in this second list by being thrust between the initial two members repeated from the first list, city and army, while pirates and thieves are dropped.

an enemy both to itself and to everything opposite and to the just" (352a). Socrates wins: justice is stronger.

This second argument is central to Socrates' indirect communication to Thrasymachus and repeats what he communicated to Protagoras, Hippias, and Prodicus:[36] they are "family," with shared interests whose success demands justice among its members. As a group they could be viewed from outside as thieves whose unjust enterprise steals other men's sons—justice among us thieves is a precondition of our success. Thrasymachus is attentive to what Socrates intimates, as his nuanced responses indicate. When Socrates asked, "Isn't it so?" after saying that injustice produces factions and justice produces unanimity and friendship, Thrasymachus said, "Let it be so, so as not to differ with you"—so as to make unanimity and friendship possible between us.[37] When Socrates said that within a single man, injustice makes him an enemy to himself and to the just, he added, "and the gods too, my friend, are just?" "Have it that they are," the "friend" responds, despite being an atheist. "Then the unjust man will also be an enemy to the gods, Thrasymachus, and the just man a friend." No response could be more in keeping with Socrates' invitation than Thrasymachus's actual response: "Feast yourself boldly on the argument, for I won't oppose you, so as not to make enemies of those here"—being just to a kinsman by not opposing a point he surely opposes, Thrasymachus ensures that he, they, not make enemies of their audience by appearing to be enemies of the gods. Socrates has won a kind of justice between Thrasymachus and himself, an agreement that must be Thrasymachus's acknowledgment of the kinship to which Socrates appealed.

What does Socrates' victory in the third argument add to this private exchange? An argument about "the way one should live" (352d–354a), it completes Socrates' victory by forcing Thrasymachus to agree that the just life is profitable because it leads to happiness. The third argument, after the rebuke of the first and the invitation of the second, seems to indicate the way of life Thrasymachus should teach, for it is an example of how to present the salutary case for the superiority of justice over injustice.[38] And Thrasymachus's behavior in the third argument suggests that Socrates' second argument was successful: Thrasymachus cooperates in

36. *Protagoras* 346a–b.

37. At the beginning of this argument Socrates complimented Thrasymachus on his good answer, drawing Thrasymachus's response, "I am gratifying you" (351e).

38. In this respect too, Socrates' arguments with Thrasymachus resemble those with Protagoras and Hippias and Prodicus, which culminated with Socrates recommending a salutary teaching.

the joint venture of making a case for justice; he is notably helpful, never once objecting and even offering his insight before Socrates is quite ready (353c). Justice is to be presented as the virtue of the soul that allows it to do its work well, where its work is "managing, ruling, and giving counsel" (353d)—the work for which Thrasymachus presents himself as the expert teacher.

The last words of the last conversation between Socrates and Thrasymachus are a fitting acknowledgment by each of what transpired between them alone, beyond the understanding of the others—for if in fact they are "thieves" with shared interests, their mutual understanding must be kept to themselves among these boys. "Let that be the fill of your banquet at the Bendideia, Socrates" (354a)—Thrasymachus claims to have done what Socrates asked him to do in the third argument: "fill out the rest of the banquet for me by answering just as you have been doing" (352b). He has acted as Socrates' associate, doing everything he asked, answering every question in the appropriate way. Thrasymachus ends without rancor or malice, and Socrates is gracious in return: "I owe it to you, since you have grown gentle and left off dealing with me harshly."

Socrates gave Thrasymachus good reason to listen and he listened. The salesman who wanted to leave after giving his exhibition speech stays of his own accord after being led to blush and to hear of a new possibility from a superior rhetorician who not only refrained from pressing his advantage but suggested they had mutual interests and could be friends. The gentling of Thrasymachus is the beginning of a process whose subsequent steps are noted with great economy as the *Republic* proceeds: everything that happens from now on will have one very attentive, very accomplished listener. What Socrates achieves in persuading Glaucon and Adeimantus will be a lesson learned deeply by this expert in persuasion persuaded to listen.[39] But kin or no kin, Socrates is ruthless. Tomorrow he will betray Thrasymachus's private teaching on tyranny to a wider Athenian audience, generating anger against him as a wild beast. That beast, however, was a pre-Socratic Thrasymachus, a dangerous teacher made civil by Socrates' efforts. Socrates *is* the opponent of that man, and he gets the better of him not only in the Piraeus but in Athens the next day. Thrasymachus can serve his advantage in one way only with a Socrates who is merciless.

Fully satisfied with his three arguments to persuade Thrasymachus of Thrasymachus's best way of life, Socrates stirs the inevitable dissatisfaction his arguments caused in Glaucon. He encourages expression of that dissat-

39. Thrasymachus is referred to later at 357a, 358a–d, 367c, 450a–b, 498c–d, 590d.

isfaction by the way he ends with Thrasymachus. He's been a glutton at the feast, he says, grabbing whatever he was offered before finishing what he already had; before finishing "what the just is," he grabbed at "whether it was vice and ignorance or virtue and wisdom," and then grabbed at whether "injustice is more profitable than justice." He takes all the blame for the result: "I know nothing." But it's Glaucon who knows nothing about what he most wanted to be persuaded of, and it doesn't take all that much courage for him to rebuke Socrates for what Socrates rebuked himself for, his failure to show why injustice is not the most profitable life.

The *Republic* is a chronologically later parallel of *Protagoras*. In both, Socrates confronts a famous foreign teacher in a private meeting in a rich man's house in the presence of Athenian young ambitious to rule. In both, privacy allows the foreigner to speak with relative candor of seditious matters the Athenian public would punish were it to hear them spoken in public. In both, Socrates makes the private public, betraying to a wider Athenian audience what went on behind closed doors, discrediting the foreign teacher and bringing credit on himself. And in both, Socrates' confrontation with a great sophist sets up an opportunity to speak with young Athenians already corrupted by the sophistic teaching and to make a positive case for justice. The great difference with the *Republic* will be the novelties intimated in *Charmides* a few weeks earlier: the Socrates of the *Republic* differs most from the Socrates of *Protagoras* because he brings back from Potidaea a teaching on order and on the gods and the soul that helps make its believers just.

6. The State of the Young in Athens

It's right that Glaucon intervene again, not because he's "most courageous in everything" but because Socrates led him to believe that the persuasion of Thrasymachus was for him (347e). Yet Socrates' three arguments, however useful for Thrasymachus, are anything but persuasive for Glaucon. Challenging Socrates to do better, Glaucon restores Thrasymachus's argument in a rhetorically schooled, three-part speech—Glaucon has done more than listen to Thrasymachus and his like, he has learned their *technê* and their teachings. But before he begins he betrays what he really wants: he speaks in vehement praise of injustice for one reason only: "in order to show you how I want to hear you condemn injustice and praise justice" (358d).

Glaucon first describes the being of justice as knowable through its becoming, its actual origins in a compact to pass laws to avoid injustice.

Second, to prove that the just are just unwillingly he tells a story of Gyges, who could do what he really wanted because he could make himself invisible: he seduced the queen, killed the king, and assumed the rule—he did what Glaucon thinks everyone would do if they could. Third, he polishes up two statues, as Socrates says, to prove that the wholly unjust man with a reputation for justice lives a better, happier life than a wholly just man with a reputation for injustice. Why does Glaucon give Gyges such prominence as the central and most vivid figure in his three-part speech?[40] He relates his story as "what they say," making use of a tale that Herodotus too used. Herodotus made the story the very first tale he told on his own in his history; he put the focus on Candaules, last in the previous line of Lydian kings. Candaules invites Gyges, his bodyguard, to view his wife naked in order to prove that she is the most beautiful of women.[41] Gyges is Herodotus's model just man; he adheres to what he has heard from the wise men of old that each should look only upon his own and not on the private things of another; he must be compelled against his will to perform each act in the story.[42] Glaucon's version reveals his suspicion that even the just man has secret yearnings he would satisfy were he able to make himself invisible. By making his central argument on nature (*physis*) and law (*nomos*) a tale of treachery and tyranny, Glaucon deepens both his first argument about the being (*ousia*) and becoming (*genesis*) of justice, and his final argument about the appearance (*dokein*) of justice trumping the reality (*einai*) of injustice. Glaucon, peering within, fears that the soul of man is ruled by unlawful passions, erotic passion and a passion to rule that can be curbed or contained only by fear of being seen, fear of punishment.

Adeimantus intervenes vehemently when Glaucon is finished: "What *most* needed to be said has not been said" (362d). What most needs to be said is that the customary manner of *praising* justice leads the clever to pursue a mere reputation for justice. Glaucon looked to what he thought

40. The leading manuscripts have Glaucon say "the ancestor of Gyges the Lydian," but at 612b Socrates says simply "the ring of Gyges." Kirby Flower Smith argues persuasively for excising "of Gyges" as a later interpolation into the text, which originally read "the ancestor of the Lydian," *the Lydian* being the famous King Croesus, the last king of Lydia (c. 560–546), and *the ancestor* being the equally famous founder of the line, Gyges, of whom the tale was popularly told. Smith reconstructs the popular tale by utilizing the texts of Plato and Herodotus plus other ancient sources to suggest a complete and satisfying "fairy tale" told of the famous founding of the Lydian line of kings ("Tale of Gyges and the King of Lydia").

41. Herodotus 1.7–15.

42. Herodotus thus makes his first tale display the necessity of esotericism, the wisdom of keeping hidden from the just man the unlawful sight of the private possession known by the wise to be most beautiful.

was nature, Adeimantus looks solely to opinion.[43] He indicts not the new teachers of enlightenment but old and new teachers of religion, condemning the whole of Greek education by tracing its history, the history of Greek religion. It begins with "noble Hesiod and Homer," who spoke of the gods as rewarding justice with earthly benefit. The steady decline from noble beginnings started with "Musaeus and his son," who claimed that the gods offer reward in Hades very like the earthly reward of drinking parties. "Others" then extended the gods' rewards on earth to one's descendants and added a new element to Hades: the unholy and unjust are punished there by being buried in mud or forced to transport water in a sieve. These claims of reward and punishment came to be exploited, Adeimantus states, by "another form of speech about justice and injustice" in both prose and poetry. These new teachers, emphasizing that justice is beautiful but hard and injustice sweet and easy, shameful only by opinion and law, teach that the unjust is more profitable. But even more remarkable is what they say about the gods and justice: whereas the earlier teachers emphasized the justice of the gods in rewarding justice and punishing injustice, these later teachers say the gods allot misfortune to many just men and good fortune to many bad. Armed with this teaching, "beggar priests and diviners" go to the doors of the rich claiming to possess powers of sacrifice and incantation by which they can persuade the gods to heal the rich man's injustices and ruin his enemies, "injuring just and unjust alike with evocations and spells" (364c). Such priests exploit the poets by perverting their gods, and Adeimantus runs through his history a second time, showing how they use Hesiod and Homer and "a babble of books by Musaeus and Orpheus . . . according to whose prescriptions they busy themselves

43. In *The War Lover*, Leon Craig gives an unprecedented portrait of the two brothers, making use of the whole of the *Republic* to lay out the differences between these two spirited young men. In his chapter "Sons and Lovers," he begins his psycho-analysis of the two brothers by describing the coming to be of the timocratic man as a lover of honor and a lover of victory. In "The Heart of Darkness," he elaborates the difference between these two kinds of lover, concluding that Socrates is exhibiting a fissure within spiritedness that separates the lover of honor from the higher type, the possibly prephilosophic lover of victory. In "Crime and Punishment," he analyzes the brothers' two long speeches at the beginning of book 2, showing the deepest concerns of the lover of victory and the lover of honor. Craig's sharply delineated philosophical psychology of the brothers focuses on how Socrates meets "the most challenging of pedagogical problems" (137), the perennial situation of rebellious youth testing their limits and breaking free of constraints. My own focus is different; while learning much from Craig's analysis, I focus on what is historically singular, Socrates' insight into the turning of the Homeric age and what that requires of wise policy on behalf of philosophy—and Socrates' recognition that his failures with the spirited young men, Alcibiades and Critias, required a new strategy for dealing with the young, a strategy displayed by his treatment of Glaucon and Adeimantus in their differences.

with their sacrifices." As he reaches the end of his indictment Adeimantus applies his history of the debasement of Greek religion to present events: these new priests "persuade not only private persons but cities as well that through sacrifices and pleasurable games there are deliverances and purifications from unjust deeds for those still living" (364e)—Cephalus is outside practicing his sacrifices and incantations in accord with the formula of some beggar priest, and the Athenians are outside introducing sacrifices and pleasurable games in the hope of deliverance by some foreign god.

In the second main part of his speech Adeimantus asks the fitting question: "what do we suppose [such teachers] do to the souls of the young who hear them?" He displays both his own soul and his dramatic powers by telling first what a young man with a good nature and high capacity would say to himself. Speaking in the first person he surely describes what he says to himself: the words of Pindar, of an unnamed wise man (probably Simonides), and of Archilochus encourage him to seem just while being unjust. Others object to the conclusion he draws from wise authority, and he brings one such objector right onto his stage by acting out a dramatic dialogue in which "someone" defends justice against a clever young man speaking in the first-person plural. The someone warns him that deception is hard, but the youth welcomes a challenge and claims devotion to reason—"we must go where the tracks of the argument lead." He knows the ways of secrecy and persuasion and is able to hide and "get the better and not pay the penalty." The someone objects that the gods cannot be deceived or forced, but the youth can defend his injustice with skeptical arguments but especially with the arguments of the very advocates of the gods: even if there are gods and they care about us, we know about them only from the laws and the poets, and they tell us the gods can be bought. The someone is reduced to his argument of last resort: in Hades the gods will punish the unjust. But "the one who calculates" has the perfect cynical retort: "the initiations and the delivering gods have great power, as say the greatest cities"—as says Athens by its actions outside—"and [as say] those children of gods who have become poets and spokesmen of the gods"—and persuade the likes of Cephalus.

Looking back at Glaucon's speech from the perspective on religion that his brother thinks most needs to be said, it is clear that he has arrived at a highly cynical view of religion, for he mentions gods only twice. Gyges, seducer of the queen, murderer of the king, usurper of the kingdom, is "an equal to a god among humans" (360c). And Glaucon's completely unjust man makes sacrifices to the gods and cares for the gods; therefore, "it is more appropriate for him to be dearer to the gods than is the just man" (362c).

Adeimantus ends his speech by having "this whole argument of his and mine" focus on "you, Socrates," assigning him responsibility for persuading them. He refers to "all the praisers of justice from the heroes at the beginning" till now, claiming that "no one has ever, in poetry or prose, adequately developed the argument that [injustice] is the greatest of evils a soul can have within it, and justice the greatest good" (366e). In his ardor "to hear the opposite from you," he repeats himself again and again, but he can state his challenge with exactitude and it is identical to Glaucon's plea: "show what each [justice and injustice] in itself does to the person who has it that makes [injustice] bad and [justice] good" (367b). He assigns Socrates the highest teaching office because of who he thinks he is: "you've spent your whole life considering nothing other than this" (367d). Adeimantus may not have an adequate view on how Socrates spends his whole life, but the reputation Socrates has cultivated allows him no escape from the authority Adeimantus accords him.

The speeches of Glaucon and Adeimantus are not the speeches of budding philosophers with a passion for the true; they are the impassioned pleas of young men who want to go on believing in the goodness of justice. Never once do they ask Socrates to tell them the truth about justice; they ask him for proofs that the just life is better than an unjust life.[44] "Leave out rewards," they high-mindedly say, but they can't mean it—the goodness of justice must consist in a good that is good for them. They want to believe that virtue brings happiness, that they inhabit a moral order of just deserts. What hangs in the balance for them is no theory but the very lives they will live from this point forward. In their youthful zeal they practically command Socrates to persuade them that what they want to believe is true *is* true. Socrates is again compelled, now by the life crisis of the best young Athenians caused in part by the Greek enlightenment, in part by the war and plague that put all securities into question, and in part by Greek religion itself in the way it praises the moral. Leo Strauss stated regarding this dramatic moment in the *Republic*, "the political questions of great urgency do not permit delay: the question of justice must be answered by all means even if all the evidence needed for an adequate answer is not yet in."[45] With the evidence not yet in, Socrates is compelled to act.

44. See Benardete, *Socrates' Second Sailing*, 44: "their desire to know what justice is does not arise from a belief in the goodness of knowing but a belief in the goodness of justice."

45. Strauss, *City and Man*, 106.

Having listened to the two speeches by highly capable and nearly corrupted young Athenians, Socrates reports his reaction the next day: he "had always been full of wonder at the *nature* of Glaucon and Adeimantus." In the presence of the youths themselves, however, he quoted and endorsed a poem referring to the *divine* in them—something divine kept them unpersuaded by their own arguments for injustice. As for their speeches, Socrates reports that he was particularly *pleased* with them, a reaction he did not betray to the boys; he hid his pleasure from them and claimed to be at a loss as to what to do in the face of their appeals for help. On the one hand, he said, he wasn't capable of helping out—earlier he had said explicitly that it was "impossible" to meet Glaucon's demand (362e). On the other hand, he can't not help out, and he gave one reason: it would be *impious* not to help out when justice is being spoken badly of. He reports that "Glaucon and the others begged him in every way to help out" (368c). "So I spoke my opinion." Socrates' chosen word to herald all that follows, *opinion*, lends it a hue that will become apparent only later when he draws his distinction between knowledge and opinion. Everything Socrates says from here on is a consequence of his being compelled by piety and their pleading to set out a positive opinion of justice in the face of the opposite opinion about it stated in their two speeches, the attack on justice by the sophistic enlightenment and the praise of justice by the religious tradition. A new opinion in praise of justice is demanded, and that, precisely that, enlightened Socrates will supply.

Plato made the first words of *Charmides* and the *Republic* indicate that they took place within a few weeks of each other as dialogues of Socrates' return after a long absence. Here, as the *Republic* shows Socrates' task with Thrasymachus passing into his task with Glaucon and Adeimantus, the chronological proximity of the two dialogues deepens the perspective. In *Charmides* Socrates stated his intentions on his return: to learn the state of philosophy in Athens and whether any young had become wise or beautiful in his absence. And *Charmides* showed him learning from Critias that his own pre-Potidaean philosophy had corrupted him into viewing tyranny as the best life. Critias was already around thirty in 429, and *Protagoras* indicates that he began listening to Socrates much earlier, probably when he was around eighteen or nineteen, as Glaucon and Adeimantus now are. What way of life is best? That question faced all ambitious young Athenians exposed to enlightenment teachers. The opening of the *Republic* shows that the question of the best life reduced itself to two options for the young, the just life or the tyrannical life. For Socrates himself the best way of life is unquestionably philosophy, and *Charmides* indicates that he tried to set Critias on the path to that life by opening the nature of true sôphrosunê to him. But Critias heard in Socrates' words a far different invitation that set him on the path to the tyrannical life. The many beginnings of the *Republic* culminate with the question of the best way of life where only two choices offer themselves to young men who want passionately to believe that the just life is better. Their practical choice hangs on a theoretical matter they never define in a theoretical way: they want proof that they live within a moral order that guarantees the conjunction of justice and happiness; they want to be just but they need it to pay. Finding on their own no evidence of a distributive justice in the world, they demand that Socrates prove that such justice nevertheless exists. For them, the *philosophical* life as Socrates lives it is not one of the options; for them, the philosopher Socrates spends his whole life on nothing but the question of morality; he has a responsibility to prove to them that the moral life is best.

Socrates' experience with Critias—his failure—confirmed the necessity of dealing differently with Athenian youth: it's not *philosophy* they need to be invited to but morality. Nothing can be done with Critias; he's firmly set on his path. But Glaucon and Adeimantus stand at the beginning of their choice of a life already tainted by schooled disillusion with what their decency makes them want most to believe. No longer can Socrates responsibly teach them the beginnings of disbelief in Delphi, as he did Critias, those first steps in self-knowledge meant to lead to philosophy as a way of life. The sophistic critique of religion and the misuse of religion by the religious compel Socrates to undertake the very different task of restoring confidence in religion. He now knows what the returned Odysseus learned: "his destiny is to establish belief and not knowledge."[46]

From this point on the *Republic* will show that Socrates learned from his failure with Alcibiades, evident to him before Potidaea, learned from his failure with Critias whose grounds and extent he discovered on his return, and learned from the doctor of Zalmoxis—from Herodotus—who taught him the foundations of the moral superiority of the Getae. From this point on the *Republic* will show how Socrates returned different, returned as a radical innovator in philosophy who makes philosophy itself the source of proofs for new teachings on god, soul, and the moral order of the cosmos. Beginning as it does, the *Republic* ends only after Socrates has persuaded his young audience that old Cephalus, terrorized by the beggar priests and diviners Adeimantus so abominates, was right. Philosophical authority,

46. Benardete, *Bow and the Lyre*, 152.

gained gradually through arguments with mostly welcome conclusions, substitutes for lost ancestral authority and makes reason itself seem to confirm that the world is as Glaucon and Adeimantus want it: ruled by the moral.

As the occasion of Socrates' descent to view the introduction of Bendis unfolds into a chance to speak with young men, Socrates turns mere accident to his advantage. He makes use of the presence of a great sophist and the absence of ancestral authority to force the perplexed to force him to teach them what he has seen it is necessary to teach them and what he has prepared himself to teach them; he makes them beg for the teaching he returned to give. The sophist best at arousing and taming anger, duly prepared, must witness it all, must learn how enlightenment can best advance itself. And Socrates himself must relate his private achievement in Athens tomorrow. Only with all these elements aligned can the best come to rule in order not to be ruled by the worse.

TWO:
SOCRATES' NEW BEGINNING

After the many beginnings of the *Republic* have shown exactly where Socrates is stationed, Socrates can begin. He begins at the beginning, founding a new city on human nature and using it to show what justice is. But when the city he founds seems complete and he turns to its decline, he is compelled by the collected company to make another beginning, adding measures that raise doubts about whether such a city is possible or desirable. What begins as a detour rises to the indispensable new measure that Socrates, that returned Odysseus, brought back from Potidaea. It alone can make the new city actual in the only way possible, and it is most desirable for both the city and philosophy.

7. New Gods

To demonstrate that the just life is better than the unjust life Socrates begins, with Adeimantus, to build a city in speech; they will watch justice come to be in the city's coming to be. Their city is built on the principle that each person perform the task for which he is apt by nature. It expands until it has achieved a completeness that enables Socrates to ask where justice and injustice can be found in it (371e). Adeimantus can't answer, so Socrates describes the way of life of its citizens, an austere way that compels Glaucon to protest against "a city of pigs" (372d). Enjoying the refinements of a rich man's house in civilized Athens, Glaucon allows the pursuit of justice to be interrupted by the demands of his nature. Socrates does not object to Glaucon's objection, even though he can call the city of pigs "the true city . . . a healthy city." Instead, he expands the city to meet Glaucon's desires, desires a healthy human community is bound to generate and required to satisfy; their city becomes "the luxurious city . . . a feverish city." Glaucon's desires dictate an expansion of the city different in kind from earlier expansions, for it requires a whole new class, a warrior class needed to take the neighbors' territory and resist their taking ours.

The new class of hoplite soldiers consists of those whose natures fit them for that task, those who have *thumos* or who are *thumoeidês* (375b).[47] Socrates alleges a problem: how will such natures be kept from being savage to one another and the other citizens, for they must be gentle to their own while harsh to enemies? He makes it seem a contradiction for one person to be both gentle and harsh (375d) but overcomes the alleged problem with an image: a spirited dog is gentle with anyone it knows and harsh with anyone it does not know, and that makes dogs "philosophical" beasts (375e). *Philosophy* is first spoken in the *Republic* as the attribute of a domestic animal. The guardians of the city they're founding must be by nature "philosophic, spirited, swift, and strong" (376c). Socrates thus begins his redefinition of *philosophy* by having it enter in this apparently odd way. Domestic guardians trained to regard themselves as philosophical, as knowers acting on the basis of knowledge, defend what they think they embody, and citizens will honor philosophy as part of their protection.

How can philosopher-dogs be "reared and educated" (376c)? Or would considering such rearing and educating be of any help at all in seeing justice and injustice come to be in a city? Adeimantus's earlier speech indicted Greek education for rearing and educating to injustice—no wonder he breaks in to answer Socrates' question affirmatively (376d). It is with this young critic of Greek religion who is already suspicious of its core teachings that Socrates initiates his program to reform Greek rearing and educating: he is free to criticize and reform the sacred things because they have already lost much of their sacred character for his young audience. "Come then," Socrates says, "like those telling tales in a tale and at their leisure, let's educate the men in speech." The soul is educated by "music," the things of the Muses, the nine daughters of Zeus and Mnemosune who cause humans to hold in memory the things of the ruling god. The speeches belonging to such music are of two kinds, true and false, and education begins with the false, with children's tales (377a). Such tales

47. Benardete argues that *thumos*, a common word in Homer for human spiritedness or "heart," had by Socrates' time become confined in its usage to a spirited animal like a horse or a dog: "Socrates first confronts [Homer] by taking over from him this old-fashioned word" (*Socrates' Second Sailing*, 55–56). *Thumoeidês* (high-spirited, passionate, hot-tempered [LSJ]; "with the form of" *thumos*, "*thumos*like" [Benardete]) is basic to the *Republic* but appears in Plato only three times outside of it (*Laws* 731b, d and *Timaeus* 18a).

can be subtle and educational for all levels of human maturing, for they can include, Socrates says, a hidden sense inaccessible to the young. "The beginning is the most important part of every work" (377a), says Socrates as he begins at the beginning of a child's rearing[48]—and begins as well at the historic beginning of Greek religion in Homer and Hesiod and at the beginning of all things as told by Hesiod. The very young are the "most plastic"; their unshaped souls take shape through "the model" (*tupos*) first stamped into them (377b) by stories told and retold, for souls are shaped by tales (377c). It is of the first importance that "we supervise the makers of tales"—a *we* that reduces to *Socrates* as he supervises Adeimantus in supervising both the makers of tales and the nurses and mothers who tell them. Adeimantus is initially unable to grasp just how radical Socrates' requirement is that most of the tales the poets pass to the mothers and nurses "must be thrown out"—though he will voice no objection for he has already shown that he was throwing them out himself. When he learns that the "greater tales" that must be thrown out are the ones "Hesiod and Homer" told, he asks, "What do you mean to blame in them?" (377d)—he who blamed in them the beginning of the process that made justice a mere means to the worthwhile things. Socrates blames the founders of Greek religion "first and foremost" for telling lies that are not beautiful (*kalos*) lies. "What's that?" Adeimantus asks, and Socrates says: "When someone makes a bad representation in speech of what gods and heroes are like" (377d). "But how do we mean this and what sort of thing is it?" Adeimantus asks.

"First," Socrates says, "he who told the biggest lie about the biggest things didn't tell a beautiful lie." The biggest lie about the biggest things—that double superlative—is Hesiod's story of origins, the authoritative tale about how the present order came to be. Socrates does not repeat Hesiod's unbeautiful lie but speaks only of "how Uranos did what Hesiod says he did, and how Cronos in his turn took revenge on him." The crime at the origin, the rising up of a divine son to castrate his divine father and replace him as ruler of the world, led to the next divine crime, which Socrates also refrains from describing: "And Cronos' deeds and his suffering at the hands of his son." After treating the biggest lie about the biggest things with reserve, Socrates says how he would handle such matters: "not even if they were true would I suppose they should so easily be told to thought-

48. At its end, Socrates calls the rearing and education of the guardians "the one sufficient thing for the well-being of the city" (423e); "the starting point of the education sets the course for what follows" (425b).

less young things." What would Socrates do with a truth like the one told about the god who rules the present order, that he committed an epoch-founding crime against his ruler-father? "Best would be to keep quiet, but if there were some necessity to tell"—if the discoverer of such truths found himself compelled to communicate—"as few as possible ought to hear them as unspeakable secrets, after making a sacrifice, not of a pig[49] but of some great offering that's hard to come by, so that it will come to the ears of the smallest possible number" (378a). The story of the origin of the present order, of the crime that brought it into being—what Hesiod told in an unbeautiful way—must be handled differently. Dangerous or deadly truths, Socrates implies, must be treated as unspeakable secrets accessible only to those willing to make the greatest sacrifice—not a pig, but the sacrifice of one's life to the task of learning the unspeakable truths. Artful telling and extreme sacrifice ensure that the deadly truths become internally audible only to a tiny minority—Socrates' critique of Hesiod allows him to intimate, at the beginning of his own act of founding, how he handles deadly truths like the truth of a founding crime.

Socrates issues a total prohibition on Hesiod's tale of origins because the crimes of Zeus could be used by a young man to justify himself "in punishing the unjust deeds of his father" (378b)—youths could come to think as young Euthyphro would, that Zeus is to be imitated, not simply obeyed.[50] Socrates generalizes the principle behind his prohibition on Hesiod's story of origins and extends his indictment to Homer—"it must not be said that gods make war on gods, and plot against them and have battles against them—for it isn't even true" (378c).[51] Socrates' reason for this prohibition is the same: the warriors' behavior tends to imitate the actions of those they hold highest, gods and heroes. Homer's tales may well have a hidden sense but that hidden sense is inaccessible to the young, whereas the surface features get stamped into them (378d–e). Adeimantus, critic of the poets' tales, is a most receptive audience for Socrates' restriction to beautiful tales: "If someone should ask us what they are and which tales we mean, *what would we say*?" Tell me what the beautiful tales are, Adeimantus

49. A pig sacrifice was basic to the annual Athenian celebration of the Eleusinian mysteries. Initiates went down to the Piraeus to wash a young pig sacred to Demeter on its beaches; they then carried the suckling pig back up to Athens for purification and sacrifice. Parke, *Festivals of the Athenians*, 62–63.

50. *Euthyphro* 5d–6a.

51. When Euthyphro relates Hesiod's tale of Zeus's overthrow of Cronos and Cronos's overthrow of Uranos, Socrates says he hears such tales with annoyance and asks if that is why he is facing indictment (*Euthyphro* 6a).

asks, tell me what to tell others if they ask me. What Socrates will tell him must be deeply welcome to him, for though he knows what offends him in the poets' tales and fires his indignation, he does not know what can take its place. "You and I aren't poets right now," Socrates responds, "but founders of a city" (379a).[52] How do a city's founders stand to its poets? "It's appropriate for the founders to know the models [*tupoi*] according to which the poets must tell their tales"—poets' tales follow the models laid down by the founders. This is not enough for Adeimantus: "what would the models for speech about the gods be?" *Speech about the gods: theologia.* Tell me the models of our theology, Adeimantus says, and Socrates, a founder with new models, speaks as a theologian to tell him the two basic models for new tales about the city's new gods. Socrates speaks as Homer and Hesiod spoke, and like them he includes a hidden sense.

Socrates' first model and law governs the gods' actions: "the god is not the cause of all things but of the good" (380c). Socrates makes this law seem the conclusion of an argument, his first theological argument, an argument with an oddity: Socrates only asks questions, the assertions are all Adeimantus's (379b). The god is really good; the good is not harmful; what isn't harmful doesn't do harm; what does not harm does not do evil; what does no evil would not be the cause of any evil; the good is beneficial; and the beneficial is the cause of doing well. Socrates states the conclusion Adeimantus's answers require: the god is the cause only of the good (379c). Socrates' theology begins with a law that already lies unformulated in Adeimantus's moral complaints about the tales of the gods. If the god causes only the good, Socrates can use that conclusion to abuse Homer and allow Adeimantus to feel himself Homer's moral superior and the moral judge of his gods. But that Socrates knows he's abusing Homer unjustly is evident from this fact: he acts as if Homer and not Homer's Achilles spoke the famous parable of the two jars on Zeus's threshold, one dispensing good, the other evil. Achilles speaks that parable to Priam almost at the end of the *Iliad*: each weeps for the loss of the dearest of all things to him, but finally Achilles, the passion of mourning spent in him, consoles the old man and himself with this parable of the fatedness of their grief. Plato, author of every word spoken by every character in the *Republic*, has his Socrates attribute to Homer what wise Homer put into the mouth of his most spectacular but hardly wisest character: humans can console themselves by be-

52. The word for founders, *oikistai*, is based on *oikidzô*, to build a house: founders are house builders: they establish the laws that "house" the citizens, providing the boundaries within which they think and act.

lieving that evil is fated by Zeus, wisest and most powerful of gods. Such consolation is no longer fitting: Adeimantus complained that such stories imply that "the gods allot misfortune and a bad life to many good men too, and an opposite fate to opposite men" (364b). Let the god be the cause only of the good; let the gods be as moral as Adeimantus needs them to be: the moral theology Socrates supplies Adeimantus returns to him in spoken models what was implicit in his indictment of Greek religion.

But if the gods cause only the good, how will the poets sing of sorrows and suffering? Socrates lays down explicit instructions on this inescapable human fate: if the sorrows or suffering is the work of a god, the poet must say "that these people profited by being punished" and that "they needed punishment and that in paying the penalty they were benefited by the god" (380b). Socrates' own justice does good to friends and harm to no one, but speaking as the founding theologian of the new city he begins to set out the view of justice according to which suffering is deserved punishment as a corrective, the view, first audible in the terrors of Cephalus, that Socrates will develop into a moral, punitive world order.

Socrates' second model and law governs the gods' appearing: "the gods are neither wizards who transform themselves, nor do they mislead us by lies in speech or in deed" (383a). Adeimantus could readily agree to all of Socrates' leading questions that culminated in the first law, but he starts off hesitant or confused about the second. Would a god actually change himself and pass from his own form into many shapes, and would a god deceive us and make us think he changes (380d)? Adeimantus can't say, having been raised on Homer's changing, deceiving gods. Socrates offers an argument proving to him that a god, being in every way in the best condition, would neither change nor be changed to a worse condition; therefore "a god remains forever simply in his own shape" (381c). But can a god deceive us? Adeimantus can't say and repeatedly can't say. Would a god want to lie? "I don't know." Don't you know that all gods and humans hate the true lie (*alêthôs pseudos*)? "What do you mean?" Surely no one voluntarily wishes to lie about the most sovereign things to what is most sovereign in himself? "I still don't understand." Socrates then explains a distinction among lies: the true lie and the lie in speeches. What would most correctly be called truly a lie is "the lie to the soul about the beings [*ta onta*], and to be ignorant [*amathê*] and to have and to hold a lie [in the soul]" (382b). As for the lie in speeches, it's not present in the soul but is a kind of imitation or copy (*mimêma*) of the affect present in the soul, a phantom that comes into being after the soul's affect. Gods and humans hate the true lie, "But what about this? The one in speeches?" (382c). Socrates' two questions open a speech on the uses of lying that consists of five questions in all. Its third question is: "When and for whom is it also useful, so as not to deserve hatred?" His next question sets out the first two of three possible uses of the lie in speeches: "Isn't it useful against enemies," he asks, "and, as a preventative, like a drug, for those called friends when from madness or some folly they attempt to do something bad?" This second or central of the three uses recalls Socrates' first argument that night, his example to Cephalus of a friend who had gone mad and demanded his weapon back; there Socrates concluded that it would not be just to tell a friend in that state the whole truth. Socrates' fifth question about the lie in speeches states its third use as appropriate to the kind of tales he spoke of as the beginning of education: because we don't know the truth about ancient things, "likening the lie to the truth as best we can, don't we also make it useful?" (382d). After Adeimantus's brief concurring answer, Socrates continues to ask questions, now applying his three cases of usefulness to their possible usefulness to a god. But he alters their order, putting the last first: would the god "lie in making likenesses because he doesn't know ancient things?" Adeimantus finds that ridiculous, and Socrates makes his first assertion: "Then there is no lying in a god." He then moves back to the first use: "Would [a god] lie because he's frightened of enemies?" When Adeimantus answers, "Far from it," Socrates turns last to the second use: would a god lie "because of the folly or madness of his intimates?"—his *oikeiôn*, family or household members. Because Adeimantus knows that "none of the foolish or the mad is a friend of the gods" (382e), it is easy for Socrates to assert that "Then, there's nothing for the sake of which a god would lie." Adeimantus concurs, "There's nothing," and Socrates reinforces that conclusion: "Then the daimonic and the divine are wholly free from the lie." "That's completely certain," answers Adeimantus. By this intricate argument Socrates lies usefully to Adeimantus in speech, stamping a true lie into his soul, a beautiful lie Adeimantus will not hate but love for it accords fully with what he most wants, gods whose moral perfection he can admire and imitate.

How did Socrates do it? By again building an ambiguity into an argument to suggest a hidden meaning different from the apparent one. When he first stated the second or central case of useful lying, the lied-to were "those called friends" who suffer a folly or madness. When restating that case last to prove the god does not lie, he replaced those called friends with the god's intimates—and Adeimantus knows that a god's intimates would never suffer folly or madness and need to be lied to. But what about that original class, those called friends? Wouldn't a god, the cause only of the good, lie as a preventive or a drug for the benefit of those called friends who are ignorant of the ancient things and not intimates of the god? Wouldn't a god's justice be at least as just as the human justice assumed in the first argument that night? Adeimantus's eagerness to make the gods wholly truthful allows him to conclude all too quickly from Socrates' argument that it's completely certain that there's nothing for the sake of which a god would lie. He wanted truthful gods and Socrates gave him what he wanted by untruthful argument. The lie Socrates stamps into Adeimantus's soul is no lie for Socrates' kin: they will recognize the justice of his argument. That the gods cannot lie is a salutary lie of the sort a doctor would tell a patient or a ruler a subject or a sane man a mad friend. While explaining the beautiful lie, the true lie, and the uses of the lie in speeches, Socrates lies in speech in order to stamp into Adeimantus's soul a true lie about the beings, stamping into that still plastic part a beautiful or moral lie about the highest beings. As a student of tales, armed in his soul with his new beautiful lie, Adeimantus can now be more than merely indignant about the old tales; now he has the model for new tales to believe and tell. Socrates lied when he said they weren't poets now but founders: *he* is a poet-founder. The founder's lie for this citizen of the new city is a model for what mere poets will tell all the citizens of the new city of truthful gods. Poets are always the valets of some morality[53]—except when they're founding poets like Homer or Socrates. Then they are morality's masters.

Adeimantus asked Socrates to tell him what the models for speech about the gods would be. He did not ask, "What is a god?" and Socrates never asks in the *Republic*. Instead, speaking as a theologian, he promulgates laws for gods who resemble the gods Adeimantus already knows from Homer and Hesiod but are moral models fit for human imitation. Socrates uses Adeimantus's beliefs about the gods to instill the old gods with new virtue. The *Republic* is not a philosophical inquiry into the nature of the gods but has, like Homer's tales, a hidden sense meant not for the young but for those who ask what a god is. The *Republic* is a moral enterprise of foundational intent with respect to the gods; it reforms morally what Adeimantus already knows a god is. As a reformer Socrates does not advocate return to true originals but recasts the originals by subjecting them to laws he promulgates with plausible-sounding reasons. Appearing first as the laws of children's tales and legislating how gods act in the first tales told, they govern all tales of the gods.

This is the beginning of education in the *Republic*. Beginning by say-

53. Nietzsche, *Gay Science*, ¶1.

ing that the beginning is the most important part of every work, Socrates himself went on immediately to prohibit the ruling tale of beginnings. The tale now to be forgotten told of gods' sons overthrowing the fathers who generated them. It is a true tale: Socrates begins by overthrowing Homer and Hesiod on the wars gods' sons make on their fathers. Hearing the hidden sense of Socrates' beginning, those not under his prohibition can speak the unspeakable sense: Socrates is a wise man rising up wisely against the wise men who fathered him. He begins his legislation about the gods by prohibiting public speech about the nature of his deed. Here, at what he aims to be a turning of the world in which Socratic gods replace Homeric ones, Socrates begins as he must, prohibiting the true but unbeautiful or transmoral tale of the succession of worlds as he starts the new succession. Socrates began his public career by giving Protagoras (and Prodicus and Hippias) a lesson on the kinship of the wise that both condemned Protagoras for betraying his own kin and kept his condemnation in the family. How then can Socrates begin (and end) his new education in the *Republic* by attacking Homer? For one reason only: Homer has lost his hold on—his enchantment over—the generation now rising. Adeimantus spoke the irremediable moral disenchantment with Homer's world, the world within which their fathers and forefathers rose to greatness but a world that is setting with them. Socrates' attack on Homer is justified because with Homer's world setting, a new world can rise only if Homer's is well set. Homer must be castrated, Homer must be bound, and the hidden sense of Socrates' act must not be told.

Under cover of the benign—mere children's tales—Socrates in Athens in late spring 429 legislates the principles of post-Homeric Greek religion.[54] He does it with—and for—Adeimantus, a young man raised within the decayed late-Homeric and maturing into moral outrage at its religious professionals who turn Homer's gods into their servants. Looking back from this decadence, Adeimantus can see its preludes and permission even in Homer and Hesiod. Scandalized into disbelief while wanting or needing to believe, he is ripe for new models of speech about the gods, and Socrates is willing to supply them. To lay the groundwork for post-Homeric Greek religion—to be the founder of that "city"—Socrates must give models to the poets. His models cannot be arbitrary inventions for he has no authority over the poets that could lead them to sing what he wants sung because he wants it. His models must have necessity in them; they must

54. "Since Plato and through him, religion has been essentially different from what it had been before" (Burkert, *Greek Religion*, 322).

represent what a wise man has understood to be the necessary trajectory of morality-based religion; they must represent what a discoverer of the genealogy of morality knows about the future history of religion. Laying down the law for the gods, Socrates legislates what he knows must come if it is to satisfy the moral stringency of people as decent as Adeimantus. His gods must surpass him in virtue; they must be even more judgmental and indignant than he is.[55]

Asked what the models for the gods of the new city are, the founder of the new city legislates the nature of its gods. Socrates' gods, the imaginary beings generated by a wise man's knowledge, are moral and invisible: they withdraw into an invisibility that allows them always to be judgmentally present. Demanding that all humans be as moral as they now are, they are powerful enough to punish the wicked and reward the good; they are the guarantors of the justice Glaucon and Adeimantus compelled Socrates to justify, retributive justice that sees to the conjunction of virtue and happiness.

Socrates' theology is a politics. That new politics founds the theologico-political project of Western philosophy. It does in a far more revolutionary manner what Protagoras was shown already doing in his myth in *Protagoras*: employing the already existing forms of the sacred to advance civility and enlightenment. Now that Socrates himself undertakes to speak mythologically, Thrasymachus must witness it all. Socrates pays the kinsman he is befriending a high compliment, inviting him to watch as he reeducates those Thrasymachus wanted to enlighten. Thrasymachus learns that the young men who were his quarry need the opposite of what he had to tell them, namely, that God is dead and everything is permitted. Instead, they need to be given—to have stamped into them while they're still somewhat plastic—new grounds for the permitted and prohibited, new reasons for being the gentlemen their still active decency wants them to be. Witnessing it all, Thrasymachus may see that he needs them to be the moral sheep

55. Homer himself seems to have anticipated that his gods would be supplanted by gods of a different moral temper: Theoclymenus, who arrives at Ithaca with the returned Telemachus, is a prophet of the new moral stringency of wholly invisible gods. Bearing a name that means "he who hearkens to gods," Theoclymenus utters, as Seth Benardete says, "a quasi-Biblical prophecy," because he "embodies the future role of the prophet." Theoclymenus, Benardete states most tellingly, "is a deduction of an argument" (*Bow and the Lyre*, 119–20). On the rational unfolding of a genealogy of morality in the natural history of religion that culminates in the "Incarnation" of the holy God as "the gift of God," see Leo Strauss, "Reason and Revelation," in Meier, *Leo Strauss and the Theologico-Political Problem*, 141–80. In Strauss that rational genealogy amounts to Reason's refutation of Revelation: Revelation is the understandable outcome of the logic of the "need of man" for *law*, a predictable, rational outcome and therefore not a revelation at all.

his art fits him to lead. If he sees that, he sees a possible new master in whose service he could practice his art to his own great advantage.

8. New Philosophers

Philosophy enters the *Republic* in a way that is worthy of wonder: just before he begins rearing and educating the guardians, Socrates surprises Glaucon by asking if the guardian must be a *philosopher*: "In your opinion then, does the fit guardian need, in addition to spiritedness, to be a philosopher by nature?" (375e). Glaucon is naturally baffled by this first use of *philosopher* in the *Republic*: "How's that? I don't understand." Socrates helps him by expanding the analogy he has just made with dogs and noting "a thing in the beast worthy of our wonder": "When it sees someone it doesn't know, it's angry, although it never had a bad experience with him. And when it sees someone it knows, it greets him warmly, even if it never had a good experience with him" (376a). He calls this trait "truly philosophic." Again Glaucon is at a loss: "In what way?" Socrates answers with an argument about what *learning* effects: it stamps in a powerful disposition to love what is learned and hate what remains alien. A dog, Socrates states, "distinguishes friendly from hostile looks by nothing other than by having learned the one and being ignorant of the other." Can a dog then "be anything other than a lover of learning [*philomathes*] since it defines what is its own and what is alien by acquaintance and ignorance?" "It surely couldn't be anything but," Glaucon says. Socrates thus gains Glaucon's agreement on the decisive point: behavior toward *one's own* and the *alien* is dictated by acquaintance and ignorance, by what rearing and educating stamp into dogs and humans. Socrates also gains Glaucon's agreement that love of learning (*philomathes*) is the same as love of wisdom (*philosophon*, 376a)—philosophy is the same as loving what rearing and educating stamp in. "Shall we be bold and assert that a human being too, if he's going to be gentle to his own and those known to him, must by nature be a philosopher and a lover of learning?" "Yes, let's assert it," says Glaucon. His assertion grants Socrates the right to assert that "the one who's going to be a noble and good guardian of the city for us will in his nature be *philosophic*, spirited, swift, and strong" (376c). Philosophy thus enters the *Republic* with an argument whose premise identifies philosophy and the love of what rearing and education stamp in and whose conclusion affixes the word *philosophic* to guardians of the city whose primary traits are dog-like loyalty to what's been stamped in and anger at what they're ignorant of—hardly Socrates' traits.

Philosophy appears next in the *Republic* at the end of the education of the guardians (410c–412b).[56] Between these two statements about philosophy Socrates educates the guardians through new models for the gods, a new model to supervise what poets say about Hades, new models of virtue for the heroic, and, finally, a new model for gymnastics. He ends their education by making his new model for gymnastics part of the training of the soul, not the body (410c). Glaucon needs to be persuaded: "How's that?" Socrates confuses him still more: "Haven't you observed the turn of mind of those who maintain a lifelong familiarity with gymnastic but don't touch music; or again, that of those who do the opposite?" "What are you talking about?" "Savageness and hardness on the one hand, softness and tameness on the other." Thus prompted, Glaucon can assert that "those who make use of unmixed gymnastic turn out more savage than they ought, while whose who make use of music become in their turn softer than is good for them" (410d). Socrates can then say that "the savage stems from the spirited part of their nature, which, if rightly trained would be courageous." "And . . . wouldn't the philosophic nature have the tame?" Thus reintroducing philosophy for the first time since he spoke of philosopher-dogs, Socrates prompts Glaucon to agree to a common prejudice about philosophy, that it produces an unmanly softness. And he leads Glaucon also to reaffirm their earlier conclusion that the philosophic nature is best when tame and orderly, as in the souls of the guardian-dogs.[57] Those souls must have "these two natures," Socrates avows, the spirited and the philosophic, and they must be harmonized for the guardians to be moderate and courageous. If the two natures are not harmonized, the guardians will be cowardly and coarse, and Socrates cements his final lesson in educating the guardians with memorable little portraits of the consequences of neglecting either music or gymnastics. Music without gymnastics melts and liquefies the spirit, eventually dissolving it completely, cutting out the sinews of the soul and generating "a feeble warrior."[58] And a spirited guardian who gives himself entirely to music and philosophy is made temperamental, quick to anger, full of peevishness or discontent (411b–c). "Most certainly," "Exactly so," Glaucon comments, agreeing with some vehemence that these are the vices of indulging a philosophic nature.[59]

56. At 407c Socrates mentions philosophy as blamed by an excessive care for the body.

57. From this point on in this final exchange on rearing and educating, all of Glaucon's responses to Socrates' descriptions are emphatic agreements (410e–412a).

58. Apollo applied these words to Menelaus while chiding Hector for weakness (*Iliad* 17.588).

59. When Socrates turns to the other case, gymnastics without "music and philosophy," he says they lead the potential guardian to become "a misologist and unmusical" (411d). Socrates

Socrates has thus assigned two blameworthy tendencies to a philosophic nature, excessive softness and an argumentativeness easily inflamed. And he prompted Glaucon to affirm these two popular prejudices against philosophy. By reinforcing the prejudices against philosophy, Socrates makes accessible his purpose in framing the rearing and educating of the guardians with a new definition of "philosopher": old and damaging prejudices against the philosopher are replaced by new and beneficial prejudices in his favor. Let the new city call its loyal guardians "philosophers"; free of the well-known vices of philosophy, possessing souls in which philosophy and gymnastics are harmonized, they are loyal to the stamped-in.

But while introducing philosophy as a trait of the guardians, Socrates intimates his own philosophizing. When he introduced the philosopher-dogs he referred to a thing worthy of *wonder* ($376a_2$), repeating himself to confirm that Glaucon has never *wondered* about it ($376a_6$). What is worthy of wonder is Socrates making philosophy a trait of man's best friend and most loyal trained animal, lover of its own, fierce enemy of the unknown. Socrates guides that wonder when he ends his rearing and educating of philosopher-dogs. His final point—gymnastic and music are both for the soul—begins with "those who established an education in music and gymnastic" (410c). To end his argument he elevates these founders: "I for one would assert that some god gave two arts to human beings, music and gymnastic, for these two things, as it seems, the spirited and the philosophic, not for soul and body except incidentally, but rather for these two" (411e). Why did the founding god do it? So that the two parts of the guardians' souls "might be harmonized with one another by being tuned to the proper degree of tension and relaxation." The founding god domesticated the spirited or thumoeidetic by training the exemplars of spiritedness to think of their souls as divided into a spirited part and a philosophic part and to think that their souls are most healthy when a tempered harmony exists between these two. The philosophic tames the spirited when the founding philosopher causes a fictional form of the philosophic to take up ruling residence in the spirited soul: learned pride in its own "philosophical" character disposes the spirited soul to regulate its native fierceness. And the one who did it wants the spirited souls to think a god did

describes a different route to misology on the last day of his life: loss of faith in reason's capacity to prove what the heart desires (*Phaedo* 89d). In the only other reference to misology in Plato's dialogues, the general Laches says he may seem a misologist when speech is misused by one who does not match it with deeds (*Laches* 188c, e); he makes that statement in order to introduce what he says about Socrates: knowing Socrates' deeds but not his speeches, Laches finds him worthy of noble speeches and complete frankness.

it, gracing them with the arts of gymnastic and music to train and temper the spirited and philosophic within them. Socrates ends his whole rearing and educating by elevating the one with the finest mix of the spirited and philosophical and adding, "Won't we also always need such a one as overseer in the city, Glaucon, if the regime is going to be saved?" "We need him more than anything," says Glaucon, not yet knowing the full extent of what he is granting by making the philosophic nature necessary for the rule of the city.

Socrates brought the philosopher onto the great stage of the *Republic* in a likeness to a dog, an analogy that can be enjoyed as a bit of playfulness and forgotten. But if it is not forgotten, if it is treated with the gravity due the introduction of *philosophy*, it reveals Socrates' intent in giving a new public definition of the philosopher. His new philosophers suggest who he is as a philosopher: philosophy, properly understood as wonder and popularly denounced as soft and argumentative, now appears as loyal and ruling. The founding philosopher Socrates introduces philosophy into the *Republic* in a domesticated, fictional version of philosophy in order to rule through that domestication. Let the philosopher be a philosopher-dog, a wholly domesticated predator reared and educated out of its wolf origins and loyal to what it learns. Socrates' domestication of philosophy is a lie and a truth worthy of Autolycus, Wolf Himself, grandfather of Odysseus on his mother's side (334b).

The chronology Plato gave his dialogues makes the redefinition of philosophy fully understandable as part of Socrates' new politics for philosophy. *Protagoras* showed Socrates to be aware of the precarious place of philosophy in the city and compelled to intervene with the wise and potentially powerful to secure a safe place for philosophy in the city. *Charmides* showed Socrates returning to Athens and learning that his way of sharing his philosophy turned a gifted follower into a self-serving predator, a danger to the city and to philosophy. When Socrates introduces philosophy into the *Republic* by making it a trait of the city's best defenders, he shows how he returned different: he will make philosophy safe from the city and the city safe from philosophy by stamping in new prejudices about philosophy. The philosopher who is already the best-known philosopher in the greatest city in Greece invents a wholly new sense for the label affixed to him and his always endangered kind. He extends the label *philosopher* to embrace those most faithful to what the philosopher must wonder at to take his first step. Genuine philosophy rules in the city by making domesticated philosophy seem to rule. Socrates rules by training a dog trainer.

9. New Justice in a New Soul

The rearing and educating of the philosopher-dogs nears its completion when Socrates adds the noble lie, a charter myth of privileged origins and a divinely mandated social structure that tradition stamps in as the greatest truth. The lie must be reinforced by an extreme austerity in the guardians' daily life: to insure that the dogs not become wolves they must be denied private property and privacy. And Glaucon has no objection, he who initially objected to the absence of couches in the "city of pigs" accepts the austere life of a warrior dog: he's one of their honored "philosophical" leaders. But Adeimantus objects, interrupting to ask what Socrates' apology would be "if someone were to say" that he is not making these actual owners of the city *happy*—it was their suspicion about the conjunction of goodness and happiness that shook his and Glaucon's noble convictions about justice in the first place. Socrates' apology persuades Adeimantus that they're "fashioning the happy city" and not "setting apart a happy few."

Thus completing the city in speech, Socrates looks to the problem of innovation (422a): the great innovator prohibits innovation, especially in music, because changes in the styles of music—the things given by the Muses—unsettle "the most fundamental political and social conventions" (424c). Extending his prohibition, Socrates leaves to "Apollo at Delphi" "the greatest, most beautiful, and first of the laws which are given," namely, "the foundings of temples, sacrifices, and whatever else belongs to the care of the gods, demons, and heroes." The theologian who set down new models and laws for the gods piously leaves to Apollo at Delphi the particulars of religious observance, folding his great innovations into customary practice.

Socrates can now turn to the ostensible purpose of the city in speech, telling Adeimantus, "get yourself an adequate light somewhere, and look yourself, and call in your brother and Polemarchus and the others, whether we can somehow see where the justice might be and where the injustice" (427d). This is too much for Glaucon who remembers that Socrates promised he would look for it and why: "because it's not holy for you not to bring help to justice in every way in your power." Without hesitation Socrates then gives the argument that finds justice, a well-rehearsed argument for he lays out its structure in advance: the city is perfectly good; therefore it is wise, courageous, moderate, and just; therefore, find the first three and the fourth, justice, will be what's left over.

Wisdom is easy to find: it is *euboulia*, good counsel, the virtue of the smallest number, the philosopher-dogs. Courage, the virtue of the auxiliary class, is easy to find but hard to get Glaucon to see. Socrates finds it: "a power that through everything will preserve the opinion about which things are to be feared"—namely, what "the lawgiver transmitted in the education" (429c). Courageous Glaucon can't recognize this definition even though it simply restates the loyalty to one's own and hatred of the alien that Socrates built into the guardians. "Courage is a certain kind of preserving," Socrates repeats, that preserves "the opinion produced by law through education about what is to be feared." He likens courage to dyeing color into fabric to make it colorfast, so fast that not even those lyes most effective at scouring—pleasure, pain, fear, desire—can remove it. "I accept this as courage," Glaucon says. But Socrates adds a single word that casts new light over this whole account of the virtues: "do accept it as *political* courage and you'd be right." If this is *political* courage, then "wisdom" was political wisdom, as *euboulia* already suggested, the art sophists promise to teach and hardly what philosophy seeks as the sophia of its passion. And moderation will be political moderation, and, pivotally for the *Republic*, justice will be political justice: all four virtues are defined as the virtues of citizens. But if the courage Socrates defined is *political*, what other kind of courage might there be? Socrates promises a "finer treatment" later, but the essential inference can already be made: there is a courage unmentionable in the city of loyalty ruled by its fiercest loyalists, courage to put into question what has been dyed in, *philosophical* courage. And if there's philosophical courage, there's philosophical wisdom, moderation, and justice, which will be only as visible in the *Republic* as philosophical courage is, visible only to inference.

Political sôphrosunê in "our young city" is the rule of the better over the worse (431d); it is a virtue not of a single class of the city but of all three, for all "sing in unison." The sôphrosunê that *Charmides* reports as a feature of Socrates' pre-Potidaean teaching—inquiry into common decorum and sense of shame that leads through doing one's own things, doing the good things, knowing oneself, knowledge of itself and other knowledges, to culminate in knowledge of what one knows and does not know—that sôphrosunê is present in the *Republic* only as the presupposition of Socrates' action.

Their hunt for justice has been simplified to finding the fourth of four things, the thing left over after the other three have been found. Socrates calls the hunter Glaucon to special alertness, suggesting he might catch sight of their quarry before Socrates does. But Glaucon reveals himself:

"if you use me as a follower and a man able to see what's shown him, you'll be making quite sensible use of me" (432c)—on Hesiod's scale of the three kinds of people, he's the willing follower of the man who thinks for himself.[60] Socrates declares his willingness to lead: "Follow."

"Here! Here!" Socrates shouts, as he alleges not just to Glaucon but to his audience in Athens the next day that he only now spots a track they could follow. "It's been rolling around at our feet from the beginning," he declares, withholding the identity of their quarry from his impatient hunting partner. Justice, he finally says, is "the rule we set down at the beginning," "minding one's own business and not being a busybody" (433a). Glaucon does not know how Socrates infers that this is justice. It's what's left over, Socrates tells him, the power by which alone the other three can come to be and be preserved, their only rival in importance. Socrates thus leads Glaucon to hold that justice is "the having and doing of one's own and what belongs to one" (434a). The busybody now minding everybody's business by constructing a new city with new gods and heroes, transforming the meaning of the very words citizens use for the things that matter most, transforms justice itself into what might look like a prohibition on what he's doing—except that in minding everybody's business, in ruling their words and concepts, he *is* doing his own things. The result of Socrates' "hunt" for justice in the *Republic* suggests that Socrates does what he does in the *Republic* by justice: he minds his own business by meddling in everyone's business; he does good to friends who are good without harming anyone.

Socrates now turns to justice in human beings singly, saying explicitly that he's completing the consideration with which they began: having found justice in something bigger, they more easily catch sight of it in the single human being (434d).[61] But if their route to justice through the city is to apply to the single human, the "three classes of natures" in the city must also be present in the single soul. Does the soul "have these three forms [*eidê*] in it or not?" (435c). Before showing that it does, Socrates issues a warning: "Know well, Glaucon, that in my opinion, we'll never grasp [the soul] accurately by such methods as we're now using in the argument."

60. Hesiod, *Works and Days* 293–97. The saying had become a standard reference for marking off the wise.

61. Socrates warns that if something different turns up in the single human, then they'll turn back to the city and test it. Perhaps by considering them side by side and rubbing them together like sticks, they would make justice burst into flame (435a)—and that in fact seems to be the upshot of comparing the justice of the city (and citizen) with the justice of that single individual who is the philosopher.

And he knows why they won't: "There's another road, longer and more complex, leading to it." Glaucon just said that "perhaps the saying that fine things are difficult is true,"[62] but he's content with the short, inaccurate way. That Socrates knows the longer, accurate way stands as the not to be forgotten introduction to the three-part soul of the *Republic*, which secures a salutary view of justice for Glaucon.

To prove the division of the soul into three parts, Socrates imagines an objector pressing sophistic objections. The logical exercises that overcome him lend the argument a sense of unassailable authority based on nothing less than the principle of noncontradiction; no objector can argue that a thing, if it is a unitary thing, can do or suffer opposites at the same time in relation to the same thing. Socrates' first long argument isolates desire from an inner resistance to desire: the resistance must come from a part of the soul different from the part that desires; the soul has a desiring part and a resisting part that calculates or reasons. To conclude this argument Socrates describes the desiring part, putting first a word that played no role in his argument: "the part with which it *loves* [*eraô*], hungers . . ." (439d). The short, inaccurate way to view the soul severs eros from the calculating part seen as the resistance to desire, and Glaucon says "It would be fitting for us to believe that." The longer, accurate way in which Glaucon expressed no interest must be the way suggested by Socrates' use of *eros*, the view he arrived at long before 429 and reported in the *Symposium*: the soul is eros-based, desire-based, and philosophy—not mere calculation—is the highest form of eros, a passion to understand that drives the soul forward no matter how long the road.

And next comes spirit, *thumos*, the seat of anger and pride, the belligerent, ambitious, combative aspect of the soul. Is it a separate part? Glaucon suggests that it is the same as desiring—does he experience desire as thumos? Socrates counters Glaucon's suggestion with a story he says he trusts, the story of Leontius (439e), a story Glaucon says he's heard too.

Leontius, son of Aglion—Lionlike son of Splendor—did the opposite of what Socrates did in the first words of the *Republic*: he "was going *up* from Piraeus."[63] He took the route outside the North Wall and close to it—did he take it knowing what he'd see?—and came across corpses lying by the place of public execution. He experienced simultaneously desire to see the corpses and revulsion that turned him away and made him cover his eyes—his soul suffered opposites at the same time in relation to the same

62. Socrates later confirms this saying: "fine things truly are difficult" (497d).

63. The lack of the direct article repeats the unusual usage at the opening of the *Republic*.

thing. He fought with himself but finally, overcome by desire, "he dragged open his eyes, ran toward the corpses, and said, 'Here they are for you, O miserable wretches, get your fill of the beautiful sight.'"[64] Socrates interprets the story immediately, with anger serving as a synonym for thumos: it "certainly indicates that anger sometimes makes war against the desires as one thing against something else." He expands his interpretation, making it a fight with three parties, and addresses it as a question to Glaucon: "in many other places, don't we notice that when desires force someone contrary to calculation [*logismon*], he reviles himself and his spirit is roused against that in him which is doing the forcing; and, just as though there were two parties in a civil war, such a person's spirit [*thumos*] becomes the ally of reason [*logos*]?" (440b). Socrates' question folds the vivid singularity of the Leontius case into the common occasions of spirit allying with reason to control desire, even though reason played no explicit part in the Leontius story. Socrates offers an edifying moral interpretation of Leontius's fight with himself, using for the first time the full image of a three-part soul whose calculating part enlists spirit as an ally against the desiring part. Has Glaucon ever noticed anything like that? Socrates allows him no space to answer; instead, he secures the interpretation offered as a question by leading Glaucon to rule out another possible interpretation.

Socrates presents this second interpretation of the Leontius story as something he supposes Glaucon would deny: spirit "making common cause with the desires to do what reason declares must not be done." "I suppose you'd say you'd never noticed anything of the kind happening in yourself, nor, I suppose, in anyone else." He supposes correctly, for Glaucon vehemently agrees: "No, by Zeus," he says, nobly ruling out any alliance of spirit and desire to oppose reason. Seth Benardete explains the logic of his response: "His reply, if taken strictly, means: 'I, Glaucon, swear that I never noticed it in myself or another.'" And he adds: "A refusal to admit an occurrence hardly constitutes evidence that there was no such occurrence."[65] As Benardete said earlier, it is enough "to cite the unrequited or jealous lover to know that sometimes anger sides with the desires against reason."[66] Socrates' use of Glaucon's high-mindedness to deny this actuality amounts to a strategic little maneuver to imply the true interpretation of Leontius, a nonmoral interpretation he immediately reinforces. For he

64. 440a, Benardete translation, *Socrates' Second Sailing*, 99.

65. Ibid., 101. My account of the Leontius story is heavily indebted to Benardete. Ronna Burger elaborates Benardete's account in "The Thumotic Soul."

66. Benardete, *Socrates' Second Sailing*, 100.

turns directly to two cases that seem to leave Leontius behind but in fact help interpret his act. The two cases parallel the two interpretations just given while adding the key element easily overlooked in the Leontius case, *justice*, for the corpses lay at the public executioner's, dead by the city's justice. The first case concerns a person who thinks he has *committed* injustice, the second, one who believes he is being *treated* unjustly. The person who thinks he has committed injustice, "the nobler he is," Socrates asks, won't he be less capable of anger against suffering inflicted on him by one he supposes does so justly? His nobility convicts him and forestalls anger: he deserved it. But a person who believes he has *suffered* injustice? Won't his spirit "seethe and become harsh and form an alliance with what seems just?" And won't it be able to withstand any kind of suffering, "not ceasing from its noble efforts" to conquer until it has succeeded or died—or been gentled by the reason within him like a dog by a herdsman (440c–d)? Not only does Glaucon agree to this thrilling picture of thumos fighting to the death for victory unless gentled by reason, he recalls that the auxiliaries in their city were like dogs obedient to the shepherd-like rulers.

Socrates praises Glaucon's agreement and recollection—"Nobly do you understand what I want to say"—and takes it as permission to conclude that in the civil wars of the soul, the spirited sets its arms on the side of the calculating (440e). But his second case shelters an alliance that does not fit that conclusion. When the spirit seethes in the noble one who believes he's suffering injustice, it allies itself "*with what seems just*," an alliance not with reason but with spirit's own conviction about justice: it has been wronged and has right on its side. Reason appears only as the *alternative* to victory or death, as a shepherd's possible counterforce against a seething spirit allied with noble belief in its own justice. This case fits Leontius, seething Leontius. He must have believed he had suffered an injustice and seethed in his spirit with righteous indignation, with the need to avenge himself and to gaze on the fruit of his just revenge—he took the route up into the city to observe the fruit of justice. Leontius experienced simultaneously a spirited desire to look at "the beautiful sight" of right avenged and a reasonable revulsion at what is after all a horror to the eyes—dead human beings transfixed in the agony of their dying. Leontius's thumos did not ally itself with reason to overcome desire, it allied itself "with what seemed just" to him, boiled with indignation, overcame reasonable revulsion, and enjoyed its revenge. His passion for vengeance displays the very alliance of spirit and desire Socrates prohibited, and it rules his reason: irrationally reifying his eyes, he assigns them an agency separate from himself and enjoys his superiority in blaming them. His *eyes* have not made the sight of the justly executed corpses beautiful; his eyes are the scapegoat of his thumos: thumos feasts on the beauty of punishment, on seeing evildoers get their just deserts. Leontius punishes twice; he punishes himself for punishing and is sated. "I suppose you'd say" anger never allies itself with desire, says Socrates after telling his story of anger allying itself with desire to carry out "what seems just."[67]

When Socrates concludes that "what we're now bringing to light about the *spirited*" is that "it sets its arms on the side of the calculated," he uses for the first time in his argument for the *eidê* of the soul the term *thumoeidês* (440e).[68] What he seems to suggest in his short route to an inaccurate understanding of the soul is that the soul with three eidê is a *product* of thumos, the soul generated by the primacy of thumos or anger. Thumos imagines itself independent of desire, debases desire, and presses the calculating into its own service.[69] The ground of that unity, the Leontius story suggests, is the moral passion to punish, to see justice done. In the very act of constructing reasons for Glaucon to reaffirm the goodness of justice, Socrates dares to indicate how justice can be not good. Limitless zeal—victory or death—can boil up when belief in suffering injustice gains spirit: *justice* can be the name for spirited vengeance. In the act of displaying a soul with three parts whose hierarchical harmony will be the salutary ground of his new defense of justice, Socrates intimates that spirited soul, possessed by righteous anger, usurps desire and in the name of justice presses reason into its service, unless reason can call it in and gentle it "like a dog by a herdsman"—unless a wise man acts to control it.

The Leontius story shows what Socrates is up against—and his interpretation of it shows him mastering what he's up against. He no more thinks he can eradicate the thumotic than he thought he could eradicate Glaucon's desires when they forced the true city to become luxurious and feverish. Instead, having understood the genealogy of the human soul in

67. Socrates acknowledges the actual alliance of spirit and desire when he speaks of spirit "corrupted by bad rearing" (441a). An example of the alliance of spirit and desire under bad rearing occurs at 553c–d.

68. Socrates last used the term when speaking of *thumoeidês* coming into the cities through the individuals reputed to have this trait such as those in Thrace, Scythia, and nearly the whole north (435e).

69. Benardete makes Socrates' argument for the three-part soul an example of "the hiddenness to things that metaphysical esotericism recognizes and reproduces through trapdoors in arguments." The discovery of the trapdoor in this argument Benardete attributes to Leo Strauss: Strauss turned Socrates' argument about desire upside down and discovered "that it is the presentation of desire by the thumoeidetic that has put on the mask of reason" (Benardete, *Argument of the Action*, 410).

its city-forming, city-formed character, he acts to bring it under the rule of philosophy. His interpretation of the Leontius story intimates both the origins of the soul in the passion of revenge and the ever-present danger of unrestrained belief in justice, its power to tyrannize the soul and mobilize it for righteousness. Yet his whole project with Glaucon aims to reestablish belief in the goodness of justice in a decent, thumotic youth learning to mistrust it. While laying bare the divisions in the soul that thumos created, the man of reason who has taken the long road to grasp the soul trains thumotic men to view their own ruling element as justly subject to reason. Socrates' Leontius story serves two aims: it leads Glaucon to a moral interpretation of a story he's heard and puts in plain sight the true interpretation of the story as a display of the roots and dangers of moral zeal.[70]

Having used the story of Leontius to separate spirit from desire—and sheltered a revelation within it—Socrates turns to his next step in separating out the parts of the soul, the completing or culminating step that separates reason from spirit. But he is not finished with Leontius, for his argument will cite Homer and shelter a revelation within; together, Leontius and Homer make Socrates' complete case for reason's rule over thumos. Glaucon thought that spirit could be part of desire; by contrast, he thinks that the calculating part is separate from spirit, and he offers a proof: children are full of spirit from birth and some never acquire the calculating, while the Many acquire it only late (441a). Socrates supplements Glaucon's proof: "in animals one could see that what you say is so." But Socrates has a proof for separating the calculating from spirit that looks not to children or animals but to the other extreme, the experience of the wise man. He refers to "the testimony of Homer that we cited in that other place somewhat earlier" (441b, 390e). This time he cites just one line of Homer's tes-

70. In *Zorn und Zeit* Peter Sloterdijk offers a powerful historical phenomenology of rage; basing rage in thumos, he attempts to map its place in Western history and in the present. He refers to Plato's account of thumos in the *Republic* (41). But because he can listen to Plato only "as a *Gastdocent* from a spent star" (72), only as the advocate of "Greek idealism," Sloterdijk misses entirely the depth of Plato's warning about the moral fanaticism that thumos can ground, as well as Plato's attempt to bring thumos under rational control. Despite the great merits of Sloterdijk's book—its power to instruct and entertain—its aim to set out the full history of rage and revenge is crippled by his failure to appreciate Plato's understanding of thumos and crippled still worse by his failure to appreciate Nietzsche's profound understanding of the cultural consequences of that greatest of all history-making events as described by his Zarathustra: when revenge "acquired spirit! *The spirit of revenge*: that, my friends, has been up to now the subject of humanity's best reflection." *Thus Spoke Zarathustra*, Second Part "On Redemption."

timony: "He struck his chest and rebuked his heart in speech [*muthôi*]."[71] Socrates adds a single comment: "in this it is clear that Homer poetically made one thing reprove another, what has calculated about the better and the worse [reproves] what is irrationally spirited [*alogistôs thumoumenôi*]."[72] Citation and comment complete Socrates' proof that the soul has three parts and that the calculating rightly rules with the aid of spirit over desire. But his comment on Homer spoke not simply of the calculating part but of what has calculated "about the better and worse"—about what is good and evil; having gained knowledge of good and evil, it rebukes not simply the spirited but the *irrationally* spirited. Socrates calls attention to his earlier citation of this speech which included a second line: "Endure heart, a worse thing even than this you once endured." Shortly before he first cited this passage, Socrates identified its speaker: "the wisest of men" (390a). The second line points to the whole speech the wisest of men actually made on that occasion, and that whole speech and action cast new light on Socrates' final argument for the three parts of the soul or for the rule of reason over spirit. Before and after citing it, Socrates assigns the speech to Homer, but it is a speech by Homer's Odysseus, wholly private and addressed to himself. A beggar in his own house, he lies awake in a makeshift bed on his porch devising evils in his heart for the suitors, when some of the servant girls slip out laughing and cheering one another on their way to their lovers among the suitors (*Odyssey* 20.1–8). "But the spirit [*thumos*] deep in the heart of Odysseus was stirred by this"; he is torn "in the division of mind and spirit" (9–10) whether to kill every one of them or to let them go one last time to the suitors. "His heart was howling within; and just as a bitch stands guard over her tender puppies when she fails to recognize a man, howls, and is eager for a fight, so his heart was howling within in his indignation at evil deeds" (13–16). Then come the lines Socrates cites: "He struck his chest and rebuked his heart in speech, Endure, heart! A worse thing even than this you once endured." Odysseus adds that worse thing immediately: "on that day when the Cyclops ate my mighty comrades. You endured, until mind [*mêtis*] brought you out of the cave though you thought you were going to die" (19–21). Odysseus's howling heart is instantly tamed in utter obedience to his mind in its recollection, allowing him to return to plotting tomorrow's fate of the suitors.

71. *Odyssey* 20.17.

72. In *Phaedo* (94e) Socrates uses similar wording about this passage in Homer but to argue that the whole soul rebukes the body.

Socrates calls in Odysseus without naming him at the culminating point in his argument for reason's separation from spirit and rule over it. The Odysseus to be pondered for the final step in Socrates' division of the soul that effects rational rule over spirit is this Odysseus: the wisest of men in a moment of inner conflict between spirit and mind on the night before he performs the ultimate act to found the new political order on Ithaca. Odysseus faces, if momentarily this time, what Socrates ruled out in offering Glaucon an interpretation of Leontius, spirit making common cause with desire against what reason has said must not be done (440b). The wisest of men settles his momentary conflict easily by recalling his greatest achievement in taming his heart by exercising his mind, his supreme self-control when mind restrained him from striking angrily at Polyphemus when he was eating his men and plotted a way for him and his surviving companions to escape the cave.

In Polyphemus's cave and again in bed plotting to kill the suitors, Odysseus is inflamed by spirit and desire to perform an act of punishment that would block mind's calculation of a better way. In both events spirit is indignant, boiling to punish wicked deeds. In Polyphemus's cave Odysseus checked his rage to punish by his calculation that he would then be unable to escape the cave whose entrance was blocked by a stone he could not move. Blinding Polyphemus became his plotted means of escape, calculated by *mêtis*, by mind or "no one," the name he so cleverly gave himself in devising his escape—mind calculated his escape, anonymous, impersonal, thumos-free mind. Ignited once again while plotting the fate of the suitors, Odysseus's spirit is quickly tamed by mind's reminder of his earlier restraint. Odysseus's killing of the suitors, Homer helps one conclude, is analogous to Odysseus's escape from the cave: both are acts of mind made possible only by forestalling just vengeance. Killing the suitors is the mind-defined necessity of eliminating all remnants of the old regime in order to establish the new regime of Telemachus and his associates, Odysseus's non-Odyssean heirs. His mind's capacity to check his anger shows that he—he alone—acts not to satisfy anger but to achieve the goal set by mind. But Homer makes him seem to act out of anger in punishing the shameless suitors: Homer's mind dictates that his Odysseus seem to act out of anger in order to enlist the angry, Telemachus and company who act on moral indignation as Odysseus does not. They administer as deserved punishment what their ruler Odysseus calculated to be the necessary condition for rightly founding the new order in which they will rule. They and their posterity will lionize Odysseus as the righteous avenger of unspeakable crimes, and Homer will be complicit in making mind seem a lion. Homer knew the necessity that he sing the wisest of men as a righteous avenger while keeping almost inaudible his being ruled by mind alone.[73]

Taken together, Socrates' Leontius story and Homer citation show how the one who took the long road to grasp the soul acts to take control over the three-part soul generated by thumos. Acting on the dictate of mêtis alone, anonymous mind usurps and colonizes the thumotic soul by adjusting its hierarchy: taking what nature and history have given, thumos-dominated desire which has its own reasons, mêtis conscripts thumos into an alliance with reason to rule desire. In this great act of political wisdom Socrates acts as he typically acts: having understood a great event in the natural history of the human soul, he acts, not against nature but with it, to rule the already-formed soul in accord with the interests of reason. The Homer citation points to the great deed of the returned Odysseus of the *Republic*, mind founding a new political order to establish philosophic rule over the thumotic. Plato shows Socrates acting as Homer showed Odysseus acting: each shows the wisest of men acting transmorally in the crucial moment of founding a new moral regime. Plato has his returned Odysseus suppress the name of Odysseus while repeating his words. Plato thus enhances his lovely conceit of naming Odysseus only at the beginning and end and only in reference to a forebear and a descendant: between the two namings, between forebear and descendant, stands, not Odysseus, but pure mêtis, mind and no one. Odysseus himself is absent from the *Republic*; present in his place is the Odyssean, pure mêtis now bearing the name *Socrates*. Socrates, whose justice does good to friends who are good without harming anyone, acts to reorder a punitive justice that harms; he acts out of pure calculation of better and worse, after calculating that the vast majority act and must act out of a combination of spirit and desire that rules calculation and whose roots lie in revenge and the spirit of revenge.

73. This view of Odysseus's restraint with the serving girls is found in Benardete, *Bow and the Lyre*, 124–28. Benardete placed his argument in a section entitled "The Slave Girls," the central section of the chapter "Nonfated Things." The central nonfated thing is a wise man, governed by reason alone, so ordering spirit that he can establish a new order of moral decency on a founding crime. In the central paragraph of this central section Benardete backs off this "repulsive" view and restores righteousness to Odysseus. But his reinterpretation is meant to bring into relief "the unblinking gaze of Homer, who would in this way be distinguishing the bow from the lyre": in making the killing bow the instrument of punishment, of moral payback, the lyre plays for reason alone. Benardete's blink in his moral restoration of an Odysseus glimpsed as repulsive is his repetition of Homer, his own play on his own lyre.

Having calculated that the moral prejudice is inescapable for human order, he acts to rule that prejudice.

On their surface, Socrates' story of Leontius and citation from Homer separate spirit from desire and set it under reason; this surface provides Glaucon with a moral view of his soul, moral and subject to shepherding. But Thrasymachus is present, a man who feigned righteous anger and was called in by reason, an expert on anger who knows how to rouse it and quiet it by miming it, a shepherd who thought he had a fine view of justice while knowing that shepherds serve masters. What will he think now that he has heard Socrates' analysis of the anger-based character of retributive justice? The Leontius story and Homer citation seem to represent, in part, Socrates' effort to convey to a potential friend a deeper, still more subversive understanding of justice, and to confirm at the same time that he's neither an innocent nor a merely moral man but a knower of justice who handles the truth about it cautiously with youths who must be persuaded of its goodness, its outcome in happiness. The Leontius story and Homer citation show the *Republic* advancing the two political tasks of *Protagoras*: they establish an alliance of the rational and the thumoeidetic, Socrates and the young men, and at the same time they encourage an alliance with the man of the enlightenment who thought it served his advantage to teach enlightenment to those who neither desire it nor can be trusted with it. As Thrasymachus watches Socrates come to rule the minds of the spirited young, Socrates' success helps make his case for ruling the mind, voluntarily, of the enlightenment teacher privileged to observe it and see in it a model for his own shepherding. If Thrasymachus sees that, he sees Socrates acknowledge a need for allies of a different order from the Glaucons if his task of founding is to succeed; he sees a needy master's call for allies conscious of their master's needs—his call for friends.

The Leontius story and Homer citation allow the chasm to open again separating Socratic justice from the justice natural to the city. A justice that does good without harming founds a version of the justice of sweet harm. Socrates is ruled by mêtis, eros-driven desire to understand, which took him on the long road to grasp the soul in its thumos-driven nature. The man of understanding who now acts acts as a realist who judges that the rule of "what seems just" is inescapable. His new rearing and educating—just gods, just city, just soul—create a context of punitive justice within which alone the nonpunitive justice of the wisdom seeker can flourish.

Now Socrates can finally say that the "hard swim" is over (441c) and take as proven that the soul has the same three eidê as the city. And he can fit the four virtues to the soul as he fit them to the city, justice being each of the parts minding its own business. The calculating part rules with the spirited part as obedient ally, and these two, trained in their own business, rule over the desiring.[74] Socrates tests justice in the soul by bringing in the "common standards" and showing that the just man is not the best thief, nor will he commit common crimes. Their "dream" has reached perfect fulfillment (443b), and Socrates makes a culminating speech, a little homily to reinforce their achievement. Internalizing the new beliefs about the soul, receiving into the still-plastic soul those beliefs about it to which it will stand loyal, each person becomes master of himself. And out of the new internal harmony stream actions of the only kind a being of this sort could deem appropriate for itself, just and beautiful actions that preserve and help to produce this condition (443e). Socrates' argument is complete: he has answered the plea of Glaucon and Adeimantus and given them a reason for being just that fully accords with what they begged for; justice brings happiness if justice is the harmony of the soul's three parts.

The discussion of justice complete, Socrates turns to injustice, saying that justice stands to injustice as health stands to sickness. Health and sickness is Socrates' final topic on justice and injustice (444c–e). He has brought a new medicine as he said he would a few weeks earlier: "Everything starts from the soul," the doctor of Zalmoxis told him, "and one ought first and foremost to treat that." And "he said that the soul is treated with certain incantations and these incantations are beautiful speeches."[75] Those speeches, never given in *Charmides*, have just been given in the *Republic*. The teaching on the three-part soul is the new medicine Socrates brought back from Potidaea, a teaching according to which justice is the natural health of the soul and the soul is the spring of all actions. Socrates has been true to the oath he said he swore to the doctor of Zalmoxis to treat only the one who "first submits his soul to be treated by you with the incantation."[76] Glaucon and Adeimantus submitted their souls to him, and he did what they begged him to do in a way they could not have imagined. They spoke of actions, he began with their natures, treating actions as a literal afterthought: actions follow from what the actor thinks is his nature. They said they wanted justice to be shown to be good without consideration of reward; he proved what they really wanted, that their justice would lead to their happiness and injustice destroy it. To understand their

74. Socrates gives two presentations of the virtues of the soul; the first (441c–d) omits sôphrosunê, and the second (442c–e) defines the first three virtues but does not define justice.

75. *Charmides* 156e.

76. *Charmides* 157b.

souls in the new way they had to be more than spectators as the new city and soul came to be. As co-founders they had their thumos-dominated souls remolded by Socrates' rearing and education. Socrates' success is proven when he re-asks their original question about the goodness of justice even if one "remains unnoticed," for Glaucon's answer states his new disposition toward invisible Gyges: not even "with every sort of wealth and every sort of rule" would life seem livable "when the nature of that very thing by which we live is confused and corrupted" (445a).

In his final definition of justice Socrates asked, "Isn't it proper for the reasoning part to rule since it is wise and has forethought [*promêtheian*] about all of the soul, and for the spirited part to be obedient to it and its ally?" (441e). This is Socrates' justice in action, the rule of his reasoning through his wise forethought. Socrates is just, he minds his own business in an act of great politics: by persuasive reasoning—taught incantations—his reasoning comes to rule the spirited, turning them willingly into his followers. He gives them the name they are to apply to themselves: let them call themselves "philosophers," not thinking they are philosopher-dogs. He gives them the understanding of the soul they are to live by: in them the rational element rules, ruled by Socrates. And he gives them a view of the virtues to which they can devote all their courage, all their powers of loyalty, thinking them powers of reasoning. The returned Odysseus sees to the state of philosophy in Athens by caring for all the young, all having turned beautiful in his absence.

Through the small scale of the individual soul Socrates institutes the rule of philosophy on the large scale. Honoring the limits of what nature and history grant—the thumos-generated soul—Socrates sets out to rule the soul and thereby rule the city such souls rule. The Socrates who returns from Potidaea sets in motion a new form of soul, shaping and stamping it with new models of the gods that resemble the only god, Zalmoxis, and a new model of the soul as the seat of all actions. Its remaining indispensable Zalmoxian feature, immortality, the new educator of Greece withholds until the proper moment, the last moment.

10. Compulsion and Another Beginning

Socrates has succeeded in what he made seem his main task, persuading Glaucon and Adeimantus of the goodness or profitability of justice. Glaucon thinks they could stop, but Socrates tells him "we mustn't weary" and prepares to show him the forms of vice. Glaucon has grown passive. "Just tell me" the forms of vice, he says. "Tell me what they are," he says of the five types of city and soul. "What are they?" he asks of the four forms of badness (445c–d, 449a). Socrates manages to name one type of regime, the "kingship" or "aristocracy" they've been describing, and he calls it "good and right." But as he's about to tell Glaucon the four forms of badness, he breaks off and addresses his auditor(s) in Athens, reporting his intention: "I was going to speak of [the four forms of badness] in the order that each appeared to me to pass to the other." But he was interrupted, he reports, and compelled to do something different. This new compulsion forces him into new topics that take hours to discuss, a third of the night's conversation, the central third in deepest night. After that long argument "reached its end," after the "detour," as he calls it when it's finally over (543c), he asks Glaucon to recall exactly where they were "so we may proceed on our way again by the same path." Glaucon does that, noting that Socrates had described the city as "good" at the point that he broke off, even though "you had a still finer city and man to tell of" (544a)—the city ruled by the philosopher king. Recalling that "Polemarchus and Adeimantus interrupted," he asks Socrates "to give me the same hold again, and when I put the same question, try to tell me what you were going to say then." And he puts the same question: "What are the four regimes you meant?"

Plato thus emphasizes that what follows the detour is exactly what would have been said had the detour not occurred. Socrates' whole effort in the detour is set off as something he would not have undertaken but for the interruption—he would have completed the edifying teaching on justice without "the still finer city and man." Plato thus assigns the interruption a very great significance: without it the *Republic* would have lacked what is now its very core. What is it about the interruption that led Socrates to do what he would otherwise not have done?

As Socrates narrates the interruption he makes it a repetition of the opening of the dialogue. Polemarchus again engineers a compulsion forcing him to do something different from what he intended to do—take up a topic he had mentioned in passing, a most provocative topic for young males: friends having women (and children) in common or, as Adeimantus puts it, "the begetting of children, how they will be begotten" (449d). But Polemarchus has become different; gone is his commanding manner, his warlordship, perhaps because he has become Socrates' partner in battle. Now, as he speaks for the only time after interrupting as Socrates' witness against Thrasymachus, he wants to interrupt but he has someone else do it. Again some distance off, he himself (not his slave) grabs a cloak from behind, Adeimantus's (not Socrates'); and he speaks, not aloud but in Adeimantus's ear. Socrates reports the only words of Polemarchus he heard, his last words apparently spoken more loudly: "Shall we let it go [*aphiêmi*] or what shall we do?" Letting Socrates and Glaucon go is what Polemarchus would not allow at the beginning (*aphiêmi*, 327c). Now he induces Adeimantus not to let Socrates go, because, as Adeimantus says, "in our opinion, you're taking it easy and robbing us of a whole section of the argument." "You thought you'd get away with it," he says, by treating as ordinary a most extraordinary measure. But Adeimantus misrepresents himself: "we've been waiting all this time supposing you'd surely mention begetting of children, how they're begotten" (449d). No, he hasn't. He was the one who fully agreed to "leaving it out" when Socrates cited it as the only example of what he was leaving out (423e). Now he speaks for himself and Polemarchus to allege "we've been waiting all this time" for the topic to be discussed. The matter is clearly of great importance to him: "We think it makes a big difference, or rather, the whole difference, in a regime's being right or not right" (449d), and he ends by using the language of the courts: "we've resolved . . . not to release you before you've gone through all this just as you did the rest." Austere Adeimantus, directed by Polemarchus, wants after all to hear how sex will be arranged in their city even though it has nothing explicitly to do with justice.

Did Socrates really think he'd get away with leaving out having women in common after mentioning it? Surely he expected that he would be asked to explain such a proposal, that sometime, somehow, some one of these young males was bound to ask him about this startling matter of eros dropped so casually before them and left as the only matter not to be discussed. Their act of arresting him is not wholly voluntary but a belated response to a provocation. But if Socrates counted on their passionate interest to ask about women in common, he will use that interest to speak about something outside their passionate interest: the philosopher king and philosophy. No one compelled him to speak about that, that was wholly voluntary though he makes it seem wholly a consequence of their compulsion. The core of the *Republic*, Socrates' account of the philosopher king, exists because he contrived a compulsion to interrupt the course he was following.

Glaucon volunteers his partnership in the vote to compel Socrates. And then Thrasymachus speaks up with the first of two brief speeches that are his final words that night—remarkable words bristling with significance in their brevity and showing that he, like Polemarchus, speaks differently at this new beginning than he did earlier. "You can take it as a resolution approved by all of us," he says as his first speech, presuming to speak for them all while preempting the individual votes of others by proclaiming unanimity—and including himself as part of the "all of us." You've *arrested* me, Socrates says in the plural, confirming the language of the courts they've employed. But he pleads that they have set a great deal of discussion in motion, going so far as to say he will have to speak "from the beginning of the regime again as it were." He warns them: "You don't know how great a swarm of arguments you're stirring up with what you're now summoning to the bar." He, however, knows very well: "I saw it then" and passed by. He knows the swarm of arguments he's preparing to give as he begins the regime again.

Thrasymachus then makes his final speech. Again, he speaks for all—except himself: "What, do you suppose these here have come to look for fool's gold and not to listen to arguments?" It is a fine moment when Thrasymachus speaks for the last time and, with great presence of mind, employs the very image Socrates used when he spoke to him for the first time. He intimates his seriousness to Socrates by employing Socrates' own standard of the seriousness of speeches: they're more serious than a search for gold (336e). He's different now, a willing listener attending to a Socrates now "willing to answer" (337a) and answering in a way that cannot but impress the master of oratory with the power it exercises over "these here." And if he can speak *for* all of them as he did in his previous speech, he does not speak *as* one of them as he shows in this second speech. Taken together, his two speeches invite Socrates to draw a conclusion about him: he's not their spokesman, he's their shepherd, the one who stands apart to present them. To whom? Who else but the master, the one he thus acknowledges may be the sought-for, fitting master his art stands in need of. But he too needs to hear more before he can securely draw that conclusion. He willingly grants Socrates the opportunity to do for him what Socrates attempted to do for an unwilling Protagoras: supply a popularizer of the Greek enlightenment with a public approach to wisdom that would endanger neither the public nor the enlightenment.

Now Socrates can speak the swarm of arguments he knew were entailed by that little bombshell he planted. Now everything is in place. A disparate group, united into a civil and unanimous community, commands him to speak, not knowing what it is commanding; its potential shepherd has indicated his willingness to listen and readiness to learn. Socrates' repetition of the beginning, his ostentatious display of being put under a new compulsion, shows the dramatic changes in roles that he has brought about since the first beginning in those who would compel him, young warlords and a kinsman who supposed they were enemies. The needed philosopher ruler rules before he tells them of the need for the philosopher ruler.

Now Socrates can begin to present his well-rehearsed account of philosophy's rule. That it is well rehearsed he demonstrates immediately. After Glaucon makes a short speech challenging him not to weary—the very challenge Socrates just gave him—Socrates shows unmistakably that he is launching himself on the course that will lead him into the topic of the philosopher ruler: he anticipates the complete detour by setting up the structural issues that organize it. The coming topics, he says, admit of many doubts, but they will be of two kinds, doubts about whether the things said are possible and doubts about whether they are for the best. Socrates will arrange the coming three topics as an elaborate, illuminating dance with two kinds of doubt. And he adds another feature he will make persistent throughout the detour by saying that "he fears that the whole argument might seem to be a prayer"—like doubts about the possibility and desirability of the coming three issues, their not being prayers will structure and punctuate his presentation of them.

Socrates knows what's coming; the others can have no inkling. In order to encourage him to do what he says he's hesitant about but what he in fact manipulated them into demanding he do, Glaucon assures him of their goodwill. That only increases his hesitation, Socrates says, describing the setting that would give him no hesitation: "to speak knowing the truth among the prudent and dear about what is greatest and dear is a thing safe and encouraging" (450d). But his setting is different: "to present arguments at a time when one is in doubt and seeking—which is just what I'm doing—is a thing both fearsome and slippery." He does not fear being laughed at but "slipping from the truth where one ought least to slip," where he'll not only fall himself "but also drag my friends down with me." That awesome thought leads him to the most breathtaking image in the whole *Republic: "I prostrate myself before Adrasteia for what I'm going to say*." For the whole detour with all that may be doubted in it, all that may seem a prayer, Socrates prostrates himself before Adrasteia, "she whom none can escape," Nemesis the goddess of necessity who punishes rash deeds.

This may be Socrates' most solemn speech in the whole *Republic*—"and Glaucon laughed." So great is his trust in Socrates' capacity that he can laugh at his deeply expressed care—Glaucon who naturally mistakes himself for a friend of the sort for whom Socrates fears, Glaucon who imagines he can absolve Socrates of responsibility, Glaucon who can have no inkling of Socrates' real care. The solemnity of Socrates' speech derives from the greatness of its occasion: returned Odysseus, having manipulated them into compelling him to do what he alone compels himself to do, now embarks on the introduction of a great novelty into the stream of Greek wisdom and he cannot know whether introducing the rule of the philosopher will succeed. He stands over an abyss unable to know for certain whether it is possible and, if possible, if it is for the best. He must ask himself: is it a prayer? Fearing that he will bring his genuine friends, the few wise, down with him in this boldest of projects on behalf of wisdom, he in fact offers a prayer, the most solemn of prayers and the only one becoming a philosopher: "I prostrate myself before Adrasteia." He prays the prayer of a philosopher compelled to act on the grandest scale not knowing whether he can succeed; he submits himself to Nemesis, the necessity that rules all, knowing the rashness of his deed while judging that necessity itself calls it forth.

When Socrates says he prostrates himself before Adrasteia he repeats word for word what the chorus of Oceanids counsel the wise to do in *Prometheus Bound* (l. 936). But those daughters of Oceanus and Tethys give their counsel to Prometheus, whom they've just heard say that the reign of Zeus is destined to end and he's glad. "Wise are they who prostrate themselves before Adrasteia," they say, in pious rebuke of the enemy Zeus is punishing, an enemy who foresees his victory in Zeus's doom. Wise Prometheus responds: "Worship and adore and fawn over whoever is your Lord. But for Zeus I care less than nothing. . . . Let him hold his power for his little day—since he will not bear sway over the gods for long." Socrates' prayer rings ominous when its precedent is heard, rings with the doom of the Promethean moment, for he stands with Prometheus and not with the pious daughters of Oceanus and Mother Tethys, those parents who are, as he himself quotes Homer saying on another occasion, "the *genesis* of gods."[77] Socrates prostrates himself before Adrasteia for the crime he is about to commit: he submits to unforeseeable necessity in bringing his new gift to humans, foreseeing that it will supplant Zeus and bring to an end his little day. The core of the *Republic*, that "detour" prepared by foresight, is Socrates' most daring act: he commits the Promethean crime once more, bringing to humans a gift that will bring a race of gods to its end and see to the birth of a new one.

That night in the Piraeus in late spring 429, as the Athenians introduce Thracian Bendis, hoping to cure their city's ills, the Athenian philosopher sets in motion a far greater revolution in Greek religion to cure the city's ills. He acts knowingly, obeying the pious daughters of Oceanus and

77. *Theaetetus* 152e; Socrates quotes Homer's veiled words while describing the use to which they were put by later "wise" interpreters like Protagoras who made what was "an enigma for us, the vast refuse-heap," available even to shoemakers (*Protagoras* 152c, 180c–d).

Mother Tethys in the act of obeisance they ordered Prometheus to perform. Yielding to necessity in what he knows he must now do, he hands over to necessity its unknowable fated consequences. Yielding to a past that necessitated the present moment in which he must act, he yields to an unknowable future all that results from founding the rule of the philosopher.

11. The Center of the *Republic*: The Philosopher Ruler

Before he begins to meet the new compulsion placed on him, Socrates attaches his new topic to all that preceded: they've "completely finished the man drama" and now must "complete the woman" (451c). Not only will the detour deal directly with women, it will bring the treatment of the human to a complementary, productive wholeness, for the third "wave" of the woman drama—which Socrates alone knows is coming—is the philosopher ruler. As part of the woman drama, philosophical rule must be more womanly than manly. The returned hoplite Socrates, returning to rule, rules by the nonmanly, rules over the manly by superior intelligence and strategic guile, womanly or Odyssean traits, one could say, evident in the detour where the one just subjected to superior strength has his way with the strong.

If the guardians are like dogs their tasks must be assigned without regard to male/female difference: all must have the same rearing and education in music and gymnastics. Socrates focuses on an erotic upshot, women exercising naked with men, and fixes attention on a comic aspect: even old women, wrinkled and not pleasant to the eye, exercise naked with men. He will not permit even the comic poets to laugh at this, but he does supply an objector to question the possibility of this measure on their own primary principle: "You said each must mind his own business according to nature," but woman differs in her nature and so must differ in her work (453c). Glaucon can't respond quickly, and Socrates, as if at a loss, describes the fix they're in: whether one falls into a small pool or the biggest sea, one must swim all the same. Swimming to save themselves from the argument, they can hope that some dolphin might take them on its back, as a dolphin saved the great singer Arion,[78] or they might hope for "some other unusual

78. Herodotus 1.23–24. Herodotus introduces his story of Arion by reporting that the arrival of Arion was said to be the most marvelous thing that ever happened to Periander, the ruler of Corinth.

salvation." That other salvation shows up immediately: it is "the power of the contradicting art"—that is what enables Socrates to arrive safely home, his resourceful invention of persuasive arguments, his form of Arion's dolphin. Glaucon is schooled in arguments as his long speech proved, but Socrates is the master of the contradicting art. He accuses others of not knowing how to divide things into their proper kinds, of using eristic rather than dialectic. "This doesn't apply to us too right now does it?" Glaucon asks. "It most certainly does," Socrates says: they've been guilty of eristic by not properly dividing nature into its kinds in a relevant way. He'll do that now: the difference between female and male, "the female bears the male mounts," is as relevant for a warrior's education and rearing as the difference between being bald and having long hair. This eristic dolphin carries Socrates past the objection to the possibility of the same tasks for women, and eristic then helps him show that this measure is also for the best.

They've escaped one "wave," he says, introducing the image that persists through the rest of the woman drama, and as Glaucon adds, "it's not a little wave" (457c). Only now does what they arrested Socrates for, having women and children in common, become the topic, and as the second wave, it is destined to be outdone by the third, traditionally swamping wave. When Socrates states the second wave, Glaucon says it is indeed far bigger than the first in both its possibility and benefit. Its benefit won't be disputed, Socrates suggests, but "a great deal of dispute" could arise over its possibility. Glaucon insists: "There could well be dispute about both." "I thought I would run away from [one] argument," Socrates says, "if in your opinion it were beneficial; then I would have the one about whether it's possible or not left." Glaucon is triumphant: "You didn't run away unnoticed; present an argument for both." Triumphant Glaucon will not notice how Socrates successfully runs away from the *possibility* of this wave.

The measures Socrates introduces for having women and children in common turn the city into a family with only primary family attachments: fathers and mothers, daughters and sons, brothers and sisters. That "family" fuses into a single body, a community of pleasure and pain in which all apply "my own" and "not my own" to the same things. There will be "nothing private but the body" (464d), and that will be made as public as possible. Having proven the *benefit* of this unity, Socrates opens the required next step (466d): doesn't it "remain to determine whether after all it is *possible* . . . that this community come to be among humans . . . and in what way it is possible?" (466d). "You were just ahead of me," Glaucon says, "in mentioning what I was going to take up." But Socrates veers away: "for as to war, I suppose it's plain how they'll make war." Glaucon bites: "How?" Socrates proceeds to say how in great detail, giving no sign of returning to what Glaucon said he was about to ask next.[79] So Socrates speaks of war to a decorated young warrior in a time of war, detailing just how their city will conduct its campaigns. Children destined to be the hoplite auxiliary will be taken to the battles. Cowards will be demoted and the best exalted—Glaucon and Adeimantus were counted among the best at Megara. The best will be crowned; he'll have his right hand shaken; he'll kiss and be kissed—and Glaucon adds a law on his own: "as long as they're on that campaign no one he wants to kiss will be permitted to refuse" (468c).[80] And more marriages will be arranged for him so that the most children will be born to him. And when such champions die their tombs will be cared for and they'll be worshiped like deities. And in dealing with enemies, Greeks will not enslave Greeks but only barbarians. And what about ravaging Greek countryside and burning houses, as Spartans were doing in Attica and they were doing in Megara?[81] Clashes between Greeks are "faction" and only those between Greeks and barbarians "war." Glaucon believes the city they're founding can only be Greek, and therefore, as "philhellenes" dealing with kin, they're rightly subject to a law neither to waste Greek countryside nor burn Greek houses. Glaucon is willing to make that law, but finally he calls Socrates to a halt: "Socrates, I think that if one were to allow you to speak about this sort of thing you'd never remember what you previously set aside in order to say all this" (471c): "Is it possible for this regime to come to be, and how is it possible?" Glaucon misremembers; what Socrates set aside to speak of war was whether it was possible to have women and children in common. When Glaucon asks how the whole regime can come to be, he changes the topic. Socrates has tricked him: proud to have caught Socrates running away from the question of the *benefit* of having women and children in common, he demands that Socrates take up a question that allows him to run away from proving

79. In *Timaeus*, Socrates' report on his speech from the day before outlines the city in speech from the *Republic* and explicitly comes to a stop just before this turn to war: Socrates alleges incompetence on the topic of war, giving old Critias space to tell his story of an older and more glorious Athens at war with Atlantis. The returned Athenian hoplite's speech on war in the *Republic* belies his claimed incompetence in *Timaeus*.

80. So repulsive did old Paul Shorey find the kissing law that he had to remark on its "deplorable facetiousness": "It is almost the only passage in Plato that one would wish to blot" (Loeb translation at 468b).

81. Thucydides 2.31.

its *possibility*—and its possibility was the cause of the whole detour. Glaucon doesn't notice. His objection, his revolt, shows him completely persuaded of the goodness of the new city: "I see that if [the regime] should come to be *everything would be good for the city in which it came to be*." He's been charmed by Socrates' proposals; they've put the fire in him, and he can't stand just imagining the benefits of their city, he has to know what it will take for it to come to be.

Glaucon alone—not the unanimous whole that forced the detour—now assigns Socrates a different task, and he commands it: "Take it that I agree that there would be all these things and countless others if this regime should come to be, *and don't talk about it any more*; instead, let's now only try to persuade ourselves that it's possible and how it's possible, dismissing all the rest" (471c). The possibility of the city as a whole—not the possibility of one of its preconditions, having women and children in common—is what Glaucon demands to hear. He doesn't know it but he's commanding Socrates to introduce the philosopher king, his as yet unnamed third wave. Glaucon's revolt allows the whole of the detour to fall open to understanding. Compelled to take up the question of having women in common, Socrates transforms that compulsion into an irresistible appeal to Glaucon's tastes. Whatever else the first two waves may mean as resources for reflecting on similar measures in Aristophanes, say, and for reflecting on human nature in its maleness and femaleness and what the city demands of that, one thing matters above all others as far as the drama of the *Republic* is concerned. Those measures plus the details of war so ignite Glaucon that he is compelled to compel Socrates to take up a new topic: how can the city they made in speech come to be? Socrates has compelled Glaucon to compel him to speak of the philosopher's rule.

Socrates does what he's told: "I've hardly escaped the two waves," he says, "and you're now bringing the biggest and most difficult, the third wave." Escaping from proof for the possibility of the one wave they unanimously forced him to address, Socrates takes them back to his initial statement of what led him to prostrate himself before Adrasteia. When they hear the third wave, he says, they'll recognize how fitting it was for him to be hesitant and afraid to undertake such an argument. Glaucon's response enforces that arrest: "The more you say such things, the less we'll *let you off*" (472a)—*aphiêmi*, the word Polemarchus and Adeimantus used to arrest Socrates to begin the detour. Glaucon won't let him off the new task he assigns: "telling how it is possible for this regime to come to be." And he commands urgency: "So speak and don't waste time."

Socrates takes a long time before stating the third wave, for the manner in which their city can come to be needs a long introduction. Having taken them back to his arrest, Socrates reminds them of what they seem to have forgotten: "First, it should be recalled that we got to this point while seeking what justice is and injustice" (472b). He then attaches that purpose of their inquiry to what the third wave will bring: "if we find out what sort of thing justice is, will we also insist that the just man must not differ at all from justice itself but in every way be as it is?" They've already found what justice and the just person are, but they must determine how the just person stands to what they're about to find out, what *sort* of thing justice is—the sort to be an *idea*, Socrates will say. When they have before them both the just man and the sort of thing justice is, will they insist that the just man not differ at all from what justice is, or will they "be content if he is nearest to it and participates in it more than others?" We'll be content with that, Glaucon says, not yet knowing what that entails. Socrates has introduced the two salient features of the *ideas* before even mentioning them: they are a different *sort* of thing, and things like humans participate in them to a greater or lesser degree. Socrates then describes how they viewed their task—how *he* did: "A *pattern* [*paradigmatikos*] was what we were seeking, both for what justice itself is, and for what the perfectly just man is," as well as patterns for injustice and the most unjust man (472c). With those patterns present, they could look off to the relationship of those patterns to happiness and its opposite. They would then be compelled to think that they themselves would stand to happiness as their models stand to it. Socrates thus summarizes his effort to construct patterns for them: they are the means by which he could help them erase their suspicions that the unjust life is happier than the just life.

This retrospective clarification of what occupied them for hours serves Socrates' prospective purpose: they didn't seek the patterns in order to prove that it's possible for them to come to be. Socrates thus begins to tame a Glaucon he has inflamed with passion to see the city he wants to rule come to be. Justice, the just man, the city they built in speech—all are alike in being patterns. But a painter who paints a pattern of the most beautiful human being is no less good for not being able to prove that such a being can come to be. The pattern they made in speech of the good city is no less good for their not being able to prove that it is possible to found a city the same as the one in speech. "That's the truth of it," Socrates says, and asks Glaucon to change his assignment: "how and under what condition it would be *most* possible." Glaucon must grant other concessions if even that is to be proven; only then will Socrates tell him the smallest change that would allow a city to approximate this sort of regime. Socrates pictures himself about to brave the biggest wave, "say it I will, even if, like a surging wave, it's going to drown me in laughter and ill-repute."

After so much fanfare—the fear and hesitation alleged at his arrest, his prostration before Adrasteia, the two waves building to the greatest wave, the demand by a Glaucon made impatient, the precautions about just how such a thing can be—Socrates finally states "perhaps the most famous sentence in Plato,"[82] a sentence placed at "the numerically exact center"[83] of the pivotal dialogue on political philosophy by an author who carefully considered his centers, as his *Protagoras* and *Charmides* prove. At the center of his *Republic* Plato has Socrates announce that the philosopher must rule. Socrates, the returned Odysseus, announces in the appropriately oblique way his intention on his return: to secure the state of philosophy he must found the rule of philosophy.

The first and famous sentence in the central speech is complex and begins with a long conditional clause. "*Unless either philosophers rule as kings or those now called kings and potentates philosophize both genuinely and adequately*. . . ." Thus beginning with some specificity about both rulers and philosophy, Socrates rephrases his "unless" clause immediately, speaking more generally about both: "*and this, political power and philosophy, coincide in the same [one]*. . . ." He then adds an "almost invisible" prohibition:[84] "*while the many natures now making their way to either apart from the other are by necessity excluded*. . . ." He thus imposes a double prohibition, excluding from rule natures inclined only to rule and from philosophy natures inclined only to philosophy. Unless these conditions are met, what can be expected? Socrates' first statement of the consequence introduces a matter that seems without precedent in their dialogue so far: "*there is no rest from evils, dear Glaucon, for cities nor I think for the human race*. . . ." A philosopher's rule somehow addresses the problem of evil. Only after stating this consequence does Socrates return to the issue consuming Glaucon: "*nor will that regime ever come forth insofar as possible and see the light of the sun, this one that now we have gone through in speech*."

This carefully wrought sentence at the center of the *Republic* has a remarkable structure: an inner core shares the structural feature set by the outer shell surrounding it, an "unless . . . then not" structure, with the inner appearing at first glance simply to restate the outer. And the outer

82. Shorey, *Republic*, note at 473d.
83. Brann, *Music of the "Republic*," 258, cf. 158.
84. Craig, *War Lover*, 252.

shell stays true to the issues they've been discussing since Socrates first started building a city in speech, while adding in the first "unless" clause a spectacular new claim (although rulers as philosopher dogs appeared early in their city); and the outer shell ends on the issue that most engages Glaucon, whether their city can come into being. Surrounded by this spectacle, the inner core of the sentence speaks more quietly of political power, philosophy, and the problem of evil. The outer shell draws all the attention, while the inner core with its vaguer "unless" and its different consequence lies secret and retired at the center of the central sentence. Ignoring the spectacle and focusing on the inner core allows it to emerge as the true center that alone bears the essential content. Here lies Socrates' true task in the *Republic*, a thing not fit to be uttered: *his* taking rule, not as king and not as just any philosopher, but rule by the philosopher Socrates who will rule as he knows the Greek wise ruled and with the same great end in view. The famous sentence at the center of the *Republic* is equal to the gravity of its location. *In structure*, it is a miniature of just how Socrates rules—from within the shelter of an outer appearance that looks as if it belongs in comedy, the comedy of the woman drama, in fact, for it practices a female art, the cosmetic art, an art of beguilement creating a useful appearance to serve the calculated end intimated within. *In substance*, the sentence parades in its prominent exterior an extension of the project that inflames Glaucon, while its less prominent interior intimates Socrates' actual project. Socrates will rule as woman rules, through the creation of appearance and without the ostentation or recognition demanded by males. But what is the substance of Socrates' rule? To what end does he rule?

The second sentence of the central speech is also equal to its great occasion, for it adds two elements indispensable to the core of the first. "*And this is what was causing me for so long to hesitate to speak, seeing how very paradoxical it would be to say. . . .*" So contrary (*para*) to common opinion (*doxa*) is the claim that the philosopher should rule that it caused him the hesitation he avowed at the opening of the detour (450d); speaking this paradox required that he prostrate himself before Adrasteia, ". . . *for it is hard to see that there is no other way to attain happiness, either private or public.*" Unless political power and philosophy coincide, there is no rest from evils: *rest from evils* put positively is the attainment of happiness. Socrates has seen what it is so hard to see, that rule by the philosopher alone makes possible the attainment of happiness, private and public. Here is the true core thought of the *Republic*, Socrates' insight into the one thing needful to secure and even advance human happiness.

The attainment of happiness—rest from evils—became Socrates' underlying theme very early. Thrasymachus first spoke of happiness, making it the culminating theme of his display speech on justice: the happiest of men is a ruler whose perfect injustice presses the ruled into the service of his happiness (343c–344b). Socrates' final argument refuting Thrasymachus concerned "the way one should live" and proved that the just person is happy; but then he ended by claiming that he still didn't know if the just person is unhappy or happy—*happy* was to be his last word that night for he then narrated that he thought he "was freed from argument" (354c, 357a). But his avowed ignorance of whether the just person is *happy* goaded Glaucon to speak up in dissatisfaction and mount his case for the superior happiness of the unjust, a case Adeimantus supported by showing how poets and prose writers called the unjust person the master of happiness. How should they live? If justice does not bring happiness, they will pursue their happiness unjustly. They thus assigned Socrates his explicit task in the *Republic*: demonstrate to the satisfaction of young men who have lost faith in the conjunction of justice and happiness that they in fact conjoin. To fulfill his task Socrates proved to them that there are different kinds of happiness befitting the different natures: a "foolish and adolescent opinion about happiness" that Adeimantus advocated when he tied happiness to the material possessions denied the guardians of their city (465d–e), the happiness their city grants for the majority of their citizens while granting the different happiness of the guardians, a happiness greater than that of Olympian victors because the honors are greater (465d). Happiness appears in its third and highest form only after the center; it is the happiness reserved for the one who has escaped the Cave, the philosopher who lives on the Isles of the Blessed, "happy and divine" (540c), a decidedly private happiness. But that happy man—whose happiness is independent of what Socrates now assigns him—must, Socrates says, *go down*. He goes down to achieve what the central speech stated: rule for the attainment of happiness. His reasons for rule Socrates has already stated: necessity and the penalty of being ruled by a worse. His means of rule are what Socrates will now show: he rules as a teacher of images like the images of Sun, Line, and Cave and of the whole class of images he is about to introduce, the ideas. Only the filigree of detail in this great project of teaching/ruling can properly show how the philosopher's rule offers rest from evils or the attainment of happiness, but the main point can be stated in advance. The philosopher, a private man with a private happiness, acts to secure the different happiness of the nonphilosopher, of the public, because of what he has learned about happiness: the attainment of happiness for all but the philosopher (and exceptions like the renegade or criminal) depends on belief and one belief in particular, belief in justice, belief that one inhabits a beautiful, just, and good order where good is rewarded and evil punished. To lose the possibility of that happiness is a great evil. But for a whole people to lose that possibility—for the gods to die—is a greater evil. And that greater evil portends the greatest evil: loss of the possibility of happiness on the Isles of the Blessed. Having seen the evil befalling Zeus's order, and having understood the basis of that order in words put up by a wise man, Socrates, a wise man who knows what he does not know, acts to restore the very basis of the common happiness, acts to establish a new order of the beautiful, just, and good. The center of the *Republic* in two marvelous sentences conveys and shelters the core of political philosophy: unless philosophy goes down to rule belief, there is no rest from evils.[85]

12. Glaucon, Ally of the Philosopher's Rule

No laughter drowns Socrates after he announces the third wave. Instead, when his now famous statement is heard for the first time, Glaucon reacts with shock and dismay, his response surging out of him as a threat of violence against Socrates that far exceeds any threat hitherto expressed in the dialogue. "You can believe that very many, and not the ordinary, will on the spot cast off their cloaks, and stripped for action, taking hold of whatever weapon falls under the hand of each, run full speed at you to do deeds to marvel at" (474a). The violence in Glaucon's reaction is partly Socrates' own doing: he brought Glaucon around to the tantalizing, transfixing point of hearing, right now, the one smallest thing that could be done to bring into being the city he has been willing to surrender almost

85. External confirmation of the hidden core of the central speech of Plato's *Republic* is found in Alfarabi's *Attainment of Happiness*, which shows not only that the philosopher must rule but how he must rule, through religion. Muhsin Mahdi has shown that the *Attainment of Happiness* is a dialogue with one speaker (*Alfarabi and the Foundations of Islamic Political Philosophy*, 173–95). Alfarabi speaks infrequently in the first-person plural and addresses another infrequently in the second-person singular. Alfarabi's "we" is at first we Muslims perplexed by the variety of methods we use to treat a problem but ultimately becomes those who "speak our language," the language spoken by the very few true philosophers whose rule is the precondition of the attainment of happiness. Laced into these *we*'s are infrequent *you*'s, and Mahdi shows that *you* is a philosopher in a still mutilated sense: "you" is, so to speak, a pre-Socratic philosopher. Alfarabi teaches Islamic philosophy what Socrates first taught philosophy: it must turn to political philosophy, to the "divine" and "human" sciences, in order to survive, survive by rule that understands how happiness is to be attained privately or publicly.

everything to found—his powerful taste for luxuries, his private home, his dogs and fighting cocks, his very privacy. And what could he have been expecting after all this sacrifice? Surely, that Socrates would tell him the smallest thing *he* would have to do in order to rule Athens and bring it into accord with the city for which he sacrificed so much. But Socrates tells him that the *philosopher* must rule his city if it is to become actual. Glaucon's own passion must drive his promise that Socrates will be assaulted for this claim. "If you don't defend yourself with speech and get away, you'll really pay the penalty in scorn." Socrates offers not the least demur to Glaucon's expectation of violence by men of substance; instead, he makes Glaucon responsible for exposing him to the threat. Glaucon, whatever dismay of his own might have driven his outburst, declares loyalty to Socrates in the coming fight: "I won't betray you, and I'll defend you with what I can. I can provide good will and encouragement. . . . And so, with the assurance of such an ally, try to show the disbelievers that it is as you say." The young man with whom Socrates descended to the Piraeus signs on for what he anticipates will be many battles with serious men. Socrates, not bridling in the least at battles on behalf of the philosopher's claim to rule, accepts him in the role he assigned himself: "It must be tried, especially since you offer so great an alliance."

Thus accepting the alliance he so carefully arranged, Socrates prepares for their campaign, stating exactly who they'll fight, how, and with what weapon. "It's necessary, in my opinion, if we are somehow going to get away from those you speak of, to distinguish for them whom we mean when we dare assert the philosophers must rule" (474b). His coming description of the philosopher is *for them*, the potent enemies of the rule of the philosopher, and their single weapon is a new portrait of the philosopher that will prove to their attackers that "it is by nature fitting for them both to engage in philosophy and to lead the city, and for the rest not to engage in philosophy and to follow the leader." "*Follow me here*," Socrates says. "*Lead*," Glaucon answers (474c), and he becomes Socrates' first follower to identify the philosopher as the knower of the ideas.

What Socrates teaches his ally in order to defend philosophy against the expected attack turns out to be "Platonism." The purpose of Platonism lies in Socrates' purpose in teaching Glaucon and only there: Platonism is philosophy's defense for those who attack its aspiration to rule—and through Platonism Socratic philosophy comes to rule. Here, flowing out of the center of the *Republic* with its announcement of the philosopher's rule, begins the long career of Platonism, the view of philosophy according to which the philosopher is the knower of the ideas, of the unchanging realities, the beautiful, the just, and the good.[86] The dignity and gravity of this new subject matter easily eclipse the little particulars occasioning its introduction, but these particulars alone explain the great event of the introduction of Platonism in terms of its purpose.

When Socrates says, "Follow me here," and Glaucon answers, "Lead," Socrates leads him to a conclusion that seems far from right, namely, that a boy lover (*philopais*) loves all boys. Socrates rebukes Glaucon for not remembering what they said about a lover loving all of a thing (474d), but Socrates alters what they said: he now claims boy lovers love *all* boys indiscriminately, whereas Glaucon avowed undiscriminate love for *his* boy—he ignored his defects and loved everything about him, his one true love (402d–e).[87] Don't "*you*"—lovers like you—Socrates goes on, make accommodations for all varieties like a snub nose or hook nose, like dark complexion, light complexion, or "honeypale"—isn't that very name a lover's hypocoristic, a term of endearment, baby talk? A Glaucon willing to follow where he's led hesitates about this: "If you want to make an example of me while speaking about what the erotic do, I agree for the sake of the argument" (475a). Socrates extends his generalization about lovers loving all of a thing to the wine lover (*philoinos*) and the honor lover (*philotimos*). Yet precisely the connoisseur of wines most dislikes inferior wine. And the honor lover has contempt for second-place honors or first-place honors in a second-class competition. They wouldn't invent hypocoristics for inferior wines or inferior honors. If the *philopais*, the *philoinos*, the *philotimos* all fail to fit Socrates' model in which every member of the loving class loves every member of the loved class, what about the *philosophos*, whom Socrates is defining by these means? He too discriminates, and at last Glaucon objects when Socrates defines the philosopher as "willing to taste every kind of learning readily": "Then you'll have many strange ones" (475c). And Socrates agrees: Glaucon's lovers of sights (*philotheamenes*) and lovers of sounds (*philekooi*) are only *like* the philosopher in being passionately drawn to their spectacles of sight or sound. And when Glaucon asks, "Who do you say the true ones are?" (475e), Socrates is positioned to tell him what he wants to tell him about the philosopher. But why begin

86. Socrates speaks once of the holy and it takes the place of the good (479a).

87. The exchange occurred at the end of the music education, just before Socrates turned to gymnastics. He discussed the aims and end of music education and introduced *eros* for the beautiful (402d). When he claimed that the musical ones would love (*eros*) those who harmonized the virtues and not love those who lacked such harmony, Glaucon agreed but pointedly made a place for loving one who lacked bodily harmony because of some bodily defect: "You have or had such a boy," Socrates said (402e).

by misrepresenting the lover as loving every member of his kind of loved thing, erasing all particularity in hypocoristic approval of all members of a kind? The why comes to light, nearly to light, by the end of his argument.

Who do you say the true philosophers are? "The lovers of the sight of the truth," Socrates says, and when Glaucon asks how he means it, Socrates answers: "It wouldn't be at all easy to tell someone else." But he easily tells Glaucon the key points of the doctrine of the ideas—all too easily, for if Glaucon is to defend the philosopher as the knower of the ideas, he'll have to be able to persuade those less easy to persuade than himself. Socrates therefore invents someone to get harsh with them, someone unwilling to grant what Glaucon so easily grants. To persuade that more resistant one, Socrates will assign Glaucon the resister's role. The master teacher trains his willing ally partly by easy persuasion and partly by having him role-play one who gets harsh with them.

Who are the true philosophers? In pursuit of his answer Socrates gets Glaucon to grant that the beautiful and its opposite, ugly, are two; that therefore each is one; and that the same holds for the opposites "justice and injustice, good and evil, and all the ideas [*eidê*]. Each is itself one, but, by appearing everywhere in communion with actions, bodies, and one another, each is an apparitional many" (476a). Glaucon assents without objection, and without asking for any explanation of how each of the ideas is a one that comes to appearance as a many. Socrates can then easily separate out true philosophers from their like: on one side are "those of whom you were just speaking," lovers of sights (*philotheamonas*), but he adds others, "lovers of arts" (*philotechnous*) and "the practical" (*praktikous*); on the other side he puts those "whom alone one could rightly call lovers of wisdom [*philosophous*]" (476b). Glaucon then utters his only question of the whole easy exercise: "How do you mean?" Socrates means that "the lovers of hearing and the lovers of sights" delight in "beautiful sounds and colors and shapes and all that craft makes from such things, but their thought [*dianoia*] is unable to see and delight in the nature of the beautiful itself." This key distinction, with its elevation of *dianoia* as seeing the nature of the beautiful itself, expressed with such brevity and no explanation, draws Glaucon's full assent: "That's certainly so." Wouldn't the other kind of lovers, Socrates asks, "who are able to approach the beautiful itself and see it by itself," be—*rare*? He asks Glaucon to assent not to anything about the unique *dianoia* of such lovers that enables them to see the idea, or about the precise nature of the idea they alone see—only to the rarity of such persons. He then moves to a second feature, again a mere upshot of what is said to separate out the philosopher: "the one who holds[88] that there are beautiful things but does not hold that there is beauty itself and who, if someone leads him to the knowledge of it, isn't able to follow—is he, in your opinion, living in a dream or is he awake?" "Consider it," he orders a Glaucon whom he is leading to follow a new definition of the philosopher, and he describes the state of the nonphilosopher: "Doesn't dreaming, whether one is awake or asleep, consist in believing a likeness of something to be not a likeness but rather the thing itself to which it is like?" Now he can define the philosopher: the one who "believes [*hêgoumenos*] that there is something beautiful itself and is able to catch sight both of it and of what participates in it, and doesn't believe that what participates is it itself, nor that it itself is what participates" (476d). Yet instead of asking Glaucon anything about the philosopher's belief or its object, he asks, "is he, in your opinion, living in a dream or is he awake?" "He's very much awake," Glaucon judges, believing he's able to judge what that wakefulness is. Socrates has uttered his defining distinction separating the philosopher from all others, but he was careful to ask Glaucon only about two secondary features of the philosopher: he's rare and awake. Having separated out the rare and wakeful one, he gives Glaucon firm language to identify him: "Wouldn't we be right in saying that this one's thought, because he knows, is knowledge, while the other's is opinion because he opines?" "Most certainly," opines Glaucon.

Socrates easily led Glaucon to follow his new definition of the philosopher, but his ally won't find it so easy to lead all others to follow. To prepare him to defend the philosopher against those less willing to be led, Socrates creates a little scene of what his ally will typically encounter. The one they've identified, "this one of whom we say he opines but does not know," takes on life as Socrates assigns him words to get harsh with them and dispute the truth of what they say (476d). The harsh one seems to embody those Glaucon promised would strip for action and threaten Socrates: it was "for them" that Socrates set out to identify the philosopher—for "*getting away from* them" (474b). To get away from such an opponent, they must "have some way to address him with soothing words and persuade him," and Socrates knows how to start: "hide from him that he's not healthy." They'll avoid insulting him at the outset by hiding their judgment that he's a dreamer who only opines while they know the really real. Socrates then devises for Glaucon a most elementary argument that he calls at its end

88. "*Holds*" in this statement is *nomizôn*, "to hold as a custom or usage, said of things recognized by convention or prescriptive right" (LSJ).

"somewhat lengthy" (484a), its length drawn out by Socrates' teacherly manner as he drills his pupil in the elements of the argument. "Come then, and consider what we'll say to him. Or do you want us to question him this way, saying that if he does know something it's not begrudged him, but that we would be delighted to see he knows something?" (476e). Socrates gives his ally a basic lesson in Socratic questioning: begin by accepting, seeming to accept, his "knowledge" as good coin and test it. "But tell us this, does the one who knows, know something or nothing?" Glaucon is to speak the opponent's part: the one they're trying to persuade, the opinion holder harsh with them, disappears into Glaucon. Socrates will make him reappear at the turning point of his exercise (479a) and again at its end (479e): Socrates' pedagogy dictates the words for Glaucon to use against the philosopher's opponent.

"Does the one who knows know something or nothing?" "I'll answer that he knows something," says Glaucon, proving he learned Socrates' first lesson. "Is it something that is or is not?" Glaucon gives the reasonable answer: "That *is*. How could what *is not* be known at all?" Thus prepared, Socrates poses the decisive question in a way calculated to elicit an affirmative response and grant him the premise for his lengthy argument:

> "Adequately, then, do we have it—even if we should consider it from many points of view—that what perfectly is is perfectly knowable, and what in no way is is in every way unknowable?" (477a)

"*Most adequately*." Glaucon's answer, were it the answer of a philosopher, would assert a complete ontological and epistemological optimism, expressing full confidence in the human capacity to know reality as it is. But there's no reason to suppose that Glaucon has thought philosophically about the nature of human knowing or the nature of the things to be known. Socrates is questioning not a fellow philosopher but a young ally for philosophy who needs an argument to defend the philosopher's new identity as the knower of the ideas. Socrates' question is the canny question of that most singular philosopher who, over twenty years earlier, first turned to investigate human knowing, turned to the *logoi* in order to test the capacity of the logoi to treat the causes of the beings that are philosophy's ultimate concern. His question shows what he learned about opining: it has complete confidence in the adequacy of its own "knowing." He does not ask for *his own* answer but anticipates the answer naturally given by both Glaucon and the opponent from whom they're hiding the fact that he's not healthy because he opines while thinking he knows. His question is calculated to draw as its answer the single most basic matter such an opiner thinks he knows: he "knows" that his thoughts and words faithfully represent the things.

"*Most adequately.*" Glaucon opines what philosophy's attackers opine, that they have a most adequate grasp of what Socrates himself was led to question—human knowledge of what is. Neither Glaucon nor the one harsh with them is harsh with himself. Knowing that, Socrates can ask, ask innocently, and be granted the premise he needs for his crucial argument. For Socrates makes no pause at all over what the philosopher Socrates must view as Glaucon's ontological and epistemological dream. Instead, he keeps to his lesson: philosophy's ally will deal with those like himself, those wholly persuaded of their own adequate grasp of what is; opinion dreams itself to be knowledge and is hard not on itself but on those who question *it*. "In the eyes of opinion, opinion is knowledge, and the things it opines are not likenesses but the things that are."[89] Socrates knows that all but the most rare live easily within a dream of their own grasp on reality. His argument is therefore dialectical: it begins with what everyone already knows about their knowing. From its opening premise on, this is an argument that a philosopher fashioned for believers.

Socrates' argument concerns opinion. Establishing that Glaucon accepts the extremes of being and nonbeing on one hand and knowing and ignorance on the other, he asks about "something that both is and is not"—wouldn't it necessarily lie between what is and what is not? Correspondingly, because knowledge depends on what is and ignorance on what is not, the search for opinion must look for something that lies between knowledge and ignorance. Regarding such powers or faculties (*dunameis*) and what they depend upon, Socrates makes distinctions he says are his own (477c–d). "What about you?" he asks at the end. "What do you do?" "The same," says Glaucon, who cannot have thought much at all about distinctions among the powers and what they depend upon. As a power different from knowledge, opinion must depend upon something different—upon the opinable, which cannot be the same as the knowable. So what is the opinable that opinion is *of*? It can't be what is and it can't be what is not. "Think about it," Socrates exhorts, as if Glaucon were stumped—and why not, for what could the opinable be if neither what is nor what is not? Re-

89. Benardete, *Socrates' Second Sailing*, 136. Benardete adds: "Everything Socrates says of the philosophers [here] must be the opinions of opinion. The philosopher who loves what he knows is the lover of opinion."

peating what he said before, Socrates leads Glaucon through his whole set of distinctions again (478b), compelling him to say himself that knowledge and opinion are separate powers and that what they depend upon must also be separate. He leads Glaucon back to what they said at the beginning of the argument (477a) about something lying between what is and what is not—that's the issue he says they're now resolving: they're bringing to light what they set out to bring to light. It has already come to light that opinion lies between ignorance and knowledge, but "it remains for us to find what participates in both, in 'to be' and 'not to be' . . . if it comes to light, we can justly address it as the opinable, thus assigning the extremes to the extremes and the between to the between" (478e).

And right here, bringing to light the between through easily picturable sets of extremes regarding being and knowing, Socrates brings *him* back: "let him tell me, let him answer, that good man who doesn't believe there is anything beautiful in itself and an idea of the beautiful itself which always stays the same in all respects, but does hold there are many beautiful things, this lover of sights who can in no way endure it if anyone asserts that the beautiful is one, and the just and so on with the rest" (479a). Having made Glaucon answer for this one, Socrates now pulls him over to his own side—"*we'll say*"—and dictates the persuasive speech they'll say together to that one set over against them: "Now, of these many beautiful things, you best of men, is there any that will not also come to light as ugly? And of the just, not also as unjust? And of the holy, not also as unholy?" Glaucon answers and goes on answering without saying he's answering for the one they're treating so respectfully as the best. In this didactic way Socrates gives Glaucon what he needs to persuade that other that the whole realm of the naturally lit is only a *between* world and that the philosopher alone has knowledge of the realm of light. This is the weapon Socrates marshals for Glaucon against those who run at him full speed: we must respectfully win such opponents around to the view that the philosopher is the one who alone has access to the knowable realm of light while all the rest perceive some twilit between, merely opining about the ever changing. Socrates' new strategy for philosophy—Platonism—dares to open a new space in reality for the whole of coming to be and ceasing to be, demoting it, depreciating it categorically in the face of what is, what allegedly is as always the same in every respect, the ideas in the realm of light.

Having created his easily memorized scheme of extremes and a between, and having assigned all nonphilosophic "knowing" to a between of inescapable ambiguity, Socrates moves directly to the logical puzzles sophists notoriously played with: doubles and halves, big and little, light and heavy (479b). Asking, "Can you do anything with [such puzzles]?" he shows Glaucon what to do with them, how the new view disarms them: "Could you find a finer place to put them than between being [*ousia*] and not to be?" Socrates is triumphant; they've found a place to put "the many beliefs of the Many about what's beautiful and about the other things": they "roll around somewhere between non-being and being purely and simply" (479d). No wonder Socrates is triumphant: he's shown Glaucon (and those Glaucon will show) how the ideas put the sophist in his place—and the philosopher in his, why one deserves suspicion and the other trust. And Socrates has outfitted Glaucon with a simple way to counter sophistic arguments of the sort pioneered by Protagoras with his "man is the measure" principle. Glaucon can now avow that all such contradictions regarding the beautiful, just, and good are contradictions of mere opinion and that the ideas of the beautiful, just, and good transcend opinion and are both unchanging and known by the philosopher. A great sophist who was harsh with Socrates is made to witness the creation of a simpleminded distinction between philosopher and sophist that wins public confidence for one and public disdain for the other.

At the end of his argument (479d) Socrates makes plural the one who was unable to follow them at the start (476c), "those who look at the many beautiful things but don't see the beautiful itself and aren't even able to follow another who leads them to it." Now, finally, he and Glaucon can say what they hid at the start and say it together: "we'll assert that they opine all these things but know nothing of what they opine" (479e). Having dealt gently with the one who got harsh with them, they can now tell all such opponents the harsh truth. And they can fix a name to those who at the start refused to be distinguished from philosophers: call them "*philodoxers* rather than *philosophers*." "Will they be very angry with us if we speak this way?" Socrates asks. And Glaucon, just taught to speak this way, says: "No, that is, if they're persuaded by me. For it's not lawful to be harsh with what's true." Embracing his role as a persuader on philosophy's behalf, Glaucon appeals to the law against lawless attackers. Socrates can proclaim his lengthy argument complete (484a): Glaucon has shown it was completely successful with him. When Socrates announced to Glaucon that philosophers must rule for their city to become actual, he began the first discussion of *philosopher* since he spoke of philosopher dogs to frame the rearing and education of the city's rulers.[90] That odd introduction of

90. At 456a *philosophos* is mentioned in connection with *misosophos* as part of what women share with men.

the term *philosopher* illumines the center of the *Republic*: Platonism caps the education of the philosopher dogs, allowing the philosopher to rule the apparent rulers of the new city.

And that misleading way that Socrates began his whole argument, alleging that lovers indiscriminately love every member of the class they love? Seth Benardete showed how the end of the argument brings back that beginning: Socrates repeats in the case of the many beliefs of the Many the misleading generalization he made in forming the class of boy lovers. "He collects believers of every kind into one class, and though each enters the class with a single identification of something as supremely beautiful, just, or good, the class characteristic is the lawful belief in a manifold of beautiful, just, and good things."[91] The first case misleadingly placed all boy lovers into a class that loves all boys even though Glaucon did what each boy lover does: love everything about his own boy. The final case misleadingly places all opinion lovers into a class that maintains the multitude of lawful opinions even though each opinion lover loves only his own lawful opinions, those of his city or people. Benardete adopts a word from the case of the boy lovers in order to illuminate, most enjoyably illuminate, the case of the opinion lovers: *hypocoristic*, baby talk or terms of endearment: "Socrates is claiming that there are three or four fundamental hypocoristics [beautiful, just, good, and perhaps holy] that are universally predicated of the lawful customs and practices of every city and tribe. They are the excuses uttered everywhere and always to disguise the love of one's own. They are identical in function to 'charming,' 'kingly,' and 'honeypale' as boylovers apply them." Socrates' argument for Platonism is a masterpiece of double showing: the very argument with which philosophy's allies show philosophy's enemies the salutary opinion that the philosopher is the knower of the beautiful, just, and good shows what the philosopher really knows about the beautiful, just, and good: that's baby talk, terms of endearment that all peoples inevitably lavish on what is hard, good, and holy for them.[92]

13. Platonism: Philosophy's Political Defense and Introduction to Philosophy

Socrates' argument for his ally—his little drill to train him—marks a historic moment in the history of the West: it is Socrates' first-ever argument

91. Benardete, *Socrates' Second Sailing*, 138.

92. Plato thus leaves to be discovered in Socrates' words what Nietzsche had his Zarathustra say openly (*Thus Spoke Zarathustra*, First Part, "On the Thousand Goals and One").

for what came to be called "Platonism," the philosophy that came to rule the West. The contexts Plato gave this argument in the *Republic* are indispensable to its import. *The broad cultural context* is established first: the decay of ancestral authority, the threat of sophism, and the moral yearning of disillusioned youth. *The general dialogic context* is the founding of a new city in order to find justice within it. *The more immediate dialogic context* is the unanimous demand of the collected company and their new shepherd that Socrates take up a perhaps impossible and undesirable proposal he allegedly hesitated to treat. And *the most immediate context*, at the very center of the *Republic*, is Socrates' claim that the philosopher must rule. Platonism first appears as the direct consequence of the central claim, but the narrative unity of the *Republic* requires that Platonism be seen as the ultimate response to the other contexts as well: Platonism is the teaching that solves the crisis of authority and the crisis of justice, that caps the education of the philosopher dogs who will lead the new city, that makes the new city possible in some sense, and that addresses the problem of evil, having understood human happiness. All these contexts internal to the *Republic* must be gathered to appreciate the scope of the introduction of Platonism at its center. But there's more: Plato gave the *Republic* itself a context, the little-known context he provided for those he taught to have a passionate interest in how philosophy became Socratic. For right here, where Platonism rises out of the center of the *Republic*, the chronology Plato gave his dialogues—and that alone—provides the full context for understanding the historic character of Socrates' act of introducing Platonism.

If the chronological cues of Plato's dialogues are taken seriously, one of the most remarkable results is insight into the history of the ideas in Socrates' shifting perspectives.[93] Plato saved the earliest stage for the last possible moment. In *Phaedo*, on the last day of his life, just before the last argument of his life, Socrates takes Cebes and the others in his cell back to the first philosophical events of his life. He reports that his turn from his passionate investigation of nature to investigate the logoi had as its impetus the search for an adequate understanding of cause, his "second sailing in search of the cause" (*Phaedo* 99d). Socrates launched himself by positing ideas and the participation of particulars in the ideas (100b–d); this gave him what he calls, at the end of his life, the "safe way" for understanding the cause of, say, the beautiful in things (100b–e). Reporting his first use of the ideas to Cebes on that last day and emphatically recommending that he make use of the safe way, Socrates refrains from reporting to Cebes (or to

93. See Linck, "Coming to the Ideas."

Glaucon in the Piraeus in 429) the other great event Plato made available from Socrates' youth with respect to the ideas. Plato reserved that event of recovery for the philosophically inclined men of Clazomenae who sailed to Athens after Socrates' death to learn of his conversation with Parmenides in 450 when Socrates was about nineteen, an event that must have followed shortly after the events he reported in *Phaedo*. Their exertions of recovery afford them the privilege of hearing the brash young Socrates present the ideas as his newly minted solution to the philosophical problem of the one and the many to which Parmenides and Zeno had devoted their lives—and of hearing immediately Parmenides' sobering, irrefutable demonstration that his "solution" had insurmountable logical difficulties. Nevertheless, after proving that the ideas, even if they exist, are wholly unknowable, old Parmenides told young Socrates that one who denies that there are ideas of the beings—his examples are the beautiful, just, and good—will understand nothing and destroy entirely the power of communicative speech.[94]

The two great events in the history of philosophy reported in *Phaedo* and *Parmenides* occurred more than twenty years before the *Republic*, yet the Socrates with that past teaches Glaucon a simplistic view of the ideas that he has known to be untenable since he confronted Parmenides. This is not a contradiction. Socrates' introduction of the ideas in the *Republic* is fully consistent with his earlier career in pursuit of the ideas if the difference between Socrates and Glaucon (and Cebes) is kept in mind: what briefly satisfied a nineteen-year-old philosopher until Parmenides disabused him of it can permanently satisfy young—and old—nonphilosophers, satisfy them that problems of no real concern to them, like that foolishness about the one and many, have been solved by Socrates and other philosophers who know the ideas. For them the ideas are what Socrates told Cebes they were, the safe way to think about cause. What the young philosopher Socrates was forced to move beyond can satisfy young Glaucon forever—he will not be hard on himself with respect to his opinion that the philosopher knows the ideas. It's no accident that Plato put him in the marketplace with Adeimantus to guide the men of Clazomenae to what they sailed to Athens for—what he, in over thirty years, had never bothered to ask his half-brother about, the conversation that forced young Socrates beyond the childish view of the ideas he later presented to Glaucon as the true view.

Plato made possible the recovery of a third great event in the history of philosophy—in the life of Socrates—that illuminates the argument at

94. *Parmenides* 135b–c.

the center of the *Republic*: the event reported in the *Symposium*, the only other glimpse he gives of Socrates before *Protagoras* in the only other dialogue besides *Phaedo* and *Parmenides* to be narrated by someone other than Socrates. In the *Symposium*, Apollodorus unwittingly profanes the mysteries of Socrates but in a manner that keeps them mysteries to all but the most capable of Socrates' lovers. For in his private speech in 416 to the most sophisticated of Athenians, Socrates conveyed his ultimate discoveries as what had been conveyed to him decades earlier by Diotima—conveyed as mysteries. The wise woman of Mantineia initiated Socrates into the mysteries of Eros, a daimon—not a god—sprung from, yes, resourceful Penia. Diotima initiated him into the most fundamental of all things humanly knowable, the eros-generated, desire-generated character of everything knowable, in particular, the eros-generated character of the beautiful. That mystery, accessible in the *Symposium* but not profaned there, accessible as the core of Socratic philosophizing, is kept still more hidden in the *Republic* where the beautiful, just, and good are said to be ideas, permanent, nongenerated hyperrealities known to the philosopher, according to the new definition. Still, the *Republic* opens a space for the truth conveyed as a mystery in the *Symposium* because the *Republic* introduces the ideas as the solution to a political not a philosophical problem. By having Socrates introduce the ideas in a wholly political context for a wholly political use, the *Republic* invites questioning about the ideas themselves, and a chronological study of the dialogues offers the pleasing answer: in 429 the ideas are that relic of Socrates' past that he can put to use as the basis of a safe new public teaching about the philosopher. The ideas are now a doctrine, a belief held on the authority of the philosopher by nonphilosophers. Sheltered by the assurance that admirable doctrine affords, Socratic philosophizing can continue its Eros-like striving, its endless homeless shoeless journeying.[95]

The chronological study of Plato's dialogues has one more dimension to add to the study of the center of the *Republic*: only the chronology can show that Socrates' new politics of the ideas is an improved version of his political efforts on behalf of philosophy in the pre-Potidaean dialogues, *Protagoras* and *Alcibiades I*. Like *Protagoras*, the *Republic* has Socrates report to a wider Athenian audience a conversation held in private between leaders of the enlightenment and young Athenians; once again he advances

95. Only a detailed exegesis of the three dialogues that afford a glimpse of the pre-*Protagoras* Socrates can fully account for the ideas' becoming the doctrine Socrates teaches in his maturity. I intend to treat these dialogues in the second volume of this work.

himself as the true defender of Athenian youth, securing them against the threat of foreign teachers about whom Athenians are justly suspicious. Protagoras is replaced by Thrasymachus, a more outspoken member of Protagoras's train, but Socrates again makes a plotted effort to redirect the Greek enlightenment—and the promise of success is present in the *Republic* as it never was in *Protagoras*, for the gentled and attentive Thrasymachus is about to become Socrates' friend. Still, Socrates again serves himself by being as hard on Thrasymachus as he was on Protagoras: presenting himself as a vigilant watchman of moral decency even in private, he betrays in public the shocking things Thrasymachus said in private. And Alcibiades and Critias are replaced by Glaucon and Adeimantus, less promising if more representative young Athenians, and Socrates gives them what he never gave Alcibiades and Critias, young Athenians with whom he failed: the safe philosophy of the ideas as a way of securing their shaken commitment to justice. *Protagoras* showed Socrates in glorious prewar Athens attempting to redirect the Greek enlightenment and to draw the best Athenian youths to himself; the *Republic* shows Socrates returned to war-torn, plague-ridden Athens attempting the same things in a far more ominous setting with far more radical means.

The *Republic* aims to succeed where *Protagoras* failed and *Charmides* showed how: the resolute new Socrates returns from Potidaea like a new Odysseus bringing foreign novelty designed to treat the inexorable political problems facing philosophy. At the center of *Charmides* Critias showed how Socrates' teaching about the words put up at Delphi kindled a dream of tyranny in him; at the center of the *Republic*, a Socrates who learned this consequence of his teaching acts differently with Glaucon, a young Athenian whose ambitions repeat Critias's but whose future must not. In the argument that follows immediately, Socrates defends the central claim of the *Republic* that the philosopher must rule and shows that he can do so by ruling belief. As the rearing and educating in their new city showed, the actions of the mature are directed by the beliefs about the beautiful, just, and good inculcated in youth. To rule belief is to rule what rules; a philosopher who ruled belief would be a philosopher ruler though not a philosopher king, that goatstag of the sort dreamed up by painters (488a).[96] Plato's brother, Glaucon, will not be tempted into the tyrannical

96. Descartes understood this so profoundly that he could attempt to duplicate it and succeed: philosophy rules through a believable likeness of itself, in Descartes's case a philosophy alleging absolute certitude and proving that God exists and the soul is immortal, a philosophy that parodies the absolute certitudes of the religion that threatened to crush philosophy by

dreaming of his mother's cousin, Critias, by anything Socrates says, for Glaucon participates as Socrates' ally in the first formulation of the new ruling teaching. As the first to be commissioned to persuade those who oppose philosophy's rule, Glaucon is the first of a coming army, the legion of Platonists, believers in the ideas who believe philosophers know them. What Socrates learned while he was away is what Odysseus learned while he was away: "that his destiny is to establish belief and not knowledge."[97]

Philosophy's need to rule, glimpsed in Plato's Homeric image of Socrates as a returned Odysseus, can be seen as well in the ease with which Glaucon accepts the ideas as true doctrine. Socrates has established his authority, but it takes more than mere authority to have Glaucon accept so readily a view that, as Leo Strauss said, "to begin with . . . is utterly incredible, not to say that it appears to be fantastic."[98] Strauss showed how Glaucon could accept the doctrine of ideas so easily: it is to begin with not at all incredible to *him* because he's a young Athenian reared to believe in gods "like *Dike* or *Nike* who is not this victory or that victory, nor this or that statue of *Nike*, but one and the same self-subsisting being which is in a sense the cause of every victory and which is of unbelievable splendor." Glaucon easily transfers his belief in Homer's gods from their discredited originals to self-subsistent beings called *eidê*, Beauty itself, the Just itself, the Good itself, which are, like the gods, "self-subsisting beings which are the cause of everything good, which are of unbelievable splendor, and which cannot be apprehended by the senses since they never change their 'form.'" Speaking as the theologian who already legislated new laws for the gods, Socrates introduces the ideas as new gods recognizably divine to disbelievers in the old Homeric gods. Homer, "the educator of the Greeks" (606e), ruled the age that is passing; the poet of Socrates aims to rule post-Homeric Greece just as the poet of Odysseus and Achilles ruled.

The first argument Socrates ever gives for Platonism teaches Glaucon what Seth Benardete called "a rival account of philosophy,"[99] rival to the Socratic philosophizing intimated in the steady progress mapped in *Pha-*

---

taking itself as the true philosophy. Because he understood the Platonic strategy so profoundly Descartes could, in the final sentence of the introduction of his first book—his introduction of himself—decline "the highest offices" that could be offered, decline mere kingship, for he had intimated throughout his *Discourse on the Method* that he was a philosopher who aspired to a higher rule, rule over a whole age through a new physics of which he was the master and the general. In him too philosophy and political power coincided in one, though few today recognize it. See my *Nietzsche and Modern Times*, 145–71.

97. These are the tell-all final words of Benardete's *Bow and the Lyre*, 152.

98. Strauss, *City and Man*, 119. The following quotations are from p. 120 of Strauss's book.

99. Benardete, *Socrates' Second Sailing*, 140.

edo, Parmenides, and the *Symposium*. As Benardete indicates, the rival account is not simply false, not simply a noble lie about philosophy. Instead, Platonism serves as a pointer to Socratic philosophizing because it pictures in the simplifying way of an image what occurs in natural human understanding; it fixes as doctrine what might be called "natural platonism." Benardete notes that "all ordinary understanding is to an extraordinary degree based on what everybody attributes to a Platonic theory of the ideas. . . . The reason for this is what one might call the systematically misleading character of language itself, which necessarily leads to the pseudo-Platonic theory of the ideas."[100] Language necessarily misleads, collecting particulars that are always parts of processes into classes of relative fixity named by words of varying generality that human propensity reifies into something like the ideas. Platonism as a doctrine pictures—and takes advantage of—the natural human propensity to "platonize," to treat as real the "ideas" that are an indispensable part of understanding and communicating. Platonism as a doctrine reifies the basic experiences of the beautiful, just, and good, the opinions that arrange the world morally; it lends the world a moral foundation while inviting the philosophically inclined to investigate it.[101]

Because the doctrine of the ideas is true to the human propensity to generate seeming permanence, it is untrue to what Plato reports about Socrates' singular experience; his turn to study human experience lingered momentarily over the ideas as the solution to a philosophical problem but led him eventually to discover the desire-generated character of the beautiful and the good. Platonism as a doctrine does what human experience generally does: sever those desire-generated products from the activity that produced them. Platonism mirrors in theory the natural human propensity to detach the product from the process, occluding and denying its product-character. Platonism as a doctrine gives this natural propensity to "platonize" the gift of a theory plus arguments and images to secure it against doubts; it gives Glaucon a "philosophy" of the sort to which he naturally inclines, a safe one that secures the beautiful, just, and good against doubts raised by philosophizing. Socrates' argument for Platonism counts

100. Benardete, *Argument of the Action*, 295f.

101. Nietzsche describes with great precision the misleading and ruling power of language that affects all knowing (*Gay Science*, ¶¶354–55); he calls the concept-formation process of language "the basic will of the mind" and describes the philosopher as the unwelcome one, different from all others in wanting to see the particular, the flowing, the different, the ambiguous (*Beyond Good and Evil*, ¶230). In his *Novum Organum* Francis Bacon described this misleading propensity of language and understanding along with the systematic method whereby science can offset it.

on the natural platonism of natural opining, its full confidence in its concepts of the beautiful, just, and good and their correspondence to the real. Socrates the inquiring philosopher is, so to speak, the only non-Platonist, the only one to doubt the adequacy of his concepts of the beautiful, just, and good. Doubting what others think they know, he judges it useful to philosophy that its allies sell the misunderstanding that philosophy shares the common ontological and epistemological certainty.

In its most evident educational purpose, Platonism is a safe philosophy for the leaders and followers of the new city. But Platonism shelters within itself a second and less evident educational purpose: it can become—for the rare nondreamers more driven by philosophy than by the beautiful, just, and good—the means whereby the errors of natural platonism come to sight as errors. The terminal philosophical education of Glaucon doubles as the initiating philosophical education of a few. Such a second education proves a principle Benardete defined: "nothing can be properly understood if one does not take one's bearings by the necessarily improper starting point of understanding."[102] The *Republic* places at its center—makes central—the most masterful trompe l'oeil: it embraces human knowing in its natural misleading tendency with an embrace that is taken as earnest by the earnest and as suspicious by the rare suspicious. Selling a moral likeness of itself, genuine philosophizing helps make the city safe for philosophy while inviting the rare to the rarest activity.

The *Republic* launches Platonism and does so most beautifully: on the day Athenians stream back to Athens to report on the novel sacred spectacle of the night before, Socrates brings up from Piraeus news of his own great innovations. Athenians report the introduction of a new god; Socrates reports the introduction of a new kind of god more fit for the enlightenment and for the young harmed by it. Knowing that the city dreams its beliefs are knowledge, Socrates does what's necessary for philosophy: fold philosophy into the universal dream, make a place for it in the city by bringing the city around to a false belief in philosophy. His new doctrine of the ideas is a new dream into which he draws the rising generation schooled in Homeric dreaming but losing its capacity to believe it and finding in its place only a corrosive wakefulness. Socrates brings up from Piraeus what he brought back from Potidaea, a new politics of enlightenment that will prove to be the one turning point and vortex for a whole civilization, and prove fit for renewed foundings by philosophers of the rank of Plato taught by Plato. As the sun set on Homer's world Socrates

102. Benardete, *Argument of the Action*, 413.

prepared its rise on Plato's. He knew the immensity of what he was doing; he prostrated himself before Adrasteia knowing that a time would come when Adrasteia would condemn him in order to raise what would succeed him—condemn him as he found it necessary to condemn Homer.

14. Public Speakers for Philosophy

After completing his "somewhat lengthy" argument with Glaucon, Socrates says that they've brought to light who the philosophers are and who the nonphilosophers (485a). "What's after this for us?" asks Glaucon, for whom the issue is still whether it's "possible for this regime to come to be" (471c). What's next for them is clear: are the knowers of the ideas fit to "be the leaders of the city" (484b)? Glaucon can't answer, but Socrates easily leads him to judge that the philosophers are the ones most capable of guarding the laws and practices of cities. Still, Glaucon says they should rule only "if they don't lack the rest"—in a city built on the principle one person one job, the *rest* refers, as Socrates says, to "how the same ones will be able to possess these two distinct sets of qualities" (485a). But the qualities he describes as belonging to the philosophical nature (487a) are not the distinct set of qualities of a ruler in any ordinary sense. And when he asks, "Wouldn't you turn the city over to [them]?" Adeimantus breaks in with a different objection. Socrates successfully runs away from showing his ally how it is possible for philosophers to rule—his ally won't know that it's through him that the philosopher launches and sustains his rule.

Adeimantus objects to rule by the philosophers because of what everyone already knows: philosophers are either useless or harmful and thus unfit to rule. An alliance with Glaucon on the philosopher as the knower of the ideas overcame the first objection to the philosopher's rule; an alliance with Adeimantus that makes him the persuader of the Many that the philosopher is in fact useful and good will overcome the second objection. But something in Socrates' persuasion of Adeimantus makes Thrasymachus, that famous persuader of the Many, Socrates' "friend" (498c). Given the shepherd's role that gentled Thrasymachus quietly assumed, Socrates' persuasion of Adeimantus deserves careful scrutiny for just what persuades Thrasymachus to become Socrates' friend.

Adeimantus broke in to tell Socrates that his "questioning and answering" is completely unpersuasive even if no one can contradict his argument. Those who experience his unanswerable arguments think it's just a game at which Socrates is skilled and they're not, and they go on believing that the truth is exactly what they believed before. In the present case, Socrates' unanswerable argument that the city ought to be ruled by the philosopher leaves everyone still believing that most of those who remain in philosophy after their youth become completely strange, not to say completely bad, while the few who seem decent "become useless to the cities" (487b–d). Socrates responds to the common judgment that philosophers are useless by devising an image that completely persuades Adeimantus: the philosopher is the true pilot of the ship of state but remains unused as the sailors compete with one another to persuade the ship owner that they ought to be pilot. Trusting to the image alone, Socrates issues Adeimantus a commission making him philosophy's ally against "anyone who wonders at the philosophers not being honored in the city": "Teach the image and try to persuade him." Adeimantus accepts his commission: "I shall teach him."

Socrates needs more than an image to answer "by far the greatest and most powerful slander" against philosophy: that "most of those who go to it are completely bad" (489d). First, he repeats what he told Glaucon about the "gentleman" who partakes of "true philosophy" (490a). This "sensible apology" views the philosopher as a lover who grasps "the nature itself of each thing that is," who gets near it, couples with it, and, begetting intelligence and truth, ceases from his labor pains (490b). "And you objected," saying that those who set the argument aside and looked instead at the ones to whom the argument referred would see that some few are useless while most are bad (490d). The new identity of the philosopher arrived at with Glaucon must be supplemented by the new role for philosophers to be arrived at with Adeimantus.

The very virtues of the philosophic nature play a part in corrupting him, Socrates says, as do the things considered good. But who corrupts the philosophic nature? The Many believe *sophists* corrupt it by private instruction, but the ones who say this are the biggest sophists, Socrates says, and they educate most perfectly (492a–b). Adeimantus can't believe it. "But when do they do that?" he asks, having just heard the usual charge that sophists corrupt in private. It can't be only Adeimantus who is arrested by this new identification of the sophist in the first use of the word *sophist* that night: the actual sophist present must also be startled, he who earlier made in private the corrupting claim that justice is a fraud perpetrated by the powerful for their own advantage. He will remain wordless as Socrates exonerates him and sophists generally from public blame while blaming the public that blames them. The Many corrupt the best natures, Socrates says, by what they praise and blame in public; no private instruction can hold out against the public blast of what is beautiful and ugly or noble and base. And the Many have the power to punish the young who don't conform—it would not be wrong to say, Socrates says, that only a god could save one from this corrupting force (493a).

Socrates then teaches Adeimantus—and silent Thrasymachus—just who those private corrupters are whom the public call sophists and believe to be their rivals in the art of educating. The private sophist educates in nothing but the dogmas of the Many, calling that wisdom. In a memorable image Socrates describes the famous orator Thrasymachus exactly: he learns by heart the angers and desires of a great strong beast he's rearing, learns what makes it savage or gentle, learns especially what sounds it utters and what sounds others utter to tame or anger it; he calls what he learns wisdom, organizes it into an art, and turns to teaching (493b). This is "the mighty man of Chalcedon who has gained, by art, mastery of speeches [and] become terribly clever at angering the Many, and when they have been angered, at beguiling them by singing incantations."[103] Still, though he knows the beast, he knows nothing in truth about which of its dogmas and desires is beautiful or ugly, good or evil, just or unjust (493c)—he does not possess knowledge of the three ideas Socrates claimed the philosopher knows. The sophist's knowledge is confined entirely to the city's conventions, and he calls what delights it good and what angers it bad. Socrates ends vehemently, "in the name of Zeus, wouldn't such a man be out of place as an educator?" That educator needs to be educated by what Socrates alone can give him.

Thrasymachus knows that he is a shepherd who serves some master, and Socrates has just shown him that his present master is the set of conventions to which the city is slave: servant to slaves, he makes "the Many his masters beyond what is necessary" (493d). Socrates is making every effort to appeal to Thrasymachus: he absolves him of the city's blame, acknowledges that his art is based on understanding the Many, and shows him that his art is animal training in service to the animal. By showing Thrasymachus that he knows him better than he knows himself, Socrates implicitly invites him to advantage himself by putting his art into the ministerial service of a knowing master. Socrates tries to succeed with Thrasymachus where he failed with Protagoras: showing a famous sophist a better way to serve the Many and be thought wise, he shows him that virtue pays better than vice.

Socrates continues his lesson on the threats to the philosophic nature (494a): the multitude cannot be philosophic, and it condemns the philosopher, as do sophists in their desire to please it. What salvation can there

103. *Phaedrus* 267c–d.

be for a young philosophic nature whose superior gifts the multitude will recognize and want to use? If such a youth does turn to philosophy, the multitude will blame the one who persuaded him and organize private plots and public trials against him (494e). Abandoned by her natural suitors, philosophy—Lady Philosophy—is pursued by unworthy suitors who bring reproach on her. Only a tiny remnant is spared to keep company with philosophy in a worthy way, Socrates says, giving four examples before mentioning a case that "isn't worth mentioning": his own. He avoided corruption and destruction thanks to his "daimonic sign"—he's the one of whom it could be said that he was saved by a god's dispensation (493a, 492a). His case is not worth mentioning because it's rare or unrepeatable: "for it has perhaps occurred in some one other or no other before." Socrates knows himself: he's an exception among the exceptions; he belongs to the happy few but he's different. He describes the rare experience of all the exceptions: they "have tasted how sweet and blessed a possession [philosophy] is," they "have seen sufficiently the madness of the Many, and that no one who minds the business of the cities does virtually anything sound, and that there is no ally with whom one could go to the aid of justice and be preserved" (496c). On his telling, the exceptions all did what he did: study what set them off from the common experience of the Many and study what ruled the Many. That study confirmed their aloneness in loyalty to what they alone knew was sweetest. They drew the necessary conclusion from their aloneness in happiness (here Socrates reverts to the singular): he's like a human being fallen in with wild beasts. Not willing to join them, not able to resist them, knowing he would perish before he was of any use to city or friends, he calculates a strategy of self-preservation: "he keeps quiet and minds his own business—as if in a storm, when dust and rain are blown about by the wind, he stands aside under a little wall" (496d). Socrates ends on the modest aspiration of the exception, content to live pure of injustice and unholy deeds and at the end leave life graciously and with fair hope. That life Adeimantus praises: "he would leave having accomplished not the least of things." "But not the greatest either," Socrates says, "if he didn't chance upon a suitable regime. For in a fitting regime he himself will grow more and save the common things along with the private."

It's almost visible: Socrates, that exception among the exceptions, blessed with a restraining daimonion, attempts that greater thing and is not restrained. Understanding the emergency conditions facing philosophy, he founds a regime in which private and public happiness prevail. He shelters himself behind a wall only figuratively; out in the storm making allies where he had no allies, he shelters himself behind careful speech that hides from the city the conflicting natures of city and philosopher. Having made an ally of Glaucon by planting in him a safe account of the philosopher, he makes an ally of Adeimantus by training him to advocate a regime that "knows" that the philosopher is useful and good. Socrates minds his own business: he sees to philosophical rule by being the exception among exceptions who does not withdraw to a private happiness but enlists allies as Thrasymachus watches.[104]

"Which of the current regimes is suitable?" Adeimantus asks, a natural question for a young Athenian who could well have been present when Pericles, in the winter of 431–430, praised Athenian democracy as "philosophizing without weakness."[105] "None at all," Socrates says, directing attention to "the best regime," "the same one we've described in founding the city." Socrates isolates the new problem facing the best regime: "that there would always have to be present in the city something possessing the same understanding of the regime as you, the lawgiver, had when you were setting down the laws." Adeimantus didn't set down the laws of the city in speech: he didn't have the same understanding of the regime its founding lawgiver had. Why misattribute founding and speak vaguely of "something possessing the same understanding" as Adeimantus? Because of what comes next, it seems, a matter Socrates describes as "by no means the easiest to go through": "How can a city take philosophy in hand without being destroyed?" (497d). Socrates moves from the city's threat to the philosopher to philosophy's threat to the city. He elevates the problem: "All great things carry with them the risk of a fall, and as the saying goes, fine things are hard." The risky, fine, hard thing Socrates here introduces is what naturally follows the founding of a regime, its being carried forward, its problem of *succession*. That perpetual political problem is made more acute by the danger philosophy poses to the city: how can the best regime's friendliness to the passion for truth be passed on by its philosophic founder if that passion is both rare and at odds with the city's need for edifying fictions? Misattributing understanding and founding to Adeimantus may be a clue: it's not necessary that the rarest thing, a philosopher, be continuously present for the succession of the city friendly to

104. Nietzsche describes himself as an exception among exceptions who studied the common man on the way to his deepest insights and greatest deeds; *Beyond Good and Evil*, "The Free Mind," ¶¶24–44.

105. Thucydides 2.40.

philosophy. Would it be enough that those possessing the understanding of Adeimantus be present?

How can the city of philosophical rule that Socrates is founding perpetuate itself in the feature that matters most, its harboring what could destroy it? While treating the city's danger to philosophy, Socrates invoked sophism in a way bound to get Thrasymachus's undivided attention. And right here, on philosophy's danger to the city, Adeimantus says that Thrasymachus will be eager to oppose him. No, Socrates will say, "we've just become friends though we weren't enemies even before" (498d). Socrates' description of how the city will take philosophy in hand seems intended to make Thrasymachus his friend: *Thrasymachus* seems to be the key to the problem of philosophy's threat to the city, the key to the philosophical founder's problem of succession. Thrasymachus traveled to Athens partly with the purpose of forming alliances with young political men. His first act showed that he viewed Socrates as his rival; but now, as he watches Socrates successfully forge alliances with Glaucon and Adeimantus, he is invited to think that *his* alliance with Socrates is key.

Socrates describes himself before addressing the problem he just introduced: his "eagerness" will be visible as he speaks both "eagerly and rashly." Still, his daimonion, just referred to, does not hold him back as he eagerly embarks on a risky but necessary novelty. A city can take philosophy in hand and not be destroyed only if its practice of philosophy is "just the opposite of what is done nowadays": Socrates solves the problem of succession for the city founded by philosophy by transforming the public presence of philosophy. He lists three stages of life to describe how philosophy is treated now, elaborating the first stage, that of "lads fresh out of childhood, in the interval before running a household and making money," lads like Adeimantus and Glaucon. "They approach its hardest part and then leave. . . . By the hardest part I mean that which has to do with logoi"—logoi are what Socrates turned to as a lad,[106] logoi are what Thrasymachus claims mastery of. "In later life," they treat philosophy only as a hobby. And "toward old age" they are "far more extinguished than Heraclitus' sun, inasmuch as they are not rekindled again" (498a).

"How ought it to be?" Adeimantus asks. "Entirely opposite," Socrates says and describes four stages of life. As "youths and boys they ought to take up an education and philosophy suitable for youths," and they should "take very good care of their bodies . . . thus securing a helper for philosophy." He replaces the hardest part, logoi, without describing its re-

106. *Phaedo* 99e.

placement: it seems he already replaced the hardest part with what he told young Glaucon, the easy-to-grasp view that the beautiful, just, and good are ideas known to the philosopher. As the soul begins to reach maturity, "it ought to be subjected to a more intense gymnastic"—Socrates makes no explicit mention of philosophy. "And when strength begins to fail and they are beyond political and military duties, at this time they ought to be let loose to graze and do nothing else, except as a spare time occupation, those who are going to live happily"—in a retirement of grazing Socrates again omits philosophy (498c).[107] He adds a fourth stage: "and when they die, crown the life they have lived with a suitable lot in that other place." The city that takes philosophy in hand without being destroyed seems to give no public place to philosophy after its philosophy for youths; and it adds a stage to life: well-being in the next life where before there was only Heraclitus's extinguished sun. Adeimantus confirms Socrates' expectation: he thinks Socrates is speaking eagerly. But he thinks as well that many among the hearers will also be eager, eager to oppose him, "beginning with Thrasymachus." Socrates does not report any reaction by Thrasymachus but reports his own: "Don't make a quarrel between Thrasymachus and me when we've just become friends, though we weren't enemies even before" (498d). Thrasymachus hears his name twice, once as the first opponent of Socrates' new way for the city to treat philosophy and once as Socrates' newly made friend. What follows shows him why Socrates is right, why his own advantage entails that he give up any lingering thought of opposing Socrates as a rival and become his friend instead. For the enticing speeches Socrates now gives show him how he and his art can bring the Many around to be the herd for his shepherding if he becomes Socrates' friend.

Socrates' eager speaking does not stop after he states that Thrasymachus just became his friend; he continues eagerly, suggesting that his task with Thrasymachus is a long-term project: "We'll not give up our efforts before we either persuade him and the others, or give them some help in preparation for that other life when, born again, they meet with such speeches" (498c–d). Adeimantus interrupts, startled by the "other life": "That's a short time you're speaking about." "None at all," Socrates says, "if you compare it to the whole." He returns to the distinction he just made, removing its ambiguities: "However, it's no wonder the Many are not persuaded by these speeches"—by the "efforts" Socrates just referred to of persuading Thrasymachus and the others about the new way the city is to

107. Feeling the absence of *philosophy* after the phrase "do nothing else," many English translators add on their own: "but philosophize" (as do Shorey, Grube/Reeve, Larson, Griffith, Allen).

take up philosophy. He now shows just how both Thrasymachus and the Many can be persuaded not to oppose his new way. The Many are persuaded by little sophistic tricks of speech like the ones Socrates now indulges in as he acts the sophist, inventing a little rhyming jingle: the Many have not been persuaded because "they've never beheld a token of the thing here spoken."[108] They've heard many sophistic jingles "purposely balanced [*hô-moiômena*] with one another, not falling together spontaneously as they are now." Socrates denies any artfulness in his artful speech and goes on artfully: From whom have they heard these jingles? Never from "a man with virtue perfectly 'likened' [*parisômenon*] and 'balanced' [*hômoiômenon*][109] to the limit of the possible in deed and word," and never from a man "who holds power in a city fit for him" (498e).

Attentive Thrasymachus will know what he's hearing: Socrates is telling him that to persuade the Many the professional jingle maker must be a man the Many trust, a man of visible virtue in deed and word, a man whose use of jingles could lead him to hold power in a city fit for him. Socrates has a final prescription for Thrasymachus's new speeches: the Many have never heard jingle-rich speeches "of the sort that strain every nerve in quest of the truth for the sake of knowing" (499a). Such speeches will "nod a distant greeting" to sophistic quibbling, to "subtleties and contentious quibbles that strain toward nothing but opinion and contention in trials as well as in private groups." Setting aside these practices, Thrasymachus's new speeches will put the persuasive art in the service of the love of truth, and they will be the same in private as in public. The city he persuades will think of itself as truth-loving and led by truth lovers, though no multitude can be philosophical and sophists are not primarily truth lovers.

Told that he has just become Socrates' friend, attentive Thrasymachus learns what his friend is offering: that "*other life*" into which they will all be "*born again*." That cannot be, for Thrasymachus, some dream of Hades: he's no Cephalus. Instead, it must be the city that takes philosophy in hand in a new way. When Thrasymachus speaks to the Cephaluses and their sons, the virtuous-looking maker of jingles will make being born again to another life part of his persuasive speech—he will do what Socrates does at the end of the *Republic*. The other life Socrates is offering Thrasyma-

108. This modifies Shorey's translation: "For of the thing here spoken they have never beheld a token." Shorey comments: "it's not translating to make no attempt to reproduce Plato's parody" of sophistic jingles. Socrates' rhyming of *gegomenon* and *legomenon* was prepared by *legomenois* ($498d_7$).

109. These are technical terms employed in the art of rhetoric; could they have been associated particularly with Thrasymachus?

chus, the new life into which he will be born again in the city founded by Socrates, can be his if he casts off his old life, his furtive life advocating justice as the advantage of the stronger party. Socrates leads Thrasymachus to see that justice is mightier for him: that central argument of the three arguments that first gentled his rivalry with Socrates here receives its completed form. Socrates showed him that their common enterprise can be saved only if they do one another justice. Socrates does him justice: knowing the power of his art, he makes a place for it. Thrasymachus can do Socrates justice in return: he can grant Socrates the mastery that is so evidently his and grant it because it serves his advantage. Casting off his old life, he can put on his new life as the shepherd whose art of rousing and soothing his herd wins him the public acclaim that is his due and that the philosophic master he serves neither needs nor wants. To succeed, however, he must speak as Socrates showed, speak in jingles persuading the Many, speak of loving truth, speak in trials as he speaks in private, speak of another life and seem to mean what Cephalus meant. Socrates and Thrasymachus become friends because Socrates shows him the one way in which their common enterprise can succeed. Theirs is not a friendship of equals; it is the friendliness of mutual benefit that a needy master offers a gifted servant he advantages.

Looking back from this point, one sees the useful ambiguity of Socrates' four stages of life for the city that takes philosophy in hand without being destroyed. Heard literally, the four stages make philosophy disappear from public presence after the youths have been taught the suitable philosophy of the ideas. The new city will not be destroyed by philosophy because genuine philosophy, Socratic philosophizing as unrelenting inquiry, disappears from public presence behind a sheltering wall. But "philosophy" does not disappear; it is present as what the boys learned, present as Platonism, knowledge of the ideas, assured knowledge of certain virtue. Platonism is the public philosophy of the new city, the philosophy of the philosopher dogs; as an image of philosophy it parades philosophy's virtue without betraying its ever-questing character. Platonism is Socrates' new exotericism, far more thorough than what he offered Protagoras yet still in need of enlisting sophism. Philosophy must befriend sophism, the public form of enlightenment that has understood a fragment of the deadly truth about justice: it must alter sophism because the Many confuse philosophy and sophistry. In the new city no philosopher will do what Socrates did before Potidaea—he learned his lesson with Alcibiades and Critias. And no sophist will do what Thrasymachus did in Cephalus's house—even in the privacy of a rich man's house sophists will refrain from offering the subversive view that justice is the advantage of the stronger. Because his art has an honored place, Thrasymachus will know as well as Protagoras did that it is not to his advantage to subvert the city's standards of justice—his rhetoric will be salutary and open, in accord with Platonism. No wonder Socrates speaks of Thrasymachus becoming his friend: he offers him rule in the city, a shepherd's rule serving its ruling master. Replaced in public by a philosophy for youths, philosophy itself is free to pursue in private an eros that Thrasymachus knows he lacks, the passion to grasp the nature of each of the beings (490b), beings as real as the sun and the laws and as usefully unreal as the reformed Olympians.

Socrates' open alliance with Adeimantus offers a secret alliance to Thrasymachus. He will embrace that alliance if he can calculate his own advantage. Because he is a master actor who can feign anger to move to anger and feign gentleness to soothe from anger, his new public appearance will be a natural act bringing new rewards as rhetoric justly becomes what it was already becoming, a necessary part of every public man's education. Thrasymachus is a stand-in for the whole sophistic enlightenment, the rising intellectual class that more or less easily comes to understand that the city's loyalties are to noble lies. By offering a curriculum of Platonism to the sophistic enlightenment, Socrates offers an easy philosophy for gentlemen, taught in their youth before they leave philosophy for the important matters of running a household and a city. By teaching Glaucon "true philosophy," Socrates gave Thrasymachus a model; by teaching Adeimantus how to steer the Many, Socrates gave Thrasymachus his explicit task. The new direction Socrates gives the Greek enlightenment solves philosophy's problem of succession: Platonism is the public means for transmitting Socratic philosophizing. The long intellectual history of Platonism in Hellenistic Greece and Rome would then be in part the history of Socrates' friends, the many Thrasymachuses who preserve both the city and philosophy by being that "something possessing the same understanding of the regime as [Socrates] the lawgiver had when [he was] setting down the laws" (497d). Socrates does not entrust his friendship with Thrasymachus to charm or chance; he founds the friendship of philosophy and rhetoric on self-interest; his politic persuasion of Thrasymachus offers fugitive cleverness public acclaim as wisdom.[110]

110. Could *Cleitophon* then be something quite unexpected: could it display the post-*Republic* friendship of Socrates and Thrasymachus? Socrates has no interest in Cleitophon as an associate; it is enough that Cleitophon praise his exhortations to justice. As for what the persuaded must then do in order to be just, let them go to Thrasymachus for that. Socrates' silence at the end

Having so artfully created an intimate atmosphere of communication between himself and Thrasymachus, Socrates can continue to address Adeimantus and draw his responses while privately addressing Thrasymachus whose response can be inferred. It was because the city had never yet heard such speeches, Socrates says (499b), that he was afraid to say that the city would never become perfect unless some necessity compelled the few philosophers who weren't vicious but were called useless to take charge of a city. Thus repeating his initial statement of the philosopher ruler while tying it to the only means that can make it actual, Socrates returns to the question of the possibility of the city in speech. It is not impossible and cannot be ridiculed for being "like prayers" (499c; cf. 450d, 540d), but only if "this Muse has become master of a city" (499d). That's hard but possible, he says, and describes the two conditions of its achievement. First, the Many must be made amenable by persuaders who do not quarrel with them but "soothe them and do away with the slander against the love of learning." Adeimantus—Thrasymachus—must show "whom you mean by the philosophers" and distinguish, "as was just done [with Glaucon], their nature and the character of their practice." Second, the philosopher must do what Socrates is now doing in the Piraeus: moved by "some necessity," leave the world he naturally occupies, "keeping company with the divine and orderly" (500b), and "practice putting what he sees there into the dispositions of humans, both in private and in public" (500d). With those conditions met, "Are we somehow persuading those who *you said* were coming at us full speed" (501c) that handing the cities over to the philosophers is fitting? Glaucon said that, not Adeimantus. Socrates' little mistake merges Adeimantus's objection with Glaucon's: to disarm the natural attacks on the rule of the philosopher and thereby rule, the philosopher Socrates takes two complementary history-making steps: paint the philosopher a Platonist and prepare a ministering rhetoric to sway the public.

Socrates will explicitly draw Thrasymachus in at the end of the argument, hours later as he concludes his night-long argument proving to Glaucon that justice is more profitable than injustice (589d).[111] After a long litany of what appropriately rules and appropriately serves, Socrates speaks

---

would mark his approval of Cleitophon's going to Thrasymachus, his friend who teaches a public philosophy and not the advantage of the stronger.

111. In the only other naming of Thrasymachus Socrates looked to the end of the argument: "won't our examination then be complete as to how unmixed justice stands to unmixed injustice for the happiness or misery of its possessor, in order to be persuaded by Thrasymachus that we should pursue injustice, or by the argument now being brought to light in favor of justice?" (545a–b).

of one "ruled by something similar to what rules the best man" (590c): "don't we say that he must be the slave of that best man who has the divine rule in himself?" But he recasts the meaning of *slave* if service is to the best: "It's not that we suppose the slave must be ruled to his own detriment, as Thrasymachus supposed about the ruled; but that it's better for all to be ruled by what is divine and prudent"—it's better that Thrasymachus too, the teacher of rule, be ruled this way. Socrates goes on: it's better when one has the divine and prudent "as his own within himself, but if not, as set over one from outside, so that insofar as possible all will be alike and friends, piloted by the same thing." Thrasymachus is a fit pilot if piloted by the true pilot to set over him what will remain outside him, the divine and prudent. And when Socrates goes on to speak of the law as an ally of all in the city, and of children "not being set free until we establish a regime in them as in the city" (590e), he says what his friend must attend to as the public educator Socrates is arranging for him to become, the educator who upholds the laws while teaching a philosophy fit for children. Socrates proves to Thrasymachus too that justice is more profitable than injustice.

15. Images of the Greatest Study: Sun, Line, Cave

Socrates must next speak of the "studies and practices" that will enable "the saviors to take their place within our regime" (502d)—"the greatest studies." When first mentioning the greatest studies (503e), he virtually compels Adeimantus to ask him what they are. Then, instead of telling him, he forces him to recall what was said earlier, and when he fails Socrates states what apparently must never be forgotten: with the greatest studies too they will take a short road where only the longer road can supply "the finest possible look at these things." Adeimantus is satisfied with the short road, but Socrates calls it "no measure at all," adding that "a guardian of a city and of laws . . . must go the longer way around" (504c). Soon after, when Glaucon breaks in to force Socrates to say what he thinks the greatest study, "the idea of the good," really is, he too says he's satisfied if Socrates goes through the good as he went through the rest (506d). It is almost explicit: Socrates' images of the greatest study—Sun, Line, Cave—are satisfying stopping points to nonphilosophers but goads and starting points on a longer road for those inclined to take it.[112]

112. Benardete noticed that *philosopher* is spoken just before Socrates leads into the greatest studies (503b) and that *philosopher, philosophy, philosophize* are not spoken again until after the

"Is there something greater than justice and the other things we went through?" Adeimantus asked incredulously when Socrates first spoke of the greatest studies and of "the greatest and most fitting study" (504d). Socrates calls what they went through for those virtues only "a sketch," adding that "their most perfect elaboration must not be stinted." Again he says "the greatest things." And again Adeimantus says that regarding the greatest study no one "is going to let you go without asking what it is"—*let go* being the word used three times before in arresting Socrates (327c, 449b, 472a). They should know what he is going to say, Socrates says, because they've "already heard many times that *the idea of the good* is the greatest study" (505a). They should also know that Socrates is going to say "that we don't have sufficient knowledge of it." Still, Socrates knows a lot about it. He knows that the Many hold the good to be pleasure.[113] He knows that the more refined call the good prudence.[114] And he knows two more things about the good: all want the good for what it really is and are not content with a reputation for what it is opined to be, as they are with the just and the beautiful; and the good "is what every soul pursues and for the sake of which it does everything" (505d). Socrates continues to insist on the importance of this knowledge for rulers, and Adeimantus continues to ask him to say what he thinks it is. Can it be just of Socrates to tell other people's convictions "but not your own when you've spent so much time occupied with these things" (506b)? Socrates evades: "is it just to speak about what one doesn't know as though one knew it?" Adeimantus insists: not as though one knew, but what one supposes as one's supposition. Finally, Socrates asks Adeimantus, "Do you want to see ugly things, blind and skew, when it's possible to hear bright and beautiful ones from others?" Glaucon erupts: "No, in the name of Zeus, Socrates, you're not going to withdraw when you're at the end," adding that they'll be satisfied if "you go through the good as you went through justice, moderation, and the rest." Glaucon's vehemence and his invitation deflect attention away from what Socrates actually said—was it what he actually thinks? He himself wouldn't think that what he holds about the good is

cave image (520a) (*Socrates' Second Sailing*, 92). What Benardete calls the "peak of the *Republic*" never names philosophy, another indication that the images imaging the greatest studies are a philosopher's subphilosophical similitudes serving the philosopher's rule.

113. And he acts as if their admission of bad pleasures refutes that view though he showed in *Protagoras* that calling pleasures *bad* is compatible with holding the good to be pleasure: bad pleasures inhibit long-term pleasure (*Protagoras* 351b–356c).

114. But they say it is "prudence about the good," as if we knew what that good was.

ugly, blind, and skew, but he could well think they would think so if he said it.[115]

So Socrates takes up Glaucon's invitation: he would be well satisfied to go through the good as he went through the rest. And how is that? By "leaving aside for now what the good itself is," and for this reason: "it looks to me as though it's out of the range of our present thrust to attain the opinion I now hold about it" (506e). He has an opinion about the good. He leaves it aside. This much is in range: if they're willing he'll give them "what looks like a child of the good and most similar to it"; if not, he'll "let it go." Glaucon is willing. They will not see Socrates' opinion, which they could think ugly, blind, or skew; they will see its decidedly bright and beautiful child. "Another time," Glaucon says, "you'll pay us what's due on the father's narrative." Socrates demurs: "I could wish that I were able to pay and you were able to receive it itself." Does he pay the father's narrative in what he relates of the child's?

Sun

With Glaucon again his interlocutor, Socrates first reviews what the two of them earlier concluded about the ideas. That is, having overcome Adeimantus's objection to philosophical rule, Socrates returns to Glaucon's objection and completes his account of what Glaucon is to believe the philosopher knows. The images he now presents build on earlier conclusions he here repeats: there is a beautiful itself, a good itself, and one idea of each of the manys; in each case they are to call the idea what *is* (507b). Regarding the good, Socrates begins with sight. For the sense of sight to see anything visible, a third thing is needed, the medium that holds the visible in visibility: light. "Which of the gods in heaven can you point to as the Lord responsible for this?" (508a). Which but Helios? Glaucon answers. "This then," Socrates says, "you may say that I meant by the child of the good which the good generated analogous to itself" (508b). Socrates speaks as a theologian and demotes the visible gods: the good is father to the brightest god in the sky. He spells out his father-child analogy: "As the good is to intelligence and the intellected in the intelligible region, so is the sun to sight and the seen in the visible." Glaucon needs more, and Socrates explains that the same eyes have clear sight of what is lit by the sun but dim sight of what is lit by "night lights," the moon and stars. He then invites Glaucon to think about the soul in exact analogy to the eyes: "So also think

115. Benardete, *Socrates' Second Sailing*, 156.

of what belongs to the soul: when it is fixed on what is illuminated by truth and what is, it intellects, knows, and appears to possess intelligence; but when it fixes itself on what is mixed with darkness, on what comes to be and passes away, it opines and is dimmed, changing opinions up and down, and seems not to possess intelligence" (508d). Socrates now sets out the complete analogy for what Glaucon is to say and think about how the good functions; and he turns from declarative verbs to imperatives: "This then, which provides the *truth* to the things known and gives the power of *knowing* to the knower, you must say is the idea of the good, and as the cause of knowledge and truth you must think of it as being known" (508e). And he provides the right opinion about the good: as beautiful as knowledge and truth are, it is right to believe that the good is other and still more beautiful than they. And he provides the right opinion about its otherness: just as light and sight are sunlike but not themselves the sun, so too knowledge and truth are goodlike but not themselves the good: "the condition which characterizes the good must receive still higher honor." Socrates introduced the child of the good as a god; now he orders right opinion about the good to honor it not only more highly than the god it fathered but more highly even than knowledge and truth. The lover of truth orders Glaucon to hold the good higher than truth.

Glaucon is overwhelmed, reduced to a foolish statement: "You surely don't mean it is pleasure." "Don't blaspheme," Socrates replies, holding to the sacred mood as he prepares to say something higher still about the good that fathered a god. Again he issues an order. Knowing Glaucon would say that the sun provides "generation, growth, and nourishment although it isn't itself generation," he commands him: "You are also to say for the things known, not only that their being known is present as a consequence of the good, but also *existence* and *being* are in them besides as a result of it, though the good isn't being but is still beyond being, exceeding it in dignity and power" (509b). Beyond knowledge and truth, the good must be said to be beyond being itself, beyond the ideas, which Socrates just taught Glaucon to believe had being beyond mere becoming.

Glaucon is again overwhelmed, but this time, "greatly amused," he does the opposite of blaspheme: "Apollo! Divine superiority!"[116] Glaucon keeps to the sun but names it Apollo, not Helios. An Olympian replaces a Titan[117]

116. *Diamones huperbolês*. Glaucon's *huperbolês* echoes the last word of Socrates' speech, *huperechontos*, "to be above, exceed, surpass."

117. Different names of gods "may be consciously equated as in the case of Apollo and Helios." Burkert, *Greek Religion*, 120.

in a divine superiority that reflects Socrates' new claim about the divine: superior even to divine Apollo is the Good, superior even to the serene Olympian who replaced Helios, superior to the god at Delphi, is a god of gods. Glaucon may be amused, but his little outburst does exactly what Socrates commanded. Socrates, a maker of new gods, the ideas, fashions a god beyond the gods, "the Good" construed as no one has ever construed it—a bright and beautiful name for the highest.

"You are responsible for compelling me to tell my opinions about it," Socrates says after Glaucon's exclamation, having a few moments before said that his opinion about the good was "out of the range of our present thrust" (506e). "Don't under any conditions stop," Glaucon says, "don't leave even the slightest thing out." He'll leave out a great deal, Socrates says, but nothing willingly—and doesn't leave out a name for what he commands Glaucon to think about the Good and the sun: "You must think, then, that as we say, these two things *are* and that one is king of the intelligible kind and place and the other of the visible." *King*. The philosopher arguing that philosophers must be kings has no desire to be king; instead, he crowns a king to rule in his place and for his ends. Crown the Good King of the ideas. But at the very coronation of the Good, Socrates suggests what he's doing: the sun rules over the *horatou* (visible), he says, not to say the *ouranou* (heavens) lest he be thought to sophistize with the name—he could have indulged in sophistic wordplay for what ruled the heavens but refrained. He refrained? He just named the Good the supersensible King of the intelligible that rules even the heavens. The philosopher rules by giving others names for a King beyond the heavens and heavenly rulers.

Socrates almost began his introduction of the greatest study by saying that "we don't have sufficient knowledge of [the good]." But he knows what to order Glaucon to think and say the good is: think and say the good is king of the intelligible as the sun is of the visible. Think and say the good gives permanent knowability and truth to the knowable things, to the ideas in which Socrates has just instructed his young ally. Think and say the good gives permanent existence and being to ideas like the idea of justice. The words Socrates gives Glaucon for the rule of the good provide rest from the evil of believing that justice does not bring happiness. The philosopher sees to the attainment of happiness by nonphilosophers: believe you live in a moral order secured by a kingly good that transcends even justice and holds it in being.

Socrates knows a lot about the good. He knows that the good is what everyone desires for what it really is and that the good is that for the sake of which everyone does what he does. Now he has shown that he knows that the good is beyond truth and knowledge as their cause—truth and knowledge themselves are customarily governed by the good, appearing only within the horizon drawn by what one inchoately divines the good to be or holds the good to be. And he knows that even existence and being appear within the horizon of what one holds the good to be. Socrates knows the truth about what counts as true: what is held to be good governs truth, knowledge, existence, and being. Consequently Socrates knows that the good is beyond being in dignity and power—while not existing in the way any and every being exists, it *is* in such a way as to exercise power over the beings as they come to light for humans. Socrates crowns as king the already ruling king. His coronation of the good yields to what is already true of the good and grants the good a new realm: the good, supreme ruler of the world, now holds in being the permanent ideas like the idea of the just. Socrates founds a great new piety about the good, but his own transcendence of piety is visible as the impiety of a maker of gods. No wonder Socrates said the opinion he now holds about the good lies outside the range of their present thrust: their present thrust is moral, and he sees to it that his transmoral understanding of the good remain outside their present thrust—detectably outside.

The short road leads to the bright and beautiful that secures the moral universe in the ruling principle of the Good. The long road leads through the bright and beautiful to what Socrates warned Adeimantus could seem ugly, blind, and skew. The same words that satisfy Adeimantus and Glaucon in the way they most need to be satisfied provide the unsatisfied with pointers to the longer road, to a reading of Socrates' words that finds in them what Socrates also wants to communicate. The brightest and most beautiful is far from simply a lie, for the world is ultimately judged good by the philosopher too, though its goodness would seem ugly, blind, and skew were he to describe it as he divines it. This philosopher's ultimate affirmation of the goodness of the world can arrange a moral appearance, affirming the world as it is not for those whose decency depends upon its being what it is not, a place where justice and happiness conjoin. His moral lie is a true lie in both senses: it takes up residence in their souls and it images the truth in the only way they can take as true. The new good, invisible king of the visible, rules knowledge, truth, existence, and being for the moral, and Socrates presents that rule in careful words that can lead to the truth about knowledge, truth, existence, and being.

Zeus is uncrowned, as Socrates foresaw in prostrating himself before Adrasteia. It is not Swirl that succeeds to his place, as Aristophanes made his Socrates teach; Plato's Socrates crowns the Good the new king. Here, at the theological peak, Plato's returned Socrates shows that he learned from the doctor of Zalmoxis, from Herodotus, to put up words for a kind of monotheistic, post-Homeric god of gods, giving him neither a Thracian nor any other local name. You must say that the whole is ruled by the Good. The words Socrates puts up for this new god of gods are wise words; a satisfying short way for almost all, they invite some few to the longer way, the way to the truth about what rules the world.

Line

The image of the line helps meet Glaucon's demand that Socrates "go through the similitude of the sun again" and not leave anything out. He'll leave much out but nothing willingly, he has said; but he makes no mention of the sun or the good in the line image, returning to them only in the cave image, his other image to meet Glaucon's demand.

The initial line has two unequal sections, one for the visible, the other for the intelligible, the two forms (*eidê*) Socrates just assigned kings. He instructs Glaucon to cut both sections in the same ratio as the initial cut.[118] Taking up the visible first, he says it is subdivided according to the criterion of clarity and unclarity (509d). He deals first with the relatively unclear, "images" (*eikonas*), saying he means shadows plus reflections on water and other reflective surfaces. Beginning with images compels him to refer only secondarily to "that of which this first is the likeness," the whole realm of actually existing individual beings. Not only does he make that come second, he never names its contents, never calls it the realm of the "things" or "beings." Instead, he supplies a list that looks merely partial: "the animals around us, and all plants, and the whole class of artifacts" (510a). Glaucon easily follows everything he's asked to picture about the original line and its first subdivision. Socrates then asks him if he's willing to say about this division that "with respect to truth and lack of it"—not simply clarity and unclarity—"as the opinable [*doxaston*] is to the knowable [*gnôston*], so what is made like is to that to which it is made like?" Glaucon is willing—but to what did he commit himself? Did he just agree that with

118. Socrates gives no way to determine which section of the original line is longer, but his instructions ensure that the two middle sections of the subdivided line will be of equal length. In the labels Socrates assigns at the end, "trust" and "thought" will be of equal length but "imagination" and "intellection" will be of considerably different lengths. Either imagination will be much longer than intellection or intellection than imagination, depending on whether the visible or the intelligible is longer in the first cut: could the placement of the original cut reflect a person's propensity to exercise imagination or intellection?

respect to truth the opinable-visible is *made like* the knowable? Socrates' subsequent approaches to the visible section all come through the intelligible section. Questions arise: Why approach the totality of individual beings first through their images? Why limit them to animals, plants, and artifacts? And why approach their truth and lack of it as if the opinable were the likeness of the knowable? The completed line image will suggest an elevation of *image* to the reigning mode of the whole realm of the visible.

The visible section gives way rapidly to the intelligible section, and Glaucon forces Socrates to treat its two subsections far more elaborately. Three accounts are given, a brief one by Socrates that Glaucon says he does not understand, a restatement by Socrates to help him understand, and a third by Glaucon after he admits to a still inadequate understanding—yet Socrates calls his account "a most adequate exposition." In this sequence of accounts lies the key to the line image, for Socrates' two accounts harbor a meaning not repeated in Glaucon's "most adequate exposition." Glaucon is right: he has inadequately understood. But why would Socrates approve his exposition?

Socrates begins by asking how to cut the intelligible section (510b). He answers himself with great brevity, making a "soul" active for the first time. Again, he starts with images, different images: in one section of the intelligible, "the soul, using as images that which was imitated before, is compelled to investigate from suppositions [*hupotheseis*] proceeding not to a beginning [*archê*][119] but to an end [*teleutê*]." The soul here acts under compulsion, employing postulates or suppositions it cannot examine. Socrates offers no explanations and without pause sets out the other subsection of the intelligible: "in the other, it makes its way from supposition to a suppositionless [*anupotheton*] beginning and without the images in the other [but] by means of the forms [*eidê*] themselves, it makes its inquiry through them." This curt account confuses Glaucon: "I don't adequately understand [*emathon*] what you mean by this." Glaucon's verb, *manthanô*, turns out to be a quiet guide to truly understanding the line image: for the first of four times he uses *manthanô* to describe his understanding, and as is so often the case, close attention to a tiny dialogic element leads to unexpected clarity. For Glaucon's failure to understand leads Socrates to say, "Let's try again" and to give an expanded account of the first subsection of the intelligible part while repeating his account of the second with only

119. *Archê* means both beginning and first principle. This ambiguity plays an indispensable role in the line image. I will translate archê as *beginning* except once, when Glaucon uses the word at the end of the line image.

slight variation. He begins by saying, "you'll understand [*mathêsei*] more easily after this introduction," and he uses what Glaucon already knows to explain first what he meant by "suppositions" (*hypotheseis*):

> those who work in geometry, calculation, and such things suppose [*hypothemenoi*, posit] the odd and the even, the figures, three forms of angles, and other things sister [*adelpha*] to them in each inquiry; assuming these as already known, making them suppositions [*hypotheseis*, postulates], they do not deem it worthwhile to give any further account of them to themselves or others, taking them as evident to all; beginning [*archomenoi*] from them and going through what remains they end consistently with that for which they set their inquiry in motion. (510c)

All this is obvious to Glaucon: "Most certainly; I know that."

Socrates then turns to what he meant by "using as images"—the first item in his first account of the intelligible. He keeps to what Glaucon already knows: mathematical explanations use "visible forms and fashion arguments about them, thinking [*dianoia*] not about them but about those others that these are like, making arguments for the sake of the square itself and the diagonal itself and not for that which they draw, and similarly with the rest." Socrates thus introduces the word he later uses for this subsection of the line, *dianoia*: dianoia thinks of the square itself while pointing to a molded square. Speaking of these "visible forms," the molded square and drawn diagonal, he repeats his wording about thing and image in the visible section: "these themselves that they mold and draw, of which there are also shadows and images in water, they in turn use as images seeking to see those themselves that one cannot see otherwise than with thinking [*dianoia*]." Thinking takes as images what visibly cast shadows and images—from both directions *images* take priority over actual things. Glaucon again finds this statement of mathematical practice obvious: "It's true, what you say."

The final part of Socrates' restatement of the first section of the intelligible reverts from this introduction through mathematics to his initial concise statement: "This then is the form [*eidos*] I said was intelligible." He restates the compulsion a soul is under in thinking: "a soul is compelled to use suppositions in investigating it," and restates its compulsory direction of inquiry, "not proceeding to a beginning." But now he gives the reason why: "for it is not capable of *going out* [*ekbainô*] above the suppositions"—*above* indicates for the first time that the line he is imaging is vertical. He ends the process where he began it: "but using as images those very things from which images were made by the things below"—the visible things that cast images of themselves are themselves made images by thinking. Socrates then adds a new claim in his restatement: "and these [*eidê*] as opposed to those are opined as clear[120] and are given honor" (511a). In his restatement on thinking and only there Socrates suggests a surreptitious presence of the good in the line image: thinking imports a standard that honors clarity above obscurity. With mathematics as the model this is hardly surprising. But how far does that model extend? And is clarity simply good? Can it obscure the true?

"I understand" (*manthanô*), says Glaucon to Socrates' final statement on the first subsection of the intelligible section, and explains his understanding, "you mean what falls under geometry and its sister arts [*adelphais technais*]" (511b). Socrates neither endorses this understanding nor opposes it; he simply moves on: "Understand me then . . ." That Glaucon's understanding is still inadequate may be indicated by a change he made in the referent to Socrates' word *sister*: Socrates spoke of what is sister to mathematical suppositions like odd and even (510c), Glaucon speaks of what is sister to geometry, the other technai. Glaucon's understanding narrows dianoia to the technai, whereas Socrates' mathematical models were simply images for the kind of thinking active in the whole lower subsection of the intelligible—thinking *generally*, natural thinking, as proven by what is active in the whole higher subsection: *dialectic* (511b), the uniquely Socratic form of intellecting; Socrates' mathematical examples image not just the technai but *all* forms of thinking that are not dialectic. Jacob Klein is right to understand dianoia far more comprehensively (though he does not mention that he is countering Glaucon): "In our thinking . . . be it 'technical' or 'natural,' all the things and properties of the visible world with which we deal are taken to 'resemble' (*eoike* 510d7) the invisible, yet more precise, objects of thought. It is clearly Socrates' contention that our *dianoia* makes us interpret those things and properties *as images* of *invisible noeta*."[121] *Natural* thinking, not just technical thinking, makes *images* of the things. *Images* are of singular importance in human thinking about things—an importance Socrates signaled by putting images first when describing both the visible and the intellectable sections of the line (509e) and putting images last in his final statement about the intellectable (511a). His initial list of things—the animals around us, all plants, the whole class

120. *Clear* in Socrates' conclusion is *enargês*, not *saphêneia* as at 509d; to be *enargês* is to be in *argos*, the shining, bright, glistening.

121. Klein, *Commentary on Plato's "Meno,"* 119.

of artifacts—turns out to be complete after all: *thinking makes things artifacts of thought*. Things are thought by being arranged under suppositions with which thinking is compelled to begin and which it cannot get out of and get above: when Socrates adds that thinking opines its suppositions to be clear and accords them honor, he triggers the suspicion that thinking, our inescapable access to things, inescapably obscures things while finding it good that they be clear. Any suspicion about thinking and its construction of the world through eidê remains hidden to a Glaucon who says, "I understand" while taking Socrates to be speaking only about technai.

No wonder most of Socrates' second effort to explain the intelligible deals with its first subsection: he must indicate that thinking, *dianoia*, stands in need of investigation. Thinking, natural as well as scientific and technical, must be investigated for its peculiar way of making clear and honoring what it clarifies. Thinking images; how are the sources and consequences of its imaging to be grasped? Socrates' very account of thinking already stands beyond thinking, having already moved in the direction thinking cannot move. What direction is that? And how did he do it? Answers come in Socrates' restatement of the other subsection of the intelligible, a restatement whose whole point rides on its ambiguity, a studied ambiguity suggesting to Glaucon the uplift palpable in the images of sun and cave while suggesting as well an understanding that better fits genuine Socratic philosophizing.

Socrates begins by commanding Glaucon to understand (511b): "*Understand me then, by the other section of the intelligible, to be saying what logos itself grasps by the power of dialectic*." A new agent operates in this subsection of the intelligible, no longer "soul" (510b, 511a) but *logos*, speech or reason,[122] and the activity of logos bears a new name: *dialegesthai*, dialectic. Logos investigates the suppositions present but unexaminable in thinking: "*making the suppositions not beginning points [archas] but really suppositions, that is, stepping-stones and springboards, in order to reach the suppositionless [anupothetou]*." The suppositionless is then named in a crucial phrase that focuses the ambiguity Socrates exploits: "*at the archê of all*" (*epi tên tou pantos archên*). Is this archê the ultimate First Principle of the All? To Glaucon, who's just heard the bright and beautiful image of the good as king of the intelligible,

122. I leave *logos* untranslated here; *reason* loses the indispensable tie to language; *speech* is preferable because it suggests the symbolic medium of language while also explicitly recalling Socrates' account in *Phaedo* of his turn to investigating the beings through the *logoi*, but *speech* is not a faculty of the intellect as logos is.

archê may well appear here as "the first principle of the All,"[123] that shining unity of the Good whose rule gives the ideas their intelligibility and being. Yet *archê* can be heard differently: as the antecedent to those beginning points of thinking that logos undertakes to examine by dialectic because thinking itself cannot examine its suppositions even though they determine how everything appears to—is imaged by—thinking. The first interpretation of archê leads upward to an ultimate principle of the All; the second suggests the very kind of inquiry that Socrates elsewhere says was his own form of investigation. What Socrates says next sustains the ambiguity: "*having grasped this . . .*" This could mean having grasped the ultimate principle of the All; or it could mean having grasped the necessity of investigating thinking. The crucial clause that follows has different senses depending on how "having grasped this" is understood: "*[logos] taking hold anew of that which holds it, thus goes back down [katabainêi] to an end.*" *Katabainô*: its direction is downward.[124] Downward subsequent to grasping the First Principle of the All? Or downward subsequent to grasping the need to investigate the suppositions of thinking as imaging? It is arresting that at this decisive point logos goes down—*katabainô*, that first word of the *Republic* whose next four uses will record the going down required in the cave image and whose final use records the going down in the image that brings the *Republic* to a close.[125] The decisive word appears at the decisive point of the central image of the greatest study; only in his restatement does Socrates use this verb of descent, and only in his restatement does he use *dialegesthai*, the verb for his own form of philosophizing. The conclusion seems necessary: the line image depicts the Socratic turn downward while also supplying yet another uplifting image of the philosopher. While causing Glaucon to imagine philosophy going up to a transcendent Unity the grasping of which ultimately legitimates philosophy's claim to rule, Socrates' line image depicts his own turn down to investigate thinking in its ruling presuppositions.

Socrates ends his restatement of this subsection of the intelligible: "in no way making use of anything sensed but of forms [*eidê*] themselves,

123. As R. E. Allen translates the phrase in his translation of the *Republic*. In her elaborate account of the sun, line, and cave, Eva Brann translates this phrase, "'the ruling source' of the Whole" (*Music of the "Republic,"* 194) while attesting later to its ambiguity (204).

124. The *katabainô* of dialectic contrasts with the impossible *ekbainô* of thinking (511a).

125. The nine uses of *katabainô* are 327a, 328c, 359d, 511b, 516e, 519d, 520c, 539e, 614d. Claudia Baracchi speaks of the occurrence of *katabainô* in the line image as "this *katabasis* barely indicated at the heart of the dialogue" and relates it to those that begin and end the dialogue (*Of Myth, Life, and War in Plato's "Republic,"* 96).

through them, to them, and it ends in forms" (511c). Logos employing dialectical inquiry uses eidê to investigate eidê and ends in eidê; the whole descent aims to uncover the eidê that ground the suppositions of thought. What eidê are they? Socrates' models for the eidê of dianoia were mathematical, but can dialectic examine the square itself and the diagonal itself? Instead, it dialectically examines natural thinking in its dependence on those eidê that are the actual ruling opinions and that function like the axioms of mathematics, turning beings into mere images. Socrates' mathematical models help image an ascent to the ultimate principle of the All while leaving obscure Socrates' actual descent to examine the actually ruling eidê of the beautiful, the just, and the good.[126]

Socrates' account of what logos investigates in dialectic draws Glaucon's only extended comment in their whole exchange on the three images of the greatest study. "I understand [*manthanô*]," he says, "though not adequately," almost repeating his first use of *manthanô*, his failure to understand Socrates' first account of the intelligible section (510b). He gives a reason for the inadequacy of his understanding: "in my opinion you speak of an enormous task"—his understanding will always be inadequate because he won't take the long road. He offers a summary of what he understood: "You wish to distinguish as clearer that part of what is and is intelligible that is contemplated by the knowledge of dialectic than that contemplated by what are called the technai for which the suppositions are beginning points." Glaucon's understanding of thinking restricts it to the technai and makes the difference between the two subsections simply a matter of clarity. He then shows his understanding of how each subsection deals with suppositions: "those who contemplate [the objects of the technai] are compelled to do so by *thought* and not by the senses yet because they don't consider them by rising up [*anerchomai*] to a first principle [*archê*] but [proceed] from suppositions, you think they do not possess *intelligence* [*nous*] about them even though they are intelligible with a first principle [*archê*]." There is no "going down" in Glaucon's statement, only the "rising up" to an archê that he seems to understand as first principle. He ends by further clarifying terminology: "It seems to me you call the habit of geometers and their likes *thought* [*dianoia*] but not *intelligence* [*nous*], as thought is something between opinion and intelligence" (511d).

126. Benardete, *Socrates' Second Sailing*, 170: "The suppositions of thought are the manifold of opinion treated as opinion. . . . That mathematical postulates are self-evident and consistent is their attraction; but that opinions are obscure and self-contradictory makes them the true starting-point for philosophy."

Glaucon said his understanding was inadequate. "Most adequate" is what he hears first as Socrates stamps his approval on what he said. But it's not his *understanding* that Socrates calls most adequate, it's his *exposition* (*apodechomai*), what he accepted or received from Socrates. It's fitting that the young ally Socrates is training understand the line image inadequately while knowing how to exposit the image and its terminology. Socrates gives him four words to clarify the terminology of the four forms of awareness (*pathêmata*) for the four parts of the line, this time in descending order: *noêsis* for the highest, *dianoia* for the second, "trust" (*pistis*) for the third, and "imagination" (*eikasia*) for the last. He ends by issuing an order: "Arrange them in proportion, holding that as their objects have a share of the truth, so also they have a share of clarity [*sapheneias*]." Glaucon closes the line image using *manthanô* for a fourth time, this time sure of himself: "I understand and agree and arrange as you say." Encouraged to misunderstand, *taught* a misunderstanding, Glaucon speaks a most adequate exposition: his inadequate understanding put into a most adequate exposition is a fit vehicle for true understanding.

Socrates already gave the first two of the four words and Glaucon already repeated them; the last two, however, he introduces only here at the end. *Pistis* or trust is a most illuminating name to apply in retrospect to human awareness of the visible things. *Trust* is the human stance toward the whole everyday world as it presents itself to awareness; the world gives itself to human awareness as a totality of familiar things within which we find ourselves at home in an "unfathomable familiarity."[127] The line image shows why: thinking arranges the world on the basis of its own suppositions. As for *eikasia*, it appeared first as the capacity to apprehend the shadows and reflections of actual things, the capacity to view images as images, apparently the lowest form of awareness. But *eikasia* reappeared namelessly in thinking's transformation of actual things into images for thought: as a form of awareness *eikasia* ranges over the whole world of trust; through our natural process of thinking, the apparent originals are always already transformed images of thought's suppositions. But *eikasia* is also namelessly present in the very activity Socrates is engaged in as he creates the images of sun, line, and cave. His speech following the line image begins: "After these things, then, make an image [*apeikason*] of our nature in its education and lack of education"—the cave image. Socrates' images educate in the enormous power of eikasia within thinking itself. Only dialectic can render eikasia's power transparent. And dialectic can begin only

127. Klein, *Commentary on Plato's "Meno,"* 114.

through some disturbance in the world of trust that thinking has created with its suppositions, some wonderment or unease about those suppositions and the adequacy of their imaging. Or dialectic can begin through Socrates' capacity to generate images whose internal ambiguities cause an educating unease that leads on the longer way.

There is a certain centrality to the line image even though it is one of two images in the service of explaining the sun image: the line image suggests that Socratic philosophizing is a going down to recover the suppositions of thought that make the world a world of trust. Let Glaucon understand and say that an unbroken line of ascent leads up to the timeless ideas and on up to the First Principle of the All. Let slight indications—the precise ambiguity of *archê*, the different verbs and adverbs of direction, Glaucon's four uses of *manthanô*—suggest the genuine movement of philosophical thought. The line can be thought to ascend to what it leaves out, the good as king of the intelligible. But if the line suggests the Socratic turn downward and nevertheless exists to explain the sun image of the good, then the good left out is present in some way. It was surreptitiously present in thinking's unexamined preference for clarity. But the good also seems surreptitiously present in the descent of logos to investigate the suppositions of thinking by dialectic, for with that investigation, Socratic philosophizing finds the suppositions of thinking to be rooted ultimately in the good or that which everyone wants for itself and for the sake of which one does what one does. The line image would then suggest that through dialectic logos finds the good operative in the very suppositions of thinking, guiding what it clarifies and honors. The greatest study is Socratic dialectic. Its descent leads it to the good as suffused into the very conditions of human knowing, which, *as* such conditions, are the starting point of all. The central image presents Socrates' second sailing with respect to cause as that investigation of the cause of beings as a whole which discovers their appearance as images under the suppositions of thinking ruled by an idea of the good.

Cave

Like the line image, the cave image answers Glaucon's demand that Socrates not leave anything out in explaining the sun image of the good (507e). The intimation audible in the line image is present in the cave image as well: Glaucon understands it one way while it opens itself to a more adequate understanding.

Before setting out the cave image Socrates tells Glaucon what it concerns: "our *nature* in its education and lack of education." The cave image thus expands Socrates' explanation of the idea of the good: the line image pictures thinking organizing the world, the cave image pictures education equipping thinking with content. Education in the broadest sense emerges as total immersion from birth through death in authoritative opinions, and all suffer it: as Socrates gives his initial picture of the cave, Glaucon says, "It's a strange image and strange prisoners." "Like us," Socrates says. Education was Socrates' first occupation in depicting the citizens of the city in speech: he gave new models of "education and rearing," new laws for the stories of gods and heroes sung and told from infancy on (376c–412b). The cave image shows what that education and rearing really is.

Our nature in its education or lack of education is to be bound in an underground cave, and even though the cave is open to the light across its whole width, our nature is such that our back is to the light and the way to it is hard. From childhood on, our nature binds us to see only shadows on the cave wall, exclusively shadows of artifacts except for one unique kind of shadow: those the prisoners cast of themselves. What counts as self-knowledge and knowledge of the human generally can only be of shadows that are dwarfed by the larger shadows cast by artifacts closer to the fire. Socrates goes into detail about the artifacts: they're carried along a road by porters holding them above a wall that is like the partitions put up by puppeteers or wonderworkers (*thaumatopoiois*) to hide themselves. The prisoners can have no inkling that the shadows they see are of artifacts—"of men and other animals in stone, wood, and all sorts of things"—moved about by wonderworkers. Socrates adds a final point about the porters: some speak, others are silent. Because the cave has an echo from the side facing the prisoners, when a porter utters a sound the prisoners believe the passing shadow uttered it. "In every way, then, they would believe the truth is nothing other than the shadows of artificial things." Wonderworkers play the decisive role in cave truth: the artifacts they carry, plus the speeches some of them make, create the shadow/echo world within which cave dwellers dwell and which they take as true.

Our nature in its education and lack of education includes the possibility of release and healing by nature, for Socrates tells Glaucon to consider "the release and healing from the bonds and their delusion . . . if something of this sort were by nature to happen to them" (515c). The process Socrates describes begins with an initial compulsion to which he assigns no agent; it has four components as the one released is "compelled to stand upright, to turn his neck around, to walk, and to look up toward the light." In pain and dazzled by the light of the fire, he is "unable to make out that of which he had formerly seen the shadows"—unable to make the first move of the line image and see an image as an image of something. Thus picturing the pain and perplexity nature forces on the prisoner it releases, Socrates begins his questioning, asking Glaucon first what he thinks the released prisoner would say were he to receive a certain kind of human aid, for he introduces someone (*tis*) who speaks to display the truth about the cave: "What do you suppose he'd say if someone were to tell him that what he saw before was foolishness whereas now he sees more correctly because he's nearer what is [*tou ontos*] and more turned toward beings [*onta*], and in particular, displaying to him each of the things passing by, he compelled him, asking him to answer what it is?" (515d). Socrates prompts Glaucon: "Don't you suppose he'd be at a loss and believe what was seen before is more true than what is now displayed?" "Far more," Glaucon agrees. The someone is relentless: "And then if he were to compel him to look at the light itself"—to look right at the source of cave truth, the fire—"would it pain his eyes and would he flee, turning away to what he is able to make out, and believe these to be really more clear than what he is displayed?" (515d). Help of this sort is no help at all: the one forced to look at cave artifacts and directly at cave light flees back to the comfort of the shadows. A story of release and healing ends with a turn back to a prison of shadows. Socrates later explains that someone attempting to educate this way is acting on a view of education that supposes he can "put knowledge into the soul that isn't in it, as though he were putting sight into blind eyes" (518b). That view is false for the eyes do not act independently but are part of the greater whole of the body, and for the eyes to see something that does not accord with the shadows to which they're accustomed, that greater whole must first be turned in the direction of the new. The someone compelling the released prisoner to look right at cave truth assumes too much of him, a capacity to be enlightened by looking; he does the opposite to what Socrates is right now doing as he refuses to give his opinion about the good and gives images instead.

Alternative to this sad failure of attempted enlightenment is a second way to help the released prisoner. Beginning "If however,"[128] Socrates again supplies a nameless agent—*tis*—but assigns him no speech. Instead, this agent drags the released prisoner "away from there" (*enteuthen*), leaving the cave entirely, dragging him "by force up the ascent that is rough and steep." This alternative way to compel the prisoner whom nature released is an *anabasis*, an upward way that leaves the cave without examining cave

128. The two "ifs" of the first way ($515d_{1,9}$) are offset by this "if" ($515e_4$), an "if however" (*Ei de*) introducing a second way.

truth or cave light. The agent of ascent is also relentless: "not letting him go before having dragged him out into the light of the sun." Thus does the sun omitted in the line image first appear in the images that explicate the sun image. The released prisoner dragged out of the cave suffers a disorientation similar to having his eyes forced to look at cave truth, and Glaucon, unprompted, agrees that the prisoner dragged outside would not be able to see the things now said to be true, and he is able to add on his own what he seems to have learned from the line image about the upward way: "at least not right away." Socrates tells a success story of the perplexed, almost blinded former prisoner after he has been dragged outside the cave, a wholly un-Socratic success story with no dialogue, no turn to the logoi, but instead a direct look at the things. It is the story of a second habituation as Socrates pictures the released prisoner outside the cave ascending to knowledge by repeating the stages of the line image. He again leads Glaucon on the upward way to a belief in the idea of the good and its effects. The released prisoner is able first to make out the shadows and "after that the phantoms of human beings and other things in water," then the things themselves (516a); then he turns to beholding the things in heaven and the heaven itself, more easily first at night, looking at the light of the stars and the moon, than by day at the sun and sunlight. "But finally, the sun, not its appearances in water or in some alien place, but it by itself in its own place, he would be able to look down at [*katidein*], and see it as it is" (516b). With this look down into the sun the released prisoner outside the cave can infer that the sun is the source of the seasons and the years and governs everything in the visible place and is in some manner the cause of all the things they used to see (516b). "It's clear that he'd come to these conclusions after those experiences," Glaucon answers: Yes, he'd gaze down into the First Principle of the Whole, then he'd infer the cause of every particular.

The ascent out of the cave pictures a complete causal explanation of the whole, a bright and beautiful image of knowledge of the whole well prepared by the line image. What the *Republic* cannot say is said elsewhere, in *Phaedo*: gazing at the sun even during an eclipse destroys your eyes if you don't look instead at the sun's likeness in water;[129] Socrates himself turned away from investigating beings like the sun,[130] fearing he'd ruin his eyes; he took refuge instead in logoi, looking in them for the truth of beings. The cave image imagines as accomplished what is impossible, fatal to the eye,

129. *Phaedo* 99d–e.
130. *Phaedo* 98a.

and replaced by Socrates' second sailing in search of cause. The ambiguity of the line image shows how to interpret that impossible success: what the anabasis feigns for Glaucon images Socrates' actual insight into the cave. Compelled by his nature Socrates turned to examine the fire-lit, artifact-cast shadow world of the cave, to investigate the human way of knowing and the human way of being educated. Eventually looking down into the sun that is cave fire, Socrates saw that this child of the idea of the good is the governor of all things in the visible place, giving them their *knowledge* and *truth* (516b–c); and it is the cause of all the things he and his companions used to see, giving them their *existence* and *being* (516c).

Socrates creates an image of a philosopher with a completed causal knowledge of the whole within the very image that demonstrates his knowledge of the power of images. Benardete states the insight dictating this image of cave transcendence: "a partial ascent from the cave cannot be justified in the cave."[131] Socrates, a cave inhabitant who won his freedom from cave fictions by acquiring knowledge of the good, creates a fiction of a perfectly wise cave-transcendent escapee. Knowing the way of education to be habituation to fictions, Socrates habituates to a new fiction: "Wisdom is an idol of the cave."[132] Socrates' cave image habituates to the new idol of the philosopher as wise.

The cave image, with its two ways of picturing what can happen to a released prisoner, one a failure, the other a success, models three ways of enlightenment: a failed way of compelled seeing, a fictionally successful way of a believed seeing, and Socrates' actual seeing. The first way was represented in the *Republic* by Thrasymachus: he compelled his audience to an unwelcome look right at the artifact of cave justice and right into cave fire. The alternative way to enlightenment is a successful way that brings imaginary enlightenment to Glaucon and a glimpse into genuine enlightenment for those whose nature compels them to take the longer way Socrates took. Socrates' image of philosophy as cave transcendence is the last of the images persuading Glaucon of what Socrates has been arguing for since the central sentences of the *Republic*: the philosopher must rule because he is the supreme knower. The cave image also proves Socrates' genuine seeing: having knowledge of the artifactual world fashioned by

131. Benardete, *Socrates' Second Sailing*, 178.

132. Ibid., 179. Insight into the fictional character of cave transcendence seems basic to Maimonides' modification of the cave image: human nature confines humans to a deep dark night occasionally lit by lightning flashes: day never comes and lightning flashes are experienced only by special individuals. *Guide* I Intro. (10–12). See Strauss, *Philosophy and Law*, 126f. and 65, 140 n. 16.

the good, the genuine philosopher has a capacity to rule based in nature. In the *Republic* the genuine philosopher takes rule in the way the image shows is available to him, the way of images, shadow-casting artifacts carried by others. The cave image allows the new habituations to which the *Republic* is subjecting its auditor/reader to be seen as what they are.

Socrates has Glaucon imagine the released prisoner outside the cave recalling "his first home" and one of its features: "the wisdom there" (516c). "Honors and prizes" are accorded in the cave to the one thought wise in three ways: he's "sharpest in making out what passes by"; he "best remembers which are accustomed to pass before, which after, and which at the same time as others"; and because of this he "is best able to divine what is to come" (516c). The honored wise among the prisoners are reasoners engaged in a causal analysis of the parade of shadows; our natural condition is to be not merely passive receptacles of sensory input but active interpreters of our experience, producing an ordered and coherent world for ourselves. Cave wisdom is a knowledge of causes, imaginary causes among shadows with no causal connections. The ultimate achievement of this knowledge is divinatory knowledge of the future, prophetic wisdom. Would the released prisoner envy the honors conferred on the cave's authoritative wise (516d)? Just here Socrates introduces Homer by name and has Homer speak the words his Odysseus reported Achilles speaking in Hades, words Socrates prohibited in the city in speech (386c): the one who has understood cave wisdom knows the cave to be a Hades, and he wants very much "to be on the soil, a serf to another, a portionless man." Cave-understanding Socrates, in the very act of fashioning new ruling images, has his predecessor speak the life-affirming judgment against Hades that ruled the world now passing. Socrates forbade that slander on Hades and will end their conversation fashioning a new image of Hades that on its image-surface, so far from affirming mortal life, slanders it as a moral testing-ground for punishment or reward in afterlife. Within his cave image, however, Socrates has wise Homer use his old image of Hades to speak the truth about the city: it is a Hades of ignorant conviction whose honored wise are authoritative diviners of imaginary causes praised for detecting patterns of meaning in a parade of shadows. By nature the city is the sacred city ruled by servants of the sacred themselves ruled by artifacts and the creators of artifacts.

The judgment voiced by Homer provides a perspective on the central claim of the *Republic* that rule by philosophers aims at relief from evils and the attainment of happiness: rule by philosophers can never bring complete relief from evils like the evil of ignorance believed to be knowledge. Nor can it bring complete attainment of happiness, beyond the private happiness enjoyed by those who migrate to the Isles of the Blessed. Homer's words acknowledge that evil you always have with you. Because the cave can be reformed but never emptied, what passes for education of the vast majority will always be a lack, immersion in shadows and echoes that even in the best case can only image what the philosopher knows. The *Republic*'s image of enlightenment teaches modesty in enlightenment.

"Now reflect on this too," Socrates tells Glaucon as he completes the cave image. If the released prisoner "were to go down [*katabainô*] again and sit in his old seat" (516e) and compete again about the shadows with perpetual prisoners with his eyes infected by the darkness, he would be the butt of comedy, and it would be said of him that his eyes were corrupted and that it's no use trying to ascend. But the comedy ends: "The one attempting to release and lead up, if they were somehow able to lay hands on him and kill him, would they kill him?" (517a). "Ferociously," Glaucon says. The cave image proper ends with the enlightener facing an understandable death sentence in a Hades of righteous conviction. Protagoras already knew there were dangers for the enlightener. As Socrates now turns to apply the cave image to what was said before, he has in his audience a follower of Protagoras to whom he just showed the failure of his way of enlightenment; now he confirms for him what the enlightener must do to preserve himself—and enlightenment itself—in the cave.

Applying the cave image to what went before, Socrates distinguishes visible and intelligible (517b–c) and focuses on the idea of the good as the cause of all that is right and beautiful in the visible and the intelligible. He explains education as a whole, the cave image being "an image of our nature in its education and lack of it": "Education is not what it is said to be by some who profess to be able to put knowledge into a soul where it is not present, as though putting sight into blind eyes" (518c). Socrates' view of education differs from the one held by the educational professionals; for him it is a power in the soul of each, an instrument with which each learns. Just as the eye can be turned toward the light only by turning the whole body, so the instrument by which each learns must be turned around—*converted* (*periagôgê*)—in company with the whole soul, converted from attending to *becoming* to look at *what is* and the brightest of what is, the good. Socrates thus applies the cave image to the first lesson he gave Glaucon on why the philosopher must rule, taking him back to the distinction between becoming and being in his introduction of the ideas. There is a technê for the quickest and most effective conversion, Socrates says, that turns it in the right direction—this is what the technician of education must do, not what he tried to do before, produce sight in the soul by telling the truth about cave artifacts. The other virtues of the soul, Socrates says after talking for hours about the virtue of justice, are more like habituations. What he's talking about now, the virtue of exercising prudence, seems more divine because it never loses its power but becomes useful and helpful or useless and harmful according to the way it's turned. Thus including Adeimantus's objection to philosophers' rule while drawing the lesson of the cave image, Socrates speaks of those commonly said to be vicious and wise (487d). The vision in such souls is not poor, he says, but it is compelled to serve evil, and the more keenly it sees, the more evil it works. This praise and blame of Thrasymachus helps educate an educator who has been all too successful, all too harming in working evils. The cave image with its two ways of education encourages enlightenment teachers to serve themselves by becoming accomplices in converting to the new piety toward new permanent-looking artifacts.

Socrates now turns directly to the issue that occasioned his trio of images, rule by philosophers. Those allowed to spend their whole time in the education he outlined could never adequately govern a city because "they wouldn't be willing to act, believing that they had emigrated to the Isles of the Blessed while still alive" (519c). Socrates then defines "our work as founders"—he, sole founder of the city in speech, prepares his ultimate work of founding, the step he can dare to speak because he acts as if it could realize Glaucon's dream, making the city in speech real in Glaucon's sense. Our work, he says, "is to compel the best natures" to the study of the good and, "when they've gone up and seen sufficiently, not to permit them what is now permitted"—"to remain there, and not be willing to go down [*katabainô*] again." Glaucon shows himself habituated to Socrates' lesson on justice: "Then we'd do them an injustice? We'd make them live a worse life when they're capable of a better?" Socrates blames him for forgetting and invokes the *law*: "it's not the concern of law that any one class of the city fare exceptionally well." Law "produces such men in the city not in order to let them turn in any direction they each may wish, but in order that it may use them in binding the city together." Law-abiding Glaucon yields. The philosopher Socrates then brings philosophy and law together to draw the ultimate lesson of his three images, for he says to Glaucon, "consider that we won't be doing an injustice to the *philosophers* who come to be among us" (520a). Finally, Socrates utters the word *philosopher* again, bringing to an end the long silence he observed on this word (since 503b) while creating the images through which his own rule as philosopher is effected. The word *philosopher* frames the philosopher's ruling deed of image making without ever obtruding into the subphilosophical images he makes. Socrates does more than just reintroduce the word, he tells Glaucon what they're to say about the philosophers and what they're to say to the philosophers. "We'll say" that when philosophers come to be in other cities it's fitting that they not participate in their labors, "for they grow up spontaneously against the will of the regime in each, and a nature that grows by itself and doesn't owe its rearing to anyone has justice on its side when it's not eager to pay off the price of rearing to anyone." Socrates grew up spontaneously against the will of the Athenian regime, but he addresses those who grow up under a different regime, that of the city he built in speech: "'You, however, we have begotten you for yourselves and for the rest of the city like leaders and kings in hives; you have been better and more perfectly educated and are more able to have a share in both ways of life'" (520b). Pressing his claim as educator on those he educated, the founder of the city in speech utters his commanding word: "'*Down you must go [katabateon]*, each in his turn.'" "Down I went" was Socrates' first word. Down where others compelled him to stay, he compelled himself to construct the city in speech. Having gone down yesterday, Socrates speaks the *Republic* today in Athens; as that speaker he wins the right to address the smallest minority among those who hear it, those like himself. Existing now, aloud and in public, the *Republic* is the educating "city" through which its founder won the right to utter a command to those it truly educates. Educated across centuries by the *Republic*, genuine philosophers were educated to a responsibility by their educator: You must do what I did. The compulsion cannot be the compulsion of law to which Glaucon just showed himself happy to submit. Nor can it be the compulsion of the moral, which the *Republic* has shown to be an artifact casting necessary shadows in the cave. The compulsion can only be the one to which Socrates yielded as the *Republic* unfolded: *self-compulsion* driven by the unique self-interest of the philosopher, the interests of philosophy. In the service of the rational, the philosopher goes down to be an image maker whose artifacts, in Socrates' case, extend all the way up to the ideas and the idea of ideas, heirs to Homer's Olympians and Homer's Zeus.

The "you" who must go down will do in their caves what Socrates did in his: in "the common dwelling of the others" they will "get habituated . . . to seeing the dark things" (520c). Seeing "ten thousand times better" than the prisoners, they will "know what each of the phantoms is, and of what it is a phantom"—they will know both the shadows and the artifacts that cast them. They will also know, though Socrates must refrain from saying so, just who the wonderworkers are who carry them and why it is necessary not to flaunt the truth about them, not to debunk them. They will also know what the fire is that lights the cave, what the good is, that for the sake of which their cave dwellers do everything they do (505d). They will know these things because the *Republic* helped them see "the truth about beautiful, just, and good things." Self-compelled descent by philosophers of the future allows the city to be "governed by us and by you in a state of waking, not in a dream." Socratic philosophers of the future rule as Socrates came to rule Glaucon and Adeimantus and Thrasymachus: through plausible argument and the creation of persuasive images, and through effective alliances that utilize the nature of the powerful to rule the powerful.

Why would "you" do it? Socrates ends his speech by raising that question and pointing to his earlier answer: "The truth is surely this: that city in which those intending to rule are those least eager to rule is necessarily governed in a way that is best and freest of faction" (520d). Among the wages of rule, Socrates said, is a penalty for not ruling (347a). When Glaucon didn't understand how a penalty could be a wage, Socrates said he didn't "understand the wages of the best." The best would rule, being the least eager to rule, in order not to suffer the penalty of being ruled by a worse (347c). The worse is now in full view: shadows and echoes of authoritative artifacts so rule cave dwellers that they can threaten the very existence of the best. Socrates asks the essential question: "Do you suppose those we have nurtured, when they hear this, will disobey and be unwilling to take their turn in sharing the labors of the city?" (520d). Glaucon's answer is exactly right—for an ally trained by Socrates: "Impossible. For we issue just orders to the just." Justice is wholly binding on Glaucon; for him the philosopher's rule is now a moral commandment; he willingly carries new artifacts to rule the cave. But the least eager nurtured by the least eager will go down so that philosophy will not be ruled by what rules the cave. Socrates looks to philosophy's rule over what rules the cave far beyond the temporal range of his own rule, he looks to the succession of Socratic-Platonic philosophy.

The image of the cave brings new images to the cave. An artifact now carried back and forth casts the new shadow of the philosopher as authoritative knower of what transcends the cave. The cave becomes the "enlightened" city of citizen believers who believe themselves enlightened by the enlightened wise man. Knowing wisdom to be an idol of the cave, Socrates knows it is wise to appear wise. As an image of enlightenment his cave image encourages belief in enlightenment in the midst of the sophistic enlightenment. Simulated enlightenment for Glaucon and Adeimantus gives them the gift of noble images as the enlightenment educator looks on. Friendship with Thrasymachus is imperative, but as a shepherd he is not himself the ultimate audience of enlightenment. Simulated enlightenment provides for the transmission of genuine enlightenment. One of Socrates' philosophers of the future, Francis Bacon, expressed this truth of transmission in an image: to be carried forward on the river of time, the most weighty must be tied to the light and frothy.[133]

Socrates ends his lessons on the three images by returning to the possibility of their city's coming into being (521a), a coming to be that now has both the literal sense Glaucon understands and the nonliteral sense "you" understand. It is neither possible nor desirable that the city in speech come into being as Glaucon understands it; it is possible and most desirable that it exist in speech both for Glaucon and for the least eager. Sun, line, and cave are images of philosophy that fulfill Socrates' purpose as announced in his claim that the philosopher must rule. The images are instruments of rule, means of achieving the goal for which philosophy rules, relief from evils or the attainment of happiness. In his *Attainment of Happiness*, Alfarabi, another of Socrates' philosophers of the future, expressed this with arresting clarity. After showing why philosophy must rule, he showed how it ruled: philosophy rules by ruling religion, where "religion is an imitation of philosophy."[134]

When Socrates commands "you" in applying the cave image, he marks the founding moment of Socratic-Platonic political philosophy, for his words forge his ultimate alliance, with the philosophers of the future. From our privileged late perspective it is possible to see that alliance stretch across millennia as the long history of Platonic political philosophy. Owing their education in part to the city founded in Plato's book, philosophers of the future went down as Socrates went down to a cave whose fundamental features cannot change, though its every aspect can: different perpetual prisoners, different shadows, different artifacts, different porters, even a different fire illuminating the cave and casting the shadows that envelop the human. Socrates' address at the end of the images is astounding in its brevity and range. Reducing the essential matter to a single word used first as the first word of his narration, he uses it here after his decisive images to state what "you" are to do because of what "I" did. Socrates' going down aims to permanently alter philosophy's place in

133. *The Advancement of Learning, Works* 3:291–92. Bacon knew the "rule" governing Socrates' use of images: "whatsoever science is not consonant to presuppositions must pray in aid of similitudes" (ibid., 3:407). Learning Socrates' lesson of succession, Bacon learned as well that the light and frothy, the vehicle for carrying philosophy forward, must itself be refreshed by alteration: the revolution set in motion by the Socratic Bacon conserves the most weighty, conserves philosophy.

134. Alfarabi, *Attainment of Happiness*, no. 55.

the city, to be the fountainhead of philosophy as socially responsible, philanthropic in a knowing way. Philosophy's descent is a descent with images, edifying images that serve the city in its sacred nature while educating the very few to the truth about those images.

Beginning with the *Republic* the history of Platonic political philosophy is the history of the secret rule of philosophy over religion. Down I went—Down you must go. That is the decisive event in the founding of Platonic political philosophy, the politics for philosophy that came to dominate future philosophy as Plato dared to anticipate it would when he compelled himself to go down by writing the *Republic*. It is the compulsion acted on by great Platonic political philosophers who founded the great enlightenments: Cicero in Rome, Alfarabi in Islam, Maimonides in Judaism, and in Christendom that series of modern thinkers such as Montaigne, Bacon, Descartes, who altered the light of the European cave as followers of "the wisest man who ever lived," reason's "most intimate and familiar friend," Socrates.[135] Friedrich Nietzsche knew himself to be the latest in this long line of Platonic political philosophers who knew that philosophy must rule religion. Such rule was not his innovation, but Nietzsche did make two primary innovations: given the centuries of scientific truth telling, he knew the time had come to tell the truth about philosophy itself; and he set out to fashion the new images of eros for the transitory to replace the bare ruined images of permanences now impossible and unsalutary within the marvelous surge of becoming.

As for Socrates in the *Republic*, he must still complete his night-long argument; he must display the explicit steps of his new education and add its final caution in the image of the changeling child (537e–539e) in order to shelter philosophy from public suspicion and secure endurance of the willing lie. After that he must close the detour, returning to the exact point at which they broke off; then he must trace the decline of the city and its corresponding souls to secure the superiority of the just life over the unjust or tyrannical life for Glaucon and Adeimantus. That extended argument helps do for them what Socrates failed to do for Alcibiades and Critias. That part of Socratic education, sheltering Homer-generated Greek youth from the dangers of the tyrannical life, has long since lost its urgency and is now primarily of historical interest. What has not lost its urgency, another aspect of Socratic political philosophy that makes Socrates our contemporary, is the most grave innovation still to come in the *Republic*, the seal and guarantee of his new teaching on the gods and the soul. To un-

135. Montaigne, *Essays*, "On Presumption."

derstand that ultimate innovation, which *Charmides* promised, it is enough to stride from the peak, Socrates' three images for the philosopher's rule, to the closing peak on which he chooses to end the night's instruction, the last of the incantations of the returned Socrates. No step had greater world-historical implications: we are still living out its Adrasteia-ordained consequences in our globalized posthistorical world.

THREE:
THE LAST ACT OF THE RETURNED ODYSSEUS

The *Republic* takes a long time to end. Socrates has completed his argument and Glaucon is fully persuaded that the just life is better than the unjust life, but Socrates does not stop. He seems to judge that Glaucon and his like need inducements that go beyond the argument. Dawn must be ending the short summer night as Socrates makes his last beginning. As a new day dawns, Socrates, acting wholly on his own initiative, breaks the hold of the old soul-shaping poetry with a new poetry to shape souls, a poetry ministerial to philosophy. But for the new poetry of the returned Odysseus to take root, Homer must be diminished, made to seem far less than he is. Only with Homer's sun set can the new sun rise.

16. Love and Reverence for Homer (595a–c)

The argument is over. Glaucon is persuaded and the city they founded has become "a pattern laid up in heaven" (592b). Socrates expresses satisfaction for what they did in founding the city and singles out one aspect of its founding as especially satisfying, their banishment of imitative or mimetic poetry (595a). But he begins a new discussion of poetry, the last beginning in the *Republic* and the only beginning to which Socrates is not compelled by others. Yet in his final response to Glaucon's initial series of questions he explains what he is doing in a speech that begins and ends with the same Greek word: "It must be spoken" (595b–c). What Socrates initiates, freely and wholly on his own, is compelled after all, self-compelled.

Socrates' claim that they were right in what they founded with respect to poetry goads Glaucon to ask, "In what respect?" In refusing to admit poetry into the city insofar as it is merely imitative, Socrates responds, adding that they are now in a better position to approve this refusal "since each of the forms [*eidê*] of the soul has been separated out as distinct." This too elicits a question: "How do you mean?" Socrates swears them to secrecy—"Among ourselves, for you won't betray me to the tragic poets and all the other imitators" (595b)—and raises a new accusation against imitative poetry: "all such things seem to maim the thought of those who hear them and do not have as an antidote [*pharmakon*] the knowledge of what things happen to be in themselves." What Socrates now wants them to take into their souls is a substitute for the real antidote to the maiming powers of imitative poetry, a *pharmakon*, that word from *Charmides* (155b, c, e; 157b, c; 158c) which named the new drug he brought back from Potidaea as a medicine for the health of the soul.

"What are you thinking about in saying that?" Glaucon asks. "It must be spoken," Socrates says, though inhibiting his speaking is "a certain love and reverence for Homer which has possessed me since childhood" (595b). With this confession, this rare look deep into his authentic origins, Socrates offers a glimpse into what compels him to raise again the place of poetry in the new city. For who is Homer? "He appears to have been the first teacher and leader in all these beautiful tragic things." Socrates must be counted among "the admirers of Homer" who say Homer "has educated Greece" (606e), but his stance toward Homer is singular: it is the stance of the founder of the new city facing the one he admires most, the founder of the old city. The founding poet of Greece must be countered and supplanted by the founder of the new city despite the love and reverence that have always gripped him. Socrates is compelled to take up the theme of poetry again after the argument is over because the poetry of the new educator of Greece must replace Homer's. Homer's achievement signals Socrates' ambition: to be the first teacher and leader in the post-Homeric, post-tragic things, the new beautiful things.

Socrates gives his reason for breaking Homer's grip: "a man must not be honored above the truth." For the sake of the truth, for the sake of philosophy, Socrates' new kind of comedy supplants tragedy, the comedy of the soul he brought back from Potidaea, the drug and teaching he said he got from a doctor of Zalmoxis. Socrates compels himself to complete his task, the task of a returning Odysseus: to establish the new order he brings a new religion ministerial to philosophy. Nietzsche put into words the essential compulsion behind the last great event of the *Republic*: "for a temple to be built a temple must be destroyed—that is the law."[136]

136. *Genealogy of Morality*, 2, ¶24.

17. Homer's Deed (596a–601b)

Socrates begins his criticism of imitative poetry by reintroducing the *ideas* (*eidê*). Till now, the beautiful, just, and good have served as his only examples of "the one particular *eidos* for each group of many things," but here his examples are couch and table. It is odd that artifacts of human design have "ideas" at all, and Socrates heightens the oddness by speaking of the couch "in nature" and of its being "fashioned by the god" (597b).[137] Why choose these examples? Couches and tables appeared once before: Glaucon protested their absence in the "city of pigs" (372d–e). Accustomed to reclining on couches and eating from tables, he heard Socrates praise a city in which such preconditions of civility were wholly absent. Socrates added couches and tables to the city they were founding as the first items in the whole world of customary civility that formed Glaucon's taste, a taste for the "luxurious" or "feverish" city (372e). Habituating Glaucon to think in terms of *ideas*, Socrates now reintroduces Glaucon's earlier examples with their implied inflection: couches and tables image the civil world founded by Homer, lived by Glaucon, and now being supplanted by Socrates. Let couches and tables be the model *ideas*.[138]

After determining that the craftsman makes a couch but not the idea couch, Socrates introduces a special maker who can make *everything*: "he fashions the earth and the heavens and the gods and the things in the heavens and under the earth in Hades" (596c). Glaucon is incredulous, but even he could do it, Socrates says: "take a mirror and carry it around everywhere: you'll instantly make the sun and the things in the heavens, and instantly the earth." These are only "appearances," Glaucon scoffs, exhibiting his absorption of what Socrates is giving him. The painter, Socrates says, is like an imitative artist with a mirror: he paints a couch that is an appearance of the couch made by the couch maker, which he in turn made by looking away to the idea couch—how easily the couch maker achieves what was so hard and rare earlier, access to the *ideas*. There are three varieties of couch: "the one in nature," which is the idea "that we'd say a god fashioned," the one the couch maker made, and the one the painter made (597b).

Socrates began his questioning by asking, "Can you tell me what imi-

137. The classic defense of Socrates' treatment is Cherniss, "On Plato's *Republic* X 597B" (1933). There is an extended discussion in Naddaff, *Exiling the Poets*, 67–91.

138. If the connotation of *klinê* in this passage is set by its earlier usage in the *Republic*, then *bed* is an inappropriate translation here even though it is one of the meanings of the Greek word.

tation in general is?" alleging his own incapacity to do that. Glaucon declined, deferring to Socrates (595c–596a), but Socrates structures his questioning to force Glaucon after all to tell him what imitation is and who the imitator is: it is Glaucon who says that the painter would "most fitly be called an imitator of that of which those others [god and couch maker] are craftsmen" (597e). Socrates keeps to the fiction that Glaucon is leading him: "So you call an imitator, then, the one who is at three removes from nature?" At this point he reintroduces his main concern: "So then the tragic poet, since he is an imitator, will by nature be at a third remove from a king[139] and the truth." He can then lead Glaucon to tell him that the imitator imitates an appearance and can imitate it in only one perspective of its appearing (598a), and he draws his conclusion as something Glaucon told him: "imitation is far removed from the truth . . . and that is why it can produce everything, because it lays hold of only some small element of each" (598b). The lesson he draws from the view he led Glaucon to express is that imitation has a capacity "to deceive children and unwary adults" (598c). And just here he introduces a someone who claims he has come across a person who knows every craft and everything else anyone knows and that there's nothing he doesn't know more exactly than anyone else (598d). That someone ought to be countered, Socrates says, as "a simpleminded sort who must have met up with some enchanter and imitator and been deceived." The simpleminded someone believes that the enchanter is all-knowing because of his own "inability to distinguish knowledge, ignorance, and imitation." "And now . . . don't we need to consider tragedy and its leader, Homer?" Homer reappears suddenly for the first time since Socrates spoke of the love and reverence for Homer that had possessed him since childhood (595c). It's not Homer that concerns him now, it's the simpleminded who take Homer to be all-knowing: Homer possesses the minds of others too, those unable to distinguish knowledge, ignorance, and imitation. Why did Socrates revive talk about *ideas*?—to help him, who can make such distinctions, break the grip "all-knowing" Homer holds on those who cannot. For his conclusion speaks not of what Homer knows but of what he's taken to know by the simpleminded: all the arts, all human matters having to do with virtue and evil, and all divine matters (598e). Homer is guilty only of being such an enchanter that he's taken to be all-knowing by the simpleminded. And now? Now those unable to

139. "King" (*basileus*, cf. 509d) is natural here as a synonym for the god, but that the philosopher king introduced at the center of the *Republic* is also implied seems to be indicated by Socrates' next three-tier scheme: *user*, craftsman, imitator replace god, craftsman, imitator.

distinguish between knowledge, ignorance, and imitation are to think that the philosopher is all-knowing because he knows the ideas.

Socrates claims that there is a test that can be applied to an imitator supposed to be a knower: if he is knowledgeable about the things he imitates, "I imagine he'd give far greater precedence in seriousness to deeds than to imitations and he'd strive to leave behind many beautiful deeds as memorials of himself and be more eager to be praised than to praise" (599a–b). Glaucon shows that he at least places deeds far above imitation, for he agrees, saying that "there's no comparison as to honor and benefit." Granted this elevation of deeds, Socrates can demean Homer as a failure compared with doers of deeds. He excuses Homer for not being a doctor, like Asclepius, and for not mastering other crafts, and he applies his standard of deeds only to "the most important and beautiful (noble) things of which Homer attempts to speak: wars and commanding armies, managing cities, and the education of a human being" (599d). Having listed the three items on which he will test Homer, Socrates does something remarkable: he interrogates Homer directly, addressing him as "Dear Homer" and putting questions as if Homer were present and could answer for himself—across the centuries Socrates questions Homer, inviting Homer's reply.

Homer has become the defendant in a trial. Inviting him to answer the charge just leveled that "he's third from the truth about virtue, a craftsman of a phantom [*eidôlou*]," Socrates suggests that he could claim to be "second, able to know what sorts of pursuits make humans better or worse in private or public." Unmentioned because unmentionable is the claim to be first, a maker of the eidê that all others take to be models, a doer whose deed is speech that puts up words that others take as words of the god: at Socrates' imitation trial Homer never appears as he is, as what Socrates knows him to be. "Tell us," Socrates tells Homer, "which one of the cities was better governed on account of you." Socrates as accuser puts first the central item from his list of the three most important and noble things Homer spoke of. He names the founding lawgivers of cities: "the way Sparta was [better governed] because of Lycurgus. . . . What city credits you for having been a good lawgiver and having been of benefit to them? Italy and Sicily do so for Charondas, and we for Solon. But you, *who*?" Socrates' last word to Homer asks *who*? He does not allow Homer to say who but instead asks Glaucon to answer for Homer at his trial, and Glaucon judges that Homer would have no *who* to mention. Could Homer answer *who* to his public accuser if better witnesses than Glaucon were to be called or if he were to speak for himself, speak out of the *Iliad* and the *Odyssey* to an accuser who from childhood on held him in love and reverence and who pays special attention to the hidden sense of what he says about the battles of the gods (378d)? If he could he would agree that he's no Lycurgus, Charondas, or Solon, founders whose cities are the two greatest Greek cities and cities of the Greek diaspora, far-flung colonies that established Greekness in foreign places. But he could go on to answer Socrates, if only Socrates: "I am who *you* said I was," a maker of models. As Socrates acknowledged in his earlier criticism of Homer's poetry, Homer is the poet-founder whose models stamped the world within which Greek lawgivers set down specific laws for their grateful cities. The *who* is *you*, Socrates. Socrates can credit Homer for his true founding deed, the god-making, hero-making poetry for which all Greek cities hold him in love and reverence, many people going so far, in their ignorance, as to judge him all-knowing. Homer is not the founder of any Greek city, he's the founder of Greekness whether in Sparta, the colonies, or Athens—and he taught Socrates, who credits him in the only way appropriate.

Socrates' prosecution of Homer on his deeds continues: are any wars in Homer's time remembered for being well conducted with his leadership and advice? None, says Glaucon, though every Greek general and every Greek warrior warred under the Homeric models of manliness they carried within themselves. Suddenly, a new item, absent from Socrates' first list, appears: "Are there then many ingenious devices of the sort a wise man makes, in respect to arts or any other practical matters, attributed to Homer as they are to Thales the Milesian and Anacharsis the Scythian?" None, Glaucon says. But if "ingenious devices" of the wise is taken in the sense invited at the center of *Charmides*, they include—the gods themselves. As Herodotus said, Homer and Hesiod gave the Greeks their gods, assigning them their epithets, defining their honors and skills, and describing what they look like.[140] Socrates broke into his list of three deeds by which to measure Homer to indicate a power that stands as the core of Homer's deed, his god-making power.

Socrates turns to the final charge in his apparent indictment of Homer: "If there is nothing in public then, is it told that Homer, while he was himself alive, was in private a leader in education for some who cherished him for his intercourse and handed down a certain Homeric way of life?" Socrates names one educator and way of life: "just as Pythagoras was par-

140. Herodotus 2.53. Anacharsis the Scythian is the only non-Greek example in Socrates' prosecution of Homer. Herodotus's report on Anacharsis focuses on his effort to introduce a foreign goddess and her all-night festival into his native Scythia, an act of disloyalty to his own gods for which he was killed by his brother the king (Herodotus 4.76).

ticularly cherished for this reason and his successors even now still give Pythagoras' name to a way of life that makes him seem somehow outstanding among the others?" Nothing like that is told, Glaucon answers, adding that it is told that Homer suffered considerable neglect in his own day. Socrates then judges Homer as educator in a long speech. He begins with a question according to which an educator's *knowledge* as compared with his art of imitation might be judged by his capacity to generate companions who honor and love him. He gives contemporary examples, citing the love lavished on Protagoras and Prodicus by companions who believe that only with their instruction are they able to govern their household and their city. Had Homer been such an educator—and here, at the end of the trial, Socrates adds Hesiod—would their contemporaries have permitted them to be mere rhapsodes? Wouldn't they have compelled such educators to stay with them at home or at least attended them wherever they went until they gained an adequate education (600e)? Did Homer as educator win special private lovers by what his poems exhibit of his *knowledge* as opposed to their art of imitation? That is the question. The answer is not exhausted by the behavior of the followers of Protagoras and Prodicus and what they believe of their masters as knowers. This final item of the indictment, like the first three, shows how the accused is loved, not condemned, and the identity of the lover becomes clear: the private lover generated by Homer, the companion who loves and honors his educator for his knowledge and not simply for his art of imitation, is Socrates. As a member of the smallest Homeric school, Socrates took Homer into his ownmost home, attended Homer wherever Homer led him, and gained an education on managing the household and the city that he could have gained nowhere else, for he learned from him what the greatest deeds are while learning that even those among his contemporaries who honored him for his imitations permitted him to be a mere rhapsode. "It's altogether true, it seems to me, Socrates, what you're saying." And it's true in ways that Glaucon cannot know: all four arguments convicting Homer in his eyes as a mere imitator unfit to be his educator elevate Homer into the fit educator of the educator, the teacher of what a founding teaching is that sets the models for a whole civilization.

What Socrates voluntarily adds to the night's argument legitimates the central claim of that argument: the philosopher has a right to rule based on knowledge of ultimate rule, rule through speeches that become authoritative and define the gods and the heroic, rule that Homer exercised while educating his private companions on the nature of rule. Socrates' voluntary addition displays his compulsion to break Homer's hold on them while intimating Homer's hold on him. "For a temple to be built a temple must be destroyed"—the crime at the origin is part of Homer's wisdom, part of what Socrates had to allege was "the biggest lie about the biggest things" (377e). Plato has Socrates take leave of Homer in the proper, the Homeric way: he is that lover of Homer who confirms Homer's rank while supplanting Homer's rule.

18. Homer's Children (601b–608b)

Couches and tables disappear, replaced by reins and a bridle when Socrates says his criticism of poetic imitation has so far been only "half-spoken" (601c). "Speak," Glaucon says. "A painter, we *say*, paints reins and a bridle"—*speaking*, what Socrates says and Glaucon "says with" him, runs as a background theme for the second half of Socrates' criticism of poetry. A painter paints reins and a bridle,[141] but only a shoemaker and a smith make them, and only the one who knows how to use them, the horseman, understands them (601c). "And won't we say it's that way with everything," Socrates asks; for each "implement, animal, and action" there are three arts, "of using, of making, and of imitating." He gives another example, flute playing. Like couches and tables, flutes were referred to once before: Socrates banished them from the city because flute music loosens the discipline and severity of the guardians and weakens the will (399d). Flute playing serves his new three-tier scheme of knower, maker, imitator with its new assertion that the *user* is the only knower: the flute player has knowledge of flutes, the maker who consults him has trust (601e), and the imitator has neither knowledge nor right opinion about what is bad or good; lacking that, he derives his standard from what appears as beautiful to the ignorant Many (602b). Though his examples are new, Socrates repeats his earlier claim that the imitative poet stands at third remove from reality as a knower (602c); but the *ideas*, which his previous examples served, he never mentions in this half of his criticism. Why begin the second half introducing new examples to make the old claim about knowledge and never mention reins and a bridle and flutes again? The actual topic of the second half wordlessly shows why.

That topic appears gradually in the answer Socrates gives to his own question about imitative poetry: "Over what sort of thing is it in a person that it has the power it has?" (602c). "Of what sort of thing are you speak-

141. Reins have never been mentioned in the *Republic*; Socrates spoke of a bridle when giving the reason why his companion Theages was saved for philosophy (496b).

ing?" Glaucon reasonably asks. "Of this sort," Socrates says, approaching his answer obliquely by first citing cases in which the senses naturally deceive even the most attentive observer. He then moves to intentional deception: "it's by exploiting this susceptibility of our nature that scene painting is nothing short of witchcraft, as are puppetry and many other such devices" (602d). Imitative poetry has power over our natural propensity to be deceived. But we have a natural capacity to offset this propensity: "Haven't measuring and counting and weighing shown themselves to be most gracious helpers with these things"—and Socrates frames the relation between these two propensities in terms of rule—"so that the apparent greater or less or more or heavier does not rule in us, but what has calculated and measured or weighed?" And appropriate rule? "This would surely be the work in a soul of the calculative [*to logistikon*]" (602d), Socrates says. "Of that, yes," Glaucon answers, no doubt recalling the name Socrates gave to the ruling element in his earlier analysis of the soul dividing it into three parts. Socrates reinforces Glaucon's recall by suggesting that the contrary of the measured can appear at the same time about the same things, and asking explicitly: "Didn't we say that it's impossible for the same thing to hold contrary opinions about the same thing at the same time?" "And we were right in saying it," Glaucon says (602e).

But no, Glaucon is wrong, that's not what they said earlier when Socrates stated the principle of noncontradiction as his premise for dividing the soul into parts (436b): he spoke not of *opinions* about things but of a thing itself. Socrates is inexact in his use of his earlier argument. But is he careless? He is also inexact in his next sentence: "That in the soul which opines contrary to the measures cannot be the same as that which does so in accord with them" (603a). Socrates earlier made *opining* the activity of one part of the soul only, and not of the *logistikon* which measures. And he violates his earlier vocabulary again: "That which puts its trust [*pisteuon*] in measure and calculation must be the best of the soul" (603a). "What else?" Glaucon says. What else? That to which Socrates actually assigned the affect *trust* (*pistis*), the less than best, sense perception (511e). Why would Socrates blur the precision of two of his most important arguments, his three-part division of the soul and his distinction between knowing and opining? His inexactnesses occur in his argument that poetry exploits the natural propensity to be deceived: arguing about deception, Socrates deceives; he exploits Glaucon's propensity to agree to statements that sound like what they said earlier. This late in the *Republic* it is no surprise that Socrates is a master of deception and Glaucon a willing, unknowing subject. How fitting that Socrates deceive right here: he voluntarily reintroduced the theme of poetry and is entering the second half of his criticism, the effect of poetry on the soul, the explicit topic of the second half. He begins by doing what a great poet does: Socrates, master of exactness, exploits Glaucon's propensity to agree to the inexact in order to establish in his soul a new poetry that looks a lot like reasoning.

Socrates draws his initial conclusion (603a–b): painting is like the imitative arts generally; it is far removed from the truth, consorts with that in us that is far removed from prudence, and can lead to nothing healthy or true; it is an inferior consorting with an inferior producing inferiors (*phaulê . . . phaulô . . . phaula*). He turns from painting to poetry as the imitative art that "we say" imitates humans in action. Is a human also divided in his *actions* at the same time about the same things as he was said to be in his opinions (603d)? They don't have to agree about that again, Socrates says, recalling that they already agreed about that in earlier arguments (603d). Instead, he treats something skipped over earlier: how a person of good character bears "some such misfortune as losing a son or something else he counts of utmost importance" (603e). *Grief* or mourning, the suffering caused by death, becomes the ever-reiterated focus as Socrates sets out imitative poetry's effect on the soul. A decent person is measured in his grief, they agree, and when alone permits himself things he would be ashamed to allow his peers to see and hear. Reason and law encourage him in keeping those things private, while he is pulled in the other direction by the grief he suffers (604a). Again Socrates reminds Glaucon of their earlier divisions of the soul, more accurately this time: "when a pull in opposite directions arises in a person about the same thing at the same time, we say there's necessarily two in him" (604b)—two only now, with one ready to be persuaded by law to keep calm and not get irritated or angry but let reason decide what's best. Socrates gives law three commonplace things to say to keep grief under control and adds as a fourth that grieving is an impediment "to what we need to come to us as quickly as possible in these cases." When Glaucon asks, "What are you speaking of?" he can say, "Of deliberating" and can portray the soul growing hard with itself in obedience to reason (604c). Repeatedly, Socrates tells Glaucon what "we say," giving him words for such self-rule: "we'll say that what leads to recollection of suffering and grief is irrational, lazy, and beloved by cowardice" (604d). "We'll certainly say that," Glaucon says, accepting the words he's given.

Characteristic of the noncalculative in this bipartite soul is its great variety and ease of imitation, whereas the calculative is always much the same as itself, not easy to imitate, and foreign to the experience of most. The poet understandably turns away from the calculative to win an audience through the varied and familiar. The poet is like the painter: both make something inferior relative to truth while stirring up and feeding the inferior in the soul and destroying the *logistikon* (605b). By repeating this main point at the end of the second half of his argument Socrates reinforces its unstated point: poetry works on the natural susceptibility of the soul to be deceived, a susceptibility countered only by the soul's capacity to measure. Successfully concluding the second half of his criticism, Socrates recalls its beginning: they were just in not admitting the imitative poet into the city with good laws. He ends by giving Glaucon another instance of what "we'll say": "the imitative poet also sets up a bad polity in the soul of each in private, gratifying what is irrational in it" (605b).

Even with the two halves of his critique complete, Socrates can say, "we haven't yet made the greatest accusation against" imitative poetry (605c). The two halves shrink poetry's authority while preparing this greatest indictment: "surely, that it's strong enough to maim even the decent, apart from a certain rare few, is wholly appalling." "How would it not be," Glaucon begins, but even after all he has heard, he is dubious about this charge: "at least if it really does it." Does it? "Hear and consider," Socrates orders as he opens the argument that overcomes Glaucon's last resistance and forces him to concede poetry's power to maim. Socrates brings Homer back for the greatest accusation; Homer on trial now faces the ultimate charge that he harms the decent, except for a rare few. Socrates focuses his accusation on one thing alone: "imitating one of the heroes in grief." Grief is again made primary. Homer and those he leads, the tragic poets, portray the hero indulging in long speeches of lamentation, even singing his lament and beating his chest (605d). Any tragic hero can be pictured here, but Socrates must mean above all Homer's model of the hero in grief, Achilles himself. The *Iliad* sings the rage of Achilles in grief, willing that all be lost, himself and the Greek cause, if only his grief be assuaged in vengeance at his loss of Patroclus. No wonder the first act of a hero that Socrates forbade children to hear was Homer imitating Achilles in grief over the death of Patroclus (388a).[142]

At this culmination of his argument against Homer and tragic poetry, Socrates didactically leads Glaucon to confess his subjection to poetry, how much he enjoys poetic indulgence in grief but how much he realizes that when he suffers a loss of his own he takes pride in the self-control that is "the part of a man" (605d). And he is didactic as he invites Glaucon to consider what happens in the soul's response to suffering (606a).

142. *Iliad* 24.10–12.

The poets' success is entirely reasonable because it exploits the natural and deep human desire to express passionate protest at suffering loss, but their understandable success comes at the cost of "what is by nature best in us." Socrates marshals the resources of the whole night's argument about human nature and reason's guardianship as he concludes his case. Lacking its proper education, what is best in us believes that its pleasure in the expressed grief of others "is steady gain," but the "rare few" think differently (605c). Accessible to the reasoning of the few is the truth of the greatest accusation against Homer's tragic poetry: it maims because its natural appeal naturally condemns what is best to subjection to the less than best in almost all. Socrates will expand the grounds of this greatest accusation, but its sole focus for the argument itself is grief, grief at suffering loss, grief indulged. Socrates ends his argument against Homer on the problem of suffering in the face of death and the fit way to deal with mortal suffering. He accuses not simply tragedy in epic or dramatic poetry but public celebration of the tragic view of life. Glaucon cannot yet know it, but by ending his argument on the problem of mortal suffering, Socrates prepares his poetry of a nontragic view of life: he will tell tales of a cosmic comedy in which gods make suffering meaningful by seeing to the conjunction of virtue and happiness; he will chant a new, nontragic poetry in which good is rewarded and evil punished in souls that he will make immortal.

Socrates expands the grounds of the greatest accusation by saying that the argument he made regarding the tragic holds also for the laughable. And it holds for sex and spiritedness (*thumos*) too, and for all the desires and pains and pleasures in the soul "which we say accompany us in every action" (606c–d): "poetic imitation works up things of those sorts in us. It nourishes them, watering what needs to be made more dry and sets up as ruling in us the very things that need to be ruled." And Glaucon's response to this final expansion of the charge? "I can't say otherwise"—what you say I say. What Socrates just gave him to say was a list of items concluding his greatest accusation. Sheltered within his list as its central item is thumos itself—*thumos* needs to be dried up, Socrates says, thumos which he took such trouble to isolate as a separate eidos of the soul in the earlier argument he repeatedly recalls in this new, bipartite account of the soul's conflicts, thumos which Glaucon first thought could be included among the desires (439e).[143] Homer leaves his children, all but the rare few, ruled

143. Socrates' list put the *epithumêtikoi* (desires) just after *thumos* (606d_{2-3}); two parts of the three-part soul thus appear right next to each other in his bipartite account.

by thumos, and Socrates gives his children words to overthrow the rule of thumos in the name of reason.

Only here at the end does the utter aptness of the examples become visible. Couches and tables imaged Homer's deed of creating a whole world of civility; reins and a bridle image what the souls of those raised in Homer's civility now need, subject as they were from birth to the power of Homer's music, flute music powerful to excite and depress thumos. The susceptibility of our nature to deception makes it malleable to great poets: if Homeric souls in Homer's children need reins and a bridle to restrain and redirect what Homer's flutes shaped and fed, only the user knows reins and a bridle, as only the flute player knew the flute. Acknowledging in this way that Homer knew what he was doing, Socrates claims for them both what befits the user who takes the part of the knower from the god. By imaging couches and tables, reins and a bridle, and flutes, Socrates proves his own artfulness in imitation, his mastery of a poetry of restraint and redirection.

Socrates assigns Glaucon a responsibility with respect to poetry. "Whenever you run into praisers of Homer saying that this poet educated Greece," you must love and embrace them while agreeing only that "Homer is the most poetic of tragic poets and first among them." Homer educated Greece but Socrates reeducates with a new poetry: you "must know that only as much poetry as is hymns to the gods and praise of good people is to be admitted into a city" (607a). Socrates set out the models of his new poetry of gods and heroes in his reform of stories for children, and he is about to add new measures to increase the power of his new poetry. "But if you let in the pleasure-laden Muse in lyric or epic poetry, pleasure and pain as a pair will hold dual kingship in your city instead of law and reasoning." The philosopher ruler who secretly rules "your city" rules through the apparent kingship of law and reasoning, the overt rulers over the pleasure and pain that ruled the city secretly ruled by Homer.

Let the argument just given, Socrates says, be their *apologia* for having raised the issue of poetry again, for it confirms that they were right to exile poetry: "the argument compelled us" (607b). But Poetry herself deserves an explanation: "Let us say to her, so she won't be able to blame us for any insensitivity or incivility,[144] that the quarrel between philosophy

144. Halliwell (at 607b4) notes that Aristophanes' *Frogs* (1491–99) charges that talking "with Socrates about philosophy involves 'throwing away *mousikê*', i.e. discarding the musico-poetic culture to which the theatre belongs and around which education was constructed." Halliwell, *Plato: "Republic" 10*, 154.

and poetry is ancient." Poets, ancient source of gods and heroes, accused philosophy of being a "howling bitch shrieking at her master"[145]—but if poets accused philosophers of attacking the poets' gods without giving a satisfactory alternative, that accusation cannot hold against Socrates. Nor can poets any longer accuse philosophy of the other three charges Socrates cites. But could Poetry still make a case for herself? "Let it be said that if poetic imitation aiming at pleasure should have any argument to make that she should be present in a city with good laws, we'd gladly take her back in" (607c). Socrates admits his reason: "we're well aware that we're enchanted by her. . . . And you, my friend, are you too not enchanted by her, especially when you look at her through Homer's eyes?" "Very," Glaucon grants. Socrates' appeal is not to enchantment: would it not be a *just* thing for poetry to be readmitted if she can deliver an apologia in lyric verse or some other meter, or if others could speak an argument on her behalf without meter how she's not only pleasant but also beneficial to polities and to human life (607d)? Those are the conditions Socrates gives for enchanting poetry's continued presence in the city. Can her case be made? They too will be rooting for her, Socrates says, because of "the love of such poetry that's arisen in us from our rearing in these fine polities of ours" (607e). But as long as she's not able to make her apologia, "we'll listen to her while chanting [*epaidontes*] to ourselves this argument we're making" (608a); our argument "will be our incantation [*epôidên*]" to keep us from falling back into a love of poetry "that's childish and belongs to the Many." So it's enchantment against enchantment, Homeric poetry serving pleasure (says its prosecutor), Socratic poetry serving law and reason. What appears to be the exile of poetry knows itself to be one kind of poetic enchantment replacing another, and its full case has not yet been made, for Socrates is preparing his new poetry of just reward and punishment. When Socrates returned to Athens from his long absence at Potidaea, he said he returned with incantations to heal the soul. The promised incantations of *Charmides* are chanted in hard-to-recognize form in the *Republic*. What look like reasoned arguments are incantations to rein in and bridle Homer's children, a new and sober form of music to replace Homer's flutes.

Socrates ends his apologia by saying that it is necessary "to believe what we've said about poetry" (608b). "Absolutely," Glaucon replies, "I join in saying that" (*sumphêmi*, literally, I speak with [you]). Socrates' last words of the argument proper are a summary injunction at the successful conclu-

145. Cf. *Laws* 12.967b.

sion of the argument that Glaucon, so many hours ago, insisted he supply: "Great is the contest, dear Glaucon, great, though it does not seem so, to become good or evil, so that not the enticement by honor nor by money nor by any rule and not even by poetry is worth it to be careless about justice and the rest of virtue." Glaucon ends the argument in complete assent: "I join you in saying that [*sumphêmi soi*, literally, I speak with you], based on what we have said." Wholly taken over by what they have said, Glaucon will speak what Socrates has given him to say, and he adds: "And I think everyone else would too." Glaucon will speak what they have said to everyone else, persuaded that it will persuade them too; he, Homer's child made Socrates' child, will speak to Homer's children as the advocate of what Socrates gave him to say.

Having undermined the authority of the poets who educated Greece, Socrates now ends his long night in the Piraeus reeducating Greece in a new poetry that Leo Strauss called "ministerial poetry," poetry generated by a ruling philosophy as an instrument ministerial to its rule.[146]

19. Rewards and Prizes for Socrates' Children (608b–614b)

The greatest rewards and prizes require Socrates to persuade Glaucon that the soul is immortal. He begins comparing "an immortal thing" with brief human life, forcing Glaucon to ask, "what is this you're speaking of?" Socrates replies, "Haven't you perceived[147] that our soul is immortal and is never destroyed?" (608d). Socrates' final observation as narrator—his only narrative observation in book 10—describes Glaucon's reaction: "And he looked me in the face[148] with wonder and said, 'No, by Zeus, I haven't.'" Glaucon is astonished at Socrates: "Can *you* say that?" He can *say* that if he is "not to do an injustice"—what he says about the immortal soul is a demand of his justice, of doing good to friends who are good while not harming anybody. "And I suppose *you* can too," he adds, "for it's nothing hard." "It is for me," Glaucon says. Socrates makes the hard easy for a Glaucon, who says, "I would gladly hear from you this thing that isn't hard." "You must hear it," Socrates says. Glaucon must *hear* what Socrates can *say* about the soul's being immortal. Is what he says true? Truth never arises during the argument, but when it's over Glaucon says, "What you say is

146. Strauss, *City and Man*, 136f.

147. Socrates begins his discussion of the immortal soul with the word *êsthêsai*, "to perceive with the senses": he asks Glaucon if has perceived something imperceptible.

148. Halliwell remarks, "*emblepsas* denotes a look straight in the eyes" (*Plato: "Republic" 10*, 159).

true" (611a), only to have Socrates resist and state the conditions necessary for considering what is really true of the soul (611a–b, 612a).[149] Socrates' argument for the immortality of the soul has this frame: its prologue concerns what Socrates can say and Glaucon must hear; its epilogue raises the question of truth but does not answer it.

Socrates' argument for the immortality of the soul in fact proves to be nothing hard for Glaucon, who eagerly contributes to its all too easy conclusion.[150] He seconds Socrates' claim that no one should be permitted to say that the body's evils can cause the soul to become "more unjust and unholy" and cause the death of the soul (610b). "No one," he says, "will ever show that when men are dying their souls become unjust due to death" (610c). But Socrates invents an objector to make that very claim (610c). The inept objector, granting all too much of Socrates' premise, maintains that the death of the body causes injustice, which in turn causes the death of the soul. Socrates acts as if his objector's causal sequence is reversible, requiring him to maintain that the presence of injustice in the soul kills the body (610d). Eager Glaucon, offered this absurd conclusion, leaps in to trounce the objector: "by Zeus," if injustice killed the body, it would not be such a bad thing, for it would "be a relief from evils," relieving us of the evil unjust. The objector is wrong, Glaucon proclaims, for instead of injustice killing the unjust, the unjust kill others; moreover, injustice vivifies, making "its possessor very much alive and . . . sleepless." Pleased to have stepped forward to aid Socrates in his last argument of the whole long night, having pummeled the hapless objector, Glaucon easily agrees

149. The argument consistently refers to what is spoken, not what is true. "Just speak" is Glaucon's invitation at the end of the argument's prologue (608d). The argument is about what Glaucon "says" (*kaleis*, 608d; *legeis*, $608e_5$), what Socrates says (*legô*, $609a_3$), and then about what "we shall say" (609e), what we'll never admit (*axiôsomen*, $610a_3$; *axiômen*, $610a_7$), what you, Socrates, say (*legeis*, $610a_4$), what we are saying (*legomen*, 610b), what we'll never say (*phômen*, $610b_2$), what we'll never permit anyone to assert (*eômen phanai*, $610c_1$), what someone is to say (*legein*, $610c_6$), what we shall surely insist (*axiôsomen*, $610c_8$), what you, Glaucon, say (*legeis*, $610e_5$), what you, Socrates, say (*legeis*, $611a_{10}$). Truth is mentioned once when Socrates says of the objector he supplies, "if one who says this says the truth" and spells out the impossible consequence of taking the objection to be true: he tests the truth of what his objector says, not of what he says.

150. Commentators more willing to grant Socrates' incompetence than his insincerity are nevertheless troubled by the weakness of this argument. Despite its flaws it is such a useful argument for feigning a proof that the soul is immortal that Descartes used it again in a setting where it was of use to him, and he made it even more clearly invalid for he supplied the merest nod to the premise that a nonsoul evil cannot be fatal to the soul. But Descartes stated the necessity behind the argument: to keep weak minds on the straight path of virtue, they must believe that their souls have more to fear or hope for after this life than have flies or ants (*Discourse on the Method* 5 end).

when Socrates draws the conclusion that "it's plainly necessary that [the soul] be always and, if it is always, that it be immortal" (611a).

Socrates adds that there are always the same souls because the immortal cannot spring from the mortal or everything would end up immortal. "What you say is true," Glaucon says. The *truth* of what Socrates said thus arises for the first time since he said he could say that the soul is immortal, and *truth* remains his theme for his final considerations about the soul: four times in his next four speeches (611b_1, b_{10}, c, 612a) he refers to truth and the soul, setting out the only route to that truth, a route they have not taken and will not take. "Let's not suppose this," he says of Glaucon's declaration that what he said was true, nor should they suppose "that soul by its *truest* nature is such that it is full of much variety, dissimilarity, and quarrel with itself" (611b). No wonder Glaucon says, "What are you saying?" for that is exactly what Socrates said soul is. They are not to suppose that because "it's not easy that a compound composed out of many things . . . be eternal." The soul "must be seen as it is in *truth*" (611c) and not as we now see it in "community with body and other evils."[151] Socrates speaks as one who has seen soul as it is: "one will find it far more beautiful and discern more distinctly justices and injustices and everything we've now gone through." But he does not repudiate what they've said—"we have spoken the *truth* about it as it now appears"—and he supplies an image to contrast the way the soul now appears with the way it is in truth: in viewing the soul they are like "those who catch sight of the sea Glaucus" and can "no longer easily see his original nature" because dwelling in the sea caused him to lose some of the old parts of his body and gain new ones. The sea Glaucus can be truly seen as he now is: Socrates claims true understanding of Glaucon's soul as it is, his sentence names Glaucus in the accusative—"Glaukon"—and ends by addressing "Glaukôn," the only difference being a short and long *o*.

But to truly understand Glaucon's soul is not yet to understand soul as it is; for that one must look elsewhere, Socrates says, and in telling Glaucon where, he again claims knowledge of soul as it is. One must look "to her love of wisdom [*philosophian*]" (611e)—the true nature of soul is accessible only in the philosophizing soul knowing itself—"and to recognize

151. As Leo Strauss observed, proof of the immortality of the soul has been gained without knowledge of the soul: "the situation at the end of the *Republic* corresponds precisely to the situation at the end of the first book, where Socrates makes clear that he has proved that justice is salutary without knowing the What or nature of justice" (*City and Man*, 138).

what she lays hold of and what sort of intercourse she longs for"—the soul in its true nature *longs*, it aspires in its very nature—"since she is akin to the divine and undying and what always is"—soul's kinship with what she longs for suggests that the divine and undying, what always is, shares her longing, aspiring nature. Soul in its philosophizing also shows "what she would become if she were to give herself entirely to this [longing] and were brought by this impulse out of the deep ocean in which she now is"—soul in its philosophizing is, as Socrates said in *Phaedo*, the practice of dying and being dead, of separating itself from body, the impossible condition of being lifted aware out of the deep ocean of bodily life. "Then one might see her true nature whether it is many-formed or single-formed, or in what way it is and how."

Offering that mere glance at what would bring true insight into the soul as it truly is, Socrates contrasts that with what they have achieved: "But now, as I suppose, we have sufficiently gone through her affections and forms in human life." The *Republic* offers a true view of what soul truly is in political life and the particular political life created by Homer's deed. But by suggesting that one look elsewhere for a true account of the soul as it truly is, the *Republic* ends its investigation of the soul inviting one to look to the *Symposium*, where soul in its philosophizing shows its kinship with what is as *eros*. The *Republic* in 429 encourages what a chronological reading of the dialogues does anyway: look for Socrates' definitive view of the soul in the dialogue in which Socrates privately takes the most sophisticated audience in Athens back to the fundamental point of his own learning, back to a time before he mounted the public stage in Athens with a new politics for philosophy. In the only dialogue devoted to the praise of a god, Socrates reports that as a young man he learned that the study of the philosophizing soul is the only route to a true glimpse of the soul and thereby a true glimpse of the whole of which soul is a part, the whole to which soul is akin and which is knowable to the degree that soul is knowable. Tracing his own route into an understanding of the whole, Nietzsche revives Socrates' study of the soul, "For psychology is once again the path to the fundamental problems"; and for Nietzsche too, in psychology at its peak, in the philosophical soul knowing itself, the nature of nature itself is glimpsed.[152]

The immortal soul, easily proved, is not reward enough. For the reward to be relevant to justice in mortal life—for virtue to bring happiness—there must exist agents able and willing to supply rewards and punishments. Socrates supplies those agents. But to introduce moral gods he

152. *Beyond Good and Evil*, ¶¶23, 36.

must ask permission to admit the "wages and reputations" of justice (612b) that both Glaucon and Adeimantus demanded he omit in his defense of justice. Now that he has shown that even if one had the cap of Hades in addition to the ring of Gyges (612b) it would be better to be just, he can ask Glaucon to "give back" what the two of them took away. The restoration of wages and reputations is itself a matter of justice: they can do justice to justice only by "giving back to justice and the rest of virtue the wages . . . they procure from both humans and gods" (612b–c). The just wages of justice are of two kinds: those while alive and those when dead. Socrates ends by promising rewards for justice both here and in the hereafter.[153]

Without the slightest nod to his vehement and polished restatement of Thrasymachus's view, Glaucon gives back, for both himself and Adeimantus, what they withheld: that it does not escape the notice of the gods who is just and who unjust, and that they not only notice but love the just and hate the unjust and give the best possible gifts to those they love (612e–613a). If evident evils befall one who is just, he is not to despair, because his justice "will end in some good, either in life or even in death." Glaucon finds all this "quite likely" (613b). The ease with which he welcomes such gods shows how right Socrates was about the two boys from the beginning: they were not persuaded by the sophists' critique of gods and morality (368b); they wanted what they said they wanted, reasons for believing what they so hoped about justice, that it brings happiness. They did not ask Socrates for the truth about justice because, as Adeimantus confessed, they "desired to hear . . . from you" the opposite of what Thrasymachus argued (367b). Glaucon accepts what Socrates says are the rewards humans lavish on the just—"What you say is just"—and what Socrates says assigns to the just what Glaucon earlier described as the rewards of the unjust tyrant (613d–e, 362b). Socrates then turns to the infinitely greater rewards "that await each when dead." He treats his coming tale of Hades as part of the compulsion he is under to do justice to justice; his final tale is the recompense owed justice. Glaucon's last speech of the night shows how prepared he now is to give justice its due, to make up for the injustice to justice he spoke earlier: "Do tell," he says, "there aren't many other things that would be more pleasant to hear" (614a). The last sentiment Glaucon

153. Criticism of "Socrates' 'Philistine' utterance" on rewards draws a rebuke from Leo Strauss: "Socrates, who knew Glaucon, is a better judge of what is good for Glaucon than any reader of the *Republic*" (*City and Man*, 137). The difference between Strauss and almost all readers of the *Republic* is the unwillingness of the latter to read it as what Socrates judges to be good for Glaucon and the Glaucon-like.

expresses is pleasure in anticipation of hearing the rewards of justice and the punishments of injustice.

The tale Glaucon will hear with such pleasure ends their night of talk on the most memorable tale of all, the last item in Socrates' catalogue of what the poets must speak of: "gods . . . and demons and heroes and Hades' domain" (392a). The tale releasing one into pleasant belief in the conjunction of justice and happiness in Hades includes the other element indispensable to that belief: new and dire warnings of what the unjust soul will suffer. What is heard last and heard best owing to "its spectacular conspicuousness"[154] caps the otherworldly character of Socrates' new public appearance for philosophy: philosophy endorses a moral religion of punishment and reward in the afterlife. Cephalus left his sons and their friends to Socrates' care while he tended the sacrifices he hoped would help persuade the gods to spare him what he fears in the afterlife and grant him what he hopes. Socrates proves worthy of Cephalus's trust; he takes over the children of a dying generation and gives them what they will pass on to their children and their children's children.

20. Replacing Homer's Hades (614b–621b)

Socrates ends the night's talk on a final reform of Homer that transforms life after death. He begins: "I will not tell you 'a tale to Alcinous' but rather of a strong man . . ." A tale to Alcinous was the name tradition assigned to a great event in Homer, Odysseus's long narration of his odyssey to Alcinous, king of the Phaeacians, which included his descent to Hades.[155] Socrates' words harbor a pun that marks his situation off from that of Odysseus: his is not a tale told *to* one "strong of mind" (*Alkinou*) but a tale heard *from* one who is "strong" (*alkimou*). A wise auditor is replaced by an original source who is merely strong, and the one now telling the tale did not undergo it but merely passes it on: its original reporter is no Odysseus, its present auditor, Glaucon, is no Alcinous, and its present speaker, wise Socrates, is a master of tales who began the night's talk with the young men suggesting that he, like Homer, was an admirer of Odysseus's grandfather on his mother's side. Introduced by this intricate association with and separation from the tale Odysseus told, Socrates' tale of Hades brims with reminders

154. Baracchi, *Of Myth, Life, and War in Plato's "Republic,"* 93.

155. The tale to Alcinous: *Odyssey* 9–12; Odysseus's journey to Hades: 10.487–11.640. "A tale to Alcinous" had also come to mean any long and tedious tale; Socrates avoids tedium by refraining from reporting some of what he says he heard (615a, 616a).

of Odysseus and ends with the soul of a reformed Odysseus choosing a new life for itself. The tale on the ultimate destiny of the soul that ends the *Republic* in so stunning a fashion is a tale of dubious provenance that replaces Homer's tale told by a wise man to a wise man. Yet it is a tale that a wise man passes on as the culmination of his incantations that night for young Athenians, and he promises great benefit from his tale: "it could save us if we were persuaded by it" (621b).

Socrates' word for "tale" is *apologos*, "an apologue, a fable but also an apology,"[156] a defense speech that explains. What Socrates now adds as an apologos helps do justice justice by extending its rewards. His apologos is an act of restitution, paying the debt his argument incurred both to justice and to the just.[157] By paying back what is owed to justice and the just, Socrates' apologos secures the justice of Glaucon and Adeimantus, who were responsible for the original injustice to justice.

Who is the strong man whose report Socrates passes on? Socrates names him only once, at the very beginning, avoiding his name thereafter by using pronouns and once calling him "the messenger from that place" (619b). Long-established convention names him "Er," but the only time Socrates pronounces his name it comes out "*Hros*"—a most remarkable name whose sound rings of two near homonyms, each crucial to the *Republic*.[158] The first is *erôs*, a word that differs only in reversing which vowel is long. In the *Republic* Socrates made human eros as public-spirited as possible while condemning it as a tyrant that drives the worst of men; but in the *Symposium* Socrates praises the god *Erôs* by making his name stand for the active force present in, present as, every event including the highest. The second word is *hêrôs*, hero, which differs from *Hros* only in its aspirated *eta* and long *o, omega*.[159] In the *Republic* Socrates transformed the heroic

156. Baracchi, *Of Myth, Life, and War in Plato's "Republic,"* 93. Baracchi's book illuminates the final tale better than any other writing I know.

157. Baracchi, ibid., 93–97, elaborates this point.

158. In Greek orthography *H* is the capital form of *eta*, the separate vowel in Greek for a long *e*. Socrates speaks the name in the genitive case; "Er" is the nominative supplied by later tradition. See Platt, "Plato's *Republic*, 614b." See also Planinc, *Plato through Homer*, 18: "the ancient and modern commentators alike give no notice to the fact that Plato deliberately gives the man who returns from the dead to tell the saving tale a name that in its genitive case (Hros) is similar to that of the divinity Eros (Erôs)." Craig, *War Lover*, 369 n. 7, noted this.

159. It is impossible to know just how close the name and its two near homonyms sounded in Socrates' mouth. In 403, Athens officially reformed its alphabet from what is now called Attic to what is now called Ionic. Plato's written text would have been in Ionic script with all capital letters and no breathing or accent marks: ΗΡΟΣ, ΕΡΩΣ, ΗΡΩΣ. In *Cratylus* 398c–e, Plato's Socrates makes *hêrôs* spring from *erôs* both etymologically and actually, and he speaks of their similar sounds in the old Attic pronunciation.

by revaluating the two greatest Homeric heroes, Achilles and Odysseus. That revaluation began with Socrates banning the lament over Hades that Achilles addressed to Odysseus (386c),[160] and it ends here in the final tale by elevating a reformed Odysseus while entirely banishing Achilles from Hades, a realm he ruled in Homer. Plato's *Republic* intimates what Plato's *Phaedo* makes explicit: Socrates is the new hero, the new ideal for Greek youth.

The strong man, Socrates says, was "the son of Armenius," the well-fitting, "by race a Pamphylian," a representative of all tribes reporting back to all tribes. "Once upon a time," Socrates says, "he died in war and when the corpses were picked up on the tenth day in a state of decay his was picked up sound." On the twelfth day, about to be cremated on the funeral pyre, he came back to life and "told what he saw there." "He said," Socrates begins—said to Socrates? Or is Socrates reporting what another said he said? Socrates' final tale reports a report whose transmission he leaves uncertain. "He said" his soul made a journey with the other souls killed in the war to a place where they were judged on the basis of their justice in life. Instead of the vague place Odysseus saw where all souls dwell in the same condition, the Hades he saw has an articulated geography and different fates for the souls arriving there. First the souls are judged for their justice by nameless judges—the virtue the *Republic* defines and defends appears in the final tale as the sole ground for the judgment of souls. The judges send the just into an opening above leading to a place where they are only rewarded, as if all their deeds had been just. The unjust they send into an opening below leading to a place where they are only punished, as if all their deeds had been unjust. When he himself went forward to be judged, the judges told him that he "had to become a messenger to human beings of all things there and they told him to listen and to look at everything there" (614d). In addition to souls departing, he saw souls returning through two other openings. These souls went to a meadow and camped there as at a festival (614e), greeting and telling their stories to one another, for they were returning from a thousand years of punishment or reward. Socrates shortens the report because "to go through the many things would take a long time;" but he reports what "he said the sum was." Every just or unjust deed had been magnified tenfold by being rewarded or punished every hundred years for a millennium. Examples are given to illustrate the reward and punishment, and after saying "he said other things not worth mentioning," Socrates reports a single story that adds

160. *Odyssey* 11.489–91.

harrowing detail to the chief moral lesson of the *Republic*. "For he said he was there when one was asked by another, 'Where is Ardiaeus the Great?'" He reports in direct speech what the messenger said he heard: just at the point of return, the tyrant Ardiaeus learned that what had terrified him for a millennium would come to pass: fierce and fiery men guarding the gates seized him, bound him, skinned him alive, and cast him into Tartarus forever. It is not enough that Glaucon hear the argument and calculation making the life of a tyrant the worst possible choice for a soul, he must hear, and fear, its vivid poetic reinforcement.

After seven days on the meadow the returned souls were sent on a journey; four days later they saw a column of light that stretched through heaven and earth, and on that fourth day they arrived at a place where the structure of the cosmos and its means of governance were visible to them. Necessity rules with the aid of her three daughters, the Fates, who apply their hands to the turning of the eight hemispheres that make up the whole.[161] With the whole cosmic order visible to them and the music of the spheres and Fates audible to them, the returning souls are to make the choice of the life they will lead. A prophet of Lachesis (Distributor of Lots), the Fate governing the past, arranged them in orderly ranks, distributing lots that determined the order of choice and setting out tablets on which were written the patterns of lives from which they were to choose one (617d–e). He then addressed them from a lofty platform, speaking in fell, fraught words befitting the awesome moment; his omission of articles and verbs added a "dignity and impressiveness"[162] that Socrates repeats, performing it in direct speech: "The word of Necessity's maiden daughter Lachesis! Souls ephemeral! Begins another circuit for the mortal race in death-bringing birth. No deity casts lots for you but you will choose a deity. Let him to whom the first lot falls first choose a life to which he will be bound by necessity. Virtue is without master. . . . Blame is his who chooses; god, blameless" (617e).[163] Like immortality and moral gods, freedom is required if reward and punishment are to be meted out justly to souls, and freedom to choose is what the prophet seems to ensure. But his words state only that no deity dictates the choice of lives, and the description of actual choices shows all but one to be dictated after all: all choices but the

161. Hesiod said the Fates were the daughters of Night and that she had "lain with no one" (*Theogeny* 213).

162. Adam, *Republic of Plato,* at 617d.

163. "This speech is frequently quoted or referred to by later Greek writers . . . [the final sentence] in particular became a kind of rallying-cry among the champions of the freedom of the will in the early Christian period" (ibid. at $617e_4$).

last are directly caused by the life previously lived and what was held to be good. Lachesis rules all but one.

Socrates intervenes only once in reporting what he heard, urging a lesson on "dear Glaucon" between speeches by the prophet (618b). The messenger has just said that "all the varieties of human lives" were available to be chosen, and he specifies tyrannies, lives of conventional repute, and lives without such repute. "Here is the whole risk," Socrates tells a Glaucon at just that point of risk, poised at pursuing a life aimed at tyranny and repudiating a life of conventional repute. Socrates has a single recommendation: one must, "to the neglect of other studies," be a "seeker and student" of one study alone, the study by which he might learn "*who* will give him the capacity and the knowledge to distinguish the good and the bad life" (618c). The one necessary study for Glaucon is how to find an educator, an authority to trust. Who will Glaucon choose as educator? Not Homer, whose gods hold no power over him and who, Socrates persuaded him, was an imitator of imitators ignorant of the ideas who watered the parts of the soul that need to be restrained. And not Thrasymachus, who in his rush into the void created by the departure of the educator of Greece repelled Glaucon with teachings he judged indecent if almost persuasive. Socrates is the educator who replaces the ancestral educator and aspiring new ones. The one Glaucon is to seek out and devote himself to is the philosopher who studies the inexhaustible array of the human (618c–d), equips himself to be the new guide of souls, knows the worse from the better life, and uses justice as his standard. "Adamantine must he go to Hades, holding on to this opinion" (619a). Adeimantus was emphatic in his unbelief in moralizing tales of Hades: Hades for him was the desperate last resort of persuaders of the young (366a). Socrates has so established his authority with Glaucon and Adeimantus that he can add Hades as his last resort without seeming desperate.

Returning to the messenger's tale, Socrates reports that the final words of the prophet singled out the last to choose: "if he chooses with mind" he will find a welcome life. And he ended: "Let the first not be careless in choosing nor the last disheartened" (619b). The first and the last are the paradigm choosers in the list of nine that follows, their two choices reenacting the extremes of available lives set out by the long final argument of the *Republic*. The soul choosing first chose hastily and rued its choice; the soul choosing last chose with mind and was glad in its choice. The first is nameless but "had come from heaven, having lived in an orderly regime in its former life" (619c). Experiencing itself free to choose the life it desired, it rushed to choose the greatest tyranny, but its rush shows that its freedom was illusory for it was bound by its former life and what it then held to be good. The messenger thus suggests what Socrates argued: Homer, educator of the old orderly regime, plants tyranny in the souls of his offspring. The messenger explained the disastrous choice of the first to choose by saying that in its former life it had participated "in virtue by habit without philosophy" (619d).[164] His explanation led him to generalize: most who came from above chose as the first chooser did, whereas those from below "weren't in a rush to make their choices." For this reason, there was "an exchange of evils and goods for most of the souls"—and for another reason: "because of the luck of the lot." His next sentence continues: "However, if someone, when he comes to the life here, always philosophizes in a healthy way and the lot for his choice does not fall out among the last, it's likely, based on the tidings from there," that he will live a happy life here and in the other world pass through heaven. *Socrates* has become the speaker in place of his messenger: no messenger—"he who brings tidings" (*aggellos*)—could say "based on the tidings [*apaggellomenôn*] from there" (619e). It is Socrates, then, who pronounces *philosophy* for the final time that night. In taking leave of philosophy, he does not simply say *philosophy* but couples it with "healthy" in order to promise that "based on the tidings from there" the one who philosophizes in a healthy way will be happy both here and there. The Socrates who speaks last of healthy philosophy spoke first of philosophy by making the guardian-dogs philosophers (375e–376c); in between he persuaded Glaucon that philosophy is knowledge of the beautiful, just, and good. To speak of philosophy this way is to shelter genuine philosophy within a healthy philosophy for guardians. Genuine philosophy, capturing with the most intense passion the few who need no reason beyond it, offers healthy philosophy to those whose lack of that passion puts them in need of such reasons.[165]

164. See Benardete, *Socrates' Second Sailing*, 228: "what one can be is [not] independent of what one was"; "one chooses to be oneself" where what one chooses is in fact a "perfect version of oneself." Benardete is led by inferences based on the first soul's choice to draw a conclusion about Socrates' difference from the poets. Viewing the first soul as that of Thyestes, the brother of Atreus fated to eat his own children, Benardete notes that the poets "do not make the best city the setting for the possibility of Thyestes"—the poets "cannot imagine the kind of innocence Socrates has imagined." The transpoetic innocence Socrates imagined holds that no mere citizen can be free because all are subject to the good bred into them by the city. Socrates thus holds that all are innocent, even the first soul to choose, even Thyestes, even Ardiaeus the Great.

165. Oddly, Socrates reinforces what his messenger just said and makes the happy choice contingent not only on healthy philosophizing but on the lot: "and if the lot for his choice does not fall out among the last." But the prophet told the one with the lot for the last choice not to be disheartened (615b), and the one with that lot, the soul of Odysseus, uses it to choose the best life. Neither the prophet nor the soul of Odysseus treats the last lot the way Socrates chose to; the one

The messenger calls the spectacle of souls choosing a life "a sight surely worth seeing" for it was "pitiable, laughable, and wonderful" (620a)—worthy of tragedy, comedy, and philosophy. Having described the first chooser's choice he reports the choices of eight more, naming each and listing them in pairs,[166] observing in advance that for the most part the choice was made "according to the habituation of their former life" (620a). The souls of two singers, Orpheus and Thamyras, each chose the life of a bird known for its song, a swan and a nightingale, respectively.[167] In the dispensation now dawning with the new life choices, old authoritative singers become mere swans and nightingales.

After mentioning musical animals choosing human lives, the messenger names the souls of two Homeric heroes and for the only time assigns a number to a chooser: the soul of Ajax, son of Telemon, choosing twentieth, chose the life of a lion; choosing next, the soul of Agamemnon chose to become an eagle. A character in Plutarch's *Table Talk* observes that Ajax is twentieth here because he was the twentieth shade Odysseus encountered in Hades.[168] And Agamemnon? Odysseus encountered him eighteenth: by making Ajax twentieth again and moving Agamemnon from eighteenth to twenty-first, the report invites a question: Where is Achilles, the nineteenth to appear to Odysseus? Not only is Achilles absent, he's pointed to in his absence. The greatest thumotic hero must be banished and his words condemning Hades must be forgotten (386c–387a) to serve the new teaching on life as preparation for the afterlife. The report on the souls of Ajax and Agamemnon states the reasons for their choices. The soul of Ajax was unwilling to become a human, "remembering the judgment of the arms" (620b); this is the reason Odysseus too reported: bitter memory kept Ajax from even speaking with him, so shamed was he at the memory of the Greeks at Troy choosing to give Achilles' arms to Odysseus and not to him. The soul of Agamemnon chose from "hatred of humankind be-

---

who speaks of healthy philosophy speaks as if the lot made a difference—for philosophy that is merely healthy, perhaps it does.

166. Halliwell (*Plato*: *"Republic" 10*) notes at 620a: "we know of tragic dramas either named after or involving every one of the characters mentioned . . . with the possible exception of Thersites." The messenger's insertion of animals choosing nameless human lives between the third and fourth choosers and his mention of other animals after the last places a caution on finding significance in the number of choosers or their order of choosing.

167. Thamyras is mentioned with Orpheus at *Ion* $533b_8$; see also *Laws* $8.829d_8$; *Iliad* 2.595–600. Diodorus Siculus (3.67) makes him one of three famous students of Linus with Heracles and Orpheus.

168. Plutarch, *Moralia*, 9.5.3, 740e–f; see *Odyssey* 11.543; Bloom, "Interpretive Essay," *Republic of Plato*, 436.

cause of what it suffered"; as Odysseus learned in Hades, it suffered for nothing as much as its memory of being murdered by Clytemnestra, his wife.[169] In the new dispensation Homer's greatest heroes either disappear entirely or become the mere beasts of prey they can now seem—all except for one, "the wisest of men" (390a).

The messenger's report then moves to a pair that had drawn "middle lots" and chose lives of the opposite sex appropriate to their natures. The choice of Atalanta's soul is dictated by her honor-loving nature, for glimpsing the great honors of an athletic man, she cannot resist choosing that manly life (620b). The soul of Epeius, son of Panopeus, choosing next chose "the nature of an artistic woman" (620c). Epeius was known for being the craftsman who made the horse Odysseus devised for the defeat of Troy:[170] a mere craftsman chooses the life of artistic devising. With the mention of Epeius the messenger again points to the memorable man who alone made Epeius memorable, and he then jumps directly to the final pair "far out among the last," the souls of Thersites and Odysseus. Noting briefly that he saw the soul of Thersites clothe itself as an ape, he moves to the choice made last by the soul of Odysseus. Pairing the souls of Thersites and Odysseus brings another masterful act of Homer's Odysseus to memory: by denouncing Thersites and beating him up, Odysseus caused the assembled Greeks to laugh, ending a brewing revolt and preserving the authority of Agamemnon, an incompetent ruler whose rule was saved by the shrewd speech and showy force of resourceful Odysseus.

Odysseus is the greatest man in Homer,[171] and the only one of Homer's heroes whose soul survives in human form in the new dispensation. But the soul of Odysseus that "by chance" drew the final lot has changed, changed itself, and the messenger had privileged access to that change. He knows that the soul of Odysseus went to its choice altered, for while every previous soul chose at the dictate of its former life, the power of Odysseus's former life had been arrested by mind: "by memory of its former labors it had recovered from its love of honor." Unique among souls, the soul of Odysseus transformed the ground of its choices, freeing itself by mind from what explicitly drove Atalanta, the love of honor that ruled the timocratic souls of all its great associates at Troy. Enabled by mind

169. *Odyssey* 11.405–61.

170. *Odyssey* 8.492–4, 11.524.

171. Socrates demonstrated this in his second conversation with Hippias nine years later (*Lesser Hippias*), another calculated effort to restrain a sophist by curbing his trust in righteous candor. See Lampert, "Socrates' Defense of Polytropic Odysseus."

to obey Lachesis's prophet, Odysseus's soul "went around for a long time searching for the life of a private man minding his own business [*apragmôn*]" (620c). There are innumerable private lives minding their own business, but Odysseus's soul must have searched for a very particular such life, for it found it only "with difficulty, lying somewhere neglected by the others." The whole of the *Republic* tells what its choice was: the life of philosophy lived by Socrates, a just life when justice is minding one's own business. Odysseus's soul minding its own business, investigating what it is and where it is, comes to know itself and then to know that "minding its own business" requires it to shelter itself behind a wall; no longer a lover of honor, this, the best of souls, discovers that its need for shelter compels it to rule in order not to be ruled by a worse; it rules as a private person[172] because it is willing to mind the political things only in its own city, the city "we've gone through founding, the one set down in speeches" (592a). The soul of Odysseus now sets out to rule through healthy philosophy, "philosophy" that believes it has good reason to believe in the ideas and in a moral cosmos. The Socrates of the *Republic* is the private man minding his own business whose life was chosen by the soul of Odysseus. Returning from Potidaea, Socrates returns with the soul of Odysseus having chosen the private life that compels it to rule through persuasive speech, speech that creates the new world in which "philosophy" is honored. Though not a lover of honor, Socrates compels himself to gain immortal glory for the sake of philosophy as the founding poet of the post-Homeric regime run by philosopher-dogs.[173]

The final reference to Odysseus in the *Republic* recalls its first reference to Odysseus, the only other time he is named. Homer admired Autolycus, Socrates said, Odysseus's grandfather on his mother's side. Socrates learned from Homer to admire Wolf Himself for "surpassing all men in stealing and in swearing oaths." Naming Odysseus only at the beginning and end and only in reference to a forebear and a descendant, the Socrates of the *Republic* lays claim to being the latest in the long line of Greek wise

172. In Plato's *Apology* Socrates must rebut the charge, a true charge as the *Republic* shows, that so far from minding his own business (*apragmôn*), he goes around in private being a "busybody" (*polupragmôn*) (31c).

173. Seth Benardete (*Bow and the Lyre*) shows that this transformation in Odysseus' soul took place in Homer: the post-Troy odyssey Odysseus describes to wise Alcinous shows him gradually freeing himself from the love of honor through his discovery of the nature of nature in human nature. Benardete shows too that the discovery of philosophy's need for political philosophy was Odysseus's discovery—Homer's discovery.

men that Homer said stretched back before himself: Socrates is the post-Homeric offspring of Autolycus who arises when he must, in the crisis of the death of the gods brought to life by Homer. Heir to Homer, bold as Homer, Socrates is Homerically just, surpassing all men in stealing and swearing oaths. He is the wise poet of non-Homeric gods who makes foreign Cephalus's fears and hopes respectable both for Cephalus's children and for the children of the best; he is the rational man whose poetry gives rational-sounding support to the irrational. The soul of Odysseus lives on in its next choice of a life, choosing with mind and effort to live as much-devising Socrates introducing a new teaching on god and the soul in the depths of 429 Athens.

21. Last Words (621c–d)

After the souls have chosen they parade past Lachesis and the two other Fates who make their choices irreversible. Passing under Necessity's throne, they move onto the plain of the river Lethe, finally drinking from the river, and with that drink "each forgot everything" (621a). Socrates' report annuls that forgetting, making unforgettable what is impossible to call to mind as memory. Each one persuaded by Socrates' tale will know himself as one who chose his life, and each will make his present choices in fear and hope of future divine judgment on those choices.

Having completed his *apologos* Socrates calls it a *mythos*. It is the kind of tale poets tell that shape the souls of those to whom they are told (377a–b); it is like the mythoi about Hades that moved Cephalus to fear and hope (330d) except that this one is made by a supervisor of the "makers of mythoi" (377b) to replace the false mythoi of Hesiod and Homer (377c–d). It is made by a founder who knows the models and himself became a poet (379a) and whose mythos of Hades' realm praises rather than disparages it (386b).

"And so a mythos was saved and not lost . . ." With these words Socrates begins the final speech of the *Republic*. The saved mythos is mighty: "it could save us if we were persuaded by it." It saves to a mythic salvation: "and we shall make a good crossing of the river Lethe and not defile the soul." Socrates continues with first-person-plural verbs, almost submerging himself in the collective *we*, except that he began as the singular in the collective: "but if we are persuaded by *me*." The last speech of the *Republic* names two agents of persuasion, and if the mythos saves the one it persuades, what Socrates does for the one he persuades is more complex. To be persuaded by Socrates means "holding [*nomizontes*] soul immortal and powerful to bear all evils and all goods." Those he persuades will hold or "own as custom or usage"[174] what persuaded them by argument and myth: to be persuaded by Socrates is to be made a believer. But the platitudes of the final speech sustain what the night's talk established: Socrates' words speak differently to different auditors. The believers Socrates' arguments and images persuade are of two kinds: the many who believe in what he has argued and imaged, and the few who believe that it is desirable that the many believe in what he has argued and imaged. The *we* comprehending both groups persuaded by Socrates is sustained to the end, each sharing Socrates' promise in the appropriate way: "we shall always hold to the upward path"—the upward path at the end reverses the *katabasis* of the first word that made this upward way possible—"and we shall in every way practice justice with prudence in order that we may be friends to ourselves and to the gods both while remaining here and when we carry off the rewards for it, like the victors in the games going about collecting [rewards] for themselves [*periageiromenoi*]." This rare word, used only here in the extant Greek literature, ends the *Republic* with Socrates putting the stamp of victory on his completed task—he is the victor in the highest of all games who goes about gathering to himself both those rare ones who are of his kind and those who will think themselves to be of his kind. "Here and in the thousand year journey which we have described"—he alone described that journey—"we shall fare well." Socrates' last words, *eu prattômen*, capture the double sense of justice as Socrates argued for it: we fare well by doing well, acting justly. And they sustain and seal the double sense of justice as minding one's own business and doing so perfectly as Socrates has just done, completing his night-long task of minding what is his business alone.[175] Socrates, that master of insight and artfulness, ends by uttering apparent platitudes of moral uplift the grounds of which, the need of which, and the transcendence of which he has already made available to those desiring something more than the platitudinous. And the whole saving tale is saved and not lost—it is transmitted, and transmitted as Homer's was, in words and images that ensure that it will be carried forward by rhapsodes who believe in it and whom Socrates has trained to also call themselves philosophers.

174. LSJ, *nomizô*.
175. See Benardete, *Encounters and Reflections*, 43.

Note on the Dramatic Date of the *Republic*

One event and one event only fixes the dramatic date of the *Republic*—the day the Athenians introduced Thracian Bendis as an official god of their city cult. All other issues of dramatic date must be subordinated to this because Plato put it first and made this innovation in civil religion the constantly present backdrop against which to measure the still greater innovations Socrates introduced that night. Plato made it easy and virtually imperative for contemporaries to know the date of the *Republic* by indicating in his first sentence that it occurred on that famous day when for the first time at least since the Persian Wars Athenians introduced a new god.[176] And as he did in *Charmides*, he chose not simply to state the dramatic date in his first sentence but to intimate it there and complete the identification only later: Thrasymachus, having been gentled by Socrates, declares that he should celebrate that gentling as his feast at the Bendideia (354a).

So when did the Athenians introduce Bendis? What Plato made easy for his contemporaries has become difficult for us. Modern scholars have, for the most part, argued for two possible dates, 429 and 413. Their arguments have been conducted largely without reference to the *Republic* because of the prevailing opinion that Plato is untrustworthy on historical matters. At the center of the debate rest three stones found by N. Pappadakis in 1936 on the southwest slope of Munychia Hill in the Piraeus. They are fragments, yet it is clear that they contain one (or possibly two or even three) fifth-century decree(s) of the Athenian *ekklêsia* concerning formal aspects of Bendis's celebration. The main controversy has been whether the events after the procession from the Prytaneum in the Athenian agora to Piraeus—namely, the sacrifice, torch races, and all-night celebration—occurred during the Bendideia's first appearance in 429 or were later additions to the festival, probably in 413. It seems most plausible from the epigraphic record itself that the procession and festival were all introduced at the same time and in 429.[177] Two additional grounds, independent of the epigraphic record, strongly favor 429.

First, there existed in 429 what did not exist at all in 413: powerful mo-

176. Parker, *Athenian Religion*, 170–75; Garland, *Introducing New Gods*, 99, 111–14. On the details of the Bendideia, see Parke, *Festivals of the Athenians*, 149–52.

177. For the detailed argument and the particulars of the scholarly debate, see Planeaux, "Date of Bendis' Entry into Attica," esp. 172–78.

tives for Athenians to introduce a Thracian goddess, an act that in itself, as Robert Garland says, "must have been debated at considerable length [first in the *boulê* and later in the *ekklêsia*], given her outlandish background as a quintessentially barbarian goddess and the general ignorance of the population of her claims to worship."[178] The motive was partly political: because of the northern focus of the war during its early years, Athens had strategic and imperial interests in Thrace that the introduction of a Thracian goddess into their own pantheon definitively advanced.[179] By contrast, Athenian interest in 413 was focused west, on Sicily, where disaster awaited their forces. And the motive was partly social and religious: in 429 the plague was devastating Athens for a second summer, and when Bendis came she did not arrive alone but brought her consort, Deloptes, an Asclepius-like figure associated with healing. The introduction of Bendis thus included the prayer that the gods themselves heal Athens of the plague.[180]

Second, if the *Republic* is not simply dismissed as historically undependable, the precise details of its opening prove that the Bendideia was introduced with all its main features in 429 and not 413. A main factor in the argument for 413 has been that the procession of the hecatomb from the Prytaneum to the Piraeus was a separate event from the festival at Bendis's sacred site on Munychia Hill in the Piraeus, with the procession being introduced in 429 and the festival in 413. But the wording of the *Republic* is exact, and it confirms that these two aspects of the Bendideia were introduced at the same time and in 429. After they have participated in the procession down to the Piraeus, Socrates sets out with Glaucon to return to Athens; he has to be told that at sunset there will be a torch race on horseback followed by an all-night festival (327a). "That is novel," Socrates says, referring to the torch race. But Socrates' first sentence in the *Republic* said he took part in the procession only because of *its* novelty: he wanted to see how they would conduct it "since they were holding it for the first time." In 413 the procession was no novelty: it must be 429 for the novel event to be both the procession that Socrates chose to witness because it was novel and the torch race that he says is novel.

178. Garland, *Introducing New Gods*, 112.

179. Planeaux, "Date of Bendis' Entry into Attica," 179–80. Those interests were also advanced by earlier, related acts of Athenian policy such as the alliance established in 431 with Sitalkes, ruler of Thrace, and the offer of citizenship to his son (Thucydides 2.29, 2.67.2).

180. Planeaux, "Date of Bendis' Entry into Attica," 180–81. Asclepius himself was introduced into Athens only in the late 420s (Garland, *Introducing New Gods*, 116–35).

There is another, more general consideration based on the *Republic* itself: 429 is so poetically apt for the great event of the *Republic* that while that aptness can have no power of its own to *establish* the dramatic date, it must be counted part of the evidence after 429 has been made plausible on other grounds. In what Thucydides shows is a time of war, plague, and the death of gods, the Athenian philosopher Socrates, recently returned from a long absence in the north, reports in Athens on what occurred the night before in the Piraeus: on the very night his Athenian countrymen were in the Piraeus publicly introducing their solution to their city's ills, a Thracian goddess with her healer consort, he was in a private home in the Piraeus introducing his own new medicine, medicine he had called Thracian some days before in *Charmides*. The philosopher's solution, with its teaching on a secure moral order upheld by observant gods, promises the long-term cure over centuries for the problem that the city's solution cannot even touch. Sheer esthetic fitness combines with historical evidence to secure 429 as the dramatic date of the *Republic*.

A date of 429, however, is many years earlier than the dramatic dates now customarily assigned to the *Republic* by scholars of Plato, 411 or 421. Both those dates have the disadvantage of requiring the introduction of Bendis to be irrelevant despite its being the most prominent dating event, for no evidence whatever attests to 411 or 421 as dates for introducing Bendis. Still, beginning in the nineteenth century with August Boeckh, many scholars of Plato have favored 411.[181] Others favor 421, often on the basis of the false supposition that the *Republic* took place the day before *Timaeus-Critias*.[182] Besides ignoring the impossibility of securing the introduction of Bendis in 411 or 421, both these dates face other insurmountable chronological problems such as the fact that Cephalus (and probably Charmantides) is dead by those dates. Such chronological difficulties have led some

181. Boeckh, *Gesammelte Kleine Schriften*, 437–49; some who follow Boeckh include Shorey, Introduction, *Republic*, 1:viii ("plausibly assigned by Boeckh to the year 411 or 410"); Bloom, *Republic of Plato*, 440 n. 3 ("probably around 411"); Voegelin, *Order and History*, 3:53 n. 4 ("411/10").

182. E.g., Howland, *Republic*, xii, "421–420"; A. E. Taylor, *Plato*, 264, "about the time of the peace of Nicias (421)"; Guthrie, *History of Greek Philosophy*, 4:438. The summary Socrates gives in *Timaeus* of yesterday's discussion (17c–19b) outlines a discussion similar to the first half of the *Republic*, but he emphatically stops with 5.469b, securing Timaeus's agreement that nothing more was added: beginning with the theme of warfare among Greeks and then the philosopher king, the rest of the *Republic* was not discussed. Definitively refuting the view that the *Republic* itself occurred the day before *Timeaus-Critias* is this: the Bendideia occurs in early June and the festival at which the *Timaeus-Critias* was set, the Panathenaia, occurs in mid- to late August. See Lampert and Planeaux, "Who's Who in Plato's *Timaeus-Critias* and Why," 88–91.

to conclude that the *Republic*, instead of being assigned a single date, is to be thought of as occurring "throughout the Peloponnesian war."[183] But a surrender to vagueness violates the temporal exactitude Plato assigned the *Republic*—"yesterday," "the festival . . . they were holding for the first time," "the Bendideia."[184] Temporal vagueness would be unnecessary if all the chronological issues that 429 entails can be resolved. Those issues reduce to this: *is 429 too early*? The following list indicates how the chief problems of a 429 date can be resolved, though the current state of historical knowledge leaves some residual difficulties.

The battle of Megara. Socrates cites a poem by Glaucon's lover referring to Glaucon and Adeimantus as distinguishing themselves at the battle of Megara (368a). Thucydides names a battle of Megara in 424,[185] and Diodorus describes another in 409.[186] But Thucydides also describes the Athenians undertaking major invasions of the Megarid every year from 431 to 424, and the first, led by Pericles, he counts as the largest Athenian army ever assembled in the war.[187] The Megarid invasions of 431 or 430 could easily have been the event that occasioned the praise that Socrates cites. Glaucon and Adeimantus would then have been at least eighteen or nineteen in 429.

The age of Plato's mother. If the dialogue took place in 429, Adeimantus and Glaucon must have been older than Plato by about eighteen or nineteen years, assuming the correctness of the traditional date of Plato's birth, 429. This would mean, in turn, that their mother, Perictione, would have to have been born around 465, though as late as 462 or as early as 475 is possible. This would accord well with other evidence concerning her immediate relatives: her uncle, Callaeschros, father of Critias of the Thirty, was probably born around 500; since we know almost nothing about her father, Callaeschros's brother Glaucon, a birth year for him as late as 490 is at least possible. Assuming she was born around 465, Perictione would have given birth to Plato when she was about thirty-six and to Antiphon, Plato's half-brother, when she was about forty. She would have been al-

183. Nails, *People of Plato*, 324. Nails's conclusion is based on a documentary hypothesis about the *Republic* that severs it into a number of separately composed units.

184. Leo Strauss states that "While the place of the conversation is made quite clear to us, the time, i.e. the year, is not" (*City and Man*, 62)—as if its first sentence did not say: "yesterday . . . to observe how they would put on the festival, since they were now holding it for the first time."

185. Thucydides 4.66–74.

186. Diodorus Siculus 13.65.1–2.

187. Thucydides 2.31.

most a centenarian by the time of her death[188]—unusual but not unheard of for Greeks of the classical period.[189]

The presence of Lysias. According to ancient information,[190] Lysias, one of the sons of Cephalus who listen to the conversation in their father's house, was born in Athens in 459/458 and moved with his brothers to Thurii when he was fifteen, allegedly in the year of its founding, 444/443; Lysias returned to Athens only in 411. Boeckh assumed the trustworthiness of this reconstruction in the totality of its details and used it to date the *Republic* in 411; it rules out 429, or 421 for that matter, by placing Lysias in Thurii at that time. But the reconstruction depends on an inference made by biographers centuries later that Lysias was born in 459/458, and on their further assumption that he went to Thurii in the year of its founding. A solution lies in skepticism about these inferences regarding just how 459/458 and 444/443 fit Lysias's life. If we assume that Plato is historically accurate and that Lysias was present for the *Republic* in early June 429, then a reasonable reconstruction of the whole chronology of Cephalus's family presents itself: 459/458 is correct as a significant date in the biographical tradition of Lysias, not as the year of his birth but as the year in which Cephalus came to Athens (at the invitation of Pericles); then Lysias would have been born in 444/443; Cephalus died in 428; Lysias relocated to Thurii in that year (at age fifteen) and returned in 411. These plausible dates not only remove a difficulty for 429 as the dramatic date of the *Republic* but solve inconsistencies in the biographical tradition of Cephalus's family.[191]

Thrasymachus of Chalcedon. Thrasymachus was already well enough

188. Plato, *Letters*, 13.361e, refers to her as still alive.

189. See Garland, *Greek Way of Life*, 17–105, 242ff.

190. Lysias's speech, "Against Eratosthenes"; Dionysius of Halicarnassus, *Lysis* 1.8; [Plutarch], *Vitae decem ortorum* 835d.

191. For further details on Cephalus's family, see Davies, *Athenian Propertied Families*, 588f., and Dover, *Lysias*, 42. Catherine Zuckert sets the *Republic* in 411 on the basis of Lysias's presence (*Plato's Philosophers*, 301–2 n. 43), accepting the reconstruction of Lysias's biography based on ancient sources that are anything but solid. She passes over in silence the most prominent fact for the dramatic date of the *Republic*, what Plato put first, that Socrates narrated it on the day after the Athenians introduced Bendis—there is no historical evidence for Bendis being introduced in 411. Ignoring Plato's direct statement of when the dialogue occurred, basing her whole argument for 411 on a dubious biography of Lysias, Zuckert then treats the impossibility of Cephalus being alive in 411 as a mere "counterfactual conjunction of characters . . . to remind his readers of [the] fictional character" (of the *Republic, Clitophon*, and *Phaedrus*, which Zuckert dates together in 411). But can Plato have been so indifferent to historical exactness and still mean to outfit his dialogues with historical indications of dramatic dates to guide us in reading them in the proper order? If he was inexact, on what grounds is Lysias's presence factual and Cephalus's counterfactual?

known in 427 to be referred to by Aristophanes in the lost comedy the *Banqueters*.[192] There is no ancient reference to Thrasymachus's visiting Athens as early as 429, but such a visit is not ruled out by the limited and imprecise information about his life. In 429 he would probably have been in his mid- to late twenties. It would be attractive, if speculative, to suppose that Thrasymachus of Chalcedon, a city across the Bosphorus from European Thrace but in a part of Asia that Xenophon still called Thrace,[193] was present in Athens in connection with the diplomatic relations required for the introduction of Bendis, a Thracian goddess. A visit of diplomatic purpose would be consistent with the appearance of other sophists and foreigners in Plato's dialogues during their presence in Athens for diplomatic purposes, such as Timaeus of Locri and Hermocrates of Syracuse, present during the Peace of Nicias in 421 when *Timaeus* and *Critias* are set,[194] or Hippias of Elis, present for the great diplomatic congress in Athens called by Alcibiades in 420 when *Hippias Major* and *Hippias Minor* are set.[195]

Theages. The dialogue of that title is to be dated in 409 because it refers to the departure of Thrasyllos for Ephesus, whence he recovered Colophon for Athens.[196] In *Theages* Socrates meets Theages, son of Demodocus, for the first time; he is mentioned in *Apology* 33e. If this Theages and the one in the *Republic* are the same, then the *Republic* must take place considerably later than 409, for Theages has by then become an exemplar of philosophy (496b–c). This would make the date of the *Republic* impossible to reconcile with the date of the introduction of Bendis, the ages of Glaucon and Adeimantus, the date of the death of Cephalus, etc. A reasonable solution is to posit a second Theages: homonyms are common in Plato (e.g., three Adeimantuses, two Charmideses, two Critiases), and Theages was a common name.

The Glaucon of the Symposium. Apollodorus, narrator of the *Symposium*, says that he and his first interrogator the day before yesterday, Glaucon, "were still boys" at the time the party occurred that Glaucon now wants to hear about (175a). The date of that party was 416: if that Glaucon is the son of Ariston, not only is 429 impossible as the dramatic date of the *Republic*, so too is 421. Even 411 would be ruled out: the actual date of the conversation would have to be pushed still later for Glaucon's lover to have sung the

192. Sprague, *Older Sophists*, 89.

193. *Anabasis* 6.2.17–19.

194. See Lampert and Planeaux, "Who's Who in Plato's *Timaeus-Critias* and Why," 91–95, 100–107.

195. See Lampert, "Socrates' Defense of Polytropic Odysseus," 234–36.

196. Xenophon, *Hellenica* 1.2.1–9.

praises of him and Adeimantus at a battle of Megara. To avoid having to set the *Republic* even later than 409, there is no choice but to say that Apollodorus spoke with a different Glaucon. That is not at all implausible: not only are many Glaucons attested at the time, but Apollodorus scorns the Glaucon he speaks with as a miserable sort who believes, as Apollodorus used to believe, that "everything was preferable to philosophy"—a most unlikely belief for the interlocutor of the *Republic*.

I am grateful to Christopher Planeaux for his generous help regarding the introduction of Bendis into Athens and the dramatic date of the *Republic*; the historical investigations on which this "Note" depends are his.

EPILOGUE

As an installment in the new history of philosophy made possible by Friedrich Nietzsche, this book aimed to show that Plato confirms Nietzsche's view of the philosopher in his relation to social life. The greatest thoughts are the greatest events, Nietzsche said—and Plato's thoughts belong among the greatest events in our history, for his Socrates proved to be the revolutionary figure he shows him setting out to be, "the one turning point and vortex of so-called world history" after whom "all theologians and philosophers are on the same track."[1] Nietzsche also said that the genuine philosopher is a commander and legislator[2]—and Plato shows Socrates becoming the philosopher who set down the principles and necessity of the rule of the philosopher while embodying those principles himself as legislator of the nature of the gods and founder of philosophic rule through the ideas. Nietzsche said too that all philosophers prior to the Enlightenment knew the difference between exoteric and esoteric—and Plato shows Socrates criticizing Protagoras for his inadequate esotericism, recovering the esotericism already practiced by the Greek wise from Homer onward, and founding exoteric Platonism to harbor and advance the esoteric philosophy he actually held.[3] No philosopher better embodies Nietzsche's truths about the philosopher than Plato does, not even those esoteric masters Francis Bacon and René Descartes, whose commanding and legislat-

1. *Beyond Good and Evil*, ¶285; *Birth of Tragedy*, ¶15; *Beyond Good and Evil*, ¶191.

2. *Beyond Good and Evil*, ¶211.

3. Ibid., ¶30. I set out these three aspects of Nietzsche's view of the philosopher in *Nietzsche and Modern Times*, 1–13.

ing are the greatest events in the founding of the modern world, and who were—as I tried to show in analyzing their esoteric writing in *Nietzsche and Modern Times*—schooled by Plato, however much they were compelled by their times to make the project they founded an anti-Platonism.

A Nietzschean history of philosophy is equipped to uncover the shared perspective underlying a philosophic tradition apparently filled with warring parties: the wars among the philosophers are family disputes, Socrates argued, debates among kinsmen who share more with one another than they do with any nonphilosopher. As lovers of truth they share the common enemy philosophy always faces, the love of one's own that Socrates identified and countered by making philosophy seem the defender of the primary one's own, the beautiful, just, and good that he made seem fixed universals known to your local philosopher: let philosophy seem the defender of what nonphilosophers love most. And as lovers of truth philosophers share a common aim, the philanthropic goal of securing a place for reason in a world in love with unreason, the goal Plato shows Socrates pursuing from the time he mounted the stage in *Protagoras*, on through the world-changing strategy he set forth on his return from Potidaea in the *Republic*, right up to the last day of his life in an Athenian prison cell when he intimated that the philanthropy of the philosopher must oppose the misanthropy of misologists, haters of reason whose hatred stems in part from what they fear is reason's incapacity to prove what they need to be true, that they are immortal.

The "Nietzschean" character of Plato's writings became more easily accessible in the twentieth century because of a great event in the history of philosophic esotericism: Leo Strauss recovered the full extent and character of the esotericism of ancient Greek writers in 1938 and 1939; his writings thereafter, themselves esoteric, describe the principles and necessity of esotericism and detail its practice in the greatest thinkers in our tradition from Plato to Nietzsche.[4] Strauss's aim was to demonstrate that philosophy was possible: the great philosophers were not simply subject to their times, sons of their times, as the reigning historicism argued; they were, as Nietzsche argued, stepsons of their times, transcending them in thought while communicating their thoughts in the local coin. To prove the possibility of philosophy Strauss had to reveal the truth of esotericism. He thereby effected a revolution in the history of esotericism: thanks to him, philosophical laborers like me can write commentaries like

4. See Lampert, "Strauss's Recovery of Esotericism." (I take this opportunity to say that the first printing of this essay contains serious errors introduced during the production stage, especially on pp. 79 and 82–83; for the essay as I wrote it please see the second printing.)

the one just completed that take advantage of Strauss's insights to enter some of the otherwise closed rooms in the mansions of the philosophers, private rooms harboring their most radical, most invigorating thoughts. The school that Strauss founded, preoccupied in its beginnings with mere politics except in its greatest exemplar, Seth Benardete, can have a future as a new scholarly tradition that recovers old masters for the philosophy of the future for which Nietzsche wrote the preludes, a philosophy true to the earth and in that primary loyalty both opposed to the Platonism that clouded our past and true to what the philosophers themselves held.

A Nietzschean history of philosophy aided by Leo Strauss uncovers in Plato's Socrates a politics for philosophy, a "great politics"[5] that in its most fundamental political aspect is a theology, a theologico-political teaching on the highest beings that teaches, stamps in, what the most worthy objects of emulation are. It is over Plato's theological politics that a Nietzschean history of political philosophy pauses longest. What is a god? Plato's Socrates made a god seem a being beyond becoming, a moral judge with a keen interest in our doings, eager to reward and punish, and outfitted with a transformed Hades where rewards are sweeter and punishments crueler for souls Socrates made immortal. Looking back from its privileged position almost two and half millennia later, a Nietzschean history of philosophy can trace the future that Adrasteia fated for a teaching that elevated to the highest ideal lies of otherworldly permanence for God and man. For it was the awesome fate of Platonism, a theologico-political teaching generated by a philosopher, to be captured by a religion, a "Platonism for the people" far more vivid and authentic than itself. Plato, the first European to reference the Persian god Zoroaster,[6] lost control over his teaching to one of the millennial monotheisms that sprang from Zoroaster/Zarathustra; Platonism came to be ruled by a kin of the religious novelties that Plato dared to introduce into philosophy as its political defense. When Nietzsche chose Zarathustra to give voice to the anti-Platonic teaching that affirms the eternal return of every earthly thing, he knew that he was going back to the very founder of the moral view of the universe, which Plato dared to give residence in philosophy. Through a Zarathustra recovered from the revenge against the earth that fires the moral view, Nietzsche initiated a philosophic politics with the same cultural aim as Plato's, to found a social order friendly to philosophy, but rooted now in the opposite passion, love and not hate with its attendant revenge. Like Plato, Nietzsche

5. *Beyond Good and Evil*, ¶208.
6. *Alcibiades I* 122a.

transcended his time in knowing what religions are good for[7]—what they are indispensable for as the structuring poetry of everyday life, the web of belief and value lived spontaneously by every human community as its useful, good, and holy.[8] But Plato's fate, the history of Platonism, allowed Nietzsche to see perhaps more clearly "the uncanny dangerousness" of "sovereign religion," religion not ruled by sovereign philosophy.[9]

Protracted things are hard to see whole, Nietzsche said,[10] he who had seen the whole trajectory of European spiritual life from Homer to the present: "We are the Hyperboreans. We know the road. We have found the exit out of the labyrinth of millennia."[11] Plato inaugurated his political project for philosophy within the Homeric tradition, but the sovereign monotheism that usurped his philosophy via his non-Homeric novelties managed to allege that it retained the best of the Hellenic while in fact erasing the genuinely Hellenic and overwriting it with Platonism. "The whole labor of the ancient world *in vain*: I have no word to express my feelings about something so tremendous"[12]—even Nietzsche found his feelings struck speechless by Jerusalem's victory over Athens in the spiritual warfare that dominates Western history. But his *thoughts* about that event, the words he found for the causes and strategies of that great war, show the way to disentangle the history of philosophy from the history of religion to which Plato had accommodated it.

How Philosophy Became Socratic aimed to expose the degree to which Platonism is a politics—one that successfully pictured the natural platonizing intrinsic to human thinking while intimating as well what genuine philosophy is. Exposing Platonism as politics can therefore be only half the task of recovering Plato for a Nietzschean history of philosophy, for what *is* the genuine philosophy sequestered within the politics? It is already obvious that it cannot be the philosophy stamped into the philosopher-dogs guarding the new city and that it cannot rest in the safety of ideas superintended by a Good that so easily becomes God. In keeping with the chronological arrangement Plato gave his dialogues, a Nietzschean history of philoso-

7. *Beyond Good and Evil*, ¶58.

8. *Thus Spoke Zarathustra*, First Part, "On the Thousand Goals and One."

9. *Beyond Good and Evil*, ¶62.

10. *Genealogy of Morality*, 1, ¶8.

11. *Antichrist*, ¶1. As to the future of Nietzsche's philosophy, no one has shown more clearly than Peter Sloterdijk how those futures still lie in our future. For a brief statement of one of those futures as an advancement of the Renaissance, see Sloterdijk, *Du musst dein Leben ändern*, 52–68, 176–207, 234[!], 246. See also Hutter, *Shaping the Future*.

12. *Antichrist*, ¶59.

phy pursues genuine philosophy exegetically by using Plato's display of the coming-to-be of Socratic political philosophy as an entryway into Plato's display of the coming-to-be of Socratic philosophy. In *How Socrates Became Socrates*, the second part of my Nietzschean project on Plato, I will trace the young Socrates' course as Plato set it out in *Phaedo, Parmenides*, and the *Symposium*. That course, Plato shows, led Socrates into philosophy's genuine mysteries, the mysteries of the god Eros. I willingly betray those secrets, profane those mysteries, to the degree that I am able, for they are mysteries already profaned by Nietzsche when he named the fundamental fact not after a god but with "a weakening and attenuating metaphor": will to power.[13] Plato and Nietzsche share great politics because each knew what religions are good for. But they share as well the essential paganism of all philosophy, eros for the earth, and that is the deepest sharing, for each discovered that in being eros for what is, philosophy is eros for *eros*, for being as fecund becoming that allows itself to be glimpsed in what it is: eros or will to power.

And if, living amid the spiritual ruins of a Platonic civilization, we have no hope and less desire to recover spiritual vitality through Plato's means, *his* politics of god and soul, we can nevertheless see that in wrapping genuine philosophy in politic philosophy, Plato did what Nietzsche too came to know he had to do. Nietzsche knew that he had to pass his knowledge of what religions are good for on to us, modern free minds still burnt by the religious experience of millennia; he knew that in being compelled to present his philosophy as the return of the earthly divinities Dionysos and Ariadne, he was compelled to present it in an unwelcome form to its only possible audience.[14] But he made every effort to teach that audience a new politics of gods and souls. "Oh those Greeks!" Nietzsche said to end the preface of the second edition of the book that ended his whole series of books on science and civilization for modern free minds, "Oh those Greeks! They understood it—how to *live*: for *that* it's necessary to remain standing bravely at the surface, the fold, the skin, to adore appearance, to believe in forms, tones, words, in the whole Olympus of appearance! Those Greeks were superficial—*out of profundity*!"[15] Like Odysseus, Nietzsche came to know "that his destiny is to establish belief and not knowledge,"[16] for like Homer and Plato, Nietzsche came to know that only through belief could he establish continuous access to knowledge.

13. *Beyond Good and Evil*, ¶22.
14. Ibid., ¶295.
15. *Gay Science*, Preface, ¶4.
16. Benardete, *Bow and the Lyre*, 152.

WORKS CITED

Adam, James. *The Republic of Plato*. 2 vols. Cambridge: Cambridge University Press, 1902.

Alfarabi. *Alfarabi's Philosophy of Plato and Aristotle*. Trans. Muhsin Mahdi. Ithaca: Cornell University Press, 1969.

Allen, Reginald, trans. *Ion, Hippias Minor, Laches, Protagoras*. New Haven: Yale University Press, 1996.

Andocides. "On the Mysteries." In *Antiphon and Andocides*, trans. Michael Gagarin and Douglas MacDowell. Austin: University of Texas Press, 1998. 99–140.

Bacon, Francis. *The Works of Francis Bacon*. Ed. J. Spedding, R. L. Ellis, and D. D. Heath. 14 vols. 1857–74; New York: Garrett Press, 1968.

Baracchi, Claudia. *Of Myth, Life, and War in Plato's "Republic."* Bloomington: Indiana University Press, 2002.

Benardete, Seth. *The Argument of the Action: Essays on Greek Poetry and Philosophy*. Edited with an Introduction by Ronna Burger and Michael Davis. Chicago: University of Chicago Press, 2000.

_______. *The Bow and the Lyre: A Platonic Reading of the "Odyssey."* Lanham: Rowman and Littlefield, 1997.

_______. *Encounters and Reflections: Conversations with Seth Benardete*. Edited by Ronna Burger. Chicago: University of Chicago Press, 2002.

_______. *Herodotean Inquiries*. The Hague: Martinus Nijhoff, 1969.

_______. *Plato's "Laws": The Discovery of Being*. Chicago: University of Chicago Press, 2000.

_______. *Socrates and Plato. The Dialectics of Eros / Sokrates und Platon. Die Dialektik des Eros*. "Themen," vol. 76. Munich: Carl Friedrich von Siemens Stiftung, 2002.

_______. *Socrates' Second Sailing: On Plato's "Republic."* Chicago: University of Chicago Press, 1989.

Beresford, Adam. "Nobody's Perfect: A New Text and Interpretation of Simonides PMG 542." *Classical Philology* 103 (2008): 237–56.

Boeckh, August. *Gesammelte Kleine Schriften*. Vol. 4. Leipzig: B. G. Teubner, 1874.

Boedeker, Deborah, and Kurt A. Raaflaub, eds. *Democracy, Empire, and the Arts in Fifth-Century Athens*. Cambridge: Harvard University Press, 1998.

Boegehold, Alan L., and Adele C. Scafuro. *Athenian Identity and Civic Ideology*. Baltimore: Johns Hopkins University Press, 1994.

Brann, Eva. *Homeric Moments: Clues to Delight in Reading the "Odyssey" and the "Iliad."* Philadelphia: Paul Dry Books, 2002.

———. *The Music of the "Republic": Essays on Socrates' Conversations and Plato's Writings*. Philadelphia: Paul Dry Books, 2004.

Bruell, Christopher. "Socratic Politics and Self-Knowledge: An Interpretation of Plato's *Charmides*." *Interpretation* 6, no. 3 (Spring 1977): 141–203.

Burger, Ronna. "The Thumotic Soul." *Epochê* 7, no. 2 (Spring 2003): 151–67.

Burkert, Walter. *Greek Religion*. Trans. John Raffan. Cambridge: Harvard University Press, 1985.

———. *Lore and Science in Ancient Pythagoreanism*. Cambridge: Harvard University Press, 1972.

Cherniss, Harold. "On Plato's *Republic* X 597B." *American Journal of Philology* 57 (1932): 233–42.

Coby, Patrick. *Socrates and the Sophistic Enlightenment: A Commentary on Plato's "Protagoras."* Lewisburg: Bucknell University Press, 1987.

Collins, Susan, and Devin Stauffer. "The Challenge of Plato's *Menexenus*." *Review of Politics* 61, no. 1 (1999): 85–115.

Coolidge, Francis. "The Relation of Philosophy to *Sôphrosunê*: Zalmoxian Medicine in Plato's *Charmides*." *Ancient Philosophy* 13 (1993): 23–36.

Craig, Leon. *The War Lover: A Study of Plato's "Republic."* Toronto: University of Toronto Press, 1994.

Davies, J. K. *Athenian Propertied Families, 600–300 B.C.* Oxford: Clarendon Press, 1971.

Dillon, John, and Tania Gergel, eds. *The Greek Sophists*. London: Penguin Books, 2003.

Diogenes Laertius. *Lives of Eminent Philosophers*. Trans. R. D. Hicks. 2 vols. Cambridge: Harvard University Press, 1925.

Dionysius of Halicarnassus. "On Literary Composition." *Critical Essays*. Cambridge: Harvard University Press, 1937.

Dover, K. J. *Lysias and the Corpus Lysiacum*. Sather Classical Lectures 39. Berkeley: University of California Press, 1968.

Ehrenberg, Victor. "The Foundation of Thurii." *American Journal of Philology* 69, no. 2 (1948): 149–70.

Forrest, W. G. "Athenian Generation Gap." *Yale Classical Studies* 24 (1975): 37–52.

Garland, Robert. *The Greek Way of Life: From Conception to Old Age*. Ithaca: Cornell University Press, 1990.

———. *Introducing New Gods: The Politics of Athenian Religion*. Ithaca: Cornell University Press, 1992.

Guthrie, W. K. C. *A History of Greek Philosophy*. Vol. 4. Cambridge: Cambridge University Press, 1969.

———. *The Sophists*. Cambridge: Cambridge University Press, 1971.

Hale, John R. *Lords of the Sea: The Epic Story of the Athenian Navy and the Birth of Democracy*. New York: Viking, 2009.

Halliwell, S. *Plato: "Republic" 10*. Warminster: Aris & Phillips, 1993.

Hanson, Victor Davis. *The Other Greeks: The Family Farm and the Agrarian Roots of Western Civilization*. New York: Free Press, 1995.

———. *A War Like No Other: How the Athenians and Spartans Fought the Peloponnesian War*. New York: Random House, 2005.

Herodotus. *The Landmark Herodotus*. Ed. Robert B. Strassler. Trans. Andrea L. Purvis. New York: Pantheon Books, 2007.

Homer. *The Iliad*. Trans. A. T. Murray. Revised by William F. Wyatt. 2 vols. Cambridge: Harvard University Press, 1999.

———. *The Odyssey*. Trans. A. T. Murray. Revised by George E. Dimock. 2 vols. Cambridge: Harvard University Press, 1995.

Howland, Jacob. *The "Republic": The Odyssey of Philosophy*. New York: Twayne Publishers, 1993.

Hutter, Horst. *Shaping the Future: Nietzsche's New Regime of the Soul and Its Ascetic Practices*. Lanham: Rowman and Littlefield, 2006.

Jaeger, Werner. *The Theology of the Early Greek Philosophers*. London: Oxford University Press, 1947.

Kingsley, Peter. *Ancient Philosophy, Mystery, and Magic: Empedocles and Pythagorean Tradition*. Oxford: Clarendon Press, 1995.

Klein, Jacob. *A Commentary on Plato's "Meno."* Chapel Hill: University of North Carolina Press, 1965.

Lampert, Laurence. *Leo Strauss and Nietzsche*. Chicago: University of Chicago Press, 1996.

———. *Nietzsche and Modern Times: A Study of Bacon, Descartes and Nietzsche*. New Haven: Yale University Press, 1993.

———. *Nietzsche's Task: An Interpretation of "Beyond Good and Evil."* New Haven: Yale University Press, 2001.

———. *Nietzsche's Teaching: An Interpretation of "Thus Spoke Zarathustra."* New Haven: Yale University Press, 1986.

———. "Socrates' Defense of Polytropic Odysseus: Lying and Wrong-Doing in Plato's *Lesser Hippias*." *Review of Politics* 64, no. 2 (Spring 2002): 231–59.

———. "Strauss's Recovery of Esotericism." Ed. Steven B. Smith. *The Cambridge Companion to Leo Strauss*. Cambridge: Cambridge University Press, 2009. 63–92.

Lampert, Laurence, and Christopher Planeaux. "Who's Who in Plato's *Timaeus-Critias* and Why." *Review of Metaphysics* 52, no. 1 (September 1998): 87–125.

Landy, Tucker. "Virtue, Art, and the Good Life in Plato's *Protagoras*." *Interpretation* 21, no. 3 (Spring 1994): 287–308.

Levine, Lawrence. "A Commentary on Plato's *Charmides*." Ph.D. diss., Pennsylvania State University, 1975.

Liddell, Henry George, and Robert Scott. *A Greek-English Lexicon*. Revised by Henry Stuart Jones. Oxford: Clarendon Press, 1968.

Linck, Matthew S. "Coming to the Ideas: A Study of Ideality in Plato's *Phaedo, Parmenides*, and *Symposium*." Ph.D. diss., New School University, 2004.

Lysias. "Against Eratosthenes." In *Greek Political Oratory*, ed. and trans. A. N. W. Saunders. Harmondsworth: Penguin Books, 1970.

Mahdi, Muhsin S. *Alfarabi and the Foundations of Islamic Political Philosophy*. Chicago: University of Chicago Press, 2001.

Maimonides, Moses. *The Guide of the Perplexed*. Trans. Shlomo Pines. Chicago: University of Chicago Press, 1963.

Mark, Ira. "The Gods of the East Frieze of the Parthenon." *Hesperia* 53, no. 3 (1984): 289–342.

Meier, Heinrich. *Leo Strauss and the Theologico-Political Problem*. Cambridge: Cambridge University Press, 2006.
Monoson, S. Sara. *Plato's Democratic Entanglements: Athenian Politics and the Practice of Philosophy*. Princeton: Princeton University Press, 2000.
Montaigne, Michel de. *The Complete Essays*. Trans. Donald M. Frame. Stanford: Stanford University Press, 1957
Morgan, Kathryn. *Myth and Philosophy from the Presocratics to Plato*. Cambridge: Cambridge University Press, 2000.
Morrison, J. S. "The Place of Protagoras in Athenian Public Life." *Classical Quarterly* 35, nos. 1/2 (January–April 1941): 1–16.
Muir, J. V. "Protagoras and Education at Thurii." *Greece and Rome* 29, no. 1 (1982): 17–24.
Müller, C. W. "Protagoras über die Götter." *Hermes* 95 (1967): 140–59.
Munn, Mark. *The School of History: Athens in the Age of Socrates*. Berkeley: University of California Press, 2000.
Murphy, David J. "Doctors of Zalmoxis and Immortality in the *Charmides*." In Robinson and Brisson, *Plato*, 287–95.
Naddaff, Ramona A. *Exiling the Poets: The Production of Censorship in Plato's "Republic."* Chicago: University of Chicago Press, 2002.
Nails, Debra. *The People of Plato: A Prosopography of Plato and Other Socratics*. Indianapolis: Hackett, 2002.
Nietzsche, Friedrich. *The Antichrist*. In *The Portable Nietzsche*, ed. Walter Kaufmann. 1954; New York: Viking Press, 1966. 568–656.
———. *Beyond Good and Evil: Prelude to a Philosophy of the Future*. Trans. Walter Kaufman. New York: Vintage, 1966.
———. *The Birth of Tragedy*. Trans. Walter Kaufmann. New York: Vintage, 1967.
———. *Ecce Homo: How One Becomes What One Is*. Trans. Walter Kaufmann. New York: Vintage, 1967.
———. *The Gay Science*. Trans. Walter Kaufmann. New York: Vintage, 1974.
———. *Kritische Studienausgabe (KSA)*. Ed. Giorgio Colli and Mazzino Montinari. Berlin: Deutscher Taschenbuch Verlag Walter de Gruyter, 1988.
———. *On the Genealogy of Morality: A Polemic*. Trans. Maudmarie Clark and Alan J. Swensen. Indianapolis: Hackett, 1998.
———. *Thus Spoke Zarathustra: A Book for All and None*. Trans. Graham Parkes. Oxford: Oxford University Press, 2005.
———. *The Will to Power*. Trans. Walter Kaufmann and R. J. Hollingdale. New York: Random House, 1967.
Notomi, Noburu. "Critias and the Origin of Plato's Political Philosophy." In Robinson and Brisson, *Plato*, 237–50.
Nussbaum, Martha C. *The Fragility of Goodness: Luck and Ethics in Greek Tragedy and Philosophy*. Cambridge: Cambridge University Press, 1986.
Osborne, Robin. "The Viewing and Obscuring of the Parthenon Frieze." *Journal of Hellenic Studies* 107 (1987): 98–105.
Parke, H. W. *Festivals of the Athenians*. Ithaca: Cornell University Press, 1977.
Parker, Robert. *Athenian Religion: A History*. Oxford: Clarendon Press, 1996.
Planeaux, Christopher. "The Date of Bendis' Entry into Attica." *Classical Journal* 96, no. 2 (December–January 2000–2001): 165–92.

______. Review of *The People of Plato: A Prosopography of Plato and Other Socratics*, by Debra Nails. *Bryn Mawr Classical Review* (October 2003).
______. "Socrates, Alcibiades, and Plato's *ta poteideatika*: Does the *Charmides* Have an Historical Setting?" *Mnemosyne* 52 (1999): 72–77.
Planinc, Zdravko. *Plato through Homer*. Columbia: University of Missouri Press, 2003.
Plato. *Alcibiades I*. Trans. Carnes Lord. *The Roots of Platonic Political Philosophy: Ten Forgotten Socratic Dialogues*. Ed. Thomas L. Pangle. Ithaca: Cornell University Press, 1987.
______. *Charmides*. Trans. Thomas G. West and Grace Starry West. Indianapolis: Hackett, 1986.
______. *Charmides, Alcibiades I and II, Hipparchus, The Lovers, Theages, Minos, Epinomis*. Trans. W. R. M. Lamb. Cambridge: Harvard University Press, 1927.
______. *Gorgias*. Trans. James H. Nichols Jr. Ithaca: Cornell University Press, 1998.
______. *Phaedo*. Trans. Eva Brann, Peter Kalkavage, Eric Salem. Newburyport, MA: Focus, 1998.
______. *Phaedrus*. Trans. James H. Nichols Jr. Ithaca; Cornell University Press, 1998.
______. *Plato's Parmenides*. Trans. Keith Albert Whitaker. Newburyport, MA: Focus, 1996.
______. *Protagoras*. Trans. C. C. W. Taylor. Rev. ed. Oxford: Clarendon Press, 1991.
______. *The Republic*. Trans. R. E. Allen. New Haven: Yale University Press, 2006.
______. *The Republic*. Trans. Paul Shorey. Cambridge: Harvard University Press, 1930.
______. *The Republic of Plato*. Trans. Allan Bloom. 2nd ed. 1968; New York: Basic Books, 1991.
______. *The Symposium*. Trans. Seth Benardete. Chicago: University of Chicago Press, 2001.
______. *Theaetetus*. Trans. Seth Benardete. *The Being of the Beautiful: Plato's "Theaetetus," "Sophist," and "Statesman."* Chicago: University of Chicago Press, 1984.
Platt, Arthur. "Plato's *Republic*, 614b." *Classical Review* 25, no. 1 (February 1911): 13–14.
Rahe, Paul A. *Republics Ancient and Modern*. Chapel Hill: University of North Carolina Press, 1992.
______. Review of Victor Davis Hanson, *The Other Greeks*. *American Journal of Philology* 118, no. 3 (Autumn 1997): 459–62.
Rhodes, James M. "Mystic Philosophy in Plato's *Seventh Letter*." In *Politics, Philosophy, Writing: Plato's Art of Caring for the Soul*, ed. Zdravko Planinc. Columbia: University of Missouri Press, 2001.
Robinson, Thomas M., and Luc Brisson, eds. *Plato: "Euthydemus," "Lysis," "Charmides."* Sankt Augustine: Academia Verlag, 2000.
Schiappa, Edward. *Protagoras and Logos: A Study in Greek Philosophy and Rhetoric*. Columbia: University of South Carolina Press, 2003.
Segvic, Heda. "Homer in Plato's *Protagoras*." *Classical Philology* 101, no. 3 (July 2006): 247–62.
Sloterdijk, Peter. *Du musst dein Leben ändern: Über Anthropotechnik*. Frankfurt: Suhrkamp, 2009.
______. *Zorn und Zeit: Politisch-psychologisher Versuch*. Frankfurt: Suhrkamp, 2006.
Smith, Kirby Flower. "The Tale of Gyges and the King of Lydia," *American Journal of Philology* 23, no. 3 (1902): 261–82 and 23, no. 4 (1902): 361–87.

Sprague, Rosamond Kent. *The Older Sophists*. Columbia: University of South Carolina Press, 1972.
Strassler, Robert. "Calendars and Dating Systems in Thucydides." In Strassler, *Landmark Thucydides*, 623–25.
Strauss, Leo. *The City and Man*. Chicago: Rand McNally, 1964.
______. *Gesammelte Schriften*. Vol. 3: *Hobbes' politische Schriften und zugehörige Schriften—Briefe*. Ed. Heinrich Meier and Wiebke Meier. 2nd ed. 2001; Stuttgart: Verlag J. B. Metzler, 2008.
______. *Liberalism Ancient and Modern*. New York: Basic Books, 1968.
______. *On Tyranny*. Ed. Victor Gourevitch and Michael S. Roth. Revised and expanded edition. New York: Free Press, 1991.
______. *Persecution and the Art of Writing*. Glencoe: Free Press, 1952.
______. *Philosophy and Law: Contributions to the Understanding of Maimonides and His Predecessors*. Trans. Eve Adler. Albany: State University of New York Press, 1995.
______. *Studies in Platonic Political Philosophy*. Chicago: University of Chicago Press, 1983.
Szlezak, T. A. "Die Handlung der Dialoge *Charmides* und *Euthydemos*." In Robinson and Brisson, *Plato*, 337–48.
Tarrant, Harold. "Naming Socratic Interrogation in the *Charmides*." In Robinson and Brisson, *Plato*, 251–58.
Taylor, A. E. *Plato: The Man and His Work*. 1926; New York: Meridian Books, 1966.
Thucydides. *The Landmark Thucydides*. Ed. Robert Strassler. Trans. Richard Crawley. Rev. ed. New York: Free Press, 1996.
Tuozzo, Thomas M. "Greetings from Apollo: *Charmides* 164c–165b, *Epistle III*, and the Structure of the *Charmides*." In Robinson and Brisson, *Plato*, 296–305.
Voegelin, Eric. *Order and History: The World of the Polis*. Baton Rouge: Louisiana State University Press, 1957.
Wallace, Robert W. "The Sophists in Athens." In Boedeker and Raaflaub, *Democracy, Empire, and the Arts in Fifth-Century Athens*, 203–22.
White, Stephen A. "Thrasymachus, the Diplomat." *Classical Philology* 90, no. 4 (1995): 307–22.
Woodbury, Leonard. "Simonides on *Aretê*." *Transactions and Proceedings of the American Philological Association* 84 (1953): 135–63.
Xenophon. *Memorabilia*. Trans. Amy L. Bonnette. Ithaca: Cornell University Press, 1994.
Zuckert, Catherine H. *Plato's Philosophers: The Coherence of the Dialogues*. Chicago: University of Chicago Press, 2009.

INDEX